School Library Journal's BEST

A reader for children's, young adult & school librarians

WITHDRAWN FROM STOCK

Edited by
Lillian N. Gerhardt

Compiled by
Marilyn L. Miller &
Thomas W. Downen

Neal-Schuman Publishers, Inc.

New York   London

Published by Neal-Schuman Publishers, Inc.
100 Varick Street
New York, NY 10013

Library of Congress Cataloging-of-Publication Data

School library journal's best : a reader for children's, young adult, and school
libraries / [compiled by] Lillian N. Gerhardt, Marilyn Miller, and Tom Downen.
   p. cm.
  Includes index.
  ISBN 1-55570-203-1
  1. School libraries—United States. 2. Children's libraries—United
States. 3. Young adults' libraries—United States. I. Gerhardt, Lillian
N. II. Miller, Marilyn (Marilyn Lea), 1930– . III. Downen,
Tom. IV. School library journal.
Z675.S3S291153 1996
027.8—dc20   96–23856

Table of Contents

Foreword

School Library Journal and its readers have come a long way together in the first 40 years of its publication as an independent magazine by and for librarians specializing in work with children and adolescents. The progress in this area of library service has been both helped by, and reflected in, *SLJ*'s feature content over the four decades as well as in its ever expanding materials review sections. We've grown with our readers from a single focus on the provision of a book selection tool for librarians into a leading, one-stop resource on the news, issues, information, and critical purchasing advice necessary to librarians serving young customers in both schools and public libraries.

For instance, since *SLJ*'s first issue in 1954, suburban children's librarians invented and refined the biggest expansion in any area of public library service since World War II: pre-school and toddler story hours as well as parent education programs. Young adult librarians in major city public libraries were first the heart and then the implementors of library outreach programs for the poor and for minority populations unfamiliar with public library services. School librarians and libraries came of age during these years; these librarians provided the national standards, began the move toward output and evaluation measures and were among the first to welcome and experiment with the new formats available for information delivery, from the days when paperbacks for young readers were new to library collections to today's explosion of electronic devices to enhance reading and learning.

SLJ's was on hand throughout these years as this compilation of articles and columns show providing a forum, reporting to and growing along with its readers from 9 issues each year to the monthly magazine it is today, from the smallest among the library magazines to the one with the biggest paid circulation among all the library magazines—over 40,000 subscribers with an estimated readership of over 100,000 for each issue.

Volume 1, Number 1 was published by R.R. Bowker Co. under the title *Junior Libraries* in September, 1954. Although well-received by public librarians and hailed by leaders in school library services, school librarians found it difficult to subscribe to it from their professional materials budgets because principals and school district comptrollers refused to authorize the purchase of periodicals that did not carry the words "school" or "education" in their main titles. Daniel Melcher, the founding publisher, told me that *Junior Libraries* was failing financially due to the inability to grow in circulation. Changing the main title to *School Library Journal* in September, 1961, reversed its financial standing within a year. The moral of this story is that this magazine and its stated purpose have always been held together by the subtitle which is restated on every issue: *The Magazine of Children's, Young Adult & School Librarians*. SLJ has stayed true to the declaration of its first issue, a promise to contribute to the efforts of school and public librarians working with their "common denominator," young library customers.

With that subtitle always in mind, *SLJ*'s pages are and always have been open to the newest practitioners as well as the leaders in library services to youth. From Volume 1, Number 1 forward, *SLJ*'s readers have been its main source of writers and reviewers: talented, critical, practical, contentious and creative—a very good description of the compilers of this book, too.

Dr. Marilyn L. Miller and Dr. Thomas Downen, both fledglings when *SLJ* began, are now leading practitioners as well as distinguished library educators. They've chosen articles and columns they believe have lasting value for today's and tomorrow's specialists in library services for young people. Judging their selections (without bias or prejudice, of course) I would give this book a rave review on *SLJ*'s "Professional Reading" page. And, exercising the same degree of objectivity previously stated, I call down in advance a curse of black warts on any other reviewer who might be so wrong-headed as to disagree.

Preface

Lillian Gerhardt reminded us at one time that "magazines are for the instant." That may well hold true for the bulk of periodical publication; nonetheless, when we examined forty plus years of *SLJ*, we found many articles for which the "instant" is still with us.

The purpose of this volume is to provide easy access to a selection of those "instants"—those articles, bibliographies, and featured columns that are of relevance to librarians moving into a new century of service to children and young adults. These articles transcend the time of their original publication for they address issues, trends, and practices or make statements that, in our opinion, are worth preserving in a single volume.

For example, in our present period of "restructuring," curtailment of media services in state educational agencies is a reality. David Bender's (December, 1975) "State Educational Agencies, Roles and Functions" points to the necessity for state-level educational media personnel, a need that exists now as it did then. In examining "Children's Services in a Time of Change," Pauline Wilson posed six issues that have yet to be completely answered by anyone in the profession, so that article stands as a challenge. As pressure groups continue to attempt to circumscribe what authors may write and what young people may read, Nat Hentoff's passionate response, "Any Writer Who Follows Anyone Else's Guidelines Ought to Be in Advertising," to the Council on Interracial Books for Children's Publication, *Human (and Anti-Human) Values in Children's Books: A Content Rating Instrument for Educators and Concerned Parents*, has special meaning today.

In making these selections, we dealt with four areas: editorials, articles, columns, and special features. After we had isolated what we felt were "the still timely," we identified overlap articles, articles that were localized to a very specific point in time, and articles that were good but on subjects that have probably been internalized by now. From the overlap articles we selected those we thought were the most effective for today. We deleted those for the moment only, and the most likely to be in today's mainstream of practice and hardcover publication. In our third round of review we asked ourselves this question: Will this speak to new librarians who are seeking to establish an identity with their profession as well as to our contemporaries for whom a review of the past forty years will be rewarding and challenging?

The collection is divided into seven parts plus a prologue that sets the stage for the overview look at *SLJ* and an epilogue that points to the future for the field of librarianship serving youth. Section One is a collection of thirty-three essays with the heading, Editorial Positions, and allows the reader to savor some of the outstanding editorials written by the current *SLJ* Editor-in-Chief, Lillian N. Gerhardt, along with two "guest" editors. In Section Two, twenty-one articles constitute an evolving philosophy of library service to children and youth. Section Three has nine articles that describe the diversity of children and youth served in our libraries. Five articles in Section Four describe the librarians who serve children and youth through library programs. Section Five's thirty-five articles describe and define the broad range of resources that have developed in the past forty years to meet the varied needs of our diverse youth. A broad array of library programs and services is presented in seventeen articles in Section Six while in Section Seven twenty-seven articles point out the enduring issues and events that have influenced the development of library services, programs, and resources in the past forty years.

Our end project is a collection of articles and other writings that we hope will make instructive and inspirational reading for *SLJ's* audience. We further hope that this collection will serve as a reminder of the issues and concerns that persist in the mid-nineties and that need solutions for healthy library programs for children and youth.

A last word. Lest you remind us that you would not have selected what we did, the next half-century is yours.

Marilyn L. Miller
Thomas W. Downen

Prologue

A Time of Growth

The Early Years at *SLJ*

Margaret Saul Melcher

It took me years to realize how fortunate those of us were who started working in the 1950s. Born in the depression but too young to remember any of the hardships, we entered the job market in a growing economy and rode the crest of the wave to educate the larger generation born during World War II.

So it was that at the age of 22, after one year of teaching school in Omaha, I found myself taking the helm of *Junior Libraries* (later to be renamed *School Library Journal*) when the magazine itself was a mere six months old.

Recognizing that the number of school libraries was beginning to mushroom, Dan Melcher, publisher of *Library Journal*, had expanded the section on children's work that appeared in *LJ* into a monthly magazine. Gertrude Wolff who had edited the section in *LJ* was the founding editor of *Junior Libraries*. I arrived on the scene in sweltering August weather in 1955 in a then-largely-unairconditioned New York City, with just two weeks to learn the job from Gertrude before she retired.

From Nebraska to New York City

Why was I given the opportunity at all? It was a matter of supply and demand. Libraries were being added to schools at an astonishing rate. School superintendents across the country were hard pressed to find qualified personnel for these libraries. Any librarian with the background appropriate for the job as editor of *SLJ* was being courted by school systems to coordinate their library program at a much better salary than a fledgling magazine could offer. Thus, the publisher decided to gamble on a neophyte with journalistic training.

It was a six-line notice in *Scholastic Teacher* about the Radcliffe publishing course that sealed my fate. I thought it would be the ideal way to get into publishing or get it out of my system.

The Radcliffe course was only a few years old. Those were different times. As I recall, there was only one man in the class. Few of the women were serious about the course. (Many went on to Katherine Gibbs for secretarial training.) I, on the other hand, was enthralled. This was the real world. The courses were taught by executives actually working in publishing. They sent assignments in advance that were examples of the work done in their departments. We did these assignments blind, and the instructors were able to review them before they came to the class.

All the instructors urged us to come see them in New York when we started job hunting. They said they might not have jobs for us, but they always had time to see us. I arrived in New York City with two interviews set up through the course placement service, both arranged because I had training and experience in teaching. The first was at Scholastic Magazines where there was an opening for someone to write a column of advice for teens. The second was at Bowker.

Helen Wessells, the editor of *Library Journal*, interviewed me. Then we went to lunch with Frederic G. Melcher and Dan Melcher. Frederic Melcher did the talking at lunch. At the end of the meal, to my utter astonishment, he offered me the job. They hadn't asked me many questions, and I didn't think they knew much about me. It became obvious later, however, that they had already talked to all my references. He offered me the job at $70 a week or $240 a month. I of course said yes to the offer, thinking to myself, "Well if it doesn't work out, my family will be glad to have me back."

We returned to the office and Dan, who had been silent during lunch, took me up to his office to talk further. By that time my brain was functioning well enough to calculate that $70 a week adds up to more than $240 a month. I mentioned this and asked which figure was correct. He said $240 a month. During my first week on the job Dan called to say that he had gotten approval for the higher figure. Having heard so many stories about salaries of $45 a week at prestigious houses like Knopf, $70 did not sound bad. And, it was an increase over my teacher's salary the previous year.

At the Helm

During my first day on the job Dan handed me an 11-page memo he had written that morning on the bus ride into Manhattan. It was full of practical advice, almost all of which was new to me. Things like, "don't take the time to go and see someone if you can accomplish the same thing with a phone call" and "don't call if you can accomplish the same thing with interoffice mail." It was one of my major regrets in life that I lost that memo somewhere along the way.

From the beginning the magazine was mine. I had the frightening but exhilarating feeling that no one was paying any attention to what I did. Galleys went up to Dan's office for his review, and they always came back with a thorough critique from which I learned a great deal. But, they rarely came back before the issue had already been sent to press. Bowker functioned that way in those days. The editor of each project had full responsibility.

Essentially, I went looking for help when I needed it. Dan's door was usually open. He always had time for your question, though he never actually gave you an answer. Rather, he leaned back in his chair and discussed the question, analyzing it from all angles. And, I always walked out with an understanding of all the ramifications of the problem and the ability to make my own decision.

Conferences and Contacts

The librarians I met were supportive from the start. My first library conference was the meeting of the New England Library Association in Swampscott, MA, during my second month on the job. I suspect Frederic Melcher had been on the phone to his friends asking them to take care of me. I was treated royally and had a really wonderful time. (But, it would have been easier if I hadn't had to face the task of dismantling my first Maine lobster at the banquet.)

My first American Library Association conference (in Miami in 1956) was a bit more daunting because of its size. It helped greatly that Harold Roth, his wife, and two young daughters were staying in the same corridor of the hotel as I was. Harold, who was then at the East Orange Public Library in New Jersey, was one of the friendly souls Dan, Frederic, and Helen had sent me to see as part of my orientation. Lost as I was in the maelstrom of librarians, it was so good to have the Roth family greeting me warmly whenever we met.

The problem of how to use my time, which meeting to choose when there was a conflict, how to cover the one I had missed, and the lack of time to reflect on the significance of the meetings as I attended them, bothered me then and bother me to this day when I go to a large conference. I feel lost the first three days, then I hit my stride, and at the end wish I had more time. (In retrospect, that Miami 1956 meeting looks small and cozy compared to the ALA conferences of today.)

Dan did teach me the importance of planning in advance as much as possible. I learned to set up breakfast, lunch, and dinner dates with people I wanted to meet, perhaps someone who had submitted an interesting manuscript, someone who was doing something unusual in his or her library, someone who had interesting views or strong convictions on a subject. As time went on and I began developing themes for issues, I began to bring all the contributors together, a process which I think helped them and certainly me to grasp all the aspects of the theme.

Important as all this advance planning was, the serendipitous things that happen by chance at conferences were equally important. The stranger you meet at a party or a lunch counter or a taxi stand. The late night/early morning conversation, when the barriers are down, that reveals something more about a person you already knew. All these encounters opened up new possibilities. Just meeting people, having a face to match a name, made later correspondence much easier and more productive.

SLJ's Board of Advisors

I worked with a rotating board of advisors from the field who were an enormous help once they learned that I would listen. It was a technique I had stumbled upon in teaching. When word got out that I was a good listener, mothers started dropping by to chat and as a result gave me the information they wanted me to have about their children. In time, the children themselves began approaching me to say, "My mother said I should tell you ..."

In much the same way, librarians both on my board of advisors and off, started calling and writing to suggest basic articles and book lists, either offering to write the articles themselves or advising me as to who should do it. In a profession that was essentially just beginning, the basic literature had yet to be written. A great deal of that literature appeared in the pages of *School Library Journal*.

As the years progressed I was able to plan ahead, making up proposed tables of contents for issues a year in advance, a practice which allowed plenty of time for consulting with the board of advisors and meeting with contributors. Those in the New York area I saw often. Others I met with at conferences.

The circulation of the magazine grew steadily, but not, as I recall, as fast as projected. There had been considerable opposition at Bowker to creating the new publication. Those were different times. One did not make changes lightly. There was none of the pressure for growth, for the creation of new projects, that one finds in publishing today. Any change threatened the old balances and the old alliances. Now, of course, *SLJ* is the leader in the Bowker publications.

Assessing the true readership of *SLJ* in those days was complicated by the fact that in addition to appearing as a separate magazine on its own, it was bound into *Library Journal* so that all *LJ* subscribers automatically received it. There was a feeling at Bowker that the children's department was an integral part of a public library, one which did not always get the attention from library administrators that it deserved and that to remove coverage of children's work from the pages of *LJ* would be a disservice to children's librarians. As long as the material was physically within *Library Journal*, an administrator might at least notice it as he leafed through an issue.

In truth, I didn't pay much attention to matters of circulation. I knew I was getting better, and the magazine was getting better. And, we were very busy. In those days Louise Davis edited the book reviews on her own, and I did all of the editorial work with no assistance.

Covering the Issues

The balancing of each issue so that it contained material of interest to both school librarians and to children's librarians in public libraries was always a major concern. To some extent, because the school library movement was new and growing fast, the issues that needed covering were easier to spot. Often we were saying things for the first time in *SLJ*.

With public library work, we were to some extent restating rules and highlighting new and interesting programming. At the time, the two areas were perhaps closer to one another in intent than they are now. Or, so it seems in retrospect.

It was in recognition of the fact that the magazine had two constituencies that it was originally named *Junior Libraries*. No one ever really liked the name. It was not immediately self-explanatory. It certainly did not appear to encompass service to young adults or high school libraries. As the years went on, I became increasingly dissatisfied with the name. Finally I became convinced that the name *School Library Journal* was a better fit.

It was clear by then that the growth in circulation was coming almost entirely from the school library arena. The name change was probably inevitable and would have happened without me, but I think the powers-that-be were relieved when I took the initiative in writing the memo that recom-

mended the change. The board of directors accepted my proposal immediately, and I wrote an editorial explaining the name change to the subscribers.

I stayed at *SLJ* for six years and at Bowker another two years, during which I did research and troubleshooting. Since then, life has taken me far afield. My focus now is on service to the Hispanic population, so I have little contact today with children's and school libraries.

It was exciting to be at *SLJ* in the beginning, to have the opportunity to grow with the magazine, to meet the pioneers like Anne Carroll Moore and May Massee, to watch the school library field develop, and to see Mary Gaver at Rutgers, for example, train future school librarians, help them find positions, and guide them as they learned to cope with school administrations. It was a time of growth, a time of hope, a time when people were very conscious they were shaping the future.

Part One

Editorial Positions

As any reader of editorials knows, the journalistic prerogative of the editor is sweeping. When reporting the news and selecting and organizing content, objectivity and rational behavior are the rules of the game. But the editor of a newspaper or magazine is allowed one special "perk"—the privilege of sounding off in one little corner of a particular printed world. There, bias may show. The balloons of the pompous may be pricked. Governments may be chided, heroes and heroines idealized, and local customs and foibles held up for reexamination. Opinionated retorts and indignation are permissible and expected.

In her editorials for *SLJ*, Lillian N. Gerhardt has done it all. She has verbally spanked ALA presidents, rebuked librarians for clinging to silly and outdated practices and procedures, reminded us of our history, and challenged us to renew our concern for ethical behavior. She has chided the Queen of England, the ALA's Task Force on Women, book publishers, and the sacred cow of author visits to libraries and schools. She has urged us to be better in our chosen profession, and she has used the pen effectively to gain recognition for the importance of good library service to children and young adults.

Here is a representative sample of the poignant points made on the editorial pages of *SLJ* in the past years and signed "LNG." Upon the occasion of the presentation of the Grolier Award to Lillian, Roger Sutton stated in an interview with her: "I think the most feared initials in libraryland are LNG at the end of your editorials, oft influential, oft infamous . . . " Her response was, "Wretch. I prefer to think of them as the most welcome." (Sept., 1995, p. 122.)

And here, too, last in this section, are two guest editorials. The first is a triumphant report of a "Dream Come True" by Mary Virginia Gaver in December 1962, that illustrates that "to achieve a worthwhile goal one must begin by dreaming." It tells of the over-a-million-dollar grant to AASL for the development of school libraries, the Knapp project. The second is an editorial that is worth repeating. "Shock—Past, Present, Future," a guest editorial by Regina Minudri in March, 1973, stands more than two decades later as a bit of sound advice to young librarians beginning their professional careers in service to youth in the mid-nineties.

A Spring for Selection

Back in the dear, dead days of such as Dewey and Dana and Mudge, when library service was often called Library Economics, our pioneers gave themselves joyously to the idea of spring cleaning. Their spring conference papers show that they pleasured in the details of scheduling spring inventories. There were treatises on the advantages of vacuums over dust cloths. Recipes for spiffing up spotty leather bindings were exchanged. Editorials prodded everybody to tidy up their libraries. *SLJ* believes its readers are clean clear through all year, but as a gesture to a fine old library custom, we urge that you give in to spring and clean up, possibly dispose of, your old materials selection statement.

Selection statements are like insurance policies or marriage certificates. After they've been acquired, they're seldom, if ever, re-read. Read yours over and you might be appalled at what you once promised to do. Maybe you've changed your mind. Perhaps the terminology employed is vague to the point of hypocrisy. Maybe what once appeared to be the loophole through which you intended to slip in a defense against censorship is the very gap through which censors can get in.

Examples of old public library selection statements show that some had completely committed themselves to the full curriculum support responsibilities of school libraries, either because school libraries didn't exist in their locales or those that did exist were amateur, unfunded rooms misnamed as libraries. If your written selection statement is that old, and area school library service is now a fact, then this is a good time to rewrite that statement to spell out the extent of cooperation and, we can hope, the mutual interdependence of the two types of libraries.

It's not necessary to hunt hard for a term hypocritically vague enough to serve any but a censorship purpose. There is one embedded in *School Library Bill of Rights'* second point. It asserts that one of the responsibilities of the school media center is:

> To provide materials that will support the curriculum taking into consideration the individual's needs, and the varied interests, abilities, socioeconomic backgrounds, and maturity levels of the students served.

Which schools' "maturity levels"? As applied to junior and senior high school selection, that's a gold-plated hint to censors that religious criticism, political dissent, and sex information will be handled with tongs, if at all, for patrons under 18 years of age.

Intellectual freedom is an absolute, There must be an agreed upon age at which it can begin or school libraries and public YA services must acknowledge that they actively connive at the restriction of intellectual freedom. So, define when a child is no longer a child either physically or mentally. The age could be arbitrarily designated as 12 or 13 years. The major religions allow full adult participation by then. Why not libraries? Because there is an unacknowledged agreement between the educational bureaucracy and library services to bow to the unnatural prolongation of childhood and adolescence, not only to restrain sexual activity, but to suppress and control the sometimes startling spurts of growth in intellectual capacity that occur during the early adolescent stage. "Maturity levels"? What rot. This has to be changed, for librarians cannot continue this impossible spraddling in selection statements between pious pronouncements against censorship in one set of phrases while inviting it with the "maturity levels" dodge.

There are sets of loophole words that present equal problems in misapplication or misinterpretation. Time was when the presence of terms such as "the best books," "the highest literary quality," and "the finest ethical standards" seemed only an unchallengeable affirmation of the good, the true, and the beautiful. Those terms are selection goals, however, not guarantees of the freedom to select materials for the practical use of a diverse audience. The novel that draws fire may be merely adequate, not "the best," and most vulnerable when the selection promise is "the highest literary quality." It usually draws fire because some group's concept of "the finest ethical standards" has been questioned. These terms can be and have been used against the librarians who wrote them under the impression that they had thus prevented insistence on the insertion of useless materials in their collections.

Censors use words to get and keep library materials out, not in. Why should your selection statement arm them with the words?

Complacent Clichés

The rhetoric standard to any local, state, regional, or national library association conference can temporarily unseat the wits of even the most stable librarian. After the speakers from other fields have flattered, the association's outgoing officers pointed with pride, and the incumbents viewed with alarm, it often takes days for the librarian who listened to cast off the megalomaniacal notion that libraries are the secret center of the universe and that librarians are on the verge of general recognition as the governing elite. But, fall conference time is nearly upon us, and we can fight off contagious convictions of grandeur by recognizing some of the infection-carrying phrases.

—The school library is the nerve center of the school . . .

This siren song is most often sung by speakers who come from departments of education. It's a difficult ideal for librarians to resist since it was and is *their* idea. No record exists of any of the many library audiences, repeatedly subjected to this line, rising up in wrath against the educators or administrators who mouth it—though this may be the year when it could happen. In this period of budget cuts and removal of staff, *SLJ* would be happy to report any catcalls, boos, and derisive questions which send a local school administrator cowering behind a lectern, further empty compliments undelivered.

—The school librarian is a full partner in the education team . . .

Librarians repeat this as though it were a fact. Library audiences accept it without question from the educators who come to speak at library conferences. The general public may even believe it if they ever get wind of it. Inexperienced school librarians often set out on their first jobs convinced that this is so. *SLJ*'s lead article this month ("The Great Certification Caper," p. 31-35) may help cure the idea that this ideal is the reality. Many state certification requirements appear to have been decided without reference to what librarians think is nec-essary to their education for school library service. "Full partners" don't have their skills defined and restricted by people in other specialties. Too often, the certification of school librarians effectively denies that they possess any skills as important as, or in any way equal to, those of classroom teachers. The various library associations, all the way up to ALA's American Association of School Librarians, have ignored this—they don't even have their own statement on certification.

—Innovation is the key to successful library service today . . .

"Innovation" has long been a favorite word in education and more recently in library service. It only means "something new or different introduced." Speakers who employ the word are unquestionably earnest, honest, and eager for better services to children and young people. Nevertheless, they should be held responsible for showing *why* something new or different is necessarily as good as, or better than, a traditional library service—and questioned about the connection their innovation has, if any, with library functions. For instance, last year both school and public librarians found on their conference agendas a batch of programs devoted to how to make films with students, lending loaded cameras, and editing the results. No one raised any questions about whether or not film-making ventures are an essential or peripheral library function. Instead, the questions were financial ("How do we? Where do we get funds?") and not philosophical.

This kind of rhetoric is actually dangerous. Surely, much of it reflects the basic goals and ideals of the library profession. But, instead of sitting back, collectively basking in the glory of empty words thrown out by speakers, librarians should be working together to produce meaningful realities. The time spent at library conferences is unproductive when the complacent clichés can go annually unchallenged. There is no firm evidence that such conferences cause permanent brain damage, but the suspicion remains.

A Blush for Dr. Bell

If the U.S. Secretary of Transportation warned the Motor Vehicle Manufacturers Association of the U.S. to go back to the production of Tin Lizzies as the best possible means of automotive transportation, he'd probably be driven from office as an ignorant nut.

In effect, this is what U.S. Commissioner of Education Terrel H. Bell, told the School Division of the Association of American Publishers (AAP) and children's book publishers when he urged a return to textbooks of the type and with the values of the 19th century McGuffey Readers. He also asked for more trade books like Frank Baum's *The Wizard of Oz*, published in 1900. (See *SLJ*'s lead news story.)

Dr. Bell will probably not be stripped of office. We have no history of removing educational bureaucrats for demonstrations of semiliteracy. Yet, Dr. Bell is potentially more dangerous than that hypothetical U.S. Secretary of Transportation who does not, after all, influence funds used for the purchase of cars as Dr. Bell influences funds spent for books in schools.

In describing the values he endorses in *The Wizard of Oz*, Dr. Bell said the book, " . . . has always struck me as about the right combination of suspense, which naturally appeals to children, and the happy ending that takes the edge off the spooky parts. This children's classic is a far cry from some of the current juvenile literature that appears to emphasize violence—and obscenity—and moral judgments that run counter to tradition—all in the name of keeping up with the real world."

Aside from failing to designate which books he's attacking, a cheap and irresponsible critical ploy, we are forced to question how long it's been since Dr. Bell poked into *Oz*. Dorothy, the Scarecrow, the Tin Woodsman, and the Cowardly Lion solve their dangerous encounters with fantastical creatures through murder and mayhem. Magic is reserved for their transportation. At the end of the Yellow Brick Road, they at last confront the Wizard and unmask a frightened faker, who had lightly endangered their lives to save his own neck, who is only too glad to fly away leaving a stuffed pinhead in control. Dr. Bell needs to read *Oz* again—and closely. His recommendation verges on unconscious political satire embarrassing to the administration that appointed him.

Of the McGuffey Readers, Dr. Bell told the textbook publishers these books " . . . stressed the values that Americans in the late 1800's wanted to instill in their children—patriotism, integrity, honesty, industry, temperance, courage, and politeness. We could use more emphasis on some of those values today." All that is true enough, but it's far from a complete review of the McGuffeys' values. Let's not forget the materialism of those textbooks; their sentimentality; their relentless insistence that society had no responsibility for the poor, the starving, the unemployed; their fulsome romanticization of the farmer at just the point we ceased to be an agricultural nation; their preference for literature in translation; and their failure to include the great American writers and poets of their time. McGuffey's Readers did not supply children the intellectual equipment needed for their own time nor present the social issues the children who used them grew up to contend with; McGuffey's Readers fled the real world of the years (1836 to 1890) in which they were published. Today's children can't. They still have to solve problems that McGuffey's Readers ignored.

Dr. Bell went on to say, "I think the children's book publishing industry, and the schools, need to chart a middle course between the scholar's legitimate claim to academic freedom in presenting new knowledge and social commentary on the one hand, and the legitimate expectations of parents that schools will respect their moral and ethical values on the other."

Aside from the dismally obvious fact that there is no single set of firmly agreed upon moral and ethical values among the parents in our ever-boiling, never-quite-melting, melting pot—Dr. Bell has thus implied that no boats would be rocked, no controversies would arise, if only trade book publishing goes back to the bloodless, conscience-clear murders of *Oz* and textbook publishers go back to the editorial selection methods of McGuffey, which allowed for the complete absence of any mention of the Civil War. The stench—from the moral and ethical values inherent in such guide books to such a middle course—is strangling.

Many librarians subscribe to the idea, "I disagree with what you say, but I will defend to the death your right to say it." In this instance, *SLJ* abstains from such defense. We recommend that none of our subscribers sacrifice their lives for Dr. Bell's nonexistent right to direct the content of new textbooks or new trade books. His book judgments aren't worth dying for either. A blush for him will do.

Selection "Guidelines" (Note Quotes)

Last month on *SLJ*'s editorial page, intent upon bellowing "Tally Ho" after *The Hornbook*'s mad suggestion that books for children enjoy and may be ready to begin to exert influence on general letters in this country, I made only passing reference to the current growth of groups with special messages to sell who see and are eager to seize on children's books as merely convenient vehicles for propagandizing and proselytizing their causes.

For instances: The American Library Association's Social Responsibilities Round Table Task Force on Gay Liberation has just distributed "guidelines" to publishers, and reviewers, on how and how not to present gay people in books for children and young adults. This comes with the bland suggestion that homosexuals be consulted on any ensuing books to insure that negative stereotypes of gay people are avoided. The Council on Interracial Books for Children, Inc. (CIBC) has turned the preparation of "guidelines" on how and how not to present racial and ethnic minority groups into a sort of cottage industry, for which the Carnegie Corporation has given it funds totalling $535,000 over the last four years; the latest $300,000 is to establish a resource and publication center on racism and sexism in children's literature and instructional materials. (Among CIBC's dubious creation of criteria is the flat dictum that no author of one race has any right to create characters of another race.) Study groups of the American Association of University Women, and the National Organization for Women, flushed with victories over written-to-order/ revised-to-suit textbooks, are arriving at their local public and school libraries urging or demanding that their textbook "guidelines" be willy-nilly applied to the retention or selection of general trade children's books and non-print. And, the patriotic groups. And the religious groups. And . . . And . . .

All of the causes listed above may be dear to your hearts or central to your selection problems. But, none of the above is indulged in adult trade publishing, and none of the above has anything to do with the authors' freedom to write, the publishers' freedom to publish, the librarians' freedom to select, or the goal of providing a wide variety of information to younger readers.

These "do's and dont's" lists are bids for creative control, evaluation control, and purchasing control. The critical issues are political, not literary. The justification offered is the development of humane values in children—an admirable aim, but never forget that the means urged are propaganda, and should be recognized as such even if, *especially* if, you agree with the propaganda.

Maybe the Carnegie Corporation could be wheedled into giving half a million dollars to ALA's Children's Services Division (CSD) to establish a resource center to collect, analyze, and develop evaluation criteria for judging all the "guidelines" for writing for children produced by all the special interest groups. Until then, here are *SLJ*'s:

1. Read all "guidelines" offered.
2. Do not weep, curse, or laugh; "guideliners" have feelings and pay taxes, too.
3. Find out what the organization's total program involves, who supplies their money, what they spend it on.
4. Regard with grave distrust any "guidelines" produced by an agency outside library service that promotes cause over artistic or literary merit or accuracy in presentation.
5. Regard with even greater distrust any "guidelines" produced inside library service that promotes cause over artistic or literary merit or accuracy in presentation; fanatics with library degrees are often at least five percent more knowledgeable about children's book content and two decibels louder than any member of the general public.
6. Create a file for the "guidelines" but do not call the file "Selection Guidelines" lest in your absence your newest or dumbest assistant should stumble on it and think it's policy. Call it: "Beware of Geeks Who Come Bearing Gifts." This will add the only literary touch to the file's content.

Moonshine

*W*e need to take a hard look at the rights of the young to access to information. It is an issue we have avoided for far too long. And what seems to have become our traditional stance—that it is up to parents to control the reading and viewing of their offspring—may be politically expedient but it isn't particularly principled.

The arrival of compulsory education provided one escape route for those children whose parents seemed determined to establish a dynasty of ignorance. Some parents still struggle to protect their children from education but, by and large, society has come to accept education as among the rights of the young. Society usually does things for selfish reasons, however, and this may be no more than acceptance that the need for an educated next generation to continue or improve upon what we have wrought is so important that it must even supersede the rather despotic rights we have customarily accorded parents.

The question for us, though, is do we then accept that the child's or young adult's right of access to knowledge stops when the school doors close? Do we believe that education happens only in school, that libraries are not educational, that they are less important, less relevant than schools? If we do not believe these things, then how come we do not protest as strongly when an individual parent bars the door of the library (or the adult section) to his or her child as when the governor of a state stands in the schoolhouse door and bars entry to children who seek nothing more dangerous than an equal crack at a decent education?

Something is wrong here, either with the consistency of our principles, or with our belief in the educational potential of libraries. Or is it really just a failure of nerve? Even the flag has had its detractors these past couple of decades; even apple pie perhaps has its rivals in the coke and the hamburger, but motherhood (let's not be sexist—fatherhood, too) is a fearsome opponent to challenge. Nevertheless, anything that pretends to be a national information policy must address the needs and rights and problems of all people—and all people includes the young—Eric Moon, ALA Presidential Inaugural Address, Detroit '77

In the body of his inaugural speech, Eric Moon called for the development of a national policy on freedom of access to information, the policy to be developed by the American Library Association. Moon wants an "umbrella policy," a single statement of principle that would cover the many areas of information services that are represented in ALA.

Moon's suggestion that ALA mount a campaign against the authority of individual parents over the intellectual—as well as the physical and moral—development of their own children has headline possibilities of a particularly destructive nature based, as it is, on the dubious assumption that only an ignorant parent exercises information control over his or her minor children.

Before librarians take to roasting Mom and Pop, it is better to remember that librarians, not individual parents:

- write the rules restricting reading rooms to adult use
- issue special cards that limit by age group access to materials
- close collections for "adult use only"
- impose the regulations for library loans that prevent minors' use of this service.

ALA's own house is not in good enough order on the issue of services to youth to win any attack on the power of the family unit. Instead of the tyranny of total tidiness required by a single statement on access to information of a "one-size-fits-all" pronouncement, there are more reasonable avenues to corrective action in regard to information services to minors that have not been explored by ALA or its presidents:

- ALA could join with elements of the American Bar Association through a joint committee in working to clarify which (if any) of the U.S. Constitution's guarantees apply to those below voting age, especially the First Amendment.
- ALA could endorse and publicize the efforts of physicians within the American Medical Association who are attempting to insure that minors seeking medical advice enjoy the confidentiality that adults get.

Granted, Moon's intentions toward full access to information for children and young adults are good. But, his suggestion for how to accomplish this is not Moon at his shining clearest. We can rejoice that a president of ALA has so loudly embraced the concerns of librarians working for and with the young. But, there's no sense in allowing ourselves to get hugged to death.

Moonshine: Second Run

Dear Lillian:

Differences over issues are to be expected, even among friends. Indeed, they are healthy and often productive, since they keep the debate open. But accused of a lack of clarity, I am forced to go another round in an attempt to overcome misunderstanding.

I grant that the restrictions listed in your "Moonshine" editorial (*SLJ*, Sept. 1977, p. 9) have been imposed by librarians, but the real question is why? Have librarians erected these barriers to protect kids from the sharp corners of life as it is, or have they been building trenches in which they will themselves be safe from the ire of censorious parents?

What, in my unclear way, I was trying to do was issue a call for courage, a plea that librarians act in a way that demonstrates real belief in that section of the *Library Bill of Rights* which says, "The rights of an individual to the use of a library should not be denied or abridged because of his (sic) age . . .

I think many librarians will not so act while they have the comforting escape clause provided in the interpretation of the *Library Bill of Rights* (entitled "Restricted Access to Library Materials") that "The American Library Association holds that it is the parent—and only the parent—who may restrict his (sic) children—and only *his* (sic) children—in reading matter." That is what I was referring to as one of those "rather despotic rights we have customarily accorded parents," and I assert that we cannot believe that statement and *also* believe in the right of *all* people to access to knowledge.

I concede, as I did in the Detroit speech, that this is a politically dangerous stance, but tactical expediency is the traditional enemy of principle and I still hold firmly with that ringing last sentence of the Freedom to Read Statement: "Freedom itself is a dangerous way of life, but it is ours." And us (for me) includes kids. I think we need to get on their side and defend *their* right to be exposed to the dangers of freedom from intellectual captivity.

Eric Moon
President, ALA

Dear Eric:

By the terms you chose to employ in restating the position you took on free access to libraries by minors in your inaugural address to ALA, it is obvious that you want a multifaceted issue in library service to be neatly divided between two camps of librarians: those who are responsive to your urgings are courageous, the others (by implication) craven; those who act upon your suggestion act from principle, while those who reject your suggestion do so from mere "tactical expediency."

First, it is impossible to equate your suggestion that librarians declare war on parental authority with a "call to courage." Whether or not you or I or any other outside observers agree with the parents who exert this authority over information access for their own children, their right to do so is inherent in free societies and absent in those where parental authority has been arrogated by functionaries of institutions of the state.

Second, a sense of protection toward children in their early and middle childhood years is consonant with adult responsibility in our society and has been an expected, accepted part of the librarians' unwritten social contract with the taxpayers who underwrite library services to children. Before this social contract is torn up, it would be wise to poll the members of ALA today on what they think is the proper exercise of adult responsibility toward children in terms of library services for them and at what age this protectiveness should cease.

It's not *all minors* who are victimized by regulations restricting access, it's those "kids" who make up the undefined age mass of "young adults." If ALA could agree on the age at which the "young adult" minor should have full access to all library held information, it would be easier to explain a national information policy to the public. Without such internal ALA membership agreement it would be impossible to achieve a national information policy that all librarians can support in good conscience or put into practice in their libraries.

Since a significant number of librarians have resisted for ten years ALA's policy on full access regardless of age, the soundness of the policy as it is now worded ought to be reexamined before any ALA president condemns the resistant librarians as either fainthearted or unprincipled.

Lillian N. Gerhardt
Editor-in-Chief, *SLJ*

Teeth for the "Professionally Nameless"

"I've always thought that the most important thing is to get libraries established in schools whatever the name they may be called afterwards—'information centers,' 'instructional materials centers,' 'library/media centers.' Whatever they're called, we know that they are *libraries* and that schools need them to fulfill an essential education function. But, I'm concerned now over this increasing pressure to drop the words 'library' and 'librarians' from our descriptors and from our professional standards."

This quotation is from a short conversation with Frances Henne, Professor Emeritus of Columbia University's School of Library Service. Ms. Henne has been associated as chief activist, supporter, or mentor with all the projects for the forward progress of school library service in our time. When she expresses a concern, we do well to listen.

"I'm concerned about the public understanding and support. The terms 'media' and 'media specialist' are not immediately understood, even within the profession. 'Media' connotes some form of mass communications and 'media specialist' evokes thoughts of some titans of broadcast journalism. These terms aren't communicating the idea of what we are about. Libraries have always collected more than just books. The word 'library' still works."

The question of what school libraries should be called is not a new concern for Ms. Henne. In the 1960 *Standards for School Library Programs*, for which she provided leadership, we find on page 13 the following caveat:

> The word *library* is rich in tradition, meaning, and usage, and for at least sixty years, if not longer, the definition of *school library* has always been and will continue to be, flexible in its program of services and in the scope of materials of communication contained in its collections, as it meets the changing needs of the school that it serves. A school library does not have to change its name to embrace new materials and new uses of types of materials any more than a school has to call itself by some other name to indicate that it is a continuously growing social institution.

The pressure to drop the terms "library" and "librarians" comes from the Association of Educational Technology (AECT) and that organization has been holding the American Association of School Librarians' (AASL) feet to the fire this year about its decision to use the term 'library' in its official correspondence. AECT considers 'media center' and 'media specialist' progress in definition, according to its Executive Director Howard B. Hitchens in his editorial in *Audiovisual Instruction* (June/July 1977, p. 52) castigating AASL for inserting the word 'library' before these terms.

Ms. Henne in her keynote address to the International Association of School Librarianship in 1976 said, "Collectively, school librarians are overnamed persons and hence, professionally, nameless. . . . An urgent plea is made here that we use *school librarian* and *school library*, terminology that is employed by the International Association of School Librarianship and still remains in the title of the American Association of School Librarians. . . . Unified support of unified media programs by the two national associations that jointly prepared the last two statements of national standards or guidelines has not fully materialized, and in the kind of competitive autonomy that frequently prevails, it is my belief that the American Association of School Librarians has been the one to suffer. This element of competition is by no means restricted to the national associations."

In her address, Ms. Henne touched briefly on some of the areas of competition that are really at stake in this pushing and hauling over terminology. These include lobbying and legislation for funding support of school libraries; the content of the education required for school library service; and the certification of school librarians with particular attention to career ladders. The competition to which Ms. Henne refers as a delicate point of contention can be stated baldly as competition for jobs, the control of jobs, and the control of entry to and advancement on those jobs—in *school* library service.

AASL has been cooperative with AECT to the point of near total surrender of the chief identification school librarians have with the rest of library service and the tradition from which school library service came into being. It's high time to take a firm stand against having the time-honored title *librarian* erased from the vocabularies of those who practice at library service in schools.

AASL needs to formulate a firm answer to AECT's presumptuous insistence that *librarian* and *library service* aren't good enough to describe school librarians that collect and circulate nonprint materials as well as books, periodicals, and pamphlets. AASL ought to bite back.

AASL might borrow Frances Henne's teeth.

How to Show the Queen

I was terribly disappointed in the Queen of England the other day. *The New York Times* ran a picture of her with a silly big grin on her puss and reported that she'd just been declared an "honorary man" by the Near Eastern countries which she plans to visit soon. According to the news brief, this "honorary manhood" will allow her to speak with heads of states in countries where women are neither to be heard nor seen. The story went on to note that the Queen has equipped herself with some scarf arrangements to cover her face as the custom of the Moslem states require of women.

If ever a regal grand gesture were called for by a bona fide queen, Elizabeth II's projected trip is it. Queen Elizabeth I, were she alive today would be a feminist, of course. She would have either cancelled the trip or set its standards. Even Queen Victoria, though embarrassingly inclined to puff up Prince Albert with a monotonous Little Me refrain, would in these times have the good sense to say, "We are not amused by this reduction in Our status." With such self-assured predecessors, women all over the world should be able to expect better of Elizabeth II than this glad rush of hers into expensively dowdy purdah.

Where Elizabeth II may stand personally on the issue of the equality of the sexes is not a matter of public record, which is too bad. We will probably never be told why she has chosen thus to cooperate in her own degradation. But, the question can probably be answered in a word: Money.

I imagine that Elizabeth II's advisors met any objection she may have raised to "honorary manhood," or to the assumption of nose veils with admonitions about the importance of trade agreements and oil as more important than symbolic gestures in support of personal beliefs. I'll just bet that one among them said, "Grand gestures can be frightfully costly, Ma'am," and, "When in Rome, etc."

We're hearing the same sort of arguments in support of returning ALA's Midwinter Meetings to Chicago before Illinois ratifies the Equal Rights Amendment. (See *SLJ*'s Midwinter '79 report in this issue). A Chicago hotel has hinted that they might sue ALA unless ALA reverses its decision to keep Midwinter away until Illinois joins the ERA states. This threat is based on a letter of intent, not a contract, and apparently seven months warning of ALA's change in intent is interpreted in hotel circles as short notice. Soon, ALA members will receive ballots to vote by mail on whether to fall in line with the hotel's desire for their return or to stand behind their support for ERA.

I fervently hope that ALA's members do better in their stated support of women's rights than the Queen of England did when confronted by the matter. I hope they vote heavily against returning ALA's Midwinter Meeting to Chicago.

Some friends of mine in ALA disagree with me because they believe that a letter of intent to a hotel is a contract and contract promises must be kept in spite of hell. But I think a letter of intent is just that. If it were a contract it would be called a contract. Other friends in ALA are afraid that any lawsuit would be more costly than ALA's treasury can easily bear in terms of legal fees—whatever the outcome of the suit. That's true. But, I think it would be money well spent to find out whether a big boarding house can over-ride the decisions of the chief organization in American library service about where its future meetings must be held.

Over 85 percent of ALA's members are women. Many have experienced or witnessed unequal pay to women in library services or have been passed over for advancement in favor of men less well-qualified. Most can benefit from the promises in the proposed Equal Rights Amendment.

1. Equality of rights under the law shall not be denied or abridged by the United States on account of sex.
2. The Congress shall have the power to enforce by appropriate legislation the provisions of this article.
3. This amendment shall take effect two years after the date of ratification.

The Equal Rights Amendment requires some grand gestures in support. Grand gestures can be costly, but only grand people can make them. I hope that ALA's members can show Elizabeth II how it's done.

The Reluctant Market

Of all the terms in daily use among publishers that seem most offensive, especially when used to describe the selection responsibilities of librarians, the term "market" has to go at the top of the list. Professional groups apparently resent this descriptive reduction to their cash control. I've seen the same sort of collective wince race around audiences of classroom teachers when publishers or producers herd the group and its spendable bucks into one of their "marketplace" categories.

Nevertheless, the librarians in schools or public libraries, who buy the books for children and young adults issued by the juvenile departments of publishing houses, are "the market" and always have been since juvenile publishing began in this country over 60 years ago. The only other buyers in library service whose expressed wants, needs, and standards (as demonstrated through orders placed) are as carefully studied by their suppliers are reference librarians whose willingness to purchase a new reference tool underwrites its profitability to its publisher.

This is not true of the impact of libraries' purchasers of adult books—except on college and university presses. The fiction and non-fiction titles offered on general trade publishers' lists might reach a break-even point through library sales, but their profits rest on sales to the individual book buyers. But, for general trade juvenile publishers, the sales of new children's books to libraries account for 70 percent to 85 percent of all their sales each year. The sales of so-called young adult novels for older children or young teens and the high-interest/low-vocabulary fiction and non-fiction, now published for this indeterminate age range, are nearly 100 percent to libraries.

So, the librarians who buy books for children and early adolescents are a targeted "market" for the 2000 new titles the juvenile trade publishers have, on the average, issued in hardcover each year for the last ten years. The sales record of a juvenile title to libraries increases its price in subsidiary sales as a paperback, a movie, or a television show. The release of the movie or TV program based on the book inevitably initiates or renews young readers' interests in the original edition or the paperback reprint, stimulating library reorders. This spurt in sales to libraries encourage publishers to find more

of the same sorts of books . . . and so the cycle goes. Librarians buying for youngsters are the focal point in the process.

Even when school librarians and children's public librarians are buying in groups, each one has a small individual budget and responsibility for relatively small unit collections. These librarians tend not to think of themselves as enormous influences on the quality and kinds of books that get published in hardcover and resold in other formats—but such is indeed the case. If, for two years, all the adult services departments in public libraries stopped buying new general trade books for adults, the quality and types of adult books would not be affected at all. But, if all public and school libraries stopped buying the new general trade books issued as juveniles for two years, the effect on juvenile publishing would be devastating. The 15 percent to 30 percent of the sales reported by a few houses as made through bookstores would not permit juvenile publishers to survive at their current size.

For all that is quite impressive about juvenile publishing in the United States, as compared to publishing for young readers in other countries, librarians in this country can walk tall because their dollar clout supports these publishing directions. For all that continues to be profitable but unpraiseworthy in our juvenile publishing, librarians need to be reminded that their combined dollar clout is still the chief (and sometimes the only) market at which the books are aimed. The institutional sales record will dictate whether or not more of the same will continue to be published and re-formatted.

When children's and young adult librarians cringe away from their influence as a marketplace and pick up the weak, "Who am I to judge . . . ?" argument (so briskly condemned by Linda Silver on p. 35 of our January issue), it's a naive refusal to exercise the power for good that accrues to the ability to expend library funds.

Juvenile publishing is not a juggernaut racing to run down powerless librarians. Their collective judgments are the juggernaut that faces juvenile publishing. What librarians buy in large numbers provides the momentum for more—the good or the sleazy.

You are the market, and you will get more of what you are willing to pay for.

Sulking to Oblivion

A successful sulk is very hard to pull off. It requires reliance on undependable equipment in the form of caring reactions from others. First, you must have someone who will be sure to notice that you are maintaining a moody silence. Then, that person must be relied upon to care enough (or to tell somebody else who cares enough) to go to extraordinary lengths to give you your own way. Some children can successfully sulk their parents into submission. Lovers occasionally survive the tactic's risks of inducing terminal boredom or fatal indifference. However, in twenty-five years of closely observing library association work, I have yet to see an individual or a group sulk their way to achievement, although it is attempted with what ought to be considered embarrassing frequency.

The latest, most startling, example of organized sulking comes by way of ALA's Social Responsibility Round Table's Task Force on Women. (See p. 11). It has issued a call to its 500 members to boycott ALA's 1980 Midwinter Meeting in Chicago, urging them to write their committee chairs or divisional presidents to tell them that they cannot "in good conscience" carry on ALA's work in a state that has not ratified the Equal Rights Amendment. This, despite the fact that an overwhelming majority of ALA's membership voted that this Midwinter Meeting return to Chicago to avoid a lawsuit threatened by the Palmer House Hotel if ALA failed to live up to a letter of intent to hire its facilities for housing this session.

As sulks go, this one seems particularly embarrassing because it obstinately refuses the principle of majority rule. It also clings to the mistaken notion that absence will make other hearts grow fonder of a particular cause that requires responsible presence and persuasive spokespersons to represent support for ERA and women's interests in every unit of ALA—not just its Council.

My guess, based on experience of chairs and officers in library associations, is that this sulk will affect the future appointments of any members whose absence from a working committee, because of a passionate but narrow dedication to a single cause not wholly within ALA's power to resolve, impedes the forward efforts of ALA's myriad concerns with the promotion of library service.

There are some other forms of sulking employed in library organizations that deserve discussion. My favorite is the Dramatic Departure. This occurs when an individual or group decides that the speaker has been offensive. Reticules are rattled. Folding chairs are banged aside. Toes are stepped on. Heels are clumped down. Exit doors are slammed. The result, of course, is that the field has been left to the speaker, who is secretly delighted that those who might be most challenging won't be part of any question and answer session. Dramatic Departures simply don't work, because they never get on the record.

Then, there is the Awful Silence. As a stratagem in library association activities, this one is the most corrosive of progress. The people who practice the Awful Silence never rise to express their dissent in open meetings, never respond to an oral or written request for their opinions, and never telephone or write about their concerns to their officers. They brood aloud, only to each other, that their interests aren't being served and discuss the prospect of quiet nonrenewal of membership as the best method of bringing the organization to its knees. Dropping membership, without telling anybody in charge why, is the outer limit of the ineffectiveness of the people who practice the Awful Silence. It insures that they will never be heard.

A lighter form of sulk practiced in library association circles can be called the Bypassed Pout. It goes this way: "I've never been asked to serve on such and such a committee." Appointing officers should never be left in doubt about what it is any member would like to do. They are usually too busy to notice who's hanging about looking sullen. As soon as they are elected, they need letters indicating two or three possible committees on which you promise to spend all your waking spare time. What they get as they leave office and have no more appointments to give is, "You never asked me to serve . . . " (I once overheard Augusta Baker unapologetically turn aside such a sulk with this brisk advice: "Well, honey, remember I told you it's just like marriage—if you want a proposal, you better make darn sure *somebody* knows you're interested.")

Last by not least is the Non-Join sulk. This one is based in the crackpot conviction that a library association that is not providing programs or supporting projects that reflect your interests will, without your vocal and energetic presence, somehow take notice and reform itself. It's never happened yet.

In fact, nothing ever yet advanced the cause of library service in this country on the basis of No-show/Non-speak.

"Take Her Up Tenderly..."

At a recent lecture in New York City the speaker, in a clumsy effort to compliment his audience of librarians, said that he could see no "... dowdy, little old maids with their hair in buns and their lips screwed up to say Shhh!" among his lovely listeners. He said he thought it was high time this old girl and the heavy shadow she'd cast as the awful image of women in library service were, at long last, laid to rest. Isn't that a thoughty thought?

However, we should not let Ms. Stere O. Type go to her Long Lost Library in the Sky without a statement on her genesis and development.

She was paid just enough to keep her shabbily genteel—hence the plain, dark, heavy clothes, always mistakenly believed, by working women of the past, to outlast changing fashion, to hide grime, and to resist wear and tear. That's where "dowdy" came from. . . .

Her personal budget did not permit weekly or even monthly fees for professional hairdressing—hence the severe coiffures, easy to manage alone. That's where the "buns" came from. . . .

If she married, it was considered reasonable by her public library or her school administration to dismiss her because a married woman's place was in the home. If she stayed single but was even so much as suspected of taking an active interest in the opposite sex, she could be dismissed on the grounds of moral turpitude. That's where the "old maid" part came from. . . .

Finally, her library bosses regarded silence as essential to the act of reading, so her ability to maintain quiet became the measure of her efficiency. That's where the "Shhh!" came from. . . .

She didn't keep a diary and her letters were lost; so we can only hope that at least once in her career she ran a bit wild. The best that can be said for her is that she certainly kept a lot of reading rooms open during hard times at the lowest possible cost to the public purse.

No feminist today could, or would, emulate her, but none should laugh when her despised image is invoked. The appropriate reaction is a shudder in remembrance of the conditions that created her accompanied by a surge of determination to stamp out the remains of those conditions.

The Dumb/Stupid Question

Why did the early librarians to children and why do those of today fail to rush, in large or influential numbers, to collect and promote yesteryear's serial novels for children?

When this question is asked by nonlibrarians—parents, nostalgia buffs, newspaper reviewers—it's a dumb question in that it lacks intelligent observation or background. That's regrettable, but these people can be excused for their ignorance of the history of children's book publishing and the purpose behind the establishment of public and school libraries for children.

When librarians raise it, it's a stupid question in that it exhibits a determined ignorance of a phenomenon of 20th century, library service at the level of brutish indifference.

Whether its [sic] a nonlibrarian or one of our own who asks it, a brief response is required because it's usually a hit-and-run question. The superficial interest of the nonlibrarians and the supercilious to obtuse librarians who put it usually do not permit a long and detailed reply.

Whenever I'm faced with that dumb/stupid question, I silently remind myself that " . . . the art of being kind/Is all the sad world needs." (That's precious piffle, of course, but it takes up as much time as counting to 10.)

Then I quote Arthur Prager who reread all the *Bobbseys, Hardys, Drews*, and yards of the other products manufactured by the Stratemeyer factory or its ilk, and wrote about them thoughtfully but lightly in *Rascals at Large, or the Clue in the Old Nostalgia* (Doubleday, 1971, o.p.):

> They were ultraconservative, cheaply bound, badly printed and festooned with substandard art. Their literary value was practically nil. They were repetitive and windy . . .

That's why the pioneers of children's services didn't buy series novels when they were new. Although some of them have been repackaged in library bindings or paperbacks, it's why most children's librarians won't use their budgets to purchase or promote them now.

Henny-Penny Lives

When some small, unidentified flying object whacked her on the head, Henny-Penny (a k a Chicken Licken, a k a Chicken Little) leapt to the unexamined conclusion that the sky was falling, and that she must set off at once to tell this news to the king. Cocky-Locky, Ducky-Daddles, Goosey-Poosey, and Turkey-Lurkey trustingly trooped along with her toward the palace until they met Foxy-Woxy, who coaxed them to a shortcut by way of his cave. One-by-one as they entered, he snapped their necks and stacked their carcasses— all except for Henny-Penny, who (on hearing the dying gurgle of Cocky-Locky) turned tail and scurried back to the safety of her cornyard.

There's not another word to the folk tale. No report that her Farmer told Henny-Penny to keep her cluck shut without good evidence next time and not one indication of remorse for feathered friends led to slaughter.

From the December 1980 memorandum of Judith F. Krug, director of ALA's Office of Intellectual Freedom to State Intellectual Freedom Committees:

Media Blitz
Lights, camera, action!
Film crews, reporters, broadcasters, and concerned citizens are descending upon OIF in droves. Library censorship—attempted and real—is once again big news.
"My phone has been ringing off the hook," Judy told a *Los Angeles Times* reporter on November 12. "It is the beginning of a major assault on the ability of libraries and schools to maintain free access to diverse materials representing all political, social and economic viewpoints." It seems some would-be censors are interpreting the conservative movement's massive political victory as a mandate to step up efforts to impose their own moral and social values on libraries. As Judy further stated in the *Los Angeles Times* article, "All of the pressures that were just below the surface are now coming out, pressures to remove those materials that people object to on moral grounds or because they believe the materials do not reflect 'traditional American values.'"
These pressures are coming from "people who believe that they have elected their man to the White House and

[that] our society is willing to superimpose their values on the entire nation."
The impact of this *Los Angeles Times* article has been phenomenal. The story was picked up by the wire services and then by hundreds of newspapers, and television and radio stations across the nation. Each day we have received additional calls from media requesting interviews and specific examples of censorship attempts in their local communities. And each time we have been able to furnish them with more evidence of censorship attempts.

Unfortunately, of the cases cited in this memorandum as evidence, four were well underway before Election Day, and two surfaced only after Krug's chat with the *Los Angeles Times* got picked up by other major newspapers and some network television news commentators.

The suspicion is inescapable that Krug's analysis of November 12, tells us more about her personal political bias than about any discernible mood of the country only eight days after the Republican sweep.

And, talk about phones ringing off their hooks! Why, Mercy! *SLJ* had at least seven calls about this—*Time, Newsweek,* the *Washington Post*, and CBS News called here to find out if we knew about any more recent evidence than the Office of Intellectual Freedom could supply. Then, librarians in Maryland, Texas, and California called to say local reporters for these news agencies had called them looking for action. Since nothing was doing, the reporters rattled the cages of local leaders of long since settled censorship attempts to ask if they had any plans for new censorship campaigns.

Speculation on how many newly elected, not yet inaugurated Republicans were drawn to the cause of libraries and their funding by all this is bootless and so is trying to estimate the extent of a credibility gap that may follow on this "blitz," which required so much digging after old news.

Most startling was the last line of *American Libraries* January '81 recap of the hullabaloo: "We've never been so well prepared," Krug told *AL*. "Let the attacks come."

A lot of Turkey-Lurkeys in frontline library service have to be put to the tooth to keep Krug's phone ringing off its hook, of course, but it's nice to know she's prepared for what she's waved up.

Brooding on Billboards

Billboards are primers. Children practice their newly found decoding skills on billboards and, in the process, learn a lot more about our society than they'll ever find in any easy-to-read children's book.

I had not thought about billboards as more than a blight on the landscape until I took a country walk with one of my youngest friends. He had just learned to read and couldn't stop reading. On our walk, we read—long and thoughtfully—every billboard we encountered.

The first showed a young woman in scant evening dress bent backward nearly to the floor by her dancing partner, who was arched above her—lust clear in his eyes and in the set of his hips. She told the world in print that until she started using a popular deodorant under her arms, she used to sit out every dance.

The next billboard showed a tigress of a woman lurked by a pantheresque man. She was applying a dollop of perfume to the back of her knee, leg exposed to the hip, while telling the world, "He loves me with this!"

Up the road a piece was another billboard . . . toothpaste. . . a woman in the bathroom, brushing for dear life. Through the bedroom door we glimpse a man in bed, smiling his face off, as she says that clean breath means everything.

My favorite was a billboard showing an elderly woman of some beauty. It was in two panels: in the first, before discovering a certain powder, she says she was just another lonely widow with unsightly black raspberry stains on her dentures. In the second panel, after soaking her choppers all night in a solution of the powder, the old girl confides that she is now the most swinging single at the senior citizens' weekly barn dance.

Reading the billboards, my young friend read or sounded out every word. Together we talked about the words and the pictures. I restrained myself from asking him what all these billboards meant, because I suspected he was bright enough to get the messages without my reinforcing them through speech:

- Women of all ages are stinky.
- They don't wash up to feel clean.
- They correct their vile odors with chemical sprays, oils, pastes, and powders.
- Men like the chemicals.

Take any or all of such hogwash off the billboards. Put it in a children's book. Put the children's book in a school or public library, and what you've got is a recipe for instant protest against the teacher or librarian who uses that book with children.

It's awfully hard to find the owners of the billboards, and it's difficult to get in touch with the people who animate the billboard messages for TV or who vocalize them for radio. But it is easy to get to any community's teachers and librarians and to the books and films they use with young children.

Not every question raised about the suitability of library materials for the young is an act of censorship, even when the tone employed is tinged with outrage or disgust. The ability to justify purchases for a library collection is a professional responsibility that will be tested again and again until the larger society moves past the low point of prurience to which the producers of mass entertainment and consumer advertising assign us all as they cynically manipulate the great adult dirty secret.

Until the larger society recognizes that sex, that great adult dirty secret, is constantly trailed before children by the advertising sales copywriters, professionals who work with the young will be beleaguered by parents who are making (to the only source at hand) a general protest against the elements of sales sleaze that have become the common and ever more blatant language of those who sell soap, in all its varying forms.

I do not agree that censorship—the actual removal and banning of books or films—is on the rise. I do sense in myself, and in others I've talked with, a growing revulsion at the quality of life as shown on billboards, commercials, situation comedies on TV and in movies, and at their producers, who insist that the First Amendment to the Constitution means that anything goes—anytime, anywhere.

It is hard to take up their cause—unselectively—after reading billboards on my long walk with a new and thoughtful young reader.

What's in a Name? Think about It

On page 21, you will find Ann Y. Franklin's latest state-by-state survey for *SLJ* of the many and wildly various certification requirements surrounding (or barricading) employment at a responsible level in what the general public still call "school libraries." Franklin's introductory comments include a list of more than 23 strange designations that are now applied to what the general public, bless their hearts, still know as "librarians." Although only three states use that downright, forthright, upright title—South Dakota, Tennessee, and Wisconsin—nevertheless, these states, according to their current certification requirements on the chart, certainly don't agree on what you need to know before you get that good word on your working papers.

The list is worth lingering over. I'm really torn between Hawaii and Massachusetts for my least favorite among the pompous evasions of the title, "librarian." For purest nonspeak, Hawaii has the edge, There, you're a "Basic Specialist."

Can't you just imagine yourself after a long, hard day of Basic Specializing, settling down in the sand at a luau, soaking your feet in the Pacific, fish in one hand and poi swirled on the fingers of the other, when up hulas the stateside tourist of your dreams. Not five minutes into the conversation comes (you can bet on it) a variation on the typical American question, "What is it you do for a living?" What a swell answer you've been certified to give. "I'm your local Basic Specialist," you must respond immodestly—possibly snubbing the only unmarried plumbing contractor that you're ever likely to meet. Or worse, he leaps to the wrong conclusion and offers to meet you at your place, cash in hand, as soon as he can shake his mother.

Hawaii's certification title is witlessly naughty-bad, but the one at the bottom of the list from Massachusetts may be worse. It's mindlessly haughty-bad. Imagine three people meeting at a national conference of the American Association of School Librarians, an organization that has done nothing about its field's title confusion except add to it. Each person is a member of AASL and each has taken continuing education time off from essentially the same sort of work to attend the conference. The person from Alaska says, "Hi. I'm a School Librarian in Nome," which is what these no-nonsense tundra types call themselves. The one from Michigan smiles at this quaint clarity and says, "I'm a Media Specialist in Flint." The third one, pausing for full effect, from anywhere in Massachusetts, delivers the all-time putdown-by-title—"I'm a Unified Media Specialist"—an identification that implies the Michigander hasn't got it all together and the Alaskan ain't quite in it.

As you browse through the charts, your laughter will change to dismay. Franklin puts it mildly: "Wide variation is apparent in the number (or lack of number) of hours required for in-depth study of library media. . . . " This means that all across the country it's getting more and more difficult to find among these "basic-to-unified specialists" a newly certified sort who has spent any appreciable amount of time on the study of books or film or any other materials swept under the term "media" that their states say they are specialists in (or should that be "of"?).

An AV production course, but no course in children's literature? Nobody working in a school library needs to be able to produce a film or, for that matter, to be taught how to publish a book. They do need to know: how to judge; how to select; how to purchase; why to purchase; and from whom to purchase educational materials in every format.

The American Library Association is the only nationally recognized body that can accredit programs in education for librarianship. Long ago it left requirements for school librarianship to the states' departments of education. This was a shameful default of ALA's stewardship. The proof is in Franklin's many charts—only three states even know what to name the jobs they are certifying. And even they don't agree on competencies.

ALA's Committee on Accreditation is always busy being busy with accrediting or re-accrediting library schools that are, without so much as a whisper about vocationalism versus professionalism, changing their schools' names to suggest that they are schools of information science. What's in *that* name is usually bad news for courses of study in library work with the young. Some of these have dropped (or are about to drop) such courses from their MLS programs. When they send their pleas for money to old grads, those old grads now working with children in school or public libraries ought to think twice about it before they cough up. If the alumni don't take a stand, ALA isn't going to make their graduate schools care about library professionals for children and young adults.

Talking About ESEA

We ought to start talking for the record about the reverberating impact of Title II of the Elementary and Secondary Education Act (ESEA), now 20 years old. I'd like to send somebody on the road with a list of good contacts, a reliable tape recorder, and plenty of time to capture some of the stories of the people who lived and worked through the first seven, often-wild-and-sometimes-wonderful years of ESEA Title II. That program directed federal funds to the states specifically for school library collections, textbooks, and other supplementary instructional materials.

We know that ESEA Title II changed the whole course of school library service in the United States. Between 1965 and 1968 the number of public school libraries went from about 39,000 to about 63,000 because a school had to have a library to qualify for ESEA funds. We also know that nearly 48 thousand of the schools with libraries in those years had no qualified school librarians because ESEA Title II did not mandate staffing requirements for libraries.

The near-doubling of school libraries, with less than half of them adequately staffed, was progress—of a sort that can only be described as chaotic. Chaos always produces a crazy quilt of individual stories that piece together into a bigger, clearer picture. The stories of ESEA Title II's first seven years go far beyond the growth in the number of school libraries and jobs for staff to run them properly.

No history of those years would be complete without a close look at ESEA Title II's effect on library schools, general trade publishing, children's book reviewing, and children's book distribution.

For instance, I think that the ESEA-generated demand for school librarians caught the ALA-accredited library schools flatfooted. For a time, the booming enrollment of students hoping to enter school library service became those schools' cash cows and, when the number of library positions in schools diminished, the school library specialty was allowed to erode by neglect. Now the number of school library positions is rising steadily, and, once again, the accredited library schools are standing flatfooted, while the unaccredited departments of library science in schools of education are tightening their stranglehold on the entry to school library service.

Then, take publishing—that's what the corporate giants did. Any house that had both a textbook and a children's book publishing division during the first seven years of ESEA Title II showed profits going through the roof. The corporate giants ate them up. Twenty years later, some of the giants are showing signs of indigestion caused by their publishing morsels. It was ESEA that helped whet their appetites.

Children's book publishing was never the same after ESEA. The lists went from about 1200 new children's and YA titles in '65 to over 3000 in 1970. The editorial staffs did not grow in direct proportion to this increase, but the staff hired for school and library promotion zoomed up. The publishing people tell the wackiest stories of those years—of authors whose weakest manuscripts were rushed out of trunks (where most deserved to molder) straight into print, of illustrators working day and night for four different publishers at a clip, and school principals without librarians buying every ridiculous book in sight before the annual spending deadlines.

Small jobbers, bookdealers and wholesalers opened for business and got into a vicious cycle. The schools with ESEA book money were often very slow to pay. Their suppliers borrowed at disadvantageous interest rates in order to pay publishers for more books. Some publishers were caught in the cash-flow trap, and so were some binderies. When, in 1973, the Nixon administration refused to allocate the funds Congress had appropriated for ESEA Title II, a whole slew of these companies went out of business. So did a lot of short-lived review agencies that sprang up, flourished for a time, and went defunct before they'd even enunciated a clear reviewing policy.

I can't swear to it, of course, but I think if a lot of these "Federal Funding Years" stories were put together, it might be the most compelling picture we would have of what can go both right and wrong when great gouts of federal money are suddenly tossed in the general direction of a social or educational problem. That ESEA caused as much dislocation throughout the children's book world as it did progress in school libraries, needs to be researched.

While the people who lived and worked through those years still have a good clutch on most of their marbles, an oral history project is called for.

Frances Henne—Standard Bearer 1906–1985

Frances Henne was a great teacher of librarians as well as a charismatic activist for the development of school libraries. Some of her greatest work and leadership in the '50s and '60s went into the promulgation of national standards for school libraries. The American Association of School Librarians, the ALA division she helped found, is now preparing to issue new standards. In tribute to Dr. Henne, SLJ reprints her philosophy of professional standards for library service.

Problems of interpretation relating to standards, especially national standards, arise from several causes, including faulty reading. The most common of these, and in many ways the most dangerous, is that of interpreting standards in terms of isolated parts rather than in their entirety. Most standards are very closely interrelated and interdependent, so that isolated parts can suffer from misinterpretation when removed from the total context. A quantitative standard has a direct and significant relationship to other quantitative standards; and all quantitative standards are tied to qualitative standards, which depend upon quantitative measures for their totally effective implementation.

There has always been an unfortunate tendency on the part of standards users to want quantitative standards summarized in tabular form and to have these summaries available, not only for separate viewing in the volume but also for separate distribution, isolated from the program of services, or qualitative standards. This procedure can lead, and often has led, to serious misinterpretation. Similarly, a mere list of figures, without textual rationale or commentary, can be meaningless or horrifying to those unacquainted with the contextual ramifications or to those who may be familiar with them but are seemingly unwilling or unable to relate quantitative to qualitative measures. Quantitative standards for staff have been victimized the most in these respects; this may largely explain why national standards for staff have been the quantitative standards least implemented—a critical matter inasmuch as this is the key standard on which media programs of good quality are dependent. . . .

Implementation represents one of the most important aspects of standards. In the case of national standards, effective implementation can represent the difference between their success or failure, their relatively quick translation into action or a dishearteningly long time lag. This holds true even in those many situations where national standards may form long-range goals—in this event, action and success take the form of developing planning programs for a period of time, updating state standards to come closer in line with national recommendations, and other measures.

Effective implementation carries with it the desirable attribute of involvement—not only of the professional individuals and associations most directly concerned, but also of parents, other citizens, and civic groups. . . . These activities can and have been carried on at national, regional, state, and local levels.

Regional standards, in cases where they are issued by accrediting agencies, carry built-in implementation. Mandated state standards also have this characteristic, as do related state regulations involving qualifications for federal and state financial assistance for media centers.

Implementation takes on another cast in some states—the implementation of activities and plans that lead to a revision of outdated standards, or to the upgrading of minimal requirements that are too low, or to the formulation or adoption of standards where none now exist.

National standards often suffer at the hands of individuals who label them as visionary or impossible of attainment and from those who have a personal bias against them. These attitudes frequently reflect fears—in the case of the former, fears of being unable to cope with the problem of improving conditions in the situation in which the individual is working, and in the latter case, fears that the standards constitute a threat to them and what they are doing.

Too often overlooked or ignored is the overall primary objective of standards—to provide teachers and students with the media services and resources to which they are entitled. Surely no one could deliberately reject such an objective. Surely excellence in media programs is not something to be feared.

The Appetite for Ignorance

"**I**t is *you* people through your fine work who will instill the love of learning, the hunger for information, the fascination for research. *You* are ushering in the Age of Information."

The audience was made up of librarians specializing in services to the very young. The speaker was an amiable fathead high in the ranks of the information industry, and the occasion was one of our fall library conference meetings.

Whenever I hear a speaker who has spent at least two-and-a-half minutes pondering librarianship's responsibilities to youth, I write down what they say we should be all about. It is a daunting collection.

I just wish that somebody who's gone dotty over a databank would—once in my earshot—acknowledge that lifelong learning, ready information, and respect for research is what library collections for any group, at any time, have always been about.

Away with this usherette nonsense. We've been high-stepping baton twirlers to the glacier-like creep of this Age of Information for over a century. But, those outside library service need to take a gander at what we have to go marching through before blaming us for the pace. The truth must be told. There is a voracious appetite for ignorance. And, the same telecommunication mechanisms that can deliver reliable data are employed to whet that unworthy appetite.

Somebody besides librarians has got to start believing that people can manage the information they get. In point of fact, there is a large body of people who don't believe that at all. For proof just tune in the World Series (or any kind of ballgame). The batter is up. The ball is pitched. The batter swings. He misses. The umpire signals strike one. All this has been captured on camera, delivered by satellite straight to your living room, and you saw it all. But nobody believes you did or that you can remember what you saw because some big bucks baritone comes right on and tells you: "He swung and

he missed, strike one." This does not bode well for the Information Age; it will be very costly to hire people to chant what the databanks throw up on the screens.

In addition to the idiotic repetition of inessential information, we have artists of ignorance. Consider the tremendous number of copies sold each day of what is said to be the country's most heavily read newspaper. Standing in line at my supermarket I witnessed a bright nine-year-old reading the paper's headlines aloud as we approached the cash register: "Hey, Ma! Look at this! Hitler's been seen hiding on a llama farm in Peru! They've got new proof that Jesus eloped with Mary Magdalene on the First Good Friday! And, here's a guy—swallowed a fertilized egg and gave birth to a live chicken!" Ma bought the paper.

Obviously, the boy delighted in what was offered as fact, and in the sense of learning something new. We as librarians can only hope and pray that he may go on to do pure research into the tantalizing question of why the people who give birth to live chickens always seem to live in trailer parks outside Los Angeles.

As an occupational group that is quite ready to continue at the tough assignment of goading the masses into the Age of Information, we can rejoice in a dazzling array of the nonfiction to come for young readers. The eagerness for information is stoked in well-stocked libraries. But we need to point out that this eagerness gets stopped or slowed down by the society beyond our walls—by a make-believe news happening staged in the middle of a Presidential speech, by TV docudramas busting budgets to recreate murders before the corpses get cold, by . . . the list is as endless as the appetite for ignorance is overfed.

When the heralded Age of Information finally dawns, librarians serving the young must get up very early. It may take them all day to find the rest of the adults who are able to live in it.

Ethical Back Talk

Sloppy historians may be tempted in some distant age to label the 1990's "The Ethical Decade" because of the print and video record we leave in this, the first month of the first year of the last decade of the 20th century. The word "ethics" is on every newspaper's front page and on the lips of every newscaster. This ethical din arises from grand scale thievery by legislators and stock manipulators and all the many commissions created to scrutinize big money scandals. It really ignores the fact that ethics go far beyond monotonous, Gargantuan greed.

That ethics involve more than money is especially clear in the codes of ethics drawn up by each and every profession. These generally dwell on the duties and responsibilities that accompany the occupational role and call upon practitioners to police themselves in the scrupulous observance of the principles that sustain their calling.

We're too quiet about ethics in library service. The librarians' *Code of Ethics*, adopted in 1939 and last revised in 1981 by the American Library Association is far less well-known and much less fussed over than the *Library Bill of Rights*—and that's too bad, because each of the six points in the code deserves the renewal of commitment that results from continuous re-examination and debate. The code has some obvious gaps, too. And, strange as it may seem to *School Library Journal*'s readers, children's, young adult and school librarians are widely believed to be immune to, or above, the temptations implicit in each of the code's points, except those of #2.

Maybe the attribution of nearly immaculate virtue by the general public as well as our library colleagues accounts for the unusual and prolonged silence from our sector on those moments in the course of our working days when "the still small voice within" is moved to mutter over the points that do (or don't) exist in ALA's ethical code. Refusing a reputation for spotless behavior is very hard, but somebody should.

To break the silence and shake up codified complacency, *SLJ*'s editorial page, every other month or so across 1990, will pounce on points in our ethics code with revealing stories and many questions about the "bold outrages and corrupt combinations" that booby-trap the ethical delivery of library services to the young. The series will begin in our February issue with point #1.

Code of Ethics

1) Librarians must provide the highest level of service through appropriate and usefully organized collections, fair and equitable circulation and service policies, and skillful, accurate, unbiased, and courteous responses to all requests for assistance.

2) Librarians must resist all efforts by groups or individuals to censor library materials.

3) Librarians must protect each user's right to privacy with respect to information sought or received, and materials consulted, borrowed, or acquired.

4) Librarians must adhere to the principles of due process and equality of opportunity in peer relationships and personnel actions.

5) Librarians must distinguish clearly in their actions and statements between their personal philosophies and attitudes and those of an institution or professional body.

6) Librarians must avoid situations in which personal interests might be served or financial benefits gained at the expense of library users, colleagues, or the employing institution.

(Adopted June 30, 1981, by ALA Membership and ALA Council.)

Ethical Back Talk: I

1) Librarians must provide the highest level of service through appropriate and usefully organized collections, fair and equitable circulation and service policies, and skillful, accurate, unbiased, and courteous responses to all requests for assistance.

No matter which way you slice it, this first mildly worded statement of principle in the American Library Association's *Code of Ethics* is a stunner. The fact that it leads off—and has to be said at all—tells the world that our ranks can harbor the idiotically organized, circulation poker players and service delinquents as well as unskillful, inaccurate, prejudiced and rude practitioners poised to maltreat information supplicants.

Libraries in schools of any size, for any age level, are particularly vulnerable to the plague of bad practices suggested in point #1 because they are less likely to have any taxpayers bellowing or filing complaints. In school-based library collections for the young, embattled parents seldom appear to right service wrongs or to deflect the casual or calculated rudenesses that many adults employ to separate themselves from, or to establish dominance over, children and young adults.

It's significant that "appropriate and usefully organized collections" is mentioned first because, despite invasions by computer database files and purchased cataloging, the way a library collection is stored and the access this permits to its holdings remains the librarian's chief professional secret. So, it follows that a collection badly arranged for its users' purposes becomes a matter of unethical practice—as in those K-3 elementary school libraries where the shelving goes far beyond the easy or safe reach of the tallest third grader. (A good talking point when dealing with any architects wedded to such design bizarreries as circular or maze shelving: "Alas. Your aesthetics conflict with my professional ethics.")

"Fair and equitable circulation and service policies" is an aspect of ethical library practice that merits more attention than it gets in youth services circles. I'm thinking of those public libraries where the children's department has no (or heavily restricted) use of the greater breadth and depth of information available in the adult reference department. It's a breach of ethics to fail to negotiate an equitable deal for the youngest library users in such situations. Adults whose grasp of a topic is negligible are usually served, without question, books on that topic in the children's department. They are even encouraged to *borrow* from the children's department, while too many discouragements and barricades are allowed to stand to keep the patter of little feet away from the adult information collections.

While on the subject of equitable reference services, spare a sob over the teaching of reference skills in our ALA-accredited library schools (or, as many are choosing for their married names, "schools of information studies"). A recent trip through the syllabi of reference courses offered indicates an information gap that stays wide open—the information tools and resources employed by those who work with the young are scanted or absent. Sad to say, when it comes to library services for youth among our leading library schools, ALA accreditation continues to flow to some cesspits of unfair, inequitable attention in terms both of an absence of necessary courses and in the context of existing courses.

In point #1, the commonest ethical problem in library services to the young, whether the institutional setting is a public library or school, centers on who takes precedence when both an adult and a minor are after the same item. In school libraries, on Day One, librarians tell students, "This is *your* library." A month down the road the students may hear, "Bring it back. Mrs. What's-her-face wants it on reserve." In the children's departments of public libraries, similar dilemmas arise when adults reserve and serially renew books children or young adults suddenly find on their recommended reading lists. (Children's librarians are notorious for hoisting and keeping, long past due, the latest Newbery or Caldecott Medal Award books.)

At first glance, the first statement in the *ALA Code of Ethics* seems a bit vague, like a grab bag of besetting sins from which it is easy to walk—or talk—away. Actually, it's best use is as an abbreviated blueprint for what every library policy book or manual of procedures should address. And, if your library exists without such written agreements on these matters, it's impractical (at least) and arguably unethical (at worst) to continue without getting them down on paper.

Ethical Back Talk: II

2) Librarians must resist all efforts by groups or individuals to censor library materials.

Of the six statements in the America Library Association's *Code of Ethics*, point #2 is the briefest, the most recitable, and the best known both inside and outside library service. Every year, new books are published about some historic or current aspect of its validity. Editorial pages in the library periodical press regularly preach to its text. Writers for the mass media sporadically discover it and gird it with praise. Annually, prestigious awards are presented to librarians who practice it at heroic levels of career-risk where even point #2's backsliders rise to do them honor. Unfortunately, the intensity of the admiration for point #2 has suppressed its regular re-examination and development.

Point #2 is unquestionably attractive to our best instincts to protect our institutions and the audiences they serve. From the time we first meet it in library school by way of ALA's *Code of Ethics* or its restatement in ALA's *Library Bill of Rights*, this puts us sternly on the path of saints and martyrs. It tells us: Go this Road or Walk in Shame. Forevermore, we know how we should behave when some person (ourselves included) or group tries to force material from a library's collection or circumscribe access to it. But, both guiding ALA documents are strangely, even dangerously silent on how to behave with those who would force material into a library collection or misuse a library staff and facilities to distribute materials inappropriate to the library's purpose. Point #2 is a story with only one accepted villain: the Censor. It's past time to focus on some others who can run roughshod through a library: the Zealot and the would-be business partners.

I say "strangely silent" because it was recognized long before there were public and school libraries for children and adolescents that the young have always been considered fair game by proselytizers for every sort of cause. This too calls forth the instinct to protect the library's purpose and its intended audience, but support for this from ALA's guideposts to professional behavior is nil. There is no model of library policy on the authority to evaluate and reject a zealot's gifts or on business overdoing business in the library.

The zealots' gift materials in every format can be repellently horrifying or corrodingly seductive. They can be beyond the comprehension of a youthful audience or so hate-filled that they are beneath the intellectual dignity of a human being at any age. But, point #2 of the *Code of Ethics* speaks only to the resistance to censorship, not to the fact that gift-bearing zealots often employ the same tactics as censors—blitzkrieg invasions of your working day, hostile publicity and steady pressure on governing boards and school administrators. It's a strange gap in the Code.

I call it a dangerous silence because we have something relatively new to manage: the idea that businesses are, in every instance, the benevolent partners of educational or cultural institutions and often baselessly and recklessly confident that they can do the jobs better than trained teachers, librarians, or museum staff. Just such a case recently came to ALA's Council calling for it to take a position on a brute-sized business deal that may yet affect ALA's public librarians just as it already confronts ALA's school librarians. It involves the offer of free installation, in thousands of classrooms, of expensive television equipment—plus the delivery, free of charge, of a daily news program.

"Free" needs some definition in this case. Instead of paying money for the wiring and the TV sets, school administrators pay with the time and attention of their teachers and students, who must watch the program every day whether they want to or not. The programs carry commercials, invade the freedom of teachers to teach, truncate teaching time, and involve required use of unselected materials. Council was silent on all these matters, opting instead to limply reiterate the importance of written selection policies. It took no stand on forcing the use of materials, on accepting gifts tied with inappropriate strings, or on administrators who bargain away the reading, viewing, or listening time of the young in exchange for equipment they can't afford, simply because they failed at their first function: to win tax money to get it.

Point #2 in the *Code of Ethics* didn't help Council in this case because it exists as an arrow without a bow. ALA's Council Committee on Professional Ethics needs to furnish the missing half of point #2—an equally noble statement on the duty of librarians to resist the resignation of their selection/ acquisition responsibilities to any individual or group, and to ensure that their libraries' users, young or old, are not bartered for free equipment, materials, hamburgers, or whatnot.

Ethical Back Talk: III

3) Librarians must protect each user's right to privacy with respect to information sought or received, and materials consulted, borrowed, or acquired.

The third point in the American Library Association's *Code of Ethics* has three distinct aspects: the one the general public knows about, the one librarians seldom, if ever, talk or write about, and the one that gets completely (usually happily) ignored.

The general public knows that librarians want court orders whenever federal or local police want to go snooping through a library's records in pursuit of evidence of actual or suspected criminal activity. The general public knows about this because heroic resistance to G-persons and DAs and sheriffs on the part of library directors gets prominent, praiseful notice from both the library and the general press.

The aspect of point #3 that librarians seldom, if ever, talk or write about is staff gossip about patrons. The silence on this underscores how extremely difficult it would be to locate and to prod into speech or print a practicing librarian who has never traded survival information about patrons who misbehave or hissy speculation on those who exhibit odd-to-weird tastes in their reading or research interests. It is a fact that we tell each other quite readily what a badge-bearing snoop would have to pry out of us with a warrant.

Last but not least (in *School Library Journal's* admittedly biased view), the ignored aspect of point #3 is the eagerness with which librarians serving children and adolescents will tell all they know or have observed about a young patron's reading tastes and skills to any parent, concerned adult or teacher who indicates even the mildest interest in the young person's use of the library. (The grand exceptions to this tendency toward the invasion of the privacy of the very young are young adult services specialists in public libraries who regularly witness how much essential hygiene, sex and marriage law information libraries must supply without interference to the young when parents or schools don't—or won't.) However, the whole idea of privacy in our society seems reserved to adults. Only minors who are the perpetrators or victims of criminal acts regularly get privacy protection of these records.

This aspect of point #3 deserves more attention than it's ever been given in print. I've searched the literature back as far as it goes; specialists in library services to the young have been, and continue to be, urged to make parents or education colleagues full partners in the effort to develop reading habits or tastes and research skills. Most librarians working with young people could not, I think, be easily persuaded that there is anything wrong or hurtful in sharing what they see and know about young readers with others perceived as helping adults.

But that's not what the *Code* says—and therein lies the problem. Codes for any professional or occupational group are intended to call forth uniform compliance. As with so many other concerns in library service—classification, preservation, fines for overdues—we have to ask, even demand, as a specialist group, "Where do we fit? How does this fit with our purposes, and our functions?"

Point #3 is quite easy to practice when you equate it only with resisting police attempts at invasions of privacy. Virtuous directors and department heads can keep inevitable staff gossip within bounds through regular reminders about the responsibility for safeguarding the dignity of those served in any library. (It's a guilt trip; librarians should never leave home—for work—without it.) But, specialists in services to the young deserve at least a background statement absolving them from its total observance.

Furthermore, such a background statement requires some guidelines on how and when and with whom these breaches of point #3 or appropriate. The ability to ignore point #3 in this way—with pleasure and job satisfaction—is something the rest of library service should recognize as an admirable rather than a naughty practice of librarians serving the young.

When you come right down to it, fending off the FBI is easier than stonewalling a concerned parent or teacher who wants to help in the serious, positive work of helping young readers to grow. While this claim would not sit well in a background statement to point #3, the statement would show us off at our professional best—between the lines.

Ethical Back Talk: IV

4) Librarians must adhere to the principles of due process and equality of opportunity in peer relationships and personnel actions.

Point #1 of the American Library Association's *Code of Ethics* lifts the veil on six ways librarians must police themselves in the provision of responsible library services.

Point #2 inspires devotion to the resistance of censorship.

Point #3 admonishes librarians to protect library users' privacy.

Point #4 just lays there in the lineup like a dead lox dredged from the introduction to a library staff personnel procedures manual.

It's probably there because the ethical codes of the major professions are the starting points for later codes, and those historical guidelines for the conduct of doctors, lawyers and the clergy contain statements on how they should behave toward each other, the responsibility for monitoring entry to their profession, and the duty to help ensure its competent practice.

As it is stated, point #4 in ALA's *Code* speaks only to how to behave to other staff members within a given institution, ignores admission to the ranks and stays mum on the matter of competency checks. Point #4 is simply not up to the task it was intended to perform: that of guiding librarians on how to treat other librarians in every specialty under any circumstances.

Comparison of point #4 with its beginnings in the first ALA *Code* of 1939, the revision of 1975 and its present statement in the 1981 revision suggests that it is the result of a series of evolutionary accidents. Point #4 is the platypus of ALA's *Code*—unlovely to look upon and confusing as to purpose, intent and application.

In the 1939 *Code*, point #4 began as a long passage dictating "Relations of the Librarian Within His Library." This is heavily weighted toward supporting the authority of administrators and safeguarding the library rather than those who work in it. (When you remember that this statement was adopted in a period of trade union victories over owners and managers, it provides a startling contrast to the political coloration of ALA today.)

In the 1975 revision, point #4 emerged as: "A librarian has an obligation to insure equality of opportunity and fair judgment of competence in dealing with staff appointments, retentions and promotions." While this version is still narrow to the workplace and overly directed to library administrators, it looks good in comparison to point #4's 1981 restatement; the addition of such personnel manual doublespeak as "due process" and "peer relationships" neither adorns nor clarifies.

Point #4 needs work to make it more all-embracing, lift it off the backs of administrators, and take it beyond the walls of individual libraries. Point #4 is most commonly breached, I think, outside a library or away from its administrative offices in ways the statement is too narrow to convey.

For instance, library educators seem exempt from point #4. Nevertheless, what they do in terms of their classes affects other librarians. Dropping admission standards to swell enrollment and passing grades for future unmanageables ought to be perceived as maltreatment of library practitioners and an ethical no-no of endless consequence to the profession.

Another example is those letters of reference for colleagues who may or may not be fellow library staff members. The field has always been full of complaints from employers stung by written assurances on the competence of wackos the letter writer wouldn't hire or rehire at the point of a gun.

Another example involves grade-mates in a conspiracy of silence before library administrators in order to keep a lovable incompetent on the job through increasingly lazy (or crazy) years. Unless librarians have been lying to me in large numbers for a long time, there is hardly any big school district, academic or public library that hasn't harbored one of these local legendary cuckoo birds with colleague support.

Other occupational groups or professional callings have enforcers—official committees empowered to discipline and/or lift licenses to practice when their fellows behave stupidly or odiously. Librarians have only their own consciences to check against their own, unenforceable code. Armed with consciences as sensitive as mimosa plants and hearts as pure as Ivory Soap, they need the sort of point #4 that speaks to all inter-professional behavior such as this variation on the Golden Rule: *Librarians should do unto all other librarians as they would have the others do unto them.*

That would spread the guilt more evenly up, down and across the ranks—like a good ethical code should.

Quotable Quotes

Intellectual freedom is an absolute. There must be an agreed upon age at which it can begin or school libraries and public YA services must acknowledge that they actively connive at the restriction of intellectual freedom—*May 1972*

As often as *SLJ* has and will again decry the practice of super-caution in the selection of books and other materials that begin to introduce alternative life styles, information about sex, criticism of religious and political beliefs, or any other issue that produces extreme emotional reactions in adults, we do not believe that librarians can or should supply anything and everything that is produced to children.—*February 1973*

Reviewer silence on potential problem passages in books is only golden to their publishers and authors; it serves library selectors not at all.—*May 1976*

Simply check to see whatever the publisher is praising the most about the book on its inside flap, don't believe a word of it until you've read the book, and then deny it in your review if you must—and often you will.—*September 1976*

What librarians buy in large numbers provides the momentum for more—the good or the sleazy. You are the market, and you will get more of what you are willing to pay for.—*May 1979*

It is past time for our associations to reaffirm in the strongest possible terms to the widest possible audience that library selection and materials purchasing oversight is a non-transferable professional skill that should not be turned over to amateurs—and never shared with suppliers.—*May 1981*

The children's book publishers' catalogs are never subjected to the same sort of critical reviews that librarians perpetrate upon the books these catalogs display. . . . [They] are almost all beautiful to look upon, . . . but still too short on hard facts to win any awards for top-notch consumer information. —*March 1982*

School administrators, at the moment, find it easier and more attractive to pay for the costly machines than to protect the positions and pay the salaries of library staff.—*April 1982*

It seems that the least understood aspect of library book selection for children is the extent to which the librarians serving them create and prolong the interest in any new children's book.—*April 1983*

The plain truth about library book budgets for younger readers is that these are not rising at nearly the same rate as the increase in the average price of one new hardcover book. —*March 1986*

Population minority groups on their way to becoming majorities in some areas need picture books with which both children and their parents can identify. Too few of this sort are being published today and too few live on the publishers' backlists.—*September 1987*

In selling books to libraries it's not, apparently, a question of what the market can bear—but rather a statement of what the market must bear.—*March 1990*

The difference in attitudes toward reviewing fiction versus nonfiction is the difference between Love and Respect. We tend to fall in love with good picture books and novels . . . we tend to respect knowledge and hold the best nonfiction in awe.—*November 1990*

Belligerent taxpayers opposed to paying more for public services are prone to be dismissive about the reading needs of ethnic minorities.—*January 1991*

School Library Project 2000

In talking with a group of newly-minted school librarians, I was sorry—but not surprised—that not one of them knew about the Knapp School Libraries Project. They knew all sorts of other wonderful things—how to build instructional modules, how to dart into databases and emerge with a forehead full of information, how to mult media . . . I know that they are going to be darn good at this work. Nevertheless, I felt sorry that in the race to get through all the coursework, the history of school library service in the U.S. is scanted. The Knapp Project is one of our bigger, better moments of just 30 years ago.

The purpose of the Knapp Project was to show how well-stocked, well-staffed school libraries could enrich the lives of students and faculties. In December 1962, the Knapp Foundation provided a million dollars to start the project, which was to span five years. It was administered by the American Association of School Librarians and Peggy Sullivan was appointed its director for the life of the project. Its four main goals (paraphrased) were to: demonstrate in a few schools how much a state-of-the-art school library could add to a school's program; offer in-service education to the school's faculty via a connection with a nearby college or library school; organize visits to these selected school libraries to show other librarians, education administrators, legislators, and taxpayers what a really good school library actually looked like; and, evaluate the effectiveness of the demonstrations.

The initial emphasis of the Knapp Project was on elementary school library service. As you read the appalling news of Rochester, NY's dumping all its elementary school librarians (News, p.10) we have had additional news, too late for publication, on other wealthy suburban New York areas in the process of cutting out all of their librarians from elementary schools through high schools. It's the sort of bad news that calls for another such school library project. The new one should have a segment built-in on what happens to school libraries when their librarians are removed. (We can predict the rate of collection and service deterioration, but the public does not know this and the bean counters need proof.)

When the Knapp Project was proposed, it was not greeted with total, boundless, enthusiasm. As I recall, for every supporter responsive to the leaders in school library service at that time, there were just as many naysayers who used every shopworn phrase that has ever been employed to kill a big project in its cradle stage: "The project is *too* big." "We haven't got the staff." "A good idea, BUT . . ."

Any such new project would have to be bigger, involve schools at every level, include every component of the new information technology and, according to Dr. Jane Anne Hannigan, "It would have to emphasize ongoing measures of the effectiveness of school libraries on student achievement as well as their capacity to enable teachers to teach more effectively." Hannigan believes revisiting a school library project with stronger research underpinnings enhances the production of new guidelines (read "standards") for school library service. She called it "a sexy research possibility." Sexy research in library service? As soon as I finished blushing I asked Hannigan what "sexy research" is since the erotic potential of research escaped me. It means: needed research that hasn't been done before for which the results can be used for more than one purpose. (OK, whatever turns you on.)

While librarians are quite good about sharing their information with each other, we have little experience with getting our best news before the wider public. A school library project aimed at preparing and equipping schools for the year 2000 and beyond would need a lot of planning for publicity far beyond our own ranks. Thirty years ago, the state-of-the-art was film and the Knapp Project called for and produced . . . *And Something More*. Now, we'd need videos from news-bite length to full-blown TV programs. The longer we look back at the Knapp Project, the more compelling becomes the urge to use it for the basis of another, thoroughly updated attempt to show the world what well-stocked, well-staffed school libraries mean when the talk of politicians and professionals turns to forecasting high quality education for the future.

Philistines in the Inner City

Does a town need separate public and school libraries?

David A. Bennett asked the question above in his opinion piece "Rescue Schools, Turn a Profit" in the *New York Times* (June 11). He's the president of Education Alternatives, Inc., which has been signed by Baltimore, Maryland to run nine of its inner-city schools. (Critical readers will translate this to "low-bid contractor moves in on minority, at-risk neighborhoods with a high percentage of single parent households and a low percentage of political/community involvement, uncertain jobs, and high crime rates.")

"How," Bennett asks, "do you save schools, save money, and increase revenues?" The first part of his answer: "Reduce the number and the cost of noninstructional staff members; collaborate with government to avoid duplication . . . " and then, with monotonous predictability he poses the question, "Does a town need separate public and school libraries?" I discussed Bennett's worn-out question with Julie Cummins. As the Coordinator of Children's Services at New York Public Library and a leading advocate of cooperation between public and school libraries, Cummins said, "The answer to Bennett is an emphatic, 'Yes!'"

"While the intent of suggesting that public libraries serve as school libraries is to save money, the reality is that it would be more costly," Cummins continued. She talked about costs that would have to be shifted from one publicly supported institution to another. She estimated that public library acquisition budgets would have to be tripled to build curriculum-structured collections, professional and clerical staff quadrupled, and existing space for young people expanded. "This muddling of the separate missions of public libraries and public schools does not prove to be the wisest use of the taxpayers' dollars. Notice that as often as the question of duplication has been raised, experience, evidence, and common sense have always prevailed."

Cummins pointed out that school libraries guarantee ease of daily access for their students and the assignment of their mission to a public library could diminish or eradicate the public library's greatest contribution to ensuring a good start for young readers—the preschoolers' programs that schools and their libraries are not equipped to provide.

"The best and most cost-efficient strategy for public libraries and public school libraries involves cooperative efforts to strengthen and develop the resources and expertise of both—cooperative reviewing of books and nonprint materials, joint education campaigns such as workshops for teachers and parents," is Cummins's view of the reasonable use of taxpayers' money.

Notice that the goal is cost efficiency—not savings or profits. This is the sort of vision of public education that inner-city children and young people need at a time when the Babbitts and the Bennetts of the bottom line arrive with Philistine questions that only begin with a question about public libraries and school libraries. That question leads to others just as benighted:

• Where there are parks, should inner-city children have school playgrounds and sports facilities?

• Where there is a locally supported orchestra or a Neighborhood Music Association, should inner-city children have school-based music instruction?

• Where there are public art galleries and museums, should inner-city children have school-based instruction in arts and crafts?

• Local hospitals have psychologists and psychiatrists, should inner-city children have these noninstructional service professionals as part of their schools' package? Guidance counselors? Nurses?

• To all of the questions above, the answers should be (to quote a sage) "an emphatic, 'Yes!'" Then we can get to the more important questions Bennett doesn't touch:

• How much does his company make on chopping down services to inner-city kids?

• How much does he take home?

• Will the education of inner-city kids join garbage as one of the public services most often contracted-out to private companies?

• When will this country agree on the national purpose of public education and how much it owes to all its children?

Choosing vs. Begging

School Library Journal has always received requests for any duplicate review copies we might have on hand. However, it is our impression that the number of these requests had quadrupled over the last five years. Hardly a month goes by without multiple pleas to ship (at *SLJ*'s expense) any new children's books we can spare.

Some of the letters are silly: "Children's books are always a popular door prize at our club members' annual banquet, so please send as many as you can as soon as possible."

Some letters are presumptuous: "Since you get review copies from publishers without charge, the least you can do is give the extras to our organization, which will pass the books on to children's hospitals at Christmas."

And, some recent letters are alarming: "We have no book budget for our school (or public) library. The children need books. Please send all your extra titles to . . . " These come on forms that have probably been sent to every house listed in R.R. Bowker's *Literary Market Place*. It's alarming, because librarians are *not* licensed to panhandle.

Long ago *SLJ* resolved the problem of what to do with duplicate copies of review books. Once a quarter, these are sold to a secondhand book dealer; the money received is allocated to a special account, which is used for such projects as the purse and the administrative costs of the annual Margaret A. Edwards young adult author award of the American Library Association's Young Adult Library Services Association.

SLJ chose this course because we really do believe in the necessity for careful book selection for children. Our editors condemn the trivialization of the professional responsibility to select children's library materials knowledgeably by way of these institutional forays into beggary. We disdain the idea that something—anything—is better than nothing in handing over just any book to young people.

Of course some of the review copies we sell are very bad books by any measure. But, their resale is a Buyer Beware choice and cannot be compared to institutionally condoned dumping of free junk upon the young.

Children's book publishers tell me that they, too, are besieged with growing requests for free children's books, requests that come from not only the general public but from libraries. Most of these begging letters (some even come by FAX, I was told) go straight into their waste baskets. However, other such requests are treated as windfalls.

It works this way: a natural disaster like Hurricane Andrew strikes—or an unnatural disaster like the Los Angeles riots. Libraries are wrecked. Private and public agencies call on publishers for help. The publishers have warehouses with unsold children's books. Like spaghetti Westerns, these can be categorized as the good (the few) the bad (more) and the ugly (most); many will never make it on merit in sales to libraries or bookstores. So, the publishers clean out warehouse inventory, which is a taxable ongoing expense. The proportion of good books to schlock will be idiosyncratic. The value of the shipment will be estimated. A large tax deduction for charity will be made. Thus, the publishers turn a probable loss into profit. (Don't blame them for this. It's exactly why publishing is called a business, not an art.)

The authors of the books publishers give away *en bloc* and cease trying to sell are not consulted and do not receive any part of the tax deduction windfall. It's a dip into public tax money and a slip away from the authors' contracts, but it's quite legal.

When librarians ask for money to buy books for children, that's called fundraising and, when the money is in hand, leads to book selection. Pleading for free books is called panhandling, mooching, or beggary. Since beggars can't be choosers, librarians who beg free books can't really be selectors. That's not only unethical, it's worse. Forfeiting selection responsibility is professional suicide.

ALA's youth services divisions have been silent on the issue of book beggary in the ranks. Too bad. More outspoken leadership and guidance on the matter is needed right now than the annual production of lists of books recommended for purchase.

Not for Publication

A body of dark lore is growing in library circles about author visits. Occupational horror stories told after hours. Strictly off the record. No names named. No teller to be identified. Nothing said for publication. In brief, all the elements of who, when, where, why, and how considered essential to the credibility of a news story or a factual article are refused. But, the stories continue and get taller all the time.

Examples abound. Last week, I heard about an author speaking at a public library who abandoned the promised topic but got the promised pay. Last month, an author appearing at a school spoke scornfully to (and about) the students and generally misbehaved—but got paid anyway. Last year, there was the one about an author/illustrator who had a public tantrum when informed that the drawings made during the course of the talk could not be sold on the premises of a tax-supported institution. That one got paid, too.

It's always astonishing to hear *how much* some of these visitors get paid, even those who are superb before a young audience and behave like angels throughout their visits. Many stellar creators keep their fees for visits high in order to discourage invitations that invade their creative worktime. But, the $2,000, $3,000, $5,000-and-up price tags we hear about get paid often enough to inflate the fees for lesser lights. Parent-teacher organizations are asked to contribute. Public library friends groups get tapped. Local service clubs and businesses often help with donations. The contingency and program funds of school principals and public library directors help make up the fees.

These visits are big business now—a business that has grown over the last dozen years or so. The positives of bringing living, breathing authors and illustrators together with their young readers have been emphasized again and again in print—and often in *SLJ*'s pages. Yet, nobody has published a word questioning the essential weirdness in scraping together fees for author visits that sometimes match or outstrip the amounts of money allocated to purchase new books for young readers.

Children's book publishers helped to start this author/illustrator visit business, but they are not now in the habit of paying all or even part of the freight for such appearances. When they talk (again, emphatically *not* for publication) about the boom in these visits, they are skeptical about the direct impact such visits have on book sales, but concede that they benefit at least indirectly from better general public awareness about new books. Publishers do not often wander far from financial considerations.

Librarians do not seem to center on these considerations enough. This probably accounts for the fact that we seldom hear, among the stories of author visits gone awry—which range from amusing to the hair-raising—about contracts. What we hear about are informal "letters of agreement." Such letters do not have a lot going for them under the law when you are tempted to withhold pay for outrageous behavior.

For instance, one common misadventure of this kind involves the creative celebrity who has extracted a promise for housing, meal, and travel expenses. Neither party has mentioned that this is just for the speaker-guest. Stories are legion about such guests arriving with an undisclosed entourage of spouse, kinder, aged parents and even pets in tow—all expecting to be housed, fed, and (sometimes) sped on their way to and fro via one of the more expensive means of transportation.

Since the staff of publicly supported institutions can call upon the services of a community's legal counsel, it makes good sense to ask that a simple but binding contract be drawn up and signed before promised fees are handed over or questions of additional expenses wreck harmonious relations between guest and host. (Following this good advice is not guaranteed to cut down on the supply of cussed author/illustrator visit stories that are so much fun to tell—and to hear—off the record. It will just alert all parties to such agreements that good will is not limitless in any business arrangement.)

The other course this editorial suggests is as obvious as it is difficult to implement, but long past due: keep the library's annual budget for new books on the table when fees for author/illustrator programs are determined. The disparities showing up between skinny book budgets and fat program fees are never amusing at all.

Marching on the Information Highway

"Information highway" has had a nice togetherness ring to it ever since Vice President Al Gore proposed the National Research and Education Network (NREN). His father had led the way with his successful push for overdue legislation during WWII that got this country out of the mud and connected by a system of national highways, arguing that these were essential to the swift deployment of troops in case of enemy invasion. It was a great achievement, but only much later it was recognized that special interests had overwhelmed the planning. The superhighways had no cinder paths for horses, no bike tracks, no footpaths for hikers, and no rights-of-way for the installation of rapid modes of public transit. In brief, they were not for all people—just those with cars and trucks or buses.

Jacqueline Mancall wants to see that the mistakes of history are not repeated in the construction of an information highway. Mancall, newly installed Vice President/President-elect of the American Association of School Librarians (AASL), has stated her priorities for her 1994-95 presidential year. High among these is insuring a real voice for public education in the policies adopted for NREN. Mancall will need all the help she can get on this. She is sure to get it from other education associations. This will present AASL with an unparalleled opportunity to strengthen and broaden its coalitions with other organizations serving the education and information needs of young people.

Strangely and incredibly, Mancall will have a tougher time enlisting full and active support from AASL's parent organization, the American Library Association. While ALA is on record in favor of NREN, it has dithered in pressing for any active role in the formulation of policies governing access to NREN's promised information lode. Furthermore, when and if ALA bestirs itself on the subject of NREN, the organization's history does not suggest that the access concerns of K-12 schools will be foremost or pursued diligently.

Evidence that ALA does not provide a vigorous, united front on library services to young people abounds. Just this last year, ALA's Council silently permitted another ALA division, the Public Library Association, to kill off the "Billion Bucks" proposal to supply children's books to libraries in advance of a pilot study to test its viability. Two years before that, when the youth services divisions combined to draw the greatest number of resolutions directing national library services to youth from the Second White House Conference on Library and Information Services, ALA's council endorsed these with so notable a lack of rejoicing, discussion, or debate that it was hard to distinguish its endorsement from sullen acquiescence. Last May, when James H. Billington, the Librarian of Congress, successfully faced down the objections of the Supreme Court to immediate access to the papers of the late Thurgood Marshall, ALA lauded his defense of the rights of scholars and journalists to read them but did not protest Billington's offhand equation of "high school students and casual tourists" in describing those who would not be permitted access. Another example is the administration of interlibrary loan policies, often designed to prevent use by young people—a long-term ethical mess to which ALA has paid scant attention.

Mancall and AASL's quest for the provision of an assured footpath for K-12 schools on NREN's information highway does not set out from a house in full agreement on the rights of access to information by children and adolescents. That's outrageous. Mancall and AASL should not have to mount rearguard persuasive action to combat the slumbrous or arrogant indifference of fellow professionals willing to reflect the general public's ambivalence toward the young rather than lead it up an information highway planned for all people.

CashSpeak

Librarians test very high on verbal skills. That's why the military coaxed so many into cryptography during WWII and after. Years ago, when the University of California-Berkeley annually tested the verbal skills of its thousands of entering graduate students, the library school students always, to the chagrin of the law school students, came out on top. For many years, until the paper disintegrated, I treasured a clipping from a State Department newsletter that said that librarians attached to foreign service agencies became proficient in other languages more swiftly than other specialists assigned abroad. Unfortunately, it is a fact that librarians find it difficult to make themselves clearly understood in the only language that taxpayers in revolt wish to use or hear: CashSpeak.

Librarians tend to be very long on courtesy and very short on crisp cost analysis of the materials they work with and the expenses involved in the expertise and services they provide. Librarians serving the youngest library customers are the most tongue-tied of all when it comes to talking about money. Perhaps this is because we get too little to speak of before it's gone. However, CashSpeak is the language of the land. Public and school librarians must learn it to survive. Let's start with a subject everyone thinks they know about, especially those revolting taxpayers who say, "When we need books at our house, we buy them."

The worst term papers, as any teacher will confirm, are those that cite and regurgitate only encyclopedia articles. The cost to institutions for the top three encyclopedias is just over $3,000 in their print formats. (The computerized or CD-ROM versions cost considerably more.)

An average term paper, one that may pull a C or B grade, usually involves two encyclopedias, a dozen nonfiction adult titles, at least four magazine articles, and a couple of pamphlets. Again, using average prices for print formats: The two encyclopedias cost over $2,000. The books, at an average price of $40 each, cost about $500. Employing an average annual subscription rate ($35) for popular magazines, add $200. Pamphlet prices have gone sky high. Say $10 for each and you're probably about right. If any materials in the bibliography had to be obtained via interlibrary loan from a research library, the costs (borne by the borrowing and lending institutions) can run as high as $30 for each transaction. then, add another $500 for the purchase and subscription prices of bibliographic tools for finding books, magazines, and pamphlets.

Expressed in cold CashSpeak, even a run-of-the-mill high school term paper is going to cost more than $4,000 for just the library resources employed. (Prorating the costs of school and public librarians' pay, plus cataloging, plus storage and maintenance costs, would run beyond the length of this page, but you can bet it would be more than another $1,000.)

In front of me is a term paper graded A+. The high school junior who wrote it last year made extensive use of both his public school library and his public library. The bibliography is twice as long as for those papers graded C or B. The lowest possible costs assigned to the print forms of the library materials listed (plus the bibliographic finding tools that had to be consulted) make this an $8,000 term paper.

No householder with a teenager on hand, no householder revolting against an increase in local taxes, is likely to assume the costs of even the worst sort of term papers. Alas, the teachers who assign the term papers are just as unlikely to know the basic costs of the materials employed. And, so are their school administrators. It's time we told them.

If you suffer under the delusion that talking about money is somehow unprofessional, watch for one thing as the arguments on the plan for national healthcare overwhelm the news media. See if you can find a physician who blushes or stammers during a discussion of costs and benefits.

Big Names & Small Books

The number of children's books by prominent adult book authors or big-name entertainers seems to be growing. It isn't that every celebrity has a good story for children inside them just whining to get out. It's about what it has always been about—sales potential increased by the power to pull free publicity far outside the reach of small budgets assigned to new children's books by their publishers.

This sort of head-hunting among the *glitterati* is not new. Virginia Kirkus, who founded the children's book department at Harper in the late 1920s, once told me she tracked on stars of the lecture circuit that flourished in that era and tried to persuade them to write for young people. "I looked for people who *did* things—explorers, mountain climbers, animal trainers. They would be interviewed by the newspapers and on the radio at their lecture stops, and so there was the extra sales help you could count on." She couldn't remember any title acquired this way when she told me that, which may say quite a lot about the historic general quality of such books coaxed from the highly visible.

Helen Jones, who was the longtime children's book editor at Little, Brown, told me about fishing for children's book authors among bestselling adult authors back in the days when adult bestsellers had almost nothing to do with sex, money, power, or drugs. Such trolling of the adult trade lists could be treacherous. "You might suspect that one of the better known novelists could write a really good book for boys and girls and that it would sell to the adults who liked their books." Well, she found one in-house, baited the hook, and got called for poaching by the author's adult book editor. Hissy fits in the boardroom and hard words in the hallway followed. Jones lost her taste for it but said the practice was widespread. It helped sales in bookstores.

Another early way into print via a children's book came from the owners and officers of publishing houses. Peggy Lesser, who began her long career as Doubleday's children's book editor in the '30s, recalled some of the shop talk exchanged at Children's Book Council luncheons in those days.

"When the big boys came back from rubbing shoulders with the politically or artistically prominent, the children's book editors learned to duck them for days because they'd come with ideas for story development from people who would never make it to their adult book trade lists. It could get very sticky." And, as is the nature of hierarchical business, some of these deals were made to stick over the protests of the children's book editors.

So, the doors of the publishing houses have always swung open easily for BIG NAMES, and spurts of initial sales have kept succeeding generations of children's book publishers prodded to add these names to their lists. The extra publicity afforded has not been marshalled to a heavy duty barrage, and the books have not been particularly problematic in children's public or school library book selection.

Expect that to change. As giant entertainment conglomerates vie to take over publishing houses, the possibilities in cross-marketing their wares are endless. It's time to think about the selection policies that can be affected if children's books by celebrities—and all the calendars, toys, posters, and tapes that can be loaded onto them—are steadily hyped into every home via TV and radio outlets controlled by the conglomerates, sung attcha or chatted up by their celebrity authors.

Our pioneers in library services to children managed to withstand being swamped by earlier waves of less heavily publicized crossovers into children's books by insisting that purchasing for and using new books with children requires a steady commitment to excellence—in the best interest of and for the development of children.

Such sales resistance wasn't easy in earlier days. It isn't easy now, and it's on its way to getting harder. But, this care for the use of children's time and their growth will always be central to the professionalism librarians serving the youngest bring to their specialty.

It may be that any sort of celebrity can get a children's book published somewhere, but it takes skilled librarians to put together collections worthy of children.

Dream Come True

A Guest Editorial

Mary V. Gaver

The opportunity which the Knapp Foundation Grant (*see* "The News," p. 20) brings to the cause of school libraries is like a fairy tale come true to those of us who have been working during the past years on the development and implementation of the standards. And, indeed, to me it does illustrate that to achieve a worthwhile goal one must begin by dreaming.

My own participation in this work goes back about eight years when four of us—Frances Spain, Virginia Mathews, Frances Henne and I—were gathered one wintry night in a Newark restaurant to hold a post-mortem on a workshop for teachers and librarians which the Rutgers Library School had been conducting. Out of this session came an *ad hoc*, self-constituted "Fantasy Committee" through which we set ourselves the assignment of outlining all the steps we thought necessary to the achievement of the kind of library service, both school and public, which children and young people need today. My memory is that we outlined projects that came to a total of something in the neighborhood of 10 million dollars, a real fantasy even in terms of the Knapp grant.

However, the point is that since that night many of the things we listed in our plan have come true; and dreams like these, by us and by many others, have had a small part in realizing the exciting developments of the past few years—the completion and publication of the standards themselves, the grant from the Council on Library Resources, the budget allocation from Congress for a children's literature specialist at the Library of Congress and now this munificent grant from the Knapp Foundation.

It is appropriate to point out that the catalyst in this most recent development was William Nichols, editor of *This Week* magazine, who in his capacity as chairman of National Library Week called to the attention of Mr. Stouch of the Knapp Foundation the "book gap" of which three-fourths of the children in our schools are victims. Through the resources of men and women of vision like Mr. Stouch and his associates on the Knapp Foundation Board, we now have a tremendous opportunity for experimentation to improve the educational resources of our schools.

The object of the program is to demonstrate school library services to the full extent of the standards. The philosophy of the *Standards for School Library Programs* (ALA, 1960) is that the kinds of service desired in a school determine the quantitative provisions which are necessary. The Knapp grant now provides an opportunity to demonstrate what we could do if only we had the money to pay for it!

The project will: 1) demonstrate the program made possible when a school library is provided with the quantitative facilities described in the standards (personnel, materials including the cost of commercial processing, quarters if needed); 2) provide in-service education of the faculty and library staff of the demonstration school, by contract with a neighboring college or library school; 3) organize visits to each demonstration school by "teams" of librarians, educators and citizens from other communities; and 4) evaluate the effectiveness of the demonstrations. The grant also provides for the prompt production of a film on the elementary school library, which will fill a particularly serious gap in our available resources.

The tremendous lag in the development of elementary school library programs led the committee to emphasize these first. However, it was held equally important to demonstrate the excellent programs of service in secondary schools which adequate personnel and other resources could make possible. At the same time, we did not believe it would be feasible to initiate so ambitious a program in more than a few schools at a time; the approval of the grant for a five-year period, therefore, makes it possible to spread the project out, which we hope will make for better chance of success. It was particularly gratifying to find that the Foundation Board was as interested as the school librarians in discovering ways to decrease the lag between the trial of an educational invention and its application in practice in all schools.

As soon as possible, an announcement will be made inviting applications from schools for consideration in the experimental program for 1963-64. The line forms to the right!

Shock—Past, Present, Future

Regina Minudri

Most of us have at last accepted long hair. We've adjusted to bare feet, mini- and maxi-skirts and the braless look. We're getting used to the idea of alternative schools and self-directed learning. Some have even accepted four-letter words like love (with all its variant spellings.) We've managed to cope with ecology, health food fads, transcendental meditation, home crafts, back to nature, communes, political semiactivism, student protest, and rock music. It wasn't easy for most of us, but somehow we accepted and survived the flower children. The Sesame Street graduates will be here soon, but are we not ready for them?

The children of change, chapter two, are predictable insofar as their needs and demands will be vocalized and visible. To meet them we must develop ourselves. Geraldine Clark (p. 76) cites the pressing need for middle-management training for school librarians. This applies equally well to public librarians. Anne Osborn (p. 78) speaks to the point of understanding the psychology of young adults and recognizing their unique dilemmas. On the job training and in-service training (p. 79–80) are cited as necessary to all levels of library service.

Library schools are not meeting these needs, and most libraries haven't developed these capabilities within their institutions. Workshops and mini courses at local, state, and regional conferences, as well as at ALA, can provide postgraduate insight and can do better than "show and tell" programs to motivate and stimulate the thinking of both young adult librarians and administrators to understand and respond to future demands. The Strategy for Change Task Force on Education of Librarians can give us assistance and young adult librarians need to be aware of their reports and then adapt their recommendations, whenever possible, to local needs.

My observations of teenage newcomers lead me to believe that we are in for some eventful years. (If you think the 60's were fun, just wait for the 70's to take hold.) We must be prepared for kids who are honest and up front, who will reject quite vociferously what doesn't attract, and cling most faithfully to what they like. Fashions will change; clothes will still be outrageous, but minds will be more open, as a result of more fluid and more responsive education. The coming young adult will be a potentially potent community force. Vocal and visual, these kids will expect—as a birthright—the things we only dream about.

As in the past, we will have to earn their respect. It won't be easy. They won't be willing to bide their time—because they are used to instant everything (from food to news). Minorities will make even heavier demands on our services, realizing that what we've done for others in the past must also be done for them. Specialized services must be increased and expanded. We will have to meet and greet our new young adults within their own framework, for they will not recognize ours as being valid for them.

The young adult librarian equal to the challenge of the new young adult will also be different, in many ways, from the present generation. This person will not put up with the rigamarole and red tape we endure. This person will devise methods that we haven't yet discovered. This admirable soul will be as conversant with all aspects of media as we are with books, though print will undoubtedly retain its importance and impact. The new young adult librarians will go forward, will be less hesitant than we, and will, I hope, have the guts to follow through with their good ideas and ideals.

Those of us entrenched in young adult work may indeed find ourselves left behind, by both the new young adult and the new young adult librarian. We should be—unless we can grow, change, adapt, and respond. Young adult services throughout the country are in a state of flux. Some are being absorbed by adult or reference services, others are dying quietly without benefit of clergy. This is not necessary, nor is it a foregone conclusion. Young adults are still here, no one can deny that, and there are new faces to be seen every year. With the lowering of the voting age, increased services and better programs are even more vital. The new voters need information, and we are just the people to give it to them. Young adult services are only as dead as they want or allow themselves to be. Young adult librarians of today and tomorrow—those who are prepared to meet the challenges—will find an audience waiting.

Part Two

Philosophy and Support for Library Service to Youth

The emphasis in library service forty years ago was on bringing children and books together. A concern with defining mediocrity and the need of kids to read for healthy development underscored this emphasis. In 1967, Mary Gaver posed the question: "The school library: an intellectual force?" For the next three decades librarians tried to answer that question by talking about freedom of inquiry, by describing the broad array of services needed in public library children's departments, and by defining the relationship between cognitive development and student research. The answer was further broadened when Bill Summers described a contemporary vision of libraries that included technology as a major resource for meeting the information needs of youth. Then, in April 1994 "Kids Need Libraries" offered us the definitive description of good library service needed to help children and youth meet the demands of the next century. But the development of a philosophy is brought full circle when Michael Cart asks the critical question "What literature?"

You Need Good Libraries to Teach Reading Today

Nancy Larrick
Education Director, Children's Books, Random House

A new library-centered plan for teaching reading is being advocated by many leaders in the field of education who report dramatically successful results in terms of children's progress and their interest in reading. Briefly stated, this new teaching technique is a plan whereby each child selects the book he wants to read and then proceeds at his own pace with his teacher helping him individually.

For the child this procedure means reading the things he is interested in without being pushed or held back by other children, and it means getting the help he needs when he needs it.

For the teacher it means increased pupil interest, greater freedom to work with individual children, and the satisfaction of seeing more children reading better.

For the librarian it means a new crop of library patrons who are brought up using the library and making the most of its treasure stores.

What is this new trend? Educators refer to this new trend as *individualized reading* because the emphasis is on the needs of each child and the help which can be given to him individually. Many who have tried this plan for teaching reading insist that it is not difficult even with a large class and that the dividends paid off in increased pupil enthusiasm more than repay the first upheaval and adjustment to a new plan of teaching.

Instead of meeting with a small group of ten or twelve pupils, the teacher meets with one child at a time, hearing him read for a couple of minutes, helping him with his special problems, and making a record of his progress. If she finds that three or four need the same kind of help, she will gather them together in one corner for a few minutes of special coaching. But such groups are completely flexible, with constantly changing personnel and purposes. While the teacher is helping one or two children, the others are reading silently or working on related activities.

When contrasted with the usual plan of three or four reading groups per class, this plan has many distinct advantages:

Each child selects the books he will read; therefore he feels greater interest in what he is reading and makes a greater effort to succeed.

Each child reads at his own pace; therefore he is not held up by and does not hold up others who might have been assigned to his reading group under previous arrangements.

Each child is taught the reading skills when he needs them; thus he sees these skills as important and worth achieving.

Because the individualized reading program is based on children's free choice of reading materials, it has occasionally been confused with what is sometimes called "free reading" or "recreational reading." A child may use the same library books for both kinds of reading and may put the same enthusiastic drive into both. But to the teacher there is a great distinction—individualized reading to her means a time for instruction and development of skills, while recreational reading means reading for fun and relaxation with little or no instruction from the teacher.

Without a goodly array of library books the individualized reading plan cannot work. Its success depends upon the psychological advantage of letting children choose what they want to read and letting them find the books they feel are within their reach. The word-of-mouth recommendation from one child may be enough to send several others after the same book as their next selection. This kind of momentum could never have operated in the old scheme of things where every child was reading from the same page of the same reader, whether or not he found the content interesting.

Only those who have worked with children can appreciate the terrific drive that grows out of a child's curiosity or interest. A new radio station in one small town brought a deluge of questions from the fifth graders. What was the tower for? Why were local programs clearer than those originating out of town? What connection did the local station have with network programs? Capitalizing on such questions the teacher and librarian helped children find books and pamphlets about radio and television so that they could read further and bring in their findings.

In another school, *Life's* science feature on dinosaurs appealed to one third-grader so much that he brought a copy to school, along with all the excitement and curiosity that a nine-year-old can generate. This was what he wanted to read—and no one could stop him! With that driving determination, he soon had many others fired with the same subject. The result was that a group of eight boys read everything they could locate on dinosaurs and the strange beasts of the past. Some of them pushed their reading skills to cope with books on a fourth and fifth grade level. For them reading was fun because it had a purpose that grew out of their own driving interest.

Range of Reading Skills in Each Grade
(Adapted from chart by W. C. Olson)

BOOK LEVEL		GRADE					
Grade	Age	I	II	III	IV	V	VI
N.S.	5	x	x	x			
Kg.	6	x	x	x	x		
1	7	x	x	x	x	x	
2	8	x	x	x	x	x	x
3	9	x	x	x	x	x	x
4	10		x	x	x	x	x
5	11		x	x	x	x	x
6	12			x	x	x	x
7	13			x	x	x	x
8	14				x	x	x
9	15					x	x
10	16						x

In both of these situations the teacher and librarian made the most of children's interests. They encouraged them to read books about the subject that was hottest at that moment instead of prodding them to read the next story in a textbook which did not stir their interest or answer their most urgent questions.

A number of studies have been made of children's interests. One of the most significant findings is that children's interests change as our society changes. Therefore some of the things that were of great interest to ten-year-olds in 1940 might not be so important to ten-year-olds in 1954—and television that was never listed in a 1940 study would probably rate a top place among children's choices today. Furthermore, the choices and attitudes of city children are known to be quite different from those in a small rural community. Thus, it seems apparent that we cannot accept research findings about children's interests without asking how recently the study was made and in what kind of community.

All of this points to the importance of teacher-librarian co-operation in determining what children are most interested in. Frequently teachers have asked their pupils to fill in a brief check list or questionnaire about their hobbies, activities, most urgent questions, favorite stories, favorite radio and TV programs. And in many cases the alert librarian can pick up some further hint that will help the teacher find a special interest on which to build a reading project for some particular child.

Yet the interests of the child are only one determining factor in his search for the right book. He wants it to be an interesting subject, but he also wants it on his reading level. In an uncanny way he will reject one book after another in his search for "the right book." He has no measuring rod to determine the reading level of the book, but he knows when it is right for him and is much happier when he has had a hand in determining whether the book fits him.

Just what range of reading levels can the teacher and librarian expect to be in each classroom group? The most authoritative answer to this question seems to be that given by Willard C. Olson of the University of Michigan in *The Packet*, service bulletin of D.C. Heath and Company.

Thus, according to Dr. Olson, a typical group of fifth graders will be reading on nine different "book levels"—Grade 1 through Grade 9 (read down under V). Children in such a classroom will need books on as many levels if they are to read easily and comfortably and if they are to progress naturally. Certainly it would be a farce to expect all such children to read from one reader or even to read from books on the three levels selected for slow, average, and fast groups.

The new individualized reading program is a library-centered program. It presupposes a wide variety of books in some accessible plan where children can browse and make their own selections. How well they choose their books will depend in part on the way the books are introduced and displayed. If the librarian has been able to introduce certain books to one class through storytelling, reading aloud, or capsule summary, she has alerted those youngsters to the possibility of those particular books. If she has displayed the jackets or perhaps children's evaluations of the books, she may be able to reach still more youngsters. If she has given teachers an opportunity to explore new books, she may be able to enlist their support in advertising her wares. And because they know something of the books in advance, children will be able to make their selections more easily and more effectively.

With such a program, learning to read becomes a great adventure whereby children explore the world of children's books and sample the joys of reading.

What NDEA Has Done for School Libraries

Mary V. Gaver, Professor
Graduate School of Library Service, Rutgers University

The request to evaluate, as of October 1959, the effects of the National Defense Education Act on the purchase of trade books by school libraries has proved to be a frustrating and only slightly hopeful assignment. Frustrating, because the discernible results up to the present are so annoyingly small and scattered—and encouraging for both school librarians and publishers because of the great possibilities for better provision of learning materials for boys and girls.

The direct effects of the NDEA on school libraries stem primarily from the provisions of Titles III, V, and VIII in the subject areas of science, mathematics, foreign languages, guidance, and vocational education. In each subject area, money may be spent for printed materials (not textbooks), *if* the state plan specifies this and *if* the local school librarian is on the job. Simplified to the nth degree, the Act provides grants of money on a matching basis for programs of education in these subject areas; the initiative, however, is assigned to the state departments of education and by them to the local school districts to choose to spend the grant or any part of it on printed materials.

The difficulty in evaluating results at the present time arises from the following facts: (1) the reports for the first year's operation are just now being compiled; (2) the preliminary report from the U.S. Office of Education for June 30, 1959 does not show a breakdown for library purchases; (3) much of the first year's appropriations was, in many states, rightly used primarily for the purchase of equipment; and (4) the provisions of the Act leave the purchase of trade books for library purposes almost entirely to local initiative—and therefore results are much slower to be seen.

In an effort to secure some advance picture of possible results of the Act, the writer made a survey of a small number of states, with the following results:

West Virginia

In West Virginia, the president of the state library association writes that under their state plan printed materials other than textbooks "may be purchased." At a recent meeting of education personnel in the state, it was indicated the "library books could be included but emphasized that this would be the case during the enrichment phase rather than the basic phase." The same source writes that in no case has he "been able to find that the school systems have been told specifically that library books may be included." Furthermore, no li-

brarians were appointed to the "committees which drew up the basic equipment lists at state level." This information is quoted in this way, because it is probably typical of the conditions in some of the other states where strong library leadership, as through a state supervisor of school libraries, is lacking.

New Jersey

In New Jersey, one of the most decentralized states in educational administration, there was no overall participation in the development of the state plan by practicing school librarians, although the state school library consultant did participate in state planning. References to pertinent bibliographies were included in the directions to local school districts. In the case of this state, new state positions were created for supervision in the NDEA areas of emphasis and the first annual report is now in process of compilation. The New Jersey state consultant has stated that a scanning of these reports reveals a "surprising inclusion of purchases of library books."

Indiana

In Indiana, another state with school library supervision, advisory committees on each subject in the NDEA included a school librarian in each case. Georgia Rankin Cole, the consultant, has distributed a number of excellent guides for purchase of trade books. A report from another source estimated that where grants to local schools amount to $10,000-$12,000, in the best situations somewhat more than 10 per cent of the amount was spent for printed materials. One advantage of school librarian participation in such state committees is that information about the procedure and the possibilities under the Act is more widely and more quickly disseminated.

Washington

In the state of Washington, where there is at present no state supervisor but where the state school library association has been very active, the association was asked by the State Department of Education to compile lists of library materials for guides in NDEA purchases. This was done but no information has yet been received as to the results.

Florida

Florida has a strong state plan which points out the need for better instruction materials in the schools and sets standards for the selection of trade books. Preliminary reports for the first year from Audrey Newman, the state supervisor, show about $50,000 available at the secondary level and $25,000 at the elementary level for printed materials under the state plan.

Hawaii

In Hawaii two tremendous developments occurred during 1959 for the advancement of school libraries—the establishment of the position of director of school library services and a sizeable increase in the appropriation for school library books to $1 per child or a total of $172,000. Carolyn Crawford, the first appointee to the new position, reports that neither development was directly due to NDEA; the Hawaiian school librarians had worked actively for these increases and they came in the same year as NDEA.

She reports, however, that through the cooperation of other state supervisors there is strong motivation of school librarians to spend money allotted under NDEA for materials in science and mathematics. They are making heavy use of the booklists of the American Association for the Advancement of Science (1515 Massachusetts Avenue N.W., Washington 5, D.C.); results are more easily obtainable in Hawaii because of the high degree of centralization in their school system.

North Carolina

North Carolina has the best and most carefully worked out state plan seen by the writer. A report from Cora Paul Bomar illustrates the excellent results which can be attained in a state where there is strong leadership and good working relationships on the part of librarians with specialists in the subject fields. Among the results of the NDEA reported for this state are: (1) establishment of a state materials center; (2) increase in status of state staff and addition of new state level positions; (3) excellent coverage in the state guides on standards for printed materials to be purchased, with little use of specific lists of titles; (4) emphasis on evaluation of the library in relation to the total education program, as a basis for selection of the materials to be added.

These states are cited here only as examples; no attempt was made to secure an overall survey. If these states are at all typical, they indicate a likelihood that the results of the NDEA on the purchase of trade books for libraries have ranged from meager in some states to sizable in others. The extent of influence of the NDEA will probably have a high correlation to the working relationships between school librarians and their colleagues in education, especially principals and superintendents, as well as the ability of leaders at the state level to see and spell out the opportunities for library development through this act.

The long term implications of the Act for trade books were stated by one state supervisor to be "a marvelous opportunity and a grave responsibility"; they were stated by a high official of the National Education Association to be a "great frustration." They certainly provide a great opportunity to develop programs and secure richer book resources for school libraries in these critical subject matter areas. The frustration arises from the limitation of the subject matter fields and the fact that so much depends on initiative at the local level where action is always slow and particularly slow in states where state supervision of school libraries is lacking.

Needs Highlighted by the Act

What are some of the needs which have been emphasized by this first year of work with the provisions of the NDEA?

It is obvious from a look at the fall booklists that many publishers are already aware of possibilities for many new kinds of books to meet the needs in the areas highlighted by the NDEA. Many new aspects of science and mathematics are being treated; new kinds of books for teaching an interest in, or developing facility in, foreign languages are appearing; many more fine stories are being translated from foreign languages and made available in English. We still need more good books at all levels on specific aspects of subjects. Possibly one of the greatest needs is for more adequate provision of books treated in an adult style, for use with the more capable young person studying the subjects emphasized by NDEA. As advanced placement programs, and other forms of emphasis on work with gifted young people, become better established, school libraries must provide for their needs far more adequately than in the past.

There is particular need for better provision of materials in the field of vocational education. Although programs are possible in this subject area, no report seen by the writer mentioned this field as one with which school librarians were working. Attention has already been called to the real needs for new materials in this field by the library consultant for the Connecticut Bureau of Vocational Education, who particularly urges the provision of a "Standard Catalog" for this subject area (*see* "The Function of the Library Program in Today's Vocational School." Anna C. Moore, *School Libraries*, Jan. 1957).

School libraries need to make far more adequate provision of professional materials for teachers in all these subject areas. Listing of professional materials is one of the strong points of the *Purchase Guide* (*see* JrL, Sept. '59, p. 24) and constitutes also one of the new emphases of the forthcoming *Standards for School Library Programs* (ALA, 1960). The inclusion of these materials in the provision of the Act provides a real opportunity for school librarians to indoctrinate their colleagues with the potential services of school libraries to their subject area.

The Act also points up dramatically the need for publishers to keep good titles in print. Although the power of a listing in the *Children's Catalog* to keep a title in print is proverbial, it is also true that many useful titles have been allowed to become unavailable. Allied to this is the fact that we have outgrown in our demands the present sizes of the *Children's Catalog* and the *Standard Catalog for High School Libraries*. These two basic tools have maintained a stable size only by dropping titles in order to add new ones. With the emphasis in new curricula, in programs of study, and in the provisions of the NDEA on such subjects as foreign languages and mathematics, it is now essential to find ways of increasing their scope so that a greater variety of titles may be listed. The expansion of our basic bibliographies should lessen to some extent the necessity for dependence on special subject lists.

The brief survey reported here also points up the quite obvious need for leadership in school libraries at the state level in all our states. Two-fifths of the states still lack this fundamental provision. This need is evidenced, in one way, by the greater awareness of the needs of school libraries in these states where such an official is working. It is also evidenced by the extent to which states can rely on criteria and standards for selection, rather than on specified lists of trade books. Certainly greater freedom to adapt to local needs can be achieved where selection does not have to be limited to a specified list.

The benefits of such leadership can be spread to other states through publication of articles describing the operation of NDEA state plans; several of these are reported to be "in the works" and, if not, it is strongly recommended that they be prepared and published.

Need for Qualified Personnel

Finally, the greatest need highlighted through the NDEA operation is for well qualified personnel—for school librarians who know their materials in these fields, who know how to work with teachers to get books in use, and who are capable and effective in working with administrators to get printed materials included in state and local plans. The correlation of the findings of the NEA study on *The Secondary School Teacher and Library Services* (*see* JrL, Mar. '59, p. 123) should be noted, in relation to the subjects emphasized by the National Defense Education Act. With the exception of science, all the subject areas represented in the NDEA rate toward the bottom of the list in amount of use by teachers, in the judgment by teachers as to the importance of library materials for their subject, in the rating by teachers on the adequacy of their school library collections, and in the extent to which teachers of these subjects encourage students to use the library.

When you come right down to it, whatever furthers the implementation of the new school library standards will also further the implementation of the NDEA for school libraries and will, inevitably, sell more trade books for publishers. ALA has given a high priority to all programs of implementation of standards and the American Association of School Librarians, as a division of ALA, is concentrating all its efforts on implementation plans for its *Standards for School Library Programs*, to be published by ALA in February. The Woman's National Book Association, whose members work directly in publishing, can share in this double implementation by seeing to it that textbooks in the field of education contain strong treatments on the use of library resources in teaching and on the administrator's role in supporting and developing school libraries.

It appears quite likely that for the United States as a whole the sums spent for trade books through NDEA have so far amounted only to peanuts; they will stay at that level unless librarians work far more effectively with administrators and teachers than they have in the past.

Bibliography

Guide to the National Defense Education Act of 1958. Carlson, Theodora E. U.S. Office of Education (Superintendent of Documents, Government Printing Office, Washington 25, D.C.)

Improve Your Teaching with Books through the NDEA of 1958. American Book Publishers' Council and American Textbook Publishers' Institute (24 West 40th Street, New York 18).

Library Opportunities in the National Defense Act of 1958. American Library Association.

Purchase Guide for Programs in Science, Mathematics, Modern Foreign Languages. Chief State School Officers, Ginn and Company. $3.95.

The National Defense Education Act, a Preliminary Report for the Period Ending June 30, 1959. Library Services Branch, U.S. Office of Education (Department of Health, Education and Welfare, Washington 25, D.C.).

"The NDEA, *School Librarians and School Libraries."* Mahar, Mary Helen. *Wilson Library Bulletin*, 31:737-80, June 1959.

The Essence of Learning

Louis Shores, Editor-in-chief of Colliers Encyclopedia and Dean,
Florida State University Library School

Of course all librarians are educators also. But school librarians are educators in a unique sense. In some ways the school librarian is nearer to the educators' firing lines than his colleague in the college or university library. For one thing, the school librarian must be evaluated and certificated by the state agency first as a teacher. For another thing school librarians are virtually required to identify themselves with teacher organizations. Consequently, it is no surprise that school librarians as individuals have membership in the National Education Association as well as the American Library Association. But it is a real tribute to the American Association of School Librarians that it is the first division of ALA to gain divisional status in NEA as well. If any official recognition of the fact that librarians are also educators is necessary, we at long last have it, thanks to the school librarians.

Somehow, this achievement, the first all-librarian division in the colossal NEA, is a triumph for the whole library profession. It signals a long delayed recognition of the role of librarianship in education. Here is a symbolization of the fact that libraries not only support classrooms and librarians aid teachers, but that libraries, and librarianship in its own right, may present an educational philosophy espoused by no other segment of the pedagogical profession.

For many years my library soul has protested against the subordinated position assigned by professional education to librarianship. Tragically, too many librarians have acquiesced and even pen-lashed in the journals certain colleagues who did not appear to be up on the latest researches in child psychology and pedagogical method. I recall a certain university librarian colleague of mine who was forever repeating the shibboleth, "Books must follow the curriculum." One day the principal of the demonstration school, mimicking him, said to me, "Often as I walk down the hall thinking of our curriculum I am conscious of the fact that something is tiptoeing behind me."

The time has come to challenge this educational dogma. I recall how many times I have worked with curriculum developers who always ended by saying, "Now that we have a curriculum constructed will you develop a list of books to go with it?" In the article I wrote for the *Saturday Review* (March 22, 1958) which they made the editorial for the first National Library Week I said, "The book is the composite of man's communicability, his evidence of life."

I repeat this here and add *the book is the composite of the school curriculum.* Rather than the book following the curriculum, I believe a better course of study would result if the curriculum followed the book.

Nor is the curriculum the only pedagogical area in which we should assert ourselves. I believe libraries have within them the very essence of learning. With due respect to the scientific studies of child psychology, I hope that neither the psychologist nor the librarian will ever conclude that now at last we understand precisely how children learn. Indeed, the more I read in psychological literature the more I doubt some of the principles of learning espoused there.

Of course I can be put in my place summarily by pointing out that none of my theories has been scientifically demonstrated. But I am afraid I will persist stubbornly that the scientific method has as often as not led to mistaken conclusions. Study the history of education for evidences of reversals in theories about learning. Or compare debates among contemporary Watsonians, Freudians, Koffkans, Deweyites, and others. In my book there is still one to be heard from: J. B. Rhine. I agree with him that psychology has been too busy with physiology. It is parapsychology alone that considers the body less and the psyche more.

I have just experienced on Broadway that moving miracle of Helen Keller. On one occasion her teacher exclaims "Obedience is the basis of understanding." And we have been through that in education. A little later as she struggles with the blind, deaf, mute child she cries out in despair, "But obedience is not enough for understanding." With the pedagogical book before her at night after the child has at last fallen asleep, she masters all the psychology that science has been able to muster. Conscientiously she teaches touch spelling by the best scientific method. But yet there is no understanding in the child, nor real comprehension. "O, God," she prays. She herself had just conquered her own blindness. "O, God, you owe me a resurrection. Or do I owe you one? How do I teach understanding to a child short three of her senses?"

I shall not spoil the play or the book for you. The miracle transcends the scientific method. It has nothing to do with child psychology. It is out of this world, not in the trite sense of the colloquialism, but because in Hamlet's words, "There are more things in heaven and earth, Horatio,/Than are dreamt of in your philosophy." And these things come from meditation, and introspection, and inspiration. They belong to those eons that make our three score ten on earth sink into insignificance. And a scientific method bounded by the five senses of one of the tiniest planets in the universe simply doesn't have a chance of understanding. It behooves education to observe diligently the chief school unit that nourishes imagination and provides the atmosphere for meditation. *No scientific study will ever discover how many miracles of understanding are created in the school library.*

As a librarian, too, the whole professional literature of reading readiness has irritated me. It is probably scientifically sound. The accent seems to me to be in the wrong places. "Delay reading," conclude some investigators, "until the child is ready." This strikes me as a negative approach. With a librarian's bias I would advocate, "Expose babies to books as early as possible, even pre-natally. Let the infant be born in the presence of books, and do not let a single day pass that the baby and the book are not contiguous at least for a few minutes. The physiology will adjust to the psyche, I believe, without injury to the eye."

Nor can I refrain from resisting the pragmatic foundation of much of our educational philosophy. "Learning by doing" is a phrase popularized from the writings of John Dewey. It has been translated into the activity school. As an example, the child learns Latin by constructing a model of the Roman forum. Said the Latin teacher in my school cafeteria as she jumped up from lunch, "Since we've gone activity, I can't stay away from my room too long for fear the children will annihilate each other with hammer and saw." Taking a cue from *Orbis Pictus* we now illustrate everything, making sure that abstract ideas become concrete images. I am sure that my friend Edgar Dale who has done so much for reading had no intention of placing the book in an unfavorable position among instructional media. Yet many an audio-visual teacher so presents his "cone of experience" that students conclude the printed word is the lowest form of educational communication. Dr. Dale has himself said otherwise in his *Challenges to Librarianship*.

I have long been an advocate of audio-visual media in libraries. In 1935 I introduced the first audio-visual course ever offered in an accredited library school. Florida and Florida State University Library School have for years championed the union of school libraries and audio-visual centers. In *Instructional Materials* (Ronald 1960), my latest book, I attempted to introduce the teacher to the whole range of learning resources at her disposal in a well-stocked school library or materials center. I cannot say better than I have said in that book (p. 100) that we must never underestimate the importance of abstract learning through the medium of the printed word: "What we must never forget is that there are still some children who learn better and more through reading than through almost any other kind of activity."

For a final contribution librarians have to offer to education, I turn to my reference specialty. Over the door of our former library building at Florida State University are the often quoted words, "The half of knowledge is knowing where to find it." I assume, therefore, if the nation's schools will make it possible for the librarian to perform her reference function, half of the job can be done right in the library.

Of course, I believe that. And much more, too. Reference is the very essence of learning. I think I chose the profession of librarianship at the ripe age of 15 as much because of a

reference discovery as for any other reason. We were studying magnetism in physics. As in preceding chapters of the textbook, I was suffering from lack of understanding. In despair I went to the library where I accidentally developed an approach that was novel to me. I consulted two encyclopedias and the indexes of four science books. Somewhere in those six references I found one that kindled my individual pile of dry fuel. A fire leaped up and in a flash I began to understand how the molecules arranged themselves. I read on and on for contrast and comparison, and even for contradictions. This was the element of learning. For me, understanding was born in that school library. I went to class with the first confidence I had ever had in physics. My recitation, especially when I pointed to a contradiction in the text, brought gasps from my classmates. My *A* was assured.

From this reference experience I gradually built a learning approach that helped me in college as well as in high school. Stimulated by my experience in magnetism, I made it an unfailing rule to begin each term with a reference overview of all the subjects in which I was enrolled. Because the encyclopedia is the composite of almost all of the other reference book types, I began by overviewing the subject of each course in one or more of the good sets. Unknown to me then, I had discovered the perfect preface to learning. The overview enabled me to anticipate what the teacher would teach in that course. If she developed the subject as I had been led to believe it should be developed by my reference book reading, I was properly gratified. If she did not, I would compare her treatment with the one I expected, and differ or accept. In any event I was learning, forcing myself to try to understand.

Comparison and overview are only two of the aspects of the reference approach to learning. Who will gainsay the elements of documentation and bibliography, of spot checking and verifying, of the many habits of scholarship that are by-products of reference-book handling. You can see why the fourth R for me has always been *reference*.

I must restrain myself from developing further this reference devotion. My thesis is larger than the mere half of knowledge. When Carlyle wrote that the true university is a library, he was not merely providing a commencement quotation for an orator. He believed as I wrote for my address "The Library Arts College" (*School and Society* 1935) at the American Library Association meeting in Chicago during the world's fair, the potential for learning in the library is greater than the potential for learning in the classroom.

This I believe today more than ever, after nearly four decades of library and education work. This I reassert to you my colleagues. And to the school librarians among you, especially, I add, we have an unparalleled opportunity. Our Sputnik-frustrated nation is casting desperately for a panacea to our real and imagined educational deficiencies. Through the National Defense Education Act they voted partial confidence in instructional media. Our schools are now ready, even if out of the desperation of national dissatisfaction, to turn to us as never before.

I pray God that we librarians will have the courage and the wisdom during these critical years ahead to harness the tremendous potential of libraries in the interest of better learning.

Taming the Young Barbarian

Margaret Edwards

Robert Benchley began one of his essays, "One day last winter as I was thumbing through some snow in my attic, I found . . . ." I don't remember what he found but I was reminded of thumbing through the snow when, only a few weeks ago, I summoned the strength finally to open the door of a little room upstairs and sort out the incredible collection left over from 30 years at the Pratt Library.

When I did finally sort out the membership cards for 1957, the thread with no needle, the medicine for an illness long since cured and notes from budget meetings of the last 10 years, I found a residue of paragraphs and pages that dealt with reading clipped or copied from various publications. These, and the train of thought they started, I should like to thumb through with you.

In his book, *Against the American Grain*, Dwight McDonald notes, "Although we have the highest level of formal education in the world, fewer people buy and read books in this nation than in any other modern democracy. The typical Englishman with far less education reads nearly three times as many. If he leaves school at 14, he reads as many books per year as our college graduates . . . . In 1955 [a Gallup poll revealed that] half of our high school graduates and one fourth of our college graduates did not read a single book."

As a member of a citizens' committee concerned with school libraries, I have read the recently issued Deiches Report with the greatest interest. The situation as regards reference work is serious to say the least but even more alarming, it seems to me, is the statement in the report that many students' books are little more than a means of preparing a lesson and getting good marks. The fact that most of the reading done in connection with schoolwork has not been enriching and meaningful enough to lead students to read on their own means that books and reading are not affecting the quality of citizenship here as they must. If a fourth of the college graduates and half the high school graduates in any given year in this country do not read a single book and if many of those who do read one or two are reading on a low level, the public library in America is not the dynamic force it should be, to put it mildly.

Of course we shall never make readers of all the people but we should be able to do as well as the democracies where the public library is not so advanced as ours. Why is it that in most large cities where libraries are as good or better than they are in other localities, only from five to 10 per cent of the adults are registered? Why do Americans read so little at a time when knowledge and understanding are so essential?

There are many reasons: the complexity of modern living, the demands made on parents who deliberately exploded the population, the speeded-up tempo of every passing day, and other reasons the trained sociologist could point out.

Yet we know that even under the pressures of modern living, people find time to do the things they really want to do. They view thousands of banal TV programs; ride for hours on Sunday afternoons in crowded traffic, getting nowhere; they sit idly on public conveyances, staring out the window; or they play endless games of cards because all these things seem better ways of spending time than reading. No one ever made reading seem important or interesting and many people fail to stumble on this idea unaided.

As for the students, Dr. Lowell Martin says that they read to complete an assignment, to please the teacher and get a better mark that will help them get into college; but that ends the matter for a majority of the graduates. If Dr. Martin is correct, few of these students have learned from their schoolwork that a book is to read. This shows up in the low percentage of adults registered with the library and may be one of the reasons Dr. Martin found little objection on the part of adults to the teenagers taking over the library.

I believe we are agreed that it is the function of the public library to make books available to people, that anyone who wishes to read standard books in any general field might expect to borrow them from his library. Here are books to enjoy, to think about, to use in solving problems included problems related to school assignments. But is it enough for a library to provide material only for those who seek it? Or should it penetrate the community to foster an attitude everywhere toward reading and cultural growth?

I found among my souvenirs that Allan Nevins said, "The best single test of a nation's culture remains what it has always been since the days of Gutenberg —its attitude towards books." I also found an old yellowed clipping from a Baltimore *Sun* report of a commencement address by Dr. Fosdick at Johns Hopkins. He was discussing the differences between civilization and culture by saying, "Civilization is easily handed down. Contrivances invented in one generation are taken for granted as a matter of course in the next. But profound spiritual culture is not so easily transmissible. . . . So it commonly happens that while the outward apparatus of civilization piles up and moves on, there is an appalling lag in spiritual culture until mankind stands as it stands today, with vast implements to use and the old barbarian using them."

The old barbarian reborn with each generation is the responsibility of the church, the school and the library. To civilize him is our charge. The library does this, not just by helping him solve problems, but by selling him the idea of reading books that will change him. The barbarian, the nature boy, walks our streets by the thousands, unchallenged by the culture in books. When half the country's high school graduates do not read a single book a year, the library is not fulfilling its mission.

An excerpt from an article by Elizabeth Bowen in the *New York Times Book Review* of August 31, 1958, seems to say what it is we want books to do to people:

> We require to be transported, to transcend boundaries—not . . . merely . . . to "escape" but out of a necessity for enlargement.
>
> We have within us a capacity, a desire, to respond. One of the insufficiencies of routine existence is the triviality of the demands it makes on us. Largely unused remain our funds of pity, spontaneous love, unenvious admiration or self-less anger . . . .
>
> We need to marvel. Overhung as we are by the nominal, concrete "marvels" of our century—the triumphs of science, the masterworks of technology—we are creatures of numbed fancy and stunned senses. . . . . Yet we await, it seems, the storyteller's cry of "Behold!"
>
> A story may act on us while it runs its course, and for that time only. . . . Another story, when its nominal end is reached, is only at the beginning of its term of life; from now on, it will continue to make growth, extend, deepen. Rooted in our imagination, it induces reflectiveness. In itself an experience, it stays at work within us, affecting experiences we may later have.

How often this magic of the book described by Elizabeth Bowen has been demonstrated to individuals on the library floor and to classes in the city high schools by skillful, disciplined young adult librarians. Slow, manual-minded shop boys have burst into applause at a 15-minute recital of poetry, amazed that poetry could mean so much to a man that he would memorize whole pages of it. Accelerated classes have been intrigued at a discussion of those three ruthless women —Becky Sharpe, Eustacia Vye and Scarlett O'Hara—or by a comparison of the three introverted heroes of *The Way of All Flesh, An American Tragedy* and *Of Human Bondage*. Fairly dull classes have been fascinated with a description of the teenager's life in Russia, with recommendations of four or five recent books from which the information is extracted. The recreation of the childhood and youth of the lonely, unloved, ugly Eleanor Roosevelt has led to a better understanding of a great woman as well as to an interest in biography. Time after time, teachers have said that after these visits a wave of reading has swept over the school.

The young adult librarian performs with equal skill inside the library where he works to keep each individual up to the highest level of reading compatible with his interest and ability, where he provides a sounding board for the young reader who wishes to discuss what he has read.

In March of 1957, Dr. John F. Fischew, then superintendent of the Baltimore Public Schools, wrote an editorial for his staff newsletter entitled "On Making Horses Thirsty" which I had added to my collection. The item concludes:

> We shall serve neither the needs of society nor the welfare of our people if we resort for excuse to the old saw about leading a horse to water. Children are not horses. With wise and sensitive guidance many can be persuaded that the water of learning is good for them. The best teachers are always able, having brought their charges to the water, also to stimulate a healthy thirst.

Jessamyn West has said, "I believe that short of lifesaving itself there is no more blessed act on this earth than the spirit-saving act of putting into the hands of a hungry child a book which will sustain him imaginatively, feed him morally and refresh him esthetically."

So I repeat what I have already said. The present crisis in reference work with school assignments is acute and must be faced but we must do more than help the young barbarian pass his courses in school. The awakening of his mind, the enlargement of his spirit, the quickening of his understanding through books are still the greatest contributions the library can make to him and his city and his country.

" . . . adolescents should be taught to realize that they constitute only a segment of society, and not a universe of their own, and . . . one of the ways of accomplishing this is through books. I am encouraged as a practicing high school librarian to note a trend in that direction . . . . The readers in my school . . . are asking for more and more adult nonfiction and mature fiction." —*Marjorie Hoke, "Out on a Limb," published by the Illinois Children's Reading Round Table.*

Underway:

The Knapp's Project's First Year

Peggy Sullivan

Retrospection, introspection and direction of the Knapp School Libraries Project are an unlikely combination. The day-to-day running of a project which has generated strong national interest and enthusiasm allows not much time for looking back, and all too little time for planning ahead.

Yet the plain title of an ordinary mimeographed sheet produced almost two years ago is proof that there were those who had both foreknowledge and foresight to stimulate an interest and continuing concern for the future of school libraries.

The title? "Project: To Demonstrate the Educational Value of a Full Program of School Library Services."

In that statement of intent on a proposal which won the interest and financial support of the Knapp Foundation, Inc., lie the answers to many questions which have been raised about the Knapp Project in its first year.

A mountain of correspondence (some 25 items directed to the Project office daily), a sheaf of applications (more than 200 thus far), a great deal of talk (by the planners, the participants and the watchers) and miles of travel (much of it by the Project director)—these already are parts of the past. What is there to show for them?

When two schools were selected last June for participation in Phase I, immediately many groups became interested in seeing for themselves the library programs that had merited this recognition from the Knapp Project. Even during the summer of 1963, when both the Central Park Road School in Plainview, New York, and the Marcus Whitman School in Richland, Washington, were expanding their library facilities (at school district expense, not Project expense), requests for visits began to come—and a few visitors arrived unannounced.

The funds provided by the Project were still in the process of being spent for materials and, sensibly, both schools had planned to spread the expenditures through the early months of the 1963-64 school year, when teachers could share in the selection of materials and when the purchase of nonprint materials could be coordinated with the instructional program of the schools.

These first visitors were, in some instances, disappointed. But the seeds for their disappointment were ones they had sown themselves, in their anticipation of seeing the ultimate in elaborate physical facilities and fullblown program. They viewed, instead, school libraries in the active process of stepping up their formerly good programs, of absorbing new staff, of adjusting to new quarters and, yes, of being accustomed to carrying on excellent programs under the continually probing eyes of curious, knowledgeable visitors who write us:

"We were impressed by the central role played by the library in the school, so that very effective teaching resulted from close liaison between librarian and teacher. We were impressed with the children's free access to the library, especially at noon, and with other frequent periods of browsing, studying, reading, listening to records, running films in individual booths, etc."

"We were received graciously; we saw teachers and children in action in the classroom; and we had a chance to ask questions and find out about the inner workings of the school library."

The large numbers of groups requesting funds for visits to the Phase I schools provide one guide to the interest in the Project. Hundreds of requests made it necessary to be selective of the groups which receive funds. Among the groups receiving grants for travel was one made up of members of a citizens' committee and administrators of a city school district. They described their interest in developing better financial and operational support for the system of elementary libraries by seeing "what operations and administrative assistance are needed to bring our system up to standards. . . ."

From another school district, where only one elementary school library has space larger than a classroom (and that one is in a new building under construction) will come a group "to observe a demonstration of new ideas in library service; to see a way of remodeling a building to create space for a modern library."

Yet even in our most golden dreams, we must admit that the numbers of people directly benefited by the Knapp Project as participants in a demonstration center or visitors to such centers will be small. What of the school librarians who will never see a Project school? What of the superintendents and principals who will persistently brush brochures into wastebaskets or scan them with suspicion, because all "giveaways" are suspect? What of the parent who is honestly puzzled when asked to support a plan for tax support of a school library program?

The school librarian who will not ever see a Project school may be one who labored over the preparation of an extensive application for the Project, and wrote: "Our application will be mailed from the superintendent's office. I am very happy to have finally completed it. It has been a wonderful experience for me and a profitable one for all of us who have been involved. I wish to personally thank you for giving us the opportunity to participate in the Project thus far."

A superintendent, sharing the same kind of interest, wrote: "We are pleased to have the privilege of applying for consideration. I know of no other program that has the potential of contributing as much to the total school program as does this project. The pressing needs in all areas of the school program, as well as the lack in general understanding of the position of the library, has limited the growth of libraries in [our state]. It has been difficult to secure the financial support necessary to establish and maintain them. It is very pleasing to see the increased interest and development."

The Knapp Project itself is one indication of this "increasing interest and development." The fact that the officers and board of a foundation, inured to many pleas for aid, considered this Project worth $1,130,000 proves that. And the bulk of that sum will be allotted directly to the individual schools and teacher-education institutions taking part in it, as well as to the visitors selected to receive travel grants to Project schools.

The Project is unusual in selecting individual schools for participation and in relying on the leadership, organization and potential of the school and school system to develop the library program to its best. For example, librarians in schools selected for Phases I and II had clear ideas of how they wished to spend the funds available for books. The Project did not supply a standard or recommended list of titles, nor did it specify the means or sources for orders. Realizing that a school library functions best when it serves the needs and demands of the staff and students in terms of the instructional program of the school, the Project recommended only that the money for materials be spent in subject areas or grades where it was needed.

Further, since an implicit goal of the Project is that the schools be stimulated to maintain ever after the same levels of support provided during the period of the schools' participation, the staff members employed with Project funds are selected and employed in the same manner and on the same terms as they would be by the local school district. And the terms of agreement between the Project and the school call for continuation of the present financial support for the school's library program, so that the expenditures may be maintained at least at that level once the Project is done.

If we were talking of mythical schools, all cut to a precise pattern and staffed with paper-doll people, each with a given role to play, we might arrive more readily at predetermined conclusions. But we have glibly stated for a long time that the library is the heart of the school. It is indeed an organic part of a whole, volatile being—the school. And in any school there will be changes that affect the library.

Transfers or resignations of faculty members will require the orientation of new teachers to the library program; budget cuts within the school district will curtail some elements of the program; progress in curriculum development will place demand for new materials on the collection, and will cause some materials to be used much less or not at all. To all these changes the good school library is responsive, and these and other changes may alter slightly the character of the library.

There is always the glimmering, will-o'-the-wispish hope that there are places where such changes do not occur and where improved program, facilities, budget and staff will encounter no obstacles. Even if such places existed, would they be good demonstration centers? I doubt it; they would be too stagnant.

It is less than a year since the two schools selected for Phase I were notified of their selection. The schools just chosen to participate in Phase II (see "The News," this issue) are beginning to assign responsibilities among their staff members. And the preliminary steps in preparing Phase III applications are being followed in dozens of secondary schools. Only three schools will eventually participate in Phase III, but we sell the Project short if we fail to realize that it gives to the total personnel of every applying school the much needed opportunity to evaluate their present progress and to develop their future plans.

According to the plan for the Project itself, four of the five years, two of the three phases, are yet to come. It is heartening that response has been so immediate and so enthusiastic. It is promising that schools midway in, or just beginning their participation in, the Project have good plans for evaluating their development.

Best of all, it is stimulating that there are problems yet to be solved, answers yet to be found and questions yet to be asked. A year-old Project with a four-year future can ask for nothing more.

In Full Swing

Peggy Sullivan

I t was hard to believe that the Knapp Project, so rich in "firsts" and innovations, could be terminating one of its activities; but the Chicago meeting this March of the project advisory committee did mark an end, as the last three schools were chosen, for Phase III of the demonstration school library programs. As in the first two phases, the same complex appraisals had to be made—of the school library programs as they complemented the instructional program; administrative and community support; the quality of the library staff; the potential for developing an instructional materials center identified with the school library operation; and the advantages of the schools as demonstration centers.

In a sense the task was easier. Only 62 high schools from 20 states had entered the final competition for Phase III, though many more had expressed an interest and sent in their preliminary applications. Having had two years, however, to prepare themselves for applying, these schools were readier for the close scrutiny that would be given them by the advisory committee.

At the same time, the broadening of interest was notable in the applications which had been prompted by teacher-education institutions eager to coapply with neighboring high schools. And, as more librarians and administrators recognized what these demonstration programs would contribute to their own localities, we received many letters supporting the applications of specific schools, or suggesting that we include certain types of schools: junior high schools, which are often overlooked in programs directed to secondary schools; or schools in nonsuburban, metropolitan districts. In its choice, this year, of senior high schools in Oak Park, Illinois, and Portland, Oregon, and a junior high school in Provo, Utah, the advisory committee has again committed itself to making the Knapp Project as far-ranging as can be reasonably expected.

"When Losers Are Winners"

The advisory committee knew there would be many reactions to its choices; personal disappointments on the part of dedicated librarians and administrators, bitter hints that some applicants had not received fair consideration, wonder that a certain school, known to the inquirer, had not been selected. The last reaction is the easiest to answer: the school itself, having its own administrative problems, and obliged to set priorities in the areas it seeks to develop, may have decided not

to apply. As for fair consideration, we can only affirm that each application was examined meticulously. The opinions of state school library supervisors were actively solicited. Advisory committee members and the project director commented on visits or firsthand knowledge of the school, the school district, and the teacher-education institution. Nevertheless, only three schools could be selected; 59 had to be disappointed.

In this respect, it can only be hoped that many will feel as Mrs. Pauline Houck did when her school, the Mary McClelland School in Wayne Township, Indiana, was turned down in Phase II. The Knapp Project, she writes, focused attention on school libraries in the township. Teachers' colleges have helped to emphasize the need for good school libraries. "Of all the advantages gained from applying for participation in the Knapp Project," she concluded, "by far the greatest was the necessity of appraising and evaluating our library program, and formulating future plans and goals."

Other librarians have derived these indirect benefits. If admiration is measured by imitation, the exciting new demonstration school library program in Connecticut is a boost for the Knapp Project, and a means of extending the idea of demonstration libraries to influence other schools.

With the vast network of communication that has surrounded this project—the generous interest of the library and educational press, the day-to-day reports from Project school visitors and staff—it is important sometimes to focus on the single, telling incident. I remember a student teacher hurrying back to a classroom at the Marcus Whitman School in Richland, Washington, clutching her fresh transparencies and saying, to no one in particular: *"That's* what I like about this school—You give me what I need to teach!" Another memory arises from a conversation with an elementary school principal in Virginia who had just seen the Project film *. . . and Something More.* She said, "You know, that part about the children acting out the story from *The Phantom Tollbooth*—that gave me an idea. We've never had anything about books in our May Day celebration, but there are lots of stories we can have plays about. We'll do it this year; and the library will be taking part in May Day, just the way it does in everything else we do at school."

We have had a surprising response even with the "readiness visits" Phase II schools held early this year, months before their collections, staff, and facilities were ready for full-scale operation. To help us organize Phase II, groups of schoolmen and community leaders were invited to make a "dry run" to see which of the scheduled activities would be most helpful for them in future visits. A member who observed the Allisonville School in Indiana this March wrote: "The Allisonville school library project is well on its way to being an excellent demonstration of good school library service. The school is ready to receive visitors after a few changes have been made in their plans. One of the most encouraging aspects is Mr. Sellmer's (the principal's) insistence that this library program is not just for three years, but for 50, and that he would like to have a third full-time librarian!"

Measures of Success

Visits to Allisonville and the other Phase II schools will be planned extensively for the 1965-66 and the 1966-67 school years. Every effort will be made to grant project travel funds to those with the potential and interest to bring home ideas and work toward making them come alive. Our heavy growing mailing list hints that once again competition for these travel funds will be great and the results of the visits far-reaching.

In the three remaining years of the Project there will be a continuous need for evaluation. The most valuable gauges would be those which measure the specific gains of children who have used school libraries "beefed up" with Project-funded materials and staff. These are also the results most difficult to isolate and quantify. In Richland, library skills tests were given to children at the Project school and a neighboring school which had maintained the same level of library service as had been available before the Project; but both schools' students scored so high, above the 99th percentile as established by national norms, that the measure had little meaning. Dr. Donald Barnes, field worker for the Project school in Indiana, has run a week's test to measure children's skills in various areas related to library use. He will repeat it at intervals in the two years to come, to measure improvement. Yet for him the most surprising results have come from an inquiry directed to students in elementary education at the cooperating Ball State Teachers College. When asked to choose which of several kinds of assistance they would most like to have in their first teaching jobs, the students overwhelmingly gave as first choice a centralized library with a qualified librarian.

Going It Alone

Another measure of effectiveness will be the degree to which improvements are maintained in the schools soon to be withdrawing from Project participation—the Phase I schools in Plainview, New York, and Richland, Washington, which will be "going it alone" after next month. They will have to decide on budget allotments to continue support for their individual school library programs, while also spreading some of the benefits derived from Project participation to other schools in their districts. The district schools will be making new and heavier demands, dramatizing needs that were only incipient until the Knapp Project raised one of their schools to the position of serving as a model.

In any measurement of outcomes, it is the teachers' conviction of the need for the library program that will determine the permanence of improvement. During a visit to Richland in February, I listened with interest to a junior high school teacher, representing his school faculty, earnestly requesting priority for the employment of clerical assistants in the libraries of other schools, pointing out, "We've seen what can happen at Marcus. Now, we want the same freedom for our librarian." This request cannot be written off as the expression of a librarian's empire-building complex; it established the link between the library and the faculty, as well as the fact that the Marcus Whitman School was affecting its neighbors within the community, not just its many visitors.

In looking for results we must be cautious and honest. With every day that goes by, I am made more aware of how intermeshed are the effects of many opportunities—the publication of *Standards for School Library Programs*, the wide-ranging influence of the School Library Development Project, the greater potential for growth in areas where active library recruitment and professionalism have kept closer pace with needs. The Knapp Project has established some patterns of its own, but it is of a piece with these overall patterns too.

One of the most reassuring events this year was the reaffirmation by the Knapp Foundation of its faith and continued support, not merely of the developments to date, but in our plans for the future. These include, in addition to the demonstration school activities, plans for publications, such as a report on Phase I, and sponsorship of institutes, in other Project schools, similar to the one held in Richland, Washington, in February. This institute brought together faculty members of teacher-education institutions throughout the state, calling their attention to the developments of the school library and the implications that ready availability of instructional materials could have for teachers—in their own education, in in-service programs, and all programs designed to help them teach better. Better teaching as a result of better libraries—that, after all, is what the Knapp Project is all about.

"The First Work of These Times"

Statement from the Library Services Branch U.S. Office of Education

With the passage of the Elementary and Secondary Education Act of 1965 (ESEA), the Federal government has added an estimated $1.3 billion to an already sizable investment in education. Title 2, for the purchase or lease of learning materials, has the most direct relevance to library programs (the pages that follow give a detailed breakdown of its terms), but librarians should consider other features of the Act as they relate to library service.

Title 1, with the biggest share of ESEA funds, authorizes grants for programs serving the special needs of "educationally" deprived children, working on the assumption of a link between economic and educational deprivation. The Federal government will give a school district an allotment equal to half of its state's 1963-64 per pupil expenditure for each "deprived" student in that district (a student coming from a family that the 1960 census found to be earning $2000 or less); however, a district may not receive a Title 1 grant amounting to more than 30 percent of its current operating budget.

A host of library or library-oriented programs are suggested under Title 1: for purchase of supplementary instructional materials, special audiovisuals, recordings of classical music, poems, addresses; expansion of libraries in major disciplines; after-school study centers and libraries; library, curriculum, and instructional media centers providing modern equipment and materials for "disadvantaged" children; mobile learning centers and libraries; home oriented bookmobiles; resources for remedial programs (especially in reading and math), English programs for non-English speaking children, and enrichment programs to be held Saturday mornings and in summer. Staffing, materials, equipment, some construction can be paid for with Title 1 funds, though Title 2 money may be coordinated with Title 1 applications.

To obtain its funds, the school district submits a local plan and application for funds to the state education agency for approval.

Title 3 supports educational centers and services that *supplement* individual school programs in terms of quantity or quality, and that will benefit the entire community—preschool children, dropouts, adults—as well as students. Here again, many library-oriented services are eligible: a model school library (perhaps along Knapp Project lines); centralized library service in research and reference, ordering and processing, or after-school use, to serve all the schools in a district. A supplementary center can maintain materials for which a single school has limited need (specialized books, a wide range of audiovisuals, living things, etc.) or equipment, including a/v equipment, which a single school needs only occasionally. It could maintain a production facility with staff and equipment to develop teaching materials; provide library resources for the advanced, remedial, or specialized courses that would be taught in the centers; or establish mobile educational services for rural areas, migrant worker camps, etc.

Public libraries are among the many agencies which qualify for representation on the planning team, but it would be best not to wait to be invited. Contact the district school superintendent now, offer your services, and ask to be represented on his planning committee. Project applications will be sent from the superintendent's office to the state education agency for review, then to the Office of Education for approval. Grants will be made directly from the Office of Education to the local districts, and funds may be carried to the next fiscal year.

Details on state and local variations in planning for ESEA funds should be available now, or soon, from district school superintendents, and from the coordinators of the various Titles at the state education agency administering ESEA. Write also to the USOE legislative branch for copies of the act and other data.

Revolution in Our Schools

by John Fogarty, Member of the U.S. Congress (D) from Rhode Island

School libraries are caught in the middle of a whirlwind. Never before have people relied so decisively on formal education to reach their goals. As the industrial revolution depended on the human body, the electronic and the nuclear revolution will depend increasingly on the power and flexibility of highly trained intelligence. At the center of this educational whirlwind is the electronic processing of knowledge and its immediate transmission to the point of need.

In this revolution it will become increasingly difficult to tell a librarian from a teacher—any kind of librarian at any level from all kinds of teachers at all levels. Learning, after all, is exclusively an individual process, and in recognition of that fact more and more emphasis is being placed on individual instruction. Teachers, librarians, or machines can only assist in making it as efficient and productive as possible, and in doing so their roles will overlap more and more.

Individualized instruction has always been the fundamental concept behind libraries: "the right book for the right reader at the right time" still sums up the best basis for developing library service. As this concept pervades educational theory and practice, only the means, not the ends, will change and develop. Educational technology will soon make it possible to bring the best teacher, the best book, the best educational experience to each student.

The size and urgency of the job demand innovation, flexibility, and prompt action. We must shorten or eliminate the lag that has existed between the best library practices anywhere and all libraries everywhere.

The Knapp School Libraries Project has been an indicator of things to come. The Oak Park High School in Illinois has combined Knapp project funds and an ESEA Title III grant to develop electronic retrieval of concept films in the library through a joint effort of teachers, librarians, administrators, and private industry. The library is building 175 carrels in which students can dial selections whenever convenient. In fact, a child at home in the evening will eventually be able to dial programs on his telephone or TV set.

This kind of development, as it proves effective, should be picked up promptly by other schools to meet their needs. But we must identify effective techniques more swiftly to equalize their impact on all students.

For this purpose, a network of regional educational laboratories is being set up by the U.S. Office of Education. It will help local school districts assess their own educational programs and practices, develop or identify new methods to improve them, and put worthwhile innovations into effect. Many of these laboratories will be studying the potential of projects like Oak Park's in solving educational problems. When the educational improvement justifies the cost of the equipment, the center will develop demonstration projects. The laboratories will also determine whether the content has been adequately evaluated, and will recommend successful programs to local school districts.

The work of these laboratories is an extension of research conducted by the Office of Education for years. But now they will bring research results to the schools themselves, giving the experiments a practical orientation which will help speed up and focus the entire program for educational improvement. The federal government will continue to carry on a wide range of research and development programs from basic studies in cognitive psychology to development and evaluation of educational techniques, disseminating programs to local school districts.

Technological advances can make their greatest contribution to educational improvement, if we maintain a close working relationship between the "hardware" and the "software" people. It is clear from the many weddings of publishers and electronics firms that industry is becoming increasingly aware of this need. But the partnership must extend also to all in industry who depend on the human resources which our schools develop, and to all those in education, including librarians, who must understand the society for which our youth are being prepared.

These developments have enormous implications for the training and skills of school librarians. They will be called on to work closely with teachers in arranging schedules and facilities for individual student projects. New programs will call for a new approach to selecting and using library resources. Librarians will be serving as liaisons with the community, helping children learn to analyze and solve many local problems. Just as the public library has a responsibility to the general public for stocking current materials on community problems, the school library must keep students informed on current issues—on mental health, water pollution, conservation—so they may learn to be active, interested citizens. School librarians should help children search through materials for conflicting points of view. They will be asked to act as good public relations and information officers, to prepare picture exhibits, lecture series, and informational pamphlets to relate the modern world to academic subjects. The school library will become the first place a child turns to for information, and the school librarian should be far ahead of him in learning his needs.

It will be a tremendous task to reorganize and reshape many of our school libraries to meet such demands. The concept of the library as a center for individual and group research on historical and contemporary problems will naturally cause the physical facilities of the school library to change. It will contain projectors, computers, tape recorders and consoles to enable students to use library resources to maximum individual advantage. Computers will hold both accurate, cross-referenced indexes for information retrieval, and factual informational data. Students will use tape recorders to record their own oral presentations and to listen to research tapes.

This kind of school library requires a new kind of school librarian. Library schools and inservice programs are giving increased attention to school library education. Many library schools now offer courses in the school library as an instructional materials center. Institutes and workshops teach librarians about new skills, new materials, and new equipment. For example, a model elementary school library in Warwick, Rhode Island, funded under ESEA Title III, will be used to train librarians, teachers, and school administrators from all over the state on an inservice basis. The school is in a poverty area.

Besides library school improvements there must be more school librarians. Present standards for staffing are too low for today's instructional programs. More young people should be encouraged to become school librarians, and classroom teachers and other qualified adults recruited to librarianship.

Librarians now in service must also be used more effectively by providing supporting personnel. Routine tasks, if performed by library clerks, aids, or technicians, free librarians for crucial curriculum-related activities.

In assessing the role of the school library in the entire educational community, we must not overlook the potential of Title III of the Library Services and Construction Act of 1966. This title, which provides funds for interlibrary cooperation, will include school libraries in library networks designed to provide maximum access to materials needed by all library users. This provision will directly supplement both ESEA and the Higher Education Act to bring focus and direction to our library efforts.

The movement of the school library from a book-centered agency on the fringes of the educational program to one that supplies the broadest range of instructional materials has radically altered its role in the school. It has moved front and center, and now must become a dynamic new force in the whole picture of elementary and secondary education.

The School Library: An Intellectual Force?

by Mary V. Gaver, professor of library service at Rutgers University,
and president of the American Library Association

A force is "anything that changes or tends to change the state of rest or motion in a body—the capacity to convince or to move." Many school librarians and the learning centers they administer are, of course, forces in the school community; others are dangerously like the library in Bel Kaufman's *Up the Down Staircase.* But are they an "intellectual force?" "Intellect" is defined as "the sum of the mental powers by which knowledge is acquired, retained, and extended, as distinguished from the senses." So whether the school library is in fact an intellectual force in its school community will be determined by the degree to which its staff and the resources it administers allow knowledge to be acquired, retained, and extended.

I'd like to explore first the extent to which, as I view them, school librarians and the school library are in fact an intellectual force, and, second, some of the problem areas in which our professional associations must become much more effective in order to extend our influence.

I'm sure many of you are familiar with Muggles, that unreconstructed rebel from Carol Kendall's *The Gammage Cup*, and the maxims she spouts on every occasion. Several of her maxims seem appropriate to the theme. For example, "If you don't look for trouble, how do you know it's there?" and "When something happens, something else always happens." And finally, "Even a wood mouse can nibble a large hole." So let's start with "If you don't look for trouble, how do you know it's there?" by examining the pros and cons of the school library as an intellectual force.

The tremendous expansion of collections and staffs, improvement in services, growth in number of elementary school libraries, and most of all, acceptance by many leaders of the essential nature of the school library within education, show that it is a real force. A short six to eight years ago, when Dr. Trump accused school libraries of being on the fringes of education, we had to search to find a group of educational leaders who would go on record as being in favor of school libraries, in order to provide promotional material for the AASL standards implementation program. This February, we have U.S. Commissioner of Education Harold Howe saying in an interview:

> What a school thinks about a library is a measure of what it thinks about education. The school which sees education as something which it does to students will

have a small, well-patrolled, attractive, and unused library. But the school which thinks of education as something which it helps students to do for themselves will have a large, actively used library in which the kids are moving about, learning from books and from each other, and creating an atmosphere of people in pursuit of something.[1]

Last fall Robert McNamara, Secretary of Defense, stopped in the middle of a Congressional hearing to ask, why was he talking about the war in Vietnam? The miserable state of the school libraries in the District of Columbia was much more important! And educators in recent years have been saying that you simply can't have a good reading program in an elementary school unless there is an excellent school library.

Another pro. I know of no greater force operating in the library field than the twin activities of the School Library Development Project and the Knapp School Libraries Project, the first financed by the Council on Library Resources and the second by the Knapp Foundation of North Carolina. these two activities have sparked a real major improvement in the quality of leadership shown by librarians and state school library associations throughout the country. The first formal report of the Knapp Project, *Impact: The School Librarian and the Instructional Program*, is just off the press, and will, I trust, help to deepen the project's influence.

A third pro. The contribution made by school libraries to the acquisition, retention, and extension of students' knowledge, especially in the content areas of the school curriculum, is, of course, a very obvious illustration of the school library as an intellectual force. As the dean of the Rutgers library school commented, "If it isn't an intellectual force, what good is it?"

Although the impact of the school library in this particular respect is, in fact, something on which we have little objective evidence, there are some significant findings in the research on elementary school libraries which we carried out at Rutgers a few years ago. The study found that children make greater educational gain, as measured by the Iowa Test of Basic Skills between grades four and six, when they have a full library program for their entire school experience with at least one full-time librarian for every 500 students.

Fourth pro. The great progress that has been made in developing libraries as instructional materials centers is of itself a recognition of the library as an intellectual force. It now seems axiomatic that it is not the format in which a piece of material appears which makes the difference, but its intellectual content. This applies to the enormously popular paperback book as well as to the new 8mm film loop. It is the paramount argument for broadening the library collection's scope and services to include all materials in all forms, when the intellectual content is appropriate to the community served by the library.

There are many other examples of the school library's effectiveness as an intellectual force: its contributions to the spirit of inquiry and independent learning, to the new advanced placement programs, or to the upgrading of curricula at all levels. And there is the tremendous potential force which we now possess in President Johnson's appointment of a National Advisory Commission on Libraries and his recent selection of a school librarian, Mildred Frary, to that commission.

And now for the cons. "If you don't look for trouble, how do you know it's there?" Are there evidences that school libraries are not an intellectual force? I think so.

The most recent study from the U.S. Office of Education on occupational characteristics of school and public librarians, with data only three years old, reports that only 56 percent of the *school* librarians have either a graduate or a professional degree. More disturbing than this, however, is the finding that 61.7 percent of the present school library manpower pool completed work on their highest academic degree in *1949 or earlier*. If you bring it down to the time of Sputnik, this last figure becomes not 61.7 but 75.6 percent. In other words, only a quarter of our group secured their highest academic degree since the revolutions in science, in curriculum, in automation, and in technology which have changed the whole nature of education and of librarianship. Hardly great potential as an intellectual force!

Another con. Several leaders have accused librarians in general, and it is true of some school librarians also, of being passive and apathetic in simply providing material for those users who choose to come to their libraries. The well known Fiske research study carried out in California found school librarians in the sample complaining of feeling isolated in their professional work and subordinate to the opinions and decisions of the school administrator. And, too many of us take refuge in doing a meticulous job of selecting materials without planning the services necessary to introduce those materials to the reluctant or unhabituated reader.

A third contrary point, which members of the Knapp Project advisory committee discovered in evaluating the grant applications: A disturbingly large number of the applicants, including some schools finally selected, evidenced little understanding of the importance and value of nonprint materials in today's instructional programs or had made little progress in implementing this concept. This low level of comprehension of the "IMC" idea was shown in total lack of provision of nonprint materials; failure to understand how to catalog, store, and circulate materials not in traditional book form; insufficient comprehension of criteria for evaluating such materials; and paucity of ideas on how to use them in the instructional program. No doubt the money under new federal programs has changed this in some schools, but not all, I am sure.

A final contrary point which I must cite is the failure of librarians as a group, including school librarians, to use "the research approach" to our work. We must look at the school library objectively, and consider its needs and what we can do to improve its effectiveness without defensiveness. Too frequently too many of us do what one of my colleagues calls thinking with our viscera rather than with our brains.

It has never seemed to me that school librarians recognize or exploit adequately the true intellectual content of their profession—the mastery of the literature of a specific subject field, the control of its bibliography, the means of access to the field, the peculiar nature and needs of the community we serve, and the history and development of the production of the media of knowledge. All these and not the courses in how-to-do-it (important as they may be) are the true elements of intellectual content which determine the peculiar contribution of librarians, including those who specialize in work in the schools.

Now, having looked for trouble, let me briefly enumerate a few of the areas of activity which seem to me to be of particular importance for the school library or professional association intent on being an intellectual force.

First, in the area of evaluation of services. Services, to me, are the whole purpose for which collections, physical facilities, even personnel are provided. The collections are not an end in themselves; if we claim that the library is an intellectual force, we must think of the library's program as an entity, as important as the school's curriculum, a body of services which must be constantly measured, evaluated, and improved.

When Congressmen ask (as they surely will) how effective federal money has been in improving the impact of your school libraries, how will you answer? The question is already on the minds of Congressmen, and is showing up in Congressional hearings. Can you tell them how many more disadvantaged children have been reached, by what services? What evidences of "impact" can you cite? Is your program of services more varied than it was before the Elementary and Secondary Education Act? Have you been able to provide a sounder balance between the six program areas listed by Dr. Frances Henne in the *Standards for School Library Programs*? Do teachers in all subject departments of your schools make more effective use of library resources? In what ways has your program been effectively adjusted to meet the needs of the new curricula being carried out in your schools? As Muggles said, "When something happens, something else happens." It is our professional responsibility to evaluate objectively the impact of ESEA and other federal programs.

Another critical area is that of training the student in work-study skills. Frances Henne, in the May 1966 *School Libraries*, outlined the need for a really new approach to this major program area:

> The current emphases in schools on self-directed learning, inquiry, and independent study all too often con-

tribute to an automatic solidifying of these established methods, with little or no critical evaluation of their current appropriateness. . . . In the viewpoint of many school librarians, the mere process of locating and finding materials in the library holds little intellectual benefit for students and time thus spent is wasted time. The many processes involved in what students do with materials—evaluation, synthesis, reflection, thinking, appreciation, or whatever—are the important factors, not the searching, locating and assembling of materials. . . . [Critics of Mr. Freiser's provocative program in Toronto would do well to study the implications of *that* statement.] Deploring the spoon-feeding of students, as librarians so frequently do, may actually mean deploring the more intelligent use of a student's time and efforts; and self-directed study or learning is not necessarily synonymous with self-directed finding of materials.

The experience of such demonstrations as Project Discovery, Shaker Heights Large Group Instruction, and the Knapp project is that it *is* entirely feasible for youngsters to enter seventh grade fully competent to use the public library and the high school library with mastery. When this happens generally, the responsibility will really be on the high school library to provide sophisticated instruction and guidance—far more like the kind described in Dr. Knapp's Monteith Library Project than like the watered-down courses in how to use three kinds of catalog cards that still prevail in too many schools.

What I have been recommending is the hard intellectual task of measuring and evaluating the impact of the services for which libraries—and our jobs—exist. It is not easy to carry out, but it is essential, if libraries are truly to make an intellectual contribution to our schools.

Second, I recommend the establishment of effective and continuing channels of communication between professional associations, especially between the state library association and the state chapter of DAVI. John Gardner, who has written so tellingly on many aspects of organizational work and leadership, states that we must "create better channels of communication among significant leadership groups, especially in connection with the great issues that transcend any particular group." It is this recognition of common goals which can make us truly an intellectual force.

Occasionally, we need to remind ourselves that as a growing and increasingly specialized profession, librarians are the people to whom we are demonstrating. The good will which every librarian has for other branches of librarianship needs expression in honest critical reactions to other kinds of librarians in our own neighborhoods. We have had opportunity in recent years, notably in 1963's Conference-within-a-Conference, to focus national attention on common problems, but no national organization can satisfy our need to talk with each other. The Knapp project provided such an example by involving all branches of library service. Public librarians, special librarians, state librarians, library science faculties, and college or university librarians, cooperated as members of local advisory committees to project schools. They report being en-

lightened as much by the problems discussed (similar to the ones they encountered in their own jobs) as by the solutions which they helped to achieve.

Turning to the Department of Audiovisual Instruction, the February 1967 issue of its professional journal *Audiovisual Instruction*—an entire issue devoted to the "Functions of Media Specialist"—makes a particularly valiant, and I think, effective effort to reach a meeting of the minds between the school librarians and the media specialists, or the bookworms and the gadgeteers. In the editorial, the president of the American Association of School Librarians, Dr. Richard Darling, states:

> The several associations with responsibility for educational media—DAVI, AASL, NARB and others—have failed, except intermittently and with faint hearts, to recognize that they have common purposes and common goals. Basic to their programs is the desire to secure the best instructional materials to improve the education of boys and girls. Yet from our various starting points we have approached this mutual goal with mistrust for one another and with zealous concern for our own rights, privileges, and status.

This argument is comparable, it seems to me, to the argument between the bibliographers and the information scientists going on in the upper reaches of the research library world. It is becoming increasingly obvious that a meeting of minds is essential, even if that resolution starts only with an uneasy truce. In some states, Michigan and New Jersey, for example, continual joint meetings have been held by school librarians, audiovisual specialists, and curriculum specialists. And AASL and DAVI have taken a major step very recently in the decision of the two boards to carry out the revision of the new standards jointly.

A third recommendation. We know there is a real shortage of manpower, possibly more acute in school libraries than in other kinds of libraries. As serious, if not more, is the need to upgrade the skills of those librarians already working in school libraries—skills in such areas of new importance as management of library operations; supervision of school library services; evaluation and use of the newer media; and use of automation in library operations.

Read carefully, in the March *ALA Bulletin*, the speeches given at the special program at Midwinter on continuing education; they are full of suggestions for state school library associations. I have been dreaming of highly structured annual meetings for state associations, perhaps with carefully planned series of short courses on specific topics needed by practitioners in the field; many of them could be focused on interpretation of new and valid research, which might eventually lead to some recognition, for completion of a post-graduate course, like the fellowships or certificates awarded in other professional fields. If the legal, medical, and other professions can do it, then I see no reason why librarianship can't. One by-product of such a program might be greater skill on the part of school librarians in job analysis, budget preparation and presentation, and scientific management of technical processes.

This would help provide more clerical and technical aid, releasing professional manpower for professional duties, with some decrease in the number of professionals needed to run school libraries.[2]

Last, we must give more attention to a problem of great significance to school librarians which will challenge all the objectivity and intellectual capacity we have. This is the challenge of inequality of educational opportunity in all our states.

The public library world was shaken a few years ago by the so-called "Access Study," whose findings were angrily denounced by many spokesmen, especially from the metropolitan areas. A similar study of schools, including significant data on school libraries, has been prepared by the U.S. Office of Education at the direction of Congress. Known as the Coleman study,[3] published both in research form and in a more popular summary, it is being widely discussed in university and government circles, and is worthy of your careful study. It documents the charge of discrimination against minority groups (Mexican, Negro, Indian) and substantiates the fact that we favor white Americans. Their schools have more books per pupil, more full-time librarians, and (for elementary schools) more central libraries. These data are reported by census region—metropolitan and nonmetropolitan.

Correction of the problems pointed out in this most significant study will be a matter for the schools as a whole, not just librarians. But for librarians it will require special attention: attention to evaluation of specific books and newer media, to long-range planning for library development, to evaluation of programs of service, particularly in terms of true accessibility.

"Even a wood mouse can nibble a large hole." The four challenges I've described—evaluation of programs of service, effective communication between professional associations, upgrading of the manpower pool, and correction of present inequalities in educational opportunity—are all, I believe, crucial to the achievement of our goal. When we have met them, we will be able to call ourselves a true intellectual force in the school and the community.

References

1. *SLJ*, February 1967, p. 28; *LJ*, February 15, p. 842.
2. This year's edition of *School Activities and the Library*, a brochure from the ALA publishing department, features my article on the manpower crisis, which goes into this problem in greater detail.
3. Coleman, James S. *Equality of Educational Opportunity*. U.S. Office of Education, 1966. For sale by Superintendent of Documents, pap. $4.25.

October 1972

If That Don't Do No Good, That Won't Do No Harm

the uses and dangers of mediocrity in children's reading

by Sheila Egoff

My title, despite its very modern flavour (it is becomingly ungrammatical), is actually taken from an ancient English folk tale, *Tom Tit Tot*. Some of you may know the story better from its Germanic counterpart, *Rumpelstiltskin*. In the English version, the key phrase—"if that don't do no good, that won't do no harm," resounds throughout the story as the policy whereby the heroine, a greedy and witless girl, guides herself into one predicament after another. In the end, of course, she lives happily ever after, but anyone over six years of age is left wondering whether this successful outcome is because of, or in spite of, the heroine's laissez-faire philosophy.

And what has this to do with the current state of children's reading? I suggest, and you'll realize now how very artful indeed my title is, that the dilemma represented in *Tom Tit Tot* is the crucial issue in current writing for children. All of us concerned with children's reading—writers, publishers, editors, teachers, booksellers, librarians, parents—all of us must decide whether to stake out our ground on the basis of careful planning or laissez faire, of principles versus expediency, of guidance as compared to permissiveness. "If that don't do no good, that won't do no harm," is there perhaps merit in mediocrity?

This dilemma, of course, is by no means new. A friend of mine used to claim that it was the compelling interest of football players' exploits as recounted on cornflakes boxes that started him on his reading career and that it was by a purely simple and natural progression from this point that he ended up by taking Schopenhauer and James Joyce to bed with him.

Now, to extrapolate from the particular to the general is a widely practiced, if somewhat suspect, form of reasoning. My friend, the cornflakes man, maintains that what he did anyone else can do—that, in short, the road to Dostoevsky always begins with *Dick and Jane*. And, you know, up to a certain point, he is right. He is a compulsive reader—as indeed, I would guess are many of you right here in this audience. Compulsive readers are like termites—they devour any book in their path, telephone directories and government publications included, and they have serious withdrawal symptoms when their bookish diet is somehow denied to them. There are even, I may add, specializations in compulsion—people who are perfectly normal about reading except when they are in a hammock or a bathroom. My prize for the most interesting variant in obsessional reading goes to the one book man, as ex-

emplified by old Gabriel Betteredge in Wilkie Collins's *The Moonstone*. Betteredge made a lifetime's preoccupation with *Robinson Crusoe*. "When my spirits are bad—*Robinson Crusoe*. When I want advice—*Robinson Crusoe*. In past times, when my wife plagued me; in present times, when I have had a drop too much—*Robinson Crusoe*. I have worn out six stout *Robinson Crusoe's* with hard work in my service."

Well, this kind of addiction is a bit unusual all right, but it helps to make my point: the book addict *is* unusual and little purpose is served in generalizing from his case. The reader who begins with "cornflakes" boxes is, I'm afraid, more apt to move on to "super sugar crisp" boxes than to anything else.

Let me go on then to the more typical situation. The average child reads, outside of school books, perhaps a book a week, assuming of course, that he has a conscientious mother and that his father watches enough football games to prevent junior from monopolizing the set. For the eight years between ages six and 14, that makes a total of about 400 books. (If you are questioning my mathematics, I've given the child a week off each year for measles, mumps, etc.) Currently there are about 6000 children's books published yearly in the English language, give or take a few hundred for reprints, different versions, etc. Many of the previously published books, of course, are still available, so the child has, according to *Children's Books in Print*, perhaps 41,000 titles to choose from. Of this number two and one half percent are excellent, 35 percent are perceptibly sludge and dross, and the rest are in between, that is, mediocre. (The percentages, by the way, are purely of my own derivation, but I can vouch for their accuracy on the basis of my own infallible emotional reactions. A fine book sends me rushing to share it with anyone I can find, child or adult; a mediocre book sets my teeth on edge, and a poor one makes me laugh.) So, and here's the grand summation: if the number of mediocre children's books extant is 62 1/2 percent of 41,000 or 27,000, and if the child reads 400 books overall, he has a very good chance of having spent his childhood in reading nothing but mediocre books.

Does this matter? There will be many who say that it doesn't and despite my personal prepossessions—you'll see that I'm already giving away my ending—I will admit that they have a considerable case.

They point out, first of all, that reading is a basic operation, and a child needs print simply for practice, if nothing else.

Demosthenes practiced too. He practiced orations in order to eliminate his speech defect. But it was the pebble in his mouth, not the noble rhetoric that really did the trick. Similarly, reading for utilitarian purpose need have little concern for style and content. Yes, I concede, it is practice that makes the perfectly skilled reader and it doesn't make much difference what he practices on.

Along with reading for practice goes reading for progress. Most of us here today have advanced in life because we can absorb reading material quickly. We can take courses, retrain ourselves, write reports and briefs, and so on. I think it is safe to deduce that reading has always been deemed useful and if it weren't, I doubt that the technologically backward nations would be spending so much time and money on literacy programs.

The reverse is also true. Reading for pure pleasure can be just as artless as reading to develop literacy. We listen to the radio, watch TV, swim, ski, sail, or gossip just for the fun of it and do not berate ourselves for doing so. If a girl wants to spend a good deal of her time reading nurse stories, is it any different? Is it any worse? Reading for recreation needs little content and no defense, or at least, so say the esteemed scholars on the University of British Columbia faculty from whom I borrow my murder mysteries.

Then of course, there is also the argument that goes this way. "How can anyone discover what a good book is who has not experienced the bad?" I love this line of reasoning because it is so comforting. It enables me to overeat, come late, sleep in, and give poor classes for how else would I know the right thing to do? Still, rationalizations aside, there *is* something to this line of reasoning. Good judgement derives ultimately from experience in comparison, and it is no accident that some of our finest works of art juxtapose the beautiful and the grotesque.

But these are all classical arguments; do they still hold true for our own time? More so than ever, I'm afraid. You have merely to examine the Report of the President's Commission on Obscenity to realize that the rights of the individual are now fiercely defended, even if it is only the right to do something foolish or repugnant. In the present atmosphere of "doing one's own thing," there is noticeable hesitancy for anyone to make a qualitative decision for another person. I met with considerable opposition a couple of years ago in my classes in children's literature when I stated that the Bobbsey Twins and their like were not worth acquiring by a public or school library. (And I gave some pretty good reasons, I assure you.) However, my view was interpreted as an infringement of a child's freedom to read and I was roundly abused by my class. Now four or five years ago not only would the students have been more afraid of me as a teacher, but they would also have almost automatically conceded the right of a person in charge of public funds to have a very definite say about what materials are put into a public institution. What the students were arguing for is called in librarianship "the demand theory of book selection" which is to be translated as "give people what they want." "Let's be truly democratic," they tell me, which means, I suppose, that one person's literary taste should carry no more weight than one person's vote.

In many cases this attitude has induced fear in those who should be in a guidance role. Fear of not being popular; fear of taking issue where one's authority could be rejected; fear of one's judgments being judged and found in error. A person in this position tends to withdraw from the difficulty and adopt the principle "Safety first." How frequent is such yielding to popular pressure? No one can supply precise statistics, of course, but we have a clue of sorts in the somewhat similar situation that prevails regarding censorship of so-called "controversial books." Marjorie Fiske's study of California librarians showed that a *majority* were guilty of self-censorship—that is, they refused to buy or, having bought, hid away, those books which they feared might arouse public outcry. And perhaps the saddest aspect of the whole affair is that many of these fearful librarians managed to deceive themselves into believing that they were merely following community standards!

Fiske's study was conducted in the 1950's when the pressures came from the right. Nowadays, the potent pressure comes from the left. It calls itself, in library circles at least, the movement for "social responsibility" and the reasoning is not without some considerable validity. It goes this way. Our society has disadvantaged groups. They are in a desperate situation that will call for desperate remedies, in matters of reading as well as in matters of economics. Worry not therefore about the maintenance of standards but find something, anything, that will bring them inside the library: cartoon movies, rock concerts and "easy books."

I have a good deal of sympathy for this point of view. It may well be that the tastes of middle-class librarians are not appropriate for the needs of slum children. What troubles me, though, is the strong element of condescension which I see implied in this attitude when it equates "easy" with "inferior." What the disadvantaged don't need surely is disadvantaged materials. When you can offer them *Sounder* (William Armstrong, Harper, 1969)—which is a poignant, believable story of a black family that has meaning for readers of every colour—why give them *Tessie*? (Jesse Jackson, Harper, 1968) (which has no relationship to reality). If *Pennington's Seventeenth Summer* (Maureen Daly, Dodd, 1948) is available, why read *Count Me Gone* (Annabel and Edgar Johnson, S. & S., 1968)? (While Pennington derives its plot from the nature of the hero's character, *Count Me Gone* is simply a piling up of rather lurid incidents).

However, I will admit that finding books that have both simplicity and substance is no small task. And this, of course, is *exactly* the virtue of mediocrity—if you can persuade yourself that almost any book will do, you avoid the large and nervous-making labor of selection. No blood, no sweat, no tears, Ché sera sera and let the blurb be my guide! This, of course, is *exactly* why I am suspicious of this philosophy. Hesiod, back in the eighth century B.C., already recognized the problem when he said: "Badness you can get easily, in quantity; the road is smooth and it lies close by. But in front of excellence the immortal gods have put sweat, and long and steep is the way to it, and rough at first. But when you come to the top, then it is easy, even though it is hard."

It takes some considerable hard training to be able to run

a mile, to weld metal, to split the atom, to write *Crime and Punishment*, to read the *Bible*. Once the skills are mastered, then the results seem effortless. Working on skills should in no way preclude the effort to reach a goal of excellence. James Ryan did not run the mile in 3:51.1 after mediocre training.

Unfortunately, many writers and reviewers for children advocate almost the opposite approach. They concentrate on the age and the reading ability of a child as defined by tests and grades. For instance, have you noticed how many children's books of the 60's begin by giving us the actual age of the hero or heroine as if only the reader who is actually that age will enjoy it? The publishers, in their blurbs, hasten to categorize the book by age or grade, in case the author hasn't made this clear. And, of course, reviewers compound it all. For examples, I quote: "*children* may find this book touching, but to an old skeptic it is banal and unrealistic—highly compressed sentimentality." Or "as a serious work of art this novel has little to offer, but for *young people* whose understanding of this period has been clouded by the confused rhetoric of our own times it has an undeniable value." I suggest it is the reviewer who is confused. This confusion may be understandable, however. Since so many children's books are written for extraliterary purposes it is not surprising that they are reviewed with condescension. Anything is good enough for the young. A reviewer of an adult book might well say "this is a scholarly study of Lord Byron" or "this is a readable biography of Lord Byron," but they wouldn't say, "this isn't a very good book on Lord Byron, but it might be enjoyed by a truck driver with a grade 12 education," or "this is a great book, but only for a mature university graduate in English."

Well, let me ask my main question: "Does it matter what children read as long as they read?" The answers are curiously mixed. Many people would balk at deliberately giving a child a poor book; others would balk at a controversial book. Relatively few, I fear, worry about giving a child something which is simply less than the best.

"If that won't do no good, that won't do no harm." Reading something is better than reading nothing.

Put in that way, such an approach is hard to controvert. But why put it that way? The choice is not really between something and nothing but between various kinds of something—between something so-so and something wow!

As I see it, there are two major facts about children's reading. The first is that whatever mediocre books do, good books can also do—and much better. The second is that mediocre content and style in a very real sense subvert the essential role of children's books. In effect, they deny the medium itself—the book—the opportunity to work its own special kind of magic, to make the kind of particular contribution that the book alone can make.

Let me explain. A book is often a vehicle for recreation and entertainment, but it is doubtful whether it is particularly well suited to such a purpose. Unless the writer is skillful, the effort required in reading may be more trouble than the entertainment is worth. In any case, reading as pure recreation has no special claims. Is there really any more virtue in reading Earle [sic] Stanley Gardner than in watching TV's Perry Mason? However, make the content not one of entertainment value only but also one of depth of thought and emotion and the book wins hands down. No other medium is so fitted for the development of complex ideas and characters, to the building up of the rich texture of life. This is the contribution which is preeminently the book's alone to make and I am distressed when it is used for a much lesser role.

It is obviously valuable to work to improve reading skills, and there are many ways of doing this, but there is another saying besides "practice makes perfect" and that is that "you can keep on practicing your mistakes." There is a difference between literacy and literature.

The role of literature is to help develop the individual and it takes a good book to do this. A poor book takes a child and puts him back a step or two, a mediocre book takes a child and leaves him where he is. A good book promotes an awareness of the possibilities of life, the universality of life, the awakening of response.

And yet, some of us expect this to be done by the mediocre. We say we want the best for our children—in housing, education, medical care. But, when we have a choice, we are quite willing to abrogate any responsibility when it comes to putting things into their minds. Content doesn't matter to us, nor does style or characterization or any of the other indeterminate qualities that make up a fine book. Those of us who are librarians talk a great deal about enticing children into libraries, and of starting "at their level." This is as about a ludicrous idea as that old 19th Century one that libraries would wean the workers from the gin palaces.

What do we do when we deliberately provide the mediocre? (we do a lot of it accidentally and inadvertently anyway). My point is over deliberate provision, that is, to do it when we know better. First of all we underestimate children. And we should remember that slow learners and poor readers may be just as interested in *ideas* as quick readers. As a matter of fact, they may have more original ideas and minds because they haven't been clobbered by mediocre ideas picked up in mediocre books. And why is it assumed that the reluctant reader is also potentially a social deviant, particularly in need of moral lectures?

Secondly, the mediocre rarely gets challenged by adults. And if children are constantly presented with mediocre books, how will they know a *good* book when they run into one? You remember, I hope, the argument that children won't be able to judge the good if they are not exposed to the poor. My questions is, if they get only mediocrity, how can they judge the good?

Thirdly, the mediocre builds laziness into children. At an age when they are best prepared for challenge it is unjust to deny it to them. Is it because some of us adults don't want to disturb ourselves with challenges that we find it easier to direct children away from them? So often we all find it easier to settle for second best. As far back as 1924, Alice Jordan, then supervisor of Work With Children at the Boston Public Library, recognized this problem when she said, "mediocrity in books for children is more universal and more baffling to combat than sensationalism."

We speak eloquently about the world commonality of children. Most of us as student teachers and librarians have read Paul Hazard's *Books, Children and Men* (Horn Bk., 1960) and have believed it. That is, we have seen a vision of children around the world being linked by their reading—African children, American children, Finnish children, and Turkish children being linked by common reading experiences—in translation, I'll admit. We have wanted the best children's books of each nation to cross boundaries to speak to the children of other nations. Well, if we settle for mediocrity we must give up this vision. Mediocrity is antithetical to commonality. Mediocre books, because they inevitably present a narrower view of life, will simply not translate well, nor will they carry well into another culture. More importantly, perhaps, as far as North America is concerned, the very abundance of the mediocre will prevent the best from rising to the top.

We give in to mediocrity in another sense when we are hipped on format as opposed to content. We look for a book with a sturdy binding, wide margins, large type, and lots of pictures. On one hand we want children to read, for all the reasons I have indicated, and on the other hand we judge books by their closeness to the pictorial media. Print itself, it seems to me, is the last thing some of us want in children's books. The result has been that we have a generation of children who shy away from a page of solid type.

There are no perfect books in the world, and certainly not every book deemed outstanding appeals to everyone. Not every so-called "good" children's book appeals to every child. And there is no reason why it should. But throughout the years and including our own time, the small percentage of children's books that have something to say to a child and say it well would still run into several thousands of books. Surely they are enough for any one childhood.

I'm sure you have noticed how respected the people are in our society who deal with the physical and emotional needs of children: child psychiatrists, pediatricians, social workers, dentists who specialize in children's teeth. (Come to think of it, orthodontists may be respected most of all because they charge so much!) These people are deemed specialists and we assume that they know what they're doing. Teachers and librarians who deal with children are less apt to be put in the specialist category by parents. The reason may be that many think the material we deal with is *childish*. When we ourselves fail to distinguish between what is "childish" and what is "childlike," I feel that this criticism is generally correct. Perhaps our own reading has failed to convince us of the difference; many adult books are childish; a good children's book is childlike. But if we haven't had a good dose ourselves of the best in literature, we are unable to make the distinction.

Many parents begin by not caring about the preschool child. A little book from Woolworth's is good enough. And second-rate picture books are even bought for our schools and public libraries. Quite a few people have warned us against this approach. *Proverbs* XXII, 6, says, "Train up a child in the way that he should go: and when he is old he will not depart from it." Well, the Jesuits also made a maxim out of this idea: "Give me a child for the first seven years, and you may

do what you like with him afterwards." And Lenin believed this. Speaking to the Council of Education in Moscow in 1928, he said, "Give us a child for the first eight years, and it will be a Bolshevist forever."

I think we have also trapped ourselves into another false premise—that it is easier to read a mediocre book than a good book. Literature—to be good—doesn't need to be heavy. As a matter of fact, it is a safe guess that any children's book that requires inordinate effort on the part of the reader is not excellent. Sheer readability is a prime criterion of excellence in children's books as it is in adult books. Take the first words of *Moby Dick* "Call me Ishmael." And the first line of Leon Garfield's thriller *Smith* (Pantheon, 1967). "He was called Smith." You simply can't wait to read the next sentence in either book—and both sentences are simple enough. A child interested in horse stories surely doesn't need a whole string of the mediocre such as Hazel Peel's *Easter the Show Jumper* (1965) in which a bad rider ends by winning the Horse of the Year Show, with the horse out of control most of the time. Two excellent horse stories K. M. Peyton's *Fly-By Night* (World, 1968) and Vian Smith's *The Horses of Petrock* (Doubleday, 1965) are most exciting, fast-paced stories with a genuine sense of reality to them. Good old *National Velvet* is surely still worthy of a child's attention.

I also think we should have a little more respect for children in regard to the books of information we give them. Many surely induce sloppy thinking, again because we think that anything is good enough for a child. Here is a quotation from V. M. Hillyer's *A Child's History of the World* (Childrens, 1951). "After Queen Elizabeth had died, Raleigh was put in prison. . . ." Actually he was imprisoned by Elizabeth for about five weeks, which fact intimates a lot about Queen Elizabeth as well as Raleigh.

And in 1970 a book was published on the voyage of the Manhattan by Bern Keating called *The Northwest Passage* (Rand). The blurb reads: "but not until man reached the moon did his earthbound contemporaries sail through the ice-choked Northwest Passage and bring to reality the dream of transpolar commercial shipping." The publisher may think he has avoided criticism by the use of the word "commercial." But the facts should be straight. The Royal Canadian Mounted Police ship made the voyage both ways in the 1940's. This book gives it 4 1/2 lines with the dates wrong. The Norwegian ship which made the voyage first rates a line and a half.

By this time you may have realized that I want to promote excellence in books for children, but you may be confused on my stand on the bad versus the mediocre. Well, let me say this—as long as I have the excellent I prefer to cope with the bad rather than the mediocre. The bad is easily recognizable and therefore more combatable. The bad also has its amusing side and who wants to be without a joke. It's no accident that Batman, Mrs. Miller, and Tiny Tim were fads several years ago. Bad taste somehow has its own peculiar charm. Nowadays we are in the counter-culture of the granny gown, the grotesque antiques, and the fringed buckskins. But we all recognize that this is more or less antiestablishment and a bit of a "put-on."

But it's that great gray area between the good and the bad that is so stultifying. Generally speaking, the bad stuff in reading—the commercialized series, the sensational mysteries, the sickening romances—are at least not pretentious and a position on them can easily be explained or discussed with a child. What I principally object to are all our dreary, smug books about growing up and coming to terms with oneself, that purport to be "with it" and are merely another brand of conformity; all the books on race relations that are little more than a condescending, inverse form of racism; all our books of dull facts that take the excitement out of science, or history, or other countries. It's really hard to explain one's stand on this "ho-hum" stuff unless you take each book individually and put a better book up beside it. Tolkien rather than Frank Baum, Sendak rather than Nan Agle, O'Dell rather than Wojieckowska, Patricia Wrightson instead of Jean Little.

Excellence is surely our goal in all that we try to achieve in life. Why eliminate children's books? Are children's books and so therefore children too *humble*, too insignificant to be taken seriously? The words of John W. Gardner can be applied to children's reading: "The society which scorns excellence in plumbing because plumbing is a humble activity, and tolerates shoddiness in philosophy because philosophy is an exalted activity, will have neither good plumbing nor good philosophy. Neither its pipes nor its theories will hold water."

It's the mediocre that drags us all down to a common denominator; common is fine but does it have to be the lowest? It's mediocrity that deprives us of judgment; it's mediocrity that closes our minds to new ideas; it's mediocrity that particularly deprives us of a sense of humor.

So—I suggest in conclusion—let kids have the good stuff. Let them have the controversial. If a book is controversial there are strong opinions about it pro and con, and this is exactly the area where the young should have a chance to make up their own minds. The bad they will find around them and will recognize, having had a dose of the good. But let's give up mediocrity. I can't say that it doesn't work; the problem is that it works all too well. "If that don't do no good, that won't do no harm." Perhaps this is right—mediocre books do no harm in the sense of actual damage. But they do do harm in the sense of deprivation—the subtraction of opportunity to know and experience the best. Slum children are not the only ones who are deprived. Lacking genuine nutrition, you can starve on a full stomach.

Like the girl in Tom Tit Tot, a child, with a little bit of luck, may climb out of a distressing situation. But unless we can guarantee that the children in our care have long golden hair and are also able to uncover the secret of magic names, I would suggest that we teachers and librarians abandon the principal of "if that don't do no good, well that won't do no harm." Instead we should take our cue from Matthew Arnold: "I am bound by my own definition of criticism: a disinterested endeavour to learn and propagate the best that is known and thought in the world."

Children's Services in a Time of Change

by Pauline Wilson, Associate Professor, Graduate School of Library and Information Science, the University of Tennessee, Knoxville

This past year, articles have appeared in the library press about problems in children's services. The writers claim that children's services have been denigrated or diminished within the library system. And the decline of the use of children's services has been used as justification for the elimination of children's services coordinator positions. In addition, children's librarians have been criticized for devoting too much time and too much attention to children's literature and too little to other important matters affecting services.

Blame for the trouble has been variously assigned. To assess the situation, it is important to differentiate between factors over which children's librarians have some control and can be held responsible and those that they cannot control and therefore cannot be held responsible.

Certainly the conditions primarily responsible for the slump in children's reading and a resulting lag in children's services are not due to what children's librarians have done or have failed to do. The root causes lie within changes that have taken place in society. These changes have become the subject of serious concern by parents, scholars, writers, and others. For example, in the field of education (of which libraries and children's libraries are a part) perhaps the first note of alarm was sounded in 1963 with the decline of the Scholastic Aptitude Test (SAT scores)—a decline that has continued to the present. In this period the scores fell 49 points on the verbal portion of the test and 31 points on the mathematical portion. Among other things, the study, reported in *Education U.S.A.* (August 29, 1977, p. 377), found that there has been "less thoughtful and critical reading demanded and done" in schools and that "careful writing has apparently gone out of style." The study noted "a lowering of education standards" evidenced by "a greater tolerance of absenteeism, more social promotion, less homework, and watered-down textbooks." Important contributing causes in the home and society were single-parent homes, deleterious effects of a "decade of distraction," and 20-35 hours per week of TV, according to the study.

Overall, the study findings present a picture of troubling social changes that ultimately became cumulative and were reflected in classrooms. Such change could hardly fail to be reflected in the library—an agency concerned with reading comprehension, self-expression, and verbal ability.

In her recent book, *Every Child's Birthright: in Defense of Mothering* (Basic Bks., 1977), Selma Fraiberg states that the first two years are crucial to a child's later intellectual and emotional development. This is because, during the first two years, a vital process known as bonding occurs if the infant receives appropriate mothering. If the child does not receive such care, bonding may not occur or may be impaired. Children lacking mothering show a "consistent type of mental retardation," in Fraiberg's opinion. The ability for abstract thinking and generalization is impaired. And language development may be "grossly retarded." Once having occurred, such impairments, while they may be ameliorated by treatment, tend to be permanent.

Fraiberg is concerned that such retardation might befall increasing numbers of American children. More children are being warehoused or put in "baby banks," as Fraiberg calls child care centers. She apparently believes that, with a few exceptions, it is unlikely that such children will receive the care they need if bonding is to occur and, thus, mental and emotional impairment may be their fate. Only a moment's reflection is needed to realize the ultimate effect such an outcome could have on children's library services. Children with retarded mental development are not so likely to become library users.

We can find other signs of change and conflict. For example, we live in a society that has a need to paste bumper stickers asking "Have You Hugged Your Kid Today?" on cars; a society in which child abuse appears to be increasing. Or consider the case of role models. Today's children no longer have heroes and heroines, men and women who are worthy of emulation. Instead they are given shabby substitutes: media personalities, entertainment idols, and sport stars. Celebrities whose behavior, made public in the media for all to see, is often tawdry. Their experiences range from arrest for traffic violations to drug abuse.

Other trends, such as the declining birth rate, could be cited as contributing to a decline in the use of children's library services. Enough have been cited, however, to make clear that blame for the slump in children's services cannot all be laid at the feet of children's librarians. These changes, however, do provide the context within which children's librarians now must work, and it should be recognized that they make the children's librarians' jobs more difficult.

Along with these societal changes already mentioned, changes have also occurred in libraries and in the work of librarians. The diminishing use of children's services has been used to justify or threaten diminution of financial support by library administrators, strapped budgets that they must stretch further with every upward move of inflation. With every budget cut or threat comes a renewed criticism of children's librarians for spending too much time on dealing with children's literature and not enough time working with the practicalities—practicalities such as determining goals and objectives, preparing and justifying budgets, and pursuing measurement and evaluation techniques.

The role of children's librarians is a good place to begin in a consideration of the criticism of children's librarians and their preoccupation with children's literature. An ambiguity in defining that role is well illustrated by the remarks John Rowe Townsend made to an audience of children's librarians and persons from publishing as reported in *Horn Book Magazine* (June, 1977 p. 346-7):

> By book people, I meant people who are professionally concerned with books: authors, publishers, reviewers, and, by and large, public librarians. By child people, I meant people whose main concern is with children: parents, teachers. . . . For book people, the book tends to be the center of the picture. . .they are interested primarily in what the book is going to do for him or her rather than in the assessment of literary merit or in placing of books on the map of children's literature.

Is this true? Are children's librarians *book people* rather than *child people*? Is the role of the children's librarians that of literary critic or otherwise? Certainly a considerable number of children's librarians give that impression through their seemingly total immersion in children's literature. How could the business of children's librarians be children's literature when it is the business of authors, illustrators, publishers, and editors?

Would it not be more correct to say the business of children's librarians is the development of children through the use of the library materials and programs? The business of children's librarians should be the development of the child's intellect, imagination, empathy, reading skill, self-expression, and so on; to help form or shape children in desirable ways.

Many people and many agencies are involved in guiding children to adulthood. By themselves, schools cannot do the job, nor can the churches, nor can the libraries, nor can the family. All these contribute something different, each in its own way. The public library provides books, pictures, and storytelling, and programs of various sorts in a non-coercive environment and in an easy manner, quite different from that of other agencies such as schools. The public library's contribution, in fact, is possible because of this very differentness.

Here then, is an area in need of attention from children's librarians—a better definition of the role of children's librarians. Perhaps it is only a question of emphasis or a better balance between concern for servicing children and concern for children's literature. Once the role is analyzed, it must be clearly articulated to administrators, and to the library profession as a whole.

The second area in need of attention is the clarification of the role of children's librarians as it relates to the defined goals of children's services. Since children's services contribute to the development of a child, that contribution should be forcefully articulated. Marshal supporting facts about how children learn, about how children develop and relate these facts to children's services showing the logical linkages between them. Then present your case straightforwardly in a no-nonsense manner, free of any hint of sentimentality. Sentimentality should be avoided for it trivializes children's services—present the service on its merits.

When presenting children's services goals to other librarians, offer them evidence of how a library-use habit develops; how people become readers. Although some needed evidence is not available, and some evidence is only suggestive or inferential, a reasonable case can be made. Consult reading studies and the public library-user studies. Having assembled all the evidence, the goals of children's services, and the definition of the role of children's librarians, examine the role within the context of societal changes. Remember that librarians, including academic librarians, need to be aware of what is occurring in children's services and why, for these developments may well foretell what the future holds in store for them.

A fourth area in need of attention from children's librarians is improvement of the impression they convey to other librarians. This problem also has its roots in the relationship between children's librarians and children's literature. Too much talking about children's literature and the virtual exclusion of other interesting topics of conversation conveys a bad impression. Constant conversation about children's books creates an impression that a restricted little in-group is excluding others. Another undesirable impression is that children's librarians know little about other library departments or about library service as a whole or at worst, do not care to learn. To be able to converse intelligently with other librarians in other specialties on library topics other than children's literature is vital.

Another aspect of this problem of conveying an impression stems from the unusual amount of homage paid to authors and illustrators of children's books by children's librarians. It is not difficult to get an impression, for example, that the reason the Association for Library Service to Children (ALSC) exists is to hold luncheons and dinners for the purpose of giving awards to authors and illustrators of children's books. This, of course, is not true. Nevertheless, a reading of the reports of the annual and mid-winter conferences of the American Library Association gives this impression. Are there not other worthwhile activities of the ALSC that could be given a similar amount of attention?

Children's librarians have a propensity to put on programs featuring authors and illustrators and bill them as "conferences." When sponsored by a library school these affairs are labeled continuing education programs. Perhaps some are, but just as often they would be more accurately billed as "entertainments," for they represent a gathering of hobbyists who have assembled together to ride their favorite hobby horse—children's literature. They are a consumption activity like going to football games or to the theater. This is not to say that these programs lack value. From the point of the author, illustrator, and publisher they are sales promotion events. From the point of view of the sponsor, they are excellent public relations devices because they are crowd pleasers and outdraw regular continuing education programs. They are fun, they are easy on the intellect and attendees can pretend to high, holy seriousness in the name of continuing education while having an enjoyable time. To be fair, one must admit that some learning does undoubtedly occur. Nevertheless, education is *not* what many of these affairs are about. When all the luncheons and dinner programs and conferences are added together and the official nature of them—stamped as they are with the imprimatur of ALSC or a library school—is considered, a certain impression emerges. An edifice is created—a pantheon in which the god and goddesses of children's librarians—authors and illustrators of children's books—are enshrined. I do not suggest an abrupt halt to these affairs. What I am suggesting is more perspective and better balance. Evaluate the purpose of each program, and its worth to library service for children, giving it no more time than its worth merits.

There is work to be done in children's library services. It seems likely that some of the effort and energy going into criticizing, selecting, and celebrating children's literature will need to be redirected toward solving some of these problems. Can it be done? One would think so, but critics tend to cast doubt. Peggy Sullivan remarked: "It may be good that children's . . . librarians are so engrossed in their real work that they neither have the inclination nor the competence to chronicle or analyze their efforts . . . " That children's librarians have the inclination to solve these problems can be taken as a given. The ongoing conversation about the problems that have been appearing in the library press is evidence that inclination is not lacking but competence may be. How such a condition of non-competence has developed and how it might be overcome are matters that must be addressed.

First, what competences are lacking? In general terms it would seem to be the ability to analyze a situation into its component parts, the ability to distinguish what constitutes evidence and what does not, the ability to apply such evidence to the explanation and solving of problems, and, finally, the ability to express such analysis in clear coherent terms to others so that understanding results. Solving some of the problems of children's services noted in this article will require using these skills. In addition, there is the problem of apparent lack of specific knowledge of how to set goals and objectives, how to measure and evaluate library services, and how to prepare, present, and justify a budget.

Presumably children's librarians are to learn all of these things in library school and if not done there, presumably in a continuing education workshop, institutes, and so on. But are these skills, in fact, learned in sufficient detail to become genuinely useful for children's librarians? How many children's librarians attend workshops on the formulation of goals and objectives? How many attend workshops on measurement and evaluation? Does it occur to children's librarians that such workshops are appropriate for them to attend? Does it occur to library administrators that it would be appropriate to send the children's librarian to such workshops? On the whole, the answer to the foregoing questions is probably

no. If this is the case, provision of such workshops for children's librarians ought to be a major concern of the ALSC. Continuing education designed to given children's librarians the analytical and managerial skills they need is more likely to strengthen the position of children's services and children's librarians than any number of affairs devoted to further discussion of children's literature. Of course, children's librarians must have a good understanding of children's literature. But a thorough knowledge of children's literature no longer seems sufficient. Librarians must acquire specific analytical and managerial skills. This concern can be addressed by ALSC, state associations, and others concerned with strengthening children's services and offering continuing education opportunities.

Another area of the children's library field in need of attention is library education. Library school is where the syndrome of over-attention to children's literature begins. It is passed on to students who, in turn, take it with them into the field thus reinforcing existing definitions, attitudes, values, and work habits.

Generally when a student enters library school, he or she will be asked to indicate a preferred area of specialization. Those expressing interest in work with children will be assigned as an advisor to the faculty member who teaches children's literature. This faculty member will remain the student's advisor throughout his or her stay in library school. If the faculty member is strongly partial to children's literature to the point of ignoring or slighting other areas of the curriculum, the student may not be advised to take needed courses and may be advised to take too much children's literature, whether as literature per se or in another form such as reading guidance and storytelling. In these courses the faculty member's values and attitudes toward children's literature and its relationship to children's services will be transmitted to the student, as will the faculty member's view of the relationship of children's services to the rest of the library. If that view is a parochial or insular one, this insularity and narrowness will be transmitted to the student who, in turn, will reflect these views in their work experiences.

The effect of the advising and teaching processes may be further heightened by the fact that children's literature courses are fun, and students may choose to take as many as possible, for who is not enchanted by children's books? Children's books are like peanuts—one could go on and on consuming them and never getting one's fill. But one must question whether this process does not at some point become dysfunctional. It becomes an indulgence, rather than a learning experience. It takes a strong-willed advisor to hold out against such a determined student (especially when the courses the students choose are one's own).

There is yet another factor that may result in students over choosing children's literature courses and under choosing others that might be more beneficial. That factor is comparative ease. Children's literature courses are much easier than courses involving research methods, statistics, measurement, and evaluation.

Children's librarians presently may not see the relationship between such courses and their day-to-day work or see the relationship between such courses and their present apparent inability to analyze and solve their problems. I'm not suggesting that children's librarians conduct research, for that is not their job nor is this the purpose of these courses. Their purpose is to help children's librarians acquire skills—the basic methodology and basic problem-solving skills they need to identify and solve problems that arise in the library. It is possible that many children's librarians are graduating with a library education that is inferior to that of other librarians because these kinds of courses have been excluded on the basis that children's specialists do not need such training. When this happens, a second-class librarian is created. One who may be unfamiliar with technology, unfamiliar with management techniques, unfamiliar with the relationship between the library's budget and policies and its political and social environment. In short, this omission produces a librarian who is left outside the mainstream of public library service. Some of the responsibility for such a situation must be attributed to the library school faculty in charge of children's services, but not all of it.

Some of the responsibility belongs to children's librarians themselves and to their professional organizations. Sometimes it seems that no one is more critical of their schools and education than librarians. But at the same time, it also seems that no one is less informed and has less genuine understanding of what it takes to produce quality education than librarians. Quality education is not arrived at by adding to the curriculum all sorts of technique and reading courses designed to remove every anxiety and uncertainty from every librarian under every possible circumstance forever and ever. Librarians as a group seem to have the notion that education is a substitute for experience; that they should emerge from library school fully prepared to meet each and every new situation that might arise throughout their careers. They haven't grasped the fundamental understanding that education is preparation for experience; it is not a substitute for it.

Given an understanding of that statement and given the additional fact that the library master's degree is a one-year program, it can be seen that some choices will have to be made and some of them will be difficult choices. A wise choice may mean that children's librarians will have to read more children's books after they begin work and fewer while in library school, to allow time to acquire new skills. The goal to be sought is a combination of courses that will produce a children's librarian equipped with transferable and long-lasting skills. Some questions to be considered are: How much children's literature needs to be taught? One quarter or two? Is a course in historical children's literature necessary or desirable? Does reading guidance have to be taught as a separate course or could it be incorporated in the literature course? How long does it take to teach storytelling? One quarter of a semester? Why not combine it with another course, such as reading guidance? It is for children's librarians and their faculty members to determine the answers to these questions in light of present and future needs.

Assuming that the right solutions can be determined, the next step is to implement them. There may be some difficulty here. Whether the curriculum change in library schools can be made depends upon the library school faculty responsible for children's services. For example, how can those responsible for teaching children's services understand the place of analytical skills in the training of children's librarians if they have no knowledge of those skills; if they have never been trained in them? And if they have no understanding of the place of such skills in the education of children's librarians does it seem probable that they would try to change the curriculum to fit changed needs? It is possible, but it is not probable.

It has been asserted above that librarians may have little understanding of what it takes to produce quality education. This is the key to all the problems. It is also an assertion librarians seem to forget. Quality education requires as its first condition, quality educators. Faculty cannot teach what they do not know. All the pedagogical methodology in the world will not mask or take the place of lack of substantive knowledge. Therefore, if librarians want to improve library education they must begin at the beginning by insisting on quality faculty in library schools. However, an appropriate academic education is not a panacea, for it simply provides the minimal condition. Its absence, however, merits closer examination. Without appropriate academic preparation and without research and writing, it is doubtful that faculty can or will contribute to solving such problems as have been identified here in children's services. Solving such problems requires much thought, research, and it certainly requires writing and publication. It also requires criticism—criticism from the field, discussion of ideas and possible solutions by members of the field in order that such ideas and solutions can be refined, corrected or augmented. That process is necessary if consensus is to be reached. Thus, everyone having an interest contributes, but the faculty have a particular responsibility in the process with their primary responsibility being the tasks of writing and research. Those tasks are an integral part of the function of all university faculties. The faculty of library schools are no exception. Library school faculty members who are presently spending their time serving on committees and boards of the professional associations and in holding conferences on children's literature must realize that such activities will not relieve them of their responsibility for research and writing.

I've identified six areas in need of attention from children's librarians, their faculty members, and their association: a clearer definition and articulation of the role of children's librarians, a clarification of the goals of children's services, preparation and presentation of a good case setting forth the worth and place of children's services and children's librarians, a need to correct the impression children's librarians convey to others, a determination of the appropriate education for children's librarians to enable them to meet changed circumstances, and, a better understanding of what constitutes quality education, why it is important, and how it may be achieved.

Indeed there are problems to be solved in the children's services field and when the solutions are found, the debate will diminish.

Information Services in Central Children's Libraries

by Mae M. Benne

In 1977 I completed a year-long study to identify the role and functions of the central children's library in large metropolitan public libraries. Of particular interest was how this department had been affected by changes in the central city and in administrative patterns, and by priorities set in response to financial problems besetting large urban centers. Twenty-seven libraries in all regions of the United States and two in Canada were selected. Interviews were conducted with the central children's librarian, the coordinator of children's services, and any other staff who had direct administrative responsibility for the central children's library. The information and reference services section of the report of *The Central Children's Library in Metropolitan Public Libraries* (Univ. of Washington, 1977) will be summarized here.

The central children's libraries served the general and specialized needs of users who ranged from scholars—engaged in the study of children's literature or reading—to children—seeking information for school reports. At the time of the interviews, 22 libraries recorded reference statistics while the others took samplings as indicators of use. Among those who had collected these statistics in 1970 (the base year used in the study), all showed increases ranging from 17 to 961 percent. (This high increase may be due to inadequate statistics in earlier years.) In many instances the libraries were providing advisory service in addition to information for both children and adults.

Because children also require access to adult collections, chiefs of central libraries were asked if their access to subject departments was equal to that of adults. Seventeen said it was; for several respondents, children's unrestricted use represented a new policy. Ten believed access to be less for children, with reasons ranging from the reluctance or inability of staff to serve children as effectively as adults, to the policy of four libraries requiring children to have signed permission forms to use other departments. In 13 libraries, children needed signed permission or referral forms to borrow adult materials. Children's access to the reserve system was considered equal to that of adults in 23 libraries, but three libraries did not encourage reserves from children.

Many children's librarians indicated that children were somewhat apprehensive whenever they were referred to a subject department for information not found in the children's library. The physical remoteness of the subject departments, the children's reluctance to go through one more interrogation, and the possibility that they could be bypassed at a busy department were cited as concerns. Eleven respondents telephoned ahead to the department if the child was alone, and eight gave the child an informational slip for the designated department.

Collection policies supported information services in most systems, although reductions in staff often eliminated the expertise or support for using these services effectively. For the most part, the collections were limited to printed materials, with recordings the most common AV material reported. In 27 libraries, the central children's library served as a repository and assumed total or partial responsibility for historical materials. Reference works in children's literature were acquired by 22 central children's libraries, and nearly one-third were assigned the major responsibility for foreign language titles and local/regional materials.

With one or two exceptions, users would not have found materials on current reading theories, curricula, or child psychology, although half of the central children's librarians identified these materials as those most commonly asked for among the requests they were unable to fill; nor would users have found information on local organizations, such as foster grandparents or tutoring programs. Information on recreational or cultural programs were more likely to be available than on social or educational agencies.

In 10 systems, information on community organizations was maintained centrally as part of an information and referral service, and in nine others, this type of information was centralized in a subject department. From an economic standpoint, a central service covering a full range of community resources would appear to be desirable. However, it was interesting to note that the involvement of children's staffs in the planning stages had been minimal or nonexistent. Respondents in two libraries commented that when a telephone information center was established, the staff was surprised to discover that children were among the users.

Bibliographic access to collections was usually through a card catalog in the central children's library. Several libraries had maintained special indexes to short story collections, folk literature, songs, handicrafts, etc. With staff cuts and trade indexes giving partial coverage in several of these subjects, many of the files were not current. However, in one system which had provided no subject access to children's fiction, the central children's staff added subject cards.

Until the 1970s, only six central libraries provided full

access (author, title, subject) to children's titles in the main catalog. Three others had only recently begun this practice. Ten libraries provided author-title only, two provided full access to nonfiction, and eight provided no access to children's materials through the main catalog. Unfortunately, informational signs giving the range of materials in the catalog were usually not in evidence. Several libraries were planning book or microform catalogs which would make children's materials more accessible. One library intended to integrate all materials—adults and children's—in a single listing; however, another chose to continue to exclude children's titles as an economy measure.

Without catalog access to alert potential users, dependence upon staff and public awareness of resources is necessary. The exchange of information about new acquisitions useful to both children and adult users was a regular practice in only four or five libraries. In many libraries, the architectural legacy from the early 1900s has not given the children's library high visibility. In several libraries it was easier to reach it from an outside entrance. Moreover, there was practically no exchange of central children's staff with other central library departments or with children's librarians in the branches. While there were valid reasons for this, the result was a further isolation.

These, then, were some of the circumstances that operated to keep the resources of many central children's libraries a secret from all but the most persistent and knowledgeable public and from the adult services staff, as well.

The School Library as the "Principal Locus" of Freedom of Inquiry

Eli M. Oboler, University Librarian Emeritus, Idaho State University, Pocatello

After many years of evading the issue, the U.S. Supreme Court has finally ruled in a case (*Island Trees Board of Education* v. *Pico*) involving the question of the limits of the authority and power of local school boards in dealing with the holdings of school libraries. By a "plurality" decision, the court held that the First Amendment *does* impose "limitations upon the discretion of [a school board] to remove library books . . . from a school library." The Court also maintained that there was "a genuine issue of fact whether [the board] might have exceeded those limitations."

The important point for school librarians is that the Supreme Court is now on record on two important issues: "The right to receive ideas follows ineluctably from the *sender's* First Amendment right to send them . . . ," and, " . . . the right to receive ideas is a necessary predicate to the *recipient's* meaningful exercise of his own rights of speech, press, and political freedom." And students—the "respondents" in this case—are entitled to their own First Amendment rights; they "do not shed their rights to freedom of speech or expression at the schoolhouse gate," a quotation from an earlier case, *Tinker* v. *Des Moines School District* (1969).

It is true that in previous dissents a minority of the Court has disagreed, but under *stare decisis* the verdict stands until, some day, a new majority of the Court hands down a new verdict in a new case. However, it is most interesting that the minority opinions all seem to agree on one point—that the school board's decision regarding which books should be in a school library are *not* subject to review by the federal courts.

Chief Justice Burger, in disagreeing with the plurality opinion as written by Justice Brennan, claims that the plurality, in finding that students have a " 'right' " of access to particular books in the public school library," are proclaiming a new, unprecedented doctrine. He states, "There is not a hint in the First Amendment, or in any holding of this Court, of a 'right' to have the government provide continuing access to certain books."

Justice Brennan's formulation has one lovely sentence for librarians. After citing a statement from *Keyishian* v. *Board of Regents* (1967) which says that "students must always remain free to inquire, to study, and to evaluate, to gain new maturity and understanding," he says, "The school library is the principal locus of such freedom." Tell *that* to any parent or school administrator or school board member who wants to keep or remove controversial ideas from *your* library!

Brennan is certainly well aware of the problems local school boards will have in interpreting his decision. He leads off his discussion of this particular point by stating, "We do not deny that local school boards have a substantial, legitimate role to play in the determination of school library content." But, of course, the question is: Just what are the "limitations upon the discretion of [school boards] to remove books from their libraries"? He cites several Supreme Court cases which bear on the powers of a school board:

> "*Keyishian* v. *Board of Regents* (1967): "The First Amendment . . . does not tolerate laws which cast a pall of orthodoxy over the classroom."
>
> *Epperson* v. *Arkansas* (1968): Re-affirmed the federal courts' duty to "apply the First Amendment's mandate in our educational system where essential to safeguard the fundamental values of freedom of speech and inquiry."
>
> *Mt. Healthy City Board of Education* v. *Doyle* (1977): "Recognized First Amendment limitations upon the discretion of a local school board to refuse to rehire a nontenured teacher."

What these decisions—and the current one—say, in essence, is that local school boards are *not* above the Constitution; their "broad discretion in the management of school affairs," recognized in numerous Supreme Court decisions, is not to be confused with absolute power. To be specific, the Brennan decision says that "discretion may not be exercised in a narrowly partisan or political manner." It goes further than that in stating categorically, "Our Constitution does not permit the official suppression of ideas."

Justice Blackmun says, "It is beyond dispute that schools and school boards must operate within the confines of the First Amendment." He focuses on one idea: "We must reconcile the schools 'inculcative' function with the First Amendment's bar on 'prescriptions of orthodoxy'." His solution is stated very simply: "School officials may not remove books for the *purpose* of restricting access to the political ideas or social perspectives discussed in them, when that action is motivated simply by the officials' disapproval of the ideas involved." The Island Trees Union Free School District's Board of Education characterized the books as "anti-American, anti-Christian, anti-Semitic, and just plain filthy." That certainly *sounds* like "official disapproval of the ideas involved"!

Justice Blackmun goes on to give some reasons which *could* justify book removal or selection *"without outside interference"* (italics added). These include instances "when the first book is deemed more relevant to the curriculum, or better written, or when one of a host of other politically neutral reasons is present . . . and even absent space or financial limitations." He uses the *FCC* v. *Pacifica Foundation* (1978) case as precedent for allowing "a board to refuse to make a book available to students because it contains offensive language," and cites *Pierce* v. *Society of Sisters* (1925) as justification if "the ideas it advances are 'manifestly inimical to the public welfare'." Another acceptable reason for book removal or non-selection is "because it is psychologically or intellectually inappropriate for the age group." Finally, he says, "Of course . . . school officials may choose one book over another because they believe that one subject is more important, or is more deserving of emphasis." All this might be summarized in his statement, "Educational reasons are appropriate; ideological ones are not."

The Court's June 25, 1982 "slip-opinion" (No. 80-2043) is well worth adding to any school librarian's shelf of books to help fight would-be censors. Although it certainly does not contain the last word that will be said on the subject of school library censorship, the Brennan opinion is incontrovertibly the currently operative judgment on the issue.

School Library Media Programs & Free Inquiry Learning

by Daniel Callison, Assistant Professor, School of Library and Information Science,
Indiana University, Bloomington

The American Library Association's Task Force on Excellence in Education report, *Realities: Educational Reform in a Learning Society*, summarizes the basic relationship between school media programs and free inquiry learning:[1]

> Good schools enable students to acquire and use knowledge, to experience and enjoy discovery and learning, to understand themselves and other people, to develop lifelong learning skills, and to function productively in a democratic society. Libraries are essential to each of these tasks. In libraries, students learn how to locate, organize, and use information that will expand their horizons and raise their self expectations. Librarians are teachers, and they serve both students and teachers.

More directly, the report uses one statement which provides a working definition of the instructional role of the modern school media program, "School libraries serve as learner-oriented laboratories which support, extend, and individualize the school's curriculum."

The report, of course, was in response to *A Nation at Risk*, the government statement on public education. Little, if anything, which supports the use of free inquiry or discovery learning could be noted in the government report. And, as has been addressed in the library literature over the past two years, very little of its content draws upon library services for enhancement of public education. Other statements on education have discussed extensively the need for student-centered activities which capitalize on a vast variety of literature and concrete experiences. Holt,[2] Silberman,[3] and Barth[4] are a few who have, in the past two decades, addressed both the need for discovery learning as well as the barriers and complications which prevent its becoming a reality in our schools.

Adler & the Paideia Group

Mortimer Adler and the Paideia Group have issued three publications since 1982.[5] Each document provides a refined outline for public education; the last two include specific responses to criticism of the proposals as well as extensive lists of basic resources necessary to implement the proposals. Adler's group moves the student through three instructional approaches; from the didactic instruction, found in lectures and textbooks to coaching or supervised practice, and on to the highest level of idea and value exchange provided through the means of Socratic questioning. This third level requires not only skilled and knowledgeable teachers, but resourceful information specialists. Although Adler's group does not define what an information specialist is, school librarians who have accepted and practiced the professional role of teacher are essential to the inquiry process. This role is not just a teacher of information location, but a teacher of information use and presentation. The school media specialist is a teacher who approaches both student and fellow teachers with intent to involve both groups in active participation of searching for answers to individual questions and sharing with others the information obtained and the method of searching.

Carnegie Report

Ernest Boyer followed in 1983 with the Carnegie Foundation for the Advancement of Teaching's report *High School: A Report on Secondary Education in America*.[6] The "agenda for action" proposed by Boyer's group includes these points:

> Teachers should use a variety of teaching styles—lecturing to transmit information, coaching to teach a skill, and Socratic questioning to enlarge understanding. But there should be a particular emphasis on the active participation of the student.

> Textbooks seldom communicate to students the richness and excitement of original works. The classroom use of primary source materials should be expanded.

> All students, during their senior year, should complete a Senior Independent Project, a written paper that focuses on a significant social issue and draws upon the various fields of study in the academic core.

Within this extensive agenda, Boyer also calls for teachers to establish themselves as role models by demonstrating that they have the skills of information search and inquiry. The group calls for the renewal in the teaching profession. Preparation for teaching should include expertise and emphasis in a discipline area in addition to general education methods, and a fifth year (post-undergraduate) of study in writing, research, and organization of information. In practice, Boyer's group calls upon school districts to establish more seminars in the secondary schools so that teachers become responsible for in-depth discussion and teacher-managed research of the issues as well as helping students through independent study projects.

Papert's Developments

Seymour Papert has pioneered the application of computer technology to the free inquiry process through the development of the LOGO programming experience for children.[7]

More than any other computer language, LOGO is the experience of managing technology based on student-centered experimentation. Following his own interpretation of Piagetian theory,[8] Papert has established a process for allowing the teacher and student to explore logic and communication *within* the advancing technological world while moving the programming experience beyond the standard curriculum. In his *Mindstorms*, Papert tells us " . . . teaching without curriculum does not mean spontaneous, free-form classrooms or simply leaving the child alone. It means supporting children as they build their own intellectual structures with materials drawn from the surrounding culture."[9] Most importantly, the child has the opportunity, the encouragement and the guidance, if necessary, to experience acting upon his or her own environment rather than the technology acting upon or dictating to the child. Rote drill may serve an entry level or remedial purpose in training and establishing the common tools for a knowledge base. Education begins when the child is placed in an environment in which he or she can experiment, document experiences, adjust and correct problems, and share the results with peers.

Media Specialists as Teachers

Davies,[10] Rossoff,[11] Wehmeyer,[12] Haycock,[13] and others have provided discussion and models for the school librarian as teacher. A recent survey of school librarians which questioned the role of the media specialist in instruction found confusion and a wide variety of opinion concerning the extent of involvement desired by librarians in instructional design.[14]

David Loertscher[15] has provided the most concrete argument for the instructional role of the school library media specialist. Not only is the role presented as exciting and rewarding, but Loertscher argues that the perception of the school media specialist by fellow teachers and administrators is crucial to the future existence of the school librarian as a professional. Without establishing oneself as a model and leader in the educational process, passive book-tending will lead to further cuts in media center staff and budget. Moving into a strong teacher-management role for the purpose of educating students and fellow teachers in search and information utilization skills sets the media specialist in the critical center of the free inquiry process.

In order to manage this shift from reactive clerical support to the position of interactive educator, Loertscher defines several stages of instructional input. Basically, these steps range from information support of immediate information demands up to formal development of course requirements and identification of information needs. As the role of the media program is shifted from one of limited enhancement to a necessary element integrated into the curriculum, the media specialist becomes not only a team teacher, but a curriculum developer. This progression is not new to the school library literature, but seldom is it practiced in the field.

Loertscher provides the reasonable approach. Today's media specialist, voicing constant cries of being understaffed and undersupported, moves into the instructional role over a period of time. He or she attempts to achieve a higher level on the instructional involvement ladder as experiences are evaluated, support groups are established, and the media specialist matures with responsibilities under his or her command.

The shift to this model of teacher first, and librarian second, will take time.

Free Inquiry Learning

Over a decade has passed since Edward Victor summarized the major elements of the inquiry approach to teaching and learning in relationship to teaching science in the public schools.[16] However, these elements are basic to all disciplines in which the student becomes the primary person acting on the learning experience. The teacher moves to the role of observer and determines, from a holistic view, when to move in order to give guidance, consultation, and evaluation.

For the school media specialist, this poses two major concerns: First, accepting the role in which he or she is established as teacher of students and fellow teachers. Second, knowing when to capitalize on an environment which lends itself to the free inquiry approach (i.e., the school resource center). The media specialist as teacher must not only be concerned with demonstrating expertise as an instructor, but must resist the traditional classroom routines which prevent free inquiry learning from taking place.

Element One: Inquiry lessons are carefully planned. This element is presented first to clarify a misconception. Free inquiry learning exercises require a great deal of advanced planning and trial. As much as possible, the teacher must consider how far the student will be able to go with an experience. Options must be posed, questions tested, and problems anticipated. Because various levels of interest and ability will be present within any group, students should be allowed to take the experience in a variety of directions. Most often, the planning stage may involve several weeks, if not months; it requires that the experience be evaluated and revised at each step of the way.

Planning includes involvement of several teachers and other resource professionals. Brainstorming to examine the potential of the student experience and the possible outcomes is essential. Free inquiry is not a free-for-all plan, but one which must be tailored to the resources available. The media specialist can move to ensure success by expanding the resource availability and concentrating on a few, well-planned, free inquiry experiences each year. To allow for positive impact, the experience must have concentrated effort from all teachers involved. Such energy input means that the free inquiry experience may not be possible in all disciplines, and it will not be possible throughout the school year.

Element Two: Inquiry lessons follow a general pattern. Learning objectives common to the entire class of students may not be present and probably not measurable at all times. However, set objectives for individual students are measurable. Often these objectives are established between student and teacher on a day-to-day or week-to-week basis. The student writes a reaction or evaluation of his or her performance, as does the teacher. The student and teacher may attempt to summarize the experience orally, but written documentation is a stronger communication device. The written record should be followed by discussion of the experiences among the students and teachers for all to hear and react. Students can get a sense of how far others may have gone in the experience and set their own future goals for additional free inquiry experiences.

Element Three: Inquiry learning is highly process-oriented. The student should have the means to document what he or she does, and should begin to understand that record-keeping is an important part of the entire learning process. It establishes a concrete map reflecting where and when one has started and ended. Important, observable skills result: students will demonstrate a record of measuring, classifying and analyzing information. This record stimulates a sharing of the individual experience with others.

Element Four: Teaching and learning are question-oriented. Experimentation is based on being able to formulate questions and then determining a method to answer them. One must also determine adequacy of the answer and, with all limitations in mind, raise other questions which need to be answered as well. This cycle for exploration is not limited to a chemical laboratory. The student's opportunity to explore questions and options should be present in the humanities, social sciences, and vocations, as well as the sciences.[17][18]

In the application of this element to the information search, the teacher-media specialist may establish an environment in which the student begins to question the authority of sources and to cross-reference facts and figures. The student should be encouraged to answer questions using more than one source, and he or she should be able to locate additional opinions and facts which confirm or reject the answer. Traditionally, library skill exercises have been valued as "advanced" if the student has moved beyond the card catalog and a guide to periodical literature to the use of the general reference collection. The information search experience should progress beyond this initial stage to the definition of concepts, not just facts and figures. The student should contact experts through letters and interviews. Relationships among events, people and places are established beyond the textbook and encyclopedia when access to many materials is available through library networking and guidance from information managers is present.

Element Five: The teacher is the director of learning. Certainly there will be checkpoints in this process where the teacher can observe that the student has reached a specific level of ability and is ready to move on to a more challenging experience or a completely different set of experiences. For some students, constant monitoring and observation may be necessary. The free inquiry approach, however, is reached when the student has attained the basic skills and is ready to venture out on his or her own. Then they must be allowed to "fly" without assistance and learn, in most cases, from their mistakes. There are frustration levels for both teacher and student, of course, but too many valuable experiences are cut short in order to save time when the real learning has not yet taken place. More importantly, the critical learning experience will not be internalized if the student is fed the answer or solution to the given problem too soon. Challenge and process are the end products of the free inquiry approach, not specific correct or incorrect answers. Without such challenge, the search experience is lost for future reference when the student meets the same problem again, on his or her own.

Element Six: Time is not of prime importance, but timing is. The standard blocks of classroom time (one hour units, six times a day, five days a week) do not lend themselves to the free inquiry approach. This structure does reinforce training methods which allow for repetition of facts, drill on brief and incomplete definitions of issues, raising problems with clear-cut solutions, and conditioning the student for the same routine, day in and day out. Even major industries are beginning to break that cycle with staggered work schedules, time-sharing, and opportunity for worker input to management. This is one of the most difficult logistical problems to solve in the public school in order for free inquiry exercises to take place.

Can a morning be set aside, a full day—every Monday, for instance—for the next two months? Demands for mass scheduling and regimenting reject such possibilities. In realistic terms, all the best public schools seem to be able to do is declare some program a special event and limit that activity to a few select students. Usually this involves the two extremes of the ability scale—the mentally disadvantaged or the talented and gifted.

Element Seven: Students are teachers too. There is also the variance in the time it may take some members of the class to complete the free inquiry experience. This problem is, and will always be, present, even in the lecture format. Some students need immediate review of the material after presentation; others are able to move on to new things.

The teacher can manage the situation so that peers help each other. There is a point in free inquiry exercises where the more accomplished students become advisors to the slower groups. In other words, the students who have reached their own goals for the exercise before the given time limitation may move into one of two options. First, they may be directed into another experience from those held in reserve by the teacher for such situations. Second, they may work with other students to assist them or to advise them. It is important, however, not to allow the student in the second option to revert to a position of being the one and only source of information, much as the teacher is in most lecture format approaches. The student's most valuable role in this second option is that of explaining his or her own experience and of providing a model for others.

Element Eight: Peer interaction is necessary during and following the experience. A team approach is the strongest method in the free inquiry exercise.[19] This team is composed of two members only, not a group of four or ten. It means companionship without the cumbersome dynamics of too many individuals and the increased chance that a student will become lost (or try to become lost) in the crowd. The team approach allows for verbal communication during the experience, sharing experiences and reactions, dividing responsibilities, compromising on logistics and conclusions. A high percentage of the end product should belong to the individual so that the experience remains personal. The team approach lends itself to the search for information in the traditional manual search through the print materials. It also tends to encourage students to stay on task longer in working with new experiences, using new technologies.[20]

Element Nine: The end product is shared with others. Students are often placed in the position of submitting their work to one judge—the classroom teacher. Free inquiry should encourage a sharing of student findings with other students, teachers, and above all, parents. Many special events which have included the free inquiry process can become presentations at the school's open house or happenings scheduled especially for the parents of children involved in the project.[21]

The immediate sharing of ideas and findings should take place in a debriefing of the entire class as members of the teams report, formally or informally, of their experiences. The teacher manages this discussion by identifying and listing, with the help of the students, common and unique findings as well as common and unique problems encountered. Bulletin boards in the classroom and the library provide the opportunity to display these summaries which can be illustrated with photographs taken during the project. Of course, this is just touching on the possibilities for sharing the results of the free inquiry event.[22][23]

Element Ten: Some students and teachers may demonstrate a desire to learn more. Jerome Bruner defined the act of discovery in his classic article nearly 25 years ago.[24] His comments are basic to the inquiry approach, as seen in this statement, "Our aim as teachers is to give our student as firm a grasp of a subject as we can, and to make him (sic) as autonomous and self-propelled a thinker as we can—one who will go along on his own after formal schooling has ended." Bruner, taking us beyond the application of simple yes and no drill training or the simplistic answers given in textbooks, writes,

> " . . . the child is now in a position to experience success and failure not as a reward and punishment, but as information. For when the task is his own rather than a matter of matching environmental demands, he becomes his own paymaster in a certain measure. Seeking to gain control over this environment, he can now treat success as indicating that he is on the right track, failure as indicating he is on the wrong one."

The key to measuring the success of free inquiry learning through the media program is observation of students who formulate their own questions. They extract and summarize the issues and show us they not only can raise the question themselves (which is a major leap), but know where and how to pursue the answer. We may not be able to measure satisfaction or enjoyment in the student- or teacher-learned process, but media specialists should record those occasions when the active process of the free search takes place. Those happenings are the result of the teacher-media specialist successfully implementing the media program as a learning laboratory.

Media Center's Commitment

As the media specialist broadens his or her role from one who reacts to immediate information demands to one who begins to interact with teachers and students in the development of free inquiry experiences through the use of the media center resources, contacts and facilities, the teacher-media specialist may find that energy must be invested in the following areas to a larger extent than ever before.

• *Networking:* In order to obtain all necessary materials to support free inquiry projects, materials may need to be located in other collections. Although students will need to practice

much of this information location on their own, the media specialist will need to "dry-run" topics in order to determine workability of the project, especially if the media specialist is unfamiliar with the topic.

• *Flexibility:* Use of the media center must be flexible in terms of space and time. It may be that the entire center will need to be devoted to just the one free inquiry project for several days or weeks. Tables and chairs may need to be moved out or rearranged, floor space may need to be cleared, and special small group work stations established within the media center or classroom. Loan of materials may need to be controlled in some cases to allow all students access to them. Loan of equipment will need to be flexible and open to students. These young researchers may need to use equipment outside of the security of the media center in order to gather information or produce a visual record of their findings.

• *Cooperation:* Team-teaching will be essential. Free inquiry experiences may involve only a few meeting times, or may involve most of the semester. Whatever the case, the classroom teacher and the teacher-media specialist must find a common ground for understanding the division of tasks and a willingness to share evaluation of the experience. Both must be advocates of the project to the school administration. It is not only a positive team effort the administration should see, but the principal should be aware of positive experiences from the students and parents as well.

• *Concentration:* The teacher-media specialist will find that for this project, and the few others which may be worked into the media center over the year, there must be a concentration of time and effort. Other routine activities must be assigned to clerical staff or postponed.

• *Financing:* In order to "seed" and encourage the project, the teacher-media specialist must consider investing in special materials to support the project. A major commitment of 10 percent of the regular media center budget is not unreasonable, along with a commitment of some funds from the department associated with the project. In addition, the classroom teacher and the teacher-media specialist should plan on approaching parent organizations or even the school board to request additional funds. Students are often the best promoters of the experience in these situations. A one-year pilot program should not only be evaluated in terms of what is learned, but in terms of what is needed for growth.[25]

• *Community:* An effort to involve community members should be made whenever possible. A community base which shares in the experience will help to create support for future projects. Some of the strongest free inquiry projects involve the exploration of the community, its history and its special people. This provides students an opportunity to identify with their home environment.[26]

• *Encouragement:* The teacher-media specialist must make an open and visible effort to encourage the use of the free inquiry approach. Media specialists need to capitalize whenever possible on getting classroom teachers to use materials beyond the standard textbooks. Continued consideration must be made towards designing activities which allow the student to search information data currently available at his or her level. Constant observation must be made of the students' attempts to practice the information search and the successes and failures they experience. Continual presentation of the results, involving students who progress not only in basic information searching skills but who begin to formulate their own questions and search out their own answers, must be given to those who view the public education system with a critical eye.

Implementation

Successful implementation of the free inquiry approach to student learning requires that the school library media specialist accept a role slightly counter to his or her traditional information tasks. The media specialist helps and encourages both students and teachers to raise questions, not simply respond to a single question with one initial answer. Media specialists encourage the thought process by supporting the patron's attempt to reach out for more knowledge with one question's answer leading to further questions. The magic of the process is that it is an endless cycle which can be explored within unique and personal interests, and yet shared with others.

Implementation requires the ability of the student, teacher, and the media specialist to see beyond the basic skills of information location and presentation to the higher levels of information analysis and criticism.[27]

Implementation requires constant attempts at communication and cooperation between the media center staff and the classroom teachers. Equal responsibilities must be accepted in instruction and evaluation of students.[28]

The major items on the professional educator's agenda for instruction excellence are opportunities for lesson revision and planning for changes in the curriculum in order to allow for free inquiry-based lessons.

References

1. American Library Association. *Realities: Educational Reform in a Learning Society*, 1984, p. 4.
2. Holt, John. *How Children Fail* (1964). *How Children Learn* (1967). *The Underachieving School* (1969). Pitman.
3. Silberman, Charles E. *Crisis in the Classroom: The Remaking in American Education*. Random. 1970
4. Barth, Roland S. *Open Education and the American School*. Agathon. 1972.
5. Adler, Mortimer J. *The Paideia Proposal: An Educational Manifesto* (1982). *Paideia Problems and Possibilities* (1983). *The Paideia Program: An Educational Syllabus* (1984). Macmillan.
6. Boyer, Ernest L. *High School: A Report on Secondary Education*. Harper and Row. 1983. "An Agenda for Action," p. 301-19.
7. Public Broadcasting System. *Talking Turtle*. From the NOVA series. 1984.
8. Papert recommends: M. Boden's *Piaget* London: Harvester Press. (1979); H.E. Gruber and J.J. Voneche, editors of *The Essential Piaget* (Basic Books, 1977); and two of Piaget's original works: *The Child's Conception of the World* (Harcourt, Brace, 1929) and *The Child's Conception of Physical Causality* (Harcourt, Brace, 1932).
9. Papert, Seymour. *Mindstorms: Children, Computers and Powerful Ideas*. Basic Books. 1980. p. 31-2.
10. Davies, Ruth Ann. *The School Media Program: Instructional Force for Excellence*. Bowker. 1979.
11. Rossoff, Martin. *The School Library and Educational Change*. Libraries Unlimited. 1971.
12. Wehmeyer, Lillian Biermann. *The School Librarian as Educator*. Libraries Unlimited. 1984.
13. Haycock, Ken. "Role of the School Librarian as a Professional Teacher." *Emergency Librarian*. May-June 1981. p. 4-11.
14. Coleman, Gordon J. "The 1975 School Library Media Standards: What the Practitioners Think." *School Learning Resources*. Sept. 1984. p. 17-19.
15. Loertscher, David. "School Library Media Centers: The Revolutionary Past" and "The Second Revolution: A Taxonomy for the 1980s." *Wilson Library Bulletin*. Feb. 1982. p. 415-21.
16. Victor, Edward. "The Inquiry Approach to Teaching and Learning." *Science and Children*. Oct. 1974. p. 23-6.
17. DeRose, James V. "The Teacher is the Key." *Science and Children*. Apr. 1979, p. 35-41.
18. Piaget, Jean. "Development and Learning." *Journal of Research in Science Teaching*. v. 2. 1964. p. 176-85.
19. Webb, Noreen Marie. *Learning in Individual and Small Group Settings*. Dissertation. Stanford University. 1977.
20. Callison, Daniel. *A Simulation of Random Access Video Technology: Reaction to Premastered Multi-Media Interactive Programmed Instruction in a Children's Museum Free Inquiry Learning Environment*. Dissertation. Indiana University. 1983.
21. Printz, Mike. "Topeka West's Students Honor E. T. Mom." *School Library Journal*. Apr. 1984. p. 33-4.
22. Patrick, Retta. "School Library Media Programs Today: The Taxonomy Applied." And Janet Stroud. "Library Media Center Taxonomy: Future Implications." Both in *Wilson Library Bulletin*. Feb. 1982. p. 422-33.
23. Harste, Jerome, et al. *The Authoring Cycle: Read Better, Write Better, Reason Better*. A videotape series with study guide. 1985. Heinemann Educational Books, Portsmouth, N.H.
24. Bruner, Jerome S. "The Act of Discovery." *Harvard Educational Review*. Winter 1961. p. 21-32.
25. Callison, Daniel. "Justification for Action in Future School Library Media Programs." *School Library Media Quarterly*. Spring 1984. p. 205-11.
26. Sitton, Thad. "Bridging the School-Community Gap: The Lessons of Foxfire." *Educational Leadership*. Dec. 1980. p. 248-50.
27. Vandergrift, Kay E. *The Teaching Role of the School Media Specialist*. American Library Association. 1979.
28. Cleaver, Betty P. and William Taylor. *Involving the School Library Media Specialist in Curriculum Development*. ALA. 1983.

Performance Standards for SLM Centers: Taking the Initiative

Peggy Sullivan, Dean, College of Professional Studies, Northern Illinois University, DeKalb, Illinois

At the time of Frances Henne's death, the editor of *School Library Journal* described her as "a charismatic activist for school libraries."[1] She was that and more. Perhaps her most enduring legacy will be the role that standards have played in the development of school library media programs. One need only review *A Planning Guide for the High School Library Program*, which she coauthored in 1951,[2] to realize that, even then, she was keenly aware of the close relationship between planning and evaluation of library programs, and of the significance of standards in program development. It is almost too bad that the impression made by some of the American Association of School Librarians' standards statements, to which Henne contributed so significantly, was based so much on the quantitative aspects of standards. She herself had to point out in 1972: "Too often overlooked or ignored is the overall primary objective of standards—to provide teachers and students with the media services and resources to which they are entitled. Surely no one could deliberately reject such an objective. Surely excellence in media programs is not something to be feared."[3]

Unfortunately, in the library world, standards for school library media programs have been characterized by tables of numbers, ratios based on school sizes, and other quantitative measures. At the time when some of these standards were developed, they were overwhelming, controversial, challenging, maddening. But they captured attention and contributed to significant change. When school libraries received their first, direct federal assistance from the Elementary and Secondary Education Act of 1965, it was possible to identify their major needs and to plan to assist them effectively because national standards existed. Some other programs in schools were not so well prepared, and they did not enjoy the benefits of federal support to the same extent.

But times change. So do attitudes toward standards and their development. In recent years, public libraries have made it appear that performance measures are their invention. By contrast, school library media programs seem to be stuck in the past with a set approach to the development of standards, and no very clear ideas among school library media personnel about how performance standards can be utilized.

Jim Liesener has provided good grounds for an approach to performance standards in school library media programs. He has defined that approach as two-fold: identifying fundamental problems and questions to be addressed by any prac-titioner, and developing approaches, processes, and techniques that could be employed in any situation to assist practitioners relate these problems and questions to their specific situations.[4] However, a lot of practitioners don't read Liesener and a lot of those who do don't understand what he is saying. The failure to understand is rooted as much in his style as in their unwillingness to study him carefully enough.

F.W. Lancaster is another author who has not been thoughtfully enough studied by school library media personnel. He has not concerned himself specifically with public library service to youth or in schools, but he has been concerned with the measurement of library service, giving one of the simplest, clearest definitions of the difference between effectiveness (measured by how good the service is) and benefit (measured by how much good the service does).[5]

Creative thinking is needed to relate some of the measures suggested in *A Planning Process for Public Libraries*[6] to school library media programs. It's all too easy to dismiss them as subjective, to view them as applying to a different kind of public and therefore inapplicable, or to discount the very firm links their designers have made with such areas as need for community knowledge, surveys of users, setting of goals, etc. Even a broad-brush sketch of examples of performance measures outlined for public libraries can help school library media personnel realize how applicable they are to their settings.

Determine overall citizen satisfaction,[7] suggest the authors of *A Planning Process for Public Libraries*. They may already regret that reference to "citizen," which omits many library users and nonusers who may be residents or library users even if they are not citizens. But the intent is to get a sense of overall satisfaction, obtainable from general comments about the library, what the school newspaper says about it, where it fits in various programs of the school. *Finding out what the perceptions of nonusers are* is a good deal more difficult. There is probably no kind of library with which individuals have had less experience, but about which they are sure they are quite knowledgeable, than the school library. To take just one segment of the community, interviewing librarians who live in a school's community to discover what their views of the library media program are would be likely to open up questions about how the library has presented itself and to suggest ways it can more assertively and more accurately report its accomplishments to its public.

Public librarians are naturally interested in *registrations* of borrowers, but that is a meaningless statistic for some school library media programs. The point is to get some sense of what the penetration of the service area is. That includes finding out to what extent students and teachers can use the school library without having to rely on other sources for school-related reading and research in a variety of media. The population to be served by a school library media program is almost inevitably easier to define than that of a public library, but it may be complicated to determine *the extent of penetration*. One of the points, important in regard to the extent of penetration of the service area, is for school library media programs to have a clear sense of what public the service area actually includes. Are teachers to expect to find in their own schools or at a district center *all* materials needed for their own professional continuing education? Should they be able to review a variety of texts and other materials? Similarly, is it expected that other libraries which are truly accessible for students should supplement what the school library offers or provide most recreational materials, or is the school library media program recognized as their full resource?

User satisfaction must be measured with some objectivity. It is not enough to cite the satisfied user who reports happily on what he has found or what he wishes had been available. It is important to discover what users expect, to determine what they have a right to expect, and then systematically to provide means, which may be surveys, suggestion boxes, or discussions during library instruction periods, to give users the opportunity to comment on the extent of their satisfaction with the program.

Habit and tradition are probably nowhere more prevalent than in the determination of *user service hours* in school library media programs. After an initial spurt of interest in providing afterschool hours of service, many programs have dropped the practice. Even with shortages of personnel, it may be that a review of the best hours for students to use the library would suggest different patterns for media program openings. Boldness and creativity might suggest that, if one end of the school day is a better time for users to get to the library, the library's hours might be extended in that direction, even if they were shortened at the other end.

In regard to *use of facilities and materials*, there is little difference in the measurements appropriate for school library media programs and those appropriate for public libraries. Patron observation is cited by *A Planning Process* as a good means of achieving some sense of this performance measure. There is nothing new about that as far as school libraries are concerned,[8] but there is some question about how systematically and consistently school library programs have followed relatively simple means of observations.

Almost every library program suffers from the frustration of not having good counts of use of materials within the library. *In-library circulation* and *circulation outside the library* may be counted and evaluated the same ways in school library programs as in public libraries, and *A Planning Process* provides good information about this. Its suggestions on *availability of materials* are also useful, and it notes that "it is quite possible to have an unsuccessful search, but a satisfied pa-

tron."[9] In regard to both availability of materials and *time delays in obtaining materials*, school library media program personnel may need to evaluate what their own expectations and mission are. Too often, it may be assumed that the time of students is virtually limitless, or, on the other hand, that if materials are wanted only for an assignment that is being done at the last minute or within a very rigid time frame, it is simply not possible to accommodate students on a reasonable basis in their terms. Performance measures call attention to the delays endured by users and potential users, so they may be useful to call attention to the need for more regular review of needs and efforts to satisfy those needs for materials.

Reference service in school library media programs is likely to be of good quality and favorably evaluated by users. Telephone questions are negligible in number, but less is known about real user satisfaction with reference service and the librarians' own views of their performances. A concern with performance measures may help to identify what these are and what they could and should be.

Users and nonusers alike are probably the best judges of the *attractiveness and accessibility of library facilities*. Those who work in a facility are sometimes the last to be aware of its shortcomings which may be corrected. They may be aware of problems of location within the school, of structural defects or programs, or difficulties caused by traffic patterns and noise. However, users of the library media center may note inconveniences of arrangement or location of materials, seating patterns, and other features which can rather readily be improved as a result of applying this performance measure.

Users' assessment of *staff availability* and *staff attitudes* need to be sought and interpreted. One of the benefits of getting users' views of staff availability is recognition of the fact that even limited staffs may have more flexibility in how staff may be assigned to public service desks than may be immediately apparent to staff themselves. Both staff and user groups may have creative ideas for improvement of availability and attitude that can be discovered through thoughtful use of performance measures.

There are some special characteristics of school library media centers that may affect appropriate application of performance measures. The population of users tends to be more fixed than in other kinds of libraries. There is of necessity an emphasis on encouraging users to become independent or fairly self-sufficient in their use of libraries and media, so that the appropriate emphasis may be on that educational aspect rather than on simple decisions to provide more convenience, and characteristics of the program need to be considered within the school setting. The selection of hours for openings, the arrangement of the facility, and other aspects of control are different when the media program is a part of a school rather than an entity in itself. Similarly, in regard to such matters as the perceptions of users and nonusers, there may be confusion between the reputation that the media program itself has earned and the reputation of the school as a whole. One area where school library media programs have a history considerably longer than that of many public libraries, the use of volunteers in public service and other aspects of the program, the public relations value of such volunteers may outweigh some limitations they place on service.

School library media programs have a long and strong history of working to achieve appropriate standards. Leaders in school library media programs ought not be dismayed nor distracted from developing and achieving performance measures for school library media programs. Much can be adapted from the recent literature of public librarianship, much developed from earlier publications in school librarianship. But, essential for all of these are creative decisions about the implementation of performance measures in school library media programs.

References

1. Lillian N. Gerhardt, "Frances Henne—Standard Bearer 1906-1985," *School Library Journal* (Feb. 1986).
2. Frances Henne, Ruth Ersted & Alice Lohrer, *A Planning Guide for the High School Library Program*, American Library Association, 1951.
3. Gerhardt, "Frances Henne."
4. James W. Liesener, "Systematic Planning in School Library Media Programs," in *Planning for Library Services: A Guide to Utilizing Planning Methods for Library Management*, ed. Charles R. McClure. Haworth Pr., 1982, pp. 97-112.
5. F.W. Lancaster, *The Measurement and Evaluation of Library Services*, Information Resources Pr., 1977, p. 372.
6. Vernon E. Palmour, Marcia C. Bellassai & Nancy V. De Wath, *A Planning Process for Public Libraries*, American Library Association, 1980.
7. Through this section, italicized statements refer to examples of performance measures cited in *A Planning Process for Public Libraries*.
8. Peggy Sullivan, ed., *Realization: The Final Report of the Knapp School Libraries Project.* American Library Association, 1968, pp. 206-207.
9. Palmour, *A Planning Process*, p. 122.

Cognitive Development and Students' Research

Carol Collier Kuhlthau, Assistant Professor, School of Communication, Information and Library Studies, Rutgers University, New Brunswick, New Jersey

Many times, teachers don't have a clear understanding of what abilities are required of students to be able to complete library research assignments. They don't really know what difficulties students will encounter. For example, requiring fourth graders to do an indepth, focused, research paper using multiple sources can be extremely discouraging, if not practically impossible. It requires considerable participation with an adult—usually an anxious parent.

Librarians can help teachers by becoming more aware of the stages of cognitive development in children, and they can suggest alternative assignments when the abilities required in the assignment are clearly beyond the children's current developmental level. Research assignments get children into the library. The specific assignment determines how the children will use the library. What they learn about using the library depends, to a large extent, on the assigned task. Assignments can be broken down into smaller segments or tasks to develop a sequence of skills. The skills needed in using information (i.e., the ability to read, reflect, summarize, paraphrase, extend and present ideas) can be developed in a sequence of assignments which incorporate skills needed for locating information, such as using the card catalog, indexes and reference tools.

Knowing something about the Piagetian stages of cognitive development can help to design research assignments that promote satisfying learning. Child development is generally divided into four levels: early childhood; middle childhood; pre-adolescence; and adolescence.

Early childhood begins with about age two and ends at seven. Kindergarteners are in the midst of this preoperational stage, and third graders are emerging into the next stage. Preoperational children are what Piaget terms "egocentric." They are individualistic, self-centered, and have a limited interest in what others are doing. They play alongside one another instead of together, (called parallel play), and speak *at* each other rather than to each other (egocentric speech). They want to please adults, are generally affectionate and need warmth and security. Reading and writing are their primary tasks in school, and they need library materials and activities to help them to develop these skills.

Middle childhood occurs during the ages of eight, nine and ten, when children are normally in third through fifth grade. At this stage, they can perform what Piaget calls "concrete operations." Although children can do a great many mental tasks, their thinking is grounded in concrete experience. They are now able to categorize and classify items, two abilities which are very important in using a library. They want to know more about a lot of things, and can pursue research assignments requiring one or two sources of information. Properly designed, these assignments can build the ability to recall, summarize and paraphrase information.

Preadolescence includes ages 11 through 14—children who are in middle or junior high school. In Piaget's terms, this is a time of transition, when children are moving away from the concrete operational stage into the final stage of formal operations. In this stage, youngsters can think in abstract terms, can generalize, and can form a hypothesis—all of which are essential for most research assignments. Most do not reach this final stage until they are in high school; some not until even later. Assignments can be designed to guide this age group through the steps of locating information on a focused topic and then combining the information gathered from a variety of sources into a meaningful presentation of ideas.

Adolescence includes ages 15 through 18. According to Piaget, the formal operational stage of cognitive development commonly emerges between 12 and 16. Students' ability to think abstractly enables them to gather information from a variety of sources and combine it into a cohesive presentation. This complex and difficult process must be practiced successfully to be mastered, and students need a framework and guidance to achieve proficiency in using these skills in libraries.

When research assignments match stages of children's cognitive development, they are more satisfied with their learning, more confident in their ability to use the library, and more interested in using nonfiction and reference books in seeking information.

Sources

Elkind, David. *Child Development and Education: A Piagetian Perspective.* Oxford University Press; 1976.

Kuhlthau, Carol Collier. *School Librarians' Grade-by-Grade Activities Program: A Complete Sequential Skills Plan for Grades K-8.* Prentice Hall/The Center for Applied Research in Education, 1981.

Singer, Dorothy G. & Tracey A. Revenson. *A Piaget Primer: How a Child Thinks.* New American Library, 1978.

Saying It Louder

by Dorothy Butler

Several months ago I started to think about what I might say to you today, and found myself in something of a quandary. Your brief was generously wide, inviting me to "feel free to be anecdotal"—a clear sign that the writer of the letter had read my books and knew about my tendency to gossip. Of course, the letter also drew my attention to the fact that the concern of this conference was to find more and better ways of "making the connection between books, babies, and libraries."

"What can I possibly say that hasn't been said already?" I asked my daughter, Chris, who I was visiting at the time. "Nothing, probably," she answered with brutal economy. "You just have to say it *louder*." She was, of course, quite right. We are not short on *theory* in this field; it is the tools with which the theory might be implemented that we seem to lack. I spared Chris my depressing suspicion that the outlook is less than rosy—that those of us who have been saying for years that children must make early contact with books if the glue is to stick are hardly even holding our own, let alone making headway. She needs all the strength and good cheer she can conjure up in her busy life as teacher, counselor, wife and mother of three school-age children, not gloomy prognostications from her own mother.

Let me pause for a moment, though, in case you feel that this address could turn into a lugubrious lament. Let me offer my first anecdote, gleaned in this same daughter's home a few minutes after the above conversation.

Some of you may recall my reference to a two-year-old called Anthony in the early chapters of *Babies Need Books*. This once chubby little chap, now a skinny, near-thirteen-year-old, is in his first year at high school. He is the eldest of Chris's three children, and, because he is one of my favorite people, I care very much that his new school, which he entered only a few weeks ago, should prove to serve his needs as well as his first school did. So I asked him how things were going.

Quite unself-consciously, he showed me an exercise book in which he is obliged to record his impressions of life in general, and school in particular, as part of his English language course. I read his first entries with interest. With the fluency I might have expected from this particular child, Anthony had touched on his personal concerns about making friends and getting used to new routines. What took my attention and touched my heart immediately, however, was his early com-

plaint that the school library was not, in the first week, open at lunchtime; in the second, his satisfaction that it *was*; in the third week his exasperation that it was never, apparently, to be open during mid-morning break; and in his latest entry, the hope that it might be possible to organize a petition for the reversal of this outrageous injustice!

Now, this is a boy who loves camping and tramping, makes energetic use of his bike and skateboard, builds and repairs things with skill, swims and plays cricket and soccer with style. That *books* owned and borrowed are part of Anthony's very being is his own good fortune. One can see how they both support and extend his experience of people, and the world. Surely, this is what we want for all children.

Before I settle down to consider the ways and means by which libraries—and schools, too, I believe—must address themselves to the recruitment of the babies and toddlers in their neighborhoods to books, I should like to look a little more closely at the benefits of a book-based life.

On all fronts we hear of the advantages to children of electronic equipment, the purchase of which, by schools and libraries, inevitably reduces the funds for buying books. The unique capacity of the book for transmitting nourishment to the mind and spirit is increasingly unrecognized.

Facts are seen as all-important—and the easiest way to produce a fact is to press a button. T.S. Eliot in his plea: "Where is the wisdom we have lost in knowledge? Where is the knowledge we have lost in information?"

There is strong justification for the fear that most of the population is not aware of any loss. How can one experience loss if one has not experienced possession? And herein lies our greatest problem. How to tell such people that electronic contraptions cannot perform miracles, that the state of children's minds and imaginations is more important than the equipment in their schools or homes—and that language is the magic component? Language—the raw material of thought, the tool used by that incomparable computer, the human brain, to reflect, deduce and innovate—has been, in my lifetime, swept aside, subordinated, as an instrument of education, to inert machinery which, we are supposed to believe, will solve all our problems. Resourceful, expansive, living language, adequate for the purposes of Shakespeare and Galileo, Dickens and Einstein, is judged inadequate for the purposes of the modern world.

The ironical truth is, of course, that the highly literate child is likely to be the one who performs best on the computer keyboard anyway, not to mention his other greater exercise of discrimination in television and video-viewing. The child whose access to books is assured and accepted sees things in perspective, and is unlikely to be seduced into dull dependence on a flickering TV screen. This child is likely to recognize the shoddy—to employ a developing faculty of judgment, to want to tap the diverse resources of the *real world*. That there is an inherent unfairness in this must be admitted. Deprived of the literature of their culture—their birthright, that unique source of information and pleasure—many millions of the world's children are exposed to the crippling effects of the all-too-readily-available television screen. For these children, ours is a crime of both omission and commission.

At the State University of New York in 1984, Robert McNeil said of this influence: "I think this society is being force-fed with trivial fare, and I fear that the effects on our habits of mind, our language, our tolerance for effort and our appetite for complexity, are only dimly perceived." I could not help but smile nostalgically at McNeil's use of that old phrase *habit of mind*. Does anyone know what it means any longer? My parents' generation used it to describe the flavor or bent of an individual's habitual thought processes. Not only has the expression disappeared, nothing has taken its place. *I.Q.* is quite different.

Kathleen Jamieson, communication professor at the University of Texas, might have been speaking of my country, as well as of yours, when she said recently that "the nation's cultural education now is commercial advertisements and prime-time sitcoms and dramas; there isn't the kind of depth and richness that a study of history, the Bible, Shakespeare brought into cultural literacy in the past. And so, the grounds on which we are building argument [and here she was referring to making of political and social decisions], is in some way substantially impoverished."

The truth is that many millions of children will be condemned to the new so-called "visual literacy" (which does not include books as we have known them in the past); their sentence has been determined by those features of the world we have created which will coarsen their tastes with banal images and strident sound in the earliest and most impressionable days.

Babies and small children need precision, beauty, lilt and rhythm, and the opportunity to look and to listen, both at will and at length, as well as to touch and feel and smell. Words are finely tuned instruments which must be encountered early if their shades of meaning are to serve the developing intellect and emotions. There must be a two-way flow. There is no substitute for the loving exchange between adult and baby, each determined to communicate by whatever method springs to mind and hand. Lifelong habits are entrenched in this apparently simple exchange.

In *Babies Need Books*, I said that "books can be bridges between children and parents, and children and the world." That simple statement, made nearly ten years ago, has been said and resaid countless times in the years between. I was certainly not the first to say it, in one way or another; my early parenthood, beginning over forty years ago, was enriched and informed by the work of my countrywoman, Dorothy Neal White, and by notable Americans such as Paul Hazard, May Hill Arbuthnot and Ruth Hill Viguers, with the English writers and critics Margery Fisher, Roger Lancelyn Greene and others on hand when I needed them for reference. What they all gave me, more importantly, was the priceless gift of stimulation, reaffirming my own conviction that children's very beings would be nurtured and sustained through story, and that the adults in their lives had a central role to play in the process.

In those halcyon days, through the fifties and sixties (which saw such a burgeoning of children's literature on both sides of the Atlantic), I imagined that we needed only time, hard work and faith. Within another decade or two, the children of the world, deluged as they were with books of irresistible attraction and quality, would all be *reading*—voluntarily, joyfully, responsively. That this sort of reading pre-supposed fluency did not strike me as a problem. I believed that motivation—determination to be numbered among the "real" readers—was the vital accelerant into the perfection of necessary skills. (I still believe this.) And these were heady days! We seemed to have solved the problem of book provision. Paperbacks appeared in the thousands; picture books in all their magnificence were suddenly within reach of ordinary families. The more idealistic of us envisaged a time soon to come, when every ten-year-old would have a paperback novel protruding from the hip pocket of his or her jeans.

Somehow, it didn't happen. Surprisingly, the provision of books was not the cure-all my generation expected it to be. I am haunted by a vision of a million bored children, their backs turned to a mountain of books—glorious books which would set their eyes sparkling, their hands grabbing, if only they could be encouraged to wade in.

We must face the fact that we have somehow failed to forge a link between these children and reading. For whatever reason, the connection is not there. What has gone wrong?

If we (and, of course, teachers) consider school-age children, we must admit that our efforts will be successful only part of the time. Producing children who perform to their own age level on a reading test is not the same thing at all as producing "real" readers. The real reader knows no barrier between page and mind; the book ceases to be a thing of wood pulp and printer's ink and assumes a nature of its own. To quote Aidan Chambers:

> . . . Literature in print transcends time and place and person. A book is a time-space machine; a three-dimensional object that has shape, weight, texture and smell, and even taste. And compressed into those abstract marks made on paper, it carries, by a mystery we still do not understand, a cargo of the deepest knowledge of one person delivered directly to the most secret life of another, who may be many hundreds of miles away and many years of time distant.

A thought occurs which is laughably obvious if we come to consider it, but is commonly overlooked: the book as we know it has not changed in form or function since its invention. The first person all those centuries ago who abandoned the awkward rolled scroll, apportioned work to pages, and finally bound them on one side so that they could be read in smooth succession, must have been a genius. Only the invention of the wheel compares. And like the wheel, which has never changed in shape, the book has never altered in basic form. As a vehicle for that mysterious "cargo of the deepest knowledge of one person" (to use Chambers's expression), it performs impeccably.

Why, then, do we find it so hard, in our modern setting, to ensure that books are received by children—seen by them—as conveyors of wonder, delight and excitement? This is not the place to examine this question in depth. Suffice to say that modern children, seduced from birth by a society which dazes while it entertains, ignores the omnipotence of language as a force of life, and scorns old-fashioned notions like the deferment of gratification and the gathering of wisdom—these children are receiving shabby treatment from those they trust. We are to blame. We find it hard—impossible in some cases—to weld child and book together because we don't do it soon enough. We allow other pernicious influences to gain sway in children's preferences and then, panicking, cast around for someone or some institution to blame.

Our commonest object of censure in this connection is the school. Yet we know from our own experience, from the findings of research and conclusions of commissions, that children who come to school with active minds, well-developed capacities for self-expression, and burgeoning vocabularies seem to slide into reading effortlessly, naturally.

The process should be natural. In learning to read, being "at home" with books, knowing how they work to convey information and to tell stories, is the fundamental first step. Learning to read, in Marie Clay's phrase, is "getting the message." Children will extract "the message" from written prose with the same determination they use to glean meaning from spoken language—if the game can be shown to be worth the candle. And it can be—as it is for the lucky children who fall into the category described above, those for whom books are playfellows and bedfellows from babyhood. We must find ways to reach the babies and toddlers of our world if we hope seriously to increase the ranks of the real readers.

Our only direct route to children that don't read is probably through parents—and for "parents" one can usually read "mothers." Of course there is reason for satisfaction—for joy—if daycare centers and nursery schools include books in their programs. But, like schools, they are institutions that children go to. Real and lasting impressions come from the home. Certainly there are those children who will seize the first book they ever encounter in nursery or primary school, hurl themselves into the reading game, and astonish everyone by embarking on book-centered lives.

They are the exceptions. For every such child—and the phenomenon occurs in the art and music fields, too—there are thousands of children who could have been recruited, and were

not. These children are exposed to books at school, may be involved in lively reading programs run by dedicated teachers, but they still bypass books and settle for the uncertain, often mindless gratification of the television screen.

Evidence abounds that lasting changes must be generated in children's homes if they are to occur at all. Short-term effects certainly flow from school programs energetically pursued at every level—and we can be surprised, on occasion.

Let us never become so disillusioned that we abandon any avenue. But until we can reach into homes, and actually change the nature of their influence on children's development tastes, it is unlikely that we will markedly change the proportion of readers in our community. In fact, in the face of the growing influence of factors already mentioned which combine to convince children that reading is a dull and difficult pastime—certainly not an attractive occupation for out-of-school leisure time—it is likely that the situation will worsen.

I believe that public libraries constitute a unique bastion in this dismal scene. Their one overriding advantage is that they actually exist for the purpose of meeting the assumed reading needs of every member of the community they serve, regardless of age, sex, race, social class or intellectual level. This is not to say that libraries have in the past accomplished this, or that they are all doing so now. But the capacity to serve, however under-realized, still constitutes a powerful potential tool for the reversal of trends in people's lives.

But, still, *potential*. Why not *actual*? What would we need to do to empower libraries to play their real, intended role in people's lives? Particularly in children's lives?

Let's look at public libraries—and of course, my conversance is with those in my own country. We have made enormous strides in the physical attributes of the libraries themselves. The high-ceilinged, cold, awesome buildings of my childhood have been replaced with warm, light, welcoming complexes in which the children's department, even if small, has cushions on the mats, books in low bins for easy access, and puzzles, puppets and stuffed toys to make small borrowers feel at home. The children who do come—remembering that babies and toddlers must be brought by parents—exploit these benefits to the fullest. Little can be said in criticism of the system from the point of view of these privileged children.

Librarians then? In my day they tended to be austere, unsmiling people dedicated to preserving books, rather than to serving people—and children must have posed problems in rooms ostensibly devoted to scholarship, rooms in which notices on the wall said, starkly, SILENCE.

My own children had much better luck, encountering that priceless blessing, a kind and friendly librarian who remained in place from the days of their babyhood until their passage into adulthood. Indeed, the garden around the Birkenhead Library was later named the "Nell Fisher Reserve"; I never drive past without remembering her. My grown children acknowledge her as a strong influence on their lives.

Miss Fisher had her own way of reserving a special book for a special child; she would rummage under her desk, and then slip it almost furtively into a child's hands: a secret treat, no less. Once, one of my children came in from school with the news that he had to walk back to the shopping center to buy some India ink for the map he was drawing. He had passed the shop, but had had no money with him. He was ten years old and the winter evening was already drawing in—but off he went. An hour later when I was starting to feel a little worried, he came in and his face was shining. "Miss Fisher had *Pigeon Post* for me!" he said jubilantly. "Good," said I. "Did you get your ink?" His expression changed to one of ludicrous dismay. "Heck! I forgot!" The lure of the library had been his undoing—but the influence of Arthur Ransome on his life more than compensated, we both believed, though we did not discuss the matter. (A friend down the road lent him some India ink and I ultimately took *Pigeon Post* into custody against an all-night stand, which might not have included map drawing.)

We all have our favorite tales to tell; but we are the favored ones—"on the side of the angels," as Forster would describe us. For each of us there are many thousands who do not see their local library as an extension of their living rooms, who do not pass on the comfortable habit of library visiting to their children. And it is from parents that children will learn, whatever the lesson.

We can safely say, then, that in your country and mine we have excellent children's libraries, suitably furnished and well-stocked (though no library ever has enough books, and provision is seldom high on the list of governmental priority.) In the main, we have well-trained librarians who understand children's needs and are increasingly accepting of children as they are: noisy, sometimes insubordinate, setting no great store by order or timetable, but also honest, friendly, and full of such willing good cheer that the heart sometimes aches for them, given the state of the world we sentence them to live in.

The problem, then, does not lie predominantly with personnel or institutions. It is one of connection. There seems to be an invisible wall between a huge section of the populace and the libraries which hope to serve it. The seduction of apparently easier, all-too-available entertainment is not merely a deterrent to library enrollment, either. It is a cause of a crippling complaint which will keep its sufferers from books for life: the inability to read fluently enough to make the exercise worthwhile.

One is not *reading* in any rewarding sense until meaning pours, without apparent effort on the reader's part, from page to mind. I like J.B. Kerfoot's analogy of responsive readers taking the text for their scenario and producing it on the stage of their own imaginations, with resources furnished by their own experience of life. This sort of reading is like listening, another skill which—alas!—is being eroded by the day in our society. Further, the reader must "reach out," in Martin Buber's phrase, to meet the author, if maximum satisfaction and understanding is to be achieved.

The active use of mind and imagination required for this sort of reading demands an investment of self, an assumption that the rewards will be positive. How hard this is to implant if those other lures are given full rein in the early years, without competition from the experience of story between covers! How easy, if print and picture have been shared, with delight, from birth!

Last year, when she was two, my granddaughter Bridget asked me for "Humpty Dumpty" from her *Mother Goose* book. "You find it," I said, busy with something else. Quite soon, "Here's Humpy Dumpy" said Bridget, having found the right page. But she was pointing to the text, not the picture! "You read it," I said then—and she did, her finger moving indiscriminately over the words, without a glance at the picture. By heart, of course, but with total, untaught understanding of the way written language works to produce meaning.

And so we go round in circles. Children must expect to become readers—*want* to become readers. Observe the example of adults who read with enjoyment, and who have time and space in their lives to read, before they are likely to embark on the long hours of "practice" which will ensure the sort of fluency which this state demands. We know what the requirements are; we know that children exposed to written language from birth are unconsciously noting the patterns, the conventions of the text. They have a head start, but it is an advantage which only a close adult can confer.

Even once school days begin, children spend more than three times as long awake, in their parents' care, as they spend at school. It is parents who are powerful. They must be reached, convinced, and helped to exercise this power. And, in this connection, enlightened public libraries which have no "age of entry" have a clear advantage over schools to reach and influence. Achieving this access must be the concern of every public library which hopes to continue to exist. Bluntly, if the readers dry up, the libraries close down!

No prescription will suit all situations; methods and programs will be as various as the people and institutions involved. High on the list must be the raising of public awareness that "reading matters," that books are unlikely to become part of a person's entrenched way of life unless encountered early, and that school entry as a time to meet books is too late by five or six years.

Most important, those authorities who are seen by the public (however mistakenly) as oracular, must be persuaded to utter convincing exhortations on the subject of books and reading to the community at large. Campaigns run by local governments, backed by business interests, supported in principle by schools and in practical ways by libraries, to reach the parents of newborn babies in maternity hospitals—with vigorous follow-up—might be expected to bear fruit. And indeed, have done so already. I know of several energetic programs; the Orlando Public Library's "Catch 'em in the Cradle" venture first alerted me to their possibilities.

We still need, in all societies, the conversion of governmental authorities to the view that the funding of such schemes is a matter of national importance. We know that children are the citizens of tomorrow; that the horrifying problems we have created on social and environmental fronts will be theirs, not ours, to cope with. Why then, do we still treat children as second-class citizens, whatever lip service we give to our concern for them? As a society, we undervalue children; worse, we work very hard to divest them of their inexhaustible energy, their fresh creativity, their astonishing faith in us.

Empowerment of parents must be central to any scheme

for change in children's lives, and this must mean more than access to financial help. Somehow, parents must be persuaded, not only of their responsibility to their children from birth, but of their own incomparable power in their children's lives. Parents must be brought to believe further that this power to influence has nothing to do with the wish to influence. They will influence their children, whether they intend to or not. They must be convinced that their love for their children will be their children's greatest strength, that unconditional human love is the most priceless of all human gifts, and that the capacity to give it has nothing to do with wealth, position, or education. They must come to know that their children will learn from them the capacity to love and relate to other people and that no other lesson will ever be as important as this one.

Frustratingly, one of the greatest stumbling blocks to success in this project is *simplicity*. Great changes are thought to require complex technology and huge sums of money. The simple triangle of parent, child, and book is not easily accepted as the passport it actually is to the essential qualities of life: the human capacities to love, laugh, and to learn. This is not likely to begin to change until support for a "Books from Birth" campaign is given, with appropriate fanfare by the "powers that be." This, while only a start, would be an important one.

Our lobby, therefore, must be to these "powers" as well as to parents. Ways must be found—and will be found—if our resolution is strong enough, our case conclusive enough, our voices heard often enough.

Children are our greatest resource. They must be helped to grow strong in spirit if our world—their world—is to become a better place. Their own survival may well depend on it. You and I know that this strength can flow from books, that language is the key to our humanity, that narrative language is the vehicle by which we order our thoughts, and that these are the things we must give our children. Our cause is not peripheral to the urgent causes of the world; it is central.

C.S. Lewis said that "through literature we become a thousand people and yet remain ourselves"; and I think my grandson, an ordinary kid in baggy beach shorts and yellow tee-shirt in Auckland, New Zealand, is simultaneously Jason among the Argonauts in search of the Golden Fleece; Chas McGill in wartime England, desperately concealing a Nazi gunner from parents and authorities, imperceptibly growing up amid the anguish, thrill and futility of it all; Beric, Rosemary Sutcliff's "outcast" in Roman Britain, knowing rejection, starting to understand prejudice—but courage, and love, too—and Sam, on his side of the mountain, determined to make his own, solitary way. Then three-year-old Bridget, his cousin, astride the verandah rail, chanting "Rumpeta, rumpeta, rumpeta," clearly inside the skin of one of that assorted band which accompanied the Bad Baby on his rollicking adventure on the elephant's back . . .

A boy and a girl, ten years apart in age, looking at the world through other people's eyes, yet seeing clearly with their own.

Once again Aidan Chambers says for me what I want to say: "While we can tell each other what is going on inside us and be told what is going on inside other people, we remain human, sane, hopeful, creative. In short, we remain alive."

A Vision of Librarianship

by F. William Summers

L *eading off SLJ's annual Educational Technology Issue, Bill Summers touches on such crucial issues as changes in the role and functions of staff, fees for specialized services and delivery of information, and costs for implementing and maintaining local and state networks.*

The opportunity to speak on a topic like "A Vision of Librarianship" is a very welcome one because it inevitable invites one to speculate about the future. For an academic, speculation about the future is a favorite activity. In fact, one of the hottest fields in universities today is Future Study. I believe the reason that academics are so interested in future study is that they are unable to explain the past or influence the present—and thus the one easy option open to them is to speculate about the future.

Another attraction of speaking about the future is that you are unlikely to be called to account for your prophesy. Depending upon the age of the audience and the time period in which you cast your remarks, a certain percentage of the listeners will not be around to comment on your accuracy and another healthy percentage of them won't remember what you said. So the chances of someone coming up to you and saying, "Back in 1989 you said such and such would happen and it didn't!" is fairly remote. Of course, there is also the possibility that you won't be around either, which gives you almost 100% freedom in talking about a vision of the future.

If you want an interesting exercise in evaluating the accuracy of these kinds of presentations, go back and take a look at a little pamphlet, *The Impact of Technology on Library Buildings*, produced in 1967 by a group called Educational Facilities Laboratories. EFL called together a rather large panel of experts to tackle this subject because there was at that time a lot of argument among facility planners that libraries could be built much smaller than in the past, since microforms and computers would shrink the need for house collections. These experts were predicting a 20- to 25-year time frame for this, so it is now possible to assess how accurate they were. Aside from missing the development of the microcomputer, they didn't do too bad a job. I'd say it is roughly equivalent to making a prediction in 1941 about the end of World War II and having to say that, aside from the atomic bomb, I had it about right.

In this presentation I will not say very much about technology for two very good reasons: 1) I don't know a lot about

library technology, and, 2) I am more interested in the results of library technology than in the technology itself.

What I do want to talk about are two matters which I believe are crucial to the information health of our country and to the societal value of these wonderful creations we call libraries. The first is the challenge that we face in trying to embrace technology without losing our basic values and how technology can alter those values. Secondly, I will examine the kinds of changes we can expect in the basic nature of library service by the time we reach the 21st century.

Despite our beliefs to the contrary, technology is not neutral. You do not introduce new technology into anything, including libraries, without some risk of altering the organization and its mores and values. Systems make their own demands. No matter how much we try, we inevitably wind up doing something in a certain way, not because it is the best way or the most humane or sensitive way, but because the system demands it. For example, libraries in some instances have had to choose two or three loan periods for materials—not because their users would not have preferred six or eight or even an infinite number of loan periods, but because the software program could only handle two or three. A great deal of what we put in the accepted format for computer-stored catalogs is there not because it matched the needs of users, but because it matched what the computer could do at the time we did it.

I am not saying that these were necessarily bad decisions, but they demonstrate that technological systems are not value-free, and that dealing with them does impact upon our values. The great challenge which we must meet in the future is how to find ways to get all that we can from technology in the form of speed, convenience, accuracy, efficiency, lower unit costs and all of the other wonders it can bring us, and how to do so without having that same technology alter the values which our institutions seek to serve.

I would like to stop at this point to identify some of those values on which technology will have an impact and the threats posed by the increase of technological developments.

1. *Respect for the individual.* Of all the things which librarians do well, perhaps the best is that we show respect for each individual who comes to us. We train (or try to train) librarians to accept that the most limited inquirer with the fuzziest inquiry is just as important as the most sophisticated scholar with the most intriguing and specific inquiry. We don't

always succeed in inculcating this value but we try, and that is perhaps what is important. As we move, for example, to artificial intelligence systems, it will be difficult to ensure that we build systems which will be tolerant of the timid, inarticulate, non-specific inquirer. It will be difficult because the system will probably work best and easiest for the knowledgeable and precise inquirer. Human interacters have, at least, the capacity to adjust their behavior to the inquirer. The expert artificial intelligence system will not have this capacity unless we insist that it is provided, even though it may be quicker, cheaper and more efficient to design one without it.

2. *Privacy of the individual.* Librarians have done a great job thus far in ensuring that their library systems will protect the privacy rights of individuals. However, as information systems become more complex (and especially, as they become more remote and more interactive), protecting the privacy of circulation records will become more difficult. Also, the benefits to others of gaining this information may increase. The ability to gain access to the online transaction records of a special or research library could be very valuable to a competitor or an enemy.

3. *Equality of user needs.* One of the basic principles of American librarianship has been the belief that the needs of one user are equally important as those of another user. By and large, libraries have done a good job of observing this principle, one which is difficult to defend and preserve. It is difficult, in academic and school libraries, not to let the needs of the faculty and administration become paramount to the needs of the students. In public libraries it is difficult not to let the needs and demands of adults—who, after all, pay the taxes—become more important than the needs of children. As we build and layer systems in the future, it will be necessary to be very militant about preserving this value. Technology will certainly give us the opportunity to make gradations in the response of the system dependent upon the age or category of the user. If we yield to the temptation to use this capability, we run the risk of altering dramatically the basic character of the institutions which the systems are being created to further.

We already have seen some tendencies in this direction. Most university librarians could not argue that professors do not receive more or better interlibrary loan service than do freshmen. Few public libraries could argue that children and youth receive the same interlibrary loan service as adults. Thus far, at least, we have based these distinctions upon rationalizing the use of a limited resource. But soon there will be the opportunity to internalize these distinctions into a system, and we need to be very careful about the assumptions upon which such systems are built. Just as we are careful about what values are inculcated into our librarians in training, so must we be careful about what values are incorporated into our systems. It should also be noted, of course, that interlibrary loan is a limited resource only because that is the way we have chosen to build library systems.

4. *Freedom of purpose.* It has been said that the library is one of the last refuges of the individual in our society. The library is the one place where individuals can go for their own purposes and not have to account for themselves. We have people in our libraries making some inquiries for purposes that society might find highly noble, but also, possibly, very unsettling.

One of the possible dangers of future systems will be their great capability; once it is there, someone will be tempted to use it. A university librarian once boasted that a new circulation system could, if asked, print out a list of every book borrowed by a faculty member over the previous year. When asked whether he intended to use this capability, the answer was no. But suppose the President wants to use it, or the legislature, or the FBI?

5. *Freedom of access.* American libraries have set their greatest value on ensuring freedom of access to information. With few exceptions, we do not place guards at the door to control who enters the library; nor do we limit people's access to information once they are inside the library. But we face a future in which less and less of the information will actually be in the library, and more and more of it will be accessed electronically, sometimes at relatively high cost. Will we be as willing to provide free access at that time? Already we are having serious discussions about how to pay for access to remote data bases. Will the problem be any less serious when the data base is in the library but with a high unit cost for each access? We are willing to hand all users the *World Almanac* or the *Statistical Abstract*, without questioning who they are or what they want to do with them, but will we be willing to do this when those sources are on an internal data base?

6. *Access to government information.* One of the things U.S. libraries have done for a long time and done very well is to provide public access to information by and about the government. Now that information is increasingly being treated as a commodity, there is a growing tendency in government—cheered on by the private sector—to want to pass on the cost of disseminating that information to patrons in the form of user fees or via a private sector vendor. More and more government publications and data bases are being privatized, and public access to this information is increasingly restricted to those who can and will pay for it. We can expect this trend to continue and intensify. In many instances, the information is published in print form and made available to libraries, but it is also processed and put into data bases by online vendors who then charge for access to the value-added product.

We will very likely see this process continue, and the government will be pressured to cease the print publication, since it undercuts the market for the value-added product. As this happens, libraries will find it necessary to pay high costs to provide public access to information that they once received free as a matter of public policy. This type of marketing has been somewhat restricted by the fact that most government information, at present, cannot by copyrighted and must be made available on equal terms to all who want it. We can certainly expect that, in the future, libraries will have to wage strong and ongoing battles with government agencies and with private sector publishers in order to uphold the goal of the library as a principal point of citizen access to government information.

It is already clear that the present levels of technology introduced into libraries are changing the ways in which these institutions perform their service. The technology which is on or just beyond the horizon will have the capacity to affect the nature of library service in dramatic ways. Before identifying and discussing some of these fundamental changes, I must tell you at the outset that I do not necessarily think they are all desirable or that all of them should happen, but I nevertheless believe that they will occur.

• Libraries will move from a function of collecting materials in anticipation of user need to one of acquisition upon presentation of need.

Almost from their very beginnings one of the basic functions of librarians has been to select from the mass of available information those sources which it has anticipated a given body of users will need, and to organize these collections and have them ready for the users. Thus, a major professional preoccupation of librarians has been with ways to anticipate what these needs might be and with processes of evaluation and selection of these sources. A large part of library school curricula and discussions at professional meetings have focused upon methods of community analysis to discover these needs. Also, these meetings detail the processes of book and information selection to identify the most usable, most reliable sources so that they will be available when the users want them. Lately, we have realized that no matter how good the staff, no library with limited resources could meet all needs and have thus created networks of various types. Library systems have poured large sums of money into processes to facilitate interlibrary cooperation so that they could obtain the needed information they were not able to pre-select or pre-purchase.

Already, some libraries have largely abandoned this predemand selection function and rely primarily upon their ability to acquire information when the need is presented. The clearest example is the special library, which maintains a relatively small collection and goes outside of its own resources to obtain most of the information its users need. Another example can be found in the so-called "information entrepreneurs," who maintain virtually no collections of information of their own but who go out and find, principally in other libraries and in commercial delivery services, the information which their clients need.

With the advances in communication and transportation of information soon to be available, more and more libraries will move in this direction. They will pre-select less of their information and will obtain more of it through relatively rapid means when the need is presented. Library schools will devote much less attention to community analysis and selection principles and much more effort toward developing the skills of information acquisition and understanding the relative value, reliability and costs of obtaining information from various sources. The function of maintaining a large retrospective collection will pass to a few great "national" research libraries and to the relatively few other institutions whose administrators wish to emulate them. Most libraries will maintain relatively small collections of frequently used information and will obtain other items as needed. This shift will make a profound difference in the skills required of the library staff and in the ways in which the library spends its resources.

• Libraries will shift from a process of identification of information sources into the delivery of information.

One of the principal uses of a commercial data base is for the purpose of identifying a group of sources, usually books or journals, in which we believe the information the users seek may be found. The user then goes to these sources and searches through them to determine if the needed information is actually present. In the future, people will be increasingly impatient with this process and will want intermediaries not to simply identify sources but to actually extract the information from the sources. This is the function which the information entrepreneur now provides; increasingly, people will wish and insist that libraries provide it. This change will profoundly alter the ways in which libraries do business. They will, for example, be required to have staffs with much greater subject expertise than they are now required to have. Those staffs will also be required to interact with users in ways which are radically different from the interactions of the present. We do this now to some extent in providing ready reference, in which we actually extract the information from the source and deliver it to the patron. In the future we will do it to a much greater extent and in much more complicated searches. I once encountered a patron in the State Library of Florida who asked, "What kind of library do you run here?" When asked for a clarification the patron replied, "Is this the kind of library that if you want to know just a little bit they will tell you, but if you want to know a lot, you have to find it for yourself?" We can expect that in the future users will find materials for themselves less and less; more and more the library staff will tell them.

• Librarians will see a change in the nature and depth of subject analysis.

One of the early claims for the value of computerizing library records was that it would provide for much greater subject analysis than manual systems. I haven't analyzed it, but I have the distinct impression that the level of subject analysis in library catalogs hasn't changed much from pre-computer days. The subject headings on an OCLC record are probably no more complex than those on an old Library of Congress catalog card. Libraries simply have not exploited the subject analysis potential of computer-stored bibliographic records. If you want in-depth subject analysis today, you go outside the library and pay for it—either directly, to a data base developer, or indirectly, through one of the data base aggregators such as BRS or Dialog. In the future (principally because of the two changes previously noted), librarians will do subject analysis of the materials to a much greater extent than at present. Since the library will contain fewer resources it will be important to get the most out of them; we will want to search them in the most efficient ways. We will certainly do Boolean searching and key-word searching in full texts—and probably find that many more ways are yet to be discovered.

This change will also cause a major shift in the number and nature of personnel needed in libraries.

• We will witness a change in the nature of library staffs.

At present, a relatively high percentage of library personnel have backgrounds as library generalists; that is, they are familiar with the basic processes in libraries even though they may work in a technical services or public services context and are specialized to that extent. Libraries also employ relatively few subject specialists, particularly if the library has subject departments. But the bulk of the staff are generalists, and even those who are not see themselves as librarians first and subject specialists second.

In the future we can expect that this will reverse and the larger portion of the staff will be subject specialists, many of whom will identify much more with their subject specialty than with the field of librarianship—if they identify with librarianship at all. This shift will have a very great impact upon the ways in which we staff libraries, upon their personnel policies and upon the way the profession is practiced in this country.

The change in the staff complement will also have a significant effect upon the organizational structure of libraries. The typical library organization chart today is relatively vertical, with a director and, commonly, associate directors for public and technical services, and a number of staff specialists in personnel, finance, systems and other functions reporting to the director. As staffs become much more subject-oriented, and as automation proceeds, we can expect that these organizational charts will become much flatter, encompassing fewer administration levels. We can also anticipate that the distinctions between technical services and public services will continue to blur and may perhaps disappear. Subject specialists will focus on both the input and output side of the organization and will be responsible for most of the classification and subject analysis of material going into the library. Library staffs will increasingly function on a team or task force basis. We have seen much of this already, as most libraries have utilized staff task forces to plan for automated systems within the library.

Along with the staff, the library building will also change. Two very noticeable changes will be the disappearance of the card catalog and the shift of the technical services function to another site outside the library building. When the card catalog is computer-stored and displayed on terminals (or optical disks or whatever may come along), there will be little need to house the technical services function, which will be essentially an office and production operation in $100 per square-foot space. The same will probably also be true of the budgeting and financial accounting operations. With all these functions on-line, they can be housed in much cheaper space than those devoted to housing collections and service staff.

Another likely change will be increased pressure for departmental libraries in academic institutions. With less emphasis on building the total collection and greater emphasis on acquisition from a variety of sources—coupled with telefacsimile and other rapid means of document delivery—the traditional arguments for the large central library will become less tenable. Added to the increasing emphasis upon subject specialists, this will suggest that it makes a great deal of sense to detach the library subject specialists and to house them along with the instructional and research specialists in the disciplines in which they serve. We already have this system in law, medicine and science, and it will develop in other disciplines as well.

• A portion of the cost of specialized information will shift to the users.

Inevitably (and regrettably) we will witness a shift of a portion of the costs of specialized services and information to the users. The American Library Association is opposed to this principle, as are most librarians, and I hope that we will be able to prevail. But ultimately, that may not be possible. Most libraries, either directly or indirectly, are supported by public funds. There is and will be greater pressure upon public funds to pay for all of the services which society needs and demands. At the same time there is considerable public pressure against increasing public expenditure. Given the demographic mix of our population—the growth in the proportion of retired people, for example—we cannot expect those pressures to lessen. We cannot expect that the costs of operating libraries will decline. Any funds saved by reductions in local acquisition and in automation of technical services will be more than offset by added staff in subject specialization and by the costs of acquiring information from external sources. Costs of participation in the wide variety of consortia, networks, resource sharing groups, etc., to which libraries will need to belong, will increase dramatically along with the higher costs to be paid for more rapid delivery of information sought by users. Libraries currently face the dilemma of not adding needed data bases because they can't afford them and don't want to institute user charges. That dilemma will intensify, and inevitably (and again, regrettably), will come down on the side of instituting charges for services beyond certain minimal levels.

How will we square these kinds of economic necessities with the traditions of free library service? The only choice appears to be in the same way we now do it for a variety of other services—through state and federal subsidy. In public and private higher education we now have large programs of federal and state grants aimed at equalizing the access of poorer students with that of wealthier students. We do the same thing in medical care. The original purpose of the Library Services and Construction Act was to equalize the access of poorer rural areas without library service to larger urban areas which already had it. We will need to find a way to do the same thing with information access to ensure that the access to information services of less-affluent citizens is equal to that of those who can pay their own fees.

• There will be a greater reliance on local and state networks than on national networks.

Almost every state in the nation is now at work building its own network. They can afford to do this for three reasons. First, the cost of computers and computer storage has declined to the point that it is affordable. Second, the cost of telecommunications needed to reach national networks has increased dramatically. Third, the technical expertise necessary to build such networks is much more widely available than it was 20 years ago when Fred Kilgore began the development of OCLC.

As these state and regional networks develop, the national networks will inevitably be faced with changes in the ways in which their services are used and in their cost factors. As the function of obtaining local bibliographic data and interlibrary loan information is transferred to local networks, the national networks will find that their services will be used principally for retrospective materials, specialized materials, and/or materials that are difficult to locate. Maintaining a large data base for these purposes will have much higher per-use costs than maintaining a data base in which the costs are spread out over a much greater variety of services. The costs of maintaining the data base are relatively fixed and, as the nature and number of uses decreases, the unit costs will inevitably rise. The problems caused by these shifts for the national data bases will also be intensified for their regional organizations, such as SOLINET. As the states come to be able to rely on their own data bases, the regional organization will decline in importance to them. These shifts will not take place in a short period but will be gradual over time.

In the short and middle term the national data bases may be able to thrive with an "all or none" policy (i.e., a library must either put all or none of its records into the national data base). But that strategy cannot be successful in the long run because some of the larger states may well be able to go it alone or to form their own networks with other large states. These developments will cause a great deal of turmoil in the national, regional and local structures and will likely not settle down for a long time. Competition in network services has reared its ugly head and will not soon be put to rest.

• **All types of libraries will be included in networks.**

Over the next five to ten years we will see increasing pressure for the inclusion of all types of libraries in networks. To date, networks have been affordable by only the largest academic, public and special libraries. As costs decline and as the number of advantages of network affiliation increase, we can expect that more of the small libraries will insist upon being included in these networks. Organizers of the state network being built in Florida, for example, are under great pressure from the legislature to include the state's community colleges. Right behind them are the public libraries, who rightly feel that if state resources are to be put into the creation of a network, their needs should be included. School libraries are also beginning to move into networking and will need to be included in these statewide resources.

These pressures will be difficult, if not impossible, to resist—and logically, there is great reason not to resist them. For many years our assumption about smaller libraries was that their inclusion would not bring many unique resources to a data base because their collections largely duplicated one another. However, study after study has concluded that this assumption has little if any validity. Even the smallest library brings a relatively large percentage of unique items to the network data base and makes it all the richer. When we couple the resources which inclusion of a broader array of libraries would bring to a network, along with more rapid means of moving information from point A to point B, then there is little reason not to make the networks as broad as possible. As the economics of network participation change, we can expect that a greater number of libraries will seek participation in networks.

There is another possible scenario which suggests that these smaller libraries may find it more economical to buy a commercial compact storage system (such as the compact disc or one of its successors) and bypass the network stage altogether. As I have suggested, this would be a loss to the concept of networking. My hunch is that resolution of this issue may turn to a greater extent on matters such as attitude, value and institutional image than on technology. The large networks will need to seek ways to make their systems economical for these smaller libraries and further, to make them feel like valuable participants not second-class citizens.

• **Networks will place a greater emphasis on information delivery than on its identification.**

For the most part, our networks have focused on the problems of identification of information rather than upon its delivery. The computerized systems can help us to identify the location of a wanted item very quickly, and the interlibrary loan sub-systems have resulted in some time savings in delivery of the interlibrary loan request. But our systems for the delivery of information itself have not kept pace with the rapidity of the identification systems. In another context I have suggested that to some degree our systems thus far have only served to increase the speed at which we can frustrate users. We can tell them where the material is at electronic speed but the delivery methods are unsure and still take days, or even weeks. We can expect this to change rapidly in the not too distant future. The speed and quality of telefacsimile is improving while the costs are declining; therefore, it will soon be possible for a great proportion of library information to be delivered from external sources relatively rapidly. These systems will work well for the delivery of small amounts of information but are probably not yet feasible for the delivery of complete documents or entire books.

The dream of whole text on-line systems for a great proportion of needed information is still some time away. These systems are feasible where the body of information is finite and the rate of consultation very high (for example in law, or in fields such as business, in which the economic interest is very great). They will also likely be feasible for fields where social value makes the cost a secondary consideration (such as health and medicine) but probably are some time away for fields in which the body of information is very large and the rate of consultation relatively low, or those in which there is no great economic or social incentive. We certainly have the technical capability to build a whole-text data base for the Chaucer scholars, but the economics of doing so will probably dictate that it won't come about soon.

As all soothsayers say at some point, my crystal ball is growing cloudy. But in closing, there are several points I would like to reinforce. I happen to believe that the professional world in which we are now living and working is on the brink of an expansion not unlike that which occurred in the 1950's. On all sides we are seeing major public investments in buildings and in systems, and there are growing shortages of personnel to do critical jobs. Despite some of the concerns I've raised, I believe that the time for the things for which libraries stand has come round again. That does not mean that there are not serious questions that need answers. We live in an era in which technology will let us do just about anything we wish to do. How we will do it will no longer be the important question. Critical questions for the remainder of this century will be: What should be done, for whom should it be done and under what circumstances?

When I look at our world, I do not see a world in which the population is yearning for more technology; they are searching for values to help answer the serious problems which technology has already given us. No student escapes from FSU's library school without hearing me say, usually more often than they wish, that the difference between great librarians and poor ones is not in what they know about the stuff of librarianship—its technology, if you will—but rather in the attitudes, values and spirit they bring to the problems before them. It is those values which we must seek to preserve in the years to come.

Kids Need Libraries

School and Public Libraries Preparing the Youth of Today for the World of Tomorrow

Preface

"Youth constitute a global resource of the first magnitude."

Javier de Cuellar, U.N. Secretary-General
International Youth Year, 1985
"United Nations Chronicle Perspective," *U.N. Chronicle*,
January 1986

"As a nation we face a paradox of our own making. We have created an economy that seeks literate, technically trained and committed workers, while simultaneously we produce many young men and women who are semi-literate or functionally illiterate, unable to think critically and untrained in technical skills, hampered by high-risk lifestyles, and alienated from the social mainstream."

*Turning Points, Preparing American
Youth for the 21st Century*
Carnegie Council on Adolescent Development
Carnegie Corporation of New York, June 1989

"Far too many Americans today are growing up at risk. The majority of poor Americans are children, with one out of every four children under the age of six now living in poverty. We rank at the bottom of 20 industrialized nations with respect to infant mortality rates. Children whose families cannot find housing are now overcrowding shelters for runaways. And homeless children and families now constitute 30% of those without shelter. This year one out of every four students will leave high school without a diploma. In some of our inner cities 75% of all young people will have dropped out of school before they turn 16 years old. . . . We do strategic planning for every other area of critical importance. We have long-term plans for the military. . . . We have long-term plans for our nation's highways, bridges, and tunnels, because they provide the infrastructure for our democracy. . . . Children are the future security for this country and the future infrastructure for our democracy. So it is about time we work on getting a comprehensive plan for the 63 million Americans who are children."

Christopher Dodd, chair
Senate Subcommittee
on Children and Families,
introducing the Young Americans Act, 1986.

"In an era of high-pressure lobbying, political action committees and single issue voting, children and youth have few effective advocates . . . none [of whom] can make the major political contributions of which big business and many large organizations are capable. Children do not produce; they do not influence foreign trade or jobs or the stock market. They cost money. They do not have clout or the means to strike or to close down workplaces. They do not even vote, and many of the parents and other adults who should be representing them at the polls do not bother to vote either."

Barbara T. Rollock
Public Library Services for Children
Library Professional Publications, 1988.

Introduction

Planners of the 1991 White House Conference on Library Information Services (WHCLIS) have identified three themes. All three apply to youth, the voters and leaders of the future.

Library and Information Services for:

- Productivity
- Literacy
- Democracy

These themes are particularly important in the last decade of the twentieth century. Only by addressing the issues inherent within these themes will we successfully meet the challenges of the twenty-first century. Some of these challenges are:

This document was prepared by Virginia H. Mathews, Judith G. Flum and Karen A. Whitney on behalf of the three youth-serving divisions of the American Library Association: American Association of School Librarians (AASL), Association for Library Service to Children (ALSC), and Young Adults Services Division (YASD). It is to be used at all levels of activities relating to the second White House Conference on Library and Information Services

Ed. note:
The Omnibus Children and Youth Literacy through Libraries Initiative which was the top priority of the 2nd White House Conference on Library and Information Services in July 1991 was based upton this policy paper.

- Improving our ability to compete in a global market.
- Finding solutions to mounting environmental threats, not just to our country, but to the entire planet.
- Rejuvenating citizen participation in our democratic process.
- Solving the literacy problem to empower individuals to cope with rapid social and technological change.

The Preamble to Public Law 100-382, approved and signed by the President on August 8, 1988, calls for the second White House Conference on Library and Information Services and provides for the states to conduct Governors Conferences and other pre-WHCLIS activities leading up to the national conference to be held in Washington, D.C., July 9-13, 1991. This preamble cites, among other findings, five that are most relevant to consideration of our youth issues and recommendations.

- Access to information and ideas is indispensable to the development of human potential, the advancement of civilization, and the continuance of enlightened self-government;
- Social, demographic, and economic shifts of the past decade have intensified the rate of change and require that Americans of all age groups develop and sustain literacy and other lifelong learning habits;
- Expanding technological developments offer unprecedented opportunities for application to teaching and learning and to new means to provide access to library and information services;
- The growth and augmentation of the nation's library and information services are essential if all Americans, without regard to race, ethnic background, or geographic location, are to have reasonable access to adequate information and lifelong learning;
- The future of our society depends on developing the learning potential inherent in all children and youth, especially literary, reading, research and retrieval skills.

How Libraries and Librarians Can Help Kids Meet Their Needs for the Future

Youth today face many challenges as the twenty-first century approaches. They are the decision-makers, workers, and parents of tomorrow. Many kids lack the necessary support

---

WHAT LIBRARIES NEED TO HELP KIDS PREPARE FOR THEIR FUTURE

Upgraded school and public library services are essential for all American youth from infancy to age eighteen.

A State and Local Checklist

State and local areas differ in major issues, levels of library service, and strengths and weaknesses of school libraries and services to children and young adults in public libraries. Each state must develop priorities and potential legislation based on its specific issues and local needs, involving children, young adults, and their advocates in the process.

The checklist below is designed to help you assess specific gaps in meeting the needs of children and young adults in school and public libraries. If you answer "no" to any of the following questions (or parts of questions), you will need to develop proposals for consideration by the delegates at your state's pre-White House Conference.

❑ Yes ❑ No   Are all public schools required to have libraries and to have them staffed by a certified school library media specialist?

❑ Yes ❑ No   Do all public libraries in your state have a program of service to children staffed by a professional children's librarian?

❑ Yes ❑ No   Do all public libraries in your state have a program of service for young adults up to age 18 staffed by a professional young adult librarian?

❑ Yes ❑ No   Do librarians serving children and young adults in your state receive salaries comparable to salaries of other professional librarians? Do they have equal opportunities for career advancement?

❑ Yes ❑ No   Does your state have a network for sharing resources that will provide access for all citizens to the resources of school, public and special libraries?

❑ Yes ❑ No   Are libraries placed accessibly in communities and funded adequately to provide convenient hours of service?

❑ Yes ❑ No   Do school and public library policies and practices adhere to the concepts of intellectual freedom and the American Library Association's Library Bill of Rights?

❑ Yes ❑ No   Is there a state-level school library media consultant within the State Department of Education to provide leadership for school library programs in the state?

❑ Yes ❑ No   Are there state-level children's and young adult library consultants within the State Library Department to provide leadership for public library programs for children and young adults in the state?

❑ Yes ❑ No   Do all children and young adults, regardless of geographic location or physical disabilities, have equal access to the information resources of the state?

❑ Yes ❑ No   Do the collections of school libraries adequately support the schools' curricula?

❑ Yes ❑ No Do the children's collections, young adult collections, and general collections in public libraries adequately meet the educational, recreational, and personal needs of all youth, regardless of race or national origin?

❑ Yes ❑ No Do school and public library collections maintain a high level of currency by providing resources that have been published within the past three years, especially in subject areas such as science and health where currency is essential?

❑ Yes ❑ No Do children and young adults in your state have free access to electronic databases?

❑ Yes ❑ No Do all school and public libraries have fax machines to facilitate resource sharing? Do all school libraries have telephones?

❑ Yes ❑ No Do all children and young adults have free access to computers in school and public libraries?

❑ Yes ❑ No Does your state dedicate a percentage of state educational funds for school library media programs? Do school library media programs in your state receive money through P.L. 100-297 (the *Hawkins, Stafford Elementary and Secondary School Improvement Amendments of 1988*)?

❑ Yes ❑ No Has your state dedicated a percentage of the public library grant monies it administers to programs serving children and young adults? Has your state offered other incentives to libraries to develop services for children and young adults?

❑ Yes ❑ No Does your state have certificate requirements for school library media specialists for elementary through high school? Are they based on *Information Power: Guidelines for School Library Media Programs* approved by the American Association of School Librarians (AASL) and the Association for Educational Communications and Technology (AECT) in 1988?

❑ Yes ❑ No Do graduate library and educational programs in your state, accredited by the American Library Association or National Council for the Accreditation of Teacher Education (NCATE), offer courses that prepare librarians to serve children and young adults in public and school libraries? Is the preparation consistent with the competency standards published by the Association for Library Service to Children, the competency standards published by Young Adult Services Division, and the guidelines published by AASL and AECT?

from family, school, and society to avoid drugs, AIDS, poverty, suicide, pregnancy and other obstacles to becoming productive, thinking citizens. Access to information, ideas, and hope can be a powerful catalyst for good in the lives of children and young adults.

School and public libraries and librarians, when adequately equipped to do the job, can be that powerful catalyst in a young person's life. These libraries offer complementary and mutually reinforcing programs for children and young adults from infancy to 18 years of age. For children and young adults in school, the library media center, which carries out its important role in structured learning as its first priority, also meets the personal, recreational and informal learning needs of many children. The public library provides the transition from babyhood into formal learning, resources and services for personal information and recreation, and the transition from structured learning into self-determined lifelong learning. When both types of libraries are well-supported, they can team up to provide a seamless information and enjoyment resource.

School and public libraries and librarians cannot solve all the problems youth have, but they can and do make a significant difference. Our society needs citizens who are literate in the fullest sense, so they can be imaginative, productive, involved in self-government, and command their own lives and contribute to the lives of others. For this to happen, kids must have some of their needs met by adults and be empowered to meet the rest themselves. Caring about kids and treating them with dignity is essential; it ignites a sense of hope, and belief

in the future, and provides a measure of protection against self-destructive behaviors that often tempt youth.

What follows are examples of how libraries and librarians can help children and young adults meet their needs. Some contributions are made by one type of library serving kids, but most are made by both at different times and in various degrees.

KIDS NEED:
The belief in a worthwhile future and their responsibility and desire to contribute to that future.

LIBRARIES CAN:
- Offer resources, displays and programs concerning local, national and world-wide issues of today and tomorrow to encourage curiosity and interest in the democratic process and in finding societal solutions.
- Provide positive role models in real life and through books, videos, and other resources to inspire and to give shape to aspirations and goals.
- Offer resources that help youth think about and plan their futures.
- Encourage youth to get involved in the community and to become advocates for their wants and need.

KIDS NEED:
A positive sense of self-worth.

LIBRARIES CAN:
- Listen to youth, treat them with respect and dignity, take time to understand them and serve as facilitators and catalysts.

- Answer all reference questions or requests for resources without judgment and with confidentiality.
- Demonstrate a trust and belief in youth that almost no other institution in society can match by affording children and young adults all the rights and privileges of adults in the library, including library cards, access to the entire collection, and supporting their right to read.
- Provide opportunities for young adults to participate significantly in and contribute to the library and the community, individually and through advisory groups, giving them the opportunity to explore their strengths and skills.
- Provide resources and activities to children and young adults that lend perspective to their place in history, race, ethnic group and family.

KIDS NEED:
The ability to locate and use information and the awareness that this ability is an essential key to self-realization in the Information Age.

LIBRARIES CAN:
- Encourage curiosity, highlighting the delight of discovery.
- Collaborate with classroom teachers to design learning activities that teach students to locate, evaluate, and communicate information effectively.
- Teach children and young adults the skills needed to search for information both within the library and outside it, the use of reference sources, including databases, computers, fax machines, and other technologies that can be used to store, transmit and locate information.
- Maintain an up-to-date community resource file for children and young adults that contains information about community services that assist youth with personal and family issues, as well as information on clubs and activities for youth.
- Link the resources of the library with those of other agencies and institutions to promote the concept of an ever-widening array of information and ideas.

KIDS NEED:
Preparation to use present-day technology and to adapt to a changing technological world.

LIBRARIES CAN:
- Instruct children and young adults in the use of computers and other technologies that can enliven and encourage learning.
- Provide free public access computers with an array of software for youth to explore.
- Offer opportunities to use a variety of information technologies that store, transmit, and retrieve information.

KIDS NEED:
Equal access to the marketplace of ideas and information.

LIBRARIES CAN:
- Provide equal access for all youth to all library services

and to all information resources regardless of the content or technological format.
- Instill the concept of intellectual freedom by demonstrating its principles through resources, policies and services.
- Reach out to all children and young adults in the service area, including at-risk youth, by providing opportunities for them to benefit from the resources available in the library.
- Collaborate with agencies serving hard-to-reach youth, such as child care services, by providing books and other materials and by offering training for staff and parent volunteers in the use of these items.

KIDS NEED:
The ability to think critically in order to solve problems.

LIBRARIES CAN:
- Engage youth in discussions about books and other materials, examining opposing viewpoints and compromises, how characters made choices, and how problems were solved.
- Help children and young adults to monitor their thought processes as they locate and use information.
- Assist children and young adults in developing search strategies when seeking information and doing research.
- Provide resources that enable children and young adults to explore issues of importance to them and offer options for personal decision-making.
- Encourage and assist teachers in developing resource-based learning experiences for youth.
- Provide developmentally appropriate resources for children and young adults as they progress in their abilities to think critically.

KIDS NEED:
The ability to communicate effectively—to listen, to speak, to read, and to write.

LIBRARIES CAN:
- Provide language experiences in listening, talking, and playing with words and word associations for even the youngest children, building a foundation for storytelling, booktalking, viewing and reading aloud in older children and young adults.
- Initiate and coordinate with teachers school-wide projects that help students sharpen reading and word skills.
- Sponsor school-wide initiatives such as Drop Everything and Read (DEAR) and Sustained Silent Reading periods during which everyone in school, adults as well as youth, reads a book of choice for enjoyment.
- Sponsor Read-Out events inviting community celebrities to read passages from their favorite books and Read-a-thons inviting the whole community to spend a day reading together.
- Provide opportunities for youth to practice reading and

communication skills through summer reading programs, lapsit programs, storytimes, book discussion clubs, contests, peer tutoring, debates, and book and music reviews to share with peers.

- Ensure that youth learn to use production equipment such as computers, video recording, and other means of recording, expressing and disseminating their perceptions, observations, opinions and aspirations.
- Develop cooperative school and public library programs to encourage children and young adults to enjoy reading.

KIDS NEED:
Preparation to live in a multicultural world and to respect the rights and dignity of all people.

LIBRARIES CAN:
- Offer resources to even the youngest children, that show people of varied ethnic and racial backgrounds and cultures and life situations in order to broaden their understanding of other people.
- Provide multilingual resources and staff who can communicate with the different populations in the community.
- Demonstrate, with stories and visuals, that human failings and human capabilities relate to individuals, not to classes or categories of people.
- Present programs and displays celebrating cultural diversity.
- Create intergenerational experiences, using library resources and programs, that help youth and older adults better understand and value each other.

KIDS NEED:
The desire and ability to become lifelong learners.

LIBRARIES CAN:
- Encourage youth to explore their interests to lead them to new discoveries.
- Promote curiosity and questions and help children and young adults find answers, highlighting the delight of finding out and knowing.
- Reinforce family involvement in learning by showing parents how to carry out learning activities at home.
- Support child-serving agencies in reinforcing good learning habits and sharing self-learning activities for children.
- Provide safe, welcoming places for children and young adults to gather with friends to enjoy library resources or to be alone to pursue personal interests.
- Demonstrate that a library is a laboratory for learning to learn, providing practice in self-determination and the setting and achieving of personal goals.
- Entice youth to visit and use the library through booktalks, outreach activities, and by developing interesting learning activities with teachers and other community leaders.

KIDS NEED:
Creative ability to dream a better world.

LIBRARIES CAN:
- Expose children and young adults to a wide variety of ideas, concepts, and experiences through a diverse collection of resources, speakers, exhibits, and events that broaden their view of the world.
- Stimulate imaginations with stories, things to touch, dramatic play, music, puppets, crafts, projects, and resource people.

Current Status of the Nation's Library Service to Youth

Present resources, staffing and facilities are not satisfactory to do the job outlined above! At the time when they are needed most, many school and public libraries have had to cut drastically their direct services to children and young adults. Informational and guidance programs for parents, teachers, community youth workers and other caregivers have been cut. These are the very programs that can help develop healthy self-esteem, a secure literacy habit, and learning confidence in children and young adults.

Elementary school libraries, many of them established or strengthened in the 1960's and early 1970's, have withered and shrunk in collection size, quality, and program of service. Many have no professional librarian. Middle school and high schools have fared little better. The latest figures from the U.S. Department of Education National Center for Education Statistics (1985-86) show that schools with library media centers spent fewer 1985 dollars per pupil (adjusted for inflation) than were spent in 1958. The same set of statistics shows that although 79% of the public schools had some portion of certified staff, in many cases this was shared between two or more schools. Since state certification requirements vary greatly, the fact is that only 64% of public schools had the services of a full-qualified library media specialist.

In public libraries, the situation is much the same. Many children's and young adult librarian positions have been eliminated. Positions that do exist often go unfilled because fewer students in graduate library schools are being prepared for children's or young adult positions. Two recent Fast Response Statistics Surveys (FRSS) of young adult and children's services, conducted by the U.S. Department of Education, show that over 50% of public library users are under the age of 18, while one of every four public library users is between the ages of 12 and 18. Only 11% of public libraries have a young adult librarian to provide services to this age group with very special needs. In fact, only 79% of libraries serving 1000 or more users a week have a children's librarian, even though children's services builds an essential base for literacy and information use.

National Proposals Recommended for Action at WHCLIS II

All the proposals below are national in scope and recommended as future legislation to better serve children and young adults in school and public libraries.

- Enact a School Library Services title or act to:
  1. Establish an office within the U.S. Department of Education responsible for providing leadership to school library media programs across the nation.
  2. Create federal legislation to provide demonstration grants to schools for teachers and school library media specialists to design resource-based instructional activities that provide opportunities for students to explore diverse ideas and multiple sources of information.
  3. Establish grants to provide information technology to school library media centers.

- Enact a public library children's services title or act to include:
  1. Demonstration grants for services to children.
  2. Funds for parent/family education projects for early childhood services, involving early childhood agencies.
  3. Funds to work in partnership with daycare centers and other early childhood providers to offer deposit collections and training in the use of library resources.

- Enact a public library young adult services title or act to include:
  1. Demonstration grants for services to young adults.
  2. Funds for youth at-risk demonstration grants, to provide outreach services for young adults on the verge of risk behavior as well as those already in crisis, working in partnership with community youth-serving agencies.
  3. Funds for a national library-based "Kid Corps" program for young adults to offer significant, salaried youth participation projects to build self-esteem, develop skills, and expand the responsiveness and level of library services for teenagers.

- Create federal legislation to fund the development of partnership programs between school and public libraries to provide comprehensive library services to children and young adults.

- Establish and fund a research agenda to document and evaluate how children and young adults develop the abilities that make them information literate.

- Require categorical aid for school library media services and resources in any federal legislation which provides funds for instructional purposes.

- Develop federal legislation to establish a nationwide resource-sharing network that includes school library media programs as equal partners and ensures that all youth have access, equal to that of other citizens, to the nation's library resources.

- Develop federal legislation to fund school and public library demonstration intergenerational programs that provide meaningful services (such as tutoring, leisure activities, sharing books, ideas, hobbies) for latchkey children and young adolescents in collaboration with networks and such private associations as AARP, which address the interests and needs of senior citizens.

- Enact federal legislation to fund family demonstration literacy programs that involve school and public libraries and other family-serving agencies.

- Create legislation to fund discretionary grants to library schools and schools of education for the collaborative development of graduate programs to educate librarians to serve children and young adults.

- Provide opportunities, perhaps through the National Endowment for the Arts, for potential authors from minority cultures to develop their abilities to write stories and create other materials about their culture for youth.

- Ensure that all legislation authorizing child care programs, drug prevention programs and other youth at-risk programs include funds for books and library materials, to be selected in consultation with professional librarians.

What's in a Name?

Caroline Shepard, Youth Services Consultant for the State Library of North Carolina

There is a debate going on in many libraries today that has grave implications for children's services. It centers around what our mission, our philosophy of service should be. Are we librarians or information providers? These two roles are not mutually exclusive, but they are certainly drifting apart in these times of rapidly expanding technology.

The term librarian implies someone who is book-centered. Many futurists have predicted the extinction of those librarians who remain hopelessly tied to the dinosaur of the book. On the other hand "information provider" conjures up images of power brokers, people on the cutting edge of new technology, with the money to support their habit. These professionals emphasize using technology to target the power elite of the community. After all, technological resources are a perfect way to appeal to a community's powerful members—voting adults with the authority to approve or deny budget requests that make it possible for us to buy all those computers in the first place. If we dazzle our patrons with electronic resources, maybe we can finally shed our traditional image as dowdy librarians.

Which philosophy is correct? Librarians have traditionally been associated with books but, now that we're faced with a multitude of technological formats, there is dissension in the ranks. Should we stick with books or abandon them for the technological marvels of the future? And, what impact will our decision have on youth services?

In true librarian fashion, we are still trying to be all things to all people. But, this is not possible and never has been. We must therefore set priorities, emphasizing some services while downgrading others. We simply cannot afford to do it all.

The most obvious implication of any shift to the information provider concept involves budgets. If libraries plan to be serious contenders in the information delivery business, we are going to have to increase allocations to acquire and maintain the latest in information delivery systems. We will have to make a commitment to invest in the hardware, software, and staff necessary to access the ever expanding world of databases, online services, and CD-ROM products.

While the profusion of information sources often seems infinite, however, our resources are not. Libraries have to live within their budgets and still manage to find money for the technology necessary to fill sophisticated information requests. In the reallocation of resources, youth services seem to be an easy target. Book budgets are constantly shrinking, and professional positions are increasingly viewed as a frill. Nonprofessionals can entertain the children as well as professionals—and for a whole lot less money—say many of today's decision-makers. Why pay a children's librarian for a professional program of service when what you really want is someone to read stories?

Children's librarians are often seen as having a missionary zeal for their profession. While this is an admirable quality, it also works against us. If we are willing to work with a smaller staff and for less money, we shouldn't be surprised when administrators see our departments as the perfect place for cost-cutting. We need to be vigilant in not only rendering professional service for professional salaries, but also in making administrators aware of what they are getting for their budget dollars.

More insidious than the downgrading of budgets and positions, however, is the devaluation of the entire concept of youth services. Information providers are concerned with just that—providing information. Where does learning to read fit into this formula? Is booktalking considered a form of providing information? Children's librarians perform a variety of functions, and many have nothing to do with bits and bytes of data. We are laying the groundwork for a lifetime of literacy. We introduce children to both print and non-print resources. We are nurturing life-long library users.

Children seem to be the "in" thing right now. Everyone gives lip service to our nation's children, but not many are willing to put their money where their mouths are. It is a fact that children and teenagers are a low priority on the national agenda. This priority is being mirrored in our public libraries. Too often, children are simply regarded as future workers and voters, as if their value is dependent upon their reaching the age of 21. Children deserve more than this. At the very least, they deserve the status of current—not just potential—members of society.

The public library is a democratic institution serving all segments of the population. Certainly, if the library can use technology to gain power and prestige in the community, the youth of that community will be better off. But, let's not forget them in our head-long rush to become information brokers. New technology is expensive, and many libraries are jumping on the bandwagon. We must remember that we cannot invest in information resources at the expense of children today and expect them to lavish us with power tomorrow.

What Literature?

by Michael Cart

Have you noticed an intriguing irony at work in the world of children's books? Although complex in all of its constituent parts, its essence is simply this: legions of librarians, teachers, authors, and others who take books for young readers seriously have labored strenuously for years to induce the rest of the world to see that "children's literature" is not an oxymoron but a valid way of describing a body of work that can lend itself to the same lofty level of criticism that literature for adults traditionally has. And, more importantly, the term suggests that books for children can provide the same pleasures, stimulations, and challenges to their readers as their adult counterparts do. Yet today, (here's the irony), after several generations of elevating our expectations of children's literature, a growing chorus of voices seems to be calling instead for its degradation, for what might be crankily described as its "dumbing down," for its demotion from the penthouse of aesthetic and intellectual experience to the bargain basement of mere passive pleasure, by decreeing that the kind of artistry that we used to look for is suddenly too arcane to be apprehended by young readers of the MTV generation. And therefore, instead of being a hallmark of excellence, art is now considered an impediment to readers' appreciation. In other words, in the competition for kids' attention, literature is declared a loser. This is distressing in concept but even more disturbing in practice if it means that literature might also be a loser in the on-going competition for the shrinking library dollar. And here irony is joined by paradox: At a time when there is ever LESS money available for books, publishers are producing ever MORE titles to choose among. Since works of literature are traditionally labeled "for the special reader," and since it is the popular perception that there are fewer special readers in an era of shrinking attention spans and diminishing reading skills, and since libraries try to serve the greatest number of potential patrons, what happens to literature? My concern is that the answer will be expressed in a simple equation: diminished expectations of readers plus diminished dollars = death of literature. In these terms the old sedate debate over quality ("give 'em what they need") vs. popularity ("give 'em what they want") assumes a newly passionate, life-and-death urgency.

The capacity of books to change lives, to humanize their readers, and to civilize them cannot be overstated. Giving literature a chance to do this good work is a challenge, of course, and requires the belief on the part of those who produce it (writers, editors, and publishers), evaluate it (reviewers and critics), and make it available (librarians, booksellers, and parents) in the innate intelligence of young readers. There was a time when this was accepted as a matter of course. Forty years ago, Walter R. Brooks (creator of Freddy the now-out-of-print pig) said, "Children are people—they're just smaller and less experienced. They are not taken in by the smug playfulness of those who write or talk down to them as if they were dullwitted and slightly deaf." Ironically, it is the very same undervaluing of young readers' capacities that seems to have doomed the Freddy books, at least, to out-of-print obscurity, an editor having recently explained to me that, at an average length of 250 pages, they are simply too long to capture and hold the interest of today's attention-span-challenged young readers. (This is not an altogether new phenomenon, alas. When I rhapsodized in a 1987 *SLJ* "Up for Discussion" piece about Pat O'Shea's brilliant *Hounds of the Morrigan* (Holiday, 1987), a librarian wrote to complain that I had been somehow derelict in my responsibility by failing to mention that *Hounds* is, indeed, a very long book: "At 465 pages," she said, "it daunted my two most-ardent fantasy readers.") Challenges of length are visiting not only books for older readers. Margaret K. McElderry, in her recent Frances Clarke Sayers Address delivered at UCLA, expressed her concern at the growing number of complaints she is hearing about too-long picture book texts. Betty Takeuchi, Past President of the Association of Book Sellers for children, who was in the audience, agreed that as a bookseller she is hearing the same chorus from parents who call for shorter and shorter texts. I would only say, in response, that books need to be as long as they need to be.

Of course, a book does not have to be long to be good. Francesca Block's *Weetzie Bat* (HarperCollins, 1991) and Cynthia Rylant's *Missing May* (Orchard, 1992), two very different but equally brilliant books, are only 88 and 89 pages long, respectively. Gary Paulsen is lately doing wonderful things with the novella as a literary form and—to my mind—the three most satisfying works of literature to be published in 1992—Bruce Brooks's *What Hearts* (HarperCollins, 1992), Budge Wilson's *The Leaving* (Philomel, 1992), and Anne Mazer's *Moose Street* (Knopf, 1992)—are all collections of short stories.

Indeed, a book as short as a picture book can be a marvel of artistic challenge and opportunity. David Macaulay's *Black and White* (Houghton, 1990) is a classic example of what literature should do: provide an interactive opportunity for readers (something that MTV cannot do), stimulate their imaginations, and invite them to think. It is an artistic antidote to the likes of the cretinous Markie Mark who, strutting about in his Calvins, bellowingly enjoins the MTV generation, "Yo, move your body!"

More civilly, Macaulay invites readers, "Yo, move your mind!" Which experience will prove the more productive and enduring pleasure? I wonder. The mind is the most wonderful toy that kids can have. And books can show them how to play with it. The appreciation of literature, however, is not something that is in-born. It is something that is learned. And this lesson cuts to the heart of the adult's responsibility.

I have been dismayed to hear librarians say of a book, "Oh, I put that book in the new book bin and it just sat there." Or to dismiss a book like *Moose Street* because it lacks the visceral immediacy of, let us say, a best-selling Stephen King melodrama as a "shelf-sitter" (a phrase which I have come to recognize as a code for "a work of significant literary merit"). This dismays me for several reasons. First it presumes that youngsters are innately equipped to recognize works of literary merit. (To argue that they aren't, by the way, is not to impeach their native intelligence but only to say that they do not have the training and reading experience that adult professionals do.) Second it seems to me to be an abdication of professional responsibility to simply drop a book into the new book bin and walk away.

I know, I know. Budgets are shrinking, staffs are being cut ("slashed" may be a more accurate word in too many sad cases), the few remaining librarians aboard are being forced to do the work of legions, and how do you find the time to give individual reader's advisory attention to every kid who comes through the doors? Not to do so, however, turns the library into little more than a self-service supermarket. And this is one area where kids as consumers are NOT equipped to help themselves.

Adults, however, read reviews and rely more heavily on them now than perhaps ever before. Reviews are probably the most powerful single factor in librarians' purchasing decisions. This visits unusual responsibility on review media and reviewers—first, to give attention to works of serious literature and, second, to bring the same critical tools and context that reviewers of adult books ideally bring to their task. Unlike popular fiction, literature is vastly more than plot. And so its review must be more than a simple retelling of a story. When incident is alluded to, it needs to be in the context of character. Remember what Henry James said in "The Art of Fiction"?

"What is character but the determination of incident. What is incident but the illustration of character?"

This is beautifully demonstrated in *Moose Street*. To look at the choice and artful organization of the incidents that inform its text is to see how character can drive a narrative and give it a coherent thematic life—more specifically, it is to empathetically apprehend the painful spiritual isolation of the outsider and the physical pain of the abused child and to see how love can bridge the gap of isolation and visit redemption on two lives worth examining.

And worth trying to understand. Books like *Moose Street* and, especially, *What Hearts*, require the readers' attention. They are not passive but active experiences, they are implied dialogues between readers and writers. How to approach them has been summarized by Mortimer Adler in his *How to Read a Book:* " . . . With nothing but the power of your own mind you operate on the symbols before you in such a way that you gradually lift yourself from a state of understanding less to one of understanding more."

Understanding is at the—well, *heart* of *What Hearts*. Some reviewers have complained that its young protagonist, Asa, may understand too much, that he is too intelligent for his years, but that misses the point, I think. Asa has to be preternaturally wise so that gradually, subtly through the operation of his intelligence and the incidents that he contemplates, he will learn that his intelligence, no matter how overarching, is by itself insufficient to give the strangers who fill his world (he is also an outsider) faces. The companion his mind needs to do that is compassion, love, *heart*. Only then can his feelings emerge "to do some work in the world." Only then can he be a complete person.

Complete persons are complex. And *What Hearts*, like *Moose Street*, is a complex work of fiction, dealing equally in ideas and emotions and demanding close attention and interactive involvement from its readers. In return, it rewards them with an experience that enriches both their minds and their hearts. As a work of literature, it is illuminating and life-enlarging. In its challenges and rewards it is a fully realized work and expands the parameters of children's literature at a time when, sadly, books are apparently to be judged not by the quality or capacity to challenge, but only by their "immediacy" and ability to "grab" their readers.

Unfortunately, as Asa observes, "grace is given, not always received." It is incumbent on us adult readers and reviewers and librarians to share the graceful prose by writers of serious fiction with young readers so that their writing can do some work in the world. To do so doesn't only honor the books. It honors young readers, as well, with respect for their own Asa-like intelligence and their capacity to become complete individuals.

Part Three

Our Clients: Children and Youth

Who are the clients of public youth librarians and school library media specialists? They are the bright, the slow, the ethnic minorities, the young people, the native or foreign born who speak English as a second language, the blind, the institutionalized, the home schooled, the children who live in shelters, and the young people who are gay. They are all ours, and librarians have written during the past forty years with compassion and creativity about designing programs and services to meet the information needs of all of our clients.

September 1971

The Plight of the Native American

Rey Mickinock

There are apparently three kinds of people in this hemisphere: those who believe Leif Erickson discovered America, those who think Cristoforo Colombo stumbled upon it, and those who know America was never really lost.

Obviously, most Americans of Scandinavian descent support the first view and those of Latin descent the second; the third is composed of those who wish their ancestors had told Leif, Cris, and a few dozen other explorers to "climb back into those disease-ridden, rat-infested tubs and go right back where you came from." Several million misconceptions of native Americans might have been avoided, not to mention the diseases the non-Indian brought with him. From Squanto's wiped-out Patuxets of New England, as reported in Willison's *Saints and Strangers* (Toronto, McLelland, 1945, o.p.), to the Ona, of whom three women remain, and the Yahgan, with only a handful left, both of Tierra del Fuego, as told in *National Geographic* (January 1971), many tribes were infected with measles, smallpox, and other diseases for which they had not previously needed immunity. From the Midwest to California, before and after the Civil War, the disease-spread continued. Quite a range for our conquering hero.

The misconceptions? These are spread by such children's "easy" books as Tillie S. Pine's *The Indians Knew* (McGraw, 1957), whose illustrator, Ezra Jack Keats, spoils a reasonably well done work by mixing hair styles of the Eastern tribes with the tipis of the West, the pottery of the Southwestern tribes with the travoix of the North. How is the Indian or non-Indian child to believe in the intelligence of the people with such drawings? Would you put a kilt on a Hollander? Or wooden shoes on a Scot? By the way, find a true Scot and ask him if he's "Scotch," then step back and listen, taking care there are no ladies present. Mr. Keats' "Willie" may be beautifully done but he seems to know as little as most whites about Indians. LeGrand Henderson is no better in his *Cats for Kansas* (Abington, 1948) illustrations when he shows a number of braves stretching a rope across the track to stop a train. His idea is most imaginative, but picturing four of the 15 men in the war bonnets of chiefs is unforgivable. No warrior who has counted as many coups as that would be involved in such labor. Nor does he identify any coup by nick, cut, or paint. Only such Chiefs as Red Cloud, of the Oglala Sioux, who had 80 coups in his lifetime, would be entitled to wear such a bonnet as Mr. Henderson puts on the four men. Any Hollywood costume department would have known better. Four chiefs for 11 braves?

Perhaps, for understanding, it would be best to read such books as Mari Sandoz' *These Were the Sioux* (Hastings, 1961), reissued as a Dell paperback. *These Were the Sioux* ranges from the mother's gentle, foolproof method of teaching the 14 day-old not to cry, to the explanation of old He Dog who, at 92, told Miss Sandoz, "It is well to be good to women in the strength of our manhood because we must sit under their hands at both ends of our lives." Dr. Spock's readers could take lessons from Sioux children in the matter of crying, and of hunting begun at the age of four. Where the white man scoffed at the Indian woman's "drudgery" in carrying the bundles of dried meat and hides, managing the tipi, the children and the dogs in travel, and arrogantly reviled the "brave" who carried only his bow, arrows, and lance, any reasoning observer should know that man, in the days before the horse, had to walk ahead into the unknown, unencumbered and in command, if the group was to survive an ambush, or if he was to find a sudden opportunity for a kill of game that might provide many meals for his family, as he had been doing for thousands of years.

In marriage ceremonies, an "old one," usually female and related or borrowed from a family that had an "extra," was always expected to live in the couple's tipi, treated with respect as the bride's helper and teacher, who knew her place and was conveniently silent or absent when discretion required. The groom became a part of the bride's family, whatever the tribe. The practice still exists, though circumstances vary. Roger Talmadge, Chief Little Eagle, is a Sioux (he would prefer to be called the guttural, "Duh-koh-tah," their word for "allies"), is married to a Winnebago princess, and is Chief of the Winnebago tribe, at Wisconsin Dells. Fifteen tribes in three divisions make up the Dakota Nation.

Divorce was easy, but not taken lightly. If a woman wanted a divorce, she merely threw the man's possessions out of her lodge; if a man didn't want his woman anymore, he carved a giveaway stick and tossed it to whoever he thought might want her next, though the catcher had a choice until he or another decided to make it permanent. Divorce was fairly common, for nothing could make a Sioux, male or female, do anything he or she didn't want to do. Ann Landers may wish to make notes.

Biographic Lies, Authentic Fiction

In another of Miss Sandoz' books, *The Horsecatcher* (Westminster, 1957), readers can learn of the Cheyenne and also something of the neighboring tribes, accepting this as authentic fiction. It is somewhat different from Elizabeth Coatsworth's *The Last Fort* (Holt, 1952), in which she calls killing the enemy "counting coup," where in truth merely to *hit* the man with the hand, bow, or coup stick was the highest possible honor, while killing him usually counted as nothing unless he was touched first. In ABC-TV's *The Immortal* this January, Italian-American Sal Mineo, playing a pseudo-hip Navajo, spoke of counting coup on "the white guy," a practice unknown in that tribe, although he may have been joking about it, as something he had read. Any plains Indian could look at a man's headdress and tell all the brave deeds that man had done by the way of the feathers, or by the wolf tails, ermine, or weasel skins he wore according to the tenets of his tribal custom.

In John Bakeless' *Fighting Frontiersman* (Morrow, 1948, o.p.), Daniel Boone, when trailing Indians, is said "to know exactly what they were going to do next . . . would soon do thus-and-so . . . as invariably they did!" (p. 5); yet on page 164, Mr. Bakeless' Indians withhold the peace pipe from the whites at the "peace council" and easily trap Boone and nine others. Overlooking this internal inconsistency, one may note that, as an example of what is accepted as biographical "truth," at least as listed in Hannah Logasa's *Historical Non-Fiction* (McKinley, 1968, p. 158), this work may be interesting, it is still hardly factual. Mark Twain would have classed Bakeless with James Fenimore Cooper. It is incredible that such tales are accepted by young readers, degrading the race, not the man.

(And in the meanwhile, the fact is universally ignored that the Puritans—the *Puritans*!—first began the practice of scalping, in 1637, by offering rewards for scalps, with the ears attached, of their enemies, and that the English, by proclamation, reaffirmed it, in 1755!)

One may find more authenticity, again, in works of fiction. Evelyn Lampman's *Half-Breed* (Doubleday, 1967) is a story of the Crow Indians and the white mountain men who sometimes lived among them, married, and perhaps tiring of the settled life, left the tribe, not always taking their wives and children along. It is sincere, deep, with courage, truth, and shortcomings intermixed according to the people involved. Mrs. Lampman writes of the problems of "half-breeds," living with the non-Indian, the bigotry of all ignorant people, and the quiet intelligence of family love.

The prologue to the paperback edition of C. Fayne Porter's *The Battle of the 1000 Slain* (Scholastic, Starline School Book Service, 1969, abridged from the 1964 Chilton title *Our Indian Heritage: Profiles of 12 Great Leaders*); should be most enlightening to a reader unfamiliar with the contributions made to American culture by Indians—among these more than half the cash farm crops grown, all the medicinal herbs known to man, and many novelty items sometimes counted as staples. At the circus or ballpark, the vendor hawks his wares, "Popcorn, Peanuts, Crackerjacks, Chewing gum!"—all first used by the Indian. Only the wasted containers were invented by the white man. The starving Pilgrims kept starving in the midst of plenty, refusing to eat the clams the Wampanoags tried to persuade them to dig, in 1620. The cahuchi, the "weeping tree," furnished balls and other playthings for Indians centuries ago. Today it is cultivated by Firestone.

The Truth about Custer

In the matter of Custer, the gathering of misinformation about him, his motives, his orders, his behavior, and the result of the battle and related skirmishes have been done to death. When the lie is big enough and told often enough, it is believed. A careful analysis should reveal that Custer's men and all the Indians involved were victims of "progress," something, not much contested until recently. No matter that the financial panic of 1873 delayed these events for three years by stopping the Northern Pacific railroad at Bismarck, named for that famous leader in an attempt to bring German money into its coffers; no matter that Custer's 1874 expedition to verify the Black Hills gold discoveries drove thousands of reservation Indians up into the Rosebud country and that even his great exaggerations brought no new investors for that railroad. No matter that this predecessor of the Burlington Northern brought about the political necessity of driving the western tribes from their homelands. No matter that Custer tried to attack a minimum of 4000 warriors, or that, if he had approached the three miles of tipis as he tried to, he would have had to face as many as 10,000 men, that there may have been 15,000 Sioux, Cheyenne, Arapaho, and others, led by dozens of "Generals," many of whom had already bloodied various army units. No matter that he lost only 225 men, which may have been only because that was all he had at that particular place. No matter that it was another unit of his Seventh Cavalry that mowed down the women, children, and old men at Wounded Knee in 1890. It only matters that the white man's greed for money and land caused the many deaths, and the ensuing loss of the homelands of the western Indians. Ecologists were a hundred years late.

Read Mari Sandoz' *The Battle of the Little Bighorn* (Lippincott, 1966), the nonfiction account not colored by any admiration for "Longhair"; or Ralph K. Andrist's *The Long Death* (Collier-Macmillan, 1969); which tells in detail of the short-haired, saberless Custer and some of his political problems as only an editor of American Heritage can; or Vine Deloria, Jr.'s *Custer Died for Your Sins* (Avon, pa. 1970), the new Indian best-seller; or the 93-page National Park Services handbook on the Custer Battlefield National Monument ($1.25, U.S. Department of the Interior) with Robert Utley's text and Leonard Baskin's "very non-G.I." drawings, all of which prove whose "last stand" it really was.

Other books of verified accuracy and intelligent perspective would include—

Betty Baker's *Walk the World's Rim,* and *Killer-of-Death* (Harper, 1965, 1963)

Christie Harris' *Raven's Cry* and *Once Upon a Totem* (Atheneum, 1966, 1963)

Florence Means' *Our Cup is Broken,* (Houghton, 1969)

Mary Warren's *Walk in My Moccasins* (Westminster, 1966)

Mari Sandoz' *The Story Catcher* (Westminster, 1963)
Hal Borland's *When the Legends Die* (Lippincott, 1963)
Thomas Berger's *Little Big Man* (Dial, 1964), probably better known as a film
Dan Cushman's *Stay Away, Joe* (Stay Away Joe Publishers, 1968).

A good policy might be to check out the particular author first, then read the works in the area desired. Most public libraries can produce the greater share of these. In spite of many good books by some Eastern authors, generally avoid those who "live and love in New York" and claim to write about our "noble" American natives. It is a verifiable fact that there are fewer Indians east of the Mississippi river than Sitting Bull directed at the council preceding the Custer episode, which gets it down to less than 15,000. There are even fewer with knowledge much better than the Hong Kong tribes, whose souvenirs are everywhere. New York Public can provide much authentic material, but the Indian mind is difficult to capture on paper, especially for one who may never have been beyond 125th Street.

In *Textbooks and the American Indian,* a 1970 publication of the American Indian Historical Society, 32 Indian scholars, students, and native historians effectively take apart over 300 books used as texts in public, private, and even Indian schools. Not one could be approved as a dependable source of knowledge about the history and culture of the Indian people in America. To repeat, *not one*! Yet, all these books are currently being used in our schools. A defective automobile is recalled. Ralph Nader, where are you?

On page two, *Textbooks and the American Indian* presents a copy of the "Memorial and Recommendations of the Grand Council Fire of American Indians," which tells yesterday as it is today, taking the white man to task for unfair books, unfair attitudes, such as "when the white man was victorious, it was a battle; when the Indian won, it was a massacre," and "If the Custer battle was a massacre, what was Wounded Knee?" The Memorial was given to the Mayor of Chicago in 1927 and printed in the Congressional Record on May 11, 1928. Forty-three years have had little real result.

It is said that the Indian doesn't talk much, that he has little to say to the white man. The Indian talks only when he wants to, sometimes says only what he thinks the white man wishes to hear, says Fayne Porter in the epilogue of *The Battle of the 1000 Slain.* Yet the day is ever-changing, and today's Indian is also changing, but carefully selecting the ancient ways to cling to, and only some of the new, rather than making any blanket acceptance of the non-Indian way. In 1868, Chief Red Cloud told his people how to become wealthy like the white man: "You must begin anew and put away the wisdom of your fathers. You must lay up food and forget the hungry. When your house is built, your storeroom filled, then look around for a neighbor whom you can take advantage of, and seize all he has." (This is from Mr. Andrist's book, on page 134.) Yet the Indian cannot shed his religion or his heritage. The mixing of the ancient and the new is called "adjustment," and it can be an eerie experience for a tourist to attend a western movie in, say Battleford, Saskatchewan, and slowly come to realize that some "Indians" are being applauded and some cowboys or cavalrymen jeered at, that the silences and cheers are coming in places he is not used to, and that not all the warwhoops are on the screen, even if the movie isn't in "3-D" and "surround-sound." May Cherokee Burt Reynolds make as many movies as did Iron Eyes and Eddie Little Sky, for they were uncountable.

To quote from *Textbooks and the American Indian*: "Everyone has the right to his opinion. A person has also the right to be wrong. But a textbook has no right to be wrong, or to lie, evade the truth, falsify history, or insult and malign a whole race of people. That is what the textbooks do."

"There is a difference between a book for general readership, and one accepted for classroom use. In the first case, the individual has a choice, and this choice we must protect. The student has no choice. He is compelled to study from an approved book. In this case, we have a right to insist upon truth, accuracy, and objectivity."

Estelle Thomas in *Gift of Laughter* (Westminster, 1967) gives this line to one of her Navajos: "Washing*tone* [The government was always called that] is inclined to stare out over the Big Waters too much."

Whether it be a textbook in the field of government, history, geography, or whatever, a television program of any kind, a movie, western or otherwise, a radio or newspaper story, or even somebody's latest attempt at fiction, let us all "Pass . . . up . . . the forked tongue, please!"

Postscript

If anyone has to make a choice of what to read, and that person has a real desire to learn of Indian attitudes, the Indian sense of reality, let him begin with Vine Deloria, Jr.'s recommendations (all of these have been previously mentioned): Dan Cushman's *Stay Away, Joe,* Hal Borland's *When the Legends Die* and Thomas Berger's *Little Big Man.*

And end with mine:

Ralph K. Andrist's *The Long Death,* Mari Sandoz' *These Were the Sioux* and *The Battle of the Little Bighorn,* Vine Deforia, Jr.'s *Custer. . . ,* Estelle Thomas' *Gift of Laughter,* and Mary Warren's *Walk in My Moccasins. Custer Died for Your Sins* is the single choice for anyone who will read only one; although the Indian favorite is *Stay Away, Joe.*

And do you know what the Indian used to call America before the white man came? "Ours."

Me—Gway—Ch (Thank you.)

Equals Or Enemies?
Librarians and Young Adults

Lillian L. Shapiro

The argument persists that there always was a generation gap—a period called by Maia Wojciechowska "the rotten years"—that young people were "always like this." Supportive evidence is offered from mythic sources, e.g., the legend of Cronos, as well as in more modern psychology texts. But to say that differences and tensions always existed between parents (or other adults) and their young is not the same as saying *these* young people in the second half of the 20th Century are just like those growing up in an earlier era; it is to discount the impact on people of the social forces and economic conditions of a specific period in history. I have been rereading chapters of *Centuries of Childhood: A Social History of Family Life*. It is a reminder that all institutions change[1] and, surely, we know that social customs are different today from those observed in the 1930's and 1940's. Ariès traces the changes in attitude toward the child from his place in the medieval family through several centuries and shows how recent, comparatively speaking, is the discovery of childhood as a distinct phase of life. In the second quarter of this century, those sociologists and educators concerned with studying the developmental stages of humankind, employing terms like "adolescence" and "teen-age," settled on "youth" for that person who is no longer a child and is not yet an adult. In library parlance we refer to that group of individuals as "young adults"—trying to bridge both worlds. The age limits defining this group vary from writer to writer and librarian to librarian, but in my remarks I have in mind that young adult who is in senior high school. While the secondary school does include the junior high school student, it is my aim to show that the older student is in a much more frustrating situation.

Growing Up Affluent

During a more sheltered era (at least for middle class youth)—without the ubiquitousness of television—a certain amount of innocence was still observable in high schools *boys* and *girls*. (Note how anachronistic those words seem in 1973.) Walk into any high school today and try to think of the group you see as anything but *men* and *women*. Add to the physical characteristics of these well-developed young people the experiences many of them have had, not only vicariously obtained through films and television, but also through living on their own or in one-parent families. If seeing life clearly in all of its difficulty, and often brutalization, compels one into assuming at least the appurtenances of adulthood, if not its actualities, then young people of 15 to 18 years of age today are a far cry from the adolescents we were some 30 years ago. They are different in every way except physically—and biologists have stated that even that process appears to have speeded up. A backward look on my own high school days in a less affluent society makes me realize how few choices we had those days. Curricula were highly structured and tracked, and courses for college preparation left little room for electives. Some of you may recall the four years of English, three years of history, two and a half years of math, two years of science, three years of one language and two of another, with Latin often one of those required.

A study was made from 1930 to 1938. It involved a comparison of the performance of high school students who followed the traditional college prep program and those in the progressive schools which allowed freedom in selecting curriculum areas. Generally, the study indicated that the students who had the freer choices were superior in their performance in college.[2] Yet so little diversity was permitted that even the seeming success of the Eight Year Study brought great change in high school education.

For many of us in those years, the need to gain economic independence for ourselves as quickly as possible or to assist our families limited our choices in terms of professions and length of time available for getting ready to earn. Acting and singing and other exciting, self-realizing futures were necessarily eliminated since they rated very low in security factors. So we became teachers, with a few doctors or lawyers where family finances permitted such a possibility. This serious decision about a lifetime involvement was made without examining too closely who we were as individuals; we could not afford the luxury of choosing among options.

The Choice "Overload"

At first glance, our young adult today appears to have many choices—in kinds of curricular offerings, in types of school, in varieties of career openings, even in the choice to remove oneself from the assembly line leading through college. For academically successful students, there have been, until recently, many scholarships, grants, and other opportunities to pursue. In some cases a kind of "overload" situation resulted, like adding that last electrical appliance without converting from a 110 to a 220 line. Result—everything stops. Paralysis. Some of our most able young people do not know what they wish to do or what the good life for them should be. Experimenting with various life styles, with drug cultures, religious sects, with militant stances, and radical politics, our young adults are, at one and the same time, the *subject* of sermons despairing of their irresponsibility and self-destructiveness, and the *object* of envy on the part of their elders (who should be wiser) because of their freedom of dress, sexual codes, and refusal to make permanent commitments to job or family.

In actual fact, however, most young adults are far less free than they may appear or than we tell them they are. Choices are still limited in most schools if you intend to go to college or even just to remain in high school. These young men and women are still fairly silent partners in the educational process. For example, student government, on examination, shows up to be a paper organization with the expected result that it is mainly ignored by the majority of students in any given high school. Student activities—plays, lectures, publications—need to be approved by faculty advisors, not only to avoid libelous or inflammatory statements, but through adult fear of too much frankness and openness. I do agree that one may not behave in such a way as to cause a dangerous situation—dangerous, that is, in the sense of shouting "fire" in a crowded auditorium. But students would be better served if encouraged to set up their own guidelines. The fact that a community is composed of many segments is, I am certain, an idea capable of being understood and respected by young adults. The key is the arrival at acceptable procedures after free and open discussion among students, administrators, teachers, and parents—not evenly weighted among those groups, since one would expect then a three to one polarization.

Much has been written about minority groups in our society, among them, young adults. What Friedenberg has to say about this is very revealing: "What is surprising is that the sons and daughters of the *dominant* adult group should be treated as a minority group merely because of their age. Their papers are in order and they speak the language adequately. In any society, to be sure, the young occupy a subordinate or probationary status while under tutelage for adult life. But a minority group is not merely subordinate; it is not under tutelage. It is in the process of being denatured; of becoming, under social stress, something more acceptable to the dominant society, but essentially different from what its own growth and experience would lead to. Most beasts recognize their own kind. Primitive peoples may initiate their youth; we insist that ours be naturalized, though it is what is most natural about them that disturbs adults most."[3]

To *appear* to be free and *not* be is frustrating in so acute a fashion as to turn one to extremes of violence at one end of the spectrum or apathy at the other. Any person caught in a middle-management job, for example, can describe the schizoid element of such a predicament. How much worse, then, for the young person who does not even have the comfort of knowing he is doing it to earn some money. The situation is even further exacerbated by what the society grants in theory and rescinds in fact. You are freer to choose among electives, but not free to decide no high school at all. You are free to vote but not free to decide what you will read about the election alternatives (the two parties may be represented in library resources but not likely all the other possibilities out to the radical fringes). Ironically, if you are over 17—an average age for a high school senior—in New York City, you can see *Last Tango in Paris* but you probably cannot get *Down These Mean Streets* (Knopf, 1967) in your friendly, neighborhood school library.

Does this mean that in the field of communication we consider films *less* provocative or stimulating than books? In the absence of scientific data and based only on empirical observation I would dispute that. Compare your reaction to viewing Anthony Burgess' *A Clockwork Orange* (Ballantine, 1971) with reading it. Such films as *#00173* and *The Hand* stir up very strong emotions about totalitarianism, and *Glass* describes more movingly than an economic tract the difference between technology on an assembly line and artistic handcraft.

New Youth in a New World

I hope I have persuaded you that young people are *not* the same today as they always were. The world is not the same as it always was. Attitudes toward what is morally right are different; carriers of information and entertainment are different; man's control over the problems presented by Mother Nature have been transformed into worry about his control over the problems presented by Old Man Technology. How then is it possible to expect young adults to read, hear, and see what we did 20, 30 years ago? The situation is interesting, too, in terms of the cyclical rejection and acceptance of certain forms of behavior. J. H. Plumb, British historian, explains our difficulties with youth today this way: "Rarely do we look far enough into the past for the roots of our present problems. This revolution of youth has been building up for decades because we forced the growing child into a repressive and artificial world—a prison, indeed, that was the end product of four centuries of Western history, of that gradual exclusion of the maturing child from the world of adults. We can now look back with longing to the late medieval world, when, crude and simple as it was, men, women, and children lived their lives together, shared the same morals as well as the same games, the same excesses as well as the same austerities. In essence, youth today is rebelling against four centuries of repression and exploitation."[4] One must admit that this exclusion applies most to the middle-class young adult.

Among the problems in young adult library service today is that those adults who work with youth, especially in schools, are the products of a society which has set up rigid divisions between child, youth, and adult. Unquestioning and undeviating respect for authority, a highly valued principle, is antithetical to education which supposedly encourages a pursuit of the truth, a mind free to explore among all kinds of information in order to find one's own answer. Modesty in language and behavior cannot be an aim of education in a world where the "beautiful people" set one example of what is desirable dress and activity, all this highly visible in the mass media, and the poor, dying all their lives, although less visible in the media, certainly are an influence by their presence in schools. Middle-class youth, who are a majority in our public schools and libraries, cannot be sealed off from the mores of both of these segments of our society.

Exposing Youth to Freedom

In their statement of the Library Bill of Rights, librarians say that "minors" should have free access to all materials. In the September 1972 *Newsletter on Intellectual Freedom,* p. 125, we read, "In today's world, children are exposed to adult life much earlier than in the past. They read materials and view a variety of media on the adult level at home and elsewhere. Current emphasis upon early childhood education has also increased opportunities for young people to learn and to have access to materials, and has decreased the validity of using chronological age as an index to the use of libraries . . . The American Library Association holds that it is the parent—and only the parent—who may restrict his children—and only *his* children—from access to library materials and services. The parent who would rather his child did not have access to certain materials should so advise the child."

In a public library, then, the whole range of adult materials would be available for young adults. But what of the school library? If the librarian there practices self-imposed censorship under the guise of protecting youth, then we see a case of unsatisfactory library service. If the library working with young adults is concerned with what will offend a particular adult in the community—teacher, parent, or school board member—it is not an agency which is recognizing the breadth of competence and sophistication represented among the clientele it serves. The criteria for selection are as they always were: timeliness of topic, authority of writer, etc., etc. as we learned in Lib. Sci. 214. The principles for selection have not changed; the social times have.

It is quite sad, then, and, in my opinion unprofessional, for librarians to threaten cancellation of subscriptions to reviewing media when they disagree with *some* of the choices included among the reviews. Such letters have appeared regularly, written by librarians and, worse yet, *teachers of prospective librarians.* In *SLJ* (May 1972, p. 61), a high school librarian complaining about *Down These Mean Streets* misstates the original review and overlooks the caveat which was included in the review. Also in *SLJ* (November 1972, p. 53),

another librarian says that she does not feel kids should be "subjected to literature which is going to pile more personal problems on them" since they already have so many personal problems!!! Of course, when she wonders about the suitability of Malamud's *The Tenants* (Farrar, 1971) and, even more surprising, Sylvia Plath's *Bell Jar* (Harper, 1971), *I* wonder what is in that library's collection. Her complaint is that these books "are really not written for high school students"—as I presume Shakespeare and Chaucer were. In that same issue of *SLJ* two library school instructors say that, "It will be necessary to point out in our classes that the books reviewed and recommended by the San Francisco Bay group may well be of interest in their local region but *may have no valid concern or interest elsewhere in the nation."* (Italics mine).

Can any one in this world of instant and universal news delivery really believe that in the United States anywhere there are young people not affected by and exposed to youth "fads" and movements? Of course not all young people have joined the "Children of God," but they are surely aware of the religious movements attracting thousands of their peers. The complaints of our protective librarians seem to imply that books which are provocatively honest, brutally frank, or bitingly critical of our times are the only ones available for our young adults. Fear not! *Beany Malone* (Crowell, 1948) still lives.

Exposing Librarians to Youth

What is painfully clear is that school librarians (I keep thinking it is less true of young adult specialists in public libraries) are fearful of the consequences of honesty. Young people, in fact people of any age, seek human contact. On that basic premise it would seem important for librarians who work with young adults to be more open, approachable, receptive, and nonjudgmental. Equally important is the need to arrange times and programs to discuss books and films. Many books really *must* be talked over. It would be difficult to gainsay the fact that Nikki Giovanni's books should be in young adult collections, but there are poems in her anthologies that demand discussion to help ease misunderstanding and pain to some of her readers.

We know what that means. It mandates the reading of titles on topics of importance to young adults. It means making possible opportunities for talking things over, as in discussion clubs, book groups, open forum sessions on current issues. A young adult librarian's day is difficult. I know. But let's set our priorities more wisely. Some of our activities can be eliminated; in this case neatness will *not* count. Let our desks look a bit like the city dump; let the catalog be less than perfection; let the shelves be, perhaps, not always in apple-pie order. Let there be time for reading the special timely titles, for seeing the controversial films, for knowing about and publicizing the TV programs "relevant" to the YA's world. And let there be time and place to discuss these with our public. I think this contact keeps *us* more alive, too. Just becoming older does not necessarily mean becoming wiser.

References

1. Ariès, Phillipe. *Centuries of Childhood: A Social History of Family Life*. Random, 1965.
2. Aikin, Wilfred M. *The Story of the Eight Year Study*. Harper, 1942.
3. Friedenberg, Edgar Z. *The Dignity of Youth and Other Atavisms*. Beacon, 1965.
4. Plumb, J. H. "The Great Change in Children." *Horizon*. Winter, 1971.

"There are no *other* children"
Special Children in Library Media Centers

Eliza T. Dresang

David is six years old. He is deaf, severely retarded, emotionally disturbed, and he spent the first three years of his life locked in a darkened room. A fictional character in a tale from the distant past? No. David is a real child, now living in Madison, Wisconsin with a foster mother and father who love him very much. He attends the Lapham elementary school, enjoys learning in a classroom with an experienced teacher, joins in playground games with 350 other handicapped and nonhandicapped children, and makes a weekly trip to the media center. David happens to live in one of the states and school districts that has led the way in the education of exceptional children.

The Exceptional Education Law, which became effective in Wisconsin on August 9, 1973, was a forerunner of the national Education of All Handicapped Children Act (PL 94–142), passed in the fall of 1975 and slated to become effective by 1978. These laws mandate that handicapped children with exceptional educational needs be educated in the least restrictive environment. The application of these laws means that many children who formerly received no public education or were segregated in separate buildings are now attending school with "typical" children and, as much as possible, are integrated into regular classrooms. (For a more detailed explanation of PL 94–142 see "We Can Grow," *School Library Journal,* May 1977, p. 44 and *Early Years,* May 1977, p. 35–73).

In the fall of 1976, Lapham Elementary School was singled out by the National Association for Retarded Citizens as one site for the filming of *The Great Yellow Schooner to Byzantium,* which the association has distributed nationally without charge, as part of its effort to increase awareness of what can be done when administrators, teachers, and students work together to provide the optimum education for everyone. (The "Great Yellow Schooner" is a school bus and "Byzantium" is a place where, according to the poet Yeats, everyone reaches his or her highest potential in life.) The handicaps of the 100 "special" students at Lapham may be physical, cognitive, or emotional and are recognized as only a part of the total makeup of each child. Much effort is put into emphasizing the unique abilities and meeting the individual needs of all children in the school.

Because abilities, not disabilities, are accentuated at Lapham, "labels" of various children are referred to as seldom as possible. Terms like "mentally retarded," "physically handicapped," or "learning disabled" tell us very little about a child. Labeling promotes damaging stereotypes whether it concerns racial, sexual, or handicapped groups. (See the article by Glen G. Foster and John Salvia in *The Exceptional Child,* May 1977, p. 533–34.) I have applied labels sparingly in this article, and the ones I have used here should not be taken as terms that attempt to pinpoint specific personalities or abilities. Also, my use of the terms "special" or "exceptional" does not apply to gifted children.

Before late summer 1974, when I was hired as director of the Instructional Materials Center (IMC) at Lapham, I had had little experience in dealing with handicapped people. I once taught French to blind students, but never came into contact with special children. Moreover, many of the teachers who transferred to Lapham came from schools without media centers and they were as ignorant as I about what the IMC might offer them and their students. Our first year together was one of trial and error, but much progress has been made since then. In the past three years it has become increasingly clear to me that any type of educational program must be developed from an understanding of the needs of the children.

A Fundamental Need

The first and major step in the education of a special child is the recognition of his or her right (and notice I said *right* not privilege) to be served. Librarians must not get caught up in dilemmas about whether to extend service to certain children or whether to limit service. It is the absolute right of every child in a school to receive equal consideration.

As people tour our school and pass through the IMC they have been overheard saying, "I would like to serve the handicapped students but I am already overworked, understaffed, and overextended. It would not be fair to the other children to try to serve this new group." The fallacy in this statement is that there are no "other" children. There should be a total IMC program. Media specialists must look at every child, at every need, and at every program in the school and then make across-the-board revisions in the library/media center program. They must be inventive and skillful managers of time and resources and learn to look at familiar programs in new ways.

Fear of the unknown is common to all human beings and the thought of serving children with whom we are unfamiliar can produce feelings of anxiety. The most immediate and helpful sources of information about new students are their teachers. It is essential for the school media specialist to spend time with the teacher discussing each child before a special class arrives in the IMC for its first visit (usually these classes are small). They should also discuss the group's needs and expectations. I find it imperative to continue this talk with the teachers informally before school or in the lounge and then to arrange for more formal talks as a follow-up after working with the children for a few weeks. If a child seems more baffling or more difficult to reach than others, I read his or her file and make it a point to inquire specifically about that child's problems.

Reading seems an obvious step for library media specialists in preparing for this new type of service, but the problem is what to read. Only one book, *The Special Child in the Library,* edited by Barbara H. Baskin and Karen H. Harris, has been written on the subject of library service to exceptional children. Published by the American Library Association in 1976, the book is a compilation of articles, a number of which are outdated in terms of bibliographies and methods (e.g., mainstreaming is not mentioned). It has some helpful information but cannot be depended on for more recent developments.

On the other hand, too many books and articles concerning specific handicaps are published for the untrained person to be able to select the one or two most informative about a certain disability. Bibliographies of professional literature are numerous and extensive, but these are frequently not selective. You may prefer to consult a teacher or other specialist to guide your self-education.

Misinformation can be damaging and may produce false expectations of the children. Some books, for example, state that trainable mentally retarded (TMR) children cannot read; my own experience proves that this is far from universally true. Journals such as *Exceptional Children, Teaching the Exceptional Child,* and *The Exceptional Parent* provide more current insights and more useful information.

The National Center on Educational Media and Materials for the Handicapped (NCEMMH) heads a national network of resource centers which provide information on materials, and sometimes the materials themselves, for educators of exceptional children. (See Part 6 of *The Special Child in the Library,* p. 163, for more detailed information.)

The National Instructional Materials Information Center (NIMIC) is a computerized bibliographical search service designed and implemented by NCEMMH. NCEMMH also publishes a newsletter, *Apropos,* to which media centers should subscribe. A fundamental responsibility of media specialists is to become familiar with the services and resources of NCEMMH and to convey this information to teachers.

Material Needs

There is no doubt that the physical size, shape, and arrangement of a library has an impact on its service to exceptional children. Most obviously this is true for physically handicapped students. A well-planned arrangement of furniture and shelves designed to accommodate children with special needs can promote their independence in using the library facilities.

Although the present state of restricted budgets would not permit major environmental changes in most media centers, small modifications are possible. For example, librarians can order revolving paperback racks that are only 46 inches high. These are accessible even to children seated in wheelchairs.

Beanbag chairs are favorite additions to the IMC at Lapham. After teachers in the orthopedic program saw how the beanbags could be molded to the bodies of the students, providing many more options for positioning, beanbags were purchased for each classroom. Our single, most useful piece of equipment has been the Singer Auto-Vance III. Because it has a large screen and is automatic, this machine allows a small group of children with special handicaps to gather around and view sound filmstrips without assistance. One of the next projects at Lapham is to work with the University of Wisconsin faculty in adapting our audiovisual machines for use by handicapped persons.

Special children do not need a myriad of new materials, either highly specialized or modified versions of those used by other IMC patrons. Take note of some of the filmstrips, records, and other products that many publishers are advertising for special children. They are frequently materials that we have used for years, now grouped under a new heading or title. It is important to select the most appropriate items in an IMC for each child, whatever his or her "label."

Occasionally an extension of resources is desirable. For Janice, a partially sighted, retarded student, I purchased a few extra books, some of which she can feel and smell and some with thick cardboard pages that won't rip easily. Recent acquisitions have included *I Am a Mouse* by Ole Risom (Golden, 1974), the Bowmar Manipulative Series, and a "scratch 'n sniff" book. We also use the Talking Books Program, a free program for both blind and physically handicapped people who are unable to use traditional book materials. On request, machinery and materials for the program are sent directly to the child's home or school. Complete information about both talking books and books in braille is available from the Library of Congress, Division for the Blind and Physically Handicapped, 1291 Taylor St. N.W., Washington, D.C. 20542.

It is important to note that most of the special children at Lapham can use the materials and equipment we already have and many of our regular students flock to any new item we receive for special students. Story books in sign language, published by Gallaudet College, 7th St. and Florida Ave. N.E., Washington, D.C. 20002, are popular with hearing impaired children.

After the children become familiar with media center services and programs, they should be directed to other community library resources. Plan a class trip to the public library or ask the children's librarian to visit the school. Send notices to parents or guardians to inform them about resources in the area and how their children can make use of them.

Psychological Needs

A basic need of all people is to be able to communicate. Handicapped children often require inventive ways of communicating. A teacher of a TMR class at Lapham, Linda Hughes, has a group of students who, although they can hear normally, cannot speak. As an experiment this fall, Linda began using sign language with her class. The music teacher, the gym teacher, and I used the signs we knew. Within a few weeks, a very dramatic change took place in both the behavior and learning of these children because they could finally "speak." (*Book,* incidentally, is one of the favorite signs of the class.) A high point for me came when Fred, a boy with whom I had had little hope of ever communicating verbally, turned to me and signed an entire sentence.

Some children who are too physically handicapped to sign or speak successfully, but who can read, use a communication board containing the most frequently used words in their vocabularies. They can point to a word they wish to use. When these children come to the IMC, I ask them questions that I know they can answer by using the communication board.

A final important means of communication is body language. All children are sensitive to approval, disapproval, warmth or reserve. This type of nonverbal communication is accessible to every person, no matter what his or her abilities or disabilities are, and its power should not be underestimated.

All children need a sense of accomplishment and self-worth. A media specialist is in an ideal position to recognize and reinforce positive aspects of personality. Some retarded people feel ashamed of the way they look. Evelyn Wieble, librarian at Northside Elementary School in Middleton, Wisconsin, helps retarded students at her school overcome this problem by asking them to bring small photographs of themselves to the media center. Together they make and laminate personalized book marks. Sometimes simply being allowed to do something that other children do can be a great morale booster for a special child.

Books are unknown entities to children who have spent much of their lives in institutions struggling to learn the basic skills of survival. For these children, many weeks or even months of exposure to books may be necessary before they are ready to borrow a book of their own and be responsible for its return. As the right to check out books was extended to each class at Lapham, the pride and happiness the students felt was extraordinary to behold. Julie, a TMR student now reading on a second grade level, is allowed to take out extra books because of her improved reading ability—a special accomplishment for her. All classes now regularly check out books; I have never had a retarded student lose or damage a book.

Encouraging a feeling of self-worth and accomplishment in a child means allowing him or her to be as independent as possible. Once TMR children at Lapham learn to operate the simple equipment, they use the IMC individually as a reward for successful classroom behavior. Jerry, a child with severe cerebral palsy and a fierce drive for independence, has created ways of functioning without help. For example, he operates the remote control buttons of the carousel slide projector with his chin. Jane Besant, the IMC director at Hoyt School in Madison, trains educable retarded children as IMC aides.

It is especially important not to get bogged down with traditional uses of materials and equipment or with time-honored rules and regulations which limit the freedom of certain children. Emily can write her name, but she uses half a book card each time she does it: far better to spend the extra penny for a new card than to insist on writing "Emily" for her neatly on one line.

Linda, an orthopedically handicapped teenager, has some learning disabilities. She is in a class of students who may never be able to use a card catalog without assistance. Nonetheless, I decided to introduce all students to all aspects of the IMC. So one day last year each student picked a drawer from the catalog to look up a subject in which he or she was interested. Linda picked *Friendship*. We located the first three books listed for her to check out, and during the next twelve months she continued to read books on the topic, including easy and difficult books, fiction and nonfiction. The really exciting part of this incident is that Linda had been coming to the IMC for one entire year before this card catalog lesson occurred, and had never checked out anything but cookbooks, despite my attempts to discover and promote other interests. If I had discounted her class because the students could not use the card catalog in the traditional manner, Linda might still be reading cookbooks. She has now finished all the entries on *Friendship* and has moved on to *Humor.*

Exceptional children do not want to seem "different" because they realize that in all the really important aspects of being human, they are not, in fact, different. So-called "typical" children can learn this very important fact by being with special children. In turn, special children can experience what society considers "normal" by playing and working with a nonhandicapped peer group. The interaction and togetherness of children who otherwise would have learned and lived apart is known as mainstreaming. The school media center is a perfect site for both informal and formal mainstreaming.

If an IMC is run on an unscheduled basis with children coming and going freely, informal mainstreaming takes place whenever special and regular children are present and are using the facilities together. On a recent Wednesday afternoon I observed several fourth and fifth graders working together on a research project, four second graders playing a game, a class of orthopedically handicapped children checking out books, three kindergartners reading with a parent volunteer, and seven emotionally disturbed students viewing a filmstrip with their teacher. (These students usually spend most of the day in a regular classroom and come to the IMC by themselves and once a week with their teacher.) It was an interesting picture of casual interaction and acceptance. All the children were learning something about each other.

Another type of mainstreaming can take place within more formalized or planned activities. At Lapham, in addition to using the IMC independently, the kindergarten, first, and second grades come to the IMC once a week on a scheduled basis, as do the ten classes of special children. An important operation this year has been the pairing of special and regular classes. Each week, a primary TMR class comes to the IMC along with a kindergarten class. The increase in attention span and responsiveness of the TMR children with this exposure to the kindergarten models has been remarkable. Most important, the children have become friends. Recently we had a "farm" day and acted out "The Farmer in the Dell." The children were free to choose whomever they wanted as the "wife," "child," "nurse," "cheese," etc. The children in the kindergarten chose children from the TMR class and vice versa. They do not fear one another and do not think of each other as bizarre or different.

When the IMC staff first encounter a new group of students, they find that the children need to be convinced that an IMC is where they want to be. The more severe the child's handicap, the more difficult this will be. Librarians must become salespeople. It is our professional failure, not the fault of the place or resources, if we do not find a way to convey a feeling of belonging to all the children. We must discover what they enjoy and provide these experiences again and again and again, if necessary, until the IMC becomes a happy learning environment and each visit is a treat.

This past fall some new children joined a TMR class from which the higher achievers had recently graduated. For the first three or four weeks the new arrivals constantly disrupted the old-timers in the IMC, refusing to sit in seats (something never expected of them before), and remaining completely unresponsive to all my tricks of the trade (puppets, flannel board, filmstrips, music, storytelling, etc.). I was almost at my wits' end when suddenly I smelled the aroma of popcorn coming from a room down the hall. The next time this class appeared, I had *Brian Wildsmith's Circus* filmstrip and a popcorn popper on hand. I put the popcorn in the popper, and then showed a filmstrip while it popped. Many people, myself included, are suspicious of stories about dramatic changes, but a miracle occurred— from that day forward, I had the attention of the new children. Eventually, they became interested in other things I had to offer (and, they did not expect to get popcorn each time).

Intellectual Needs

The need for intellectual stimulation, support, and motivation may be overlooked in the case of special children because they may have so many other more obvious needs. Or, this omission may be the result of stereotyping. All physically handicapped children and their families have to fight the pervasive notion that the disabled cannot learn and progress. Similarly, people tend to refer to retarded persons as having the "minds of five-year-olds" as if they are unable to learn and will always remain at that intellectual level.

Exceptional children should be exposed to the best in children's literature and artistry on whatever level they can handle. Simple folktales, for example, can be read and then acted out. One of my favorite books, *The Very Hungry Caterpillar* by Eric Carle (Collins, 1969), was enjoyed by a class of severely retarded students. After the story, Maureen Ellsworth, the librarian, taught them to make paper butterflies. Mixed-media presentations are almost always desirable, but

books should not be overlooked.

All school media librarians recognize the necessity of coordinating activities and programs with what occurs in the classrooms. With children who have some sort of impaired learning ability this is crucial, for it is through repetition that they learn. A conceptual approach—organizing units of study around a certain theme, reinforcing classroom activity with field trips—is most successful. If an unfamiliar subject is introduced, the same material should be used on several occasions.

After the emphasis I put on independence it may seem contradictory to say that one of the most important things the IMC can offer children is a group experience. Because of their unique needs, some special children, particularly those who are severely retarded, have almost totally individualized instruction. In order to enjoy movies or plays or even television, these children must learn to listen attentively as members of a group. The IMC is a perfect place for reinforcing this skill. During group time, the concept that books are a source of pleasure is also introduced. When the media specialist reads aloud regularly, the size, shape, and contents of books become familiar to children who may have once considered them strange objects.

Accurate Representation

Books dealing with exceptional children are now pouring off the presses. The media staff, even if there is not one special child in the school, need to be aware of the inaccuracies of representation and the gross stereotypes that have existed in the past or are appearing again in some of these new books, both fiction and nonfiction. "Labels," such as those to which I referred at the beginning of this article, are used carelessly. As with books portraying racist or sexist images, we should not run to the shelves with a zealous effort to discard in order to show that we are cognizant of the problem. We should learn to discriminate between the good and the poor titles now being published in such numbers, and recommend the best ones to students and teachers.

Although many books now focus on special children as protagonists, exceptional children should be included in illustrations and texts that reflect society in general. Victor Fuchs, Assistant Director of NCEMMH, has pointed out that 99 out of 100 children's textbooks and nonprint materials fail to mention that exceptional persons exist. Close to 10 percent of the population is almost completely ignored. Teachers and library media staff should insist that publishers be aware of this omission.

Teachers will ask media specialists for help in preparing a regular class to receive special children. Classroom materials must be previewed with a discerning eye before they are recommended to avoid stereotypes. Some excellent suggestions for preparing these children are also found in the May 1977 issue of *Early Years*.

Parental Support

Parents of special children, in league with organized groups of handicapped persons, have been chiefly responsible for the legislation which is now requiring education for all children.

Media specialists can provide support for these parents who have established their children's right to equal opportunities. This can be done in three ways. Perhaps the most important is to involve parents in school programs. Being a part of a "regular" school will be new to many parents and they may be hesitant to volunteer for school activities. I use parent volunteers in book fairs, in PTA programs, and on field trips and for IMC routines. Second, as the media staff become more knowledgeable about which books are helpful and accurate, they can pass this information on to parents or start a professional collection. Third, the library can provide addresses of national and local organizations offering help and service to handicapped people. Order pamphlets from these organizations to have on hand so that parents can increase their knowledge.

Serving All Children

The media center or IMC is one of the most positive things in education for exceptional children because the fundamental principle of an IMC is that different children learn in different ways. By presenting material in the medium and format most appropriate to the message being conveyed, each child can be accommodated. Remember that children who cannot see can hear; children who cannot hear can see; children who cannot understand abstraction and generalization can feel and handle and hold the concrete. Children who cannot relate to adults may relate to puppets and stuffed animals or to real animals. In the Lapham IMC we have three gerbils, six fish, and many stuffed animals and puppets. I begin almost every program by using a puppet to talk to the children.

In the IMC special children can increase their vocabularies, reinforce listening skills, and expand their knowledge of both commonplace and exotic things. For children whose mobility may be limited, vicarious experiences are essential. Perhaps more than anything else, a library media center can introduce exceptional children to lifelong sources of recreation, enjoyment, and stimulation.

Tomorrow's Scholars:
Patterns of Facilities Use

Jacqueline C. Mancall & M. Carl Drott

The task of the school library is a difficult one. Its primary responsibility is meeting the students' curricular needs with appropriate materials and services. However, students have widely varied levels of ability and differ considerably in competency. To further complicate matters, the curriculum deals potentially with every field of human knowledge. Fortunately, the school library, particularly when located in a major metropolitan area, does not exist in isolation as the sole information resource within a community. In such a metropolitan area a wealth of information resources is available, housed in a wide variety of libraries and information centers.

Recently, there has been a growing realization that students must learn to function in an information society. To do this they will have to develop skills that go beyond the use of a single library or collection. Students must develop both generalized, information-seeking skills and specific knowledge of community and national resources. A number of formal statements exist whose purpose is to explore and facilitate the concept of including school library media centers in a national information network. However, at present, the responsibility for putting students in contact with the broad world of information resources lies primarily with the individual efforts of the school media specialist (at times in conjunction with the local public librarian).

In preparing students for the information society, it is important to recognize that while much networking is still in the planning stage, community information resources exist and are, in fact, widely accessible to students (particularly students in metropolitan areas). Therefore, programs to develop student skills should take advantage of the informal development of information use patterns which has already occurred. Knowledge of such patterns can aid librarians and teachers in planning instructional services for students. By identifying present behaviors it is possible to determine which aspects of instruction of students should be encouraged. It is also possible to identify the shortcomings of the present system which could be overcome by better student training, or cooperation among librarians across institutional barriers.

Because student use is so diverse, this study focused on one particular type of student assignment—the independent study paper. Such an assignment, in which students are expected to select topics and work on their own initiative in seeking information, was judged likely to involve students with a variety of area libraries and information facilities as well as their own school media centers.

The Sample

There seems to be no economical method of identifying the population of students doing independent study papers so that a random sample can be selected. Our experimental design selected a purposeful sample of schools from which to draw papers. Six metropolitan area schools were selected—four public and two independent (private). Three of the public schools and one independent school were located within the city. One public school was in a near suburban area. The remaining independent school was a residential school in a more distant suburb. Each school selected offers a strong college preparatory curriculum and the students may be considered roughly similar in terms of academic orientation. Within each school, principals, librarians, department heads, and teachers were contacted to explain the study and to determine which classes had independent study assignments. Arrangements were then made with individual teachers for data collection. A total of 11 teachers participated in the study which involved a total of 13 classes.

Data collection involved four sources: student questionnaires, teacher questionnaires, interviews with the school librarians, and examination of the bibliographies of student papers. These data are discussed in their entirety elsewhere. The present report deals mainly with the student questionnaires, supplemented by information from the teachers and the librarians.

The Questionnaire

The questionnaire, which was developed specifically for this study, addressed the following questions:

1. *How many and which types of libraries or information agencies did students try when searching for information to use in their research papers? Did they search elsewhere?*

2. *Which of the sources provided them with the information they used?*

3. *Did they seek assistance from library staff members and, if so, in which libraries?*

4. *Did family or friends assist them in their search?*

5. *Did others search for them and provide them with the information they eventually used in their papers?*

The development of the questionnaire proceeded in several steps. The questions were designed to require only factual replies. Checklists were provided to aid the students' memories, with questions logically ordered. Questions asking for similar information were presented in similar ways. The questionnaire was pretested on a group of students. The experimenter discussed the questionnaire with the students as well as with librarians and teachers. On the basis of this test some questions were reworded and the instructions were rewritten.

An important step in the design was to check that the answers could be coded for computer analysis. For example, in question 1, each of the libraries that could be used is listed and coded as a separate yes-no variable. This arrangement permits a very flexible plan of statistical analysis.

Administering the Questionnaire

The questionnaires were administered in classes near the time when the independent study papers were handed in to teachers. Typically, the investigator briefly described the research, answered questions as the students filled in their answers, and in some classes, gave a more detailed discussion of the research project after the questionnaires were completed. In order to preserve the anonymity of the students, the questionnaires were identified by class but not by individual. Data was also collected on the bibliographies of the papers submitted by these classes. These results, which analyze the materials used, are presented in "Materials Used By High School Students in Preparing Independent Study Projects: A Bibliometric Approach" by Mancall and Drott in *Library Research* 3 (1979).

A total of 234 questionnaires were completed by students in the six sample schools. On the basis of statistical sampling, the error for this sample size would be expected to be plus or minus six percent. The present sample is purposeful, not random, hence this error figure can not be completely relied upon.

Responses

A. *Facilities Used*

Student use of libraries ranged from the use of one library by 16 students to the use of eight libraries by one student. An average student used three libraries; 15 percent of the students used more than four libraries. The distribution of the number of libraries used is shown in Table 1. Students are using a number of libraries in fulfilling their independent study assignments. Roughly speaking, about one-third of the students sought materials in three libraries. Slightly more than a third used four or more facilities. The remainder used one or two libraries.

Knowing, in general, the number of libraries in which students sought information, the next logical question concerns the type of libraries to which they turned. The questionnaire specifically measured use of the school library, neighborhood public library, regional public library, community college library, college or university library, and home library. In addition, students indicated the other types of libraries or information agencies they tried. These included private and special libraries of all types, with the questionnaire allowing for indication of the names and institutional affiliations of these libraries (special purpose institutions, private profit-making corporations, etc.). Table 2 shows the types of libraries which students tried.

Both school and public libraries were heavily used by students in this sample. In the search process most students (86 percent) tried their school library. If public library use is analyzed as either use of a neighborhood public or use of a regional public library, 89 percent used one, the other or both.

The home library ranks third in importance (i.e., number of users). This high use of the home collection (over one-half of the students) becomes a factor to which librarians and teachers might consider paying closer attention. The materials use portion of this study did not specifically identify the materials which students obtained from their home collections. Analysis of student bibliographies suggests that the home provided diverse types of materials. Specifically, home use cannot be simply attributed to consulting encyclopedias. One strong support of this finding is the fact that twice as many students used home libraries as referenced encyclopedias.

Table 1
Student Use of Libraries
(N = 234)

Number of Libraries	% of Students	% of Students (Cumulative)
1	7	7
2	20	27
3	32	59
4	26	85
5 or more	15	100

Table 2
Student Use of Libraries By Type of Library
(N = 234)

Library	% of Students
School	86
Neighborhood public	70
Regional public	54
Combined public (neighborhood and/or regional)	89
Community college	4
College/university	37
Home	56
Other (private/special)	19

College or university libraries also played an important role as information sources in the sample. More than one-third of the students searched for information in this type of library. This is in spite of several problems which such libraries present. The collections are large and sophisticated; the classification scheme may be unfamiliar (LC rather than Dewey); and college and university libraries may discourage or actually forbid use by high-school students.

Other libraries (i.e., special, private) are approached by only a limited number of these students. Less than one-fifth of the students used libraries belonging to private groups, organizations or companies, and most of this small group used only one of these private or special libraries. Science students tended to use hospital or medical school libraries, or libraries of scientifically or technically oriented institutions or companies. History students turned to highly specialized historical societies and historical records (or public records). Students pursuing legal topics turned to law libraries.

It is interesting to note at this point the types of libraries which teachers reported that they suggested to students. All teachers (11) whose classes cooperated in this study completed a teacher questionnaire. School and public libraries were specifically recommended to students by all teachers. College libraries were suggested by nine of the 11 teachers. One teacher went into a detailed description of the variety of other special, information agency resources available to students. Most teachers mentioned no other types of libraries, or suggested only one or two possibilities.

Given the number and types of libraries students used, the next question dealt with the success rate which the students reported in locating information useful for their research. Three-fourths of the students who used their school libraries found information for their papers. Public library use was also productive. Two-thirds of those who tried neighborhood public libraries found useful information, while all (100 percent) had success who used regional public libraries. Most (84 percent) of the group trying libraries in colleges or universities found information they eventually used. The same is true for materials in home libraries—85 percent of the students who indicated they used home collections used material found at home. Although only 19 percent of the students used private or special libraries, all who did found information which they put into their papers.

The questionnaire asked what help students might have received from family or friends. It also asked if the library had been used by some other person (a surrogate searcher). Most students (74 percent) reported receiving no help from family or friends. Those who did were assisted mostly within college or university libraries (27 percent of users), with a somewhat smaller number getting assistance at public libraries and at home. Searching by a surrogate was acknowledged by very few students (6 percent). Most of this type of help was provided for students using college libraries.

B. *Assistance Received*

Given the rate of success users have within different types of libraries, it becomes interesting to measure the degree of assistance students sought and received in these libraries. This study asked students if they received help, and if so, in which libraries they received it and from whom (library staff or family and friends). Analysis was not directed toward the type of help the student needed; rather it ascertained only if students reported obtaining assistance, and if so, where. A final question dealt with whether students had others use libraries for them. This type of assistance (i.e., via surrogates) was minimal. Table 3 summarizes student use of libraries.

Two-thirds of the students reported that they received help from the staff of at least one library. Although the data is insufficient to allow any speculation on why students sought help it does point to the fact that most sought an intermediary to interact between their information needs and the collection available. Most assistance (i.e., 50 percent of those using) was provided in regional public libraries and university libraries, with school libraries ranking third (40 percent of those using) as places where students received staff help. Staffs of neighborhood public libraries also assisted students (25 percent of those using this resource). Less help was provided in private or special libraries (only 18 percent of those using).

Table 3					
Students' Rate of Success/Need for Assistance					
Type of Library	% of Students Using	% of Students Finding Info.	% Receiving Staff Help	% Receiving Outside Help*	% Receiving Surrogates Help
School	86	75	40	4	1
Neighborhood public	70	69	25	10	2
Regional public	54	100	50	16	.7
Community college	4	67	22	—	—
College/university	37	84	50	27	6
Home	56	85	—	13	.7
Other (private/special)	19	100	18	18	2
*from family or friends					

This leads to a type of speculation which the data are not sufficient to answer. For example, is the need for help related to the size of the collection? Regional public libraries are of such a size that an inexperienced user would need more help than in a smaller and more familiar neighborhood public library. College and university libraries present similar problems to students. The low percentage of help (18 percent) in special or private libraries may be attributable to the fact that students who tried special libraries were largely from the class in which the teacher gave detailed instruction in the availability and use of such collections. It may be that the high success rates reported for large or specialized libraries are due to a tendency for only well-prepared students to attempt such use.

The data indicate that those students (56 percent) who used their home libraries were successful in finding information for their papers (85 percent of those using), and did so with little help. Again, one is tempted to speculate on the spin-off value of educating parents in selecting materials for home libraries. If students are indeed successfully using home collections, perhaps the most direct way to effect student use is through the home.

Differences Among Schools

Throughout this research it became apparent that there are differences among schools. These differences include access factors such as school location and availability of public transportation, school library factors involving both collection and staffing, and assignment factors such as the specific instructions given by the teacher. The sample as a whole was selected to provide a mix of these factors. The aggregated data above can be viewed as a somewhat representative cross section of metropolitan, high-school students.

This section examines the differences and similarities among schools. The small number of schools (six) means that this discussion must be treated as speculative. The average sample size was 39 students per school. Thus, for data on a single school, each student accounts for over 2 percent of the sample.

In order to summarize the most important information, Table 4 presents the libraries used by half or more of the students in each school. The most significant factor associated with the use of many libraries seems to be access, both actual and perceived. For example, Independent Suburban school is an isolated residential school. Students must make special arrangements for transportation. In such a situation it is not surprising to find low use of outside libraries. For the remaining schools, access seems to have two components: availability of transportation and student familiarity with transportation. Access to transportation is nearly equal for all schools. The metropolitan schools have somewhat better public transportation while the suburban public school had greater access to private transportation. The determining factor in student use of a diversity of libraries is the students' perception of access. The students from Independent Metropolitan and Public Metropolitan 1 and 2 regularly commute from all areas of the city. These students showed greater willingness to use a diversity of libraries. The students at Public Metropolitan 3 and Public Suburban do not have as much experience in traveling around the city. These students are less likely to leave their neighborhoods in search of information.

School library usage was important throughout the sample. The differences among schools may be more dependent on the school library staff than on the collection of materials. The largest school library in terms of budget and collection per student was Public Metropolitan 2; the smallest was Independent Metropolitan. For both of these schools usage levels of the school library are similar and are exceeded by several other schools. This failure of the collection to noticeably influence student use was also observed in our analysis of student bibliographies. In that study the school with the most outstanding vertical file collection did not show any higher pamphlet or clipping use, and the school with extensive newspaper microfilms reported no student references to them.

Interviews with the librarians and teacher questionnaires showed a strong dependence between teacher-librarian interaction and overall student use of the school library. The most

Table 4
Libraries Used by One-Half or More of Each School's Students

Library	Ind. Metro.	Ind. Suburban*	Public Metro. 1	Public Metro 2	Public Metro. 3	Public Suburban
School	84	100	95	86	59	100
Neighborhood public	—	—	95	62	90	98
Regional public	92	—	80	53	85	—
Combined public (neighborhood/regional)	—	—	—	—	—	—
Community college	—	—	—	—	—	—
College/university	100	—	—	—	—	—
Home	62	—	70	66	56	51
Other (private/special)	—	—	—	—	—	—

*residential school

active librarians were those in schools which showed high, overall library use. In the case of the suburban schools this use tended to center on the school library, while in the metropolitan area this was manifested by use of a variety of libraries. Much of this interaction is complex, including joint planning of assignments, preparation of special bibliographies, and in-class instruction provided by the librarian. The sample is too small to comment on the effect of any specific approach.

The third factor which affects the number and type of facilities used by students is the specific assignment and the teacher's preparation of the students. For all assignments in the sample, most students felt a need to use more than one library. Many students used other libraries without assistance—indication that they had already established patterns of multi-library use. The effect of the teachers' instructions was to point students toward more specialized collections or to encourage the use of a greater variety of types of materials. It appears that the more detailed and specific the teachers' instructions (for example, written rather than oral) the more likely that students would use a greater variety of resources,

Suggestions for Practice

Readers should recognize that, while the sample described above may be broadly representative of a class of students in a particular situation, local differences may produce different student-use patterns. The questionnaire approach described in this paper represents a general tool for describing the patterns in any specific situation.

Our experience with this study has indicated that a straightforward questionnaire, asking for direct, factual answers, can be constructed and administered with relatively little effort. Tabulation and interpretation of student responses is greatly clarified and simplified by concentrating on a single specific instance which is fresh in the students' minds. A concentration on factual information in a restricted number of areas gives students a direct way of describing their actions. This factual approach reserves questions of the quality of library service, or possible alternative services, to those professionals appropriately trained to deal with such issues.

Our experience with selecting samples suggests that it is not necessary at the local, school-building level to be concerned with the details of random sample selection which would be involved in a technical research project. There are two reasons for this. The first is that students are each so individual in their approach that any sample short of a complete description of the student body would be, to some degree, inadequate. The second is the recognition that this information will be used by people who have a great deal of additional knowledge about the local situation. Thus, unlike the role of the disinterested researcher, information from this type of study represents only a part of the knowledge of the local situation upon which a librarian or teacher draws in formulating educational policies or objectives. On the other hand, quantitative measurement (such as that provided by a questionnaire) provides a baseline for judgment that is more broadly representative than information gained from daily involvement with the special problems of individual students.

Local Applications

The steps for applying this type of analysis to a local situation are straightforward:

1) develop a questionnaire which directs the student's attention to a specific assignment and concentrates on factual questions;

2) discuss the questionnaire with teachers and other librarians, both to check the questionnaire for clarity and to identify those classes in which students will be preparing independent study or research papers;

3) administer the questionnaires close to the time when the papers or projects are due (in class administration is most convenient);

4) reduce the questionnaire answers to tables, using this paper as a model. For small samples, these tables can be easily created by tallying the questionnaires by hand and using a pocket calculator to obtain the necessary percentages.

While one cannot take rational action from a state of ignorance, it is also the case that simply having data does not guarantee wise action (or choices). The creation of specific programs to develop the student's access to the world of information must be a process of trial and evaluation. In fact, repeated surveys of the type described above may help to determine whether new programs have had a measurable impact on student behavior.

The specific programs will depend greatly on the local situation and on the priorities assigned to various goals and objectives. However, based upon the specific results of our survey the following are some program ideas which might be tested in developing student information awareness:

1. A concrete program in school/public library cooperation might set aside a specific time that the public library would reserve for intensive assistance to students in research topics for school assignments. For example, a Saturday morning might be designated during which specific reference tools were made especially accessible and library staff were assigned to active roles in offering assistance to students in relation to specific assignments.

In order to offer such assistance it is important that the school and public librarians agree on the objectives for the students' learning. Is the focus on the students' ability to find information, or on the students' ability to produce a paper once the information has been found? Cooperative contacts could also include descriptions of the preparation which students had received in the classroom or school library.

This particular recommendation grows out of our observation that students will be heavy public library users, but that many do not specifically seek assistance.

2. A second possible action is a cooperative effort involving the local parent-teacher organization. The focus would be the upgrading of home library collections and increasing parent sensitivity to their own role in shaping the information seeking habits of their children. A program of this type could be undertaken either in the school or public library, or both in concert. Specifically, this program might include: lists of recommended reference books for holiday and birthday giving; recommendations of pertinent criteria for selecting books or

magazines for the home; programs designed to remind parents of the availability of librarians for professional advice; and other presentations aimed at developing in parents an appreciation of the importance of information skills in modern society.

This recommendation comes out of our finding of frequent use by students of home collections, and especially, that home collections were often used in conjunction with both school and public library holdings.

3. A third plan of action would deal with shaping the assignment and the preparation given to the students by their individual teachers. One way of encouraging students to try new facilities and new information seeking approaches is by giving them clear and concrete suggestions in the classroom. The identification of specific facilities within the community and instruction in the use of specific locating tools (i.e., indexes) may be more within the regular experience of the school or public librarian than the teacher who is, by necessity, more concerned with the subject matter. Therefore, close cooperation between librarians and teachers in identifying appropriate subjects and where materials are available on these subjects will encourage the student to explore new information sources.

This recommendation is derived from our finding that active involvement of the teacher and librarian was an important factor in the use by students of a variety of facilities. Our interviews with teachers showed that this effect was particularly strong when students were given specific written instructions and detailed recommendations to community resources (including addresses and hours of operation, etc.).

Conclusions

The students in this sample show a strong tendency to go beyond their school libraries when working on independent study papers. This library use extends not only to home collections and neighborhood public libraries but to regional public libraries, academic libraries, and a variety of special collections. Within all these institutions, students often obtain assistance from librarians. Students report high success rates in all of the libraries which they use.

The fact that students use a wide variety of libraries is important to the school librarians. Students need library instruction which is not limited to a single, local resource. They need the basic skills which will be applicable to a wide range of collections. The large amount of help reported in other libraries suggests another instructional objective. Students would benefit from question asking skills which would allow them to express their needs clearly to the staff of outside libraries.

Librarians must evaluate the factors of transportation access, materials availability, and the nature of the assignment for their own particular schools. Librarians who wish to encourage student use of a variety of facilities must be willing to take an active role. Activities should include: communication and coordination with the librarians of other area libraries; assistance to teachers in the design of assignments and in the preparation of instructions for students; and contact with and encouragement for parents and parent groups in the selection of materials for home collections.

Acknowledgments

Belver C. Griffith, Raymond W. Barber, and D. Jean Rafsnider. The study was supported in part under grant G007801806 from the U.S. Office of Education. Drexel University supported the computations.

Hispanics in the U.S.
Implications for Library Service

Esther Dyer and Concha Robertson-Kozan

Librarianship and ethnicity are inescapably intertwined. In the broadest sense, the function of libraries, whether they are public, school, or academic, is to serve their communities. It is not enough for librarians to understand the specific informational and social needs of their clients, to know the community's tapestry, if you will; they need to understand each and every motif—the cultural heritages, the various languages, the socio-economic backgrounds, the socialization patterns, and the preferred learning modes of groups within the community.

The focus of this article (using demographics taken from the 1980 census) is on the socio-economic, cultural, and informational needs of the largest, most important, fastest-growing minority group in the U.S.—Hispanic Americans. Also covered is the development of bilingual education and the role of the library in developing programs which will best serve the Spanish-speaking community and its youth.

The federal government reports 14.6 million Hispanics in the U.S., a questionable figure due to language problems, a fear of immigration officers, and the failure of census-takers to adequately cover poorer urban areas. A better estimate might be 20 million, or approximately 10% of the total population. While the majority of Hispanics live in three states (California, New York, and Texas), many states claim more than one million Hispanics.

Contrary to popular opinion, the population of Hispanics in the U.S. is not a homogeneous one: 60% is Mexican in origin; 14% Puerto Rican; 6% Cuban; and 8% Central and South American. Although the characteristics of these sub-populations vary, they are linked by a common language and, to a lesser degree, by a common historical and cultural background. This article will provide a comparison of Mexican Americans and Puerto Rican Americans, since these groups comprise three-quarters of the total population.

Demographics

Virtually all Puerto Ricans (96%) and the majority of Mexicans (80%) live in metropolitan areas; only two thirds of all Americans live in metropolitan areas. Puerto Rican families live in central cities (79%), as contrasted to Mexicans, who are divided fairly evenly between the central cities (46%) and the suburbs (34%).

While the average size of the American family is 3.28 persons (generally parents and children), the average family of Mexican origin has 4.07 members, and Puerto Rican families 3.67 members. However, the normal family pattern of two parents and a varied number of children is often broken: 20% of all Hispanic families are maintained by women as single parents. Here again, subgroups differ: only 17% of Mexican families fall into this category, but 40% of Puerto Rican families are headed and supported solely by women. Naturally, family patterns greatly affect a child's intellectual and social development.

The median income of Hispanic families is lower than the norm: the average American family has an annual income of $14,000; the Hispanic family averages about $2000 less in metropolitan areas and $3000 less in other areas. The median individual income for the total population is $6900, but for Hispanics it is $1000 less. These figures do not show that 20% of all Hispanic families in the U.S. live below the poverty level. Not surprisingly, 53% of the Hispanic women with sole responsibility for maintaining their families live in poverty, with an average income of $5600 to care for an average of two or three children, and possibly a grandparent as well.

Also important are the educational and employment levels of Hispanics. While 69% of the total population in the U.S. completes high school, only 40.1% of the Hispanic population who are 25 years of age and older have done so. Only 6.7% of Hispanics as compared to the 16.4% of the total population complete college. Here again there are noticeable differences within the Hispanic population that can be traced to migration patterns. The Cubans who fled to the U.S. for political and intellectual reasons were generally an affluent and educated population; 51% of all Cubans who came had completed high school, as compared with 39% of the Puerto Ricans and 35% of the Mexicans. Both the Mexican and Puerto Ricans migrations frequently reflected the hopes of poorer classes of people, equipped with fewer skills, who were looking to find "El Dorado" by selling their labor in the U.S.

Given their educational backgrounds, the employment opportunities for most Hispanics are limited. The federal government admitted to a 6% unemployment rate for the population in general in 1979 in contrast to 8% of the Hispanic labor force. The highest unemployment figures were for Puerto Ricans: 34%. Of the Mexican population, 9% were out of work. Job level is yet another factor: while 17% of the total population are professional and technical workers, only 8% of Hispanics are similarly employed. Hispanics are more likely to be employed as service workers or operatives. Only 11% of Hispanic professional and technological workers are employed as managers. In contrast, 67% of other professional and technical workers are in managerial positions.

Cultural Aspects

In addition to the demographic and economic differences between the total population and the Hispanics, there are significant cultural differences to be considered. The urgency of this need becomes apparent when one realizes that there are few Hispanic teachers; although 38% of all teachers in the U.S. have Spanish-speaking children in their classes, less than 14% have had any training in how to deal with children with limited English-speaking proficiency.

Research studies have demonstrated that much of learning is culturally-based. For example, in 1978, a study was done of *incentive-motivation* of children of Mexican, Mexican-American, and Anglo-American heritages. Tasks that required cooperative behavior were performed best by Mexican, Mexican-American, and Anglo children—in that order. This order was reversed when tasks were structured competitively (see "Prospects for Bilingual Education in the Nation." National Advisory Council for Bilingual Education (NACBE), Fifth Annual Report, 1980–81, p. 52). Such studies have profound implications for educational development. The very backbone of the American educational system is competitive in structure, e.g., the curve to determine rank order of students, the competition to be first in line, in grade, etc. Classroom teachers accustomed to this teaching style are hard-put to adapt to more group work and find it difficult to grade group activities.

Other sources of conflict between teacher expectations, teaching styles, and the responses of Hispanic students are manifested in the differences in perceptions of time, space, personal contact, and even in defining what constitutes good behavior. Students are dubbed "good" when they can recite or regurgitate information; further, the "good" child is involved in classroom activity—he or she always participates and volunteers. But an Hispanic child on good behavior will sit still in his or her seat, will pay attention but will not volunteer responses nor ever question the teacher. All hallmarks of a "slow" or recalcitrant student.

The American school bureaucracy in general, and teachers, in particular, expect students to attend class, and expect that school work and school obligations should be of primary importance to both children and parents. Yet the Hispanic culture socializes its members to put family and community obligations before the school. So the good child is often the one who stays at home to take care of a brother or sister when needed, or who takes a younger sibling to the doctor. Thus, another indication that the Hispanic child "is not interested in school, does not want to learn" or, in many cases, "is incapable of learning as well as Anglo children." Unfortunately, these expectations often have a tendency of being fulfilled.

Fluency in the basics of English does not immediately bring about colloquial fluency. Indirect translations can often produce comic phraseology or change an intended compliment into an insult. A good example here is the Spanish "Negrito," a term of endearment which literally means "little black one." A Spanish child using newly gained English skills might well call an Anglo friend "Little Blacky"—sure to be interpreted as a racial slur at best. Parenthetically, teachers and librarians looking at Spanish language books have seen the word Negrito and have rejected excellent books because they, too, have misinterpreted this to mean "nigger"—clearly a gap in communication.

Names can be another problem. Many Hispanic students have hyphenated names, which school bureaucracies have a tendency to mutilate. In some cases, such changes can transform a very proud child into an illegitimate one by the use of the wrong name or wrong name order. There is a scene in a film on bilingual education that features a child named Concha during her first day in school. Her last name is truncated; her teacher writes "Connie" on her name tag. In addition, both the teacher and other students, who seem to interpret her language problem as stupidity, address her slowly and loudly. In a short time the child's identity and self-image are totally changed. The differences between her home and community environment, the hostility of the classroom, and the inflexibility of the schools are exaggerated in this film, but they certainly do exist. The editorial point here is that those working in schools (and libraries) must be aware of cultural traditions so they can be flexible in meeting the needs of all students and, at the very least, show respect for their traditions.

Bilingual Programs

At the present time more than five million students in the U.S. suffer from a limited proficiency in English—three million of these are Spanish-speaking. These students are not distributed evenly throughout the U.S. and in some metropolitan areas the problems are quite dramatic. More than 30% of the school children in New York City, Denver, Hartford, and Miami, and more than 45% in Los Angeles and San Antonio have limited English.

It is only within the last five years that cultural instruction and inservice training for teachers and librarians have been available to help them cope with cross-cultural problems. Proyecto LEER is a nonprofit foundation that selects, evaluates, and distributes information on Spanish-language books. Recognizing that a bulletin or review alone was insufficient to solve the cultural communications problems, this group, in cooperation with the National Endowment for the Humanities and the U.S. Office of Education [now the Department of Education], sponsored several programs to train teachers and librarians to use Spanish language materials in the curriculum.

First, two summer institutes were held, one in Philadelphia, with emphasis on the Puerto Rican heritage, and the other in Texas, with an emphasis on Mexican heritage. The original aim of the programs was to stimulate teachers and librarians to jointly develop a curriculum that dealt with Hispanic history, culture, dance, music, and art. A demonstration collection of 3000 books was made available so that participants could look at materials and develop bibliographies and projects that included published material. Experts from all over the United States were invited to address particular cultural topics. Adequate coverage was given to the processes of selection and review and to the criteria for evaluation of Spanish-language books. While an understanding of the Spanish language was helpful, it was not required, since it was recognized that most teachers and virtually all librarians working in the schools would not have Spanish backgrounds and would have to depend on community aides, bilingual teachers, and review media to help them evaluate materials. Other institutes were designed for public libraries, and dealt primarily with selection criteria, resources, and program possibilities. The lesson here is that staff attitudes and individual dedication can do much to overcome both language and cultural barriers.

Professional associations. both educational and library related, have also taken up the gauntlet and sponsored programs to help educators deal with the bilingual population. The federal government has created a bilingual network of materials development and resource centers that help teachers and librarians locate material and that provide for the special needs of children with limited English.

While much of the bilingual effort is clearly better in its theory than in practice, some exemplary programs can be found. In the Boston area, there is a project in which Hispanic teenagers tutor K-6 students in Spanish and present programs on art, music, literature, and drama. This provides not only instructional help and greater cultural awareness, but also role models for children in the schools.

Other successful programs have sought to build on the strong sense of community and the extended Hispanic family by involving parents and community leaders. One such program, aimed at preschool children, offered tutoring in English and Spanish; parents were asked to read to their children in both languages. These parents met monthly for counseling and discussion, and were visited at home by teachers. Some school programs involve development of a community resource file which lists a variety of speakers and places to visit in the community. This kind of file is particularly appropriate for libraries. A lecture series and visitation program, undertaken by a school library in Florida, invited Hispanic adults in a variety of occupations to speak to classes about their jobs.

Library Programs

While some programs are appropriate for libraries, the role of the library in the bilingual educational process is still unclear. Unfortunately, although millions of dollars have been spent for bilingual education, very little has gone to purchase books and materials—and few bilingual teachers know about or use the library's resources. For their part, librarians who do not speak the language often feel inadequate to address the special needs of Spanish-speaking students.

This situation clearly cannot continue. Virtually every librarian in major metropolitan areas and, in some states, in almost every community will have to serve Spanish-speaking children. The first step will be to augment woefully inadequate Spanish-language collections with excellent books and

nonprint materials in Spanish, and with English materials about Hispanic culture. The need for materials in a broad array of subject areas means a serious dollar commitment to service and tangible proof of official sanction and support for bilingual/bicultural programs.

Successful library programs relate to both the different learning styles and patterns of Hispanic children and to their specific frames of reference. Not only must libraries recognize festivals, holidays, and known historical facts, but they must also operate as a vital link between school, community, and family. A good beginning might be a series of talks on topics of interest to the community or simply hiring Hispanic library aides. Including older Spanish-speaking students in the process of book selection and program presentation is another beginning.

The librarian can provide teachers with adequate references on teaching/learning styles, and work with administrators ands guidance teachers to sensitize the entire faculty to the needs of Hispanic children. This is not to say that school librarians will be able to conduct workshops, but rather that they can use their organizational and information-gathering skills to develop appropriate formats and to locate and recommend speakers.

Acting as a curriculum consultant and part of the curriculum planning team, the librarian can provide the total school with the necessary support to integrate and enhance the bilingual program. Librarians, who are always resourceful in selecting and organizing materials, can obtain and distribute a number of excellent English bibliographies that review Spanish language books, including one published by the New York Public Library on books for Spanish-speaking children. Librarians can also search for representative materials about specific cultural groups: Mexican, Puerto Rican, and Cuban, to name a few. The federal government sponsors the National Clearinghouse on Bilingual Education, an agency that helps teachers and librarians locate information and materials.

For the selection process, librarians should be aware that Hispanic children have different reading interests and preferences. For instance, Hispanic children seek out more poetry and short stories than their Anglo peers, who often spurn poetry. Furthermore, the normal selection criteria of good binding, best illustrations, no cartoons, and appropriate length of sentences or reading formulas cannot be applied. For example, Disney-esque cartoon drawings are quite common and do not necessarily indicate that the books are of poor quality. While it is possible to select only the best in English literature for children and assume that they have access to a broad range of materials either at the library or the local book store, this assumption is inappropriate in the case of Hispanic children, whose access may be limited to what the library has on hand. Spanish-language periodicals, newspapers, and ephemeral materials are essential.

Other resources that should be accessible through the school library are television programs and films. The U.S. government has sponsored a number of bilingual audiovisual programs; these are available free from Far West Laboratories. "Sesame Street" is now available in Spanish and Latin American versions. "Villa Alegre" and all Spanish-language TV shows can be taped off-air for use in classrooms and libraries. Storytelling and performances in which different cultures are presented should be included in library programming and school events.

A Look to the Future

As a whole, the U.S. population is an aging population. In 1970 the median age was 27.9; by 1990 it will be almost 5 years older or 32.8 years. The birth rate has declined from 3.8 to 1.8 within 20 years. But these predicted changes in population will not be uniform either in geographic or cultural distribution. In contrast, the Hispanic population is a young one; in 1979 its average age was only 22. For the population as a whole, one in 14 is under 5 years of age, but for Hispanics, the figure is one in 8. By the year 2000, it is projected, there will be an increase of over 800,000 Hispanic children 5–14 years of age with limited English-speaking proficiency. (Two-thirds of these students will live in California, Texas and New York.) By that time, it's estimated that over 77% of the students requiring help with English will be Hispanic.

These projections have enormous implications. Bilingual/bicultural education for Hispanics will be an increasingly important factor in resource allocation, in teacher and librarian preparation, and in curriculum planning. The challenge of these demographic trends must be answered by educational policy if cultural conflict in the schools is to be minimized.

What does the future hold? One certainty is that library services to the Spanish-speaking population will be a clear challenge. Cooperation is the key to success: teachers, librarians, administrators, and members of the community all working together to elevate bilingual and special programs from mediocre measures of educational innovations to opportunities for quality education for *all children*.

Bibliography

Bureau of the Census, "Persons of Spanish Origin in the United States," *Population Characteristics* Series P-20, No. 354: March 1979.

Dyer, Esther R. "Children's Media for a Culturally Pluralistic Society" in *Cultural Pluralism and Children's Media,* American Association of School Librarians, 1978.

National Advisory Council for Bilingual Education, Fifth Annual Report, 1980–81. "Prospects for Bilingual Education in the Nation."

Pifer, Alan. "Bilingual Education and the Hispanic Challenge," in *Education for the Hispanic,* 6: Fall 1980.

Early Childhood Centers
Three Models

Ellin Greene

Within the last twenty years, public library service to preschool children, parents, and professional child caregivers has expanded to a remarkable degree. The research and writings of Benjamin Bloom[1] of the University of Chicago and Burton White,[2] director of the Preschool Project at Harvard University, which emphasized the importance of the early years in learning and the parent as the child's first teacher, and the civil rights movement which demanded compensatory educational programs for children of economically poor blacks, brought about a change in attitude toward early childhood programs.

With the initiation of federally-funded Head Start programs in 1965, children's librarians found their expertise in children's literature and storytelling in high demand by staff of these programs. They also found that the preschoolers in these programs were not used to being read to, and that simpler books, such as Munari's *Jimmy Has Lost His Cap* (World Publishing, 1954), were needed to hold their attention. In time, publishers began publishing more books for toddlers who were not ready for longer, more literary stories.

By the 1970s the traditional library preschool story-time for 3- to-5-year-olds (developed in the '30s) had been extended to younger children (18 months to 3 years old) through toddler hours and services to new parents. The highly successful "Catch 'em in the Cradle" and "Sharing Literature with Children"[3] programs started by the Orlando (Florida) Public Library are such programs. A recent survey conducted by Ann Carlson, as part of her doctoral study at Columbia University School of Library Service, indicated that public libraries in 45 of the 50 states offer some form of literature-sharing programs for children under the age of three.[4]

The quintessence of public library service to the young child is the center specifically designed to meet the needs and interests of preschoolers and their caregivers. Five such centers were identified in the literature[5][6][7] or in the files of the Preschool Services and Parent Education Committee of the Association for Library Service to Children (ALSC) of the American Library Association. All five centers opened between 1972 and 1978. They are (1) the Media Library for Preschoolers of the Erie Public Library, Erie, Pennsylvania; (2) the Preschool Adventure Library of the Cambria County Library System, Johnstown, Pennsylvania; (3) the Center for Discovery of the Public Library of Columbus and Franklin County, Columbus, Ohio; (4) the Gail Borden Public Library Children's Center, Elgin, Illinois; and (5) the New York Public Library's Early Childhood Resource and Information Center in New York City.

Interest in these centers led to a comparative study, the subject of this paper. The purpose of the study was to find out the current status of the centers, and to compare them in regard to the following aspects: (1) origin and purpose; (2) scope of the collections and types of services; (3) ways in which this innovative service differs from traditional services to preschoolers. The study also aimed to identify (1) factors that contribute to the success or failure of a center; (2) factors to consider before starting a center; (3) competencies needed by a center's staff; (4) the implications of the need for such competencies for library education.

Methodology

A two-part questionnaire was sent to the director of each center, or, in the case of the now defunct Media Library for Preschoolers (MLP), to the present coordinator of children's services.

Part I of the questionnaire was open-ended, and attempted to elicit the director's or coordinator's attitude toward this type of library service, his or her perception of the goals and objectives of the center, and opinions on the kind of education that best prepares staff for working in an early-childhood center. Part II asked for descriptive and statistical data. Data for the defunct center were obtained from the present director of the Erie County Library System; files of this center were made available, and telephone interviews with the present coordinator of children's services and former staff members of the Media Library were held.

The questionnaire and telephone interviews were supplemented by visits to each of the three centers discussed. (Two of the centers turned out to be so specially oriented—the Preschool Adventure Library was a Montessori-based program and toy-lending library; the Center for Discovery is oriented to serve "disadvantaged preschool children and handicapped children who are chronically or developmentally preschool-aged"—that it was decided not to include them.)

Profiles

• **The Media Library For Preschoolers** (MLP) was the outcome of a study made by Kenneth G. Sivulich, then Director of the Erie Metropolitan Library, and Dale W. Craig, then Extension Librarian. The purpose of their study was to discover the public library needs of preschoolers in Erie. Based on the findings of the study it was decided that a *multimedia* center would best satisfy the needs of young users, since few were readers. In an interview published in *American Libraries,* Craig states that the MLP was designed "to introduce preschoolers to the library, to channel their curiosity with stimulating media experience, and to provide an alternative to structured preschool programs."[8]

The MLP, funded by a 2-year grant from the Library Services and Construction Act, was located on the first floor of a building formerly occupied by a local bank, six blocks south of the main library and easily accessible by public transportation. A facility was selected away from the main library because of lack of suitable space in that building. Theodore Pettersen, a media specialist and library administrator with an undergraduate degree in biological sciences and a graduate degree in pupil personnel services, was appointed director. Additional staff included a children's librarian, a media technician, supporting staff, and students in a work-study program who worked up to 15 hours a week.

When the MLP opened to the public on November 20, 1972, it was hailed as the prototype of public library services to young children. Public reaction was overwhelming. Within the first three months of operation over 1400 preschoolers registered for library cards and over 7200 items were borrowed by 2400 users. The average visit to the library lasted between one and $1^{1}/_{2}$ hours. A majority (68%) of the children using the facility were between the ages of two and five, 12% were under age two, and 20% were ages five and six.

The writer's first impression of the MLP was of a large open space divided, not by walls, but by activity. A parents' lounge furnished with comfortable chairs, books and magazines on parenting, and disposable diapers and hot coffee were available. For the children there was a "Listening Cave" with a built-in speaker for music, stories, etc.; a "whatever-you-want-it-to-be" platform, designed and built by a local architect; an animal corner with live animals—hamsters, gerbils, mice, rabbits, turtles, etc.; books, toys, audiovisual materials everywhere. A former bank vault had been converted into a story hour room; the vault door was kept open so that the children could see the tumblers, and the inside of the vault was decorated with Dr. Seuss and Sesame Street characters drawn on the walls by a local artist. Children and parents were playing together; some children were watching a filmstrip based on a children's book; others were listening to a story being read aloud, or playing with toys.

Ted Pettersen stressed the importance of the environment, one in which the child and his or her parents felt free to explore, "to wonder and discover." He considered the human element the most important in the program—openness, friendliness, patience, and a love of children. The key words, he stressed, were "spontaneity and awareness of preschoolers." Pettersen defended the center's innovative and controversial feature—the circulation of live animals—saying it gave children "insight into the mystery of life" and "encouraged responsibility."

He emphasized that the Media Library was not a babysitting service: an adult must be present, and he or she was free to participate in the many programs planned for parents. These included lectures, films, and craft activities. Lecture topics ranged from selecting toys to the effects of television on children. A Parent Handbook introduced parents to the services of the Media Library. The staff compiled many bibliographies, not only of books, but also of places to visit and things to do with young children in the Erie area. Volunteers, ranging in age from 12 to 65, worked under the guidance of a local volunteer agency. They read to children, taped and edited children's literature for the "Dial-a-Story" line, conducted

---

Media Library for Preschoolers

Center: Media Library for Preschoolers, Erie Public Library, Erie, Pa.

Type of community: Urban

Population served: 125,000

Opened: November 19, 1972

Source of original funding: Library Services & Construction Act grant of $199,000 over a 2-year period. The first year's grant of $99,500 included the cost of renovation and large equipment. The second year's grant for the same amount included the cost of evaluating the project

Quarters: Downtown Erie, on first floor of a commercial building formerly occupied by a bank; six blocks south of the main library and easily accessible by public transportation

Hours open: 38 hours per week. Open Su, M, T, F, Sa, including some evening hours; on W, Th, closed to the public. Open for group visits

Staff: 2 professionals; 4 full-time clerks; volunteers

Special features: Animal corner with live animals for lending, listening cave (special environment on wheels with built-in speakers for enjoying music, stories, etc.); climbing platforms; rockers; a "whatever-you-want-it-to-be" platform; tent canopies for viewing films and filmstrips; "Parents Playpen" (equipped with lounge furniture, TV set, coffee books and magazines on parenting disposable diapers); bank vault converted into a story hour room with Dr. Seuss and Sesame Street characters drawn on walls

1982 materials budget: NA

Materials: Books, recordings, filmstrips, puzzles, toys, games, multimedia kits, live animals. (No figures available.)

Programs: Story times twice a day, craft activities, "Dial-a-story," film programs, parent/child programs, and workshops and seminars for adults

story hours, and gave programs in the creative and performing arts. The Media Library offered a course, "Exploring Childhood," for 7th to 12th graders. This offered an opportunity for students to learn about child development and experience working with young children.

When I visited the Media Library for Preschoolers in 1974, project funds were ending and the center was to be relocated in the Main Library. An information sheet for the public stated: "The services of the Media Library will continue as part of the total services of the Children's Department of the Erie Metropolitan Library once the federal funding has expired. Since the response from the community has been so overwhelmingly favorable, it would be impossible to end the service completely." The staff expressed concern about the consequences of the move and their concerns were borne out when the Main Library was unable to assimilate the innovative service in its tradition-bound setting. Today, only fragments of the collections remain.

• **The Gail Borden Public Library's Children's Center** in Elgin, Illinois opened on January 13, 1978. The library already had a strong children's program, but two grants afforded funds for additional space and resources, as well as staff to develop an innovative service and creative programming for young children and their parents. The Local Public Works Act of 1976 provided a grant for the remodeling of the library's original meeting room (40' × 52') and the addition of a sky-lighted atrium (24' × 18'), thus creating the new Children's Center. A Library Services and Construction Act grant matched funds expended from the local library budget for a two-year period; this made possible an extensive expansion of the collection and the addition of one professional and one part-time clerk. The library matched this staffing.

When the federal funds expired, the library retained the Children's Center and its staff of two full-time professionals and two part-time clerks, evidence of its support and commitment to the program. The regular library budget does not allow for experimenting, but the Center's director, Mary Greenwalt, feels there is less need for experimentation at this point. Relying on experience and user response, buying priorities have been set; fewer toys are purchased and emphasis is given to those that are used in the library, have developmental value, and which may be too expensive for home purchase. Cassette/book kits and records, the most popular of the non-book media, make up the largest percentage of the audiovisual acquisitions. The Center has acquired audiovisual equipment and a piano.

The goal of the Children's Center is "to establish a lifetime habit of library use." The director described the Children's Center as "an environment where parents and teachers can work with preschool children to create and support opportunities for intellectual and social growth . . . it is designed for adults and children communicating and interacting with each other."

The Center is located on the main floor of the library, diagonally across from the Youth Room, which serves children six years and older. When the Center first opened it served children from infants through age seven, but it soon became apparent to the staff that first and second graders are physically too big for the room and that their interests demand a wider range of books. Consequently, a major portion of their materials and activities was moved to the Youth Room. The Children's Center now concentrates on serving preschoolers and kindergarteners and their caregivers.

The Children's Center is an inviting area dominated by a playhouse/climber/slide, a favorite spot for the preschoolers but a controversial item among visiting librarians. Perhaps because most of the furniture is fixed rather than movable, the Children's Center has a neater, more orderly look than the Erie MLP. There is a pleasant hum, and the users—both adult and children—obviously feel very much at home. Like the Media Library for Preschoolers, the Children's Center is divided into activity areas for browsing among its 8000 books and over 1500 non-book items. The Parents' Corner contains a permanent collection of about fifty books on parenting which is supplemented with a rotating collection of 150 titles from the adult services department. Other materials in this section include magazines, pamphlets, and a resource file on health and

---

Children's Center

Center: Children's Center, Gail Borden Public Library, Elgin, Ill.

Type of community: Urban

Population served: 70,000

Opened: January 13, 1978

Source of original funding: Local Public Works grant in 1976. A Library Services & Construction Act grant of $410,000 over a 2-year period covered extensive remodeling in the basement, meeting rooms, art gallery, rest rooms, kitchen, and elevator as well as construction of the Children's Center. Estimated cost of Center: $117,000

Quarters: In main library, diagonally across from the Youth Services Room, on the first floor

Hours open: 68 hours per week. Open daily, and some evening hours

Staff: 4 professionals; 4 part-time paraprofessionals cover both the Children's Center and the Youth Services Room

Special features: Playhouse/climber/slide; story pit; puppet platform; dress-up cupboard; craft activity space; rockers; piano; live animals in cages (not for lending); plants

1982 materials budget: $10,000

Materials: 8000 children's books, 700 recordings. 100 filmstrips, 450 puzzles, 200 toys and games, 50 puppets, 200 books on parenting

Programs: Toddler hours, story hours for 3- to 5-year-olds, craft programs, song and rhythmic activities, film programs, parent/child programs, workshops and seminars for adults

recreational services for children available in the community, an annually updated booklet with information about area nursery schools and day care centers, and a weekly hand-out card of "Hints for Parents."

A survey made in 1979 showed a dramatic increase in the number of preschoolers and adults using the library (51% and 124% respectively), and in the circulation of books and nonbook materials (30% and 100% respectively). A recent survey, taken five years after the Center opened, shows even greater gains—the Children's Center is thriving. The library board, administration, and staff are committed to the concept of a center for preschoolers and supportive of the wide variety of activities that encourage reading readiness and media awareness for preschoolers.

The Children's Center is viewed as an integral part of the library and its services. There is space to accommodate the sounds and movement that preschool activities generate. The staff have enthusiasm, stamina, and expertise to work with preschoolers. The director has an undergraduate degree in education and a graduate degree in library science. Her assistants have degrees in early childhood, education, or librarianship. The director remarked: "We have had the Children's Center for five years now, and the staff and the public take the facility somewhat for granted. I believe the Center is an important and vital community resource. At worst the Children's Center is a babysitting service for adults when they leave to select books in the adult department; at best it is a rich learning environment for caring parents and their preschool children. It serves a significant cross-section of the community, racially, culturally, and economically. We probably do not offer as many opportunities for parent education as originally planned, but I make no apology for this. We have come to realize our expertise is in the selection and use of children's media. We sponsor workshops and seminars in this area, and we serve the media needs of two colleges, two senior high schools, and a YWCA and a YMCA and other community agencies which offer courses for parents and childcare givers."

• **The Early Childhood Resource and Information Center** (ECRIC) of the New York Public Library is located on the second floor of the Hudson Park Branch in west Greenwich Village. Its neighbors include New York University, the New School for Social Research and the Little Red School House. The community residents are politically active, highly educated, articulate, and are staunch supporters of the Center.

The Center is the brainchild of Barbara Rollock, Coordinator of Children's Services at the New York Public Library, and opened on October 26, 1978, Original funding came from a bequest by the poet and children's book author, Mary Agnes Miller. Mrs. Rollock wrote up the proposal as a one-year demonstration project. Support was so high by the end of the year, it would have been inconceivable for the library to close the center.

Much of the credit goes to the director, Hannah Nuba Scheffler, a former staff member who has a master's degree in library science and is currently studying for a doctorate in early childhood from New York University; she was persuaded to return from early retirement to set it up. Mrs. Scheffler is assisted by a full-time professional, a half-time professional, a part-time clerk, and a part-time page. An advisory committee composed of 185 persons—educators, librarians, psychologists, health care providers, and parents—lends strong support. Approximately 35 members attend the bi-monthly meetings—a nucleus—plus those who come whenever they can (some live at a considerable distance from the city). Members do whatever needs to be done, from canvassing local politicians to giving workshops or writing articles.

Unlike the two centers described in which the emphasis is on parent-child interaction, the New York Public Library Early Childhood Resource and Information Center is oriented toward serving adults—"parents (single, teenage, grand, foster, prospective) as well as those who work in the fields of early childhood education, day care, Head Start, family day care, pre-kindergarten, and who are health professionals, babysitters, family-life educators, librarians, childcare workers, teachers, and social workers." Over 14,000 adults from all over the world visited the center in 1982.

Early Childhood Resource & Information Center

Center: Early Childhood Resource & Information Center, The New York Public Library, New York, N.Y.

Type of community: Urban/suburban NYC and tri-state area (N.Y., N.J., Conn.)

Population served: 7,000,000 plus

Opened: October 26, 1978

Source of original funding: Bequest of $50,000 from poet and children's author, Mary Agnes Miller

Quarters: Located on second floor of the Hudson Park branch in west Greenwich Village. Separate entrance

Hours open: 27 hours per week; open Tu-Sa, closed Su, M. No evening hours

Staff: 2.5 professionals; 1 part-time clerk; 1 part-time page

Special features: Family Room with toys, dolls, building blocks, a housekeeping corner, rockers and rocking horses, a climber slide, playpen, plus music, art, science, and math corners

1982 materials budget: $15,000

Materials: 6000 items for adults—includes 1000 books and magazines in the parenting collection, 29 recordings, 6 filmstrips, 30 films, 4500 items for children—includes 25 recordings, 40 games and toys in the Family Room

Programs: Toddler hours, parent/child activities, workshops and seminars for adults. Parents' Hotline, video programs in process

ECRIC offers three major services: (1) a resource collection of over 6,000 books, pamphlets, periodicals, recordings, films and filmstrips on early childhood, and a browsing collection of over 4500 items tor children. The focus is on materials "that promote the child's growth in a variety of ways. especially in language development and preliterary skills."

(2) A Family Room, an area that is arranged to encourage interaction between child and caregiver. This area includes a picture-book nook, a dramatic play space, music, art, science, and math corners, infant and toddler toys, playpens, infant walkers, rocking horses and rocking chairs, and a climber slide. The area is used as a place for parents and children to play together, or for children to play in while their parents attend a workshop or seminar presented at the other end of the room. The circulation desk separates the Family Room from the "library" where the resource collection is housed and the workshop/seminars take place. There are no dividing walls, so children in the Family Room are visible to the staff or parents at all times.

(3) An ongoing program of workshops and seminars that are conducted by educators and practitioners who contribute their time and expertise to the center. Four or five workshop/seminars are held each week. Recent programs included "The Language of Stories," by Dr. Jerome Bruner; "What Every Child Needs From His Parents," by Dr. Louise Ames; and "The Cultural and Political Context of Child Development: Fantasy and Reality," by Dr. Joseph Church. An annual conference in October presents an opportunity for elected officials, civic leaders, and the general public to get together to discuss issues and policies that affect the well-being of children. The center is in the process of developing video programs for home use and establishing a telephone "hot line" service for parents.

Recently the center published *Resources for Early Childhood: An Annotated Bibliography and Guide for Educators, Librarians, Health Care Professionals, and Parents,* edited by Hannah Nuba Scheffler, with contributions by members of the Advisory Committee (Garland, 1983).

Comparisons

The profiles of each center reveal many commonalities as well as significant differences. All three centers were established in urban areas. This suggests that only a fairly large system would have sufficient budget and staff to support a center. All three required a substantial initial financial outlay and received support from either a private bequest or federal funding.

The types of materials found in the centers are similar— books, recordings, films, filmstrips, puppets, puzzles, toys, multimedia kits, and learning games. The Early Childhood Resource and Information Center has the largest collection of materials for adult users and is more a "library" in the traditional sense.

Each center is or was a facility specifically designed to meet the needs of young children. The centers were developed as media libraries, based on the theories of Piaget, Montessori, and other developmental psychologists which stress that a child's first learning is sensory-motor oriented.

Two of the three centers are primarily oriented to parent-child interaction. One, the Early Childhood Resource and Information Center, is oriented toward parents and professional child care-givers, but has a Family Room designed for interaction between child and adult. This center is open on Saturdays, but not in the evenings, whereas the defunct Media Library for Preschoolers was open on Saturday and Sunday and weekday evenings for the convenience of working parents, as is the Children's Center.

The centers offer similar programs—story times, song and rhythmic activities for the children; parent-child programs, and workshop/seminars for adults (see table). The Media Library for Preschoolers emphasized informal adult-child interaction stimulated by the media environment. The Children's Center also emphasizes informal adult-child interactions, but in addition offers structured programs for toddlers. The Early Childhood Resource and Information Center has only recently initiated a structured program for toddlers. "Mommy, Daddy and Me at the Library" consists of stories "designed to foster emerging reading skills and language development" and related activities, such as dance movement, music, art, or dramatic play. ECRIC's strength lies in its collections and its workshops and seminars which offer parents and professional child caregivers an opportunity to interact with experts in the field and to keep up with the latest theories in developmental psychology. These programs are open to the public without charge.

All three centers share a similar philosophy of service to preschoolers and their caregivers. All consider this a part of *total* library service to the community. The Media Library for Preschoolers was the most innovative of the three, both in concept and physical arrangement; it was also the only center that was physically separated from its parent organization.

Observations

Formal evaluations were conducted by two of the three centers. These were highly positive. Even where there was no formal evaluation (as in the case of the Early Childhood Resources and Information Center), public response has been highly enthusiastic. The staff of all three centers rated this type of service superior to traditional library service to preschoolers. Why, then, have two of the centers flourished while the Media Library for Preschoolers has gone out of existence?

The failure of the Media Library for Preschoolers seems due to at least three factors, in addition to loss of funding: (1) relocation; (2) loss of original staff; (3) political considerations. When federal funding ended, the Media Library was moved into the main library where the lower level of the library was renovated to accommodate it on a smaller scale. The staff was kept intact for a year. At that time the city and county libraries decided to merge. The city library had been under the jurisdiction of the Board of Education. When the city and county libraries merged, the school district withdrew its financial support. The library director (who was also the co-creator and vital force behind the Media Library for Preschoolers) found his energy and time was absorbed by the political situation and diverted from the Media Library. When both the library director and the director of the Media Library left the system, the center just faded away. Lack of suitable space in the main library building, loss of the original staff, and less staff, severely limited the program. The overall community felt no necessity for the program, but individual users still remember the service favorably and still request that it be reinstated. Mothers report that their children who used the Media Library are "different" from their other children—they enjoy reading more, read more, and use the library more frequently. Since the names of the children who registered at the Media Library are on file it would be possible and interesting—to do a follow-up study.

The necessary ingredients for success of a center seem to be: (1) a library board, administration, and a staff committed to, and supportive of, the concept of a media center offering preschoolers a wide variety of activities that encourage reading readiness. The center is integral to the library's services, not an "extra".

(2) Ample funding over a long enough period of time to establish the service in the public eye. Respondents to the questionnaire cautioned against starting a center without assurance of funding at the end of the grant period. The director of the Children's Center pointed out that once the program is established it is not any more expensive than special services offered to other identifiable library groups.

(3) A physical facility separate from but in proximity to the youth services area; space that can accommodate the sounds and movement that preschool activities generate—a multimedia environment designed to meet the sensory-motor orientation of young children.

(4) Staff which has the patience, stamina, enthusiasm, and expertise to serve preschoolers and their caregivers. This type of service requires expertise in librarianship and in early childhood education. Continuity of staff helps too.

(5) High public awareness and appreciation of the center's services—success comes through public awareness and support. The two existing centers had advisory committees which lent strong support while the centers were getting started.

When asked what are the most important factors to consider before starting a center for preschoolers, the respondents emphasized (1) community need, (2) adequate funding, and (3) qualified staff. Obviously, it is important to assess the needs of the community, to coordinate existing services for young children and their caregivers, and to be assured of adequate funding, before expanding service. Equally important, and sometimes overlooked, is the need for qualified personnel. The best educational background for staff working in a public library for preschoolers, according to all respondents, is early childhood education. Next is experience in library service with an emphasis on programming. Other disciplines checked as important were education, psychology, music, and art. Two respondents emphasized the importance of administrative ability. Staff are expected to be competent in materials evaluation (book and non-book), programming, ability to work with young children, parents, and professionals in the childcare fields. Patience, stamina, and a liking for children are basic. All respondents recommended that universities offer a joint degree in librarianship and early childhood. All noted the necessity of courses in child development, programming, administration and management, as well as courses in library material and services to young children. This response supports the literature which substantiates the need for more adequate preparation for librarians who work with young children.[9] Yet only a few of the 69 accredited library schools in the United States and Canada, judging from their current announcements, offer courses specifically designed for service to young children and their caregivers.

Research indicates that parents expect public libraries to provide service to young children,[10][11] that early childhood educators support the concept,[12] and that there is a relationship between early language experiences, adult-child interaction, play activities, and reading aloud, to the child's interest in reading and use of the public library.[13][14][15][16] The Media Library for Preschoolers may have been too ambitious, but it provided the prototype for future library service to preschoolers.

An increase in the number of young children in the population is projected for 1990. A rising birth rate, especially among older, better-educated parents who are more aware of the importance of the early years in learning, is likely to create increasing demands for high-quality library service to preschoolers. The centers now in operation demonstrate that the public library can offer a supportive but neutral learning environment for young children and their caregivers. Communities planning to construct a new library facility or to engage in a renovation (LSCA Title II funds are once again available after a moratorium of ten years) may want seriously to consider opening a Center to provide this innovative and exciting new development in library service.

References

1. Bloom, Benjamin, ed. *Taxonomy of Educational Objectives.* David McKay, 1956.

2. White, Burton. *Experience and Environment: Major Influences on the Development of the Young Child.* Prentice-Hall, 1973.

3. Peterson. Carol Sue. "Sharing Literature with Children." In *Start Early for an Early Start,* ed. Ferne Johnson. ALA, 1976. p. 100–104.

4. Carlson, Ann. A Nationwide Survey of Librarians' Practices and Attitudes in Serving Children Under Three Years of Age and Their Parents and Caregivers. Doctoral dissertation, School of Library Service, Columbia University, 1983.

5. Shannon, Linda. "Preschool Adventure Library." *School Library Journal* 23, no. 3:25–27 (November 1975).

6. Sivulich, Kenneth G. and Sandra Sivulich. "Media Library for Preschoolers: A Service of the Erie Metropolitan Library." *Top of the News* 31, no. 1:49–54 (November 1974).

7. Savage, Noelle. "Special Report: N.Y.'s Early Childhood Center Serves Mothers and Caretakers." *Library Journal* 108, no. 1:13–14 (January 1983).

8. Craig, Dale. "Preschool Library Service." *American Libraries* 4, no. 3:136 (March 1973).

9. Smardo, Frances A. "Are Librarians Prepared to Serve Young Children?" *Journal of Education for Librarianship* 20, no. 4:274–84 (Spring 1980).

10. Fasick, Adele. "Parents and Teachers View Library Service to Children." *Top of the News* 35, no. 3:309–14 (Spring 1979).

11. Young, Diana. "Parents—Children—Libraries. " *PLA Newsletter* 16 no. 4:16–18 (Winter 1977).

12. Smardo, Frances A. An Analytical Study of the Recommendations of Early Childhood Education Authorities with Regard to the Role of the Public Library in Serving Children from Infancy to Six Years of Age. ERIC Document ED160 222, 1978.

13. Clarke, Margaret M. *Young Affluent Readers.* Heinemann Educational Books, 1976.

14. Clarke-Stewart, K.A., and N. Apfel. "Evaluating Parental Effects on Child Development." In *Review of Research in Education,* ed. Lee Shulman, vol. 6. F.E. Peacock, 1979.

15. Johnson, Ferne O. "Library Services Benefit Preschoolers." *Catholic Library World* 50 no. 5:212–17 (December 1978).

16. Teale, W. "Positive Environments for Learning to Read: What Studies of Early Readers Tell Us." *Language Arts* 55 no. 8:922–32 (November/December 1978).

Home Schoolers:
A Forgotten Clientele?

Jane A. Avner

In his best-seller *Future Shock,* Alvin Toffler asked a jolting question: should education take place in school? Noting the increasing number of well-educated parents, Toffler predicted that "with the move toward knowledge-based industry and the increase of leisure, we can anticipate a small but significant tendency for highly educated parents to pull their children at least part way out of the public education system, offering them home instruction instead."[1] Toffler's prediction was reiterated by John Naisbitt in *Megatrends.* In explaining his position that the self-help movement was supplanting institutional help, Naisbitt stated: "In the 1960's and 1970's the self-help approach to education took the form of creating alternative schools; in the 1980's it will be home education."[2] Today, public libraries all over the United States are noting the presence of home schoolers in their communities. "My guess is that homeschoolers have made quite an impact, especially in the Children's Room," said one Pennsylvania mother who is educating her children at home. "After all, several of us spend long periods there regularly . . . Our children are regulars—and actively involved!"[3]

Although the actual number of children who are taught at home is unknown, estimates range from 10,000 in 1983 to 260,000 in 1986. Spokespersons of the home school movement claim that over one million children who do not attend public or private schools are being taught at home, with a parent as the primary teacher.[4] There are several reasons why exact numbers are difficult to ascertain. First, parents may teach their children at home for one or two years after which they enroll them in a school. Second, the legality of home schooling varies from state to state; in some areas the parents register their children under a simple set of regulations, while other localities make the rules for registration so complicated that the parents don't bother to do so.

Researchers are currently attempting to classify the home schoolers by asking the parents to supply information about themselves and their reasons for rejecting traditional educational channels. The families are located all over the United States, in both urban and rural settings. The majority are traditional families in which the father is the principal wage earner and the mother is at home doing the greater part of the teaching. Many of these parents are well-educated; often they have college degrees and have acquired teaching credentials. The average income varies, with more recent studies indicating a middle-class salary range.

Research shows that parents choose to educate their children at home for a variety of reasons. These families seem to separate into two philosophical camps: ideologues and pedagogues.[5] The ideological or religious group include fundamentalist Christians who are unhappy with what they perceive as the public school's "secular humanist" curriculum; they do not want to integrate secularism into their own way of life. The second, classified as "pedagogical,' are parents who school their children at home because of deep misgivings about the quality of education in formal school settings. They object to large classes and rigid curricula. They feel that children learn more efficiently and are happier on a one-on-one basis.

This two-group division is somewhat artificial; however, parents often cite both reasons for home schooling. Sometimes they teach their children at home because of the nature of their individual child. Perhaps he or she is learning disabled, or has a physical handicap, or is academically gifted. Parents may be concerned that a peer group might be cruel and taunt or shun the child. Another reason might be a significant distance from the home to the nearest school. Still another reason may be the nature of the parent. Whatever their reason or reasons for home schooling, these parents are sincerely committed to their children's education.

Throughout most of history, children were educated at home. Today, parents who make that choice are considered eccentric, radical, or even revolutionary. Perhaps this is because these parents have questioned the accepted wisdom about education: that children learn best in a school setting when taught by a professional.

Home schoolers base their beliefs on two schools of thought which have had an impact on their decision to educate at home. The first is represented by the late John Holt, the founder of Holt Associates in Massachusetts, which publishes a newsletter, *Growing Without Schooling,* directed to home schoolers. Perhaps best known as the author of *How Children Learn* (Pitman, 1967), Holt has written other books in which he criticizes the state of education. For example, in his *Teach Your Own* (Delacorte, 1981), Holt provides a handbook for parents who are frustrated with conventional schooling; he argues that learning should be integrated with the rest of life's activities, and that children learn more productively when they are extremely curious.

The second school is represented by Raymond and Dorothy Moore, both of whom are educators and religious fundamentalists. Since 1979. when their *School Can Wait* was published, they have been conducting seminars, compiling research, and directing the Hewitt-Moore Child Development Center in Washougal, Washington. The Moores argue that children are sent to school far too early. They say that before the age of eight or nine, children have not yet reached what they term the "optimal integrated maturity level," and are happier and more productive at home, with their parents as role models for socialization.

Considerations of the benefits of home schooling naturally lead to an examination of its legality under state and local laws. The right to an education is not guaranteed by the United States Constitution: the Tenth Amendment delegates such powers to the states. States, by enacting compulsory attendance laws, have sought to ensure that each child receives an education.

Historically, according to Judeo-Christian traditions, parents are responsible for the education of their children. Early in the 17th century the governing bodies in England and the American colonies saw the need to enforce the care of children by the parents so as to prepare the children for a position in the workplace. This need to assure the eventual competence of the child led to the enactment of compulsory attendance laws and to the provision of funding for schools.

In the 19th century, during the Industrial Revolution and the influx of immigrants, the states recognized an even greater need to ensure that children attend school. It was thought that the older apprentice system would not be adequate to prepare American youth for more sophisticated technical work, and the children of immigrants needed to learn English to gain an understanding of America's political, social, and economic system. By 1918, every state had passed compulsory school attendance laws.

Subsequently, states gradually shifted toward control of the school curriculum as well, instituting standards for local school systems to follow. The purpose of these standards was to allow all children access to a quality education. The U.S. Supreme Court accepted the states' role in promoting educational consistency in the schools, but on several occasions the Court prevented the states from denying parents educational choices. For example, in *Pierce v. Society of Sisters* (1925), two schools, one private and one parochial, challenged Oregon's compulsory attendance laws, which stated that children must be educated in public schools. In its decision the Supreme Court stated: "the child is not the mere creature of the state; those who nurture him and direct his destiny have the right, coupled with the high duty, to recognize and prepare him for additional obligations."[6]

In its famous 1954 decision, *Brown v. Board of Education,* the Supreme Court reaffirmed its support for compulsory attendance laws, stating that the laws "and the great expenditures for education both demonstrate our recognition of the importance of education to our democratic society."[7] The Court again ruled in favor of parental choice in 1972, when it handed down a decision in *Wisconsin v. Yoder,* supporting the decision of several Amish families to remove their children from school after they had completed the eighth grade. According to the plaintiffs, the compulsory attendance statute violated their First Amendment right to freely practice their religion. The Amish claimed that a secular high school would expose the children, as well as their parents, to censure in the Amish community, thus endangering their hope for salvation.

These Supreme Court decisions show that when considering educational issues, the Court tried to weigh the parents' interest against the interest of the state. This is also the concern of state courts. The question often asked is: "Does the state responsibility for education stand in the way of parental rights of privacy, due process and freedom of religion?" Final legal decisions often address the clarity of the portion of the compulsory attendance law that discusses an alternative to formal schooling.

Although every state allows some form of home schooling, its definition varies from state to state. The least-restrictive laws call only for notification of the school district by home-schooling parents, while the most-restrictive specify curriculum subjects and require that the home-school parent be a certified teacher. In many states the local school district must approve the family's request to conduct school at home. If the compulsory attendance statute is vague or unclear as far as curriculum requirements, interpretive disagreements are likely to enter the court battles. In the past year in Pennsylvania, for example, 50 families were involved in court disputes relating to problems they had getting local approval of their home schooling. U.S. District Judge Edwin M. Kosik of Scranton subsequently threatened to strike down the state's compulsory school attendance law if it wasn't clarified by December 31, 1988. Kosik stated that its description of what constituted a "qualified private tutor" was so vague that school district policies could be arbitrary and discriminatory.[8] On December 21, the state of Pennsylvania passed Act 169, which allows home schooling by parents who file an annual affidavit with the school district superintendent and who compile a portfolio (to be evaluated annually) in which their educational efforts are documented.

Thus it is imperative for parents to be aware of their state's stance on home schooling. Parents can obtain information about the legal issues of home schooling from several organizations: The Home School Legal Defense Association (P.O. Box 2091, Washington, DC 20013) and the National Guide to Home School Attorneys and Organizations (Christian Liberty Academy, 502 W. Euclid Ave., Arlington Heights, IL 60004).

Home schools are as different as the families who operate them; however, common characteristics can be inferred from the parent contributions to local home-schooling newsletters and from case studies done by researchers.

Many families use a prepared curriculum, such as the Christian-oriented Hewitt-Moore Program or the non-denominational study courses developed and used by the Calvert School in Baltimore. Whether religious or secular, the curriculum appears to be only a starting point; parents who learn of them usually choose to pursue their individual interests. For example, courses in the home school could lead children into the garden to study botany, or to the local zoo to study zoology, and to the neighborhood public library to get materials to supplement the curriculum.

Home schooling publications addressed to parents stress reading aloud to children, often mentioning specific stories others have used. In *The Three R's At Home* one learns of the Murphy family, who don't use textbooks or workbooks but rather, in their words, "books you find around the house, or buy at yard sales, or get out of libraries." They then read books "upteen" times and played matching games so that their children can identify specific words.[9] I found that many families begin with a mathematics textbook, but then discover that lessons can be learned through everyday experiences—shopping and checkbook balancing, for example, can help their students comprehend money management, while home repairs make for an excellent primer in measurement. In families with several children, the older children often teach the younger ones, providing both age groups with a positive learning experience.

From some of the case studies, it appears that formal learning takes place in the mornings, while independent study occurs in the afternoon. In spite of a shorter period of time for formal instruction, achievement test scores generally show that, compared to children taught in conventional settings, children educated at home test at comparable or higher levels.

How long do children go to school at home? Again, this varies. Reports of home-taught teenagers going off to college are beginning to appear in popular magazines. Other families keep their children at home just during the early years.

The public library has a responsibility to all its patrons; home schoolers are no exception. The library should be aware of both school district and state policies relating to education at home. They should welcome home schooling families and help them by stocking some of the books parents are likely to request (see list below), and by encouraging and reaching out to them. Regular programming—story hours for preschoolers, summer reading clubs and craft and film programs for school-aged children—should find a ready audience. Special programming will, of course, depend on the availability of the library's staff and time. Most important is the provision of excellent reference service. Librarians who have served home schoolers find the experience to be especially rewarding, as they watch children pursue an interest with a passion, and see parents check out armloads of books, videotapes and other media. I asked one home-schooling parent, Paula Christensen, if she used a formal curriculum in teaching her children. "The library," she replied, "is our curriculum."

The relationship between the home schoolers and the public library is not elucidated by the many guides to home schooling that parents borrow or purchase. It is, however, very clearly stated in the writings of parents and children in the home school movement. Nine-year-old Jennifer Lerew, for example, has been conducting preschool story hours at her local library in Pennsylvania for the last three years. She chooses her own books, rhymes and fingerplays, and sometimes uses a "lap theater" (which contains the characters and props for her story) that she made out of a cardboard box. Testifying in favor of home schooling at a state legislature hearing, Jennifer said of her storytelling sessions: "I am glad I am able to read at our library because it is something I really enjoy doing and because it is something I can do to help my community."[10]

Libraries situated in communities in which home school families are both visible and vocal have initiated many services to this group. In the Issaquah Library, part of the King County (WA) Library System, home schoolers have used the meeting room regularly for support group meetings. Children's Librarian Elise DiGiuseppi, who has done workshops on how to use the library, say they are well attended by homeschool children and their parents. DiGiuseppi notes that the families use more materials, including nonbook items such as videotapes and recordings, than her conventionally schooled patrons. She finds that early reading materials are requested most by the home-schooling families.

Susan Madden, young adult coordinator for the King County Library System, says that she is most impressed by the intense interest the audience shows in library reference materials and library services. She first became aware of home schoolers and their involvement in the public library about six years ago. Since then the library has supplied these patrons with assistance; an information packet is located in branch vertical files. The packet contains a summary of the Washington home schooling law, suggestions for service ideas by local librarians and useful booklists. King County also holds a workshop aimed at home-schooling parents on the use of the library; this is presented intermittently at the system's branch libraries. One of the first bits of information that workshop leaders give to the parents is how to find homeschooling materials in the card catalog. This may not seem very important until one realizes that the Library of Congress subject heading is not "HOME SCHOOLING," but "DOMESTIC EDUCATION." King County also participates in the annual Washington Homeschool Convention, which attracted over 2000 participants last year.

Given the prevalence of the two wage-earner family and the increasing number of one-parent families, it is unlikely that home schooling will ever become the norm. However, its growth in the face of contrary trends demands the attention of librarians. We can recognize and assist these families, and equally important, use this opportunity to further understand the learning process in an individual or small group setting. Armed with this knowledge, learning for all children can be enhanced.

Books for Parents

Ballman, Ray E. *The How and Why of Home Schooling* (Crossway, 1987). $6.95 pbk.
Ballman's stated purpose is to encourage Christian parents to educate at home and to describe how it can be done.
Holt, John. *Teach Your Own* (Dell, 1981). $8.95 pbk.
Holt provides the reader with his philosophy of education and draws from parents' accounts of their home schooling experiences.
Moore, Dorothy and Raymond. *Home Grown Kids* (Word, 1981). $9.95.
———. *Home Spun Schools* (Word 1982). $9.95.

————. *Home School Burnout.* (Wolgemuth & Hyatt, 1988).
The Moores give "how-to" information as well as descriptions of parent experiences in home schooling.

Pride, Mary. *The Big Book of Home Learning* (Crossway, 1986). $17.50 pbk.
This Christian-oriented source book contains personal evaluation of standard curricula as well as names and addresses for recommended materials.

Wallace, Nancy. *Better Than School* (Larson, 1983). $10.95.
A personal account by a family that chose home schooling.

Notes

1. Toffler, Alvin. *Future Shock.* Random House, 1970, p. 349.

2. Naisbitt, John. *Megatrends.* Warner Books, 1982, p. 144.

3. Letter from Sherry Sommers to *Pennsylvania Homeschoolers* #23, Spring 1988, p. 10.

4. Some general articles about home schooling are: Henderson, Nancy, "Teaching Your Kids at Home," *Changing Times* (March 1987), pp. 83–86; Kohn, Alfie, "Home Schooling" *The Atlantic* (April 1988), pp. 20–25; Lines, Patricia M., "An Overview of Home Instruction," *Phi Delta Kappan* (March 1987), pp. 510–517.

5. Many researchers have identified the two groups; the labels "ideologues" and "pedagogues" were used by Jane Ann Van Galen in her unpublished dissertation *Schooling in Private: A Study of Home Education* (Univ. of North Carolina, Chapel Hill, 1986).

6. Pierce v. Society of Sisters, 268 US 510 (1925).

7. Brown v. Board of Education, 74 S. Ct. 686 (1954).

8. Wolf, Don. "Education Panel OKs Home-Schooling," *The Pittsburgh Press* (Oct. 13, 1988), p. B4.

9. Richman, Howard and Susan. *The Three R's at Home.* Pennsylvania Homeschoolers, 1988, p. 87.

10. *Pennsylvania Homeschoolers* #24, Summer 1988, p. 3.

Shining STARS
Public Library Service to
Children in Shelters

Pam Carlson

"**O**kay, everybody got their books? We've got to go. It's almost time for dinner."

Familiar words and a familiar sight in libraries: children checking out books after a library program. But these young readers are not going home to dinner. They are going back to their cottages at the Orangewood Children's Home in Orange County, California, and the words come from staff counselors, not parents. The children are participating in "Library STARS." This program provides neglected and abused children with an introduction to the library and the ways in which its resources and services can help them to cope and enrich their lives when they leave the shelter and return to the community.

A Nontraditional Shelter

In fall 1989, Orange County Public Library was awarded a Library Services and Construction Act grant to provide library services to the Orangewood Children's Home. Orangewood is the primary intake center and shelter for physically abused, sexually molested, and neglected children in Orange County. Approximately 2500 children pass through Orangewood each year, ten percent of the cases reported to the Child Abuse Registry annually. The home provides a confidential and secure environment for the children whose ages range from two days to 18 years. A stay at Orangewood varies from a few days to over a year. Most children eventually return home, or are assigned to foster or group homes, or to a special institution.

Orangewood is not a stereotypical shelter. The architecture is Spanish Colonial, with large cottages for each age group. It has a swimming pool, playing field, and a state-of-the-art gymnasium. The community program specialist and recreation director schedule a host of activities such as game nights, field trips to nearby parks and beaches, life-skill programs for the teens, movies, and even an annual spring prom, to keep the kids busy. The year-round William Lyon School, run by the County Department of Education, serves the educational needs of the children. But even with all these resources, something was lacking—access to a library and the services most children take for granted.

Library STARS (**S**tory **T**imes, **A**ctivities, and **R**eading in **S**helters) was created to fill this need. The practical objectives of the project were to:

1) Provide weekly programs for the target group, ages five through 12, to promote books, reading, and library use;

2) Give each child in that group a book of his or her own to keep "forever and ever";

3) Purchase books to add to existing collections in the cottages;

4) Issue fine-free Orange County Public Library cards for the children's use upon release;

5) Provide training for library staff to continue the weekly programs at the end of the grant period; and

6) Produce a manual for distribution to other library systems desiring to implement a similar program.

After hiring Project Director Pam Carlson and Program Assistant Corinne Tebo, our first step was to research existing library programs to discover if any were similar to ours. We found that many public libraries have outreach programs to low-income families living in hotels and housing projects, while others provide deposit collections in shelters for the homeless. No one, however, was doing exactly what we hoped to do.

Next, we read articles profiling abused children, which helped prepare us to work with Orangewood's residents. We learned that as a result of abuse, children frequently engage in extreme behavior. They may be withdrawn or overly aggressive, easily angered or overly affectionate, defiant or compliant. Social skills may be lacking, making it hard for many of the children to function in a group setting. Education may have been sporadic or even interrupted, so many of these children read below grade level, and self-esteem may suffer. In short, we discovered we would be working with seriously at-risk children.

We realized that building self-esteem would have to be a high priority in everything we did. If we played games everyone needed to be successful. Instructions for crafts had to be simple and very clear, to avoid frustrating the less dexterous. Praise and patience would be required in abundance.

Programs for Multiple Needs

To meet our first goal during the initial grant period, weekly storytimes and library programs were held for the five-to-seven-year-olds, known at Orangewood as the "Preteens," and boys and girls ages eight to twelve, known as "Junior Boys" and "Junior Girls." Programs for both were centered on high-interest themes which varied from "Bears" to "Self-Acceptance" to "Wild West" to "Cinco de Mayo." Nonfiction themes took a look at science tricks, dinosaurs, sports, careers, animals, paper airplanes, and poetry. Some of the Junior programs involved various genres of literature including folk and fairy tales, mysteries, jokes and riddles, poetry, historical fiction, and survival adventures. Still others featured read-alouds. There were movie days when films based on children's books were shown, and the book and film compared afterward. The programs were varied to appeal to different interests and learning styles. Because of the transience of the population, each program was self-contained with no carryover from week to week. We discovered that flexibility and adaptability are necessary qualities for all staff.

Some of the programs involved professional, paid performers, although grant funds could not be used for this type of expenditure. Orangewood's support auxiliary, La Casa, funds programs and special projects for the children. John Aliberti, one of the community program specialists, enthusiastically presented our requests to the board. Thus, we were able to have a jousting tournament presented by a local dinner show in conjunction with our summer reading program. We also celebrated Cinco de Mayo, a holiday observed by Mexicans everywhere, and National Library Week in April.

Following each library activity the eight-to-twelve year olds were allowed to check out two books brought in from nearby OCPL branches. Allowing children to choose and borrow books displays an important element of trust. One counselor commented that this was perhaps the first time some of the children had ever been allowed to borrow anything. To be told that we trusted that they would return these books increased their sense of responsibility. The kids felt good about themselves each time they returned the books and were allowed to check out more.

Getting Staff Support

Learning to work cooperatively with shelter staff is important, as their support can make or break your program. Fortunately, the majority of the counselors were supportive from the start because of the good they thought we could do "their kids," and the few who had reservations were won over when they saw the enthusiastic response of the children. Staff always attend the programs since they are responsible for the children, and they deal with any discipline problems that occur.

Because of our good rapport with shelter staff, we were able to add a special series of storytelling programs to our lineup of activities. Called the "Superb Storytellers," this is a rotating group of two boys and two girls in fourth through sixth grades, trained to read stories and put on puppet shows for older preschoolers.

The training is not complicated. The storytellers are chosen on Monday and they select their stories that morning. They practice the stories in class and back in their units until Wednesday when the stories are shared with the older preschool group. Each Friday during the school's weekly awards program, the storytellers receive a special certificate and a candy bar of their choice. Although they like the candy and the chance to get out of class, the storytellers particularly enjoy this time because, in their own words, "It's fun to tell stories," and "I like the little kids; they're so cute."

The program benefits everyone. The preschoolers learn how to listen to stories and participate in an enjoyable group experience. The storytellers are building reading skills and confidence in public speaking. They also receive an incredible boost to their self-esteem. Storytellers are not necessarily chosen for academic ability; in fact, some of the least obvious choices make the best storytellers because they appreciate the chance to do something responsible. It may also be the first time they've been made aware that the ability to read is truly important. For them, the Storyteller Award may be the only positive recognition they receive while at Orangewood. They get cheers from teachers, staff, and all of the kids at the Friday assembly, as well as applause from the preschoolers after their stories.

Because of the success of the "Superb Storytellers," storytelling has been expanded to include other ages. On an experimental basis, first and second graders read simple stories and sang to the toddlers. This was not as successful as we had hoped, mainly because the attention span of the toddlers is so short, and the readers read a little too slowly to capture their interest. To allow this group to keep on reading, we now have them record their stories to make "customized read-alongs."

Our high school students read to the kindergarten through third grade unit at their Tuesday night storytime. They love the smaller children, who in turn enjoy the special attention. The teenage girls even planned and conducted a spring storytime for the older preschool unit, which included stories, a game, and an egg hunt.

Some read-along stories have been recorded by older children in both Spanish and English. Readers often add their own unique sound effects to indicate when a page is to be turned. The books and cassettes are kept in the library and may be used by the kids and teachers.

A Book of Their Own

As much as possible during the grant project, we followed the regular calendar of activities at OCPL, including Children's Book Week and of course, summer reading. Our theme for summer 1990 in Orange County was "In Days of Old, When Tales Were Told." Each child's name was displayed along the game board. To make the game easy to play and fair for everyone, we used one marker which was moved along the path leading to "Castle Read." Everyone received the same reading incentives at the same time. New children could be easily incorporated into the activity using this format and there were no disruptions when children left.

Most branches have a summer reading party at the end of their program. We were no exception, and we presented a jousting tournament on the baseball field, complete with two knights and a horse. Every child was invited to the program, from infants through high school. We also had individual parties for each of our targeted groups, where each child received a book in recognition of having participated in the reading program.

Our second and third project goals were to allow each child to own a book and to improve the small collections already in existence in the cottages. These books were purchased with grant funds, and every new child received a book during his or her first library program. Children chose their own books from titles available in English and Spanish, on all reading levels. Many children couldn't believe they would be allowed to keep the books. Often, younger children claimed to be new each week to get another book. Those who were readmitted usually still had the book they had received originally. Books were also given away at Easter, Christmas, and on birthdays.

Staff reported that the books seemed to have a powerful impact on some children. One six-year-old boy who had been sent to his room for a discipline problem, watched as the room was emptied of all his possessions to prevent his destruction of them. But when a counselor put the boy's "Library STARS" book on the pile to be removed, the child said, "No, you can't take that. It's mine. The library ladies gave it to me." It was the one thing that he was allowed to keep with him and after a while, he calmed down. The name of that book? *Harry and the Terrible Whatzit* by Dick Gackenbach (Houghton). This same boy would recommend it to the new kids as the best book to choose during the weekly book giveaways.

Even nonreaders enjoy receiving books. Being able to choose their own titles is very important, one way of being independent. Almost every activity at Orangewood is done in a group. The kids eat together, go to school together, and most have roommates in the units. The kids have been uprooted from family and friends and placed in a strange environment with people they have never met, and are expected to live that way until the court decides their fate. It's an unnatural way to live. So when the children enjoy and are motivated by something like the library programs or receiving books, it's encouraging for everyone.

In meeting our fourth goal, the distribution of fine-free library cards for children to use at OCPL branches after their release from Orangewood, we ran into some logistical problems. The mechanics held us up for awhile as we tried to decide what would be the most efficient way to distribute the cards. Because we did not know where the children would be when they left, we could not enter that address information into our patron maintenance file. We finally decided to enter the children by name only and then put a block on the card which would prevent items from being circulated before we obtained a complete address. All cards received the designation "Library STARS" to help us record circulation statistics and alert us to possible overdues. Although the cards were fine-free, we did want to retrieve as many items as possible! Notices were sent to each branch explaining how the process worked and we also sent letters to the other public libraries in Orange County as well as those in nearby Los Angeles, Riverside, and San Bernardino Counties.

The library cards are filed in specially created exit packets, held with each child's personal property until the child is released. The packets are produced in both English and Spanish and each contains a letter to the child's caregiver which explains the STARS program and encourages visits to the library. There is also a graded booklist for children, one for adults, activity papers based on Caldecott and Newbery winners, star bookmarks, maps to all OCPL branches, generic calendars of children's activities at each branch, and a simple Dewey Decimal subject list.

Keeping It Going

The grant project was scheduled to end on September 30, 1990. However, our fifth goal in the "Library STARS" grant was the continuation of weekly programs for our target group of ages five through 12. Each OCPL branch was to be responsible for conducting six programs a year. To help the OCPL staff prepare for this, three training sessions were held, entitled "Taking Your Show on the Road to Orangewood—Parts 1, 2, and 3." The sessions were structured to be fun as well as informative, and brought together Branch, Adult, and Children's Librarians for training.

The first session was an overall look at the project. Regular updates had been provided at system-wide meetings and staff were invited to visit early in the program, but now the time was drawing near for the branches to take over the project and there were a few nervous people.

The tour of the facility impressed everyone. Orangewood serves as a model of what a shelter of this type can be, due to the cooperation of the private and public sectors in the planning and building process. Being able to see firsthand all of the work that has gone into providing a homelike atmosphere rather than an institutional environment assuaged the anxieties of many OCPL staff.

Handouts at this first session included opportunities for branches to sign up for branch tours of Orangewood, and special events where we would bring the kids to the branches. There were also tips and hints for program planning to make the process as enjoyable as possible.

Training sessions were scheduled approximately a month apart to give staff time to digest what had been presented and provide feedback. Session number two concentrated on working with the Junior Boys and Girls. At this time, we spoke of ways to build self-esteem among the kids. We also had some of our adult services librarians present program ideas based on their own interests and hobbies, reinforcing the fact that they too, would be involved in the project.

The final session was geared to working with the Preteens. Various children's librarians spoke on their areas of expertise, including how to choose age-appropriate books, create and tell flannel and magnet board stories, and lead crafts and creative dramatics. A display of storytime props purchased during the grant period, including puppets, a puppet stage, games, resource books, and theme boxes, provided more ideas. The theme boxes are complete canned storytimes put together by the project assistant. They contain story books, puppets, craft materials and patterns, program suggestions, outlines, and other material relating to the theme of that particular box.

The workshops reassured many OCPL staff and allowed them to ask questions and brainstorm. The thought of assuming responsibility for the program lost some of its scariness and some eager beavers began immediately to plan their programs.

STARS Shining Brightly

With the end of the grant period quickly approaching we began to close out the grant. The final project goal, the manual to be produced and made available to other library systems, was targeted for publication in late 1992. The final narrative and budget reports were completed and the statistics were in: over 100 library/storytime programs had been presented; the Superb Storytellers group was established, 1,494 books had been purchased for giveaways and additions to cottage collections (also purchased were resource books, Scholastic Big Books, audiocassettes, and library skills and *Reading Rainbow* videos), over 200 books were donated by OCPL Friends of the Library groups, and 125 library cards had been issued.

During the last week of the grant period, a tea was held at Orangewood in honor of the "Library Ladies," at which a commendation was delivered by the Orange County Board of Supervisors. along with letters of appreciation from Orangewood and Lyon School staff. The children presented special handmade thank you cards. Even though it would continue in a modified form, it was apparent that no one wanted the program in its established format to end.

But what could be done? Lynn Eisenhut, children's services coordinator for OCPL, and Emily Jackson, programs administrator, continued to stress the value of the program to library administration. Meetings were held between OCPL and the Orangewood administration. Funding was found to continue the project director's position for one month, then another until it achieved its current two-thirds-time permanent status. Although the assistant's position could not be retained, a dedicated book budget was created. The program continues without disruption, and that is of primary importance.

Once the Orangewood librarian position became permanent, it was possible to expand the program. Toddler storytimes have been added to the existing programs, along with weekly library times for high school boys and girls. Branches are still responsible for programs at the rate of two per year. A "mini-branch" has been established at Orangewood, located in a former classroom. This library has been "adopted" by various community groups who have donated paperback racks, books, and funds to purchase books. A local library supply company donated both shelving and the labor to install it. The children can now check out books and magazines from their own library rather than have them brought in from branches.

The success of "Library STARS" can be summed up in the words of its participants. "I've learned a lot from you guys. You helped me learn how to read better. I like to read now." (Brian, age 11); "Now I can read out loud to other people." (Melissa, age 9); "I'm proud I could do things I didn't think I could do." (Helen, age 12). The children have discovered that reading can be fun and that libraries are places where they feel welcome. Because of the "Library STARS" program, the readers of Orangewood Children's Home are shining brightly.

"It's the Best Thing in the World!"
Rural Children Talk about Reading

Constance A. Mellon

When I was a library school student—at a time my adult children refer to as "back in the Dark Ages"—the main requirement in the children's literature course was to read and evaluate 100 children's books. "Evaluate" meant to read, summarize, and quote from published reviews. I now teach in a library school program and one of the courses I teach is children's literature. In designing that course, it seemed to me that something would be left out if that sole focus of the course was children's *books*. What would be left out was children. So, in my course, students read fewer books; however, several assignments require them to observe and talk with children. One assignment in particular, the reading interest survey, seems to uncover the most interesting information and to spark the most spirited discussions. The following vignettes will illustrate why.

A Family Interview

The setting for Rosa Sydney's interview was the reading room of a small branch library in a city of about 45,000. The area in which this library is located had recently been in the news. The residents, mostly poor black families, were waging a war with drug dealers and their victims to keep violence and the corruption of the young away from their streets.

Rosa sat at a low, round table with the "Price" family seated around her. As part of her assignment, she talked informally with the children of the family about their attitudes toward reading. Rosa described her experiences this way. Shaunda is an active six-year-old who loves to read. Her mother and her oldest brother read to her a great deal. Her favorite books are *Cinderella* and *Little Red Riding Hood*. Shaunda likes reading because it's fun and because she sees her mother and her brother reading.

Michael, the middle child, is eight years old. Having attended the neighborhood elementary school, Michael was concerned about what library he will be using when he returns to a different school in the fall.

Alonzo, the eldest child, is eleven, a rather withdrawn child. He thinks reading is fun, but he is getting older and his mind is on other things. Even though Alonzo's mother read to him just a few years ago, he now reads on his own. His favorite books are those related to sports.

The "Price" family displayed a high interest in reading; however, I found the reason that they had no library card heart-breaking. They had lost their card because they owed money for books.

At Summer School

Helen Nicholson was nervous when, "armed with a tiny tape recorder," she interviewed a class of rising fifth graders in a remedial summer school program. "All of these children," Helen wrote, "had been recommended for remediation by their teachers because of test scores or academic weaknesses. Frankly, my expectations for an enthusiastic response to questions about reading and books from such a group were low." As the interview progressed however, Helen found herself "pleasantly surprised."

The children prefer to read books that they select themselves (independence fairly oozed from their pores as they said so), but do admit that their teachers and librarians *sometimes* choose "pretty good" books for them to read. One little girl told me that her mother selects all the books she reads because "She says I pick out crazy books." When I asked her if she likes the books her mother chooses, she told me she loves them, "but they are too thick." I noticed that this little girl knew the most book titles, was very articulate and spontaneous in her answers to my questions, and was the only one who mentioned "poems" when I asked the children what they liked to read.

400 Children, four to twelve

During the last academic year, 24 students collected information on reading interests from over 400 children. The children ranged in age from four to twelve and were enrolled in classes that ranged from preschool programs to sixth grade. The groups included children representing almost every ability level, from "at risk" students to the academically gifted, with the majority described as "average." All socioeconomic levels were represented in these surveys; however, due to the cultural makeup of the region—eastern North Carolina—students were predominantly black or white.

Eastern North Carolina consists primarily of small towns with populations under 3000. Several larger cities, whose populations range between 35,000 and 50,000, are scattered throughout the region. Although employment is relatively high, many families subsist at or below the poverty level, particularly in the more rural areas. Schools are centralized and students are transported to and from school by bus. Public libraries outside the cities are small, with limited budgets, services, and collections.

Although most of the information was collected in schools, students also talked to children in public libraries, preschools, day care centers, and Sunday schools. Some students even invited neighborhood children into their homes. One enterprising young man conducted his interviews around the pool in his apartment complex.

Information was gathered in one of two ways: interview or written survey. Interview groups tended to be small and the techniques used ranged from informal discussion to structured trigger questions. Survey instruments were constructed from a set of sample questions handed out with the assignment. Some students combined both interview and survey in their studies. After completing their studies, students prepared reports that summarized what they had learned and also discussed their findings in class.

The primary source of information for this article was student reports, many of which were supplemented by quotes from interviews or by actual data: sets of completed surveys. To prepare the article, the reports were analyzed for common themes and for information to support and clarify these themes.

Indiscriminate Enthusiasm

The most important concept that emerged is that reading for pleasure is primarily developmental and experimental rather than genetic. In other words, pleasure readers are made, not born. Young children, for the most part, are indiscriminately enthusiastic about reading and its related language skill, listening to stories. As their ability to read and understand more sophisticated materials increases, many of the attitudes they develop toward reading depend upon the quality of the experiences they associate with it. If those experiences are pleasant and reinforcing, children are more likely to acquire a lifelong appreciation of reading. The concept of reading enjoyment as developmental and experiential emerged from the analysis of two common themes: positive experiences related to reading and attitudes toward reading expressed by children.

Positive Reading Experiences

Most of the children in this study described positive experiences related to reading. These included having stories read or told to them and various types of adult influences including modelling, reading materials in the home, and motivating activities by teachers and librarians.

Despite the literature claiming that television has become a replacement for reading aloud, the majority of the children in this study had been read aloud to. Younger children were most often read to at home, usually by mothers, although fathers, grandparents, siblings, and other relatives, as well as teachers, librarians, and camp counselors, were mentioned. Some children were read to daily, mentioning bedtime and rainy days as the most frequent times. Others were read to about once a week or on such infrequent bases as "not very

often," and "when my parents get a chance." A number of children, ranging from "half" to "a few" of those interviewed, had never been read to in the home. Older children mentioned being read to in the home, usually as young children; however, reading aloud to older children was generally done by teachers and librarians.

When asked why they liked being read to, children agreed that it was more relaxing and more interesting. "It's fun to listen," claimed a number of children. They gave reasons such as "So I don't have the work to do," "Because they will know the hard words," and "The story is easier to understand." Moreover, adults who read aloud usually do so with expression. "The teacher makes it interesting," said one child while another said she liked it, "because you can make a picture in your mind."

Some children mentioned enjoying the social experience of listening to a story: sharing it with a class or the one-on-one interaction when being read to at home. Children also pointed out that books were usually read aloud for the pleasure of those listening rather than to instruct them.

In addition to being read to, children were also told stories, usually family stories or tales about when mother or father were young. "Ghost stories" and "scary stories" were also mentioned. Helen Nicholson noted that "Mothers, grandmothers, teachers, sisters, and librarians (all females?) read to these particular children, while uncles, fathers, brothers-in-law, and stepbrothers (in addition to the females) tell them stories."

Older children, it was found, are more discriminating about the read-aloud experience. While many of them still enjoyed hearing books read, the choice of the book and the ability of the reader to make the book interesting was of concern. Children didn't like being read to when it was "boring," "annoying," "too slow," or "too loud." An 11-year-old, the only one in Cindy Solomon's group that did not like hearing stories read aloud explained, "At school they read first grade stories to me and make me feel like an idiot."

Somewhere between the third and fifth grade, children begin to prefer reading to themselves to being read to. Among Bonnie Whitesell's group, this was the majority. Perhaps, Bonnie suggested, this was because children wanted to be in control. "They could read the way they wanted to, could look at the pictures as long as they wanted to, and—as one said—skip what they wanted to."

Adult Influences

In addition to reading aloud, two types of adult influences in the home that motivate reading were identified: the presence of reading materials and the modeling of reading behavior. Children reported having a wide variety of reading materials in their homes. These included newspapers, magazines, letters, religious books (most frequently the Bible), and other types of books such as "fiction" books, "hard" books, "stress" books, teacher's manuals, and encyclopedias.

Most children mentioned some type of reading activity that occurred in the home. Parents and siblings who read model behavior for children to follow. In this study, the family member children most often observed reading was the mother. Mothers read books as well as magazines and newspapers. While some children saw their fathers reading books, usually the reading material was newspapers

Siblings, depending on their age and sex, were seen reading textbooks, comic books, picture books, and novels. Catherine Robbins pointed out that, in her group, some of the children with older siblings "noticed that girls read romance and horror books, while boys liked sports and car magazines and books." One child told Lina Christopher that "it was fun for everyone in the whole family to have a book and read together."

One point worth noting, however, is that in each of the 24 surveys conducted, there were children—usually less than one-fourth of the group—who claimed that parents and/or siblings did not read. Although this number is small, the fact that it was consistent throughout all groups is significant.

Teacher, Librarian Influence

Teachers and librarians also influence children's reading behavior. In their reports, many students credited children's positive attitudes toward reading to the teacher whose class they visited or the school librarian whose name was heard over and over in their interviews. Mary Joyner was surprised when the class of 23 second graders, mostly boys, all said they liked reading. "The words they used to express their feelings toward reading included 'happy,' 'excited,' 'proud,' 'great,' 'soothing,' 'curious,' and 'fantastic,' " reported Mary. This reaction, she felt, was probably influenced by their teacher. The teacher reads to the children every day and although it is not scheduled, takes her class to the library every day after lunch to check out a book. She feels these activities are important, says Mary, "because she realizes that not all of her students are read to at home and some do not even have books in their homes." Deborah Hurdle stated that among her group of 35 children, ages seven to twelve, were five who said that "their librarian reads to them and she was the only person who does."

Positive Attitudes

The students conducting these surveys were surprised at the overwhelmingly positive reaction to reading that they uncovered. While children universally agreed that, given their choice, they would rather play than read, the majority of children in all groups surveyed said that they like to read—many of them said that they *loved* to read—and they were able to discuss the pros and cons of reading in a knowledgeable, sometimes sophisticated, manner.

Most children seem to have strong opinions on reading. If they feel positive toward reading, they say things like, "I love it!" and "It's fun!" If they feel negative toward reading, they say things like, "I hate it!" and "It's boring!" Peggy Piercy began her interview with a general question: "What do you do when you get home every day?" All but two, she reported, responded by saying "get a snack and watch television." But when she asked if they liked books, "they all started talking at once about what they did and did not read." Peggy was particularly interested to see that "some of the quieter ones were now eagerly talking to me about reading. The enthusiasm and excitement of talking about books was seen in all their faces."

Children who enjoy reading describe it as "terrific," "interesting," and "the best thing in the world." Said one fifth grader, "If you don't know how to read, it's like you're not alive." Reading makes children feel "tickled," "proud," "wonderful," and "relaxed." Four of the ten children Lina Christopher interviewed surprised her when they said that they preferred reading to watching television. Reading was more fulfilling, they told her, "because they could use their imagination to make the characters and setting just the way they would like them to be." Lina's group of children summed up their feelings toward reading with this statement: "When you have a good book and like to read, you are never bored or lonely. The characters become friends that you can visit any time you want."

While very young children talk about the pleasures of reading, older children often associate reading with learning. This can have both positive and negative effects. "Reading helps me to get smart," a number of children claimed while others described reading as "important" for such reasons as "to do good in school," and "to find out things." Rudolph Knight noted that the fifth and sixth graders he interviewed read a wide variety of materials as they experimented with new interests and hobbies: "travel folders and road maps, timetables, weather charts, riddles, recipes, and pamphlets about products and industries. Most children said they were excited when the postman brought a letter or magazine addressed to them."

However, several of the 16 children interviewed by Pam Martin claimed they didn't like reading because their parents made them read. Pam said she asked one little girl if she knew why her parents made her read. "Yes," she replied. "So I can get good grades so that I can get a scholarship to college and my parents don't have to pay for it." I asked the other children if their parents told them the same thing about college. Most replied, "yes."

Helen Nicholson was disturbed by the pragmatic view of reading expressed by rising fifth graders in a summer remedial program. Helen recorded comments such as the following: "When you are on a highway, you have to learn how to read the signs"; "When you go grocery shopping, you have to read packages so you won't buy what you don't want"; and "When you can't read math, some people might cheat you out of your money."

Everybody's Favorites

Children not only enjoy reading, they have very definite preferences about what they read. Children said they liked animal stories, mystery, adventure, and "scary" stories, jokes and riddles, "happy" stories, and informational books on topics that interested them. Boys mentioned science fiction and books about sports, cars, real people, and real things while girls like stories about girls their own ages and collected series books, such as "The Babysitter's Club," "Sweet Valley Twins," and "Nancy Drew." The popularity of modern series like "The Babysitter's Club" seems to stem from the fact that they are about children the same age and with the same problems as their readers. Moreover, series books allow children to "get to know" the characters.

Almost every report listed magazines among the things children liked to read, with *Highlights* being the most frequently mentioned. Older girls liked looking at fashion and beauty magazines while older boys enjoyed magazines about sports and cars. Surprisingly enough, comic books were infrequently mentioned and then primarily by boys. That might be because, as two children explained, they aren't "real" books.

Many of the children interviewed were able to explain why they liked the books they did. When discussing fiction books, they mentioned characters, plot, humor, action, and realism. The two most frequent responses to the question "Why did you like the book?" were "because I was interested in [or "liked"] the characters" and "because it was funny." Mystery was a favorite "because it is fun to guess what is going to happen," and they liked science fiction because it "had adventure" and "other galaxies and planets in the plot." Books about "real things" were popular because they "tell a lot about" topics of particular interest to individual children.

Children and Books Together

These surveys and interviews, my students and I agreed, taught us a great deal about reading and children. Several of the things we discovered, while not surprising, deserve more attention than they seem to be receiving. First the fact that enjoyment of reading is primarily developmental and experiential, not innate. The majority of young children interviewed for this study expressed positive attitudes toward reading. But somewhere around the fourth grade, children became more selective about reading. They separate reading for enjoyment from reading required by teachers, they like to hear stories read aloud only if the stories are interesting and are read well, and many prefer reading to themselves rather than listening to others read.

What happens to cause the initial enthusiasm toward reading to wane? Three things affecting children's attitudes toward reading were identified: the response of significant adults to reading, the experiences that children connect with reading, and how much physical activity individual children need. As Bonnie Whitesell concluded, the children who like reading "had a history of positive experiences, such as enjoying bedtime stories when they were little, going to libraries with Mom or Dad, and learning to read with little or no difficulty." In addition, several students noted that physically active children, those who seemed to need a great deal of movement, often expressed little interest in reading. This lack of interest, they speculated, might be connected to the sedentary nature of reading.

Most poignant of all, however, was the question raised by Helen Nicholson—a question well worth the time and attention of librarians, teachers, parents, and all who care about helping young people toward a lifetime of reading enjoyment. Helen's group, a remedial class of "four boys and seven girls between the ages of nine and eleven," provided her "with some surprising information about children from low socioeconomic backgrounds"—information that caused her concern.

These eleven children, contrary to all rationalization offered by educators, do have books at home and do have parents who read to them and take them to the public library. Could there be other reasons that children lose their love of reading as they grow older? As I look into their faces, I found myself looking ahead and wondering if any of these children would one day see his or her name added to that dreaded list of "at risk" high school students who, so often, never achieve what the world seems to promise in the fourth grade.

What are the "other reasons" that lead children to lose their love of reading? From this study, it appears that adults who are significant in the lives of older children need to examine the interaction they have with children around the concept of reading. Do parents of older children think they no longer need to take time to read to, or with, their children? Has a concern with performance on standardized tests caused teachers to relate reading only to learning? Does the low priority awarded to storytelling by library educators and school administrators discourage librarians from engaging in, and becoming competent at, telling stories and reading aloud? Perhaps most importantly, are high scores on standardized tests worth the sacrifice of a lifelong love of reading?

Reaching Out to Gay Teens

Carolyn Caywood

Returning home after the American Library Association's Midwinter Meeting in Denver, I experienced a form of culture shock. After spending a week surrounded by colleagues proclaiming their solidarity in support of gay rights, I was back in a heavily military community, where the idea of acknowledging the presence of homosexuals in the armed forces was generating hysteria. Despite frequent and intense discussion of the issue in the local newspaper, its advertising department refused to run an ad announcing a local Gay Pride event, thereby prompting picketing and more letters and calls.

Curiously, there is a wide discrepancy between what the advertising department thinks readers don't want to be exposed to and what library circulation records show. Many books about the gay experience, especially those that address teenagers and their families, circulate almost as often as best-sellers. I have one tattered paperback copy of *One Teenager in 10* (Alyson, 1983) that has been checked out 44 times in the past five years. I suspect, too, that even the books that stay in the library long enough to be reshelved are consulted by many more people than are willing to bring them to the check-out desk. Clearly there has been strong community interest in what it means to be gay for at least as long as we've maintained circulation records.

The importance of maintaining a substantial, up-to-date collection of materials to serve gay and lesbian teens is underscored in James T. Sears's *Growing Up Gay in the South* (Haworth, 1991). This is a must-read book for any librarian who wants to provide service to *all* the library's teen patrons. The case studies include several teens who said they sought information about homosexuality in their libraries but either found nothing beyond medical definitions or were too embarrassed to check anything out. Yet, these same teens said that "reading material supportive of homosexuality" is essential for their self-acceptance. This need seems especially urgent in light of another of Sears's findings—63 percent of the gay teens he interviewed also reported having contemplated suicide.

An important element in materials for gay teens is the presentation of role models. Because homosexuality and child molestation are so often erroneously conflated in public opinion, it is very risky for any adult gay or lesbian to reveal his or her identity to a teen. As a result, the only positive images many teens encounter are in books or movies—and even there, they can be difficult to find. This is why informational books for teens such as *A Way of Love, a Way of Life* by Frances Hanckel and John Cunningham (Lothrop, 1979)—which profile gays and lesbians who lead well-adjusted, productive lives—are so valuable. (It is a pity that this classic has not been updated to cover AIDS, but its advice is otherwise useful.)

Librarians also should become familiar with biographies and fiction that contain positive gay role models, since these books are not easily identifiable in the catalog unless homosexuality is the dominant theme. Information on Alan Turing, for example, can be located by those interested in computers but not, without help, by those to whom it would be important to know that the mathematical genius was gay.

While there are now many books available with homosexuality as a theme, if a librarian is not careful with recommendations, teen readers can wind up with an unrelieved diet of tragedy. Mystery and fantasy are two genres that have adjusted to gay characters as protagonists. It is important to seek out a wide variety of materials that might be of special interest to gay teens.

Religion may be the most difficult area of the collection for finding selections that treat the subject of homosexuality. There are widely different interpretations of the often quoted passages from *Genesis* 19:4–5, *Leviticus* 18:22 and 20:13, and *Romans* 1:26–27; libraries must represent the diversity of these interpretations. Religious publishers offer a variety of resources for parents and family members, but these are often classed with social issues materials. *Parents of the Homosexual* by David K. and Shirley Switzer (Westminster, 1980) is one of the more heavily used titles in our collection. Since homosexual teens often fear exposure to their families, however, it is important for the library to take a strong stand on confidentiality.

Since September 1990, the American Library Association's Office for Intellectual Freedom has recorded 123 challenges to library holdings based on actual or perceived content related to homosexuality. Certainly there is always some risk involved in adhering to the principles of the *Library Bill of Rights,* but I do not assume that the fear of censorship accounts for all libraries that lack materials on gays and lesbians. No doubt, there are librarians who think that none of the teens who use their library could possibly be interested in these materials, or that reading about gays will contaminate young minds. It will not be easy for all librarians to reconcile the need to provide such materials with their personal beliefs, but the consequences of self-censored collections can be devastating.

The school environment is very hostile to a teen who is different. Low self-esteem can drive a teen to drugs or unsafe sex for comfort—or even to suicide. Library materials that offer support to gay and lesbian teens can save lives.

Part Four

Those Who Serve Our Clients

Those who help the young meet their informational, intellectual, and emotional needs in libraries need to know what competencies they must demonstrate; they should strive to meet high standards of professional preparation and should accept their responsibilities for life long learning. However, those who serve the young in their quest for knowledge of self, and others in good books and other formats today do not work only in libraries. Over the past forty years, librarians have learned that they must work with parents, teachers, and early childhood learning providers to help broaden the influence of quality resources and information seeking activities on young learners. The articles in this part address these topics. In addition, Margaret McElderry's "Remarkable Women" that appeared in March, 1992 presents a portrait of early twentieth century providers of library service to youth. This portrait serves as an inspiration to us today.

Young Adults Deserve the Best: Competencies for Librarians Serving Youth

In 1981, the Board of Directors of ALA's Young Adult Services Division (YASD) asked the YASD Education Committee to develop a list of competencies which librarians working with young adults in *any type of information agency* should be able to demonstrate. The Committee began to develop this competency statement as a guideline for library educators who are involved in training people at the pre-service level. Its applicability and audience is much wider and should also include library administrators, YA librarians, school library media specialists, and library school students. The YASD Education Committee determined through research that the following competencies are needed by the librarian working with youth:

Area I: Leadership and Professionalism

The student will be able to:

1. Develop and demonstrate leadership skills in articulating a program of excellence for young adults.
2. Exhibit planning and evaluating skills in the development of a comprehensive program for young adults.
3. Develop and demonstrate a commitment to professionalism.
   a. Adhere to the American Library Association Code of Ethics.
   b. Demonstrate a non-judgmental attitude toward young adults.
   c. Preserve confidentiality in interactions with young adults.
4. Plan for personal and professional growth and career development through active participation in professional associations and continuing education.
5. Develop and demonstrate a strong commitment to the right of young adults to have access to information, consistent with the American Library Association's *Library Bill of Rights.*
6. Demonstrate an understanding of and a respect for diversity in cultural and ethnic values.
7. Encourage young adults to become lifelong library users by helping them to discover what libraries have to offer and how to use libraries.

Area II: Knowledge of Client Group

The student will be able to:

1. Apply factual and interpretative information on adolescent psychology, growth and development, sociology, and popular culture in planning for materials and services for young adults.
2. Apply knowledge of the reading process and of types of reading problems in the development of the collection and program for young adults.
3. Identify the special needs of discrete groups of young adults and design and implement programs and build collections appropriate to their needs.

Area III: Communication

The student will be able to:

1. Demonstrate effective interpersonal relations with young adults, administrators, other professionals who work with young adults, and the community by:
   a. using principles of group dynamics and group process.
   b. establishing regular channels of communication (both written and oral) with each group.
2. Apply principles of effective communication which reinforce positive behaviors in young adults.

Area IV: Administration

Planning

The student will be able to:

1. Formulate goals, objectives, and methods of evaluation for a young adult program based on determined needs.
   a. Design and conduct a community analysis and needs assessment.
   b. Apply research findings for the development and improvement of the young adult program.
   c. Design, conduct, and evaluate local action research for program improvement.
2. Design, implement, and evaluate an on-going public relations and report program directed toward young adults, administrators, boards, staff, other agencies serving young adults, and the community at large.
3. Identify and cooperate with other information agencies in networking arrangements to expand access to information agencies in networking arrangements for young adults.

Reprinted with permission, from a document approved by the Young Adult Services Division's Directors, July 1982.

4. Develop, justify, administer, and evaluate a budget for the young adult program.

5. Develop physical facilities which contribute to the achievement of young adult program goals.

Managing

The student will be able to:

1. Supervise and evaluate other staff members.

2. Design, implement, and evaluate an on-going program of staff development.

3. Develop policies and procedures for the efficient operation of all technical functions (including acquisition, processing, circulation, collection maintenance, equipment supervision, and scheduling of young adult programs).

4. Identify external sources of funding and other support and apply for those suitable for the young adult program.

5. Monitor legislation and judicial decisions pertinent to young adults, especially those which affect youth rights, and disseminate this information.

Area V: Knowledge of Materials

The student will be able to:

1. Formulate a selection policy for young adult materials, consistent with the parent institution's selection policy, with a systematic procedure for handling challenges.

2. Develop a materials collection for young adults which includes all appropriate formats, using a broad range of selection sources.

3. Demonstrate a knowledge and appreciation of literature for young adults.

4. Identify current reading, viewing, and listening interests of young adults and incorporate these findings into collection development and programs.

5. Design and locally produce materials in a variety of formats to expand the collections.

6. Incorporate technological advances (e.g., computers, video) in the library program.

Area VI: Access to Information

The student will be able to:

1. Organize collections to guarantee easy access to information.

2. Use current standard methods of cataloging and classification, and be aware of the newest technology.

3. Create an environment which attracts and invites young adults to use the collection.

4. Develop special tools which provide access to information not readily available, e.g., community resources, special collections.

5. Devise and publicize pathfinders, book lists, displays, etc., which will ease access to collections and will motivate use.

Area VII: Services

The student will be able to:

1. Utilize a variety of techniques (e.g., booktalking, discussion) to encourage use of materials.

2. Provide a variety of information services (e.g., information referral, crisis intervention counseling, on-line data bases) to meet the diverse needs of young adults.

3. Instruct young adults in the basic information gathering and research skills needed for current and future use.

4. Encourage young adults in the use of all types of materials for their personal growth and enjoyment.

5. Design, implement, and evaluate specific programs and activities (both in the library and in the community) for young adults, based on their needs and interests.

6. Involve young adults in planning and implementing services for their age group.

Media Specialists and the Quest for Lifelong Learning

by Carolyn L. Cain

Several years ago, when I sent my fellow media specialists my annual questionnaire seeking their inservice preferences for the coming year, among the many practical and specific suggestions received was this cryptic question and comment: "How should I know what I need? You plan the programs and I'll come to whatever is offered." I was both flattered and disturbed by this honest feedback. Flattered, because it meant that someone had confidence in my ability to forecast and identify what new knowledge or skills would be needed by the school district's medial specialists. Disturbed, because it seemed unlikely that anyone in libraries and education would not be aware of areas which needed improvement in order to do a better job.

That response has continued to intrigue me because it raised important questions that needed answers. As professionals, do we really have a responsibility to define continuing education needs? Why do we find doing this so difficult? What are some effective ways to approach the task? What do we gain if we do it ourselves? Will assessing our needs always be such a difficult task?

Although there are no simple answers to these questions, my experiences in planning, experimenting, succeeding (or failing) in a variety of staff development and inservice activities designed to help library media specialists get more involved in identifying their learning needs, have suggested some areas we might look at. An examination of the continuing education literature as part of my graduate study in this field has also led to other ideas that may be useful as we examine the problem and seek solutions. It is becoming apparent that school districts and state certification or licensing agencies require more and more continuing education. The question is: If we are going to be required to participate in learning, shouldn't we have a major part in determining what that learning should be? I believe that we should, and that it is essential that we do so.

In a recent book entitled *Continuing Learning in the Professions*, adult educator Cy Houle suggests that a "zest for continuing learning and a personal responsibility for their own continuing education must be borne by all who call themselves professionals."[1] Houle defines this responsibility as taking charge of the direction of one's continuing learning, and seeing that it contributes to one's personal and professional competence.

The issue of whether librarianship is truly a profession is not part of this article, but I have taken the view that it is, based in part on an article by Shirley Fitzgibbons on professionalism and ethics for school librarians.[2] She clarified the issue by pointing out that the work of school library media specialists clearly includes many of the elements of professionalism, and therefore we should approach the field from a professional perspective. Fitzgibbons says this includes developing a positive attitude toward lifelong learning as an essential part of our education.

Additional literature in the school media field supports this view and further defines the continuing education element of professionalism with regard to what must be learned. For example, in the *Certification Model for Professional School Media Personnel* (AASL/ALA, 1975), under the competency area of the model called "Leadership and Professionalism," the following statement appears: "Engage in self-evaluation to identify the areas of need for continuing education and professional growth."[3] Also, the *Behavioral Requirement Analysis Checklist*, which came from the Knapp Project, addresses this topic in the fourth function of the section on professionalism: "To engage in continuous study and self-evaluation for professional growth."[4] Authors such as Chisholm and Ely in *Media Personnel in Education*[5] and Daniel in an article on performance evaluation[6] clearly identify the individual's responsibility for determining his or her own learning needs and for engaging in activities that will contribute to improved competence.

Whose Responsibility Is It?

Backed by such statements from leaders in the school library media field, I contend that it is critical for practicing school library media personnel not only to accept individual responsibility for identifying their learning needs, but for them to do so in a skilful and active manner. Only then will they be in a position to *insist* that opportunities be provided to meet these needs.

One important reason for doing this is the rapidly changing nature of the library media specialist's role in the school's instructional program. As this role expands and develops, it can move in different directions. Of necessity, it will reflect the training and experience of those currently working in the field, as well as the vision and challenges posed by school library innovators. It will also reflect the extent to which potential changes are understood and supported by those who must adopt them if they are to succeed, namely teachers, administrators, and the parents who demand that schools prepare their children for the future.

Today's library media specialists are shaping their own roles and are being shaped by them at the same time. Without a real sensitivity to what new skills and knowledge are needed to enable them to shape this changing role, media specialists necessarily will limit that role and prevent it from becoming a dynamic force in the educational process. Also, without a high degree of competence in several fields that were once distinct and separate (teaching, librarianship, instructional technology), media specialists may lose the opportunity to contribute attitudes toward learning itself. Skills must be broadened if the media specialist is to combine the essence of information management and access with instructional design and advanced educational technologies to create new means to enhance student learning.

There are other important but less compelling reasons why media specialists should be directly involved in identifying their personal learning needs. One stems from the fact that relatively few of us started out to be school library media specialists—we came to the profession from diverse and unrelated fields—and therefore the training and experience we bring to the job is dissimilar and often specialized. This varied background makes it difficult to assume common learning needs, and suggests that only individuals themselves can assess themselves and determine their needs. As a more broadly based understanding of media services and programs evolves, it is all the more important that each individual look for his or her own learning gaps and determine how to integrate his or her background with developments in the field.

Another way to examine learning needs is to consider to what extent school library media specialists have developed personal approaches to their work. Adult educator Malcolm Knowles's framework for library competencies includes three distinct cores: a central core common to all librarians; a middle core which will be different based on the different specialties (for example, school librarianship as different from academic or public, or elementary as different from high school); and an outer core which represents the individuals personal talents and unique approach to the profession.[7] This last is often overlooked by those in the field. While satisfactory delivery of media programs demands a certain level of basic competence and an adaptation to individual school settings, it also allows us to infuse programs with elements of our personalities, talents, special skills and interests, and even our idiosyncrasies. These become the basis of our media center programs and lend them that exciting personal touch. However, if we don't consider all of Knowles's cores in determining our learning needs, we can develop narrow or one-sided programs that tend to ignore some of the needs of our teachers and students.

One final reason why the identification of learning needs must fall primarily on ourselves as professionals is that we work alone, in what Houle calls a "related or adjunct setting." Most school librarians, media specialists, and audiovisual personnel are employed in a setting in which no others perform the same kind of work. We are on our own, so to speak, and our bosses and our clients have limited knowledge of what we are doing and what we should be doing. Therefore, the level of personal responsibility is higher for us than for others, such as teachers, whose job expectations are commonly understood and shared by a number of staff members.

Why Is This a Problem?

Once we understand the importance of identifying our learning needs and accept the responsibility for doing so, we can look for clues to why this is difficult and why we haven't done this effectively in the past. Isolation by the nature of our work setting is one of the reasons why this is a problem. Tom Galvin, speaking at the 1980 AASL National Conference, said, "The biggest problem in the school library media field is isolation, which makes appraising your own professional development difficult."[8] This isolation results in little supervisory help to assess needs, and, as suggested earlier, there are no teammates or natural peers on hand to provide feedback on performance. Few district supervisors have time to conduct extended staff evaluations; their work is usually limited to occasional observation and specific problem solving. Teachers and principals, whose understanding of media services is based on their own school experiences, are of limited help in identifying gaps in the competencies of media specialists today.

A second factor that contributes to the difficulty of identifying needs is a fear of performance evaluation. Adult educator Malcolm Knowles proposes that we view evaluation as a "diagnosis of future learning needs" rather than as a judgment of worth.[9] That way it will be less threatening and can be a tool for improvement instead of a barrier to it. We must initiate evaluations of our own performance in the process of identifying learning needs. If we are to improve, it is essential to know how well we are doing.

Another factor affecting the successful identification of needs is the lack of a clear picture of how competence is defined, what we can be expected to do, and how well we should be able to do it: before we can make assessments about performance we need to understand what constitutes good professional practice in our field. Media specialists are beginning to develop more precise and detailed statements of media competencies as education institutions and state certification plans move in this direction, but much remains to be done before we have complete and realistic standards against which to measure ourselves and the programs we seek to deliver. As indicated earlier, the changing nature of the field adds to this dilemma; the level of competence and the range of competencies are not static, nor are they universally agreed upon.

Finally, we must contend with our own feelings that we have earned our degree—we have been prepared—and in some cases we now have a "lifelong license" to practice this profession. I believe this attitude of total preparedness is diminishing as change becomes more and more the internal "zest for learning and growing through one's professional life," which Houle believes should be a part of every professional, is not something that was fostered, valued, or promoted in most of the educational programs that prepared today's practising library media specialists. We were encouraged in our training to take advantage of various learning opportunities, but the notion that professionals must undergo self-evaluations and self-assessments throughout our working careers was certainly not stressed.

How to Assess Our Needs

Let's look now at some of the approaches we might take toward identifying our own learning needs, and consider how to go about assuring that we improve our competence in the most fruitful manner.

There are four basic sources of information we can use in learning about our own performance: *self-assessment, peer review, supervisory evaluation,* and *client feedback.* Adult educator Jerry Apps identifies these and suggests that by combining information from each of them, we can gain the most realistic and helpful picture of our strengths and weaknesses.[10] I believe that we must concentrate on improving our self-assessment for reasons already stated, and that we must also learn to request and use feedback from others in a more systematic manner. The focus of the approaches presented here is on the self-assessment process, since it is central to the rest.

The first step is to distinguish between learning needs that are necessary to keep current in the field—those that will help upgrade or improve our present skills and knowledge—and those that are part of our basic philosophy or understanding of the mission of our profession. This last is especially critical; all too often, we associate learning needs with demonstrable skills and practical knowledge, ignoring the attitudinal or conceptual aspects of library media services,

Secondly, it is important to bear in mind that a "need" may be defined as something either basic or essential to practice, or desirable or helpful to improve our work. Defining the nature of the need is important because we have to choose which learning needs to pay attention to and in what order.

Thirdly, we should keep in mind that there are three levels of learning to which we can pay attention: the level of our present job and its performance, the level of our overall career development and future jobs, and the level of our overall professional performance and satisfaction in our own professional development.

One common way to start a needs assessment is to look for models of competence against which to compare oneself. Standards at the national and state levels can be helpful in determining and understanding what current leaders in the field perceive to be the competencies required for the job. Assessment of performance against standards can range from informal, using the standards as a checklist in our personal review of how well we are doing, to more formal assessments, such as those used as the basis for supervisory evaluation and improvement planning, and to very formal assessments, which are used as the basis of licensure and certification.

Strategies

1. The literature shows increasing interest in the development of new methods to aid practising professionals in voluntarily testing themselves against professional competency standards as a way of identifying areas for learning and improvement. For example:
•   An assessment center has been established at the University of Washington for helping practitioners examine their abilities and weaknesses in the area of library administration and management.
•   A joint project has been set up between a university and a professional organization in the field of pharmacy. This model, called a "practice audit model," has combined the work of the professional organization in identifying performance standards and the university as the place in which practitioners can come to evaluate themselves against these standards.[11]
•   Computerized test items have been developed to help Minnesota's public librarians test themselves in specific areas such as public relations, management, etc. Resources for learning are suggested so that areas testing as weak can be addressed.
2. Another commonly used strategy is to examine the people and programs of other schools and institutions and, through a process of informal comparison, to note programs and skills which demonstrate effectiveness. The model school and the exemplary librarian can provide role models against which others can compare themselves.

The more one reads the literature to see what is described, visits other schools and talks with other professionals, attends national, state, and regional conferences, and works cooperatively with professionals from related fields, the more models and ideas will be available against which to measure and evaluate oneself.
3. Getting into the habit of looking toward the future is a third strategy to employ in identifying learning needs. Anticipation and planning are important aspects of the media center's responsibility if it is to fulfill its role. Contact with individuals at the forefront of the field is important, whether through reading the literature, attending conferences, or looking critically at what other fields are doing.

Although the programs and activities of professional organizations are likely to be more forward-looking than regular university and college programs, there is increasing effort on the part of educational institutions to offer short courses, sponsor conferences, commission speakers and position papers, etc., to help graduates come in contact with new developments within their respective fields.

Media specialists also must look beyond their own specialized field to become more sensitive to school priorities, community changes, technological possibilities, cooperative experimentation with other agencies, and the like. Maintaining contact with leaders in the community, in your own institution, and in other professions can provide useful clues to what is coming up and what is considered important by others.
4. Another strategy in needs identification is the simple but difficult task of self-reflection, or periodic personal reassessment. By taking the time to reflect how successful (or unsuccessful) the year was, or how well a bothersome problem was dealt with, we can often decide what action, if any, to take.

Perhaps there were tasks that were difficult, or which we didn't feel competent to tackle. This is sometimes painful, and often discouraging, but most often a realistic look at our own performances to determine how to improve job proficiency is a positive, satisfying experience.

5. Reflection and "hard thinking" can be enhanced by taking the next step: sharing conclusions with a close friend or fellow professional with whom we can speak openly without feeling threatened. We can come closer to knowing ourselves—and recognizing learning needs in the process—not only by looking objectively at ourselves, but also by seeing how well we perform through the eyes of others. Learning to seek and give constructive, positive feedback is a process that may take some attitude changing and skill development, but it is a powerful source of support and professional enrichment.

6. Another aspect of reflection and hard thinking is the identification of career goals and of a broader professional development than one's present job might suggest. The media specialist who looks only at what he or she is doing right now is missing an opportunity to grow and develop in other, newer directions. While we may sometimes feel that we have many more learning needs in our job alone than we can possibly do anything about, it is important not to identify only with our jobs, but to look to increased fulfillment and personal growth. Choosing a personal goal, such as getting elected to the county board, or writing that book, can mean the identification of many learning needs not having a direct bearing on our job. Fulfilling these learning needs often results in renewed enthusiasm and confidence in one's job as well as in one's personal life.

7. Finally, among the various approaches to identifying learning needs is what I call confrontation. Few of us willingly place ourselves in situations in which our ideas, values, attitudes, skills, or knowledge are directly challenged or confronted. However, these kinds of situations, whether involuntary or freely chosen, can serve as important identifiers. A change in principal or administrator, a transfer to a different job, a different co-worker, or the addition of new job responsibilities can provide us with evidence of what we don't know. Panic, a sense of despair at not knowing enough, pretending to know more than we do, and defensiveness are common responses to such involuntary confrontations. The best strategies in these instances are often the most difficult: realizing the learning need and admitting it to our supervisors, then developing systematic plans to obtain the necessary skills and knowledge.

One of the marks of professionals who are truly interested in doing the best they can is a willingness to seek out and confront situations that encourage them to identify learning needs and to grow in broadening, positive ways. Developing a career path, seeking a new job before the current one is old hat, volunteering for new experiences in which you know you will be tested or have to learn new skills, are examples of how people use voluntary self-confrontation as an invitation to personal and professional growth. Picking activities that are not directly related to the job is especially useful, as they are less threatening if there is failure or difficulty in learning. Seek-

ing out experiences and activities that challenge our assumptions, require critical thinking, suggest new approaches to old problems, and help us see ourselves in a new light can be part of a "confrontation approach" which is useful in the learning process.

Identifying Needs

There are several benefits from identifying one's learning needs. The most obvious is the motivation which it gives us to satisfy that need. The adult education literature contains much evidence that the most satisfactory and effective learning is that which is (1) based on an identified or recognized need on the part of the learner, and (2) includes a learning situation in which the learner has control of the learning, relates it to previous experience, learns at a successful pace, and makes use of the learning in a relevant manner. Self-identification is the critical first step in this process.

A secondary benefit is the fact that learning as a result of identified needs often leads to highly individualistic and creative learning experiences. Life-enriching experiences which also satisfy job-related learning needs can be a valuable outcome of the self-assessment process. For example, a learning need identified by a colleague was to improve her speaking ability. She considered a speech course, but decided instead that since she was also interested in theater, a role in a community theater production would be a much more exciting and motivating experience. She recognized that since she had as much need to overcome shyness as to learn about giving polished speeches, the informal theater experience would best meet her needs.

Finally, it is beneficial to see in what way self-identified learning is consistent with the philosophy of adult continuing education and staff development which places the learner in the center of the experience. This places the emphasis on learner-directed growth and development, rather than on outer-directed remediation and deficiency reduction. A philosophy that respects learners as capable of determining what will satisfy their own personal and professional needs enhances the concept of professionalism.

Getting Started

The most difficult part of any new task is getting started: assessing one's own learning needs and taking steps to meet them is no exception. Now that lifelong learning is becoming an accepted way of life, many exciting things are happening. Part of the excitement comes from a new respect for adults as learners. Current courses, workshops, and a variety of other learning experiences are better planned to meet their needs. And because of an increased emphasis colleges and universities are placing on continuing education programs, there are more higher education opportunities from which to choose. Private companies are also moving into this area, offering courses that range from personal development to management training. School districts and state departments of education are also beginning to take much more active roles in staff development by supporting, requiring, and offering continuing education opportunities. Given such a positive climate for the growth and improvement of continued learning opportunities, it is important for school library media specialists to get involved.

The first step, as outlined in this article, is to acknowledge personal responsibility for our continued learning. The next step is to engage in some of the identification activities I've discussed, or in those you may discover on your own. It is probable that in the future we will have better ways to critically assess our abilities and identify with more precision just what our learning needs are. For now, however, we can make good use of what is available. By examining the conference programs of national professional organizations, such as the American Association of School Librarians (AASL) and the Association of Educational Communications and Technology (AECT), it is possible to locate a myriad of learning experiences.

In addition, state-level efforts in defining competencies of media personnel, as was recently done in Texas, can provide us with a clearer picture of what we can be expected to do in a fully functioning media program.[12] Research reported in professional journals can be applicable to our own programs. Ready access to national data bases such as ERIC allows information-gathering about new developments and increases our knowledge in many media and education areas. With the rapid development of new technologies such as interactive television, video discs, cable television, computerized instructional programs, and satellite communications, it will be possible to meet one's identified learning need with a specific learning experience.

The crucial part of getting started is to become actively involved in a learning experience that will meet your needs. Locating what you want may be difficult, but there are many places to look. The library/media department of your state government has a recognized continuing education responsibility and is likely to be a good source of information on nearby programs, workshops, and courses. Your state's library and media professional associations sponsor various programs; these and other state and local events are listed in their newsletters. State regional councils and library systems often sponsor short-term continuing education activities of interest to media personnel. At the national level, some professional organizations list various state and regional activities along with national events, and the calendar or program event sections of professional periodicals often include detailed listings of educational activities.

Other major sources of continuing education are the colleges and universities within your state or region which may provide late afternoon or evening courses, programs on television or through telephone networks, independent study opportunities, summer institutes, and short courses, etc. Students not working on a degree are often given reduced rates or allowed to audit at minimal cost. Their offerings are usually advertised statewide.

CLENE, the Continuing Library Education Network Exchange, is making an attempt to serve as a national clearinghouse for information by publishing a monthly listing of continuing education activities of interest to librarians and media specialists.[13] They have also established a program to certify quality programs and to provide a computerized record-keeping system to help individuals maintain a file on their learning activities.

Finally, you may consider planning your own learning activity by obtaining a copy of Malcolm Knowles's *Self-Directed Learning* and writing up your own learning contract.[14]

It's time to take charge of determining and fulfilling your learning needs. Look into the available research and put your information access skills to work for yourself as well as for your students.

References

1. Houle, Cyril. *Continuing Learning in the Professions.* Jossey-Bass, 1980.

2. Fitzgibbons, Shirley A. "Professionalism and Ethical Behavior: Relationship to School Library Media Personnel." *School Media Quarterly*, Winter 1980. p. 82-109.

3. American Association of School Librarians, Certification of School Media Specialists Committee. *Certification Model for Professional School Media Personnel.* American Library Association, 1976. p. 17.

4. Case, Robert N. *Behavioral Requirements Analysis Checklist.* American Library Association, 1976. p. 52.

5. Chisholm, Margaret E., and Ely, Donald P. *Media Personnel in Education.* Prentice-Hall, 1976.

6. Daniel, Evelyn H. "Performance Measures for School Librarians: Complexities and Potentials." *Advances in Librarianship*, vol. 7. Academic Press, 1976.

7. Knowles, Malcolm. "Model for Assessing Continuing Education Needs for a Profession." In *First CLENE Assembly Proceedings* (Jan. 23-24, 1976). CLENE, 1976.

8. Galvin, Thomas. In "School Libraries Too!" by Susan Brandehoff, *American Libraries* 11 (1980):595.

9. Knowles, Malcolm. Speech at National Staff Development Council Annual Conference, Madison, Wisconsin, Oct. 31, 1980.

10. Apps, Jerry. "Are We Learning Anything from Mandatory Education?" *Lab World*, May 1980. p. 31.

11. Lindsay, Carl A. "Continuing Professional Education and the University; the Practice Audit Model as a Process for Needs Assessment and Program Development." ED 187298. March 1980.

12. Staples, E. Susan. "60 Competency Ratings for School Media Specialists." *Instructional Innovator*, November 1981. p. 19-23.

13. CLENE, Inc. *Continuing Education Communicator*, monthly publication of Continuing Library Education Network and Exchange, 620 Michigan Ave., N.E., Washington, D.C. 20064.

14. Knowles, Malcolm. *Self-directed Learning.* Associated Press/Follette, 1975.

Remarkable Women
Anne Carroll Moore & Company

by Margaret K. McElderry

Anne Carroll Moore was a remarkable woman, one of the small group who pioneered library work with children. She established the children's services in the New York Public Library. A native of the state of Maine and daughter of a lawyer, she had hoped originally to become a lawyer herself, something almost unheard of for a woman at that time. She planned to clerk in her father's office, but his death ended that possibility. Instead, she turned her considerable gifts—an incisive mind, a strong will, great determination, and remarkable critical abilities—toward children and books.

In those far-off days, books for children were primarily happenstances. If a writer, well-known to the adult reading public, happened to write something for children—often a particular child, as in the case of Lewis Carroll—his (or her) publisher would publish it. However, the idea of setting out to write regularly for children, or to have rooms in public libraries specifically designed for children, had occurred to very few people. In fact, children were not encouraged to come to libraries. They were apt to be noisy and a nuisance.

Miss Moore—or ACM, as she was referred to sometimes, though never to her face—believed in children. She recognized the marvelous open quality of their minds, their intense curiosity about the world around them. She saw the infinite possibility of enriching their lives, of helping them to grow through books. Books not only enlarged their store of knowledge but gave them the pleasure of sharing the experiences of other children who lived different lives from their own, though only on the printed page. Other countries, other regions, other customs, other cultures could thus be shared by a child in Harlem, or in Chinatown, or in Little Italy, even if readers never left their own locality.

Beginnings in New York

In 1934, I was a graduate from the Carnegie Library School in Pittsburgh. I had come to library work simply because I loved books and had always been a reader, so what better field to dedicate one's life to than library work? Those of us who entered library school then had a sense of service drilled into us almost daily—the importance of bringing people and books together. It was a satisfying goal. We knew that library work was not one in which to make a fortune, but if we were lucky, it would provide us with salaries on which we could live.

Since the Carnegie Library School specialized in training children's librarians, it seemed natural for me to go into that field—a decision that has continued to prove wise and gratifying through the many years since then.

However, even after four years of college and one year of graduate work in library school (which in those days gave one a second bachelor's degree—a B.S. in L.S., as it was known) it was extremely problematical as to whether those of us graduating in that June of 1934 would get jobs anywhere. There's a strong similarity between our situation as young people then and the situation of young people today just out of college.

The Great Depression of 1929 had devastated this country and the world. Men who saw all their life's work destroyed—their savings, investments and businesses vanish—had jumped out of skyscraper windows when Wall Street crashed in 1929. Banks had failed everywhere. Many people were wiped out. Government safety measures to prevent such wholesale disaster had never been thought of, or at least not legislated, up until then. All services were cut back. There was very little tax money to fund anything. People on street corners selling apples for a nickel were a common, accepted sight. They've been replaced today by the homeless. This all has an oddly familiar ring to it.

Like any disaster of such proportion, the Great Depression brought people closer together, trying to help each other, and to reach out to strangers, as much as possible. The family unit was still pretty much intact. Wholesale divorce and extra-marital relationships had not yet changed the patterns of our society.

So, there was the Carnegie Library School graduating class of 1934 about to be launched on the world, eager for work. Toward the end of our last term, Frances Kelly, then director of the school, announced to us that the newly established WPA, Works Progress Administration, under which government-sponsored activities provided jobs, might help us. Some great things came out of the WPA—priceless photographic records of Southern rural life which was totally poverty stricken; remarkable murals on the walls of many public buildings; work camps; and such things. So there might be some hope that we could earn some kind of a living in the field of work we'd chosen, since a bit of WPA money was being given to libraries.

I discovered a novel way of finding a job, but it's not one I would recommend. Like many, many young people, then and for a good many years thereafter, I wanted to live and work in New York City. Surely, there Life would begin! There was theater, music, ballet, opera, publishing—all the things one read and dreamed about. When Miss Kelly discussed my possible future with me, and I expressed my strong desire to come to New York and work in the New York Public Library, her response was: "We don't like our girls to go there unless they have family living in the city."

That response will give you some idea of how far away and long ago 1934 was. Imagine any library school administrator today giving such "professional" advice! Well, there was a cousin of my mother's living in the city, so I figured I qualified and Miss Kelly gave me a letter of introduction to Anne Carroll Moore. I carried it with me when my mother and I drove to New York on a visit, to spend the week between the end of my exams and the graduation ceremony.

The Central Children's Room

And here is my unorthodox way of getting a job. I planned to see Miss Moore and present my letter on the last day of my New York visit—typical young idiocy to leave such an important thing to the last minute. The day before, in an accident, my mother had broken her collar bone and been hospitalized, so she could not drive back to Pittsburgh with me for graduation. I saw Miss Moore late on that morning and then had to drive back to Pittsburgh, at once. Later on, Miss Moore told me the reason she hired me was because she thought anyone who could drive so far alone must be all right! I hope I had some other potentials for a career in library work, as well as being able to drive.

So, on July 1, 1934, I reported for work at the 42nd Street Library—hired for two months only, because that's all the funding there seemed to be. I discovered my first assignment was the Central Children's Room, then in the main library, to the left as you come in the 42nd Street entrance. One can't compare it with the bright, attractive, modern Central Children's Room now in the Donnell branch of NYPL. The two are vastly different, each with its own character. Helen Masten, then the head of the room, was on vacation. Maria Cimino was in charge that month. Mrs. Rodzianko was also on the staff—a beautiful White Russian exile whom Miss Moore had met in Lord & Taylor, where Mrs. Rodzianko was selling dresses, and whom Miss Moore had the great good sense to lure to the library. I once saw a photograph of Mrs. Rodzianko taken when she was a very young woman in an evening dress she had worn at the Imperial Court, with a jeweled diadem in her hair, and she was breathtakingly lovely. What an experience it was to a brand new children's librarian to work with these gifted, sophisticated women.

Maria Cimino, a singer and an exceptional storyteller, guided me through that month. The greatest—and most embarrassing—mistake I made still stays in my memory. A very nice looking older man with bushy eyebrows and twinkling eyes came to the circulation desk when I was staffing it alone and asked to take out the book he was holding. I asked for his library card, which in those days had to be stamped, but he said he would just take it out "on his name." Totally nonplussed, I had to go into the Reading Room and ask the staff member there what to do. The man turned out to be the Director of the Library, Harry Miller Lydenberg. You can imagine how I felt!

The Central Children's Room was not too busy in the summer, so I had a chance to gain some familiarity with the marvelous Reading Room collection. Miss Moore had set up there, and in each branch library children's room, rich collections of books special for their literary value, for their illustrations, or for their design and bookmaking. Many of the books were in foreign languages—imported to serve the needs of New York City's multinational, multiracial population. Times change, and a number of years ago, the branch Reading Room collections were disbanded and the books discarded or auctioned off. They had served their purpose, though I was sad to see it.

On to Harlem

My next assignment was in Harlem, at the 135th Street Branch Library on the corner of Lenox Avenue. What a memorable experience that was. Augusta Baker was the head of the children's room there but, like Helen Masten at the Central Children's Room, Augusta was on vacation. Priscilla Edie was her wonderful deputy. For a WASP—White Anglo-Saxon Protestant—as I was (and am, I guess! Can one ever grow out of it?)—no experience could have been better. As almost the only white person on an otherwise black staff, a staff that would take me to a neighboring restaurant sometimes for lunch or dinner (when we worked at night) where I would be absolutely the only white, I realized quickly what it felt like to be a minority. Only no one ever treated me the way the black minority has for so many years been treated in reverse situations—and all too often still is.

Harlem was in its heyday then—with gifted writers and poets and musicians and artists. The children who came to the library were a joy to work with, responsive to all kinds of books, great to read aloud to and to tell stories to. Believe it or not, Arthur Ransome's books about English children and their sailboats on the Norfolk Broads, were great favorites with many of the children to whom they'd been skillfully introduced. So much for reading only about your own small world!

I learned many lessons there. A small girl returned a book one day with the corners of it badly chewed. I scolded her gently for letting her puppy chew the book, and I couldn't understand why she kept smiling quite happily. Only after she'd left the desk did another staff member enlighten me. It was a rat that had chewed the book's corners, and the little girl was delighted that I thought she had a puppy.

Assistant to Miss Moore

From 135th Street I was moved back to the main library, to be the junior assistant in Miss Moore's office, the famous Room 105. It was a large room, all the way to the left of the Fifth Avenue entrance. The room had a warm, brown, cork-tiled floor. To the left as you came in was Miss Moore's large desk, given a modicum of privacy by a standing leather screen. To the right of the door were three desks, one belonging to Mary Gould Davis, who was the Supervisor of Storytelling in the library system, another remarkable woman. She was very different from ACM in many ways, but that fact was indicative of Miss Moore's perception about people and her willingness to appoint to the staff people of great diversity in background and personality. From the beginning, Miss Moore had recognized storytelling as an integral way of bringing books and children together at an early age.

One of the other two desks in Room 105 was occupied by the person officially known as "the Assistant to the Superintendent of Work with Children." It was filled by Marjorie Burbank when I came there, a wonderful woman, immensely capable and calm (of great importance in that office) and blessed with a tremendous sense of humor (also essential in a job that entailed a good deal of stress). The third desk was for the junior assistant who was I on that July 1, 1934 day.

The only telephone for the office was on a corner of Miss Moore's desk. Each time it rang, the junior assistant had to rise, get to it quickly, and say "Miss Moore's office." If the assistant fumbled or stumbled at all, or if, God forbid, the assistant had a personal call that took more than a minute or two—Miss Moore would clear her throat in a particular way, guaranteed to strike terror into the heart of the inexperienced. It indicated her displeasure was mounting.

When anyone came to the office, the junior assistant had to rise, go to the door, greet them, and find out who they were and what they wanted. If Miss Moore could and would see them, they could wait on a chair that backed up against the screen.

As you will have guessed, the situation was extremely formal, and Miss Moore expected perfect discipline. It turned out I was the first person ever allowed to wear a dress with short sleeves in the summer—and the sleeves came right down to the elbows. It's hard to imagine such a restriction in this day and age.

There was one occasion when I might have been dismissed. Julie Cummins, current head of Children's Services at NYPL, made me promise to tell the story, so here it is. Marjorie Burbank always brought jelly beans to the office around Eastertime, and it turned out she could perform a remarkable feat. She could balance a jelly bean on the tips of her fingers, palm upward, then hit the heel of the palm with her other hand. This made the bean jump up into the air. Marjorie would then skillfully catch it in her mouth. Well, could I do that? No! The bean would always shoot off in the wrong direction and I'd have to scramble after it. Naturally, I was determined to master this trick which, incidentally, we never did if Miss Moore or Miss Davis, or anyone else, were around.

One morning, with great concentration, I placed the jelly bean just so, hit the heel of my hand smartly, and opened my mouth wide. Miraculously, the bean fell right into my mouth, but also right down my windpipe—and there it stuck. For a few seconds, my breath was cut off, and I knew I might die if I couldn't dislodge the jelly bean, but even greater than that fear was the fear that Miss Moore might suddenly arrive and find me gagging to death in the corner!

That office was the center of the children's book world in New York City, and its influence spread across the country and abroad to other countries, as well.

Miss Moore's Vision

Those of you who have read Miss Moore's *Roads to Childhood* (Doran, OP) books know what a remarkable critical mind she had and how wise and astute her vision was. It was she who encouraged publishers to establish separate children's book departments with a children's book editor in charge, instead of sporadically publishing a book for children if a well-thought-of writer for adults happened to write one.

It was she who pushed for and achieved regular viewing of children's books in newspapers and magazines. It was she who saw the need and the great opportunity to reach out to the waves of immigrants flooding into New York from Ellis Island, hungry for the chance to give their children better lives, better educations, to whom free public libraries were an enormous gift. This situation is a familiar one today, particularly with Asian, Spanish-speaking, and Haitian peoples.

Yet, despite the tremendous importance of library service to children, which had been widely recognized by the time I came on the scene, the Great Depression had taken an enormous toll on library work, just as has happened today to library systems everywhere. Tax money to pay staff and buy books had all but vanished. I believe (though I regret I've not checked this out) that library hours were curtailed then as now—history repeating itself. Then, as now, children were hungry for books, and for a quiet place in which to read them. Further, at that time, they did not have television for a diversion, and there was no money for movies or any other entertainment.

Books in the branch libraries were unlike any books I'd known before. They had been much mended and rebound in dreary buckram. They had been read and circulated for so long that the pages felt thick, somehow, and pulpy, and they were almost gray in color, not from abuse but from the many, many hands that had held them and turned the pages.

By 1934, the worst of the Depression was over, and slowly funds for books began to trickle into the library system. At last, one could dare to discard some of the most worn-out books because there was a little money to buy replacements.

I'll always remember one occasion when (I don't know the circumstances) a special sum was allotted to the 135th Street Branch children's room. Augusta Baker would come to Room 105 and then she and I would work in the stacks, deciding what could be discarded from her collection and what new books or replacements could be bought.

To see clean, colorful-looking books begin to appear again in the children's rooms—and the excitement and pleasure of children and staff alike when the books arrived—gave us a rare uplift. It was an upbeat time to come into library work, when a sense of renewal began to spread, a realization that perhaps the worst was over.

ACM and the Publishing World

Into Room 105, Miss Moore's office, came a great variety of people. Children's book editors visited Miss Moore, sometimes to seek specific advice, more often just to get a general sense of what sorts of books were needed, what was doing well and why. The younger editors often came with considerable trepidation because Miss Moore did not mince words and could, upon occasion, be quite caustic.

But of course Miss Moore wasn't always right. Thank goodness she was human and made mistakes of judgment like the rest of us. But, beginning as a young woman who started library service for children in New York City, she had fought—as those pioneering women had to—to establish the fundamental importance of books for children. Miss Moore had fought for the provision of books that gave children pleasure as well as for their education and had earned the right to have strong opinions or to make stiff judgments upon occasion.

Mae Masee of Viking Press; Helen Dean Fish of Stokes which then merged into Lippincott; Peggy Lesser of Doubleday; Bertha Gunterman of Longmans; Louise Raymond and later Ursula Nordstrom of Harper; Alice Dalgliesh of Scribner; Louise Seaman Bechtel followed by Doris Patee of Macmillan—these were some of the callers in 105.

Then, too, there were people from abroad who wanted to learn more about the remarkable system of public library work with children in the U.S. (epitomized by the New York Public) so that they could promote something similar in their own countries. Dr. Valfrid Munch-Peterson from Denmark was one such visitor who came more than once. She spent a lot of time studying our ways of working and then started something similar in Denmark.

Authors and illustrators often came to call in 105, as well—mostly those whose work had passed muster with ACM, I must say. Ruth Sawyer Durand, author of the Newbery winning *Roller Skates* (Dell), James Daugherty (whose *Andy and the Lion* [Viking] was read aloud by Mayor Edward Koch a few years ago in the Central Children's Room, here at Donnell), the d'Aulaires, Bob McCloskey, are only a very few of the visitors that come quickly to my mind.

Of course, prominent librarians from other cities, and reviewers and critics of children's books, like Louise Seaman Bechtel in her later years, and Bertha Mahoney Miller of the *New York Herald Tribune* and *The Horn Book*, respectively, visited from time to time.

Spreading the Word

The New York Public Library then was a mecca for all who had some connection with books for children. In later years, when I was no longer on the library staff, as I traveled to other parts of this country, again and again I would meet people in libraries who had worked here and then gone elsewhere, taking with them the principles and beliefs and standards Miss Moore gave to her staff. What this library meant to New York and to the country as a whole is a proud heritage.

Despite her sternness, Miss Moore also had a great sense of celebration. She liked to make an occasion whenever possible. Sometimes, those celebrations took place in Room 105. Then, there were always crackers and a whole big cheese of some sort, and candlelight all around—even if the occasion happened while it was still light outside. Children's librarians from the branches would be invited and the room was mercilessly crowded and—in my memory—overheated! I confess that those of us who worked in the office rather dreaded these parties because, when they were over, we had to scrape up the dropped crackers and bits of cheese that were scrunched into the floor by many feet!

One of the truly celebratory events was then, as it is now, the appearance of the annual list of outstanding children's books. To this event, held in the Central Children's Room, always around four o'clock of a November afternoon, invitations were sent out to each author and artist whose work was included on the list, to editors and publishers, to reviewers and critics. It was a stellar audience that gathered. There was always at least one guest speaker—an author or an artist, or both.

The next morning, the children's librarians came to the Central Children's Room for (if possible) a repeat of the previous afternoon's program. On the afternoon occasion, the staff could see the children's book editors—some surreptitiously, some openly—checking to see what if any of their titles had been judged worthy of inclusion on the list. Editors are now given a little advance notice! It is an important list and it travels around this country.

It seems to me, in retrospect, that we worked every night for a month in 105, deciding which books to include and then writing appropriate annotations for them, typing it all, and finally getting copy to John Archer, a wonderful man who was head of the library's print shop. I am sure this process is still very much the same today as it was then.

The pursuit of excellence was Anne Carroll Moore's constant concern—excellence in staff performance as well as in books to be recommended and bought for the library. Her drive and her constancy imbued the staff with the same desire for excellence. All the new books came in to Room 105 then, just as they do to Julie Cummins's office today, for review and consideration. Though the total output of new books in any calendar year in those long-ago days was not nearly as large as it is now, there were exceptional books, good books, and a lot of dross, just as today, only in greater numbers. Exceptional books now, as then, are not necessarily popular books, but they are books of special quality that should be celebrated and introduced to readers.

Frances Clarke Sayers

Inevitably, the time came for Miss Moore to retire. Her long reign—the only word that's appropriate for the many years of her leadership—was over. She had established standards and built expectations that would not be easy to uphold or fulfill. The choice of successor was made by Miss Moore herself—Frances Clarke Sayers. Mrs. Sayers had worked in the Central Children's Room years before as a very young woman. This was an inspired choice.

Some of you may have known Frances. She was as different from Miss Moore as could be. Her personality was more relaxed. Miss Moore had had to fight to make her dream a reality. Frances Sayers had to fight other kinds of battles, and did so most effectively. She upheld the cause of excellence—by inspiring her staff, by sharing with them the best in books of all sorts; those meant for children and those meant for adults. She lured many people to come and speak to the staff, people like the great Norwegian novelist, Sigrid Undset, author of the Kristin Lavransdatter books (Random), and Louis Mumford, when his book about his only son's death from a brain tumor, *Green Memories* (OP) came out.

Miss Moore was a spare, quick-moving New Englander, born and bred. Frances was the embodiment of all the old Southern qualities of charm and elegance, stemming from her Galveston (TX) childhood. Both women were devoted to quality in books and had the ability to inspire others to share their dreams.

Within a few years of Frances Sayers' arrival at 105, my tenure ended. And so must this reminiscence of "the olden days," as children say. Those of you working in the library share a proud heritage, often under great difficulties but never more important to uphold than now. It is easy in retrospect to see the beginnings of this work. It is satisfying to know that the great tradition still flourishes. The prospect that it will endure is a joyous one.

Frances Sayers gave an eloquent and moving speech, called "Lose Not the Nightingale" at an American Library Association conference in New York City in 1937. In it she used Hans Christian Andersen's story *The Nightingale* as her metaphor. She was championing the cause of good books and of reading. At the same time she was decrying certain methods of education that were putting the techniques of reading before the remarkable act itself—the act of reading books that can stretch the mind and make the imagination soar; against the idea that children can only understand books about things they have actually experienced. Frances's speech sums up the principles on which library work with children was founded—which continue to this very day to be the heart of the matter:

The power of responding to the intuitive and the poetic is greatest in childhood. Rob children of this power, and you rob them of an everlasting anchor and refuge. It is on this intuitive knowledge that our emotions are built, and without emotion, no amount of experience will suffice. Experience is not enough. There must be the emotional ability to realize that experience . . . If we let go the fashions, the theories, and the trends in reading; if we read and re-read the great books; . . . if we lose no opportunity to share with children these books that have possessed us, irrespective of their ages, their seeming ability, or disability, trusting in powers beyond tests and measurements . . . the power of the writer, the power of our own sincere, spontaneous enthusiasm; if we demand of publishers and writers and artists the best they can give; if we can wake in children a response beyond their immediate need—if we organize to accomplish these things, we shall never, never lose the nightingale.

A Shared Responsibility
Nurturing Literacy in the Very Young

by Barbara N. Kupetz

Upon his "graduation" from kindergarten, Jonathan, my talkative five-year-old neighbor, announced with pride, "I'm all finished with kindergarten and pretty soon I'm going to first grade. I'm gonna learn how to read there."

Learning to read is an exciting time in the lives of children. Their new ability to make sense of the printed symbols on a page allows them to take exciting journeys and meet marvelous new characters. Like Jonathan, many people associate first grade with learning to read, since that is the time most children experience their first "real" reading classes and become familiar with such educational terms as "vocabulary," "comprehension," and "reading group."

No one would dispute the importance of these critical first-grade experiences. But, why do so many adults view reading as a skill that magically appears when children reach the age of six? Children don't just come to first grade and suddenly learn to read. There is a great deal of activity that must occur prior to formal schooling in order for children to become good readers.

The responsibility for this activity must be shared by all of us who work with children if we expect them to enter school ready to learn. Early childhood educators, parents, caregivers, and public librarians all have a responsibility to identify opportunities for early encounters with literacy and to make sure that all children have the chance to participate.

Read Early, Read Often

Research over the last several decades indicated that children begin learning to read long before their first-grade reading experiences. Before they are able to decode words and actually "read" the printed word in the conventional sense, children are becoming readers in their earliest days. They are constantly exposed to print both in books and in their environment. And, they are beginning to develop a love for the rhythm of language and an aesthetic sensitivity to illustration that will carry over into their reading years.

When we talk about using books with young children, most of us think of the preschool years—and we should. Book experiences are critically important for three- and four-year-olds if they are to establish good habits and preliminary literacy skills.

Studies have shown, however, that it is equally important for infants and toddlers to have pre-reading experiences. The benefits of this kind of activity include helping children's eyes to focus; helping them recognize objects and develop sensory awareness; reinforcing basic concepts; and providing the opportunity for physical closeness so critical to young children's emotional and intellectual development.

A recent study under the sponsorship of the National Institute on Education gathered a panel of reading experts to synthesize their research findings regarding the development of reading. This National Commission on Reading concluded, "The single most important activity for building the knowledge required for eventual success in reading is reading aloud to children."

Librarians and others have vital roles to play in encouraging early childhood literacy. There is much we all can do to ensure that every child, even the very youngest, is exposed to the necessary learning opportunities.

How Children Become Literate

The beginning of literacy is multi-faceted and involves more than just learning certain technical skills. Becoming literate means acquiring a set of attitudes, behaviors, expectations, and understandings that begin early and may appear quite unlike conventional forms of reading instruction.

I recently spoke with a young mother who listed her reasons for not reading to her 16-month-old son and three-month-old daughter. She thought her children were too young to understand the story, they were too rough on books and tended not to take care of them, her son didn't like to sit still for a whole story, and she didn't think she would do a very good job of reading anyway. All of these are common responses from parents who think their children are too young to begin literacy development.

In some respects, the mother's response is correct. Very young children are not comprehending the story in the same way a five-year-old does. But, the sound of a reader's voice gets an infant's attention even before the child can focus on the pictures. The warmth and security of being held and the melodic, soothing sound of an adult's voice make for a pleasurable combination. Even when a children's book is not available, adults can use their voices effectively to read *any* printed material. At this early age, the words are not the most important part of the book-sharing experience.

Two-year-old Catherine loves hearing a story. Her father recently read her the book, *Chicka Chicka Boom Boom* by Bill Martin and John Archambault (S. & S., 1989). A few hours after hearing the story, Catherine came into the kitchen with her book and said, "Mommy, I can read to you." She found a spot in the center of the kitchen floor, held the book correctly on her lap, and began to flip the pages as she changed, "A meets B and B meets C. I'll meet you at coconut tree. Chicka, Chicka, Boom, Boom. Enough room."

Catherine's pretend reading and the reenactment of the behaviors of reading makes it clear that she is interested in reading stories. Of course, she is unable to read in the conventional sense, but she pretends to know. Playing with reading is one way she learns about language, words, and books. Already she is familiar with such book-handling skills as turning pages and progressing from left to right and top to bottom. Most important, Catherine loves a great many things about reading, including the sounds and rhythm of language, the illustrations in the book, and the special time she spends with adults when they share books with her. These early reading experiences, which Catherine has been having since birth, lay an excellent foundation for her later literacy development. As she begins to make sense of the symbols on the printed page, she will be an eager participant in "real" reading.

Catherine is surrounded by adults who understand the value of these early encounters with books and do all they can to provide such experiences. What can we do for the child who is not so fortunate?

A Shared Responsibility

Most teachers expect parents to provide some home experiences for young children to support their literacy development in school. Many parents, however, see this as solely the responsibility of teachers. Children who are missing the at-home literacy activities their age-mates are experiencing are at a distinct disadvantage.

One might assume that book experiences are a part of the daily routine at Head Start or other day care centers. But, the fact is that some of these facilities share books and literacy experiences infrequently, in many cases because they are understaffed. This is especially true of programs serving infants and toddlers.

Given these gaps in literacy education, many children need better access to early reading experiences than they are now getting. This is where the librarian comes in. Many adults think children do not need to encounter librarians until after they begin to read. But, the role of the librarian goes beyond that of directing children to books by a particular author or reading a story aloud. Librarians are important players in literacy development, sharing the responsibility of providing enriching experiences for very young children so that literacy can develop and flourish.

What exactly does this mean for the community librarian? Public librarians can be an essential resource not only for children, but for parents and teachers as well. They can build their collections to include materials appropriate for children of all ages (including very young readers). They can make themselves accessible to parents and early childhood professionals who need guidance in book selection.

Librarians also can provide an important function for the parent who feels uncertain about sharing books with his or her child. They can model for parents "how" to read aloud, help them develop their own literacy and their confidence in reading aloud to their children, and encourage them to show their children that they themselves enjoy the experiences of books.

Offering the Right Materials

Following are some of the genres and formats librarians might focus on in choosing materials to meet the special needs of young children and their parents:

Rhymes: Since young children are so focused on the sound the reader makes, books that contain rhythmical verses, such as "Mother Goose" rhymes and lullabies, can be very comforting to a child. When parents learn them, these kinds of rhymes can become part of infant feeding, rocking, bathing, and even diaper-changing.

"Point and Say" books: These books can be used when infants are ready to begin focusing on pictures of simple objects (at about two to four months). They provide opportunities for parents to engage in conversation with their children as they name the animals, people, or objects on the page. Although the youngest child may not be able to respond with recognizable words, after a time of adult pointing and naming, the child will begin to point to the pictures to which the reader refers.

"Touch and Smell" books: These books let infants and toddlers use their senses as they participate in the reading experience, offering flaps for a child to lift and peek under, mirrors to look into, textures to feel, and flowers to sniff.

Boardbooks: For parents who complain, "Reading to my baby is frustrating because my child tries to eat the book instead of listen to it," offer them a boardbook. The heavy, laminated cardboard pages in these books are designed precisely for the abuse a baby has to offer. Public libraries should be prepared with an ample supply of these nearly indestructible books for the very young to explore. If we hope to immerse children in books and provide many rich reading experiences, we cannot supply books only to quickly pull them away for fear of damage.

Library Outreach Programs

Libraries also can help by providing outreach programs that encourage area nursery schools and day care centers to bring young groups into the library. In this way, even children in understaffed facilities can receive the quality literacy experiences they need. Such programs also help young children begin to see the library as a place to gather for information, find materials, and, of course, experience reading pleasure. Children are never too young to get library cards and enjoy book-related activities at the library.

Library outreach programs are especially important for children who might not otherwise have access to any literacy experiences at all, such as homeless children or those living in public care facilities. In addition to being at an educational disadvantage, these children have a great need for some of the emotional benefits that early literacy activities can provide, such as the development of self-esteem and a sense of belonging and social acceptance.

Collaboration Is the Key

Literacy development begins long before children embark on their formal education. Without question, first grade is an exciting time for children like Jonathan, but earlier literacy activities (such as those experienced by Catherine) can be equally exciting—and essential.

Learning to read is a process in which a great many individuals play vital roles. Through collaborative efforts among librarians, parents, teachers, and day-care providers, young children can have the variety of early opportunities and the continuity of experiences they need to nurture their literacy development. We must all work as members of a team if we hope to nurture children and facilitate their development as lifelong readers.

A Fair Accompli

by Sharon A. Ahern

Parents selecting a preschool program for their children are faced with a confusing array of choices. In our community, the options include playgrounds, traditional part-time nursery schools, full-service day care centers with a preschool curriculum for three- to five-year olds, and two different programs offered by the public school system. While some parents gather information about preschools through the neighborhood grapevine, many visit the children's room of the library looking for help. After several years of referring parents to the phone book and the local school department, I faced this issue for the first time as a parent two years ago.

As a working parent I found it difficult to make phone calls and visit schools to gather the necessary information and weed out unsuitable programs. When I shared my frustration with another parent, she commented that she wished there were preschool fairs like the college fairs we went to as high school students. The idea for the Preschool Fair was born. Sponsored by the library's new Family Center, the fair would be an active way for the library to fulfill its goal to provide parents with the informational support they needed to care for their children.

I began by making a list of all the possible preschool options within a 20-minute drive of the library. I phoned the schools on my list (about 30) and described the program; nearly two-thirds expressed interest in participating. I learned that many of the schools in our area have late winter/early spring open houses and registration periods (for programs beginning in the fall), so I reserved the library's large meeting room for a Saturday in late January. In early November I sent out letters inviting all preschools in the area to register by phone the first week of December (before the holiday rush). I sent out press releases to local papers and the cable TV station to get the word out to any small or new preschools I may have missed.

In the weeks leading up to the Preschool Fair, I contacted the National Association for the Education of Young Children (NAEYC) and ordered copies of some of their pamphlets to distribute to parents. The total materials cost was less than $30. NAEYC also sent along two dozen copies of their catalog for me to pass out to the preschool reps. Our staff prepared a bibliography of selected titles on early learning, school readiness, how to choose a preschool, and current issues in education.

Finally I selected books and magazine articles for a display of library materials at the fair.

Publicity began while the fair was still in the early planning stages. Once I knew that a number of schools were interested, I sent out press releases to several monthly papers. An earlier press release captured the interest of a local reporter who wrote an article on the fair for a daily newspaper. I also promoted the fair in the library column of our town's weekly paper.

Our staff prepared flyers and sent them to the school department, which distributed them to all children, teachers, and other employees in the school system. I used the town census to determine which families with preschool children did not have school-age children and mailed flyers directly to them. Flyers were also posted on church, store, and small business bulletin boards around town. The local cable television station included the Preschool Fair on its community calendar for the entire month of January. Many patrons remarked about having heard about the fair "on TV."

The morning of the fair was sunny and clear (weather is always the first big hurdle for a January program in New England). I arrived early to set up the library's book display and handout table. Representatives from the 12 schools arrived about 30 minutes prior to the library's opening to set up their assigned tables. Several brought balloons for the children, and two brought small TV/VCRs to show videotapes. (They had called ahead to ask permission. I said it would be fine as long as they brought everything they needed—including extension cords.) All of the schools brought handouts describing their program, schedules, and fees.

We knew that many parents would bring their children to the fair. I also knew how difficult it would be for parents to talk with school reps and attend to their children at the same time, so we set up a children's activity table in the center of the room. A library volunteer put out art materials, puzzles, and a display of popular picture books, reading to the children and supervising them during the program.

The success of the Preschool Fair far exceeded our expectations. More than 100 families attended the three-hour fair. Several months after the event, we were still receiving phone calls asking for copies of the handouts as well as numerous requests to make the fair an annual event.

Our second Preschool Fair took place in January of this

year. We knew we were on to a good thing when inquiries about the fair began coming in the previous September. Many people had heard about the event and didn't want to miss it this year. Again, attendance exceeded 100 families—not bad when there are fewer than 250 households in the area with pre-school-age children. The fair provided parents with easy access to the latest information on an important subject. The library benefitted from the popular program, too: we fostered new relationships with area preschools and made contact with parents who had not been regular library users.

Part Five

Resources for Youth

The number of learning resources for youth has exploded in the past forty years. This fact makes collection development indisputably one of the most important and challenging functions a librarian performs because it is through this performance that books and other resources are provided for discovery by young people or to fulfill a young learner's specific information need.

Collection development is an ability that requires many skills and a broad knowledge of many subjects as well as knowledge of the users to be served by the materials selected. Since its beginning *SLJ* has been a valuable resource for collection developers, for, in addition to the "Book Review," a comprehensive, or in the words of the editors, " . . . the country's most complete source of critical reviews for each year's new trade books for children and young adults," a large block of *SLJ*'s articles and columns addresses the multi-faceted dimensions of collection development. This section provides a selection of these articles and columns published in the past forty years.

Eroticism and the Art of Film

by G. William Jones

I would like to look upon screen eroticism from an artistic point of view. If motion pictures, the world's newest and most pervasive art form, are going to press toward their own artistic maturity, all artificial barriers against their serious treatment of all areas of life must fall. A few months ago when I was in Houston, I found that there was a Museum of Modern Art right across the street from my hotel. The sculptures of Rodin were there, about 40 or 50 of them. Rodin created many excellent works, not only the Thinker, but many works which are erotic, almost in the extreme. I was standing there looking at all these sculptures, when in came two nuns with about 20 pre-school toddlers. They were bringing them in to see the sculptures. I began to muse, "What is the difference between bringing them in here to see all these nudes in all these various positions of love and taking them down to a movie theater in town in which they can see the same kinds of nudity? Why here and why not there? What are the real reasons?" One of the strongest ones that I come up with is that these people trusted Rodin's sculptures to be "art"; and they trust "art" to be uplifting, sensitizing, making wholesome. They trust art to be "good for you." But perhaps these same people did not trust the film to be a work of art, and would feel that sexuality on film, no matter how integrally presented, would be a negative experience—especially for their young wards. In our country especially, motion pictures have been traditionally looked upon as merely an entertainment form, and only very recently have many people begun to look upon them as even potentially an art form.

There are, of course, a lot of other reasons why people might find sexuality in other art forms to be quite appropriate, but not find it so in motion pictures. One other reason why sexuality in the film may be much more threatening than on canvas, or in the forms of sculpture, may be simply the gigantic size of the picture. We look at a piece of art work on a page and it is not very threatening to us, no matter how erotic it may be, so long as we know the work to have been executed by an artist whose name we recognize. But if it is thrown large before us on the screen, somehow it seems to overpower us and therefore, perhaps, may seem to be more threatening.

But excellence in artistic treatment seems to thrive under the same kind of conditions in which trashiness also can thrive. Limit the trash and you limit the art. What is the dividing line between trash and art? I have to confess that many of the movements that are very well established in modern art, I thought were "trash" when I first came upon them. In my first contact with Pop art, I thought, we were really being put on. But now I appreciate much of the Pop art as a celebration of the beauty and grace of the ordinary.

Education, I think, is the most dependent and reliable tool with which we can help each person to be his *own* discerning and discriminating divider between the real and the phony, between the truth and the lies. By the time a modern high school student graduates, he will have seen 500 films, at least; he will have spent more time watching TV than he will have spent in the classroom. In the average American home there are more TV sets than there are homes with indoor plumbing. This average American home's TV set is on for an average of more than six hours a day, 365 days a year. And in the midst of this, what are we doing in the schools? We are still teaching literacy—and very well we should—but we are not teaching "cinemacy," the art of being a discerning viewer. Marshall McLuhan, whether you love him or not, says that the only defense against "media fallout" is the understanding of media, and that we are doomed to being in the power of the media unless we understand their magic. Once we understand them, they are no longer magic, and we can use the media rather than their using us. Why not teach cinemacy, then, as well as literacy?

I would look, then, upon screen eroticism for a democratic point of view, a point of view determined by my being a citizen of a country which I love very much, which has the best experiment going in all the world, in what it means to be a country, a cooperative national community. The irony is that antieroticism seems to be a safe political platform nowadays, but that if anybody who espouses such a platform gets pushed into a corner where he begins getting more specific, he is very likely to appear more and more anti-American. The reason I say this is that we have constitutionally guaranteed freedoms, such as the First and Fourteenth Amendments, and any person who wants to restrict these freedoms is forgetting, or ignoring, our Constitutional basis as a country. I find that in our society, we may be guaranteed more freedom than many of us want, that pleases many of us. A sort of a qualification for this is that I think almost everybody wants these freedoms for *himself*; it is the other guy having this freedom that we worry about. But in America, one might almost say that we are condemned to be free "whether we like it or not, and that we must learn to deal with all the kinds of problems that come with freedom," a much different set of problems from that which comes from suppression. We seem to want sometimes to trade our fellow citizens' heritage of freedom for a mess of restrictive pottage. The danger, however, of restrictions upon those constitutional freedoms is that in suppressing *lies* about sex, the *truth* about sex will also be suppressed. For want of a suitable net, for want of a board of censors, which has the superhuman ability to divide unerringly between sexual truth and sexual falsehood, we are liable simply to suppress *all* information and artistry concerning sex, leading to what has been called "the conspiracy of silence" about sex. And this conspiracy of silence has greater possibilities for social harm than the problem which it seeks to correct. Plus, I am concerned about the short distance between repression of sexual expression, or "sex speech," and the repression of political expression.

I am no supporter of pornography, I am no friend of the pornographer, regardless of how some people might throw accusations at some of us on the Commission. Pornography is a lie about the human experience. I know of no better work existing now than Drs. Eberhardt and Phyllis Krumhausen's book called *Pornography and the Law*, in which they draw very finely a definition between "pornography," on the one hand, and "erotic realism," on the other. "Pornography" is full of clichés and exaggerations that are lies about sex. But "erotic realism" is the truth about sex, a representation much like Henry Miller's depictions, in which sex is not all glamorous by any means and elements which are an integral part of the reality of sex, but which are antierotic and nontitillating, are included.

I am not a supporter of pornography, but I *am* a supporter of the arts' ability and freedom to depict, in depth, with candor, and with integrity, the entire gamut of human relationships, including the sexual. I foresee a time in which our country, sick with sexual crimes and sexual distortions of all kinds for many many years, will become healthy in this way. Depictions of nudity will become so common (as they are even now) that no one will snicker obscenely at the depiction of the human body, or shout "For shame!" and try to cover it up. Information about sex; good, straight, and complete, will be so immediately available to normally curious adolescents at the moment they are concerned about it, that the pornographer will have lost his market once and for all, for pornography lives on ignorance and repression. So free will men be to produce and obtain, if they want, depictions of erotic realism that it will have lost its appeal as a forbidden fruit—which was always the largest part of its appeal, anyway. I already see this happening among our high school and college youth, who, unlike their elders, cannot be interested in a movie by the promise of nudity, or once in a movie, cannot have their flagging interest renewed by intrusions of gratuitous sex or violence. They find such things disgusting; they find them a bore.

Having seen the human body, having had access to magazines like *Playboy*, since they were little children; having seen *that*, they are ready for some more relevant social commentary or some serendipitous revelation of artistic quality. Having been raised with the screen only a fingertip's length away, they are much more discerning and demanding about their screen fare than those of us for whom it was a sometimes-Saturday privilege. In fact, they have an open-mouthed wonder at the rest of us, which I find sometimes irkingly condescending, about the kind of movies which turn us older folk on. They say, "Man, what's *your* problem?" It is a strange switch, when *they* become concerned about *us* because of our weird appetites, and because we keep the box office thriving for films like Russ Meyer's *Beyond the Valley of the Dolls*. We older folk assure that there will be more films produced like this because we respond to them at the box office. The kids are also aghast at our apparent liking of violence for the sake of violence, violence as entertainment. But if there is something that disgusts this age group even more, it is someone trying to tell them what they can or cannot see.

I asked a class of mine the other day, "How many are in favor of any form of motion picture censorship?" Only one in 120 held up his hand. He clarified himself with "for those over 30!" The other day I asked a group of Girl Scouts, "What do you think of the 'R' classification for movies?" They said, "It's a good thing, because parents need someone to interpret the films to them." And I would add that the "R" classification is a good thing if it causes parents to go with their children to see films which depict controversial issues, if it means that they will go home and talk about the films together. Such film-based conversations have the possibility of one of the best bridges available to us today. Motion pictures are a live channel into the attention of young people, which the elders could well use as a basis for dialogue with their estranged youth.

After several years of study on the effects screen-mediated violence has upon social behavior, I am really not too worried about the effect screen content, whether it be violent or erotic, can have upon its viewers. The supposition that it can have antisocial effects is based on a "monkey see, monkey do" theory of man, which I find dishonorable: it is certainly not a Christian view of man. Instead, there seem to be defense mechanisms which are built into us from a very early age, which protect us from intrusive media presentations which might try to change us. First there is "selective exposure"—we do not expose ourselves to that which we do not wish to be exposed, and we know before we go into a movie how we are to be confronted. There is also a mechanism for our defense called "selective perception"—we only perceive that which reinforces our pre-existent standards, particularly in the deep things of life, like social controls. We also have "selective retention"; we tend to forget first and quickest that which disagrees with positions we treasure, and we tend to remember that which has reinforced us in our feelings that we were right to begin with. The effects of the screen, if any, are best pointed up to us by McLuhan, who speaks of the electronic signal which closes the intervening spaces, making us citizens of the world, making us into a "tribal village," making us eye-witnesses of Viet Nam; and which not too many years away will bring the classroom and office into the home. What will be the effects of that, and how shall we plan for it? The screen, which educates more effectively than the classroom; the screen, which will connect the home with an information storage and retrieval center so that any written work can be instantly punched up and read out electronically.

The visual media shall soon, under the joint consultation of church, school, and home, become the servants of sexual education, for the whole family. The whole truth plainly stated and as available as it needs to be, will be within the instant grasp of each person.

"And they shall know the truth, and the truth shall make them free"—free from ignorance *and* free from pornography.

Crisis Information Services To Youth
A Lesson For Libraries?

by Carolyn Forsman

Young adult services in public libraries are being threatened with extinction. The elimination of separate departments and of their specially trained librarians in Chicago, Montgomery County, Maryland, and other library systems may signal the beginning of a national trend. The New York State plan to give the school library sole responsibility for services to youth is another step in this direction.

At the same time a new phenomenon, the Crisis Intervention Center, which provides counseling as well as information and referral services to troubled youth, has emerged within the last four years in hundreds of urban, rural, and suburban areas: Anchorage, Atlanta, Denver, Des Moines, Long Island, and Long Beach. Your community probably has one or soon will. Crisis Centers explain themselves by such evoking names as Hotline, Switchboard, Free Clinic, Rapline, Help Line, No Heat Line, Y.E.L.L., Rescue, H.I.P. (Help Is Possible), Somebody Cares, We Care, Inc., Listening Post, Night Line, Drug Aid, Y.E.S. (Youth Emergency Service), Community Youth Line, Your Information Unlimited. Crisis Centers are there to serve the needs of youth ten to 25, not only as students, but as whole persons.

The history and development of young adult services has yet to be written,[1] but young adult librarians have always taken pride in their ability to change with the times, to be sensitive to their clientele's needs and to be innovative in services and programs. Perhaps we can learn from the Crisis Intervention Center new ways to serve the young adult in his complete range of information needs.

Crisis centers in philosophy, organization, services, training methods, publicity, and insight into youth's problems contrast sharply with the whole concept of library service to young adults. They suggest possible new roles and directions for libraries and librarians.

The Crisis Center developed as an alternative to traditional community mental health and medical services. And because information and referral are an integral part of its concept, Hotlines, Switchboards, and Free Clinics can also be looked at as an alternative to traditional library service to young adults.

As with any new phenomenon, the definition of terms used to describe it are often not clear, concise, nor consistent with each other. However, agreement seems to be growing that the term "Crisis Intervention" includes three fairly distinct types of crisis services: Hotlines, Switchboards and Free Clinics.

A Hotline is an emergency anonymous telephone service for young people in crisis providing a listening ear, with referral to agencies and professional backup when necessary.

A Switchboard is primarily a telephone and referral service as well as a message center. Unlike a Hotline, it may also have a walk-in or drop-in facility for visitors.

A Free Clinic is basically a walk-in center that provides direct medical services. It also has facilities for individual or group counseling in both medical and nonmedical problems, such as birth control and the draft.

An example might better explain the relationships and differences between these facilities in a community. A teenager thinks she is pregnant. If she calls the Switchboard she will be referred to the local Free Clinic for a pregnancy test. At the clinic, in addition to the free test, if she chooses, she will be counseled on birth control methods as well as possible solutions to her immediate situation. She might also be counseled on her relationship with the father. If she calls the Hotline instead of Switchboard, a nonjudgmental anonymous voice will direct a few questions to determine if she might indeed be pregnant, and also refer her to the Free Clinic for a test. The listener will not advise her to have an abortion, nor to marry the suspected father, nor otherwise tell her what to do. He will instead, in a series of questions and replies, let the caller discover the options for herself. The Hotline will more likely be used for this type of problem since Hotlines emphasize and specialize in interpersonal and individual psychological needs. Switchboards tend to satisfy more concrete needs, such as food, housing, transportation, and information on political and leisure activities. If a call to the Hotline requests a place to crash for the night and the caller is over 18, he more than likely will be referred to Switchboard. If he is a minor who's run away, the listener will encourage the youth to question his action in terms of himself and his family.

Hotlines, Free Clinics, and Switchboards do not advocate or encourage illegal behavior, including the harboring of runaways without the parent's permission, or the use of drugs.

In certain crises, the person is not in any state to be referred to another agency, no matter how logical it may seem. Persons experiencing a "bad trip" on drugs or contemplating suicide or who are in other life threatening situations, and who call in a state of panic, are handled by whichever of the three services he or she happens to call.

Switchboards

Switchboards and Free Clinics arose out of the counter-culture of white alienated youths. The first Switchboard began in the summer of 1967 in San Francisco to serve the Haight-Ashbury community as a message and referral service. Its prototype was the old "Central" switchboard in American communities which not only connected telephones, but was also a source of solutions to human problems. Its initial use was primarily as a crisis and problem center (what the Hotline now serves) but it soon expanded into a "community resource center." The Switchboard, with the help of its community, created a "human resource file," a list of people willing to teach and to share their skills and knowledge with others. The philosophy is to help people control their own lives by providing them information to make their own decisions. Other files developed to further this goal show the extent of Switchboard services: Jobs, Housing, Transportation, Buy and Sell, Music, Theater, Education, Messages.

A Switchboard is usually reached by telephone (San Francisco had 150,000 calls in their first two-and-a-half years). Its number will be found in a local alternative newspaper listing of frequent phone numbers. Some have a walk-in service, where visitors can read bulletin boards for notices on survival, politics, the youth culture pleasures, or leave and pick up messages. The message service is also used by parents of runaways as a possible point of contact.

In all cases dealing with youth, his or her privacy and confidentiality are respected. Switchboard workers are volunteers from the community who try to make decisions in a democratic manner. When there is a coordinator, he or she has no more rights than the volunteers. Often the staff lives together as a collective. Switchboards are funded by donations from the community including local ministries.

The manuals of the Berkeley and San Francisco Switchboards detail the philosophy, services, and policies of two of the oldest and most stable information services to the youth community.

Free Clinics

The First Free Clinic opened in Los Angeles in November 1967 as a drug treatment center for the free community. The philosophy of the Free Clinic movement is to treat the whole person; and so, it was natural that it would extend its services to include counseling on birth control, abortions, diet and nutrition, and drugs, as well as such nonmedical areas as the draft and law. Counseling is performed by community volunteers, professional and nonprofessional.

A client who enters the clinic is assigned a "facilitator" or "advocate" who is responsible for seeing that his or her needs are met by doctor and/or counselor. The facilitator is there to determine the person's needs, to put him at ease, to refer him to the right services(s) and to post-treatment follow-up.

Free Clinics are supported by donations, foundations, and federal dollars. The latter are sought reluctantly because of the restrictions often attached. Like Switchboards, decision-making is communal or by a board of directors composed of volunteers, the few full-time staff on subsistence salaries, and members from the community.

Free Clinics are loosely organized into a National Free Clinic Council, which facilitates communication via national meetings and a journal.

Hotlines

The use of community volunteers, the nonbureaucratic organization, the sensitivity to community needs and the ability to adapt and expand services in response to these needs, are significant features of Hotlines, as well as of Switchboards and Free Clinics.

While the Free Clinics originated in response to the drug problem, Hotlines evolved from suicide prevention centers and the community mental health movement. In 1958 the Los Angeles Suicide Prevention Center opened its telephones and doors to answer the *Cry for Help*," described by E. S. Schneidman, its founder, in the book by the same name. Experience and research indicated that most of the persons responding were not contemplating suicide but were nevertheless in a "crisis" situation, i.e. a point of extreme stress in which a decision must be made, but the person feels immobilized and unable to cope and is liable to behave in a self-destructive manner.

Adolescence is a "crisis of status discontinuity," socially, psychologically, and physiologically,[2] and in April 1968 the Los Angeles Children's Hospital began its Hotline for Youth. Hotline, the "port of call for angry, frightened, and frustrated young people."[3] Hotline, a personal, anonymous, emergency telephone service for young people in crisis.

Interdisciplinary Approach

Crisis intervention is a human problem and is therefore the responsibility of no particular profession or discipline. Though it arose out of the medical community, it soon aroused the interest and cooperation of professionals from the fields of psychology, psychiatry, therapy, health education, social work, pastoral counseling, nursing, and even law, anthropology, biostatistics and logic, but not librarianship. Its multidisciplinary approach is paralleled by the multi-service functions of Switchboards, Free Clinics, and Hotlines.

Confidentiality

Implicit in the provision of crisis intervention services is an atmosphere of Trust, as one hotline is aptly called. To engender this, a potential source of financial support will be refused if it threatens the center's credibility. There can also be no trust without confidentiality.

The relationship between the caller and listener on the Hotline, between patient and counselor at the Free Clinic, and between person and staff at the Switchboard is confidential, whether adult or minor. Respect for the confidential nature of the client-Crisis Center relationship when the client is a minor is a unique feature of Crisis Centers. "We are responsible to the youth who come in, not to their parents." Hotlines, in particular, can guarantee confidentiality to both the caller and the listener by means of the anonymity of the telephone. In fact, the location of a hotline is often kept a secret to protect both parties. Should a parent inquire as to whether and why his or her child has used the Hotline, the listener can honestly reply that he doesn't know and can explain the Hotline's purpose.

Can public and school librarians honestly make the same claim with respect to their circulation records? How often are they guilty of telephoning a parent even prior to a teenager's or child's use of materials on, say, sex and drugs?

Alternatives

Hotlines do not advocate drugs, but neither do they preach their evils. Free Clinics are not pro-abortion, but neither will they moralize to an unwed parent. Switchboards do not encourage runaways, but neither do they turn them in. A nonjudgmental approach toward the client characterizes the variety of crisis services to youth. They do not judge the person, nor do they recommend one solution, but for each of the range of alternative solutions, crisis centers do try to evaluate and recommend the best resource, whether it be a person, agency, book, or pamphlet.

For example, an unwed pregnant teenager, during a telephone encounter might discover that abortion or adoption are among her alternatives. The listener would not judge her predicament, nor ask her how she could have been so cruel to her parents, etc. If the caller should consider adoption, she would be given a list of recommended adoption agencies and homes for unwed mothers. In contrast, if the same young woman had asked a librarian, she might very well have received a short sermon or even an unintentional casual remark about the *badness* of her condition. Then the librarian might have handed her an outdated health and welfare directory for her to evaluate by herself!

Or if a young man were contemplating shooting heroin or smoking marijuana and let the librarian know this, it would not be surprising if he were told about the evils of drugs in general. But the librarian would not feel responsible for misinformation in any book or pamphlet the person might find by himself and would probably not feel confident to recommend one title over another. A Hotline or Free Clinic worker would discuss with him the possible consequences of drug use and would be prepared to recommend a particular book that had been evaluated to contain accurate information in a nonsensational way.

Hotlines do not advise, but they do more than listen. The aim of a crisis line is to provide constructive alternatives to a problem, to help the caller examine it from all angles, making use of his own resources to the fullest extent possible. If it is necessary, to go beyond this, the listener will "patch-in" to the telephone line, from his file of human resources in fields relevant to youth, a lawyer, doctor, psychiatrist, or minister, who has volunteered to be on call as a professional back-up. Alternatives might also be sought from the community resources file for the caller to contact later himself. Crisis centers hope to alleviate the immediate crisis, but also, just as important, to prepare the caller to deal with future crises, to become a better problem-solver. The repeat caller to a Hotline is a problem and is not encouraged.

Contrast this to the dependency relationship implicit in library services, e.g. "hooked on books," "book bait;" not only is one encouraged to frequent the library, but once inside, he is expected to have to "ask the librarian" to utilize its resources to the fullest. The reader's adviser hopes that a satisfied reader will return to him for additional advice.

Volunteers

Hotlines are operated primarily by volunteer youth. In the mental health services community, aides were used initially because of the shortage of professional manpower. Experience proved them to be more than an inexpensive second-best substitute. Their knowledge of the community and similarity to the clientele were qualities that the professional could not substitute with skill, and they became recognized members of the mental health team. It was only natural that youth would have a similar role in helping troubled peers who did not use and were not reached by traditional facilities.

Though the structure and organization of Hotlines is more varied than that of Switchboards and Free Clinics, even the most traditional, those organized by mental health and religious associations, have a youth advisory board and utilize teenagers and college students as volunteers.

Other Hotlines are sometimes part of a City Youth Agency, a University Counseling Center, or are nonprofit corporations. Support comes from their parent organization, if there is one, as well as from civic groups, personal donations, benefits, and foundations and federal grants. In any case, their budget is miniscule compared to that of health or information services in their community.

Problems

An analysis of the problems that are brought to these centers is possible because of the detailed records kept of each contact, whether by telephone or in person. A data log sheet will include age, sex, marital status, and first name; the degree of the crisis, the attitude and approach the listener took; whether the problem was resolved by referral, professional back-up, or went unsolved; and where the caller heard about the service.

Though no systematic analysis exists at this time comparing one center to another, a general picture does emerge from inspection of the records of several crisis centers. Most calls involve inter-personal relationships: mainly boy/girl, peer, or family conflicts. Problems arising from an internal mental state, especially loneliness and depression are the second largest category. Suicidal calls are listed separately and are relatively few in number, though they are the most serious and have the greatest impact on volunteers. Medical problems, including drug information, drug overdose, tripping, pregnancy, venereal disease, and other sex problems rank third. Only about ten percent of the calls are drug related. Questions about the legal status, rights, and obligations of youth, including the draft, runaways, parental support, and marriage make up the next significant block. School-oriented problems occur less frequently, but enough to be a category. Only a small percentage of problems involve employment or housing.

Crisis Centers do not give advice, including medical or legal advice. Volunteers are not engaged in the practice of medicine or law without a license, but they are nonetheless able to serve youth in many sensitive areas with legal and medical implication, especially runaway, sex, and drug information. The possibility of legal suits has been raised both by Kahn[4] and Leviton[5] on hypothetical and empirical grounds and dismissed by both. It's these very sensitive areas that public and school libraries have feared to tread.

Crank calls, including put-ons and obscene calls, are generally treated seriously. The rationale is that the caller has a problem but is afraid to reveal it, perhaps even to himself.

Compare this attitude to the library's response to a "troublemaker," which not infrequently is to ban him from the building.

In every Hotline, female callers predominate over males, between two to one to as much as five to one. But boys, when they call, have more specific problems than girls, who comprise almost all of the "lonely" calls.

The average caller is about 16, though older at college crisis centers. In one county, 16 percent of the callers were 12 or under. If this is not an unusual number of preteen calls, what implications are there for the present boundary in libraries between children and young adult services at 13 or 14 years, or the programs and materials in the children's room? Should the territorial boundaries in both libraries and library associations be re-drawn to include 11- and 12-year-olds in Young Adult Services? Should junior novels be written, reviewed, and selected with the ten to 14 rather than the 12- to 16-year-old in mind?

Many Hotlines receive over 2000 calls a month. In the Washington, D.C. area alone, over 50 Hotlines, Switchboards and Free Clinics were identified as providing a configuration of listening, counseling, and information or referral services to young adults. This is not an unusually large number for a metropolitan area. The combination of many centers, each with a potential large volume, indicates the possible, if not actual, impact of these services upon other information and referral services.

Referral Files

A referral system of community agencies and professionals is an essential element of any crisis center: Hotline, Switchboard, or Free Clinic. The degree the problem can be matched to referrals is one measure of the effectiveness of the center. Before an agency is used, as much information as possible is collected about it, including the identification of a particular contact person, so that a client is told who to see and not just where to go. Sometimes, an agency is checked out by means of a fake call.

Crisis Centers rely on users to improve their files. Volunteers are guided to ask the person for feedback on how helpful the referral was. If the center is unable to provide the information needed, he might be asked to call back and make the files more complete should he discover other sources. This mutual learning process also takes place between the center and the agencies themselves. The crisis center influences and educates professionals and agencies in more effective ways of handling the problems of young people, while the professionals and agencies provide training and expertise. Both user and agency feedback to the Center provide a mechanism for the continual up-dating of the files' "vital" information. The data sheets also encourage the search for and development of new referral resources.

Advocacy

Crisis centers not only intervene in individual immediate crises, the "band aid" function, but work to prevent future crises in a community. With the data collected on user problems and the follow-up and feedback provided on referrals, they function as a social indicator of the needs and gaps in community service. Perhaps the hours or regulations of an agency inhibit or prohibit its use by potential clientele, or there may be no agency at all that is concerned, or maybe a local ordinance on minors' rights needs changing. With data in hand and a constituency of community groups and professions behind them, the crisis center is a powerful persuader to appropriate bodies to alter services or regulations. Alfred Kahn[6] names this "Program and Policy Advocacy" in describing the range of services a neighborhood information center could provide.

The library could assume the function of group advocacy. Even if it is not an advocate for individuals, it could use its accumulation of "unanswered questions" to be used by appropriate groups or organizations to substantiate and justify changes in services.

Access

Since crises can occur at any time and by their nature require rapid intervention, Hotlines and other crisis centers try to be open 24 hours, seven days a week. When this is not feasible, it is the daytime hours during the week that are closed, those nine-to-five Monday-to-Friday hours when public and especially school libraries are open, since emotional emergencies tend to occur most often at night. Crisis centers seem to have no problem recruiting staff for these hours, yet libraries base their limited hours as much on the unwillingness of paid employees to work at other times as on budgetary constraints.

It is not enough to be open, a service must be made known to its target audience by any media necessary: calling cards distributed at schools, stickers in phone booths and on cars, public service announcements on TV and local radio rock stations, stories in the local paper, listing in the alternative press, posters in neighborhood stores. These are the imaginative ways crisis centers try to reach troubled youth, while parents are informed by a Center's Speakers' Bureau, PTA's, and periodic written reports to the communities. Ironically, the one point of access that has been a stumbling block is the telephone directory and the operator. Some directories require an address in order to be listed, and those Hotlines that demand anonymity have been refused a listing. In addition, there is yet no agreement by the phone company as how to list these Centers in the Yellow Pages, regardless of their name.

Training

The philosophy, services, and techniques of crisis intervention are initially conveyed to volunteers through a short training period, of not more than a dozen sessions, which utilizes role-playing, sensitivity groups, outside experts, and real crisis situations. It is necessary to understand oneself before one can help others and make oneself sensitive to the real but unstated and hidden needs of people seeking help, and so the volunteer is placed in situations which reveal his own biases and hang-ups. Authorities on subjects likely to be problems provide the information to answer these needs. Instruction in the content, organization, and update of the referral files is additional input into the volunteer's subject knowledge. The data sheets are a check that his training is consistent with the user population and its problems. Telephone techniques in particular are explained, demonstrated, and practiced through role-playing and actual supervised calls.

The initial training period, during which some volunteers are asked to drop out or do so by choice, is followed by weekly or monthly meetings to discuss problems, unanswered needs, and internal policies. Though written material plays a minor role initially, most crisis centers develop a training manual for future reference. The manuals describe the goals and services and emphasize the importance of follow-through, feedback, and up-date, so that services and resources will reflect community needs.

Is your library manual an adequate reflection of your library's stated priorities? Or does it contain more "don'ts" than "do's"? Would you be uneasy if your public read it?

Resources

Several crisis centers have indicated the desire to establish a resource library in their facilities (for reference by both staff and clientele) made up of handbooks, pamphlets, periodicals, and directories. One newsletter, the *Confederation*, mailed a questionnaire to crisis centers asking for recommended materials for such a basic collection. Materials so identified would be likely candidates for inclusion in a library's collection. Perhaps the library could provide them on indefinite loan to its local crisis center.

An information network connects the over 750 crisis centers in the U.S. and Canada. The total number is increasing rapidly, despite the high death rate for new centers. *The Exchange* has established its responsibility for the production of the *National Directory of Hotlines, Switchboards, and Related Services.* At the International Hotline Conference, regional divisions were organized. The network also consists of smaller metropolitan area councils, such as in Long Island and Baltimore, and national research centers, all of which publish newsletters or journals and hold conferences and workshops. But there is a great resistance to any strong network with regulatory powers. A proposal for national standards and accreditation was defeated in 1971, but the minimum criteria suggested: 24-hour-access, continuous training, justification of need for a service, formal evaluation to include feedback, are an accurate reflection of their importance to the crisis center philosophy.

Summary

In summary, a crisis intervention center is an easily accessible storefront or telephone community facility, counseling, advocacy, information, and referral service feeding into a larger human services network, using paraprofessionals from the community, who are peers of the clientele, with professional back-up when needed, and providing stopgap crisis services until more comprehensive and preventative services can be found.

When phrased this way, the crisis services image is parallel to storefront library "outreach" programs. Librarians are searching for new and innovative ways to reach the nonuser. Can we learn anything about changes in services, hours, personnel and training, and public relations from a similarly nontraditional service? In addition, several public libraries have gone into the information and referral business themselves,[7] so it is not entirely academic to ask if and how libraries, both school and public, should become a part of this network and cooperate with crisis centers as equals. Third, if we can accept as fact that we will never serve everyone directly and personally, can we perhaps serve our public indirectly by providing information and back-up services to the staff of our local hotline, switchboard, and free clinic, i.e. consciously serving community groups. Fourth, how can we apply the information crisis centers are collecting about the needs of troubled youth in our communities to even traditional library services, e.g. in areas such as book selection or programs.

"Every community needs a police department, a public school system, a mental health clinic, a welfare agency, a fire department, . . . and a suicide and crisis intervention service . . ."[8] Is the library ready to assume its place among these community helping services?

References

1. Braverman, Miriam. Ph.D thesis in progress at Columbia University School of Library Service.
2. Sebald, Hans. *Adolescence; A Sociological Analysis.* Appleton-Century Crofts, 1960, p. 24.
3. Bell, Joseph. "Take Your Troubles to the Hotline." *Seventeen*, August 1970.
4. Kahn, Alfred J. *Neighborhood Information Centers.* Columbia University School of Social Work, 1966. Reprinted by University Book Service, Brooklyn, N.Y., 1971.
5. Leviton, Dan & Stanley Parey. *Proposal for a University of Maryland Crisis Intervention Center, 1970.* 8p. mimeo.
6. Kahn. *op cit.*
7. Donahue, Joseph. *Public Information Center Final Report.* Enoch Pratt Free Library, February 1971.
8. McGee, Richard K. "Toward a New Image for Suicide and Crisis Services." *Crises Intervention.* vol. 2, no. 3, 1970, p. 63.

Africana:
Folklore Collections for Children

by Gertrude B. Herman

. . . Afric's Sunny Fountains
From Greenland's icy mountains,
From India's coral strand,
Where Afric's sunny fountains
Roll down their golden sand;
From many an ancient river,
From many a palmy plain,
They call us to deliver
Their land from errors chain

What though the spicy breezes
Blow soft o'er Ceylon's isle;
Though every prospect pleases
And only man is vile;
In vain with lavish kindness,
The gifts of God are strown;
The heathen in his blindness
Bows down to wood and stone . . .
(Reginald Heber, 1783-1826)[1]

Head ringing to the marching rhythm of the lusty old hymn, the child that I once was clutched her pennies in hand and dropped them, one by one, into the Sunday School missionary box, noting with satisfaction the kneeling white-robed heathen lad atop it, who nodded his black papier-mâché head gratefully as each coin clunked in to start on its appointed way to deliver his land from error's chain. The rich imagery of the hymn's words merged in my mind with Dr. Dolittle's African garden where thick-lipped, stupid Prince Bumpo lay dreaming of a white princess. Through the jungle echoed the cries of Tarzan; and all the while someone later personified by Deborah Kerr, with stiff British upper-lipmanship, was hacking her way through the bush to King Solomon's mines.

My vision was not unique. Of such lush materials the fantasy world has been woven which many American children have carried around in their heads as their image of Africa. Even as adults we have our illusions. We, who tolerate the daily body count from Vietnam and who have been able to accommodate to memory the murder of Europe's Jews, were almost disappointed when the predicted blood-bath by "savages" failed to materialize in Biafra at the conclusion of the Nigerian war. And when the heathen's wood and stone were assembled in the Metropolitan Art Museum a few seasons

back, we were astonished by the compelling power of the spiritual force and beauty revealed.

The decades of the 60's forced us to listen to many hitherto unheard voices, among them those of the African peoples. As new-old nations emerged from the collapse of colonialism, we discovered that our old images needed revision. A burst of publishing in the juvenile field occurred and continues to flourish. Works of fiction and nonfiction have proliferated, among them a considerable number of collections of African folklore, as well as picture books in which the traditional tale has provided a vehicle for the illustrator's talents. Children's librarians have welcomed the new stories, not only as a means of correcting old errors, but also of bringing to both black and white children some of the rich heritage hitherto denied the black American. But enthusiasm has sometimes outrun critical acuity, and we have tended not to apply rigorous enough standards to our evaluation of African folklore collections for children.

Few American librarians in services to youth are trained as folklorists or anthropologists; some have travelled more or less extensively in Africa; the number who can read or understand an African language is probably infinitesimal. Nevertheless, it is possible to inform ourselves by reading, viewing, and listening. It seems worthwhile, therefore, to define once more some general criteria for the evaluation of folklore for children; to identify some of the particular characteristics of African folklore; and to present a selected bibliography of recommended books.

Basically, the questions one should ask about any book which purports to be folklore are: 1) what is the authority of the book? where do the stories come from? who collected them, from whom, and under what conditions? and 2) how honestly and artistically does the literary form preserve the cultural and stylistic integrity of the original? In the case of folklore intended for children, one should also inquire: 3) how appealing will the material be to children, whether for reading or listening, and at what ages? and how does the format of the book support or enrich the content?

When one examines the question of sources and authority, one finds that many of the African collections for children are not primary material, i.e. collected in the field by the compiler. In many cases they are adaptations from literary sources, most often from the works of 19th and early 20th Century missionaries, colonial officers, and scholars.[2] Unfortunately, acknowledgment is not always made to these sources, for many of them have passed into the public domain, presenting the same opportunities for exploitation as do Grimm, Perrault, Asbjornsen and Moe, etc.

A second kind of collection is that gathered by the compiler himself, sometimes combining field work with literary sources or the work of a collaborator, in which case he usually makes a point of identifying his sources specifically and accurately.

A third kind of collection is that in which authority is very nebulous, often printed only on the book jacket, and couched in such vague phrases as "told among the Bantu people," or "the author has travelled in Africa, where he heard these stories told by village storytellers." In what language, one wonders, and in what villages? Literary sources are implied but not specified in such equally cloudy authority as "research in the libraries of Nairobi (or Accra, or wherever)."

A fourth recent and important kind of collection is that containing stories set down by native Africans. Source identification is equally important for such works, and is often supplied in introductory materials or notes.

The authority of the work having been determined, one turns to consideration of how to evaluate the written form of an oral art. Field collectors emphasize the role of the audience and the stylistic devices employed by the narrator in the transmission of oral literature.[3] In the culture from which the literature arises, the audience brings to the performance a whole complex of assumptions, past experiences, etc. The story is not new to this audience; it is interested in the plot, but more profoundly in the skill which the narrator brings to his particular rendering of it. The accomplished performer draws his audience into the experience through words, but also through music, dance, body gesture, tonal variations, etc. The audience participates by singing, clapping, dancing, hissing, taking sides in the outcomes of the story, etc. A range of multimedia devices might capture some of the essence of what appeals to the eye and ear, but the social matrix which nourishes the art will continue to allude the alien observer. As the score of a Mozart concerto symbolizes, or stands for, the living music, so the printed form of an oral narrative is but the record of a living, changing, aural event. How effectively can the adaptor translate such an experience to the printed page?

Harold Scheub, of the University of Wisconsin, who in 1967-68 was a member of the audience of over 4000 performances created by some 2000 Xhosa and Zulu artists in South Africa, has said:

> The basic problem for the translator rests with those elements of the performance which most clearly identify it as an oral work—the non-verbal elements of production . . . New tensions must be introduced into the recast work . . . The rhythmic sounds of the language have indeed been replaced by a language which is no longer itself an oral language, but this does not mean that it is not a poetic language . . . . [The translator] must be something of an artist himself, for the only way an oral

narrative-performance can survive the translation into the written word is as a new work of art.[4]

A third critical question is: how appealing will the material be to American children, whether for reading or listening, and how does the format of the book support or enrich the content? Dundes warns against ethnocentricity, "the retouching of oral tales . . . in the children's literature field where reconstructed, reconstituted stores written in accordance with written not oral conventions are palmed off as genuine folktales."[5] The elimination of unfamiliar elements and reliance upon western literary devices are common faults. The stories must retain faithfulness to the oral style and the cultural content of their African prototypes, but a faithfulness which is lively enough and dramatic enough to draw children into an unfamiliar world.

Format, including print and illustrations, ought to be attractive to children. It should reinforce the ethnic origins of the content, including distinctions in artistic motifs, colors, landscape, costume, and artifacts of the particular culture from which the stories come.

What are some of the stylistic features and story elements one might expect in African folklore? Many of the stories are analogues to familiar European stories, but they are analogues with a difference, testifying to their unique origins, each culture using familiar motifs to fabricate its own unique works of art. All African stories are not alike. Just as there are important cultural differences between Navajo and Iroquois American Indian stories, so are there important differences among the stories and artistic conventions of various African peoples. It is important not to repeat the errors made in treating all American Indian groups as undifferentiated.

As an example one might consider the Trickster stories which are to be found all over Africa. Among the Ibo the Trickster is Tortoise; among the Ashanti, Spider; among the Bantu peoples, Hare; and among the Bushmen, Mantis. The central theme of all Trickster stories is the triumph of brain over brawn. But each Trickster is distinctively Ibo or Ashanti or whatever, and the stories reflect societal differences.

> . . . All these tricksters, however, are adaptable. They are able to turn any situation, old or new, to their advantage. The tortoise, we are told, now aspires to white collar status in Southern Nigeria and attends adult education classes, while the spider, Ananse, referees football matches among the Ashanti in Ghana. (From "Tricksters and How They Differ")[6]

Some common stylistic elements of African folktales are: formulaic openings and closings; repeated songs and chants; direct conversation rather than narrative ideophones (words used to represent sounds, as "he knocked on the door—ngo! ngo! ngo!");[7] the use of repetition as adverb ("he walked a long way, a long way, a long way"); and proverbs added at the end of stories. Some story motifs are: talking animals; supernatural creatures differing from the European stock, e.g. few fairies, instead one-legged monsters, and ogres (the Hausa "Dodo," the Zulu "Zim"); magical oxen as symbols of beauty and/or power; the metamorphosis of human spirits into animals, particularly birds; heroines frequently protagonists. (Incidentally, the Dodo and the Zim are both cannibalistic, which somehow worries us more than the flesh-eating propensities of trolls or Jack's giants. Visions of missionaries in pots still haunting us?)

Implicit in all African stories are the values of the people telling them. In those parts of Africa where Islam is dominant, Muslim elements will be pervasive. The extended family and the obligations of kinship are reflected consistently all over Africa. Stories from Africa south of the Sahara reflect the force of custom, the importance of the welfare of the group, and the respect accorded to the ways of the elders.

The late A. G. Jordan, a black South African in exile and a scholar of African oral tradition, once said: "Traditional literature is the artistic property of the community." Respect is due. The emphasis in human relations books has often been, "We are really all alike." Actually, of course, we are not all alike. To understand and to value differences rather than deny it, is a more difficult, but more human concept. All people are limited by the "error's chain" of their own cultural conventions, not only superficially but on unconscious and linguistic levels. The probability is that one should refrain from attempting to interpret another culture unless one is seriously committed to acquiring particular and deepening knowledge of that culture. African life and oral literature are rich and interesting enough to inspire that kind of commitment, so that we may select wisely and interpret adequately to children.

For advice and counsel, the author wishes to thank Professors Harold Scheub, A. Neil Skinner, and the late A. G. Jordan, all of the Department of African Languages and Literature, University of Wisconsin-Madison.

References

1. *Oxford Dictionary of Quotations*, 2d ed., Oxford Univ. Pr., 1955, p. 240.
2. Dorson, Richard M., *The British Folklorists: A History*, Univ. of Chicago, 1968, p. 349-71.
   Finnegan, Ruth, *Oral Literature in Africa*, Oxford Univ. Pr., 1970, p. 26-47.
3. Finnegan, *op. cit.*, p. 1-25; Scheub, Harold, "Translation of African Oral Narrative-performances to the Written Work," *Yearbook of Comparative and General Literature*, 20, 1971, p. 28-36.
4. Scheub, *op. cit.*, p. 36.
5. Dundes, Alan, "Folklore as a Mirror of Culture," *Elementary English*, (April, 1969), p. 472.
6. Finnegan, p. 345.
7. Scheub, p. 31.

Children's Books in Translation: Facts and Beliefs

by Mary Ørvig

The farm in southern Sweden once owned by Dag Hammarskjold was the scene in 1966 of a meeting between publishers, critics, and translators from different European countries to discuss the prospects of the representatives of minor languages obtaining a hearing in major cultural contexts. Those present agreed that literary prejudice is quite common in large language areas and that people do not feel any the worse for it. There was also unanimity on many other things, including the numerous national limitations of higher literary studies in the majority of countries. There is a striking lack of concrete literary knowledge concerning a series of language areas. Another problem of cultural communication lies in ignorance of foreign environments and lack of any desire to rectify that ignorance. All were agreed, however, on the important fact that a first-class book can be untranslatable because it is on a wave length that another country's receivers cannot pick up. This is probably part of the reason for so many failures which in the eyes of the country of origin are quite inexplicable.

In this context, one of the leading critics in Sweden, Ingemar Wizelius, has an instructive tale to tell in the introduction to a survey of Swedish literature abroad. A professor of literature related how an English colleague who had called on him caught sight of the seven volumes of Schück and Warburg's history of Swedish literature on the bookshelves and saw fit to ask what this mammoth work was about. On being told he was silent for a moment and then asked: "But what is it about, *really*?" Mr. Wizelius remarks that in asking what Schück and Warburg was really about, the English professor of literature had given the international status of Swedish literary output in a nutshell.

As to children's books, one is amazed to see over and over again how readily and effortlessly one tends to generalize about the internationality of them on the strength of some classical novels which have become children's reading and a few works whose writers have had no difficulty in negotiating the international frontiers with all that this implies. Although we owe Paul Hazard a great deal, it was he, in his famous *Books, Children and Men* (Horn Bk., 1932), who first expressed some of the ideas and phrases which are almost invariably reiterated on the majority of international occasions. For example.

Yes, children's books keep alive a sense of nationality: but they also keep alive a sense of humanity. They de-

scribe their native land lovingly, but they also describe faraway lands where unknown brothers live. They understand the essential quality of their own race, but each of them is a messenger that goes beyond mountains and rivers, beyond the seas, to the very ends of the world in search of new friendships. Every country gives and every country receives—innumerable are the exchanges—and so it comes about that in our first impressionable years the universal republic of childhood is born.

Paul Hazard's book was, after all, published in Europe between two world wars, at a time when internationalism had very little concrete background. Again, after World War II his book touched us deeply because of the isolation enforced by the long years of war. Nowadays perhaps Hazard is important, above all, as a comparative literary historian and one of the first critics to place children's books in their comparative historical context. One of his greatest works, *La Crise de Conscience Européenne* (1935), was devoted to the study of major literary currents in the collective consciousness and cast light on a number of interesting literary facts.

The sentence, "every country gives and every country receives," often comes to mind. Now that the western world has opened its eyes to the fact that there are countries in many parts of the globe without a body of children's literature of their own, perhaps it is time to discard a few illusions, painful as the process may be. Thus, is not internationality after all based on a mutual give and take? For indeed, reciprocity and, consequently, true internationalism are quite small and there are many linguistic and cultural frontiers which are extremely hard to cross. Or, how seriously have we really tried?

The distribution channels of books provide an interesting subject which in the nature of things is bound up with such circumstances as war, peace, political constellations, copyright questions, and monetary relationships. Economic laws and situations play a very important part in this context. Nor should one forget the great influence of ancient cultural links on the translation scene.

There can be no doubt that many new initiatives are needed on the translation side, especially within children's literature, but also the cultural sector as such. Children's books are mostly regarded as an isolated phenomenon in the cultural exchange of different countries, which of course is as wrong as wrong could be. Some concrete problems related to the book publishing may perhaps be illustrated by the comparatively small Swedish language area, comprising some eight million people. The volume of publication in Sweden is unusually high in relation to the number of people who understand the language. If one considers the number of titles published, Swedish book publication per capita is more or less on a level with Great Britain, even though that country has the whole world for its reading public while Sweden's is less than the population of greater London. In conditions like these, book publication frequently becomes something akin to gambling. The profile of children's book publication in Sweden in 1970 was as follows: we brought out 637 titles (227 of them new editions), including 179 new Swedish titles and 175 new foreign titles, which will give almost an even balance between original works and translations. Of these translations, 212 were from English, 18 from German, 11 from Danish, nine from Norwegian and one from Czech.

Day by day it is becoming increasingly obvious that the comparatively generous and ambitious scale of book publishing which we are used to in Sweden can no longer be accommodated within the framework of a stringent market economy. Publishers have to concentrate more and more on established authors and reliable types of books. This creates difficulties for new writers and it means also that many important translations fail to materialize, especially as regards the books on the different wave lengths which need to be published regularly for many years in order to break down the resistance of the reading public, above all, books from the eastern bloc and from other new areas where children's books are gaining ground.

Certain of the circumstances relating to book consumption and the conditions of Swedish literature led to the appointment in 1968 of a Commission to consider the forms of public support to literature. The experts concerned within this commission, who have been given very wide terms of reference, are to study the need for measures at the consumption, production, and distribution levels to strengthen the status of literature in Sweden's cultural life. Confronted by the difficult economic situation within the book market, many Swedish publishers have shown a remarkable unanimity in calling for state subvention, indeed they have pointed to the need for this form of assistance, which is already enjoyed in Sweden by the theatre, the cinema, the film industry, and music. Government support to authors was channelled through the Swedish Authors' Fund set up already in 1954, when library royalties were introduced. The Fund exists to handle the royalties paid out of the public funds to the authors of books used by public libraries. The Swedish Riksdag determines the allocation to be made to the Fund each year. For the budget year 1971-1972, a royalty of 15 öre was fixed for each external loan, the royalty on reference copies being 60 öre. Royalties are paid for translations at four öre per external loan and 16 öre per reference copy. Altogether the Fund has received nine million 307.000 kronor for the budget year 1971-1972.

The above illustrate how a small country tries to surmount the crisis of its book trade so as to avoid individual isolation and the dangers of provincialism. Whether we regard books from a commercial, individual, cultural, or even social angle, we need to know more about the factors governing people's reading interests and their use of different kinds of literature. This in turn begs the question—for small language areas at least—how are translations controlled? Are the translation movements which so obviously exist really controlled at all? Children's books provide a good starting point for such an inquiry.

When the Swedish scholar, Göte Klingberg, first coined the term "children's literature regions" in a lecture given at a Unesco seminar in Denmark in 1970 on the subject of "Literature for Children and Young People as a Means of Promotion of International Understanding," he said,

> Four countries were studied, Sweden, Austria, West, and East Germany. It became apparent that Sweden, Austria, and West Germany belonged to the same children's literature region characterized by a predominant import from the English language area (that is from Great Britain and the U.S.); in Sweden, 70-77 percent (in two different samplings); in Austria, 57 percent; in West Germany, 57 percent; and further by an import of a smaller number of French, Dutch, and Scandinavian books, an interchange of books in German and Swedish, but also by the very small imports from other countries, such as the Slavonic language area. East Germany belongs to another children's book area, as Dr. Klaus Doderer has shown in his report from the research institution in Frankfurt. East German imports from the English language areas were listed to 17 percent, on the other hand, 51 percent of the books were translated from Slavonic languages and, in addition, 12 percent came from Hungary.

What is the answer? Is it a simple question of foreign politics? It goes without saying that we in Sweden belong to the Anglo-American translation area, which, however, did not start after World War II, but probably already in the 1870's.

At the Swedish Institute for Children's Books, one of the most frequent questions asked by students at library schools and teachers' colleges is: "Why this Anglo-American domination of the translation side, why not a little more from Eastern Europe and other parts of the world?" In reply, a reference is usually made to unsolved copyright problems and financial situations. The important part played by old, established cultural links in the translation context is not to be discounted, as can be seen from a visit to the Frankfurt book fair, even though the eastern countries usually put in as much of an appearance as they can manage. A great deal of information is required to make the discussion of these and kindred topics more specific and less emotional. Nonetheless, one may ask why the children's book publishers of the west do not in their turn try to visit the Leipzig book fair in East Germany, which among other things could be their gateway into the eastern book sector.

In her interesting paper *Children's Literature and Libraries around the World*, Marguerite Bagshaw has shown a real concern over the important issues:

There is much talk today of the mutual exchange of ideas and cultures from one country to another. In actual practice there seems to be little reciprocal sharing as far as cultures are concerned from East to West . . . How can we engender closer international contacts?

Mildred L. Batchelder, an authority on children's books and libraries in several European countries, was also one of the first to raise the problems of translation. In her article, published in *ALA Bulletin* (1963), "Learning about Children's Books in Translation," she touches upon many important matters, for instance:

> Tailoring children's books to their new country takes various forms. When a book comes through an English translation to an American edition, additional adjustments are made to make it conform to our national taste and style. I question whether all such changes are necessary to accommodate English editions to America, or for that matter, American editions to England.

Miss Batchelder also found "that characters are removed, incidents are taken out." "Perhaps," she concludes, "the cutting and changes were for economic reasons."

One valuable research project on children's books would be to compare original texts with translations and adaptations. It would be a good idea to start with a title published in several countries, so as to expose what is termed adjustment or discreet or overt cutting. In translations from Swedish to English and German, for instance, one may frequently find:

1) overemphasis of the basic plot, often at the expense of the real essence of the book;
2) the different climates of humor are always difficult, therefore, one often finds the elimination of all but the most elementary or slapstick humor;
3) a playing down of sensibility which often by Anglo-American standards is typically European or too profound;
4) a constant tendency to smooth things over;
5) an emasculation of content, due to an aversion to intellectual contents or conclusions in children's books.

Often the reason is to be found quite simply in the translator's ignorance, not so much of words and grammatical structure as of the images behind them. One would like to stress that differences are every bit as important as similarities when describing foreign environments. There is a dangerous tendency for differences or customs and morals to be degraded to quaint details for tourists. Yet it is a salutary experience to learn early in life that in certain parts of the world men can weep without losing their dignity or embrace each other without causing any embarrassment.

If, as Marguerite Bagshaw wrote, there is to be more reciprocal sharing between different countries through the medium of translation, we must learn more about the conditions and ways of the translation process. We should use the tools at our disposal, such as the international organizations, to find out how literature operates in different countries, for example,

starting with those belonging to IBBY. This organization should pay far more attention to translators. We need to learn more about the literary process, production, distribution, and consumption. Many of the Hans Christian Andersen prize-winners, for instance, have run into difficulties on the translation market. Let us find out why: are the books untranslatable because, as mentioned earlier, they are attuned to wave lengths which the receivers of other countries cannot pick up? Let us find out the facts about this. Without wishing to cause any serious ructions, it may be suggested that the reason for important children's books being refused—in spite of the Andersen Medal—is a very important factor for our knowledge of untranslatable books.

It is remarkable that so little scope has been given to the conditions and ways of translations in all these top level international research projects and discussions. The distribution channels of children's books and the part played by translations within children's literature of different countries are neglected fields of research. Most of the work has still to be done. We who are concerned with children's books, nationally and internationally, must study more in detail the practical results in the field of translations in different countries. Then we will have greater opportunities to make concrete observations and perhaps enter some new paths. Coprinting seemed to be an excellent instrument as far as translation was concerned, but this supposition has often been given the lie. The original idea has often been lost sight of, and a coprinted book in several languages can provide a manual of national tabus in the children's book sector, and not, as was really intended, a children's book that has broken down barriers.

The isolation of children's books must concern us all. This isolation must simply be overcome, even at the sacrifice of a few well-loved tribal deities. Children's literature must be more consciously integrated in the whole pattern of cultural life. Analyses are needed of events in the field of criticism, not only our specialized journals but popular periodicals and the daily press. The coverage given by press critics should not be determined by personal preference or the cultural and literary interest of the chief editor. Let it be said aloud and repeatedly that no serious cultural observation can exist without an interest in children's books. Children's books are everybody's business, for we all spend a quarter of our lives being children and growing up.

Translations are often said to be more important to small countries than to big ones. But national and cultural isolation is not necessarily the exclusive fate of small countries. Big countries also need to know what is important at the other side of the border, what people laugh at and what makes them cry. There are many doors which need to be opened in order to help our understanding. To popularize translations of children's books from new and different language areas is a question of breaking down all sorts of inhibitions and attitudes of which the book world is so rich. As always one has to start with the young. Translation is the strongest link in an international chain which is constantly in need of amplification and reinforcement.

Up for Discussion
From Jane to Germaine, With Love

by Regina Minudri

Esteemed and venerated colleagues, purveyors of literary treats (and treatments) to the young and not so young, let us examine the most perennial of fictional favorites, the Gothic novel. Who has not read with pleasure and a sense of escape the exciting and exacting tales concocted for our entertainment by those ladies, and a few gentlemen, who specialize in the genre? The *Random House Dictionary* defines gothic as "noting or pertaining to a style of literature characterized by a gloomy setting, grotesque or violent events, and an atmosphere of degeneration and decay."

Many young adult girls are particularly drawn to and interested in Gothic novels because the heroines are themselves quite young and also because they are usually successful in their chosen life styles. The aspects of mystery, suspense, and the soupçon of the supernatural which permeate many Gothics also lend impetus to their popularity. The similarity of structure, plot and characterization in Gothics keeps them well below the rank of belles lettres, but as escape and simple fun reading a good Gothic is hard to beat.

When pressed, we can all come up with definitions of Gothics that produce much laughter, are devastatingly accurate, and naturally put down such light entertainments with scorn. The Gothic plots make this easy. There is usually a young girl, penniless but well educated, who accepts a position as governess or companion in a large house on a deserted moor staffed by a bevy of frightened servants and a master as mysterious as he is handsome. Somewhere along the line a flaw will be discovered in the master's character. Nevertheless, he and the young maiden generally fall in love instantly—although he neglects to tell her of his love until the final pages. During the book our Gothic Heroine fights magnificently against the forces of evil which threaten the household, her charge or charges, and ultimately, herself. She is saved in the nick of time and all ends well.

Most scholarly sources list Walpole's *Castle of Otranto* (1764) as the first real Gothic novel in the sense we understand them today. Since I pretend to no special scholarship here, I prefer to think of Charlotte Bronte's *Jane Eyre* (1847) as the spiritual mother of them all and as a Gothic Summa Cum Laude, even though the novel did not originate all of the stereotypes mentioned above. What Jane does have is class, real class. She is not about to be put off by anybody or anything in the pursuit of what she considers to be her true and righteous goal: the preservation of life and limb and the security of the home, not to mention the final and firm acquisition of Rochester.

Some would have it that Gothic Heroines are the very antithesis of what the Women's Liberation Movement stands for. I beg to differ. Rather, I feel that the Gothic Heroine as depicted in novels like *Jane Eyre*, *Heir of the Starvelings*, *Nine Coaches Waiting*, or even *Rebecca* are bastions of Women's Lib insofar as they represent some of the very same ideals women admire now. These Gothic Heroines are strong, they are intelligent, they are educated, curious, and, for the most part, they are unable to accept the structures of a society which push them toward patterns of behavior they find untenable. They are not the whimpering, simpering females found in the many romantic novels so justifiably pilloried by Germaine Greer in *The Female Eunuch*.

As the Heroines, they are responsible, in whole or in part, for the movement of the novel. It is their courage which prompts them to walk through the moors, venture out into the night after the ghosts, or question the mysterious happenings in the manse. It is their curiosity which makes them wonder and investigate. It is their intelligence and education which causes them to reject the pat answers given by the male characters who are supposed to know all. Of course, some of our Heroines are frightened by what they see or seem to see, and sometimes they are misled. They are not superwomen, but they are not long deceived and have enough tenacity to ferret out the answers and bravely face the foes in their lairs. Using the strength inherent in the "weak women" syndrome, most of our Heroines are quite capable of playing on their femininity to make the best of a bad situation.

Quite frequently the Heroines of Gothic fiction are leaders in social reforms and improvements of living and working conditions for those less fortunate than themselves. What they seem to represent, and often very accurately, are some of those marvelous 19th-Century women reformers who carried such big sticks in England and who were instrumental in changing many laws and easing conditions in the slums and factories. Not only do many of our Heroines work for others, but they also realize in what kind of legal binds they find themselves with regard to inheritance, property and control of money. At first they seem willing to let husbands or guardians manage their affairs, but when circumstances reveal bungling of monumental proportions our Heroines wonder quite vocally why they should not take care of themselves. In other cases they do manage affairs successfully, much to the begrudging admiration of the males surrounding them.

If the Gothic Heroine can be seen as a prototype of the Women's Lib Movement, then it must be said that the Gothic Heroes are, almost unanimously, among the great stereotypes of male chauvinism likely to be found between boards, buckram or paper covers. They, our Heroes, just cannot understand why the Gothic Heroines do what they do, even though our Gothic Heroes frequently revere them for those very qualities which set them apart from the run of the mill secondary female characters: determination, courage, imagination, intelligence, persistence, just to name a few. The secondary female characters are not usually well developed and are frequently stereotypes which do give a certain sexist taint to the novels, but this is the distinction which makes the Gothic Heroine a separate, identifiable and admirable woman. In addition to having a certain amount of class, the Gothic Heroine has guts.

Yes, it's easy to chuckle over the lovely ladies of long ago, who moved through their worlds with grace and style and seemed impervious to the ravages of time and worry. But, in our heart of hearts, we all know that we admire them, that we (women readers at least) identify with them, and that sometimes we unwittingly emulate them. Jane, baby—you've come a long way—meet Germaine.

Twelve titles germane
to the discussion above.

The criteria for selection here was based solely on entertainment value. A definitive list of Gothic novels would take far more space than is possible. So take them in the proper spirit.

Brent, Madeline. *Tregaron's Daughter*, Doubleday. 1971. $5.95. Bantam, $1.25.
Caterina Tregaron wonders why she is haunted by dreams of a dark palazzo.

Berckman, Evelyn. *Heir of the Starvelings*. Doubleday. 1967. $4.50.
An evil master, a moldering mansion and a poor boy who is saved by the epitome of the Gothic Heroine.
Bronte, Charlotte. *Jane Eyre*. many editions.
Jane does her rebelling against narrow rules and gets Rochester in the end.
Case, David. *Fengriffin*. Hill & Wang. 1970. $5. Lancer. $.75.
A curse on the women of the family causes problems all the way around.
DuMaurier, Daphne. *Rebecca*. many editions.
Coming to the estate, Rebecca, the young and shy bride, realizes that all is not well.
Eden, Dorothy. *Ravenscroft*. Fawcett, $.95.
Two orphaned sisters are trapped and then rescued from a fate worse than death in Victorian London.
Holt, Victoria. *Mistress of Mellyn*. Doubleday, 1960. $5.95. Fawcett. $.95.
Cornwall, a creepy mansion, and murder complicate things.
Jackson, Shirley. *Haunting of Hill House*. Viking. 1959. $7.95. Pop. Lib. $.75.
Checking out supernatural happenings and ghostly phenomena.
Maybury, Anne. *Minerva Stone*. Holt. 1968. $5.95. Bantam. $.75.
Her husband wants to transform her into a kind of automaton.
Michaels, Barbara. *Ammie, Come Home*. Meredith. 1969. $5.95. Fawcett. $.75.
Ghosts, black magic and other supernatural happenings abound.
Stevenson, Florence. *Curse of the Concullans*. NAL. $.75.
A governess in Ireland faces banshees with much tongue-in-cheek humor.
Stewart, Mary. *Nine Coaches Waiting*. Morrow. 1959. $5.95. Fawcett. $.75.
In an isolated French chateau the Gothic Heroine finds that her pupil's accidents aren't quite accidental.

Books For The Young Disabled Readers

by Evelyn Goss Altemus

According to a report of the National Advisory Committee on Dyslexia and Related Reading Disorders, reading disorders affect approximately 15 percent of the children in school today. These are children who, in spite of apparently adequate intelligence and emotional stability, exhibit difficulties in learning to read within a teaching program that proves effective for most others. In an elementary school of 500 students, about 75 are disabled readers and need special help.

Ruth Edgington gives a clear definition of the dyslexic child: "He is *unable* to learn to read without special help . . . . he often confuses letters that look alike, because they face in different directions, (p-q, d-b, m-w, u-n, d-g). Also, he often confuses letters whose sounds are similar, (d-t, v-f, e-g, b-p). He may also have great difficulty with short words, especially if they are sensible when read backwards, (saw-was, on-no). Short words are harder for him than long ones, because the short words have fewer distinguishing characteristics. He often will read a word correctly in one sentence, and later on the page the same word is a complete stranger to him. He will sometimes invent or substitute a word which fits the thought of the sentence for a word which he does not recognize . . . ."

Specific Learning Disabilities may encompass other kinds of problems. Pierce H. McLeod says, "Too frequently time, space and position have little meaning to these children." and Patrick Ashlock points out that there may be difficulties with reasoning and abstractions. "This child seems to think concretely and does not 'get the idea' of the story, and cannot 'read between the lines.' " He may have trouble with sequencing of ideas. Boys are more often afflicted with Specific Learning Disabilities by a ratio of about four to one. Though varying degrees exist it is rare that the problem is so severe that people remain totally handicapped despite all efforts. Although reading disabilities tend to run in families, according to Harold D. Love, " . . . recent research indicates that 95 percent of dyslexics can learn to read if they are given proper treatment. The outlook is definitely better if the child is identified early in his school career."

Learning to read is one of the most important tasks in the early school years. Children who fail at it or for whom it is very difficult suffer incalculable loss of self-esteem. Therefore, Disabled Readers with Specific Learning Disabilities need all the help they can get. For younger children, an important source of meaningful aid should be elementary school libraries and librarians. Although problems stemming from Specific Learning Disabilities require diagnosis and remediation by trained personnel such as reading specialists and school psychologists who can offer assistance to children, classroom teachers, and parents, knowledgeable school librarians can be a part of the effort. Here are some guidelines for selecting books which these children can learn to read without inordinate frustration along with a brief, annotated bibliography. Hopefully school librarians will find the following suggestions helpful as a basis for recommending other titles.

Criteria for Books for Disabled Readers

The usually acceptable criteria of high interest-low vocabulary materials are not sufficient as a basis for selection books for children with Specific Learning Disabilities. Because these children have more difficulty with short words than with longer, more distinctive words, low vocabulary does not necessarily mean that the book will be easy; neither are books with only a few words on a page necessarily helpful. For obvious reasons, if children mix up the simplest letters and words along with the most difficult, they are going to rack up quite a high percentage of errors on any page. In general, criteria for selection should be based on the following points:

1. *Typeface*: Large, clear, easily seen type with wide leading (white space) between lines is important for disabled readers. Larger type (at least 14 pt.) allows them to see the shape of the word more clearly. Caps mixed with lower case type allow a word shape to be seen clearly. Thus, Millions has a more distinctive shape then MILLIONS. Lower case helps in differentiating between similar words, pit and tip are more distinguishable than PIT and TIP. In addition, italic and other script typefaces are harder to read and are not recommended. White type on a black background should be avoided unless the type is sans serif which minimizes loss of legibility.

2. *Appearance*: Books should be a comfortable size and shape, (not too long), with attractive covers; they should look appropriate for the children's age. Paper should not be glazed as it reflects distracting amounts of light.

3. *Subject matter*: Fiction should have a fairly direct story line without complicated subplots, nonfiction should be simple and accurate with clear concrete concepts. Humor, fantasy, and generally far-out books can present problems, but for the most part, dyslexic children have average or above average intelligence and their interests will be the same as other children's.

4. *Literary merit*: As in all recommended materials, books for dyslexic children should follow recognized standards of literary merit.

5. *Length:* Books should be short with frequent breaks—usually just a few words on a page for beginning readers and short chapters for older readers. Collections of short stories are good.

6. *Illustrations:* Pictures should be clear, plentiful, and help to elucidate the content.

Toys and Games:
"The First Reading Tool"
SLJ Interviews Edythe O. Cawthorne

"**P**lay is the chief learning activity of preschool children; toys and games are the first reading tools."

The sentence has a quotable ring to it and Edythe O. Cawthorne, Coordinator of Children's Services for Prince George's (P.G.) County Memorial Library System (Md.), delivers it with persuasive conviction. She's been saying it for many years, but it was only four years ago that she began to move toward the circulation of toys and games in the seventeen branch libraries of P.G. County.

"I considered toys, games, and realia as the logical next step in our acquisition of 'non-print' materials. And, the economy had something to do with our getting started. Parents were and are finding it more and more difficult to provide the essentials for their children, let alone toys and games. The fact that this service allows them to try out toys and games on their kids before purchasing prevents expensive disasters of the sort that almost every parent experiences sooner or later, the toy or gift that just doesn't take the interest of the child to whom it's given—that's a good reason to offer non-readers, taxpayers, and trustees for establishing toy and game loans. I think the best reason is the fact that you don't develop readers by the use of books alone. There have to be motor skills, eye development—and practice. Toys and games are not just play; play is *work* and *practice* for children, the basis of reading readiness."

As Julia Reed Palmer says in *Read for Your Life* (Scarecrow, 1973):

> Games are the best key for an older child who has given up hope of learning to read. The School Volunteers have probably taught more children to read by playing Go Fish than in any other way. A game that resembles gin rummy, Go fish is played by assembling a trick of cards all of which have the same beginning sound such as baby, bat, bear, etc. Each card has the word top and bottom and the picture of the object in the middle. By the end of two or three games, the student not only has learned the letter b and its sound, but has come unconsciously to recognize the word and when he sees "bat" on a piece of paper, can read it easily. He has learned to read without knowing it, and, surprised by success, has the confidence to go on.

"Another instance is the game Candyland, which teaches shape recognition, color recognition, and all this has to be in place before you go on to Scrabble with older children—which, by the way, provides drill in spelling and adding in a form that has children who are bored stiff by their school workbooks begging for more.

"I never claim that our toy/game lending program is more than two years old, but we really started planning four years ago and the program, as well as our procedures, took two years to evolve. We will continue to revise and modify our methods as we learn by experience. There's no huge backlog of library literature on this, but, more and more, you can hear people at conferences exchanging information informally about how they began lending toys or games or both."

When To Buy

"We started in the summer. We had some money in the Children's Services new project fund and, I suppose, we had a vision of summer as a leisure/learning time. If we had it all to do over again, knowing all we know now, we wouldn't have tried to start buying then. I'd urge any librarians considering the possibility of beginning a toy/game lending program to plan their purchases for late August, early September, and October. We discovered that the toy/game manufacturers are geared to supply the Christmas market. By late spring, the toy and game dealers are likely to be out of stock on items from the last Christmas push and some of the things listed in the last catalogs, may, by then, be out of production. This isn't true of educational toys and instructional games; there isn't the same range and variety, but these always seem to be in stock."

How To Buy

"We had everything to learn about the ordering process. For instance, we found out that games are usually sold wholesale in units of six or twelve. We've been very fortunate in P.G. County in finding a wholesale toy dealer who also has a retail store. He's willing to break a unit for us if we want an odd number, but this isn't easy nor standard practice for wholesalers without their own retail outlets.

"Another thing we discovered in shopping around for a toy and game wholesaler is that some want cash and they are unwilling to bill, or to put up with the bookkeeping of our library invoicing. We get a 30 percent discount from the retail list price.

"We began without a budget, just a few thousand from our special projects fund, but the best indicator of the program's success is the fact that our toy and game lending is now supported by an appropriation from the local tax in P.G. County's library budget" (now, $3000 per annum).

Selling the Program

"I don't want anybody to get the idea that all of the children's librarians in P.G. County were gung-ho for lending toys and games. There wasn't resistance as much as there was puzzlement and I tried to reduce that with my first general memo:

In the near future, as soon as circulation routines can be worked out, Prince George's County Memorial Library System will begin circulating educational toys on the same basis as books. There are many reasons why we think this is an important contribution to make to the development of children. We would like to share with you the thinking that led to the decision to include this kind of material in the collection.

The question has been raised about the wisdom of introducing our new project, the circulation of educational toys, at a time when libraries are asking patrons to speak out in favor of library legislation. From the point of view, however, of nonprint oriented adults to whom the library still remains virtually invisible this is a meaningful service which we would be furnishing to them. Conceivably this group would see the value of joining those telling their lawmakers, "Don't you dare cut library services now that they are doing something for me and my family!"

Families who have not been able to afford expensive learning or viewing equipment will find toys a usable library item.

If we really believe that the library exists to help each person to achieve his greatest potential, we must do everything we can to meet the needs of children during the time they have the possibility for making the greatest mental growth. As Anna W. M. Wolf states in *The Parents' Manual*:

> Education does not wait for school. It begins with the infant's first experiences of the world and with all that he senses and does. Toys and play are far more than childish pastimes to be replaced as soon as possible by serious work and lessons; on the contrary, they have positive and intrinsic values, since they furnish the materials by which a child experiments and learns much about the fundamental nature of the world in which he finds himself."—*Chapter 7, p. 186*

Selecting

"We began the collection with stacking blocks, hand puppets, trucks, planes, etc. From the start, we opted for quality toys. Early on, we had agreed that crib toys were not to be part of the collection because of the sanitary problems. We've been concerned about safety—everybody involved in toy and game lending needs to be—we try to avoid toys with sharp edges, wheels that pull off, and easily breakable plastic parts. However, our lending policy is clear—*vigilance on the part*

of parents is required. When you come right down to it, kids can brain themselves or each other with the books libraries lend. After achieving a set of selection standards (see box) you have to relax on the *understood vigilance of the parents*."

Publicizing

"After selecting the initial collection, we publicized our toy and game loans through every medium at hand: newspaper stores; local radio and TV (both daytime and evening hours); flyers; and our monthly branch calendars. We also had a series of Monday night parent/child workshops on toys and games conducted in cooperation with an adult education agency. Now *there* is something I'd like to go back and do over—with all the wisdom of hindsight!

"We did everything right but the scheduling—publicity, branch preparation, lecture participation plans—everything was in order. We thought we'd sit back and watch the fathers march in with their children. And, a few fathers *did* bring their kids. But, we were really done in by Monday night football on TV! We'll think twice about ever choosing Monday nights again.

"One of our most effective means of introducing our toys and games service has been a brochure, 'Growing Through Play' by Clair Suhr. It is directed at parents and describes briefly and clearly the role of play in children's learning at various stages and it promotes the positive effects of parents joining and sharing the fun of their children at play." (Single copies and "Toy and Game List" free on request. Send 9" x 12" envelope with 16¢ postage affixed to: Children's Services, Prince George's County Memorial Library System, 6532 Adelphi Road, Hyattsville, Maryland 20782.)

Processing and Circulating

"We make a shelf card for each toy or game and put one copy of the card on each item. We've kept preparation for circulation to a minimum. For instance, some of the best, even the most expensive, games come in very flimsy boxes, so boxed games get their corners reinforced with cloth tape. We started with a special catalog picturing each toy and game, but we've given it up as too time-consuming. The flat items submit to our photographic circulation equipment and we have special canvas bags for carrying the borrowed items away. This is important. Games and toys are bulky; you need to supply the means to get them back and forth. Because paper bags don't get returned, we chose canvas bags stamped with the library name and we find that these do come back for re-use. The loan term, the renewal privileges, and the reserve possibilities are the same as for our book loans."

Maintenance

"Our experience on returns is quite good. Toy loss has been minimal. Borrowers are very pleased with this service and the low-rate of nonreturns indicates that they are taking special care.

"We are not prepared at this time to become involved in making repairs on any damaged toys or games. We've figured that the time spent in making or acquiring the replacement part equals and probably exceeds the cost of a new item. Boxed games are opened when returned and given a quick check. Pieces missing? We rely on the borrowers to tell us (they do) and we've arranged with some manufacturers a supply of extra pieces."

In response to the question, Do you know of any school libraries with toy and game lending programs? Mrs. Cawthorne replied: "Too few with too little. There is wide recognition among educators of the effectiveness of peer-teaching and self-teaching. I can't think of any better mechanism for peer-teaching than board games. Can't you imagine teaching conversational French with Scrabble? And, school libraries should acquire and lend duplicates of every instructional game used by classroom teachers for student self-tutoring or for help at home.

"School libraries are really much more into 'non-print' than public libraries, but that awkward term usually refers to AV holdings. School librarians are missing a great opportunity to extend the education experience and bolster the curriculum unless they make part of their 'non-print' collections toys and games!"

GENERAL CRITERIA FOR SELECTING AND REVIEWING TOYS AND GAMES
(The terms toys and games will be used interchangeably)

Toys and Games Should:

1. Be safe, They should have no sharp edges, explosive contents such as caps, flammable materials, and should be shatter-proof and splinter-proof.
2. Not have parts that are intended for one-time use such as score cards; unless they are easily replicated or are available in most homes.
3. Be well constructed to endure repeated use. Parts should be well attached, not with staples, long pins, poor glue, etc.
4. Not produce food or contain eating implements.
5. Not be battery or electrically operated. Batteries may corrode and need to be replaced frequently.

Items to consider:

1. Can the game be used independently or is adult supervision required?
2. Are the instructions clear? Will they be easily lost?
3. Is the game versatile enough to allow scope for the child's imagination?
4. What are the possible uses and values of this game beyond its specified function?
5. What is the object of the game? Is it sufficiently rewarding to sustain the child's interest for the length of the playing period?
6. How will missing pieces affect the usability of the game?
7. Can the materials be returned to the container easily? Is assembling and disassembling practical?
8. Is the container sturdy?
9. Does it contain toxic dyes, especially in items which may be placed in the mouth?

Special Criteria For Preschool Toys

1. Toys should not invite chewing as a major activity.
2. Toys should be washable.
3. Toys should not have small items that may be swallowed.
4. All colors and dyes *must* be nontoxic.

Assorted Thoughts on Creative Authors and Artists

Ursula Nordstrom

The topic I was assigned is: An Editor's Thoughts on Creative Authors and Artists. I'm glad I wasn't asked for "consecutive thoughts," "well-constructed thoughts," or "noncontradictory thoughts." A lot of them don't come from the brain, but they do come from the heart.

The difficulty in trying to talk about creative authors and artists is that everything connected with the subject seems so fascinating that selection is almost impossible! I recently had a lesson in this. I was asked to write about publishing E.B. White's *Stuart Little* and *Charlotte's Web*. I began going through the old folders, which in the case of *Stuart Little* go back to 1945. E.B. White's notes to me were marvelous, and so were his comments on Garth Williams' first tentative sketches of Stuart. It was hard to sift out what might have been of general interest because even the grubbiest memos from the manufacturing department still had a sort of backstage glamour for me.

Learning from Authors

My first thought is that an editor can learn a great deal from creative authors. I'm afraid too many people think an author learns from an editor. I'm also afraid a lot of so-called Creative Editors think so, too. Of course an editor can do something for a creative author, and that is to try to create an atmosphere, a climate of openness and interest in which creative authors and artists can grow. Someone once said to me, thinking they were giving me a nice compliment, that I had done a lot for a brilliant Mr. X. I tried to say then, and I truly meant it, that all I did was not do him any harm. He was the talent, the genius, the energy; all I as an editor could do was give him room and a climate in which to grow. There's a medical axiom, "First, do no harm." That's a good thing for editors to remember. You may think that no one can really do harm to a truly creative person but I believe that a clumsy editorial approach, an unperceptive remark, can throw a creative person off balance and can do a lot of damage. This is certainly true in the early career of a creative person with a "raw and weedy talent" as Maurice Sendak once put it. I know I have been guilty of doing harm, and I regret those instances with all my heart. I think most editors would admit that they too have been clumsy and that they, too, regret those instances. Editors must listen with all their senses and try to react as creatively as possible to the ideas of the truly creative person. Thus editors can learn. And, "First, do no harm."

I remember John Steptoe's original version of the text for *Stevie*. I had seen John's portfolio, which was full of brilliant work, and had the benefit of several long, wonderful talks with him about his hopes, his thoughts, his then 16-year-old self. But when I read the first version of *Stevie*, with its black English, I said tentatively that perhaps the story should be told in a more acceptable grammatical style in order to reach the readers. John became stubborn and shook his head. He told me, "No, I want the story written this way." I'd had, as I've said, the benefit of seeing his portfolio, and in talking with him I was convinced of his tremendous talent. So I went along with him. Indeed, I had no other choice. As an artist he was convinced that he was right, and so he convinced me.

He knew black experience, and I didn't. I had to be more keenly aware than ever that unperceptive editorial suggestions could possibly harm. We've all sooner or later put our big fat editorial feet into delicate matters. Again, I regret the times when I have done this, but I'm very grateful for times when instinct, or trust, or blind faith in discerned talent kept me from harming a young author or artist.

Amiable Authors?

When I was young and scared I published some books by an author I inherited from my predecessor, Louise Raymond. The author lived in California. She simply sent in her manuscripts and we sent her suggestions. When she wanted to, she acted on them and we sent her contracts. She only wrote to me every time she got divorced and remarried to give me her new name and address. This happened several times. One day I sent her copies of her new book. She replied that she liked the look of the book, but she wondered when she was going to receive the contract. Unbelievable! I had never been so forgetful before, and I sent her the contract at once with a letter of apology in which I praised her for her forbearance in not sending me an angry letter. I told her she would receive the (then nonexistent) Nordstrom Award for the Most Amiable Author of the Year.

She wrote back, forgave me, and asked me when I was sending the award. Well, my bluff was called so I asked the production department to fix me up something, and they designed a document with, I think, a bluebird at the top and a citation designating the recipient as the Most Amiable Author of the Year.

A couple of years later one of our New York authors went to California on a visit and met the Nordstrom Award winner, who showed off my award. When the New York author came back, she telephoned me and said rather peevishly, "It seems to me that I've been pretty amiable about some of the things you've done. *I've* never won the Nordstrom Award." Well, the whole thing was too involved to explain so I had more copies made, and I gave her one.

I was silly enough to try to use it as a little ploy in difficult situations. "Careful there," I'd say to an author who was getting temperamental, "you may be blowing your chance to win the Nordstrom Award!" But I began to notice that I had very few occasions to give it. Finally I noticed that no one was even *trying* for it. And indeed, why should they? Again I learned something important from authors: Being amiable isn't necessary. Being temperamental and thoughtless and unkind isn't a prerequisite. But truly creative people should not be expected to be amiable, and I certainly learned that.

In the Night Kitchen . . . .

Talking and listening to Maurice Sendak is a learning experience. It's terribly exciting to hear him talk about the first glimmering of an idea. Long before he did *In The Night Kitchen* he began to talk to me about several things which were obsessing him.

I remember talking with him one late afternoon in the dark little studio he had on West 9th Street before he moved to his beautiful house in Connecticut. He told me he was finding himself fascinated by a print of a Winslow Homer picture. It showed a young girl in a field or garden who was wearing a starched sunbonnet. What particularly fascinated Maurice about this picture was the way the sunlight shone through the starched muslin.

Then another time when I asked him about his work he shook his head almost in puzzlement and told me he was becoming unusually fascinated by everything connected with Mickey Mouse. He was remembering his childhood love of Mickey, remembering coming from Brooklyn to Manhattan to see Mickey's movies. He was beginning to collect Mickey artifacts. He said he didn't know where all this was leading, but he was just going to follow the threads.

Another time he told me that he couldn't get out of his head a bakery commercial he'd heard over and over again on the radio when he was a little boy. The bakery advertised, "We bake while you sleep," and as a child Maurice had been delighted with the idea that while he was asleep there were bakers in his kitchen baking bread. Again he said, "I don't know what it all means, but I'll just keep on going following these threads."

In the Night Kitchen came from many levels of Sendak's mind and heart, but in it there is the starched muslin from the Winslow Homer picture in the hats of the bakers. There is the hero named Mickey and, in the background, the city where Maurice was brought to see those movies. And certainly there are the bakers baking in the night kitchen. It's a rare privilege to hear about such a book long before work is begun, and I'm grateful.

One's Younger Self

One learns that the creative writer of children's books has his or her younger self more easily available to him or her than it is to most of us. The creative writer can somehow catapult himself or herself back to a six-year-old or 12-year-old emotion and experience. This doesn't necessarily make for a complete mature, emotional adult person.

I remember years ago that I was greatly moved while talking with Margaret Wise Brown. It was after she had written *The Runaway Bunny* and *Goodnight Moon*. One day I turned to her and made myself say that I felt very grateful to her, that I had to tell her, lest something happen, lest we lose touch somehow, lest one of us die, which one of us did. "Why?" she asked. "Well," I said, "I think you're pretty close to a real genius. And I feel very fortunate to know you, to see you working and revising. It's wonderful to have this job and the chance to know someone like you." She was touched, I think. But she said that the emotional equipment that made her a good writer didn't necessarily make her a happy, emotionally mature person.

So good books often come from those whose younger selves are easily accessible to them and who are perhaps oversensitive and different and difficult. And it doesn't do a bit of harm if the editor is a little nuts, too.

Friendly and Unfriendly Thoughts

It's always so fascinating to me to see the way a creative person uses his or her emotions in books. Charlotte Zolotow, who has written so many beautiful, sensitive, and poetic books, is a good example. She is an extremely private person who does not express her emotions easily to others, but she puts them into her books. For instance, if she is lonely, she doesn't talk a lot about it, but she writes a book about loneliness, an emotion which most children feel sooner or later. She has written some very peppery books—*The Quarreling Book* and *The Hating Book*—but many of her books are based on more gentle feelings: *Mr. Rabbit and the Lovely Presents, Do You Know What I'll Do?*, the recent *William's Doll*, and the more recent *My Grandson Lew*.

But Charlotte herself is not all sweetness and light, thank goodness. Some time ago she was expressing a great deal of rage to me about someone she disliked intensely. This person, Charlotte felt, was always putting others down, was always critical. It made Charlotte furious. She was so full of all this anger that I, as her friend and editor, sought to break some of the tension by saying mildly, "You should write about it. I hate to see all this emotion lying around loose and going to waste." Sometime later I was delighted to have Charlotte put a manuscript on my desk which told about two little girls—one a putdown specialist who jars the other into independent thinking. It is *The Unfriendly Book*, to be published in the spring of 1975. This is an excellent example of the creative artist's ability to harness and give permanent form to emotions and convictions.

Love

An editor must love the creative ability. Then the editor can take anything. Creative people can, and apparently sometimes must, strike out at those close to them. Often the editor is the closest.

Of course, "love" is one of those vague words. It means one thing to one person and too many chocolate fudge sundaes to another. Recently, when we were having an unusually good year financially in the Harper Junior Department, a new member of the management came to see me to talk about the operation of our department. He asked me to what I attributed the success of the department. As a daughter of the Depression I am still insecure and fearful that it might turn out that really I don't know how to publish children's books at all. I tried to talk in a very businesslike way and said I thought we'd had the success we'd had because the House is very sharply departmentalized, that we didn't have to check with anyone else to publish what we wanted to publish, that the Harper management had kept their cotton-pickin' hands off us and so we had complete freedom to make our own mistakes and our own successes.

This broad hint against any future changes in the functioning of Harper seemed to leave him interested but not quite satisfied. He looked as though he thought that for some strange reason of my own, I just wasn't telling him everything I should tell him. All my attempts at being businesslike fell away. I said, "Well, it sounds funny—but we have to give out a lot of love. We have to love the authors and artists, even when they are difficult, and in fact we have to love each other as much as possible and be supportive of each other. And you know, we just have to have a lot of love." He left rapidly. But there it is—there has to be a lot of love.

Picture of a Problem

Occasionally people ask, "How much thought do you give to the psychological values of the books you publish? Do you think books can have a role in the adjustment to family life, self-appreciation, sibling rivalry, etc.?" Of course we think they can, but editors can make terrible mistakes if they accept books just because they seem therapeutically good for a child or because they think the writing is psychologically sound. Adults change psychological styles. This year's warm, reassuring story may be, so far as the adults are concerned, next year's mother-fixation book. For instance, Margaret Wise Brown's *The Runaway Bunny* is about a little bunny who threatens to run away, whose mother promises to come after him. One psychologically oriented review committee refused to recommend it. They thought it would give young children mother fixations and Oedipus complexes! It was a good thing we published it simply as a book we thought children would love, rather than as any sort of therapeutic agent.

As a matter of fact, the book probably does have a good effect psychologically. Creative artists know more than all the psychiatrists and certainly more than all the editors know. We must, of course, take very seriously the total effect we think books will have on children, but we mustn't publish a book just because we think it will help children avoid mother fixations. We must listen to the creative people.

I recently read *Theophilus North* by Thornton Wilder and was interested in the part where Theophilus met Dr. Sigmund Freud at a social gathering. Dr. Freud asks him, "Do you know an old English comedy, I forget its name, in which the hero suffers from a certain impediment? In the presence of ladies and of genteel, well brought-up girls he is shy and tongue-tied. He is scarcely able to raise his eyes from the ground. But in the presence of servant girls and barmaids he is all boldness and impudence. Do you know the name of that comedy?" "Yes, Herr Professor," says Theophilus, "that is *She Stoops To Conquer* by Oliver Goldsmith." "Thank you!" said Dr. Freud. "We doctors have found that this Oliver Goldsmith has drawn an excellent picture of a problem that we are now frequently discovering among our patients. Oh, these poet natures have always known everything."

Finding Authors and Artists

It isn't ever easy to find or recognize creative persons. One of the most important things for an editor is, I think, to be available and open—to let authors who come to see you feel that you are truly interested and that you have all the time in the world. An editor doesn't have to pretend to be interested, but that part about giving the impression that you have all the time in the world isn't always easy. Some come wandering into Harper with or without an appointment. That's what Ruth Krauss, Tomi Ungerer, Emily Neville, John Steptoe, Russ Hoban, and so many others did. We've found that it is important to look for the creative potential in the whole person, in the emotional vitality of the individual, and not necessarily concentrate on the particular book idea that is presented to us. Then, editors have to go out and look for authors and illustrators. Many extremely talented authors do not know that the field of children's books can offer them an unparalleled opportunity.

Truly, I believe that the most talented persons in today's book world are working with children's books. When an editor can go out and share this belief with creative people, it often results in good books. Charlotte Zolotow found Paul Zindel through the television dramatization of *The Effect of Gamma Rays on Man-in-the-Moon Marigolds* and wrote to him suggesting that he write a novel for young people. He reacted positively to the suggestion and the results were: *The Pigman, My Darling, My Hamburger*, and *I Never Loved Your Mind*. We were also proud to publish the play, *The Effect of Gamma Rays*. It later won the Pulitzer Prize for drama.

Unbeknown to us, an author of adult trade books was interested to see that a prize-winning dramatist such as Paul Zindel had written a junior novel or two. So M.E. Kerr read them, felt that this certainly was a great field, and decided to write for it. The results were: *Dinky Hocker Shoots Smack, If I Love You, Am I Trapped Forever?, The Son Of Someone Famous*, and coming up in the spring of 1975, *Is That You, Miss Blue?* Maybe someone is now reading one of M.E. Kerr's junior novels and deciding, "Gosh, this is good! I'm going to try to write something for this field." Nevertheless, we don't rely on this ripple effect or wait for authors to find us. We do go out and try to find creative people if they don't come to us.

Sitting Out This Dance

Helping authors live through unfavorable and/or unperceptive reviews is a difficult editorial responsibility. I won't name names, but a few of the very best authors with whom I've worked have gone through periods when they literally couldn't write. They thought they were finished, that nobody would care about anything that they might write even if they could. Of course, some writers' blocks do last forever, but the ones I'm remembering didn't. In such cases all an editor can do is be patient and write lots of letters expressing not pressure but continued interest and concern; in general, try to get across the idea that the editor will sit out this dance with the author who isn't able to dance just at that moment. Many years ago, I read something the great Martha Graham wrote. I've often repeated it to authors suffering through Writers' Block. "There is a vitality. A life force. An energy. A quickening that is translated through you into action, and because there is only one of you in all of the time this expression is unique and, if you block it, it will never exist through any other medium and it will be lost. It is not your business to determine how good it is nor how valuable nor how it compares with other expressions. It is your business to keep it yours, clearly and directly to keep the channel open. You have to keep open and aware for the urges that motivate you. Keep the channel open."

When a writer breaks through a block and the phone rings and a joyful voice says, "I've started. I think I've started something really good!" Well, there are few moments like it for an editor.

As for helping an author to live through a time of unfavorable or unperceptive reviews—well, everyone bleeds. There is not much an editor can do at times like these. You can try, but not always with any degree of success.

On Revisions

Most of the really fine authors and artists have the built-in discipline to revise until the work is as close as possible to perfection. Of course, this isn't always the case. After a couple of revisions an author can get too close to or tired of the material and simply become unwilling to do any more work. I've found it helpful to remind some weary reviser of the perhaps apocryphal story of the first versions of Beethoven's Fifth Symphony, which didn't contain the famous first four notes. They didn't appear until about the 19th version. Now those four notes seem absolutely inevitable and as though they were always there. As indeed they always were. Beethoven just hung in there until he found them.

Of course, a good editor does to some degree work with creative authors on revisions, though that phrase "work with" seems as pretentious to me as the pretentious term "creating editing." The most helpful thing you can do perhaps is to re-member what the author's original vision was. The author often comes in and tells an editor about the next book. Both grow excited and the author starts to write. Somewhere along the line, somehow, perhaps by being too close to the material, perhaps because writing is necessarily a lonely occupation, the author loses track of exactly what he or she wanted to say. An editor can remember the original vision and perhaps tactfully say. "Yes, but didn't you really want to do so and so?" This has to be done very gently. Again, "First, do no harm."

NGEFY

The really hard situation for an editor to handle is when a really good author writes a not-so-good book. It's often possible to say NGEFY, shorthand for "Not Good Enough for You." However, if a valued author is determined and the editor hopes the author still has other fine books to write, then the editor goes ahead and publishes the book. I think people often wonder, "Why did so-and-so publish that?" I wish there could be some code word to use on the flap copy indicating, "We agree that this isn't as good as the author's previous books, but we want to keep the author happy and functioning, and so we're trying to go along with him."

Then of course there comes a time when the hitherto creative powers of a fine author begin to wane. This is an extremely painful time for both editor and author. It is awful to see, for authors' egos balloon as authors' talents shrink, perhaps in self-protection. It is perhaps almost as difficult for an editor to know when it is time to let an author go from the list as it is to know when it is time to add a particular author to the list. But when it is done, it hurts. Of course sometimes an author lets an editor go and takes his work elsewhere. That hurts even more, and I'll drop the subject immediately.

One Final Thought

It's wonderful to realize that the books children love the most have turned out to be what most of us call the best. Many adults didn't love or recognize *Mary Poppins* (Harcourt), but children did. Children loved E.B. White's and Sendak's books, and every year there is new proof that they can take the very best books we can give them.

I've said this so often, and I'll repeat it here. We must try to remember that the children are brand new and we adults are not. It is difficult for the most devoted and sensitive adults not to sift his or her reactions to a book through his or her own adult experiences, complexes, and neuroses. All but a very, very few of us have some rather mixed up, even messy little things buried deep within us. If we let our adult reactions to certain situations negatively influence our judgment of a book written by a creative artist for children (most of whom are extremely creative themselves up until the ages of 12 or 13), we're guilty! It's one of the hardest things for editors to remember, but we must try—the children are new, and we are not.

Collecting Local History

by Esther Perich

So often the school librarian is faced with a dilemma in that regular channels to local history sources are often not accessible to students, and if obtained, are not written at the reading and comprehension level of the students. The reasons for this situation are many. The local historical society is often understaffed, thereby not able to devote considerable amounts of time to helping individual students. Quite often, though ready to provide a general introduction to the locale, the staff is not ready to serve great hordes of children, nor can the building stand the traffic. Unfortunately, historical societies have been created as "special libraries" for adults, while the school and its library are for children. In order to challenge this precedent, yet work together effectively with the established historical institution, school librarians must play important roles in collecting and preserving materials which will not only support the curriculum of the school, but will also reach out to each individual within the school community by furnishing something "just for him."

Beginning with the premise that a community (or any unit you decide to work with) which does not know its own history can be likened to a man who has lost his memory, the school librarian must begin to provide materials that fall within the students' level of understanding.

Building a collection

First and foremost in your plan should be the establishment of a picture file portraying the growth and development of the community. Sources for the file can be obtained or copied from the files of the real estate offices, local industrial organizations, and from the local newspaper morgue. Parents of students might have early pictures of the community before major buildings were erected, streets landscaped, or the terrain otherwise changed. Tell parents to root through their cellars, attics, and old scrapbooks. No telling what they might find. What might otherwise be an insignificant photo in their collection might be a valuable addition to the school's collection. Remember that photographs can be copied at little expense.

Maps play an important role in local history. The growth of the community, as recorded on paper, captivates the interest of all youngsters. They can see "what was here before my house was," or "before the school was." Topographical maps are available from the Geological Survey, 12201 Sunrise Val-

ley Drive, Reston, Virginia (22092), at reasonable cost. Air maps can be obtained from the airport. Residents can enrich this collection by the donation of their own early maps of the community, including outdated road maps that would otherwise be given to "File 13."

Each school and community has a list of "greats"—those members who spent their early years (or their lives) in the locale and went on to establish their names and reputations. An author and artist collection consisting of published books, columns of poetry, periodical articles, unpublished manuscripts, and holographic documents, by and about the authors and artists, can be assembled. In addition, slides, photographs or photocopies of original art work should be preserved. A taped interview of each celebrity may be added to this collection.

Of course, school yearbooks, newspapers, literary magazines, and underground newspapers should be part of the collection. Other primary and secondary source materials worth gathering are: directories of all types—city, telephone, commercial and fraternal, sermons, and anniversary addresses given at churches, and public speeches given by notable residents. Artifacts gathered in and about the geographical confines of the community will add special interest to the collection. These can include rubbings of cemetery inscriptions, and realia such as signs from defunct stores, retired parking meters, etc. Relevant newspaper clippings from the local paper should be clipped, dated, and kept in a scrapbook.

The establishment of an oral history project, that is, a systematic attempt to obtain historical information through interviews from citizens who have lived and participated in the growth of the area, will provide another source of historical documentation. In this way, a fuller record of their participation in the social, economic, and political arena of the community will be available. This can prove to be a most interesting project, affording actual student participation. Students may assist by undergoing training as oral history interviewers. Consult manuals, such as Willa Baum's *Oral History for the Local Historical Society* (Am. Assn. for State and Local History/Calif. Historical Soc., Nashville, 1971), or William Moss's *Oral History Program Manual* (Praeger, 1974) for information and guidance. Remember, too, there are several legal aspects which should be considered. You may wish to see the *Forms Manual*, sponsored by the Colleges and University Archives Committee of the Society of American Archivists (Phila., 1973), for sample contracts that circumscribe these problems. Oral history need not be tailored to the history of the leaders of the community but may be tied in with individual genealogy-research projects under the guidance of teachers.

Once you have begun collecting information and have a clear mind as to what direction the collection will take, a public plea for parent participation can be made through the school's communication channel. If you can get them to work on the oral history project, give donations, or obtain their permission to photocopy papers of historical value (printed genealogies, diaries, journals, memoirs, scrapbooks and photographs), a well-rounded collection can develop. Remember that each donated item should bear the donator's inscription on the catalog card, and if permissible, this should be put on the item itself.

Once your collection is established, a description of its purposes and goals should be distributed to the local paper, city officials, civic leaders, services organizations, and senior citizen groups. Not only will this show good spirit on the part of the library, but members of the community might want to add some items in their possession to the collection. Experience shows that once a library displays honorable intentions in collecting and preserving local history sources, misgivings about the care and future of donated articles are dispelled. The school will become a natural depository for all such material.—*Submitted by Esther Perica, Librarian and part-time City Historian, Rolling Meadows High School, Rolling Meadows, Illinois.*

Extending School Programs
Via Community Resource Files

by Juanell S. Marks

When the Spring Branch Independent School District in Houston evaluated its learning resources centers last year, one area kept drawing our attention. The Texas Education Agency (TEA) *Guidelines for the Development of Campus Learning Resources Centers*, stated that, "All communities have resources which can enrich the school's instructional program when they are used wisely. The learning resources center in each campus unit maintains a card file of index of community resources available to pupils and teachers. "We knew that many of our teachers used community resources, and certainly that a variety of community resources abounded in the greater Houston area, but there were no card files on indexes of these resources available in the learning resources centers. We felt the need for a community resource file, and we knew that now was the time to do something about it.

A volunteer committee made up of four learning resources specialists (two elementary, one junior high, and one senior high level) and the Coordinator of Learning Media Services met and discussed a plan of action. First, we had to determine what we would like our community resources file to contain.

The committee first established criteria for resources to be included in the core community resource file: 1) the resource should provide expert knowledge of the subject; 2) the resource should be appropriate for selected age, grade, and purpose; 3) the organization should have a policy of providing resources for schools, and these should be reasonably available; 4) the charges, if any, should be within the financial capabilities of the user; and 5) procedures for contacting or obtaining the resource would be left to the discretion of individual teachers, department chairperson, or principals.

Then, to obtain a list of community resources already being used, a questionnaire was sent to all the teachers in the district through the learning resources specialists in their buildings. On it we asked teachers to recommend community organizations, institutions, or individuals that had provided a resource person or activity that they considered worthwhile. A separate form was provided for each suggested name so that they could be sorted and alphabetized at a later date. The information requested was: the name of person or organization, address and telephone number, type of activity or presentation, and suggested grade levels and curriculum subjects. The completed questionnaires were arranged alphabetically by or-

ganization. We found that many organizations, such as Young Audiences of Houston or the Houston Fire Department, had been listed many times, and the information for each of these was combined on one sheet.

The Houston Public Library and the Mayor's office were contacted to determine if they could suggest additions for our prospective list. Some of their suggestions did not pertain to our educational programs but some did, such as the Palmer Drug Abuse Program. The committee checked the telephone directory for other appropriate prospects for the file, and ended up with a list of 160.

The next step was to contact these prospects by telephone, and the committee devised a telephone inquiry guide and answer sheet and developed interview procedures.

If the necessary information was given directly over the phone, the inquirer asked specific questions and immediately noted the answers on the telephone inquiry answer sheet. Each respondent was thanked and told when this file would be completed, in our schools, and available for use.

To get the resource file organized, we decided to use 4" by 6" index cards. Each card contains pertinent information such as the name of the individual or organization, telephone number, address, person, or department to contact, a brief description of the activity or presentation, the hours the person or activity can be scheduled, availability on video tape, transportation requirements, audience limitations for presentation or study trips, fees, advance schedule time needed, type of equipment and facilities needed, and suggested curriculum units and grade levels. Continuous revision, additions, or eliminations could be easily accomplished by using cards.

From the information on the cards, appropriate subject or subjects were assigned for each activity or type of program. *Sears List of Subject Headings* was used as the subject authority because of its availability in each learning resources center. Subject cards were prepared with cross references to names of organizations which provide resources related to the subject, so that the user could refer to the company's name for necessary information. The cards were filed in two alphabetical sections, the first being the subject cards, and the second the organization of individual names.

Rubber-footed metal file boxes were purchased for each of the district's 38 schools and its Central Professional Library; a master card for each resource entry and each subject entry was typed; and the district's publications department printed the required number of copies. Blank forms were provided so that the individual school could add to its file resources from its local community which would not be available to all the district's schools. We also provided an evaluation form to be used as needed. This can provide compliments, suggestions, reactions of students, and problems encountered, thus enabling teachers to use the resources more effectively.

The learning resources specialists presented the new community resource files to their faculties in unique ways. One news blurb to a senior high faculty stated, "Teachers, have you ever said, 'I would love to have someone come and speak to my class or club but I don't know anyone to ask'? Well, now your problem is solved. This year, for the first time, a community resource file is available in your learning resources center to help you. This file of guest speakers and field trip suggestions is arranged by subjects and organizations. It provides all the information needed to contact speakers and gives a brief description of each activity or presentation. Come by the learning resources center and share our newest addition."

Many teachers responded to the invitation—typical comments heard were, "This is great!" and "I wish we could have had this last year." We expect use of untapped resources within the community to mushroom as they and their students become aware of the exciting possibilities of community involvement made possible through these files.—*Juanell S. Marks, Learning Resources Specialist, Spring Woods Senior High School, Houston.*

Are We Selecting for a Generation of Skeptics?

by Kay E. Vandergrift

In my experience many students with whom I've worked have not been skeptical enough, that is, they are sometimes too accepting of what teachers or "authorized materials" have to say. My hope for youngsters in schools and my aspiration for those of us who work with them is that this attitude of cynicism be disproved by our actions, specifically by our evaluation and selection of materials, and that their habitual doubts and questions be transformed from an apathetic to an active skepticism. I believe that part of our job as media specialists is not only to evaluate and select materials but to help students develop the critical skills which will enable them in turn to evaluate and select those most valuable for their own purposes.

In focusing our attention on the development of this form of active skepticism, we might do well to keep in mind John Dewey's definition of criticism as "judgment engaged in discriminating among values," so that students, and ourselves, don't fall into the trap of thinking of criticism only as fault-finding. From this vantage point, evaluation itself goes beyond just searching for value according to specific criteria but actually helps to develop, in the critic, the very capacity to value something.

Criticism is a cumulative, developmental process which starts at a very early age when children begin to group like things together and to make choices from among them. Thus, the preschooler who understands enough about the various types of stories to ask for another "once-upon-a-time" story, is already a practicing critic and hopefully well on his or her way to recognizing excellence and developing the capacity to enjoy it. Even in the elementary school, and certainly by the time students reach secondary school, they should have learned to be critical and skeptical consumers of materials available in the media center and elsewhere. We [media specialists] should have helped students to realize that no maker of materials ever says all there is to say about a topic, that one's values in some way always come through in the materials produced, and that the producer's intent is to keep the consumer interested, perhaps using all the tricks available to get users to turn the pages, advance the filmstrip, or listen to the entire recording. A student who understands this will not be content to rely on a single source for information and will approach another's ideas and opinions with an active and healthy skepticism.

Media specialists, building collections for these active young skeptics, must first distinguish between *evaluation* and *selection*, knowing that even those materials rated highest on their evaluation scales might not always be appropriately selected for a particular collection. These two words are so often linked together in the literature of our profession that we sometimes lose sight of the fact that evaluation and selection are two separate processes, each with its own set of criteria. The evaluative criteria for specific types of materials are usually more clearly identified and more readily available, so that I will focus my discussion on criteria for selection in developing a particular collection. In so doing, I have chosen to look at five critical components of selection which I have called: 1) Selection and the Child; 2) Selection and Teaching/Learning Strategies; 3) Selection and the Curriculum; 4) Selection and the Balanced Collection; and, 5) Selection and Bibliographic Access.

My first category of criteria for selection is entitled "Selection and the Child" rather than "Selection and Children" to remind us that, although we are, of necessity, most often concerned with abstract concepts of children based on generalizations of age, sex, I.Q., etc.; we can, in selecting materials for a particular collection, at least look at the characteristics of the children who will be using that collection and may even at times select for a given child. I might add here, perhaps parenthetically, my concern that much of what we have done in the name of that great god "individualization" may have been an instrument of de-personalization in our schools. Sometimes our very enumerating and categorizing of all the objective data about a given child so captures our time and our attention that we are prevented from seeing those subjective qualities which make that child a unique human being.

Using all the data available to us about individuals in the school and whatever personal knowing we have about the unique human beings represented by those individuals, we begin to select materials according to our most informed hunches about what users want and need. Even when students and teachers are actively involved in the processes of evaluation and selection, much of the decision making is left to the media specialist.

Libraries should provide materials to confirm young people's life experiences, help them recognize—in history, in story, and on film—people, situations, and settings familiar to them. But we need materials also that do more than just confirm what youngsters already know; we need those that, through their own excellence and insight, actually illuminate users' lives and help them to understand their own place—and their own value—in the world. A fine collection of materials also extends students' knowledge and understanding of the world by taking them beyond the boundaries of their own time and space to imaginatively encounter ideas, people, and places they could not know otherwise. These materials, too, illuminate the understanding of self as they help users identify common aspects of the human condition unbounded by time or space. Thus, the school media center collection should be the source of great adventure—and great joy—for students.

I'm quite sure that none of us would select materials for a school media center without first considering the interests of the students who are to use the collection. I believe, however, that we do frequently fail to consider the levels of interest with which human beings approach ideas and information. What does it really mean to say that a child is interested in anthropology? Is that student interested in a simple definition, in getting assistance for a class assignment, or in searching for additional information about something he saw on TV last night? Or has that student already exhausted all the resources of your collection and now is asking for more advanced or specialized information? The varying levels of interest represented here are obvious—from the surface curiosity to some degree of personal concern to a deep and long-term commitment. Yet how do we take these differences into account either in our selection policies or in our interaction with students? If the media specialist is himself committed to the study of anthropology, the collection he has put together will probably be able to meet all but the most specialized needs of students in this area. The danger here is that this particular media specialist may overwhelm students, and perhaps even drive them from the media center, with more information than they really want to know. She or he can be like the over-eager parent who takes out all the sex education books and goes into detailed explanations of human reproduction when the young child asked "Where did I come from?" just to find that the child only wanted to know whether he was born in New York City or Chicago.

On the other hand, media centers frequently stock large numbers of materials on a particular topic, but a close examination of those materials might show that they serve a very narrow range of interests within that topic. For instance, I would guess that most elementary schools have a quantity of books on dinosaurs. There does seem to be a fairly consistent interest in this topic, at one level or another, among students in about the second grade; but how much material do we have available for the child who sustains that interest for the next four years he uses that media center?

A final concern under the label "Selection and the Child" is that of the rights of children and adolescents. We are all familiar with the statements published by ALA and other organizations concerned with such rights. The intellectual freedom movement has focused our attention on the rights of young people to information about sex, drugs, abortion, etc.; and most school districts have come to grips, in one way or another, with

access to this type of information. But there are other topics about which students are concerned and have a right to know. Can the student who wants information on the latest religious or political cults find this in our media centers? For a particular young person it might be just as crucial to find out about the "Moon children" or the "Jesus freaks" or Hare Krishna sect as it is for another to get the phone number of the nearest abortion referral center. And even more critical for some young people is the right to survival information, that is, such things as hard information on welfare, legal rights, medical aid, and suicide prevention. Even those of us who advocate the child's or the adolescent's right to all this information have a great deal of difficulty keeping our own biases from intruding in the selection process and thus limiting access to that information which the child or adolescent does indeed have a right to know.

A second category of selection criteria to be considered is "Selection and Teaching-Learning Strategies." Educational philosophies and, in fact, many of our views of schooling have undergone significant changes in the last two decades. Open education, the discovery method and modes of inquiry in the disciplines are all commonplace expressions to us now; and whether or not we advocate their practice, we can not escape having been affected by them in the ways we think about young people and about schools. Some districts have considered these "innovative" practices and have rejected them, but even more have institutionalized some of the newer structures while maintaining practices in direct contradiction to the philosophies they espouse. One of the most subtle of these is the selection and distribution of materials in the school media center. Students who are asked to inquire or to discover, that is, to practice an active and positive skepticism, are sometimes prevented from doing so by the use of bibliographies, reading lists, or specific instructions that set limits inhibiting inquiry. In addition, the materials themselves may be limited or one-sided. How many of our media centers give equal and unbiased information on the issues surrounding the Arab-Israeli conflict or our own Civil War, for that matter?

A major inhibitor to the practice of the discovery of inquiry method in schools is the lack of primary sources available to students. It's difficult to see situations afresh when one has only others' preselected facts and judgments from which to work.

Let us move on now to a consideration of "Selection and the Curriculum." What I would ask you to do here is to examine more closely the specific content of the curriculum guides, textbooks, or courses in your school so that you might select materials which truly match not only the methods of instruction employed but the actual topics of study as well. I heard a story recently of a second-grade class that was studying Indians. The media specialist in the school collected various kinds of materials on Indians and sent them to the classroom, told Indian stories to that class during story hour and even began to construct a wigwam with some of the children. It was only after all this that she discovered that the class was not studying Indians in general, but the Hopi tribe in particular. All the materials she had sent to the classroom were generic in nature with only one or two specific, and not very informative, references to the Hopi; and her own Indian activities with children were not at all representative of the people they were supposedly studying. Those of us who heard the story laughed but none of us too heartily for each could remember a time when we'd been in a somewhat similar situation. Media specialists cannot afford to accept convenient labels or what is going on in the school curriculum. They must dig beneath the surface to uncover what aspects of content are really important to students and teachers and search for materials that support and add to what is going on in the classroom. For younger children especially, this is often difficult to do because too many of the materials do, in fact, present general rather than specific views of their topic, and the bibliographic tools may not give the information really needed for selection.

Although our primary concern in curriculum is for the intellectual content, we must also remember that all curricula include practical and aesthetic content, that is, they focus on specific skills or abilities and on human feelings as well as on ideas. These aspects too, should be considered in our selection policies. Of particular interest throughout the country right now, is the whole question of moral education and values clarification in the schools. If these programs are advocated in schools, how can media specialists select materials to support them without impinging upon the rights of students or inflicting their own biases on the users of the materials they select?

Even at the skills level there are curricula concerns to be considered in selection. Do we, for instance, purchase attractive trade books in mathematics which use different computational procedures or notations than those taught in the school? Would your answer be the same for materials produced for primary students just learning math as it would be for advanced high school students? Or, in the physical sciences, do we search for materials on experiments that not only encourage students to inquire but also advocate the use of the same equipment and the same procedures as taught in their science classes?

A fourth category "Selection and the Balanced Collection" is, of course, a part of all that we've been discussing, but this is so important that it merits attention on its own. We've been looking at balance in content to meet individual and personal needs of children in terms of curricular content and teaching-learning strategies. An obvious area of concern which we have inferred only in passing, is that of balance in format. Not only do different learning styles require different forms of materials; but if young people are to be skeptics and inquirers, they must have access to similar messages in different formats so they can make informed judgments about how meanings are shaped by the containers which carry them.

Since we've been focusing most of our attention on instructional materials, let us now examine this whole question of balance as it relates to the selection of nondiscursive or imaginative materials provided primarily for the students' entertainment and enjoyment. Do the users of our media centers have access to toys and games, posters, photographs, paintings, models and sculpture, in fact, to the whole range of materials recommended in *Media Programs: District and School?* Considering only print, do they have available to them a variety of books, periodicals and pamphlets: beautifully bound volumes and inexpensive paperback editions; novels, poetry, drama, and short stories as well as nonfiction; traditional as well as modern tales; and fanciful as well as realistic views of today's world.

These are only a few of the options in the world of print. Nonprint has comparable options in software and additional considerations in the selection of the range and types of machines which make the content of the software available to users. On the one hand, media centers need inexpensive and portable recorders, players, and projectors for students to check out and use away from the center. On the other hand, they need equipment of sufficient sophistication and technical excellence to accommodate the quality of the material. The equipment used and the environmental conditions in which films are screened in many schools makes that viewing experience about equal to listening to the finest stereophonic recording on a $10 record player. Media specialists must reconsider certain aspects of their selection policies or at least to raise such questions as, "Do we exercise as much care in selecting the quantity and quality of equipment used as we do in choosing the materials they display?" and, "Do we adequately involve teachers in the process of selection or at least keep them sufficiently informed about materials we are considering for the collection?"

The fifth and final component of selection to be discussed is that of "Selection and Bibliographic Access." If we take seriously all that we have been discussing concerning young people in schools, we must admit that the standard selection sources often do not suggest materials dealing with non-school topics, which students want and certainly have a right to know. Nor do they frequently provide the kind of information which allows us to match materials to an educational theory or to particular teaching or learning strategies. It is understandable that a publisher trying to market materials would describe them in generic terms to appeal to the widest possible audience, but this lack of specificity seems inexcusable in the selection tools of our profession. Moreover, generalized descriptions of content have conditioned many of us to accept such subject headings without question as we select materials. For instance, we read an interesting review of a book about snakes and sometimes even decide to add it to the collection without knowing whether it deals with snakes in general or a particular poisonous snake found only in one region of the western United States. The computer obviously makes the storage and retrieval of this kind of specific information possible, but neither National Commission on Libraries and Information Science (NCLIS) nor any other agency seems to be taking the informational needs of children and young people seriously.

The standard catalogs and periodicals will probably remain the basic sources of information for the building of a school media collection—alternative views of society, of young people, and of education may never be fully represented in them. We must turn to alternative sources such as those put out by the Feminist Press or the Gay Alliance, to local distributors of information on survival and regional resources, and to special interest groups whether they be political or religious sects or crafts cooperatives. In addition, we need to visit toy stores and museums and attend film festivals in order to keep abreast of materials we are not likely to see reviewed in our bibliographic tools. We must also keep up with the popular media to help identify current issues and interests among our users. Television for instance, not only stays on top of, but may even initiate topics of immediate concern.

If it appears from all of this that I expect only supermen and superwomen to serve as media specialists in our schools, perhaps I do. But have any of you read your job description lately? If schools serve as a kind of controlled environment for young people in the process of trying to make sense of themselves and their world, surely those who in any way determine what is accessible to students in the media center have a super responsibility. Young people represent an infinite capacity for new ideas and new actions in the world, in fact, for a new world itself. Too often schools stifle originality and encourage uniformity by forcing students to concentrate on the reproduction or regurgitation of someone else's prepackaged ideas. Those who learn to retrieve and store information without developing the capacity to discriminate and choose from among it; that is, to practice an active and healthy skepticism, may well become slaves to second-hand or ready-made opinions.

The Pleasure Principle: Where Is It in Kids' Art Books?

by Shirley M. Wilton

There is much talk these days of the development of visual literacy in children and the use of picture books to teach art appreciation to young children. The proof of the pudding in art education, however, is the appreciation children may develop for the fine arts and, in particular, for painting. Unfortunately, there doesn't seem to be any rush toward art books in libraries, nor is there a surge in the publication of juvenile art books to stimulate children's interests.

The fact is children are not taught to love great art. They learn about form, texture, and composition; they are offered every kind of art experience from finger painting to macramé, but they don't know how to enjoy the best paintings and sculpture.

The responsibility of passing on an enthusiasm of the fine arts is most often left to individual art teachers, or classroom teachers, or librarians who try to work it into a curriculum which allows little time or opportunity to encourage "appreciation." Art is a going concern with adults, and so libraries stock beautiful oversized books with full-color, glossy plates and even circulate framed pictures which can be enjoyed at home. But when teachers and librarians turn to juvenile lists for books to interest children in art, it's quite a different story. Few of the art books for youngsters are truly introductory books; only a handful offer children an experience in seeing and responding to great art. Instead of serving their appropriate audience, most juvenile art books seem to buttress the misconceptions that many adults have learned from their own art experiences. Four misconceptions which beg for a healthy airing are: the mystique of the museum, the hang-up on art history, art as an intellectual activity, and the obsession with creativity.

The mystique of the museum: There is a staunchly-held misconception that "real" art is to be found only in museums and, for a true "art experience," children must see an original painting or piece of sculpture. From this assumption comes the idea that a good art book teaches readers to identify, rather than enjoy, masterpieces. Facts about artists, about techniques, about historical periods often accompany the illustrations in the belief that they will help children enjoy the originals when they finally see them.

Reproductions are often in black and white and rather lifeless looking, again with the idea that children will view the original work in person. Of course, the impact of first seeing a famous painting in books cannot be denied, but how many children will have an opportunity to visit the great museums of the world? The only art most kids will ever see is in reproduction, and they will not necessarily be the poorer for it. Although reproductions are secondhand art, they need not be second-rate. Quality photograph and art reproductions enable children to view the whole world of art; to see in juxtaposition, frescoes, paintings, sculpture from every historical period. Art books should not be museum catalogs; instead they should—and can be—primary art experiences. Quality reproductions, imaginatively selected, can create a "museum without walls," to borrow the title of André Malraux's book (Doubleday, 1967).

The hang-up on art history: Although the study of art history can add a valuable dimension to the enjoyment of painting, it is wrong to assume that art can only be fully appreciated if viewed as a developmental process, from cave painting to 20th-Century art. The interest in art as history places too great a premium on the art book author's narrative. The paintings and works of art, often beautifully reproduced, become merely illustrations for the text rather than the central focus of the book. There are excellent art history books for children: e.g. Janson and Cauman's *Art History for Young People* (Abrams, 1971), Craven's *The Rainbow Book of Art* (Collins-World, 1972), and Ruskin's *History in Art* (Watts, 1974). None of these, however, is useful as a first introduction to art.

Because of the traditional historical view of art, many children's books have been needlessly chained to a chronological order. Chase's *Looking at Art* (Crowell, 1966) has many merits, but the black-and-white photographs and the arrangement of the pictures into a chronological survey of Western art makes its title a misnomer. In Behrends and Kober's adult book, *The Artist and His Studio* (St. Martin's, 1974), pictures of working artists are displayed in chronological order so that the paintings illustrate periods of art history, rather than variations on a theme.

Art as an intellectual activity: Thinking of art as just for "eggheads" is another pitfall. The belief that art appreciation is based on an understanding of the elements of art has led to a number of books which are essays in aesthetic theory. They can be enjoyed only by young adults and older children who are already knowledgeable enough about art to understand discussions of critical analyses. Moore's *The Many Ways of Seeing: an Introduction to the Pleasures of Art* (Golden Pr., 1963), are both rich in thought and handsomely illustrated but would scare off young children. In contract, Barr's *Wonders, Warriors and Beasts Abounding* (Doubleday, 1967), groups pictures relating to four subjects with a text which amplifies rather than dominates the pictures.

The obsession with creativity: The compulsion to develop creativity in children has led to the false assumption that art appreciation should lead inevitably to the desire to express oneself, in the same way that watching a tennis match should make spectators long to seize a ball and racquet. And so, many art books emphasize techniques and materials and include a final chapter filled with do-it-yourself ideas. For example, in *How Artists Work* (Lion Pr., 1968), Belves and Mathey begin with a discussion of art objects in terms of techniques and end with photographs of children sculpting.

Given these caveats and criticisms of available books, what should be the nature of the art books on both school and public library shelves? In the first place, instead of rattling off facts or teach principles of art, art books for children should be picture-centered so as to entice and intrigue children. Chase's *Famous Paintings* (Platt & Munk, 1962) is an excellent example of a book having full-color reproductions that capture the eye. These are accompanied with a brief text plus smaller black-and-white pictures of similar scenes for comparison. *Enjoying the World of Art*, (Lion Pr., 1966) by Belves and Mathey, is also full of colorful and lively pictures with a text that is simply a brief guide to the plates.

The series of "Fine Art Books for Young People" published by Lerner, which groups pictures according to subject matter (cats, demons, cities, or ships), offers readers a good, visually-oriented format.

The titles of Glubok's *Art of America* series (Macmillan) and her books on the art of other cultures are also picture-centered. Although the framework is a historical survey and all the reproductions are in black-and-white, the author chooses arresting art works and writes about them with contagious enthusiasm.

In the second place, there should be many more introductory books of art for younger children. As librarians, we emphasize the variety of art styles in picture books, but we do not take picture-book age children one step further toward the enjoyment of fine arts. And yet it is possible to find paintings on subjects to intrigue the very young which can be presented in unintimidating formats. The 1975 *Childcraft How and Why Library*, published by Field Enterprise, has done it. Volume 13, entitled *Look Again*, is a colorful and exciting presentation of art for elementary grade children, including many pictures and a minimum of text. This book should be more accessible (and obtainable) than it is as part of a reference set.

In *Brueghel's "The Fair"* (Lippincott, 1976), a new book by Ruth Craft, a single painting is presented in its entirety in separate details, all in full color. Read-along verses catching the sights and sounds of a fair, accompany the pictures and unobtrusively add verbal color to the visual treat. The plan of the book is inventive, and the simplicity of presenting a single masterpiece is so appropriate for young children that it should provide a pattern for many more books.

As a third suggestion, why not use famous paintings to illustrate picture books, poetry collections, or any of the many kinds of books that are apt to be used by children not looking for art books specifically? For example, works of art illustrate Dunning's anthology of poetry, *Some Haystacks Don't Even Have Any Needles and Other Complete Modern Poems* (Lothrop, 1969), and art works are also used in the first volume of Summerfield's poetry anthology, *First Voices* (Knopf, 1971).

In a few picture books, specific works of art have been the inspiration for the illustrations. The pictures in Yolen's *The Bird of Time* (Crowell, 1971) were drawn by Mercer Mayer from his knowledge of Brueghel's paintings. Lasker's *Merry Ever After* (Viking, 1976) is a wonderful distillation of Medieval and Renaissance art works. Such books offer interested librarians grand opportunities to introduce children to whichever of the originals in reproduction can be rounded up for comparison.

The fourth and last recommendation is that there should be more books dealing with the kinds of art to which children relate most directly, namely folk art and contemporary art. The first is naive and childlike in its simplicity and directness, and can spark children's interest because the paintings are so much like their own.

Children can also relate to many contemporary artists, and it is appalling that there are so few introductory books on modern art. It is almost as though adults are afraid that children brought up to appreciate Marc Chagall, Paul Klee, or Joan Miro will never come to admire da Vinci's *Mona Lisa*. There is, however, a notable exception, a book entitled *Going for a Walk with a Line* (Doubleday, 1959) by Douglas and Elizabeth MacAgy. It is a happy little adventure through the world of modern art in which the authors play with the words and pictures, breaking them apart and bringing them together, leading children to look—the first step toward liking and learning about art.

It may be necessary for adults working with children to first educate themselves in the art of our own age. There is no better way than through fine introductory art books prepared by authors who see themselves not as essayists or educators or historians, but as willing and enthusiastic guides to a fascinating visual world.

Acquiring Foreign Children's Books

by Lucretia M. Harrison

Acquiring foreign children's books can be exciting and rewarding, but be warned! Starting such a collection is sure to be frustratingly slow, expensive and fraught with disappointments. If you are nevertheless determined to have a collection of foreign children's books, the most important step is to plan ahead.

First, identify a real need on the part of your prospective users. A casual interest in exotica can be fulfilled in less strenuous and expensive ways. Decide who is to be served by this large investment of money and professional time. Will it be a working collection, circulating to foreign-speaking children, or will it be a research collection serving adult students of children's literature, the social sciences, education, and national cultures?

The answer to this first question leads to other questions regarding the scope of the collection. What languages are to be collected? Will the collection be organized on the basis of languages or cultures? Remember that English is the language of literacy in many Third World countries. Spanish is the language of many different South American, Central American, and Caribbean cultures. The U.S.S.R. recognizes several official languages. Switzerland recognizes three. Canada, Austria, England, and Scotland also have foreign cultures, although their children's books are written in English. Portuguese and Brazilian cultures are quite different, although they use the same language.

Then there is the question of age orientation. The more broadly you interpret "children's books" the larger your project will become and the more money you will need to commit, both in purchasing and servicing. Restricting the collection to books for younger children is much less ambitious because neither the selection nor the cataloging of picture books and simple story books is difficult compared to cataloging materials of diverse subject matter, social and political relevance, and ethnic significance.

Political conditions may prevent any appreciable collecting from a particular area at a particular time. Will you therefore omit it from your master plan.

Are you going to limit this collection to books? If not, what other media would it be appropriate to include? This may have to vary as you research and discover the production conditions in various countries. Have you considered the problems involved in cataloging non-book materials in a variety of languages?

To what extent are you going to purchase additional reference materials, such as bilingual dictionaries and other professional tools, to service the collection or to extend its usefulness?

After you have developed a fairly clear picture of potential users and the kinds of materials that are needed, it is time to decide on a cataloging policy. Most American libraries undertaking such collections will not have appreciable bilingual or multilingual staff, so it may be foolish to omit English-language cataloging even if you expect your patrons to be fluent in other languages. Descriptive cataloging in the form of English annotations will enable English-speaking staff members to help patrons seeking materials in another language. Catalog cards printed in a foreign language can be interfiled easily enough in a general, English-language catalog if the foreign language uses Roman orthography or is transliterated into the Roman alphabet. However, if you collect considerable amounts of non-Roman print, it may be wise to establish a separate catalog for use by those familiar with the language and its peculiar filing conventions. Bilingual book cards and spine labels will also make it easier to shelve and circulate the books.

Publicity is important in bringing a foreign language collection to the attention of its intended users. Children in particular may not be able to read or speak English. However, conspicuous posters or newspaper ads in their native language will attract them like magic! This is especially true of the non-Roman alphabets. Public service television and radio spots will have the same effect. Publicity materials written by literate volunteers in the respective languages will act like magnets in attracting users. Even children who do not read or recognize the language will be intrigued by its mysteriousness, ask about it, and become proud purveyors of information about the foreign language collection.

Another "fall out" from publicity is the attraction of local people who can read and write different languages. Among them you will find not only boosters who will help advertise your collection but also enthusiastic volunteer readers who can assist in preparing annotations for books your staff members cannot read because they are unfamiliar with the language. At my center, books given to volunteer readers were accompanied by a simple questionnaire which asked:

1. Is this a story the author made up?
2. Is this a book of one or more traditional tales from a particular place? If so, from where?
3. Is this an information book? If so, what is the subject?
4. For what age child do you think this was written?
5. Would it be enjoyed more by boys or by girls? Or would it make no difference?
6. What, in your opinion, is the most important thing about this book?

Volunteers were also asked to make a diagram of the title page (and of the verso where appropriate), translating every word into English and placing it in the same position as it appeared on the title page of the book. This provided a real boon to the cataloger. We soon learned that in many countries copyright information appears at the very end of the book, rather than on the title page or its verso.

Other Hurdles

Consider the dealers from whom you will be ordering materials. Only very large institutions are really prepared to engage in foreign book trade. Most librarians must rely on United States book deals to supply foreign materials. Their prices depend on a continuously fluctuating rate of money exchange and reflect the expense of ordering, shipping, invoicing, and handling books in more than one language. These costs, like the costs of refined cataloging, can in themselves exceed the purchase price of a children's book. And political considerations and conditions intrude into foreign trade. For instance, trying to supply natively produced reading materials for refugees from areas in a state of war or revolution is a sure exercise in futility. Vietnam, Cambodia, and Angola have not yet begun to carry on normal free trade with outside countries. Ordering from the Near East is not only seriously hampered by outbreaks in Beirut, Lebanon (the erstwhile center of the book trade in the Near East), but also by sabotage and the disappearance of shipments from that part of the world.

American librarians, accustomed to a publishing industry that pours out over 40,000 U.S. titles annually (of which 2,500 or 5 percent are juveniles), will be appalled by the publication statistics in other countries. In 1970 Egypt's total annual book production was 2,142 titles. In 1971, South Africa published 2,600 titles; Canada, 4,200; and Greece, 2,212. Few if any countries dedicate as large a percentage of their publishing effort to juvenile books as does the United States. Not only are fewer titles produced, but the production runs in foreign countries are also small by United States standards, and additional printings are not common. It is obvious that unless a librarian has fresh information and can order quickly, many books on order are likely to be out of print by the time that order reaches the foreign supplier.

Librarians are well-aware that buying books sight-unseen is risky, even in our domestic market. A librarian may be in for quite a shock the first time he or she sets eyes on a seven- or eight-dollar import from India or one of the poorer South American countries. Even the Mediterranean countries, which produce many very beautiful children's books, also print quantities of reading materials for children using low-grade papers and inks and inferior bindings. These qualities do not make them inexpensive to deliver to your library, however.

How do you find out what specific children's books in particular languages are actually available for purchase and which of these might merit inclusion in your own collection? Children's books are typically ignored, overlooked, or at best slighted in the majority of foreign reviewing publications. But, very few such publications are freely available in this country anyway. Larger research libraries may subscribe to some specialized European children's book reviewing media, published, of course, in the respective national language and sent by surface mail some weeks after publication. Even if you do gain access to some of these and manage to select and order from a dealer who is able to import the titles you have chosen, don't think your problems will be over when the shipment arrives in your library. Who is going to check these strange, unintelligible entries on the invoice against the contents of the box (if you are lucky enough to have them arrive in a box)? And is your cataloger eagerly waiting to undertake the exciting challenge of cataloging exotic foreign languages? Will asking for a double set of cards, one in English and one in the language of the book, help the cataloger? Is there a file clerk who knows an article from a preposition in all the designated languages? Where are you going to shelve the processed books when they are ready for use? If put in a far corner where they won't confuse other patrons, they will be overlooked by everyone; if placed in a prominent location to catch attention, they will probably be in constant disorder because few people will understand how they have been arranged.

Why not visit a library that has a foreign books collection? The Boston Public Library recently embarked upon a very ambitious program of acquiring foreign children's books. You may want to attend the library's annual Children's Books International exhibit each spring.

The Information Center on Children's Cultures of the U.S. committee for UNICEF in New York City is another fascinating and informative place to visit. Make arrangements in advance so that the staff will be free to consult with you. The New York Public Library also has extensive collections of foreign children's books, both for research and for circulation. Contact the children's services department to plan visits. For other parts of the country, write to the children's services office of your largest city's public library system and to your state library. Inquire about existing collections of foreign children's books that you might visit and where you can confer with professional staff members. Contacts like this can save many a misstep or wasted experiment. They can also result in continuing communication and cooperation over the years to come.

Unfortunately there are very few lists of recommended, current foreign children's books available in the United States. At this writing, the most accessible, perhaps, are the bibliographies appearing irregularly but frequently in *Booklist*, a reviewing medium published twice monthly by the American Library Association in Chicago. These lists of foreign children's books are published with the encouragement and assistance of ALA's Committee on Selection of Foreign Children's Books, whose purpose is to inform American librarians of currently available and recommended children's books from every part of the world. The committee works in close cooperation with domestic dealers who supply *Booklist* with the approximate prices at which they will see the listed titles.

Combined Book Exhibit, Inc. works with the dealers to produce annual exhibits at ALA conferences of all the books listed on *Booklist* bibliographies published in the previous year. This exhibit provides librarians with an opportunity to see the books and to order them if they wish. The dealers are encouraged by the committee to purchase ahead so as to have a reasonable supply of books at hand by the time the list is published and the orders start coming. Due to the vagaries of international trade, this does not always work smoothly. Brisk sales may deplete dealer supplies and reorders may or may not be filled by the foreign suppliers. All of which explains why it is advisable even with this source to order as promptly as possible. Titles may remain available over a long period of time, but then again, they may not.

Of course, librarians are free to order these books from any dealer, not just those listed at the end of a particular bibliography. In fact, finding a domestic dealer in foreign books who is compatible with the needs of your particular collection is an invaluable asset; you may well ask that dealer to supply you with items from *Booklist* bibliographies.

A second source of annotated lists is *Bookbird*, the quarterly journal published in Vienna by the International Board on Books for Young People (IBBY). Subscriptions must be paid for in Austrian schillings. You can buy a bank check for the exact amount, with the dollar cost depending on the monetary exchange rate on the day you buy the check (plus a bank charge).

This most valuable journal carries articles about children's literature, authors, and libraries in various parts of the world, as well as reports on outstanding books being published in member countries. The annotations and reviews (in English) are full and informative; titles are printed both in the original languages and in English translation. Other features include news of IBBY and of BIB (Biennial of Illustration in Bratislavia), the organization which mounts a comprehensive exhibit of current children's book illustrations from all over the world and awards prestigious prizes. This quarterly is crammed with information any foreign children's book collector needs. And, like most worthy enterprises of its kind, it is just barely keeping afloat financially. *Bookbird* needs your money just as much as you need *Bookbird*. I strongly urge you to subscribe! You may also be interested in becoming a personal member of Friends of IBBY. The *Newsletter* alone is worth many times the price.

For those with a strong interest in Spanish language materials, a subscription to the Bulletin of Projecto Leer in Washington, D.C. is worth far more than the 15¢ postage to request it. The project is currently supported by the Breaks for the People Fund and the bulletin is available for the asking. In addition to annotated lists of recommended Spanish language materials (both for adults and for children), the *Bulletin* supplies annotated lists of domestic dealers. The project is deeply involved in research and in setting up regional workshops for professionals concerned with Spanish American materials.

If your patrons include children who read Spanish and need materials in this language, don't overlook domestic publishers who publish in Spanish as well as in English. Keep your eyes open for these books in regular trade channels, as they are easily available and are oriented toward the Spanish American child. Special Chicano-oriented and Puerto Rican-oriented lists appear in publishers' catalogs as well as in *Booklist* from time to time. Don't hesitate to let U.S. publishers know that children's books in other languages are in demand!

The UNICEF Information Center on Children's Cultures also provides service to those seeking any kind of information about and for children around the world and issues many free leaflets for the sole cost of a stamped, self-addressed envelope. The center responds to requests for selected lists in difficult languages (such as Swahili, Portuguese, Hindi) that specify a particular scope, such as age level. For more accessible European languages the center recommends particular national reviewing periodicals. These periodicals can sometimes be found in large university or city libraries but for small beginning collectors subscriptions to several of these would be very expensive. Many are not immediately useful—some are annual; all are slow in arrival. They require a good knowledge of the language in which the reviews are written. Librarians in large libraries that do subscribe to one or more of these sources will sometimes be helpful.

The UNICEF Center has an especially useful list (revised annually) of the names and addresses of book dealers (domestic and foreign), arranged by world regions and by specific languages or countries.

Books in Other Languages, published by the Canadian Library Association, also provides lists of reviewing media and lists of dealers, both domestic and foreign. It is in book form and serves adult collections as well as children's. (Unfortunately, the expensive format prohibits annual revision.) The introduction offers useful ideas about many aspects of foreign book acquisition. The author particularly cautions librarians to write to unfamiliar dealers before sending their first order—addresses change uncomfortably quickly, language facility varies (especially when dealing with foreign firms), and a firm's interest in and commitment to handling children's materials is often not clear from bibliographic or even advertising sources. A domestic dealer who is really sympathetic to your collection and who has developed good rapport with foreign dealers is perhaps the most valuable asset you can find with regard to getting the books you want into your collection.

Another important periodical for collections oriented toward research is the American journal of children's literature research, *Phaedrus*. Scholarly articles of historic, social, literary, and artistic significance to children's literature, worldwide in coverage, share space with bibliographies, both American and foreign.

A great deal of authentic foreign culture can be injected

into your regular English-language collection by buying generously from lists of foreign children's books that were written originally in English. India and many emerging African countries have established English as the language of literacy. Native authors are encouraged to write culturally valid works in English for children, young people, and adults. These materials are immediately useful to Americans of all ages who are interested in the cultures of these countries. And all your linguistic problems within the library are eliminated. British and Australian books need only be given geographical subject-headings to be recognized as foreign children's books.

Building a Mini-collection

If your library wants a representation of foreign children's books on hand but is not interested in committing money, staff, and space to the project, an attractive display area could do.

A minimal cataloging system could be built on the accession-number principle, making the classmark serve as a symbol for the collection, followed by the accession number and the language of the particular book. Two cards might be sufficient, a main entry and a subject card giving the English name of the language of the book. Both cards could be filed in the main catalog.

The books themselves might be on permanent display, from which visitors could borrow for reading room use only. If the display is arranged basically by accession number, it's easier to shelve the books or locate specific titles. Acquisition for such a collection could be confined to a few especially attractive suggestions from *Booklist* bibliographies plus occasional shopping by the librarian and the inevitable donations from patrons who know and enjoy the collection. This small operation would involve little professional time and minimal expense.

Do's and Don'ts of Collecting Foreign Children's Books

Do plan the scope of your collection in advance.

Do plan policies and procedures for cataloging and processing materials.

Do contact the nearest large library that has had experience with foreign children's books for guidance and cooperation.

Do begin acquisition with reliable U.S. sources, such as *Booklist*, UNICEF's Information Center on Children's Cultures, and Proyecto Leer.

Do develop foreign professional contacts through *Bookbird*, Friends of IBBY, and other channels.

Do correspond with an unfamiliar dealer before placing an order.

Do develop a good, cooperative relationship with one or two U.S. dealers who can supply the materials you want.

Do find local bilingual citizens to help with descriptive cataloging and annotating.

Don't bite off more than you can chew at first. Experience will make gradual expansion comparatively easy.

Don't expect quick results. You will suffer delays in selection, ordering, receiving, checking in, cataloging, shelving, and even in developing significant use of the collection.

Don't use selection tools more than about a year old, except as last resorts.

Don't expect that the poor quality of some foreign papers, inks, and bindings will be reflected in low cost.

Don't expect books from foreign countries to meet U.S. standards for library acquisition, either in bookmaking quality or in literary cultural viewpoint.

Don't promise your users specific titles or types of materials before you receive them.

Don't purchase direct from foreign dealers unless your library is experienced in foreign acquisition.

It's Not Just a Game

by Margaret Tassia

The frustrations of teaching library media skills to disinterested students has long concerned school library media specialists who would like to see students using reference sources and libraries enthusiastically and effectively. Yet, in spite of the introduction of various teaching strategies, librarians find that the negative attitudes students have toward libraries and library media skills are hard to change. The challenge to motivate students remains. Educational games that are designed by the school library media specialist to meet the needs of students, present library media skills in a manner that will motivate them and is one method to actively involve students in your lessons.

Alice Gordon in *Games for Growth* defines a game as "any simulated contest (play) among adversaries (players) operating under constraints (rules) for an objective (winning)."[1] Educational games can be defined as games in which players reach the desired educational objectives or goals.

Games allow students to: experience the immediate consequences of their actions; experience a sense of controlling a situation; become actively interested in the educational process.

Games also allow for physical and mental participation; accommodate a wide range of student abilities; remove librarians from the position of having to judge children on the basis of their (the librarian's) expectations.

Educational games are an effective and innovative teaching method for school library media specialists. Creating games to meet the needs of students is not easy, but it can be highly creative and rewarding. Perhaps one of the easiest ways to learn how to construct a game is to play an existing one. Study the game, play it, and evaluate it. The experience of developing a game—the analysis and the decision-making—is probably just as important, if not more so, as utilizing a fully-designed one.[2]

School library media specialists (and students) can develop games to meet their specific needs by following this model. The steps need not be followed in sequential order, but they can serve as a useful starting point and a checklist for the process of devising an appropriate and interesting game.

Game Construction

- *Step 1. Develop the Theme*

The initial step is to define the theme. It is essential that it relate to the existing curriculum and have a "real world" application. Start with the library media skills sequence and determine the areas in which students will be actively involved. Will the student player(s) see a relationship between the game and the application of the skill in a real instructional situation? Does the subject or theme fit into the school's educational program? Is it of significant educational value to warrant game construction? These questions should lead to some preliminary ideas.

- *Step 2. Determine Goals.*

Precisely define the concepts, information, and processes students should attain. The purpose of the game must be made known to the students. Without a precise goal, students may lose sight of the educational value of playing the game. State the time and spatial boundaries so that they represent real world parallels. It is helpful to state your goals in terms of behavioral objectives. Is the purpose of the game to review or reinforce? Motivate or challenge? Advance concept building or decision-making?

- *Step 3. Determine the Format*

The decision of which technique or format to use will depend upon the goals, needs, and abilities of the students. The objectives will also help to determine just what format to use. In deciding on the appropriate format, consider all options that will support learning objectives. One word of caution—do not let the game format overshadow specific learning objectives.

Pearson and Marfuggi in *Creating and Using Learning Games* suggest that "surprisingly little of the rich heritage of game forms and potential varieties of gaming forms have been exploited."[3] A few suggested gaming forms are:

> **Board games** graphically represent the process under study, and provide an easy way for players to keep track of their resources and their opponents. Ray Glazier refers to these more traditional types as "gamey-games,"—those games that require a good deal of hardware (i.e., spinners, dice, boards). This format lends itself to more factual or easily quantified subjects.
>
> **Role play** is used primarily in games that teach processes involving bargaining, negotiating, or other human interactions. The human factors of persuasion, power, planning and strategy, decision-making and "psyching out" the actions of others are emphasized. This format is particularly useful where qualitative factors are important.

When deciding on a format, consider the competition involved. Will the game be competitive or non-competitive? Educational games seldom have cut-throat competition—where one person wins everything and everyone else loses. Competition has two sides: a) an expression of power or the need to lead, to exert; b) an expression of achievement or the need to do something well.

Most games reflect both kinds of competition, and are categorized by the terms "zero-sum" and "non-zero-sum" games. "Zero-sum" games are based on a fixed number of points. One players' gain is another's loss. Chess and tic-tac-toe are examples of "zero-sum" games since these are most likely to express power motivation. "Non-zero-sum" games yield as many points as a player can accumulate through skill or luck. This type of game offers each player an opportunity to achieve the highest score without having to beat an opponent point by point. In this situation, winning is relative—not absolute. Some examples of this type of game are bowling and jacks. These games usually require achievement motivation.[4]

- *Step 4. Design the Equipment*

Game equipment should relate to established theme and goals. It should be attractive, functional and durable. Introduce an element of chance in the game. Will you use dice, spinners, playing cards or coins? The use of chance (in motivation) has a definite function in a learning game. Pearson and Marfuggi state that chance provides a learning topic in itself, as an introduction into the study of mathematical probabilities; creates uncertainty in the challenges presented to the players; provides an equalizer for unskilled players, therefore, it minimizes the fear of failure.[5]

- *Step 5. Define the Players' Roles*

It is necessary to determine the number of players, their roles, and the resources (material or equipment) available to them. Perry Gillespie, in *A Model for the Design of Academic Games*, discusses several role types: a) individual roles, in which a person reaps the rewards of consequences of that behavior (or actions); b) maintenance roles, in which a player acts as a messenger, a referee, or administrator; c) task role, in which a player must perform a specific task to win (i.e., use a dictionary, etc.).[6]

- *Step 6. Determine the Rules*

Rules can make or break a game. Effective learning takes place when there is active participation, so start a game with a minimum of preliminaries. While complex rules reduce enthusiasm for the game, vague, or incomplete rules can lead to frustration. Be exact about how the game is to be played. The best advice is to make the rules brief but clear. Tell each player what to do, who will interact with whom, and what transactions will take place, and what the playing time will be.

Gillespie outlines seven classes of written procedural rules.

1) Initiation and Termination—state when a game begins and ends;
2) Deployment and Disposition—indicate who, where, how, and when a player can move;
3) Communication—indicate if any kind of communication is permitted, restricted, etc.;

4) Arbitration—indicate how disputes will be solved;
5) Intervention—indicate if, and how, chance is introduced;
6) Enforcement—indicate how infractions are covered. Rules of restitution, regression, or repulsion are stated in the beginning of a set of directions; and
7) Rules of Outcome—indicate what conditions have to be met to win.[7]

- *Step 7. Test Run*

There is no substitute for playing the game to iron out specific problems. David Zuckerman and Robert Horn, in their *Guide to Simulations-Games in Education and Training*, suggest several things to watch for:

a) Amount of time devoted to each playing period.
b) Are the instructions clear? Are any changes needed?
c) Did the players accept their roles easily?
d) Were any of the players inactive during play?
e) Did the players have fun? Were they emotionally involved in play?
f) Does the game meet your educational objectives?[8]

- *Step 8. Debriefing Evaluation*

Winning or losing does not constitute an evaluation. It is always necessary to evaluate the entire procedure. Schedule time for students to discuss what they learned, what difficulties they experienced, what goals they met by playing the game, etc. To begin the discussions you may ask, Why did you win? Why did you lose? In what way was the game like or unlike real life?

References

1. Gordon, Alice. *Games for Growth: Education Games in the Classroom*, (Science Research Associates, 1970), p. 8.
2. *Ibid.*, p. 122.
3. Pearson, Craig & Joseph Marfuggi. *Creating & Using Learning Games*, (Education Today, 1975), p. 16.
4. *Ibid.*, p. 19.
5. *Ibid.*, p. 20-21.
6. Gillespie, Perry S. *A Model for the Design of Academic Games*, (University Microfilms, 1976), p. 78-85.
7. *Ibid.*, p. 93-102.
8. Zuckerman, David & Robert Horn. *Guide to Simulation-Games for Education & Training*, (Information Resources, 1973), p. 43.
9. Pearson & Marfuggi, op. cit., p. 24.

A Sample Game

"Silly Safari" which follows was devised utilizing the model for constructing an educational game. This particular game has been used with students from ages 7 to 10. Their ease in using encyclopedias as a source of reference for all kinds of classroom activities is evidence that *Silly Safari* has proven to be an effective educational tool.

Theme: Encyclopedia usage for locating facts about the jungle as a geographic region.

Goals: To integrate the skill of using the encyclopedia reference source for the study of the jungle.

The specific educational goal is to guide students in using the encyclopedia as a source to locate general background information

Scope: Time of play—1/2 hour or until the board is completed. All questions relate to various animals, plants or minerals found in the jungle.

Techniques: *Silly Safari* is a board game of the race/chase variety. Players record their progress by moving markers along a track. Each player begins with the same advantage and the first to complete the course wins the game.

Equipment: The board design reflects the jungle theme. The illustrations not only add to the game's attractiveness but imparts information about the topic. Notes inserted along the course introduce chance, in addition to facts of jungle life (i.e., alligator swamp—lose one turn; find some rare medicinal plant—take a short cut, etc.).

The question cards also relate to the jungle. Students are asked to identify the subject on their card as an animal, plant, or mineral. As an introductory lesson, students are asked to locate specific details to acquaint them with the topic.

Another element of chance is introduced by shuffling the question cards. Since the cards are of different value (animal = 1 point; plant = 2 points; mineral = 3 points), there is chance involved in what card is drawn. Player's Roles: (Number of Players—two to six)

In *Silly Safari* each player will use the encyclopedia and skim the article related to the card drawn to locate a correct answer. (Usually the encyclopedia will state in the first few paragraphs whether a word is animal, plant, or mineral). The referee (another capable student, or parent volunteer, or library aide) encourages each student to locate the information as fast as possible by using guide words at the top of the pages, the volume indicators on the spine, or the index volume. The referee checks each answer to be sure the player located the cor-

rect information in the encyclopedia before moving a marker on to the next question.

Rules:
1. Each player begins at *start*, selects the top card and reads the question.
2. Next the player locates the word in an encyclopedia and skims the article to decide if it is animal, plant or mineral.
3. Before proceeding check the answer with the referee.
4. If your answer is animal, move one space; if plant, move 2 paces; if mineral, move 3 spaces.
5. As soon as a player moves another card is drawn from the top of the pile.
6. The first player to progress completely around the board completing the "safari through the jungle" wins the game.

Debriefing:

Both the classroom teacher and the library media specialist can review the facts students learned concerning the jungle and what steps they used to locate the information.

Game Potentials

Games have only recently been accepted as educational tools, but their potential in teaching students is yet to be realized. School library media specialists should investigate this method for actively involving students in the learning process. Educational games contribute to a student's decision-making ability, social interaction, and positive self-image. Games motivate students to participate regardless of their intellectual abilities and games provide immediate results.

And, they don't cost a lot of money to construct. One note of caution—library media specialists might be challenged to come up with more innovative games to hold the interest of their students.

Sing Me A Story

by Helen Gregory

We play games, jump rope, dance, relax, exercise, take showers, worship, marry, march, live, die and are buried to music. Early experience with simple music prepares children to enjoy more complex and subtle forms later on. Musical training deserves as much time and attention as the development of skills in color identification or animal recognition. Picture song books can encourage such exposure.

The Caldecott committee laid its blessing on the form when Rojankovsky won the coveted award for his illustrations in Langstaff's *Frog Went A-Courtin'* (Harcourt, 1955). It followed naturally that, in the 60s, publishers produced more song books than they had in the 50s until, in the 70s, their proliferation seemed unending. This boundless production provoked a strong critical reaction. With so many tacky examples on the market, e.g., Pam Adams' *This Old Man* (Grosset, 1975), the books began to be considered a rip-off. But to say that the entire genre is worthless is to toss the gems with the junk.

What, then, should selection standards be? If we are to consider picture song books "real" picture books, they must meet the following criteria generally considered in evaluating picture books:

1. High quality illustrations in a style and medium suited to audience, subject, and lyrics. Pictures should relate directly to the song. If the text tells a story, however sketchily, the artwork should help fill it in. The predominant picture song book audience is very young, and tends toward literal interpretation.
2. An imaginative and well-written text. Although a well-plotted narrative is desired and is common in ballads, when that is not possible a unifying thread may suffice.

But a first-rate picture song book is not only a "real" picture book; it should also be a first-rate song.

3. The music needn't be printed with the pictures, but should be available for reference somewhere in the book. It is also helpful to have a simple piano accompaniment with indications of guitar chords. (Beginning guitarists appreciate diagrams as well.)

It is amazing that many song books don't include a simple melodic line. Several elaborately illustrated and otherwise attractive books disqualify themselves on this score, e.g., Susan Jeffers' *All the Pretty Horses* (Macmillan, 1974), Janina Domanska's beautifully lush *Din Dan Don It's Christmas* (Greenwillow, 1975), the Zemachs' zany *Mommy Buy Me a China Doll* (Farrar, 1975), and A. B. Patterson's colorful *Waltzing Matilda* (Holt, 1970) to name a few. The omission might be understandable for such familiar songs as "The Farmer in the Dell" or "London Bridge Is Falling Down," but it is an easily avoidable nuisance with any song which is not universally known or which has a great number of variants. Furthermore, we tend to take for granted that our own culture is universal when, in actuality, even one region of the country is far from aware of what any other region considers the common culture. Which brings us to four more items on our growing list of requirements:

4. Well-known verses ought to be included, at least in an addendum, unless there are too many to enumerate, in which case a note is in order.
5. If the English is difficult in any way, for example, regional slang, there should be a glossary.
6. If the lyrics are in translation, the original should be shown as well. Not everyone speaks English exclusively. Parents who wish to share the original version of an old song with their children may not remember the precise wording. And language students find songs a helpful supplement to their studies.
7. If there is a game that normally attends a song, or if there are many variations of melody or lyric, notes are helpful. Folk songs have a history. These notes needn't be intrusive or extensive, but they should be available for readers who want to know more.

Last but not least:

8. Good pacing is a prime factor. The balance of pictures and text, important in any picture book, is more important in a picture song book which should flow uninterruptedly at an even rhythm, allowing readers to sing the text and turn the pages at a speed that does justice to the illustrations. It might bore children to have too many lines per page and not enough happening, but it's a catastrophe when they have to stop singing in order to see the pictures. Of course, singers may memorize the verses or fake a chorus to fill in, but such methods of coping only draw attention to the basic flaw in the book's composition.

Following is a partial bibliography of some of the better known picture song books currently in print that meet most of the above standards. While there are some excellent picture books based on songs, e.g., Gauch's *On to Widecombe*

Fair (Putnam, 1978) or Hazen's *Frere Jacques* (Lippincott, 1972) which paraphrase, elaborate upon, or re-invent the story of the song, frequently including the song itself as an afterthought, they are not included. We are considering books that enable us to *sing* the story, not simply to tell it.

To save space, information on musical notation will appear with publication data. "Music" indicates melody only. Piano and guitar accompaniment will be mentioned if they are present. "Diagrams" refers to guitar chords. The list is alphabetical by titles of songs.

Adventures of the Three Blind Mice. John W. Ivimey. Nola Langner, illus. Scholastic Book Service. n.d. Music. $.85.
The many, rarely sung verses comprise an interesting tale. The music supplies entrances for second and third voices, if anyone should be in doubt.

Always Room for One More. Sorche Nic Leodhas. Nonny Hogrogian, illus. Holt. 1965. Music. Glossary. Notes. $5.95.
A jolly song about generous Lachie MacLachlan who burst his house with guests. Several lines per page give singers time to take in the Caldecott award-winning illustrations. The delicacy of the artwork makes this a better choice for lap than large group use.

The Cat Came Back. Adapt. and illus. by Dahlov Ipcar. Knopf. 1971. Music with piano & guitar. $5.39.
The rollicking tale of an indestructible cat in a large, colorful format. Not for the non-violent.

Catch a Little Fox. Beatrice Schenk DeRegniers. Brinton Turkle, illus. Seabury. 1970. Music. $6.50.
Variations on a folk theme, with built-in suspense on each page. You have to turn mid-sentence to find out what animal has been bagged, mouse, cat or frog, but best of all, dragon. Droll drawings in charcoal and red pastel.

The Fox Went Out on a Chilly Night. Peter Spier, adapt. Illus. by adapt. Doubleday. 1961. Music with piano & guitar. Notes. $4.95.
Rich, autumnal colors tell the adventures of the fox, hunting his family's dinner.

Frog Went A-Courtin'. John Langstaff, retel. Feodor Rojankovsky, illus. Harcourt. 1955. Music. Notes. $6.50.
This familiar edition has big, colorful pictures that make it ideal for large groups, with detail to hold the lap singer. Line-a-page moves along at a nice clip, but not too fast for comfort.

Go Tell Aunt Rhody. Robert Quackenbush. Lippincott. 1973. Music with piano. Notes. $6.95.
Eleven, verses, mostly funny starring the old gray goose who is a living legend in her lifetime and the greatest American since the American eagle. Hidden pictures which don't tell the story but add to it, rebuses, puzzles, and a party page (although the point of "gander punch" is elusive at best) make this a treat. A great rainy-day book.

Hush Little Baby. Margot Zemach, illus. Dutton. 1976. Music. $6.95.
The slapstick drawings are fun, suiting the desperation of the lyrics if not the tranquility of the tune.

The Laird of Cockpen. Sorche Nic Leodhas. Adrienne Adams, illus. Holt. 1969. Music. Glossary. Notes. $3.95.
The comic wooing and winning of Lady Jane: the lady changes her mind (obviously not a member of NOW, but then, how could she be?) Written to one of the oldest Scottish melodies in existence.

The Little Drummer Boy. Ezra Jack Keats. Illus. by author. Macmillan. 1968. Music. $5.95.
Occasionally there are too few words to linger adequately on a page, but Keats' rich illustrations carry to large groups. No notes are necessary for this popular carol.

London Bridge Is Falling Down. Ed Emberley, adapt. Illus. by adapt. Little. 1967. Music with piano. Notes. $4.50.
Eleven verses (three additional are appended) with illustrated game instructions that take nothing for granted. A short history of the bridge is included, with the guard's uniform and flowers identified. Authentic ink and pastel watercolors.

London Bridge Is Falling Down. Peter Spier, illus. Doubleday. 1967. Music with piano & guitar. Notes. $5.95.
Eighteen verses, with authentic and detailed ink and watercolors and extensive notes on the bridge's history. While this has the edge over Emberley's on verses, there is not much repetition and both editions should be welcome in most collections.

Oh, A-Hunting We Will Go. John Langstaff. Nancy Winslow Parker, illus. Atheneum. 1974. Music with piano & guitar. $6.95.
It's enormous fun to find out what's to be done with each of 12 entertaining animals captured, including an armadillo and a brontosaurus. The rhymes were devised by school children.

On the Hearth. Gabriel Lisowski. Holt. 1978. Music. Notes. $5.95.
A translation of a well-known 19th century Yiddish lullaby by Mark Warshowski. Lyrics in English, Yiddish and Hebrew, nicely balanced with fine line pencil drawings.

One Wide River to Cross. Barbara Emberley, adapt. Ed Emberley, illus. Prentice-Hall. 1967. Music with vocal harmony & guitar. Notes. $5.95.
Excellent block prints provide lively illustrations of the Biblical characters.

Skip to My Lou. Robert Quackenbush, adapt. Illus. by adapt. Lippincott. 1975. Music with piano & guitar. Diagrams. $6.95.
This may be his best songbook. Bright, vivacious cartoons illustrate the 10 best known verses (there are 150 in all). Clear and thorough instructions for the game plus a short, prefatory history are included. Best of all, is the whacky storyline of a wild engagement party.

Soldier, Soldier, Won't You Marry Me? John Langstaff. Anita Lobel, illus. Doubleday. 1972. Music with piano & guitar. Notes. $4.95.
A spirited rendition of the humorous dialog song, with one question and answer per double-page spread.

There'll be a Hot Time in the Old Town Tonight. Robert Quackenbush, adapt. Illus. by adapt. Lippincott. 1974. Music with guitar. Notes. $6.95.
Quackenbush always does his homework, and this book begins with a short history of the great Chicago fire and ends with a fire survival plan and instructions on escaping a burning building.

The Twelve Days of Christmas. Ilonka Karasz, adapt. Illus. by adapt. Harper. 1949. Music. $5.79.
The standard edition, finely designed in soft colors to carry the medieval theme. Even the type selection is perfect. A first choice if you need the music.

Jack Kent's The Twelve Days of Christmas. Jack Kent, adapt. Illus. by adapt. Parents. 1973. Music on endpapers. $5.41.
Taking lyrics literally, provides the oft imagined absurd accumulation of gifts to the developing dismay of the giftee: 12 partridges, 22 turtledoves, 30 French hens, etc. There is a useful double-page spread pause to catch breath on the last line while the suitor searches for his love among geese, eggs, drummers, bagpipers, etc. Zany.

A Wart Snake in a Fig Tree. George Mendoza. Etienne Delessert, illus. Dial. 1968. Music with guitar. $4.95.
For monstrous fun (12 days of raining/ 11 lizards boiling/ 10 devils dancing . . .), Delessert's monsters are supreme.

When I First Came to This Land. Oscar Brand. Doris Burn, illus. Putnam. 1974. Music with piano & guitar. $5.95.
Brand's cumulative song of pioneering deserves notice for its lively tune and good-humored lyrics. Warm, sepia illustrations capture the mood.

Yankee Doodle. Richard Shackberg. Ed Emberley, illus. $.95. Prentice-Hall 1965. Music with piano & guitar. Notes. pap. $.95.
If you can afford only one Yankee Doodle, this should be it. Excellent notes by Barbara Emberley include a recipe for hasty pudding.

Networking & School Library Media Programs

by David R. Bender

What is the role of the school library media program in networking? No issue presses more heavily upon people involved in network planning than this one, for schools have been excluded far too long. What is the mission of networks? Who is to be served? How are they to be served? Is the network to be defined in terms of the conventional, traditional, isolated approaches to information sharing or is there to be something different and new? Other questions can be asked in the planning stages—questions about financial matters, characteristics of delivery patterns, and governance structures are three which readily come to mind.

As Cosette Kies has so wisely stated, "Only with perpetual watch will the successful program continue to be successful."[1]

In developing our cooperative program activities, we need to have a clear purpose in mind. What is our program, activity, or model to look like? However, we must be careful not to let the model get in our way. In order to get a handle on what we are about, we do need a structure—a plan, a mission, goals, or call it whatever you want. Our program objectives must determine our organization or else the organization will determine our objectives. We might keep in mind a statement made by Robert Kennedy, "Our good luck we make, our bad luck we endure."

We must become involved in a comprehensive planning venture. Comprehensive planning is a process of designing programs and allocating resources in order to achieve specific objectives, then modifying and improving those activities through continuous evaluation of how well the objectives are being reached. It requires the use of all available and applicable planning techniques, extensive involvement of those affected, and mechanisms for monitoring and coordinating program activities. In order to survive, a program must be monitored, evaluated in terms of its performance, and upgraded wherever possible.

Remember for whom we are designing programs. What are our clientele's specific needs, and how can we most efficiently and effectively fulfill their needs? By the age of five, before most children enter school, they have learned a language, can imagine the unknown, can create music, poetry, art, and have learned well over 50 percent of all that will ever be learned. As we work with each patron, and especially with each child, let us keep this in mind. We must also remember that, just as success is never final, neither is defeat. Let us work with each patron according to his or her needs regardless of age. All of our patrons need our services. For example:

> Early childhood is a time for children to have experiences which will expand the imagination and lead to wondering and questioning, experiences which will later become the basis for the formation of . . . concepts. It is a time for children to handle things, to test out ideas, to see the results of their actions, and to think about how and why things happen as they do. This implies the need for a rich environment, but the provision of materials is not, by itself, enough. The child also needs to have someone say, "What would happen if . . . ?" or "Have you tried it this way?" or "Put this here and that there and see if it makes a difference."[2]

The person who discovers the magic of the library is on the way to a lifelong experience of self-education and enrichment. Let us not prevent this from happening—whatever you can do, do it!

It is services, not words, which make the library media program a source and force for educational excellence. It is achieving the five Rs:

> The *right* material for the
>   *right* person at the
>   *right* place at the
>   *right* time, to be used in the
>   *right* way.

The patron doesn't really care how you achieve the five Rs, so long as they receive what they need.

Excellent use of media should provide access to necessary information, helping people make well-informed decisions from alternative possibilities. The ability of media to humanize learning and reinforce people-to-people contact must be emphasized over the technological capacity of media. Indeed, the most basic skill of all is the skill of relating well to others.

A philosopher once said, "It is not at what we are looking that is important but from where we are looking that is." Activities which involve school library media programs in information networking certainly substantiate this aphorism. We have all heard too frequently that the inclusion of schools in any networking system will place a disproportionate drain on the resources of the system and that they will contribute very little in the way of resource sharing. I do not believe that this is true. Writing in the Fall 1977 issue of *School Media Quarterly*, Audrey Kolb and Jo Morse also help lay this notion to rest—"Let there be no mistake, the primary thrust of this . . . is that networking is of value to schools and that schools have contributions to make to networks."[3]

Network Considerations

Let us explore several items which require further exploration. Because of the many variables which are involved in fulfilling the needs represented by school library media programs, no arbitrary set of guidelines will exactly fit all of our programs. However, prior to entering into any cooperative arrangements, nine principles need to be considered and agreed upon by all participating groups, these are:

1. *The purpose of networking*. There must be agreement as to what the purpose of networking is. Is it the improvement of library media services for all users? If it is, then the sharing of resources and services becomes a primary goal. To facilitate the accomplishment of this goal, the network must be built upon access to all of the informational resources of academic, public, school, and special libraries within its scope. Each library must continue to perform its primary function, which is to serve its immediate clientele, while making available its resources and services to the other members of the network.

2. *The philosophical framework of each body considering cooperative activities*. It is extremely important to investigate, study, and analyze all the characteristics of the groups entering into an agreement. If you cannot reach agreement or resolve conflicts regarding all visible issues, do not enter into cooperative arrangements, for numerous unforeseen events will occur which will be troublesome. Having studied thoroughly the available information regarding the groups entering into cooperative activities, sound judgments based on facts, not emotions, can more reasonably be made.

3. *The political setting*. What are the governmental constraints placed on each member? How "political" must the individual members be in order to survive? Is there support (legal and financial) within the governmental structure for the cooperative endeavors?

4. *The social surroundings*. Look at the total environment and all the issues which will be involved. Do the people you are serving accept your notions of cooperative activities? Remember, all groups involved must accept the concept of cooperative activities, and this means give and take on everyone's part.

5. *The economic situation*. Many times people look on cooperative activities as a way to save money (sometimes known as "fiscal fever"). However, once begun, if successful, they will require more revenue than previous arrangements. Therefore, consider carefully what kind of financial support is available. From where are the funds going to flow? Who is going to act as the fiscal agent for the cooperative

projects? Remember to examine and scrutinize programs in terms of cost effectiveness and accountability.

6. *The administrative organization*. The participants will have to decide on how the activities will be coordinated, managed, and supervised. This often means that one group may have to relinquish some of its autonomy, a threatening concept for many. Remember the major goal is better services for the user.

7. *The legal basis for cooperative involvement*. Are there any laws within your state which prevent the establishment of this type of activity. Before any group enters into cooperative activities, an agreement, a project statement, or some written document should be prepared. This official document should outline the specifics of the project in enough detail to answer the concerns and needs of the participants.

8. *The natural areas in which cooperative activities can be undertaken*. Look for the obvious. As you begin to explore possibilities, attempt to select something which will provide you with quick, positive results. Do you undertake as your first project something that is quite involved, will span a long period of time, require large sums of resources (human, space, money, and materials) and considerable supervision.[4]

9. *Staff commitment to cooperative endeavors*. Is present staff size sufficient to carry out cooperative activities, or will additional staff be needed? Does the necessary expertise exist? Will inservice or continuing education programs be conducted? Perhaps, in some places, only selective retirement will save us!

Joint Programs & Services

School library media programs must be included, where appropriate, in cooperative program activities. For without them nearly 50 million children and young adults enrolled in the nation's public and nonpublic schools will be under-served or unreached. In addition, the informational needs of these students, parents, teachers, administrators and support personnel will be denied access to the information resources they'll need.

Individualized instruction, independent learning programs, and other teaching methods require that users have immediate and easy access to a wide range of services and materials that meet the varied needs, interests, and abilities of each student. The school library media program is a service to the school's instructional program and serves as a teaching component of that program, too. The library media specialist must be an integral member of the school's instructional team, working cooperatively with administrators, teachers, students, and members of the community in the evaluation, selection, and use of resources that support and enrich learning activities. The library media staff must also be able to develop and deliver a program of activities that satisfy the learning needs of those using the services of the program.

Today's school library media specialist functions, foremost, as a teacher with a secondary role as information provider. Being a teacher does make the school library media specialist's role different from other librarians. However, there still exist many commonalities. As librarians, we are all information managers because we all assist our many users in using information the best way possible in order to manage their present and cope with their future needs. The media convey information to people who must, in turn, process and use it according to their specific needs. Everything we pick up, feel, read, look at, listen to, or otherwise become involved with has the potential to stimulate, educate, or sedate, depending upon how we use it. Our concern must be the best way to make necessary information available and in helping individuals and groups make sound decisions about the information. So, while differences do exist between libraries and librarians, our common concerns and mutual interests must bridge these differences.

Cooperative activities are not new to school library media personnel. Jointly developed and cooperatively-sponsored activities are in operation throughout the country. However, most of these activities have occurred via informal arrangements, thus making their continuation somewhat less than certain. For a change in personnel could bring an end to such cooperative endeavors. Also, such arrangements usually exist at the local levels, without any sharing on a regional or state-wide basis. Examples of these activities include:

1. informal meetings between public and school librarians to address mutual concerns
2. exchanging lists of collection holdings
3. jointly planned summer library programs
4. joint compilation of community resources
5. joint planning of community programs
6. joint material evaluation, selection, acquisition, and processing programs
7. placement of public library book catalogs in school libraries
8. joint development of storytelling groups to improve techniques and skills
9. reciprocal borrowing and lending of materials
10. class-orientation visits to the public library
11. book talks by public librarians given in the school
12. providing the public library with curriculum guides and units of instruction
13. inservice programs designed around topics of mutual interest and concern
14. production facilities for materials
15. preparation of union lists or catalogs
16. access to specialized and computerized data bases
17. joint film cooperatives.

I am certain that, collectively, we could expand this list and provide numerous examples relating to each of the 17 items. However, the success and continuation of these activities rests with the individual commitment of staff members who are willing and eager to engage in inter-institutional activities.

Multitype library cooperatives that include school library media programs at various service levels can be found in Colorado, Illinois, Indiana, Maryland, New York, Oregon, Wisconsin, and Washington. It is almost impossible to search the literature to identify and locate information about existing cooperative activities. And, when found, usually the information contained in the article is descriptive rather than analytical and is of little value. We need such cookbook information, but we need to know more about how these projects operate, how they are evaluated, and more specific recommendations and conclusions concerning how the activities may be carried out.

Media Specialists' Roles

Many school library media specialists are reluctant, just as others are, to become involved in networking, while some already involved remain jealous of their territorial rights and are reluctant to include others in their activities. It is time for such attitudes to die. What is needed is communication and cooperation, not a battle to hold on to "our own." Darrell Van Orsdel, in his article, "Cooperation with Results: Ramsey County Library/Media Centers Serve All," states that when librarians from different types of libraries begin to communicate, the age-old belief that each type of librarianship is different begins to disappear.[5] There is commonality among all our roles and functions regardless of where they take place. We all experience similar difficulties in providing services to our primary users. School library media specialists share and face many of the same problems as do the staffs of community college learning resources programs. Special and academic librarians share in dealing with specialized collections which are needed to fulfill users' requests. All types of libraries are faced with similar staff, budget, and facility problems. While mindful of our primary roles, we should build upon our commonalities and get on with the task of providing "every individual . . . with equal opportunity of access to that part of the total information resource which will satisfy the individual's educational, working, cultural, and leisure-time needs and interests."[6]

There is one other sensitive issue which requires attention. None of the noble goals we seek will happen until library media educational programs offered by colleges and universities are examined with an eye toward change. Many programs provide little opportunity for continuous planned interaction among students aspiring for employment in different types of libraries. The artificial barriers built around these various domains must be torn down. Unless they are, much time will be wasted for the training period of preparation for the profession is also the time to develop attitudes favorable toward cooperation. Persons involved in planning and conducting inservice and continuing educational offerings should include all types of librarians in their programs. This, again, will assist in opening up new and yet unexplored cooperative activities.

Cooperative activities emanating from any system or network should not be designed to supplant the existing library media program. The services provided should increase the offerings of a single library, therefore supplementing existing operations.

An unpublished report, "The Role of the School Media Program in Networks and Interlibrary Cooperation," developed by the American Association of School Librarian's Committee on Networking, provides information of substance. Divided into two sections (Needs & Potential Benefits; Strengths

& Potential Contributions), the report lists the potential contributions that school library media programs can bring to networking. And the report further delineates how networks can aid school library media programs in providing for the unique needs of students and teachers.

Challenges to Be Met

It's not an easy task but school library media specialists must become informed about multitype library activities and other cooperative networks, for they need to help the teachers, principals, administrators, board members, and parents understand the benefits to be derived from participating in a cooperatively developed network. This article briefly described possible potential expectations and aspirations of school library media programs and networks. The technology and resources are available and yet our number one challenge still remains people—their attitudes, their notions, their fears, their emotions. The day when these can be overcome will be the day a national network will become a reality. For we should remember that, as library media professionals, there are far more things we can do than we have supposed. This must be our attitude. We must concentrate on what needs to be done. What we can do. If everything remains important, then nothing is. We have to collectively decide what is important.

Our worst mistake is to come to a dead stop just because our future is unclear. It will never be 100 percent clear. Erica Jong in *Fear of Flying* provides us with an excellent insight of the future by stating that, "It's only when you're forbidden to talk about the future that you suddenly realize how much the future normally occupies the present, how much of our daily life is usually spent making plans and attempting to control the future. Never mind that you have no control over it. The idea of the future is our greatest entertainment, amusement, and time-killer. Take it away and there is only the past."

However, we must also guard against the crazies who tell us exactly what is to happen. For no one has the mystical powers to predict all future events. Take great care to distinguish between those who are interested in innovation and change as a means to better deliver user services, and those who are attracted to anything different only because it is different, or who are against anything already established simply because it is established.

Although we have ignored them too long, the changes we are facing are not abrupt. I have noted an acceleration of movement in bringing libraries of all types into cooperative arrangements. Now I'm waiting for this movement to broaden, to become responsive, and to be more concerned with *client needs* rather than *institutional territoriality.*

References

1. Kies, Cosette. "Projecting a Positive Image through Public Relations," *School Media Centers: Focus on Trends and Issues*, No. 2. Chicago: American Library Association, 1978.
2. Howe, Ann C. "Childhood Experience in Science," *Instructor*, January 1975.
3. Kolb, Audrey and Jo Morse. "Initiating School Participation in Networking," *School Media Quarterly* 6:52, Fall, 1977.
4. American Association of School Librarians. *The Role of the School Media Program in Networks and Interlibrary Cooperation.* Chicago: AASL Committee on Networking, September 1978.
5. Van Orsdel, Darrell E. "Cooperation with Results: Ramsey County Library/Media Centers Serve All," *Wisconsin Library Bulletin* 71:113, May-June 1975.
6. The National Commission on Libraries and Information Science. *Toward a National Program for Library and Information Services: Goals for Action.* Washington, D.C. NCLIS, 1975.

Reading, Imagination, and Television

by Dorothy G. Singer

The potential for imaginative play and creativity may exist in all children. Why some people develop these gifts and why others do not intrigues the social scientist. Looking back at the lives and childhood experiences of great artists, writers, poets and musicians offers us some clues and allows us to search for some common denominators that existed in their early childhoods and nurtured budding talents. Vladimir Nabokov's rich use of language and fantasy episodes, for example, may be traced to childhood experiences where make-believe games and his exposure to books played important roles. Nabokov learned to read in English before he could read Russian. His earliest "friends" were "four simple souls in my grammar, Ben, Dan, Sam, and Ned," although the book focused on three-word sentences such as "Who is Ben?" and "Here is Dan." Nabokov's rich imagination endowed these characters with physical attributes and personality traits of the various people who worked on his estate. Nabokov also remembers the pleasant moments with his mother as she read to him in English every evening at bedtime. He recalls how he leafed through picture books before he learned how to read, and most important of all, he remembers the great discovery of some books stored in the attic of his country home. Eight-year-old Nabokov carried them down to his room by the "armloads," and his deep friendship with books was firmly established.

Not only Nabokov, but Tolstoy, Ibsen, Shaw, and Milne, remembered the childhood games they played, the importance of books in their lives, and a key person—whether parent, relative or teacher—who prompted and encouraged their imagination and curiosity.

Today, the important member of the family may be the television set rather than the parent. Indeed, television occupies a large part of children's daily lives. Preschoolers spend about three hours per day watching television while elementary-school-aged children spend from four and a half to five hours per day (Lyle and Hoffman, 1972; Singer and Singer, 1979). George Gerbner (1979), Dean of the Annenberg School of Communications at the University of Pennsylvania, found that before a child enters school he or she will have spent more time in front of a TV set than is spent in his or her entire school career.

Television has been accused of interfering with a child's acquisition of language skills and reading, and of impeding his or her imagination. In actuality, there is a paucity of empirical evidence that can substantiate these claims. Although there are numerous articles dealing with television's effect on aggression, only more recently have researchers begun to critically examine the relationship between television, reading and imagination.

Imagination & Vocabulary

Our work at the Yale Family Television Research and Consultation Center has focused on television and the development of imagination in preschoolers. We find, for example, that children who watch the least amount of television, but who engage in make-believe play are the most imaginative children. They are also rated by research observers in the nursery schools as cooperative, persistent, and more joyful than those children who are heavy television viewers. These results have been found with two different samples of children— middle class, and lower class. Each sample was studied over one year's time. We have found, too, that children who are light television viewers have more imaginary companions than children who are heavy television viewers.

The data on imaginary companions is quite interesting. For example, we found that television characters played an important role in a child's choice of an imaginary companion. Both boys and girls named their companions after television characters, but while the girls were willing to use male and female characters as "friends," the boys only used male characters.

We have also looked at the language structure of preschoolers in order to determine the relationship between television viewing and the acquisition of language. Milkovich and Miller (1975) found that elementary-school-aged children who were heavy TV viewers had a less-advanced syntactic structure than those children who were light television viewers. We found similar results with the preschoolers we studied. The light viewers in one sample of middle-class children used longer sentences, more adjectives and adverbs, and more future tense verbs than the children who were heavy television viewers. These children used nouns, pronouns, and present tense verbs. They tended to label objects, and use shorter, less complicated sentences. We found that the light television viewers were more imaginative than the heavy television viewers. The children who engaged in make-believe games were actually learning more mastery skills alone than were children who spent considerable time in front of television sets or who played only physical games such as climbing or swinging.

Our study shows (Singer and Singer, 1975) that make-believe play may have many benefits for a child such as developing a capacity for imagery, flexibility, and empathy. Pretend play helps a child to concentrate, to learn sequencing, to delay gratification, to develop a clearer distinction between reality and fantasy. We have found that make-believe play leads to vocabulary growth. Two studies by Corinne Hutt (1979) in England, and one by Sarah Smilansky (1975) In Israel have substantiated this. They have found that through the encouragement of make-believe play by teachers or parents, children made significant vocabulary gains. Just think of all the words a child needs to play a fairy princess—crown, wand, castle, moat, gate, dragon, witch, and more. If the child does not know the word, an adult can supply it. Active use of the words in play reinforces the meaning of the words for the child so that they become part of his or her long-range memory system.

One of our studies (Tower, Singer, Singer and Biggs, 1979) found that children who watched the slow-paced "Mr. Rogers" TV program, compared to those who watched the fast-paced "Sesame Street" program, increased significantly in their imaginative play. These children who were high in imagination also showed significant differences in their speech from those children low in imagination. A good deal of conversation during free play is egocentric, fulfilling the same functions as Vygotsky has termed "inner speech." When a child is thinking, verbalization helps to clarify ideas; the scenario in play becomes more vivid. Children who are watching considerable amounts of television do not have ample time to use language with their parents or peers. Among poor children who are the heaviest television viewers, there may also be a lack of opportunity for rehearsal of expressive language. Parents permit these children to watch a great deal of television and may not be interacting with them. Work by Cook et al. (1975) found that children who were "encouraged" to watch "Sesame Street," and then talked with their parents about the programs made the greater cognitive gains. He also determined that the gap between advantaged and disadvantaged children actually widened in terms of skill acquisition from this program. Thus, it is important for an adult to act as a mediator between program content and child if *learning* is to take place.

Visual & Verbal Processes

Although television is obviously a visual medium, there are relatively few systematic studies concerned with hemisphere functioning and television viewing. The right side of our brain seems more closely related to reprocessing in imagery of visually related material, while the left side of the brain appears to process verbal-lexical and arithmetic material. Human beings use both verbal and imagery coding systems. If children are to learn more effectively from television, they need the opportunity to rehearse the picture material, whether through their own verbalization of the content, or through parental mediation. This dual processing, visual and verbal, will help children store the material in their coding systems more effectively. Dual processing enables children to develop language and to apply these skills to reading.

Blumenthal (1977) believes that an efficient reader is an active thinker who, when reading, devotes "much greater effort to constructing internal representations on the basis of rapidly scanned cues." The reader is anticipating what comes next and scans the text for inferences to support his or her developing configurations. It makes one wonder if a person watching television forms images of the upcoming scene before it appears. We wonder, too, if persons with imagery skills store the television's picture in their memory systems more readily than those who do not have such well-developed imagery capacities.

Some researchers, Karl Pribram, among them, have expressed concern that television viewing is enhancing a strong preference for or reliance upon global visual representations. The fear is that children will become impatient with the efforts needed to process auditory verbal materials such as teachers' directions or explanations. Males appear to be more differentiated in right and left brain functioning (Witelson, 1976), and this may account for the fact that more boys have reading difficulties in school than girls. Boys do watch more television than girls, (Singer, 1979) and are therefore exposed to more visually-oriented material in which the verbal component is presented very rapidly. We do know that imagery skills help a child in conservation tasks (Adams, 1978; Fink, 1976; and Golomb, 1976). For example, if a child can envision that the pennies spread out in one row actually equals the same number of pennies placed together in another row, or the tall glass of water equals the same amount of water in a short, wide glass, he or she has less trouble with transformations of quantity and volume. In light of such results, it may be that the use of imagery training as part of a school curriculum could enhance reading as well. Each time a child reads, he or she must picture the scene in his mind. Certainly as they grow and read more extensively, there are fewer pictures in their books, necessitating more effort on their part to provide the images.

TV Exposure & Reading

Reading requires an active stance on the part of the child. Compared with television, reading poses some challenges and some decided advantages. When a child reads, he or she is in *control* and can reread a section, pace himself or herself and can stop, at any point, and elaborate the material through his or her auditory or visual imagery. There is time to look up a difficult word and still go back to the text without missing a part of the "action," as compared to television where material is presented so rapidly that if a sentence is missed it cannot be retrieved. And while television offers instant replay for sports alone, reading allows the child the opportunity to reread a treasured passage, and return to the printed page of a favorite story over and over again, weeks, months, and years later.

We ask then, what are the long-term effects of television viewing on reading acquisition? At the moment, we are following 340 children over a three-year period, attempting to assess their reading readiness, and later their reading levels in relation to the amount of television viewed since nursery school days. We are now analyzing that data, and it is too soon to know the results. We do have data on older children (Zuckerman, Singer and Singer, 1979) who are not typical of children in the same age group or socioeconomic bracket so far as television viewing *time* is concerned. This sample watched about 15 hours per week, compared to the national norms of 30 to 40 hours per week. Their pattern of program choices, however, is similar to the nation as a whole when Nielsen tables are examined. We found that those middle-class children who spent more time reading, had higher IQ's and more highly educated fathers, and watched fewer fantasy-violent programs. One of our speculations is that fantasy-violent programs provide the same kinds of excitement as fairy tales, adventure books, comics, and other popular children's books, and may, therefore, satisfy similar needs for escapism and fantasy. These results are consistent with recent findings (Murray and Kippax, 1978) which indicated that watching television tended to replace reading comic books.

Research on reading in the 1950s and 1960s (Greenstein, 1954; Ridder, 1963) found no significant relationship between television viewing and grades. These studies, however, did not control for IQ, or socioeconomic status. When these variables are controlled, the relationships between television-viewing and school achievement were no longer significant (Furo, 1971; Thompson, 1964).

More recently Hornik (1978) found that there is a negative relationship between television exposure and the attainment of early reading and general school skills. This study, carried out in El Salvador, compared children whose families did or did not own television sets. It is difficult to generalize Hornik's results with studies made in the United States, since his study centered on the introduction of television into households, not the long-range impact on children. In the United States, it is virtually impossible to find children who have not had some television exposure. As a result, studies trying to explore the relationship between reading and television are confounded by numerous variables. For this reason, we are studying a preschool sample before and during the acquisition of reading.

It seems to me that we have to take a more realistic approach and stop blaming television for all our national ills. Since the visual impact of television is so exciting and attracts children, we must begin to think of ways to combine television interests and reading. Some attempts are already underway—the use of television program scripts in the classroom, guides to *Prime Time School Television* for children in the upper elementary grades, and various instructional programs that use television as auxiliary teachers. Although the instructional programs and guides to television are available, teachers have not taken full advantage of them. Indeed, perhaps parents will have to take a more active role in controlling the television viewing of their children and in directing them to books.

Television can be used to entice children to read if parents become aware of books that are related to television subject matter or if the story itself appears in a visual form. Certainly book sales of *I, Claudius, Roots, Nancy Drew, Little House on the Prairie*, and other television produced novels increased their sales after the broadcasts. A campaign to "advertise" books will begin this fall on CBS.

It is up to parents to be sure that television is used with discretion and that other modes of information and entertainment—especially books—become a habitual part of a child's life.

Bibliography

Adams, J. S. "Pretense-play: A Study of Its Cognitive Implications." Paper presented at 49th annual meeting of Eastern Psychological Assoc., March 1978, Washington, D.C.

Blumental, A. L. *The Process of Cognition*. New Jersey: Prentice-Hall, 1977.

Cook. L. D.; Appleton, H.: Conner, R. F.; Shaffer, A.; Tomkin, G.; and Walker, S. J. *Sesame Street Revised*. New York: Russell Sage Foundation, 1975.

Fink, R. "The Role of Imaginative Play in Cognitive Development. In *Piagetian Theory and the Helping Professions*. Edited by M. K. Paulsen, J. F. Magary, and G. I. Lubin. Los Angeles: University of Southern California Press, 1976.

Furo, L. *The Function of Television for Children and Adolescents*. Tokyo: Sophia University Press, 1971.

Gerbner, G. Personal communication, June 1979.

Golomb, C. "Pretense Play: A Cognitive Prospective." In *Symbolization and the Young Child*. Boston: Wheelock College, 1976.

Greenstein, J. "Effects of Television Upon Elementary School Grades." *Journal of Educational Research* 48 (1954): 161-76.

Hornik, R. "Television Access and the Slowing of Cognitive Growth." *American Educational Research Journal* 15 (1978): 1-15.

Hutt, C. "Towards a Taxonomy of Play." In *Play and Learning*. Edited by B. Sutton-Smith. New York: Gardner Press, 1979.

Hutt, C. "Play in the Under-Fives: Form, Development and Function." In *Modern Perspectives in the Psychiatry of Infancy*. Edited by J. G. Howells, New York: Bruner/Mazel, 1979.

Lyle, J., and Hoffman, H. R. "Children's Use of Television and Other Media." In *Television and Social Behavior*, edited by E. A. Rubinstein, G. A. Comstock, and J. P. Murray (Vol. 4, "Television in Day-to-Day Life: Patterns of Use"). Washington, D.C.: U.S. Government Printing Office, 1972.

Milkovich, M., and Miller, M. "Exploring the Relationship Between Television Viewing and Language Development." Report #3, *TV Advertising and Children Project.*, College of Communications Arts, Michigan State University, 1975.

Murray, J. P., and Kippas, S. "Children's Social Behavior in Three Towns with Differing Television Experience." *Journal of Communication* 28 (1978): 19-29.

Riddler, J. "Public Opinion and the Relationship of TV Viewing to Academic Achievement." *Journal of Educational Research* 57 (1963): 204-07.

Singer, J. L., and Singer, D. G. "Imaginative Play in Early Childhood: Some Experimental Approaches." In *Child Personality and Psychopathology*. Edited by A. Davids. New York: Wiley, 1976.

Singer, J. L., and Singer, D. G. "Television-Viewing and Imaginative Play in Preschoolers: A Developmental and Parent-Intervention Study." National Science Foundation and Spencer Foundation, New Haven, June 1979.

Smilansky, S. *The Effects of Sociodramatic Play on Disadvantaged Preschool Children,* New York: Wiley, 1968.

Thompson, C. "Children's Acceptance of Television Advertising and the Relation of Televiewing to School Achievement." *Journal of Educational Research* 58 (1964): 171-75.

Tower, R.; Singer, D. G.; Singer J. L.; and Biggs, A. "Differential Effects of Television Programming on Preschoolers' Cognition, Imagination, and Social Play." *American Journal of Orthopsychiatry* 49 (1979): 265-81.

Witelson, S. F. "Sex and the Single Hemisphere: Specialization of the Right Hemisphere for Spatial Processing." *Science* 193 (1976): 425-27.

Zuckerman, D. M.; Singer, D. G.; and Singer, J. L. "Television Viewing and Children's Reading and Related Classroom Behavior." *Journal of Communication*, in press.

Porter PL Makes The Cable TV Connection

by Kathy Wendling

You don't need a large staff or a generous budget to pro-duce quality cable TV programs. Three staff members at Porter Public Library have been turning out exceptional children's programs since September 1982, when the library began its cooperative venture with the local cable station, West Shore Channel 6, becoming the first public library in the Cleveland area to produce cable television programs for children.

When cable television first came to Westlake, Ohio, in 1980, the programming director approached the library staff to ask for help in producing public service programs. We were receptive to this request for these reasons: through cable we could reach residents of the community who were not library users and who, perhaps, had no idea of the library's wide variety of materials and programs. We also knew that some people in the community might want to take advantage of our programs and services, but could not because either their time or mobility was restricted.

After considerable discussion with the stations' program director, it was decided that a children's story hour would be a relatively simple format to present via cable TV. Little did we realize the vast amount of work involved in preparing a television program! The planning began with a brainstorming session to decide on a name for the series. The children's librarian, the staff artist, and a library clerk put their heads together and came up with *Porter P. Mouse Tales*.

They decided to create a logo to represent Porter P. Mouse, and our staff artist set about adapting one of her drawings. The result was a large poster of the mouse logo, which was painted and mounted so that it could be shown on camera at the beginning and end of each program.

Meanwhile, the children's librarian was re-examining her all-time favorites, looking for stories she could tell on the 15-minute telecast. With story length an important consideration, she eventually chose 30 stories. It was necessary to write to the publishers of each story to secure permission to use copyrighted material. Most were willing to grant permission; however, some asked for a fee. We discarded the stories for which a fee would be charged and searched for others, until 26 stories had been selected. The next step was for the children's librarian to memorize each story, timing them to fit the 15-minute time slot precisely. She planned to tell two stories during each program and leave some time for chatting with the children.

Both the staff artist and the clerk worked closely with the librarian to enhance the storytelling programs. The artist would illustrate a major scene from one of the two stories; these illustrations were shown on camera while the stories were told. Appropriate props, such as elves, pumpkins, and puppets, were gathered and made ready before each taping session. This was the responsibility of the library clerk, who was designated producer of the programs. She often enlisted the aid of the entire library staff, occasionally asking them to contribute their favorite stuffed animals for props.

A live audience was the final ingredient necessary to make the shows a success. School-age children who were regular library patrons were contacted, and four to six children were invited to the studio each week to listen and react to the stories on camera. Since the programs were taped during school hours, the library had to request the parents' permission for their children to miss a morning of school. (The school personnel were extremely cooperative, as were the parents, who signed permission slips and drove their children to the TV station.)

Because we decided to tape two 15-minute programs in one session every other week, the storyteller had to memorize four stories, the artist had to prepare two illustrations, and the producer needed to prepare two sets of props for each taping. The first taping session went well, although several minor problems had to be worked out. It was apparent that two cameras were not enough, so on subsequent tapings our artist was enlisted to operate a third videotape camera, thus getting a wider variety of shots. To lend variety, different arrangements of the set and the audience of children were tried, and at each taping session, the librarians and the cable TV staff all learned more than they had before. By the end of the 13-week series, it was apparent that the programs had improved immensely in technical quality. The staffs had also streamlined production to the point that a taping session could be accomplished in a three-hour time span; two hours were needed to set up and one needed for the taping.

At the end of all this preparation, viewers were able to tune in the *Porter P. Mouse Tales* on the local cable station three times a week—on Thursdays at 10:45 a.m. and 6:15 p.m., and on Fridays at 10:45 a.m. One important aspect was the necessity of publicizing the series. This was done by publishing articles in the local papers as well as in the library newsletter. Special bookmarks and posters were made available at the library, and the area schools cooperated by announcing the programs each week.

Second Time Around

When cable TV's second season rolled around, our staff felt they wanted to create a program aimed at the preschoolers who were watching *Porter P. Mouse Tales*, so we developed a preschoolers' story and craft show. Again, this series was organized within a 15-minute time frame, but it ran for eight weeks rather than thirteen. Each weekly program had a theme: bears, snowmen, things that go, popcorn, rabbits. Highlighting the theme, the children's librarian first told a short story and recited poems and rhymes, then demonstrated a craft that centered on the theme. The audience was made up of three five-year-old children.

The planning for this series was more elaborate than the first series of storytelling. As she chose the eight program themes, the children's librarian had to consider how many preschool stories and rhymes on each subject were available, as well as their length. After making her selection, she discussed the material with the artist and producer to develop plans for scenery and props, as well as to select those crafts that could be accomplished by preschoolers within the allotted time. The artist decided to build special scenery for the programs, and created life-sized snowmen and an enormous popcorn box. Since all three staff members would, at times, appear on camera helping the children construct the crafts, they thought it would add to the professional look of the program if they wore a special costume. So they bought identical T-shirts and had our artist applique the Porter P. Mouse logo on them.

The most difficult undertaking was assembling the props for this series—in fact, this proved to be a giant undertaking. The first program featured bears. Our producer gathered together two dozen stuffed creatures and used them as props. This was highly effective—the audience enjoyed viewing the wide variety of adorable bear personalities perched around the set.

In addition to preparing a story and locating appropriate rhymes each week, the children's librarian (with the help of the producer and artist) had to collect all the supplies needed for making crafts. Paper, scissors, yarn, and glue were often used; some of the projects involved making paper bears and monkeys, popcorn pictures, snowmen hats, and stuffed paperbag rabbits. Because of the variety of activities in these programs, it was necessary to rehearse them thoroughly prior to show time. For this we set up a stage in the library meeting room, where the librarian told the stories and rhymes and practiced the week's craft with the others. Everyone worked until they could complete all of these activities in exactly 15 minutes.

On the day of the taping, the job of transporting all of the scenery, props, and supplies to the cable studio was enormous. Fortunately the producer owned a station wagon—each week a heavy child-sized table, three chairs, two stools, the appropriate scenery, props, and craft supplies had to be moved. Once everything was in place, the taping sessions proceeded

with very few problems. The first program did run overtime, however, mainly because we lacked experience in handling a participating audience. Subsequent programs, however, fit the time slot accurately, and we discovered that five-year-olds made better audience participants than older children did, because they responded spontaneously and behaved beautifully. Originally the cable people had wanted our staff to tape two programs at one session, but we insisted that would be impossible at this age level—and were proved correct.

Community Response

The response to the *Porter P. Mouse Tales* programs has been gratifying. When one mother heard the series was being planned, she said, "Oh, we're finally going to have some *good* programming on television!" Another parent told the children's librarian her children really enjoyed meeting her at the library as well as seeing her on TV. Many children said they had seen the show; the participants who served as members of the audience found it exciting to watch themselves on television. Most important, the response indicated that more preschoolers were watching the programs than were school-age children, our target audience. This was due primarily to the time of the day the programs were aired.

For the second series, the library distributed free instruction sheets for the craft activities and lists of books about the weekly theme. These had been prepared by the children's librarian in advance of each program's show date. Along with book marks and other standard publicity materials, the program follow-up information turned out to be very effective publicity devices. Each child who was a member of the audience on the *Porter P. Mouse* programs was excited to receive a specially designed certificate of participation.

The second series engendered more response than the first one because it was directed to a specific audience. After the airing of the first program in this series, one of our regular viewers said, "We really enjoyed the action in the new show. It's so colorful and lively." Many young children who came to the library after the show looked at the children's librarian wide-eyed and said, "I saw you on TV!" Their parents were generous with their compliments too—we often hear the comment, "Mrs. Denslow is an excellent storyteller."

Evaluating Library Efforts

Many staff hours went into the preparation and execution of the children's programs. After the preliminary planning, which included the selection of stories and themes, approximately six hours of the librarian's time was required for each taping, three hours for rehearsal and for contacting the children who were to be in the audience, and three hours to set up and tape the program. Naturally, the artist and the producer also spent many hours creating illustrations and sets and gathering props. The real cost of the productions can be expressed only in terms of the total time spent, since we used library funds solely for the three T-shirts and some basic art supplies.

Throughout the planning and production of each series, our library staff worked closely with the cable station personnel. Continual communication was vital, and many phone calls were exchanged to discuss details as we prepared the programs. The cable station required that we tape the programs in their studio, but the library staff had complete control over the content and length of the programs. Our first consideration in working with the three cable staff members was to keep them informed of our plans. This close working relationship with the local cable station has been beneficial to the library in many ways. Besides reaching people who are not library users, we have been able to communicate our special PR message to the general community through a new vehicle.

The cable news staff has taped portions of some of our adult programs, such as those on microwave and Chinese cooking, for use on their local news show. In addition, they have interviewed staff members about our campaign to persuade voters to pass a bond issue for a new library building. No words could communicate our crowded conditions to the public half as well as the cameras could. The station has also run 30-second messages promoting library services immediately after the *Porter P. Mouse Tales* programs.

Westlake, with a population of approximately 20,000 people, is the fastest growing suburb in the Cleveland area. It's projected that by the year 2000, we will have 50,000 residents. Porter Library plans to increase its cable involvement as the community grows; we will expand our cable programming efforts by adding programs for adult viewers. The skills and knowledge gained by our staff members as they learned by doing should provide a sound basis on which to build as we explore new cable program possibilities.

Cable TV and Libraries

If your library would like to become involved with cable television, you should contact the program director of your local cable station. Outline in detail some specific program ideas and you will likely find the director a receptive audience. Most local cable stations are required to present a certain amount of public service programming, and they are delighted to have help in this area. If your library decides to work cooperatively with a cable station, the staff must be willing to devote a lot of time and effort to the project, remain flexible, and let each person's creativity run free. Remember, money and a large staff are not necessary—dedication is!

The Cupboard Is Bare:
The Need to Expand Poetry Collections

by Jeanne McLain Harms & Lucille J. Lettow

In many school libraries, few volumes of poetry are available even though other areas of the collection are well developed. Not only is the poetry section often limited in size, but it is frequently out of date. As a result, teachers are thwarted in presenting poetry as a pleasurable experience and as an integral part of the school curriculum, and children never realize the nature of poetry. This vacuum does not reflect the current state of the art; many volumes of quality poetry are being published yearly. The list of poets writing for children has never been more impressive than it is today.

Poets respond with their imagination and the sound of language to the emotion of an experience. Consequently, they can lift an experience out of the ordinary by offering a new, intense, and often startling or surprising, perspective. Children find these imaginative responses fascinating. A teacher read aloud to her sixth-grade class Myra Cohn Livingston's haiku, "Weather Conditions," from *4-Way Stop*, in which Livingston described bees as working in striped sweaters. During the art period later in the day, when the teacher and students were discussing the use of one's imagination to express ideas through collage, one boy recalled his early experience with that poem.

Poetry offers natural invitations to identify with others, gain new perspectives, learn about language, and create meaning through responding to the affective aspect of experiences.[1] Poetry's contribution to the different areas of the curriculum is an "enduring truth." While informational works need revising to reflect advancements in knowledge, poetry's responses to emotions in experiences remain constant.[2]

With the current emphasis on literature in the curriculum, the development of poetry as a resource needs the immediate collaboration of teachers and librarians. Two pitfalls, however, must be avoided by those attempting to build or rebuild the poetry collection in their libraries and by those determining which volumes will be incorporated into the curriculum: (1) selecting, for the sake of efficiency and economy, a general collection containing a large number of poems representative of many poets' work and many topics; and (2) acquiring volumes with high first-glance appeal to insure wide circulation and a positive attitude toward the genre. In view of the nature of poetry, these criteria for selection are faulty. General poetry compilations and gimmicky verses do not convey the notion that the writing of poetry is a personal experience, nor are they necessarily a positive reflection on the genre.

Collections vs. Poets' Responses

General collections usually are organized by topics, such as nature, seasons, animals, nonsense, and make-believe. Such a categorization allows poetry to be mistakenly conceptualized as being about ideas and events rather than responses to experiences. As a result, listeners/readers do not become aware of each poet's message and style—how each poet views the world, what is important to the poet, and how each has responded to these experiences. A collection that is an exception to this practice is Lilian Moore's *Go with the Poem*. The compiler has recognized the essence of poetry by organizing the volume with such headings as "I'm the Driver and the Wheel" and "The Tiger Has Swallowed a Black Sun."

Poets are unique in perspective and in the way that perspective is represented in their work. From listening to or reading one or two of John Ciardi's poems in a collection, one might miss knowing what is special about his poetry; he wrote rollicking verse that is easy to listen to and recite.

From reading Lilian Moore's many volumes of poetry, her audience learns that she primarily responds to experiences with nature and that the imagery in these responses offers fresh, strong perspectives. One is somehow not surprised to find out that Lilian Moore had a secret garden behind her home when she lived in the city and has now realized her dream of living in the country.[3]

One marvels at how Myra Cohn Livingston has perfected her craft, using many forms and points of view and responding to the wholeness of the human existence—the positive and the negative. She says that she naturally responds to the joy in life, yet she has gradually found negatives that motivate her to protest.[4] In *Sky Songs*, she offers both the light and dark sides of sky phenomena in cinquains using the second person. An example of the joy found in the sky is related in the poems "Stars" and "Morning Sky." These poems express a sense of wonderment and delight as the poet ponders over the countless people looking at a certain star or the sky being the "earth's astrodome." A contrast in mood is found in "Smog," in which Livingston asks the earth who is making it sick with smoke, fumes, and poisons.

Some of Arnold Adoff's finest poetry is a response to the emotions encountered when people rise above the superficiality of social conventions.[5] In *All the Colors of the Race*, he describes human relationships based on love, and as a member of a multiracial, multiethnic family, he attempts to rid his own mind of bias.

Recently several poets have selected poems from their published volumes, many of which are out of print, and have presented them in a single book. These volumes are most helpful in understanding a poet's work. Karla Kuskin, in her collection, *Dogs and Dragons, Trees and Dreams*, not only presents her favorite poems, but also discusses the nature of poetry and her writing experiences. Lilian Moore, in *Something New Begins*, has selected poems from several of her works and has included a section of new poems. David McCord's compilation *A Star in the Pail*, like his earlier *Every Time I Climb a Tree*, is representative of his approach to poetry for children: it has to delight.

Strengthening the case for selecting volumes by a single poet rather than general collections is the fact that many of these recent volumes have been illustrated by fine artists. Their graphic artwork has enhanced the poets' responses to the emotional quality of experiences. Marc Simont's bright watercolors for David McCord's two compilations contribute to the enjoyment of the poetry. Leonard Everett Fisher's impressionistic paintings for Myra Cohn Livingston's *Sky Songs* not only strengthen the different emotional responses in the poems, but also contribute to the idea that the phenomena of the sky—the heavenly bodies, the times of day, and the elements of weather—are viewed from afar. This poet and artists have used a similar format for *Celebrations, A Circle of Seasons, Sea Songs*, and *Earth Songs*. Tom Feelings' black-and-white sketches collaborate with Nikki Grimes' free-verse responses to black children's urban experiences in *Something on My Mind*; their work is simple, eloquent, and in tune.

Gimmicks vs. Childlike Responses

Very little distinction between gimmicky verses and serious poetry seems to be made in schools today. Teachers and librarians often believe that they must resort to nonsense and light verse to appeal to children. As a result, children do not discover the essence of poetry. True, children enjoy laughing at humorous twists and hearing what sound-play can do to make meaning, but these types of poems are only a part of the childhood experience. Adults sell children short when they use gimmicky word play to attract them to poetry. Given the opportunity, children respond with natural delight to poetry that honestly addresses their experiences. Myra Cohn Livingston states that good poetry "promises not answers but reflection, surprise, more fruitful inquiry into ourselves and our worlds."[6]

Children's enthusiastic response to the surprise element in poetry should not lead to the presentation of nonsense that may catch children off guard, for it does not provide a genuine response to the emotions in an experience. The surprise element in poetry should extend children's cognitive and affective development as well as entertain.

Biographical Information About Poets

As part of the study of poetry with children, the lives and the contributions of individual poets should be explored. Bio-graphical sketches of all of the major poets are available in the general reference sources focusing on children's authors, such as "The Junior Book of Authors" series (Wilson), Lee Bennett Hopkins' "Books Are by People" series (Citation), and the "Something About the Author" series (Gale Research). Also, *Language Arts* includes informative articles on recipients of the National Council of Teachers of English Poetry Award in a fall issue.

By knowing more about poets, children will understand more about the nature of poetry. They will realize that poetry has far more to offer than mere entertainment. Focusing on collections of a single poet's work and on poetry with substance which expresses feelings and ideas can provide new avenues for thought and new sources for unlimited experiences. Fortunately, much fine poetry is available; the cupboard can be filled.

References

1. Jeanne McLain Harms and Lucille J. Lettow. "Poetry: Invitations to Participate." *Childhood Education*, v. 63. October, 1986. pp. 6-10.
2. Helen W. Painter. *Poetry and Children*. International Reading Association, 1970. p. 2.
3. Doris DeMontreville and Elizabeth D. Crawford, eds. *Fourth Book of Junior Authors*. H. W. Wilson, 1978. pp. 267-268.
4. Anne Commire, ed. *Something About the Author*. Gale Research, 1973. v. 5, pp. 116-117.
5. "Arnold Adoff—Profile of an Author. *Top of the News*. v. 28. 1972. pp. 152-159.
6. Myra Cohn Livingston. "The Ministry of Poetry." *Catholic Library World*. v. 58. July/August, 1986. p. 43.

Titles Discussed

Adoff, Arnold. *All the Colors of the Race*. illus. by John Steptoe. Lothrop. 1982.

Grimes, Nikki,. *Something on My Mind*. illus. by Tom Feelings. Dial, 1978.

Kuskin, Karla. *Dogs and Dragons, Trees and Dreams: A Collection of Poems*. illus. by author. Harper, 1980.

Livingston, Myra Cohn. *Celebrations*. illus. by Leonard Everett Fisher. Holiday, 1985.

———, *A Circle of Seasons*. illus. by Leonard Everett Fisher. Holiday, 1982.

———, *Earth Songs*. illus. by Leonard Everett Fisher. Holiday, 1986.

———, *4-Way Stop and Other Poems*. illus. by James J. Spanfeller. Atheneum, 1976; o.p.

———, *Sea Songs*. illus. by Leonard Everett Fisher. Holiday, 1986.

———, *Sky Songs*. illus. by Leonard Everett Fisher. Holiday, 1984.

McCord, David. *Every Time I Climb a Tree*. illus. by Marc Simont. Little, 1967.

———, *A Star in the Pail*. illus. by Marc Simont. Little, 1975.

Moore, Lilian. *Go with the Poem*. McGraw-Hill, 1979.

———, *Something New Begins*. illus. by Mary J. Dunton. Atheneum, 1982.

Visual Literacy & Children's Books:
An Integrated Approach

by David M. Considine

In 1985, a Roper Poll indicated that, for the first time, the college-educated segment of the U.S. population was deriving its news information from television rather than from traditional print sources. Videocassette records, computer graphics, and interactive video are further developments in the expanding electronic environment which testify to the growing importance of images in our lives. As this visual envelope expands, there is ample evidence to suggest that we need to be aware of it and we need to help children understand it.

Television, aided and abetted by new technology that allows multiple screenings and increases its potential to influence impressionable viewers, also needs to be understood in terms of both its form and content. George Gerbner called television "the American schoolchild's national curriculum."[1] Charles R. Corder-Bolz, in his article published in the Summer 1980 *Television and Children*, maintains that "students' awareness and understanding of national and world geography, political issues and leaders, social problems and the functioning of government, appear to be derived from what they see and hear on television."[2]

For young people to understand today's complex communication systems and tomorrow's technology, teachers must help them develop competencies in media literacy, computer literacy, and visual literacy.

Visual Literacy Defined

Visual literacy refers to the ability to comprehend and create images in a variety of media in order to communicate effectively. It is important to note that this is broader in scope than are critical-viewing skills—the ability to analyze, understand, and appreciate visual messages. As does traditional literacy, visual literacy contains the competencies of reading and writing. Visually literate students should be able to produce and interpret visual messages.

There is a substantial body of evidence to suggest that learning can be improved if teachers incorporate visualization into classroom strategies. Pressley, et al, have asserted that "there is no doubt that illustrations can and do often increase children's learning of meaningful verbal materials."[3] Gaylean holds that "teaching with imagery can help students focus on lessons, retain information, improve psychomotor skills and accept themselves and others."[4]

Although teachers and administrators may fear that visual literacy is merely another demand upon their limited time, staff, and budgets, visual literacy training, when treated as a competency to be integrated into the curriculum, can actually be achieved within existing schedules and despite limited materials and staff. Illustrations in children's books, for example, provide an astonishingly diverse means of developing visual literacy skills across a broad spectrum of the curriculum and with youngsters at all grade levels. Because these illustrations are readily available in school and public libraries and because still images are easy to view, they are a rich and rewarding initial step on the road toward achieving visual literacy.

Stereotypes

Lenore Weitzman, in *The American Journal of Sociology*, states "children's books reflect cultural values and are an instrument for persuading children to accept those values."[5] Because books for children contain and convey information and impressions, it is necessary for librarians, teachers, parents and children themselves to be aware of these "windows on the world" and the accuracy of the images they convey. In *Children's Literature in Elementary School*, Charlotte Huck states:

> Picture books frequently give children their first impressions of various ethnic or racial groups. Only when our books portray characters of both sexes, all races and all colors, in a wide range of occupations and from a great variety of socio-economic backgrounds will we have moved away from stereotyping to a more honest portrayal of literature for children.[6]

Finding examples of stereotyping in children's books and in the media in general is an excellent way in which children's books can be used with students of all ages. Older students can be taught simple content analysis, using quantitative and qualitative methods to study messages in book illustrations. They might, for example, research the number of images of male and female characters, or the number of images of black Americans, Native Americans or Hispanics that appear in books. To ascertain if the illustrations are an accurate representation of the American population, their figures might be compared to the percentages of these groups in the real population. In qualitative terms, students might examine how certain groups are depicted. For example it may be useful to see if there is a gender bias evident in the occupations, roles, tasks, and activities of male and female characters.

Once understood within the context of children's books, these methods of analysis can be employed to help children study magazine and newspaper advertising and their favorite television program. They can look at the relationship between what they read or by the spoken word and the more subtle messages conveyed by the media. Advanced students can consider how and why such messages are created. For example, do female illustrators tend to draw more or fewer female characters than their male counterparts, and are these characters more or less stereotypical than those drawn by male illustrators? Is the publishing industry more male- or female-dominated, and how does this influence the kinds of stories published? Does the fact that the majority of librarians and media specialists are female affect the kinds of quality books that are produced?

Techniques such as these promote a holistic approach to education by which students can understand everything from messages in advertising to the way Native Americans are misrepresented in Hollywood movies. Stories can be studied in English classes; the illustrations in art classes; and the ideas and accuracy of the images can be examined in social studies classes.

Reading the Image

In any picture book both the illustrations and the words should be read. In a quality book, the pictures elaborate and embellish the text. By focusing attention on book illustrations, children can attain a deeper meaning, and become aware of how images are used.

Author/illustrator Gail Haley helps to foster children's awareness of images as she travels to schools and libraries around the country. "Can a picture be noisy?" she asks as she shows a group gathered around her *The Green Man*. The dedication page is inscribed, "The story you are about to read may have happened just this way—or perhaps it came about in a different manner in another place entirely." Like most of Haley's stories, *The Green Man* is more of a beginning than an end. "Children find their own level of meaning in it" she says. "What I like to do when I meet them is to open their eyes and, through their eyes, to activate their other senses." When the children look at Claude's village and its images, Haley asks, "What do you see?" The answers come back in quickly-jumbled phrases and impressions. "What kinds of noises are in Claude's village?" Immediately, the room is filled with the sound of barking dogs, a babbling stream, a flock of sheep, a blacksmith's anvil, and children playing. Thus the richness of one image has created a sensory world—another time and a place that children can enter with an adult's guidance.

While helping children to see more clearly can expand their insight and imagination, it also has practical, everyday applications especially in driver education and in skills that require visual concentration and discrimination. Again, children's books can be used as a starting point. They can also be fun. For example, have children read *Madeline* and note

how many discover a mistake, now well-known, where Ludwig Bemmelmans drew 12 girls having dinner, even though the text says that one is in the hospital. Or, tell children that there is a mistake in Haley's *The Post Office Cat* and see if anyone can locate it. (Since the story is set in London, the vehicles should actually be on the other side of the road.) This little exercise helps children, not only to look more carefully at illustrations, but to think about why images appear as they do.

One means of directing attention to the interpretation of images is to provide viewers with several basic tools. Specific elements in a series of workshops I conduct with teachers, media specialists, administrators, and students can be used. As a first step I have participants identify an image and then interpret it. For example, a photograph of an eagle is an excellent starting point. Everyone will correctly identify it as an eagle. The next task is to interpret it, to say what it means. Few will say that it means an eagle—most will associate it with power, the presidency, the country's national symbol, etc. This process opens the way for a discussion of literal and figurative or symbolic meaning. It is important to point out that even though the image does not change, the meaning may change. The same image, in a different time and place, could represent the Third Reich or the Roman Empire. Also, a turkey means something quite different in the United States than it would in Australia. Through this simple process, students discover that even though everyone sees the same image, they do not all read it the same way.

Elements

Posture: Posture refers to body language and may include facial expressions. Children intuitively understand and can act out the way in which their expression and posture reflects their moods and feelings. Many books contain good examples of this, e.g. *Where The Wild Things Are, Moon Man, The Garden of Abdul Gasazi.*

Point of View: A particularly helpful technique for decoding film and television messages is understanding a "point of view"—the perspective created by a camera angle conveys meaning. A tilt up at an object or figure tends to make the subject strong, powerful, aggressive, etc. Tilting the camera down on the subject creates a sense of weakness, vulnerability or insecurity. This technique is evident in children's books, however, students can also enjoy finding examples in film and television, particularly in horror movies. The "point-of-view" method is used extensively for propaganda purposes.

Props: The artifacts in a frame help readers to understand something about the lifestyle of the characters and the story's time and setting. Even if they have not read a story, children who read the props can tell a great deal about characters and settings.

Position: Sometimes the position that a character occupies in a frame may indicate something about the significance of his or her role in the story. A character standing at the head of the stairs, for example, is more dominant than a figure positioned at the foot of the stairs. A character in the foreground is likely to be more important than one in the background.

Additional Tools

Artistic Style: In his Caldecott Award acceptance speech, Gerald McDermott said that it is the role of the illustrator to "nurture the development of his young audience's visual perception." McDermott's art was described in *The Journal of Popular Culture*. "He abstracts the inner core of the tale and translates the ideas into his own personal world view and visual vocabulary."[7] By focusing the student's attention upon the style employed by a variety of illustrators, a fusion can be created between art and English classes.

Appreciating art means more than liking or disliking certain illustrators or particular techniques. It means establishing a criteria for evaluation, and understanding why particular stories have been told through particular techniques. In *Wood and Linoleum Illustration* (Weston Woods), Haley explains some of her techniques and reasons for using them. *The Green Man* was painted with acrylics on heavy canvas board to suggest a medieval tapestry. *Jack Jouett's Ride* was influenced by the wood engravings of Thomas Bewick. The translucent colors of *Birdsong* referred to in so many reviews were created on a light box. Commenting on her recent *Jack and the Beantree*, Haley says:

> This is my first organic book. I actually used bits of the mountain, leaves, lichen, bark. You are aware of the woods all of the time that you are in the mountains. Everything springs from wood. That's why I decided this time around I had to paint on wood blocks. The wood was treated, and then I applied a gesso covering because by using that I could carve and incise and inscribe other textures. The fantasy of the story had to be real; had to have depth. The gesso allowed me to create a meaning beneath the surface, so that even after I had applied the acrylic paint, there was something deeper going on beneath the surface, in the same way that the story can be read on more than one level. The technique enabled me to stress the sparseness and bare board existence of the cabin where Jack lives with his mother, at the same time that I could convey the richness and warmth of the giant's home.

Children's books offer a striking variety of artistic styles and techniques. Among others, *Arrow to the Sun, The Stonecutter, The Polar Express*, and *The Girl Who Loved Wild Horses* provide an exciting array of images which can be used to promote an interest in the language arts. Perhaps students will be encouraged to explore their own artistic skills.

The Artist: Students may take a greater interest in illustrative styles and techniques if they know something about the creator behind the image. The *Presenting the Author* packets (produced by the National Council of Teachers of English), Caldecott speeches, publicity distributed by publishers, and various indexes can all be used to get information about illustrators.

The images themselves may tell students something about the artists. A well-trained eye, looking through the collective works of any illustrator, may find certain objects, settings or images repeated over and over, irrespective of the time or place in which the story is set. Talking about the characters in his books, Steven Kellogg observes, "many times they come out looking just like me." *Birdsong* has more than a passing resemblance to its creator. Also, Haley appears to be fascinated with cats. It comes as no surprise to discover that she has five at home; there is usually a cat perched on her drawing table as she works.

Visual Validity: If images serve young people as windows on the world, it is important that we help them understand how to recognize accurate representations. When illustrators depict different cultures and times, how authentic are the images? What sources do they consult to guarantee the accuracy of the period they recreate? What sources can be researched to verify whether or not these illustrations accurately reflect the time and place in which they are set?

These questions provide another way in which training in visual literature can be spread throughout the curriculum to develop student competencies in English, social studies, and in library media skills. In *Tracing a Legend: The Story of the Green Man* (Weston Woods), Haley explains exactly how she went about researching the background for the *The Green Man*, a fascinating insight that provides some understanding of where her stories come from.

Always concerned with accurately creating the language, costumes, and architecture of the time in which her stories are set, Haley conducts meticulous research. For *The Post Office Cat*, she spent hours in London's Victoria and Albert Museum. When she was creating *Jack Jouett's Ride*, she visited Jefferson's home at Monticello, the place where the real event occurred. Haley attempts to bring her stories to life by making them real:

> By studying the art, music, food and lifestyle of the people who told it [the story], I can make it whole in my mind. In the case of *A Story, A Story*, the lines and planes in Ananse's face are based upon African masks and sculpture. The textures, colors, and costumes are all based on African artifacts and the brilliance of the African landscape.

The Medium & the Message

An important but often ignored aspect of exploring images in children's books is a comparison between the books and the audiovisual products upon which they are based. The films, filmstrips, and videotapes that Morton Schindel has developed at Weston Woods provide extraordinary opportunities to explore this. For example, in *Evolution of a Graphic Concept: The Stonecutter*, Gerald McDermott explains how moving a story from one medium to another changes the way the story is expressed. (In making the transition from film to book, he also changed the image from a horizontal format to a vertical one.)

> I drew 500 different pictures to animate the transformation of the stonecutter's hut into a castle. In the book I had to communicate the entire action in just one pic-

ture . . . In the film, motion and music generate the excitement. On the printed page I had to rely on active composition and vibrant color to provide this excitement.

When audiovisual materials are used in the classroom, students' attention should be focused on more than the narrative content. To help them understand the way in which the form conveys the content, multiple screenings may be necessary. On at least one occasion it may be useful for students to view the materials without benefit of sound so that they concentrate only on what they see. Large, single-frame projection, which is possible with a film-strip projector, is a good way to have a class concentrate on reading images.

Weston Woods supplies printed materials with its filmstrips; these contain each image from the program along with the text. Such materials are invaluable when students compare the printed and the projected versions of the same story. *The Post Office Cat* filmstrip contains nine images that are not found in the book. In the book, there is an illustration of Clarence being chased out of the house by a cook wielding a broom, but this image does not appear in the filmstrip. Several lines of text have also been deleted. Some questions for students to think about are: Where did the image come from? Were they left out of the book or were they added to the filmstrip? Did the same artist do them? Why are there more images in one medium than another?

Teachers should help students understand why editing decisions on illustrations are made and how characteristics of a particular medium may affect decisions. In *The Post Office Cat* filmstrip for example, a quarrel in the post office is depicted in four frames. By positioning the camera at different distances, the producer is able to create four images out of one book illustration.

Why Visual Literacy?

A book doesn't really exist until it's read, looked at, and thought about. My picture books need the reader to fill in the blank space between one page and the next. How each reader makes a book come to life is unique. That's why books are so special.—Gail E. Haley

In this world of instant replays, freeze frames, and congressional investigations of rock videos, there is a growing need for students to be trained to understand the visual culture in which they live. While the quality of TV programming is often lamented, critical production will only come about as a result of critical consumption. Shallow processing of television and other media is not the result of any attribute of the media itself, but is derived from the expectations viewers have from it.

As the traditional guardians of quality children's literature, librarians and teachers are now in the unique position of making a lasting contribution to visual literacy by helping young people explore and understand traditional and emerging technologies through which the stories of yesterday, today, and tomorrow are told.

Referenes

1. Gerbner, George. "Television: The American Schoolchild; National Curriculum Day In and Day Out." *P.T.A. Today*, April 1981.
2. Corder-Bolz, Charles R. "Critical Television Viewing Skills for Elementary Schools." *Television and Children*. Summer, 1980. p. 34.
3. Pressley, Michael, et al. "Picture Content and Preschoolers Learning From Sentences." *Educational Communication and Technology Journal*. Fall, 1982.
4. Gaylean, Beverly Colleene. "Guided Imagery in the Curriculum." *Educational Leadership*. March, 1983. p. 54.
5. Weitzman, Lenore. "Sex Role Socialization in Picture Books for Pre-School Children." *American Journal of Sociology*. Vol. 77, No. 6. 1972. p. 1126.
6. Huck, Charlotte. *Children's Literature in Elementary School*. 3rd ed. Holt, Rinehart, Winston. 1979. p. 112.
7. Hains, Mary Ellen. "Gerald McDermott: Popularizer of Universal Myths." *Journal of Popular Culture*, Vol. 17, No. 4. Spring, 1984. p. 124.

Resources

General

Anno, Mitsumasa, *Topsy-Turvies: Pictures to Stretch the Imagination*. Weatherhill, 1970.

Anno, Mitsumasa, *Upside Downers: More Pictures to Stretch the Imagination*. Weatherhill, 1971.

Classroom Projects Using Photography: Part 1, For the Elementary School Level. Eastman Kodak Co., 1975.

Classroom Projects Using Photography: Part 2, For the Elementary School Level. Eastman Kodak Co., 1975.

Curriculums in Visual Literacy. Report of the International Visual Literacy Association Task Force on Curriculum. Iowa State University Research Foundation, 1982.

Hoban, Tana. *I Read Symbols*. Greenwillow, 1983.

Hoban, Tana. *I Read Signs*. Greenwillow, 1983.

McKim, Robert. *Experiences in Visual Thinking*. Brooks Cole Pub. (Monterey, CA.), 1980.

Television and Families. Journal of the National Council for Children and Television, Princeton, N.J.

Visual Learning Materials. Free kit for teachers. Eastman Kodak Co.

Stereotyping

Considine, David M. *The Cinema of Adolescence*. McFarland. Jefferson, N.C. 1985.

Dick and Jane as Victims: Sex Role Stereotyping in Children's Readers. Women on Words and Images. Princeton, N.J. 1975.

Ten Quick Ways to Analyze Children's Books for Sexism and Racism. Council on Interracial Books for Children. N.Y.

Reading Images

Haley, Gail E. *The Green Man*. (filmstrip) Weston Woods.

Haley, Gail E. *Birdsong*. Crown. 1984.

Sendak, Maurice. *Outside Over There*. Harper & Row. 1981.

Ungerer, Tomi. *The Moon Man*. Harper & Row. 1967.

Van Allsburg, Chris. *The Garden of Abdul Gasazi*. Houghton Mifflin. 1979.

Weston Woods. *Non-Verbal Filmstrip Package. (The Bear and the Fly; Bubble Bubble; A Flying Saucer Full of Spaghetti; Pancakes for Breakfast; Sir Andrew and the Silver Pony).*

Artistic Style

Goble, Paul. *The Girl Who Loved Wild Horses*. Bradbury Press. 1978.

Goble, Paul. *Star Boy*. Bradbury Press. 1983.

Haley, Gail E. *Wood and Linoleum Illustration.* (filmstrip) Weston Woods.

Haley, Gail E. *A Story, A Story*. Atheneum. 1970.

Haley, Gail E. *Jack and the Beantree*. Crown. 1986.

Haley, Gail E. *Jack Jouett's Ride.* (filmstrip) Weston Woods.

Hodges, Margaret. Illus. by Trina Schart Hyman. *Saint George and the Dragon*. Little Brown, 1984.

McDermott, Gerald. *Arrow to the Sun*. Viking. 1974.

McDermott, Gerald. *The Stonecutter*. Viking. 1975.

Van Allsburg, Chris. *The Wreck of the Zephyr*. Houghton Mifflin. 1983.

Van Allsburg, Chris. *The Polar Express*. Houghton Mifflin. 1985.

The Artist

Kellogg, Steven. *How a Picture Book is Made. The Making of the Island of Skog From Conception to Finished Book.* (filmstrip) Weston Woods

McDermott, Gerald. *Evolution of a Graphic Concept: The Stonecutter.* (filmstrip) Weston Woods.

NCTE. *Presenting the Author: Gail E. Haley.* (teacher's kit) National Council of Teachers of English. Urbana, Ill. 1985.

Visual Validity

Fritz, Jean. *Where Do You Think You're Going, Christopher Columbus?* (filmstrip) Weston Woods.

Fritz, Jean. *And Then What Happened, Paul Revere?* (filmstrip) Weston Woods

Fritz, Jean. *Who's That Stepping on Plymouth Rock?* (filmstrip) Weston Woods.

Haley, Gail E. *Tracing a Legend: The Story of the Green Man.* (filmstrip) Weston Woods.

Haley, Gail E. *Jack Jouett's Ride.* (filmstrip) Weston Woods.

Lobel, Arnold. *The Day Peter Stuyvesant Sailed into Town.* Harper. 1971.

Musgrove, Margaret. *Ashanti to Zulu.* illus., by Leo & Diane Dillon. Dial. 1976.

Provensen, Alice & Martin. *The Glorious Flight*. Viking. 1983.

The Medium & the Message

Deitch, Gene. *The Picture Book Animated.* (film & video) Weston Woods.

Deitch, Gene. *Animating Strega Nonna.* (film) Weston Woods.

Haley, Gail E. *The Post Office Cat.* (filmstrip) Weston Woods.

Kellogg, Steven, *How a Picture Book is Made.* (filmstrip) Weston Woods.

McDermott, Gerald. *Evolution of a Graphic Concept.* (filmstrip) Weston Woods.

Schindel, Morton. *From Page to Screen.* (video) Weston Woods.

Sharing and Preserving Family Stories

by Cynthia K. Dobrez

Because of the increasing number of working parents, we see many grandparents in the library with their grandchildren. I decided to capitalize on this situation by offering a special program in honor of Grandparent's Day (which falls on September 13, 1987). The idea was sparked by a statement of Alex Haley's in an article on storytelling, "When an old person dies, it's like a library has burned down." I designed a storytelling program in an attempt to save some of those grandparents' stories and, in doing so, perhaps strengthen family relationships.

First I compiled a bibliography of titles where family stories were shared, to be distributed during the program. Many stories used some device for sharing—a quilt, a box of mementos, old pennies, a handmade book. Next I produced and distributed a flyer to every teacher in Oak Lawn. Flyers were inserted in our regular monthly school packets and were also available at the library's information centers. Some were delivered to the Senior Citizen Center which is next door. Press releases were sent to ten newspapers. The library's newsletter also carried a notice of the event.

The program was limited to students in grades four through eight. Two weeks in advance we held registration; we asked for the child's name, his or her grade level, the name of the grandparent, and a phone number. So that they could think of stories in advance, registrants were told that the grandparent would tell a family story to his or her grandchild at the program.

While waiting for the participants to arrive, I chatted with grandparents to put them at ease. I was surprised to see that these were not the grandparents who had brought children to other library programs. For some, this was their first visit to our library.

I began the program with a short booktalk about the books I included on the handout. I told several stories, one of which was about a quilt my great-grandmother made for me. I explained that each grandparent was to tell a good family story, and gave them some suggestions—a childhood incident, a favorite holiday, what they were doing on the day their grandchild was born, what they remember about their own grandparents.

At first, the grandparents were hesitant, but the children, eager to hear their stories, urged them on. The storytelling was done one-on-one. One grandfather told about a war experience; another related a childhood incident involving a dare. One girl was so anxious to hear the stories, she and her grandmother stayed after the program ended. She left with a book of five stories about her great-grandparents' immigration to the United States and the customs of her nationality. Immediately after the storytelling, each child wrote a short story and illustrated it. Using a three-ring punch and yarn, we bound the stories into books for the children to keep.

The two generations enjoyed talking about something more than "How is school?" and "My, you're getting tall!" One admitted to his grandson, "We don't get to spend enough time together." Another asked if the library offered this type of program often. He enjoyed getting out and meeting new people. Certainly, the highlight of this program is fostering family communication, but there are other rewards: the preservation of oral history; promotion of storytelling; encouraging children's writing skills; circulation of books. Now each child has a book of their grandparent's story to share with their own children and grandchildren.

Bibliography

Clifford, Eth. *The Remembering Box.* Houghton Mifflin, 1985.
Flournoy, Valerie. *The Patchwork Quilt.* Dial, 1985.
Geras, Adele. *Apricots at Midnight.* Atheneum, 1982.
Herzig, Alison Cragin. *Thaddeus.* Little, 1984.
Levinson, Riki. *Watch the Stars Come Out.* Dutton, 1985.
MacLachlan, Patricia. *Sarah, Plain and Tall.* Harper, 1985.
Mathis, Sharon. *The Hundred Penny Box.* Viking, 1975.
Moore, Elaine. *Grandma's House.* Lothrop, 1985.
Sendak, Philip. *In Grandpa's House.* Harper, 1985.
Stevenson, James. *Could be Worse!* Greenwillow, 1977.
——— *The Dreadful Day.* Greenwillow, 1985.
——— *Worse Than Willy!* Greenwillow, 1984.

Reading Lifelines

by Hazel Rochman

In Lowry Pei's *Family Resemblances*, when 15-year-old Karen meets George at the local swimming pool, they talk about the detective story she's reading. "How come you read murder mysteries anyway?" he asks her. "Don't you think it's weird to read about people getting killed?" Karen begins to see that talking to George might be hard going, but she thinks about his question. "See, I'll tell you what it is," she says. "They're not really about murder, they're about secrets."

Karen says that she and her Aunt Augusta, an English teacher, read murder mysteries all summer: "Row upon row were paperback murder mysteries, which [Aunt Augusta] kept buying, only to discover, sometimes, that she had already read them and knew how the plot came out. I was always in the middle of one of these mysteries, carrying them from room to room and putting them down without noticing where, losing my place, losing track of the plot, wishing the current one would be over with so I could read something better."

That's one kind of reading. For all of us. Teenagers, English teachers, librarians. The comfort of secrets that can be revealed, of mysteries neatly solved. The same kind of pleasure we get from fast thrillers, shivery horror, sweet romance—expectations satisfied. What Margaret Atwood calls "thumbsucking" kind of reading. There's nothing to make you reread those books. As Karen says, you know how they come out. And, anyway, they're replaced each year by others just like them.

But books can hold you with a different kind of power. In her autobiography *I Know Why the Caged Bird Sings*, Maya Angelou describes how as a child she was raped by her mother's boyfriend. The man was killed, and, as a result of the trauma and guilt, Maya stopped talking. She was punished, beaten, but nothing happened. Then, in her segregated neighborhood of Stamps, Arkansas, an aristocratic woman, Mrs. Flowers, who made Maya feel "proud to be a Negro," helped her break her silence. Mrs. Flowers invited Maya to her home, and read aloud to her from Dickens: "It was the best of times, it was the worst of times." She lent Maya poems to read aloud and recite, and showed her the power and beauty of the human voice. Angelou says that in that sharing, she felt that Mrs. Flowers was throwing her a "lifeline," freeing her from the grim confines of her private sorrow. The best books can do that. They can be lifelines.

Maya Angelou isn't talking direct therapy here. Mrs. Flowers didn't read to her about child abuse or about the black experience. It's more mysterious than that. They read a great story in language that sang, and Maya was moved beyond her narrow self—as I am moved when I read her book. When she read aloud how Sidney Carton sacrificed himself on the guillotine for another, saying "It is a far, far better thing I do, than I have ever done"—Angelou says that "tears of love filled my eyes at my selflessness." There's pleasure in books that unsettle us, mystify us, disturb our sleep and trouble our dreams. Kafka said a great book must be "the axe for the frozen sea inside us."

We all need Karen's murder mysteries. We need the popular genres in our libraries and on some of our lists. But we also need to promote the books that endure, that could never be mistaken for each other, books that are "lifelines."

Not that enduring titles all have to be about dark personal terror. Science fiction can grab you with story or with ideas, shake you up, make you think, turn the familiar into the strange, and change the way you see things. The wacky world of *The Hitchhiker's Guide to the Galaxy* is still a joyful read, and anyone who's booktalked *House of Stairs* knows the way faces suddenly light up when they catch on to Sleator's daring leap of imagination.

In Margaret Mahy's *The Catalogue of the Universe*, Tycho has always shared with Angela his excitement for science, and they read and talk about ideas. But he thinks of himself as short and strange looking, and when she tells him she admires his brilliant searching mind, he replies (only half-jokingly), "I'd rather be tall." This is a witty, tender, and passionate story; it celebrates love that is ecstatic and powerful, and knowledge that can make you a giant in touch with the stars. As in Angelou's and Pei's books, Mahy's characters share the pleasure of reading; books are important in their daily lives.

The one thing readers don't want is a reverential attitude—the status reader described so painfully by Richard Rodriguez in his autobiography *Hunger for Memory*. In high school he worked his way doggedly through a list of "the hundred most important books of Western Civilization," reading each word of each book but often having to check the book flap to see what he was reading about.

Kendall Hailey's new autobiographical journal *How I Became an Autodidact* (1988), makes the same mistake. At 15 she decided to graduate early, avoid college, and educate herself. She read the classics, from Virgil and Aristophanes to Dickens and Gertrude Stein. But she's showing off. Her pleasure is not in the books, but in the fact that she's read them. There's nothing to indicate that anything she's read has disturbed her or changed her in any way. She's as complacent at the end as she was at the beginning. And she perpetuates an elitist view of the classics and of reading—as something removed from common experience.

Everything old isn't necessarily enduring. As librarians we dread some of those required outside reading lists from teachers who haven't changed or added a title for generations. But some of us are guilty of that too. You know the people who've been recommending and booktalking the same few books and only those few, for 20 years—never adding anything new, never changing, never reading. Most of us have a too-rigid canon of *the best*, the books we assume everyone knows are the best.

We have to accept that some of the old "bests" aren't any good anymore. There's some disappointment in re-reading for a retrospective list. Some titles we remember as outstanding breakthroughs now seem thin and simplistic—and we have to let them go. They were revolutionary in their time, and they're important in historical studies of the development of the YA novel. But they don't have much for young people today.

One reason why they've become outdated is that YA literature has become so good. And our view of young people and their reading is less condescending. YA books are no longer regarded just as "bridges" to adult reading. In fact, when you talk to adult librarians now, you don't hear the old contempt for YA books. It's much more a two-way street. Many of them tell me that, just as they give adult books to young adults, they put some YA materials on the adult shelves. In the field of poetry published in the last year, for example, I have told adult librarians about Ruth Gordon's *Under All Silences*, a work anthology of great love poems; Betsy Hearne's personal *Love Lines* ("A few lines a day will keep you company," she says in her introduction); Paul Janeczko's stunning collections of modern American poems; and the combination of the popular and the serious in *American Sports Poems*, edited by Knudson and Swenson. It seems it's just a publishing sales strategy to call such books YA.

Of course, in young adult work our interest is not in impressing adults but in reaching young people. And there are many older books, young adult and adult, that still speak powerfully to teenagers in 1988. Some of the books have direct appeal and they need very little help from us. It's easy, for example, to hook kids with a story about highschoolers who murder their English teacher.

We need immediate, exciting action titles on our lists. But it's condescending to assume that kids want *only* that. In any group there is a wide range of reading interests and reading levels, including young people who are reading at many levels at the same time. We must be sure that we don't lose the more subtle, more demanding books, books that may need us to promote them—like *Running Loose*, where a boy struggles with his conscience and his feelings. Or *The Moves Make the Man*, where a boy learns the moves you need to survive, both in basketball and with people. Or *One-Eyed Cat*, where a boy is weighed down with a guilty secret. Or *Gentlehands*, where a teenage discovers a terrible secret about his grandfather. Or *The Flight of the Cassowary*, where a teenager thinks he may be turning into an animal. Or *Beauty*, where the hideous gentle Beast asks the same question each night, "Will you marry me, Beauty?"

I recently read Zibby Oneal's *The Language of Goldfish* for the first time. What a discovery! There isn't a false moment. The suffering is intense, but so controlled, never exploitative. When Carrie finally accepts her mother for what she is, that quiet climax is one of the most heart-breaking coming-of-age moments in fiction. That's a book with enduring appeal, but it does need us to promote it. I use it in a booktalk on the outsider theme as a story of inner struggle, after books about gangs and action. I show how Carrie feels like a stranger in her own home. She tries to tell her parents about her panic attacks, but they won't listen to her. Sometimes I read from the scene in the car, where Carrie says quietly, "I think I'm going crazy," and her mother natters on that Carrie should eat a proper breakfast—until Carrie blurts out: "Why don't you listen to what I'm telling you? Why do you keep saying anemic and breakfast?"

Rereading can be just as deep a pleasure, as is discovering new ways to promote a book you've always loved. Suzanne Newton's *I Will Call it Georgie's Blues* improves with rereading: in booktalks I always focus on Newton's strong sense of ugly family secrets beneath a respectable facade—a theme which is never lost on teenage readers. Judy Druse, present chair of the YASD Recommended Books for the Reluctant Young Adult Reader Committee, approaches this book more dramatically, opening her booktalks with an introductory line that plunges you straight into the world of the book: "Dinnertime at the Sloan house is like dodgeball: you spend all your energy staying alert to keep from getting hit." That hook of tension at the family dinner table has universal appeal, a reason why *Georgie's Blues* stands up to multiple readings.

We all like the immediate and the contemporary. In most booktalks I start off with something written here and now—to grab even the reluctant readers and show them directly that books are about their own lives. But then I use an unobtrusive theme or link—secrets, outsiders, terror, love—to bring in books that may not have today's brand names or be set in the mall, or even in this country, but that still tell a great story about how we live now.

In a booktalk taking the theme of the outsider, families or women, or the genre of biography, I bring in Maxine Hong Kingston's *The Woman Warrior*, a fiercely honest autobiography about growing up female and Chinese-American in California, caught by both the ghosts of Chinese tradition and the alien ways of the U.S. I read aloud the scene where her parents try to marry her off to one of the new immigrants, the FOB's (Fresh-off-the-Boats), and she makes herself as unattractive as possible: "As my parents and the FOB sat talking at the kitchen table, I dropped two dishes. I found my walking stick and limped across the floor . . . I spilled soup on the

FOB when I handed him his bowl . . . when he left, my mother yelled at me about the dried-duck voice, the bad temper, the laziness, the clumsiness, the stupidity that comes from reading too much . . . "

That book didn't make the Best Books for Young Adults list. As anyone who's served on the Best Books Committee knows, if there's one casualty, one kind of title that gets missed, it's the serious adult book with young adult appeal. There's so much pressure to read so many titles that there's often no time to give the longer and more demanding adult materials the attention they deserve. *The Woman Warrior* is one such book this year (Toni Morrison's *Beloved* is another, more well-known example). Besides being a moving coming-of-age story, *The Woman Warrior* is important in other ways. It's about a minority experience too little represented on our lists; and it's also about something else that tends to be underrepresented—what Betty Carter, former Chair of the Best Books for YA Committee, calls "passionate" non-fiction.

Another one is *Kaffir Boy* by Mark Mathabane, a searing account of what it's like to grow up under apartheid. This didn't make the Best Books list, or any list at first. Then Oprah Winfrey found it and promoted it. Now it's a bestselling paperback. I booktalk the scene, where, as a small child, the main character watches the police break down the door of his shack and drag his father off to prison for not having his papers in order. I use this in a talk on apartheid, but also with other biographies or with stories of outsiders and terror or the Holocaust.

The list can never be final—a fixed canon of the BEST. One of the pleasures of a good book discussion conference is that it shakes you out of your stereotypes. You discover that what "everyone" (that is, everyone you know) considers the best may not even be read in other places, and that others may be excited about things you've never heard of. At the moment, there's a strange debate raging in education and reading circles about whether students should read the classics *or* contemporary titles, Western Civilization *or* World Culture. At the same time, there's the age-old debate among YA librarians about our role as nurturer—whether our focus should be on the children or on the books we select for them. Why the absolutes? Why must it be either/or? In YA reading, it's not necessary to choose one or the other; it's not a question of *either* old *or* new, quality *or* popularity, the books *or* the kids.

Stephie Zvirin's bibliography of World War II fiction in the July *Booklist* includes classic and contemporary titles, American and World Cultures, YA and adult, stories of anguish and light escape reading. In the same way, you can talk about Brock Cole's recent novel *The Goats* in the context of all the enduring stories about young people adrift in the night—from Sue Ellen Bridgers's *Permanent Connections* and Danny Santiago's *Famous All Over Town* to Felice Holman's *Slake's Limbo* and Dickens's *Oliver Twist*.

Walter Dean Myers's splendid new novel *Fallen Angels*, about American teenagers fighting in Vietnam, is very close to Remarque's German World War I classic, *All Quiet on the Western Front*. Both books are about young boys sent to fight for a cause they know nothing about. Both are quiet, controlled, written in a series of stark episodes—highly dramatic for booktalking with terse, accessible scenes that communicate the teenagers' loss of innocence as they face terror and slaughter.

I was working as a YA librarian when an 8th grade social studies teacher made me read *All Quiet*. She was teaching a unit on early 20th century history and she wanted the class to read fiction about the time, to humanize the history. She asked me to do a bibliography and booktalk, and she wanted me to include *All Quiet*. I'd never read it—though I didn't dare tell her that—and I resisted her suggestion (I thought it might be either too dull, foreign, or difficult). But she persuaded me, and I did read it. We bought bright new paperbacks of the novel and promoted it, and many kids chose it and found it wonderful.

We all have books we're ashamed to say we haven't read, young adult and adult. It's hard to get back to them. If you missed the book when you were young and didn't read it at college or library school, and missed all the excitement when it first came out, and then you heard so much about it—how are you ever going to find the occasion to go back to it?

That's why we need more book discussion meetings, nationally and locally. They make you read and go back and reread and discover. Reading is a solitary activity. But always working alone can be limiting—you get rigid or dull—or complacent like Kendall Hailey. When a book excites you, when you talk about it, you share something of who you are. The vital stimulation we get from each other gets passed on to the young people we work with—the pleasure in particular titles, old and new, the power and excitement of reading lifelines.

Technostress:
Technology's Toll

by Sandra Champion

The end of the school year was only a month away. Arlene, a popular and skilled school librarian for 13 years, couldn't understand why she felt irritable, frustrated, and exhausted. The onslaught of last-minute demands to finish research papers, reports, and book reviews had lessened; inventory was well underway; the summer reading promotional materials were ready; seniors with outstanding library fines were paid up; the staff was winding down by talking about summer plans; and, for the first time, all the numerous end-of-the-year reports would be generated by the library's new automatic circulation system. The mood of everyone coming into the library was upbeat. Yet Arlene was uneasy. She couldn't figure out what was wrong with her.

Arlene couldn't help worrying about the reports which the machine now completely controlled. She was suffering from a modern malady—"technostress"—a term coined by Craig Brod and West St. John, coauthors of *Technostress: the Human Cost of the Computer Revolution* (Addison Wesley). Brod and St. John define it as "a modern disease of adaptation caused by an inability to cope with new technologies." Technostress threatens library media specialists by attacking their physical and psychological well-being. It affects one's intimate relationships, jobs, and mental health.

Each of us has something to gain by learning to recognize the symptoms of this modern disease. If we fail to manage our rising levels of stress, we will succumb to anxiety, tension, and/or mental fatigue. How we manage the rapid changes in technology—"technochange"—and what kind of leadership we provide in this area will have a profound impact on the future of the profession.

The Techno-epidemic

School librarians have been hit hard by a technostress epidemic. Massive exposure to information assault makes librarians extremely vulnerable. Virtually all operations in information management have undergone dramatic change due to technological innovation—automated circulation systems and inventory control, acquisitions via telecommunications, information retrieval systems, online catalogs and software for cataloging, networking, telefaxing, computer conferencing, electronic mail, data transfer, interactive television, distributed processing, even major publishing advances with CD-ROM. The speed with which these have been implemented is a major cause of technostress.

School librarians must learn all the computer applications for media management and, while they apply these applications and juggle newer technologies, they must also provide for changes in the curriculum. It is the role of the school librarian to ease technological change into the educational setting while, at the same time, continue to manage traditional programs.

If only *I* had eased technological change into *my* library! Instead—eager to explore the cutting edge of technology, and committed to providing my students and staff with opportunities provided by technology—I convinced my new princi-

---

Figure 1
Symptoms

Anxiety	Fear of losing autonomy
Denial	Fear of losing promotion opportunities
Resistance	Fear of losing control over work environment
Technophobia	Fear of social isolation
Panic	Fear of change
Conflict	Fear of loss of freedom, privacy, & control
Mental Fatigue	Fear that technology will increase illiteracy
Intolerance	Intimidation by documentation
Perfectionism	Fear of inability to keep up with rapid change
Physical discomforts	Problems with relationships

Figure 2
Technostressors (Causes)

Environmental
Inadequate wiring
Inadequate electrical outlets
Poor lighting
Lack of security for equipment
Uncomfortable work spaces
Incompatible equipment
Noisy equipment
Not enough equipment to meet demands
Frequent breakdowns
Lack of maintenance knowledge
Limited software
Lack of funding
Shortage of trained personnel
Accidental loss of data

Social
Conflictual relationships
Power struggles
Hierarchical shifts
Task & role change
Job insecurity
Job fragmentation

pal to install 25 computers in the library. He agreed after I reassured him that the access lab would be open, and busy, at all times. I then had four computers installed in the library's work room so that teachers could learn what their students had already mastered—how to use them. In addition, that year the administration asked me to pilot a new automated circulation system which, I later learned, would not accommodate our large collection.

Looking back, I'd do it all over again. The greater opportunities available in the lab resulted in triple attendance, dramatically challenging our philosophy, priorities and policies—and changing not only the spirit of media services, but ourselves. Make no mistake, changing oneself is what the information age is all about. It's not about machines, programs, cables, fiber optics, networks, packet switches, laser discs, or telecommunications. It's about one's own personal response to "technochange."

Technosymptoms

In an effort to understand and cope with technostress, I run periodic inservice workshops on managing technostress. I also manage a computer lab for teachers (separate from the students' lab) for those adults who want to learn how to use computers and how to integrate them into the curriculum.

Results of my surveys, workshops, and observations over the past three years reveal that different kinds of technostress manifest themselves at different stages of involvement with new technologies. I also have observed that the majority of school librarians feel that they already have enough to do and

should not have to take on the additional responsibility of retraining to understand how to apply microcomputers to media center activities. Most feel angry that new computer-based management systems have been forced on them and they must learn on the job while conducting regular library programs.

This practice of "maintaining while training" fuels symptoms of technostress. Yet as technological advancements lead to a redefinition of the role of school librarians, they also give them an opportunity to take a leadership role in instructional design and teaching. The operation and storage of the technology is all under the care of the school librarian, who is responsible for creatively interlinking the technology so it best serves the learning needs of individual students. School librarians will find that knowing the software and hardware markets will help maintain their traditional leadership role in curriculum design.

Obviously, the very nature of our job is stressful. In all of the workshops and in all of my informal discussions with school librarians, every professional disclosed, without exception, a problem that created degrees of technostress. Although technostress is an individual response, I find four general personality profiles dominate school media specialists' collective response to technology. Each of the general personality types, listed below, have exhibited behaviors that produce technostress signs and symptoms listed in Figure 1:

(1) The resistor: denies the new; values the old.
(2) The experimentor: tries new ideas scientifically.
(3) The lover: tries anything new; loves everything new.
(4) The manager: thinks, plans, chooses selectively.

First, the causes (called technostressors) are different for every professional; individual responses are also different. Each person must analyze environmental factors, attitudes, behavior, and what control may be exerted over them. We must then identify technostressors, determine how they may be controlled, examine our responses to each technostressor and, wherever appropriate, we must reconstruct our individual responses.

Managing Stress

I will highlight a number of skills required to manage both change and conflict. Effective management reduces technostress—and therefore, increases pleasure—in one's work. If you, as the manager, believe change and conflict are opportunities, you will be able to convince others to think this way also. (Of course, this will take time and persuasion.)

The first step in management is to meet the challenge of technology head on, not deny that computers are a part of the library profession. Our job has changed in the last decade, and it is time to change with it. Those who resist change and persist in following the same, now-outmoded procedures will be eliminated by the advent of technology; job descriptions will be rewritten as more and more technology becomes implemented. Understandably, a librarian who has been practicing management skills with expertise for a number of years will not readily assume another angle of vision toward his or her job performance. The long established organization of the

Figure 3
Attitudes Toward New Technologies

Responses	Translation
"Computers are just a fad."	I am uneasy about computers.
"We've always done things this way."	I am afraid of changes
"I run things around here."	I'm losing control.
"Computers are my enemy."	I'm going to lose my job.
"Computers cause more work."	I'm already working too hard.
"The technology keeps changing."	I can't keep up with change.
"I know this job better than anyone."	The computer knows more than I do.
"My experience makes me invaluable."	My experience means nothing now.
"I'm in control of my environment."	Electronic environment controls me.
"Computers are just tools."	The old way is easier.

work place, often informal, changes dramatically when technology takes over fundamental library operations. What once was for the most part, an invisible, undocumented power structure no longer exists. Knowledge of the technology is the key to power; power and control, once exclusively in the hands of a selected few, filters down to those receptive to change.

Secondly, focus on the person, not on the machine. Much of the power of the workplace has shifted to computer software. For a while, in a strategic move to either survive in one's position or to avoid a takeover of job responsibilities, an information manager becomes machine-centered. Once this happens, other people in the work situation suffer. Additionally, the informal day-to-day behavior that determines the communication, productivity, and success of operations is dramatically altered by a manager's need to respond to a machine instead of to people who need responses. The manager's focus on matters of the machine results in less communication with others. Some employees feel abandoned; others detect indifference on the part of the manager.

Third, you must devise a strategic management plan. As stated before, the best way to deal with technostress is effective management—and effective management begins with the age-old art of thinking. Thinking about change and thinking about what raw data means and how it can be used is a primary responsibility for every information manager. The aim of technology is to solve human problems and to improve the quality of our lives. At the same time, however, with each new solution an entirely different set of problems emerges and, for a while, the quality of our life seems threatened.

Fourth, three fundamental stages to successful technostress management must be considered in adapting to change: (1) How one *perceives* technochange and how one *interprets* it; (2) how one *feels* about technochange; and (3) how one *copes* with technochange. The information manager must also be a technostress manager. Failure to recognize that every change imposed by new technology generates varying degrees of technostress automatically results in the failure to effectively manage change. To succeed, the information manager has to recognize that technology will, by its nature, result in changes in (1) the environment; (2) relationships; (3) self-imposed

Figure 4
Behavioral Tendencies (Effects of Change)

External	Internal
Lose data due to carelessness.	Panic
Purchase poor software and/or hardware.	Fear of being found out.
Criticize everything about your work.	Anxiety.
Expect perfection of self and others.	Fear of failure.
Demand instant results.	Frequent mistakes.
Interrupt long conversations.	Tension (tight muscles).
Depend on the computer.	Fatigue
Decrease time spent with people.	Feeling of alienation.
Increase time talking about computers.	Unexplained sweats.
Develop problems with relationships.	Confusion
Gain weight sitting at the computer.	Back pain.
Talk compulsively about computers.	Neck pain, eyestrain.
Think about sabotage.	Anger.

emotional pressure; (4) the power structure; and (5) the role of the school media specialist.

Fifth, the staff should become a high-tech/high-touch team to create a sense of involvement and establish mutual goals. No one can understand all of the technologies at once. Approaching change with group support can be an adventure as well as a great reducer of technostress.

Sixth, experienced computer users complain about dense documentation all the time, so don't let documentation discourage you. Try to solve problems with the help of staff; talk to other users about their solutions; send a key staff member to a demonstration of the computer; call for technical support. You can avoid problems and save yourself hours of frustration by calling for help when you need advice.

Seventh, be alert to technostressors in your environment so that you can readily identify them. These change as your expertise grows and as new problems emerge. As stated, you must examine your responses to the technostressors and then try to manage the ones over which you have control.

Eighth, get support from the computer enthusiasts in your school and users in the community. A support system is important for both professional and personal growth. Sharing problems often leads to creating solutions. It is reassuring to know.

Actual Technostress Victims

Carla, a 32-year-old high school librarian, armed with strong recommendations, an advanced degree in library science, and a successful track record for the past ten years, made the final round in interviews for a coveted position as head of media services in a school only ten minutes from her home. Feeling that the dream job in a beautiful library was hers, she was floored when she learned the district had hired someone else—someone with a degree in computer education, not in library science.

Bernice, a 48-year-old elementary school librarian, was determined to automate her new library. Still remembering her failure to successfully automate another collection, she was determined to avoid mistakes made the first time. First, using some of her limited funds, she purchased a highly recommended circulation system for an Apple computer. She spent the rest of the money on a commercial service that would undertake the data entry project. After months of painstaking care to make the shelf list accurate, she mailed it to the company and left on a well-earned summer vacation. Upon her return, Bernice was greeted by a new principal, who told her that he had purchased a beautiful IBM for the library and, since he had been so generous, he didn't want to hear any more requests for money. Bernice realized she would have to tell the principal that she had spent thousands of dollars already for the software and for data entry designed specifically for the Apple.

Pressured from the district to purchase an index on CD-ROM, Eugene, a 40-year-old high school librarian, decided it was time to hop on the high-tech bandwagon. Reluctantly, he cancelled the traditional print index to magazines, invested $2000 for a subscription to CD-ROM, promoted it, and surrendered valuable space to accommodate accompanying hardware. He then waited for the highly touted CD-ROM player to arrive—and waited for ten months. Meanwhile, frustrated teachers delayed assigning required research reports to students. Eugene eventually discovered that some administrator, deep in the bureaucracy, had challenged the price of the CD-ROM players and demanded that three competitive bids be submitted, delaying the purchase of hardware while three bids were submitted. Bureaucratic efforts to save money also resulted in loss: ten other schools spent a total of $20,000 for laser discs they couldn't use because they had not received the CD-ROM players. (In the end, the district only saved a sum total of $50 on the players.)

Carla, a seasoned librarian who was always on the lookout for improvement in standard procedures, eagerly ordered a scanner after she was promised that her inventory time could be cut by two-thirds if she purchased a portable, hand-held scanner which would rapidly download the information to the main circulation system. She used the last of her library fine money to do so. Another librarian, who agreed with her decision, assured Carla that she had bought a remarkable, incredibly simple-to-use timesaver. But, when it arrived, Carla could not get this miracle device to work! After two months of troubleshooting, the problem was finally uncovered. Although the dip switches were set according to specifications in the manual, they were reversed at the factory when they were positioned on the interface card.

John, an elementary school librarian, was known throughout his district as a masterful storyteller. Caught up in the excitement of stories, John often ran out of time during scheduled classes so he allowed students to check out books by signing their names and the book's barcode number on a legal pad. He found it easier and faster than using the automated system installed by the district. Although books circulated and were returned on time, the circulation statistics generated by the automatic system showed that books were not circulating. The next year, John was transferred to the district's technical services department.

Emerging Technologies
A Roadmap for Librarians

by Marlyn Kemper

They're faster, newer, better. Featuring abbreviations and acronyms that are filtering into everyday language, e-mail (electronic mail), DTP (Desktop Publishing), LANs (Local Area Networks), and fax (facsimile or telefacsimile) have been dubbed the hottest advances on the digital landscape. The introduction into the marketplace of these new computer communications, technologies, electronic publishing products, and information delivery systems has brought about a corresponding wave of advertising hype, press coverage, and a profusion of announcements claiming each new technological breakthrough the most significant yet. Every device promises to be more sophisticated, simpler to use, and less expensive than any other.

The challenge, for library practitioners, is to establish these dynamic, innovative, and exciting technologies as central contributors to productivity in the library setting. Unfortunately, these sweeping changes are engendering great confusion, which stems from having to evaluate a huge array of new commercial offerings and technological "solutions." It's a rough world out there for anyone attempting to make an educated buying decision.

I recently conducted a telephone survey with randomly selected public library systems across the country in order to find out how some of the larger systems were handling the new technologies (see list of libraries, Figure 1). Although glitches in software applications, hardware, and user training programs had cropped up periodically, I found that, on balance, users are reasonably pleased with their acquisitions and/or plans for future action. Other topics covered in the survey, such as projected use, availability, selection, and applications of the four technologies are presented in a descriptive format throughout this article.

Among the library systems queried, implementation of innovative technologies was not geared toward enhancement of services for any specific client population. While youth services librarians could employ leading edge technologies to enhance on-the-job productivity, staff specialists generally were assigned the control, maintenance, operation, and integration of these technologies into the fabric of the library environment. Still, though monetary constraints make using these new services something of an impossible dream for many youth services librarians, awareness of the array of projects underway and on the drawing board will enable them to more critically appraise and assess what role these products and services can play in their organizations.

Electronic Mail (E-Mail)

Electronic mail (e-mail) involves the electronic transmission of textual and graphic information. While electronic message transmission can involve many technologies including fax, voice, and mailgram, in recent years electronic mail has been associated with the transfer of messages between users of networked computers. A popular alternative to conventional delivery services, electronic mail results in rapid information exchange and turnaround. Within the library setting, electronic mail can be used for special applications such as time sensitive messages; memos and reminders; longer text projects including budgets, reports, manuals, policies, and documents; and business transactions including invoices and purchase orders.

Twelve of the 17 participants in the telephone survey have the capability for e-mail transmission. The Atlanta Public Library and Chicago Public Library have e-mail capabilities available on circulation systems. The Boston Public Library has e-mail functions associated with the cataloging system. The Denver Public Library, a member of CARL (Colorado Alliance of Research Libraries), a multitype academic and public library cooperative, has e-mail as a result of participation in that network. The Cuyahoga County Public Library, Hennepin County Library, and Broward County Library have e-mail capabilities that are available on inhouse networked computers or through outside linkage to municipal or county government agencies.

E-mail messages can be sent by telephone lines, coaxial cable, and satellite links. Instant message delivery, quicker message/reply turnaround time, flexibility, elimination of time-zone problems, and increased communications efficiency (a reduction in "telephone tag," the game in which a series of calls go unanswered as each destination person is away from the desk or out of the building), all make e-mail advantageous.

In order to use electronic mail as well as other emerging technologies effectively, the youth services librarian should know what users are doing currently and the way in which new tools can assist them in becoming more effective in their work environment. Those computer-based messaging systems used to handle electronic mail can be applied in the following areas:

- Document creation and maintenance. With e-mail, electronic documents can be created, formatted, edited,

Figure 1
Public Libraries Surveyed, Spring 1988

Atlanta (GA) Public Library
Electronic mail (e-mail) operational; Desktop Publishing (DTP), Local Access Network (LAN), Telefacsimile (fax) planned

Baltimore (MD) County Public Library
E-mail, DTP, fax planned

Boston (MA) Public Library
E-mail, LAN, fax operational; DTP planned

Broward County (FL) Library
E-mail, DTP, LAN, fax operational

Chicago (IL) Public Library
E-mail, LAN operational; DTP, fax planned

Cuyahoga County (OH) Public Library
E-mail, DTP, LAN operational; fax planned

Dallas (TX) Public Library
E-mail, DTP, fax operational

Denver (CO) Public Library
E-mail, DTP, LAN, fax operational

Free Library of Philadelphia
E-mail, fax operational; DTP planned

Hennepin County (MN) Library
E-mail, DTP, LAN operational; fax planned

Miami-Dade (FL) Public Library
Fax operational; e-mail, DTP planned

Orange County (FL) Library System
E-mail, LAN operational; fax planned

San Antonio (TX) Public Library
E-mail, DTP operational

San Diego (CA) Public Library
E-mail operational

San Francisco (CA) Public Library
DTP operational; e-mail, fax planned

Tampa-Hillsborough County (FL) Public Library
Fax operational; DTP, LAN planned

Tulsa City-County (OK) Library System
Fax operational

---

printed, filed, and searched and can take a wide range of information formats including data, graphics, voice, and video.

- Decision-making. Analysis, presentation, and retrieval of data from files throughout the library can be used for the formation of inhouse policies and guidelines.
- Personnel productivity. Through the storage and manipulation of e-mail data, tickler files that provide reminders to the user (i.e., indicating that a report is due on a certain date), calendars, and to-do lists can be constructed to enhance staff effectiveness on the job.
- Organizational communication. Everyday tasks can be accomplished effectively through sending a document or message.

Within the electronic mail network, a computer provides a broad array of capabilities including:

- An electronic mailbox. Recipients do not have to be present in an e-mail environment, since all messages are collected in the user's electronic mailbox and can be scanned at their convenience. An electronic wastebasket supplies recipients with the ability to purge a message from the system.
- Text retrieval and preparation. In an e-mail system, the sender, with the aid of text editing capabilities, can alter a message before it is sent to a recipient or transmit a document originally written in a word processor environment.
- Distribution lists. Lists of recipients for specialized distribution can be maintained, thereby enabling individuals to be sent messages in their areas of interest.

- Communication acknowledgment. The sender can be provided with confirmation that the message has been sent and received by the recipient. Generally, the e-mail system has the capability to store a message for delivery at a specified time in the future.
- Management tracking. Messages can be tracked in an e-mail system since the computer can be programmed to keep data on the time the message was sent and the number of characters contained in the message. Reports can be generated indicating the total number of messages sent within a particular timeframe.
- Filing functions. Messages sent by e-mail can be stored and retrieved for work enhancement.
- Security. System security based on the use of encryption and passwords ensures that only those recipients who should have access to messages do in fact read them.
- Message disposal. Users of e-mail systems can have the option of discarding a message, saving the message, leaving the message in a mailbox, or adding a note to the message prior to rerouting it to other recipients.
- Ease of use. Systems are simple even to the unsophisticated user.

Desktop Publishing (DTP)

One of today's most exciting microcomputer topics is desktop publishing (DTP). Desktop publishing involves creating, editing, and arranging text electronically through the use of a personal computer or a workstation that enables the user to import or enter text and graphics on a monitor, rearrange and edit the different elements, and ultimately print them out on a dot matrix or laser printer. Scanners capable of converting photographs and drawings into digitally stored images that can then be incorporated into the document are increasingly popular desktop publishing peripherals.

An entire desktop publishing configuration calls for the following components:

- Personal computer or workstation. Because of the storage requirements of most desktop publishing software, the user generally needs at least a personal computer with a hard disc. If many graphics are to be used and a large volume of pages published, the square wafer of silicon known as the 80386 microprocessor chip (which places minicomputer potential at the personal computer user's fingertips) is recommended.
- Special monitor. The resemblance of the screen image to the printed page reflects the monitor's resolution capabilities.
- Input devices. A mouse or scanner can be used for bringing line art, existing logos, and photographs online.
- Output devices such as laser printers.
- Software packages. Generally, the PC packages include a WYSIWYG ("What You See Is What You Get") display on which the user can view and make adjustments in page format, character spacing, and font size. The user also has the capability to import graphics and text created in other programs, integrate these texts and graphics into a single document, and print the output on a high resolution laser printer.

Recognizing that compatibility conflicts can be generated because of the volume of hardware required for a desktop publishing system, hardware manufacturers are now bundling composition packages with their equipment to create complete desktop publishing solutions.

Tasks that can be accomplished effectively in a desktop publishing environment include:

- Formatting or document appearance. Desktop publishing programs enable users to specify page layout, set a piece of text in a certain font, float text around an image, employ sophisticated automatic hyphenation and justification, and kern (or fine-tune) the spacing between letters and words.
- Text editing and graphics design. Special features include writing and style verification, bibliographic citation placement, spell checking, creation of cross references and indexes, automatic page numbering and table of contents generation, incorporation of scanned graphics, and precise control over the placement of elements such as the location of multiple fonts in multiple sizes anywhere on the page.
- Interfaces. New systems (including Bestinfo's Document Manager System, Ultimate from Composition Technologies, and Archetype Designer from Archetype) allow networked users to transfer files back and forth.

A document's information content is more than the text and graphics that it contains. The way in which information is presented is frequently just as important as what is stated. It is at this junction that desktop publishing technologies are having significant impact. The capability to manipulate text without having to rekey it has dramatically changed the way documents are created and disseminated.

In the desktop publishing environment, graphics and images can be scanned into the computer; textual material can be captured as keystrokes and stored. Pages are laid out employing the computer's memory instead of scissors, paper, and glue. (For this reason interactive systems that display something resembling the printed page on the computer's monitor are the most effective systems.) With electronic publishing, a document can be typeset at a cost equal to that of a text-only typewritten document.

Fourteen of the 17 public libraries surveyed intend to use desktop publishing for generating bookmarks, catalogs, booklets, newsletters, press releases, community announcements, pamphlets, calendars of events, and materials for formal and informal presentations.

PC-based publishing tools enable youth services librarians to save money and time once needed for cutting and pasting documents together by hand and sending printing jobs to professional typesetters. The appeal of control over document production and the publishing process by one individual, generally the author, has contributed to the emergence of desktop publishing as this year's catch phrase.

Local Area Networks (LANs)

A combination of evolving technologies, economic circumstances, and the need to improve access to decision-making data has led to the utilization of local area networks (LANs) as cost effective solutions for optimizing information interchange. LANs involve the interconnection of a wide range of equipment, either within a single building, or among a number of buildings within a limited radius, such as a university campus.

Local area networking is a relatively new phenomenon, and presently no single universally accepted definition of LAN exists. Nonetheless, a few general concepts help to clarify matters. A LAN is a prviately owned, user-administered communications facility extending over a limited geographic area (generally not exceeding 10 kilometers). Typically operating at a very high speed ranging up to 10M bps, a LAN can be customized to support many types of equipment. A LAN acts as the high technology glue for binding together terminals, printers, fax units, microcomputers, modems, e-mail, licensed software, and voice and video functions.

In designing a LAN, one should consider the overall network architecture including conformity to international standards, as well as several basic technical concerns, including the network's physical medium and transmission technique; its topology, or the logical arrangement of its stations; and its access method, or the way it arbitrates among its stations for the use of the shared medium.

- Technical concerns. Three media are presently practical in terms of cost and performance: twisted copper wire, coaxial cable, and optical fiber. There are the same number of basic LAN topologies: bus, in which stations

Figure 2
Steps for ET Deployment

Problem definition.
1. Determine existing needs or potential deficiencies.
2. Identify types of emerging technologies (ETs) and assess suitability in supporting applications.
3. Provide initial answers to the following questions:
What are the costs involved?
How will the ETs be integrated into the existing environment?
What are the human and nonhuman resources needed to support the ETs?
4. Discuss goals and objectives.

Feasibility study. The feasibility study is designed to establish with greater accuracy, precision, and certainty the potential of the project and its likelihood of success. Types of questions that should be considered by the youth services librarian are included in the checklist that follows:
1. Can total costs, including equipment, facilities, and materials for the new technology, be determined?
2. Can total delivery costs for the proposed ET, including acquisition, hardware, and maintenance costs, be determined?
3. Will utilization of the ET culminate in annual savings over existing systems?
4. Are personnel skilled in implementing, operating, and maintaining the ET available?
5. Are administrators with the necessary expertise on hand to manage and supervise ET activities?
6. Are patrons and staff likely to be supportive of the ET?
7. Do key decision-makers display a positive attitude toward the ET?
8. Is support for use of the ET widespread or confined to a few individuals?
9. Are staff and administrative expectations concerning benefits of the ET reasonable?
10. Is the organizational structure flexible enough to deal with the disruption triggered by the installation and testing of the ET?
11. Is there a formal mechanism for handling procedural or policy modifications necessary to accommodate changes triggered by the ET?
12. Is there a designated authority, who has responsibility for implementing, maintaining, and operating the ET?

On the basis of the feasibility study, a determination is made to implement the new technology or discontinue the investigation. A report can be presented to management detailing such factors as developmental costs; dollar resources needed; recurring costs; equipment, space, and personnel required; anticipated outcomes of the project; expected problems and limitations; organizational and personnel changes; and benefits.

Definition, design & implementation. A narrative description of the work to be achieved is prepared, including:
1. Project objectives
2. Funding constraints
3. Implementation schedule (startup date, end date, and major milestones)

Implementation is a testing and standardization effort so that operations can proceed smoothly. Steps include:
1. Verification of specifications
2. Final preparation of procedural reports and policy
3. Creation of plans to operationally support the ET
4. Identification and management of resources needed to facilitate installation.

Conversion & evaluation. Modifications may be minor, involving only maintenance, or major, such as a call for redesign and redevelopment. Once conversion has taken place, the ET can be evaluated in terms of the following criteria:
1. Reliability
2. User perception of quality and service
3. Frequency of discrepancies or errors
4. Software and hardware performance
5. Vendor support

Staff training & development. Investing in a new technology does not guarantee successful operation. A new technology disturbs and changes an environment, triggering stress and discontinuity. The following can spur acceptance:
1. Assign clearcut, relevant job responsibilities
2. Involve personnel responsible for implementation in the decision-making process
3. Reassure staff by supplying up-to-date and pertinent information

are arrayed along a single length of cable; ring, in which stations form a closed circle; and star, in which a central node connects to each station and all communications between one station and another station pass through the central node. The techniques by which the network allocates transmission rights among its participating stations is known as the network's access method—its mechanism for controlling traffic. Generally, access control can be centralized (in which terminals are polled in sequence for their transmissions), or distributed (in which each station participates in controlling the LAN equally).

- Network architecture. The exact definition of functions that a computer network and its components perform is its architecture. Explosive LAN development has been accompanied by a strong market pull toward an open network architecture requiring equipment vendors to follow generally agreed upon standards, thereby enabling end users to mix and match network equipment. This movement toward standardization has culminated in the development by the International Standard Organization (ISO), of OSI (Open Systems Interconnection) Reference Model. The OSI Reference Model provides a basis for interlinking dissimilar systems to facilitate information exchange.

Nine of the 17 participants in the telephone survey that have installed or are planning to implement a LAN consider the LAN a useful tool for supporting a variety of applications including circulation control, word processing, cataloging, OPAC display, electronic mail, and file transfer.

The Boston Public Library has implemented a small-scale Novell-S(tar) LAN to streamline administrative tasks. The Chicago Public Library's LAN (also small-scale) is located in the Computer Assistance Reference Center. The Cuyahoga County Public Library has a small-scale LAN operational as part of its Hewlett Packard System and also participates in a large-scale LAN through membership in Cleve-Net, a metropolitan area network.

The Broward County Library and Miami-Dade Public Library are members of SEFLIN, the SouthEast Florida Library Information Network. SEFLIN, a multitype library consortium serving the 3.2 million residents in Florida's Dade, Broward and Palm Beach Counties, is presently exploring the possibilities for creating an extended LAN to provide a communications framework for resource and data sharing among multiple hosts and devices in a heterogeneous communications, computing, and applications environment. In creating this extended LAN, key objectives include low-cost, high-quality transmission capacity for expansion at small incremental costs, and technical capability for supporting emerging and changing service demands.

With its ability to incorporate diverse functions, a LAN supplies a framework for strategically implementing applications involved in institutional planning, growth, and development. The capability for linking incompatible software and hardware systems easily and quickly is a powerful mechanism for connecting resources between all sectors of the information community.

Through a LAN, messaging, resource sharing, and storage and delivery of decision-making data are expedited, thereby enhancing the user's access to accurate and timely information as well as the ability to communicate effectively with others inside and outside the organization.

The advantages of linking systems through extended LANs are that each library can select the best available system for each function, individual libraries are not tied to one vendor or source, and the interaction among functions is kept to a minimum so that the performance of one function does not affect another. The need to share processing and information resources knows no bounds. Extended LANs make it possible for libraries to exchange time critical information, schedule group events, and work together to perform resource sharing tasks to enhance the range of services provided to the patron base.

Facts on Fax

With its capability for transmitting graphic and alphanumeric data within an institution, among buildings on a campus, or to distant sites across private transmission links, telephone lines, microwave relay channels, and satellite, facsimile is one area of technological advance that has already had a profound impact on libraries and will continue to affect library activities even more in the future. Facsimile is one of the oldest image-oriented message transmission technologies. The terms facsimile, fax, and telefacsimile are used interchangeably.

Facsimile technology has great potential for a wide range of library applications including document delivery and message transfer. For most types of documents, fax output quality is now excellent. High resolution systems can reproduce legibly the small type fonts found in journal articles, government publications, and research reports.

A stand-alone fax machine becomes operational once it is connected to a telephone line. Fax functions by scanning a page and transforming text and graphics into dots per inch (dpi). These lines are subsequently converted into tones of differing frequency so that they may be sent via a communications line and subsequently retrieved to reestablish the original signal by another fax unit. Generally, the communications line is the public telephone network. Upon receipt by the fax machine, the tones are translated to dots per inch on paper generally through a thermal printing process, thereby resulting in practically instantaneous transmission of a page from one locale to another.

Facsimile technology is characterized not only by its speed, but by:

- Easy installation. A fax machine can be placed wherever a telephone outlet and power are available.
- Input flexibility. Maps, photographs, sketches, charts, and text can be retrieved and transmitted.
- Minimal message preparation costs. Messages need not be rekeyed for transmission by fax.
- Operational simplicity. Following a brief instruction session, a fax device can be used by paraprofessional and professional staff. Generally, fax calls for only as much of the user's attention as is necessary to insert the document.

All but two of the 17 public libraries surveyed have purchased a fax or are considering fax implementation. The use of telefacsimiles facilitates resource sharing, improves timeliness of document delivery, provides access to other libraries by mitigating the handicap of distance, and offsets inflation or lower operating costs by shared use of collections and staff expertise.

The Atlanta Public Library drew up plans for fax units to link the convention site with the Central Library for the 1988 Democratic National Convention. The Baltimore County Public Library, meanwhile, has designed a proposal for Project RFD (Rural Facts Delivery), a project which will enable the 19,738 residents of rural north Baltimore County to access information resources beyond the limitations of a collection of 6,000 catalogued volumes by utilizing onsite and remote electronic resources such as fax units, desk top copiers, CD-ROM, and workstations. Target clientele for this project, which has the support of the school system and local community groups, include local high school students and area farmers.

Another project developed by the Baltimore County Public Library, Project Tristar, will use fax and electronic mail in five library branches, four Baltimore County public middle schools, and four high schools to facilitate a timely exchange of information about school assignments. Teachers will be encouraged to supply assignment-related information two weeks in advance of each due date. This material will be faxed or e-mailed by the school librarians to the appropriate library branches. To facilitate long range planning, the school system will provide lists of curriculum topics to the Baltimore County Public Library's information and programming office. Fax and e-mail will be further used to communicate information on meetings and inservice workshops. By June 1989 students should be able to use electronic resources routinely to locate previously inaccessible bibliographic material and full text information appropriate to their information needs.

The combination of enhanced service and monetary savings makes fax a valuable asset. Fax units now have phone dialing features and computer memory, and in addition to getting less expensive, smaller, and faster, fax units can now be linked up on networks (standards permit rival brands to communicate rapidly).

Advances in electronic circuitry and microprocessor technology have allowed vendors to place much of the functions of stand-alone fax machines on a single board that can be plugged into a personal computer. Declining prices and a slide-in circuit known as a PC fax board for desktop personal computers have triggered the emergence of the personal fax era.

Fax development responded to users' demands for greater transmission speed and capacity. Advantages of using fax in the library environment include enhanced reliability, faster response time, better supported facilities, and internetworking capabilities for multiple remote locations.

With more and more materials becoming available and the costs of operations skyrocketing, youth services librarians have to come to terms with the fact that because of a lack of funds, any semblance of self-sufficiency has become an impossibility. As a consequence, fax-based networks will play an expanding role in facilitating data exchange.

Preparing for Tomorrow

There are many and varied benefits of these technological tools, including reduced costs, enhanced job performance, improved utilization of materials, more effective resource allocation to handle unexpected increase in demand, and end user satisfaction. The creative use of these technologies can make the volume of knowledge, which yearly grows exponentially, more manageable, thereby benefiting both the institution and all its clientele.

As indicated in Figure 2, the "Strategic Management Plan," new services based on the deployment of emerging technologies require careful planning before full-scale implementation. Successful project management calls for using strategic planning techniques for dealing with human-machine interface considerations, operation and management, and policies and procedures.

Planning for staff training is a key element in the deployment process, a major mechanism for ensuring a successful program. Benefits of an effective training program include increased output and creation of a more positive work environment, thereby leading to enhanced library services. The right combination of aid and support encourages youth services librarians to expand and explore the application potentials available in new technologies.

A Selected Bibliography

Black, Uyless D. *Data Communications and Distributed Networks.* Second Edition. Englewood Cliffs, New Jersey: Prentice-Hall, Inc., 1987.

Goldberg, Cheryl J. "Desktop Publishing's Inexpensive Upstarts." *PC Magazine* 7 (April 12, 1988): 92-125.

Johnson, Jeff and Beach, Richard J. "Styles in Document Editing Systems." *IEEE Computer* 21 (January 1988): 32-43.

Kemper, Marlyn. *Networking: Choosing a LAN Path to Interconnection.* Metuchen, New Jersey and London: Scarecrow Press, 1987.

———. "Local Area Networking: The Management Problem." In *The Library Microcomputer Environment: Management Issues,* pp. 187-206. Edited by S. S. Intner and J. A. Hannigan. Phoenix, Arizona: Oryx Press, 1988.

Ryan, Donald J. "Making Sense of Today's Image Communications Alternatives." *Data Communications* 16 (April 1987): 110-115.

Stanton, Tom; Burns, Diane; and Venit, S. "Page-to-Disk Technology: Nine State-of-the-Art Scanners." *PC Magazine* 5 (September 30, 1986): 128-177.

Vallee, Jacques. *Computer Message Systems.* New York, New York: McGraw-Hill Publications Company, 1984.

Wiener, Hesh and Houck, Vicki. "Facsimile Networking with Personal Computers: A Shopper's Guide." *Data Communications* 17 (March 1988): 130-145.

Mass Market Books:
Their Place in the Library

by Barbara A. Genco

Sesame Street, Who Framed Roger Rabbit? The Berenstain Bears. Nancy Drew. Sweet Valley High. Librarians today are faced with tough choices in book selection. How can we balance the pressures of mass culture against our goals for appropriate library collections? As major purchasers of books, do we merely succumb? Do we welcome these books uncritically or do we bar the door against the encroachment of mass culture, as damaging and threatening to "good books." Can "good" and "bad" books coexist within a public library children's room?

Library administrators often make veiled and direct references to circulation figures. Parents ask for the books that their kids see in K Mart. First graders clamor for the newest "Berenstain Bears" entry, while pre-teen girls cluster around the "Sweet Valley High" books, swapping favorites. Do these specters fill us with dread? Do we see ourselves and our rooms as the last bastions of pure, quality reading choices for kids? Must we continue to try desperately to keep that unruly monster, mass culture at bay?

As book selectors and experience balancers of meager children's room budgets, how can we begin to approach the selection issues raised by these commercial and often highly successful and popular products?

One approach is to consider these items as separate genres unto themselves and then apply conventional selection goals. In the classic introductory text *Children and Books*, 5th edition (Scott Foresman, 1977) (the needs are expressed a bit differently in subsequent editions), Sutherland and Arbuthnot address Maslow's hierarchy of needs and explore how many of these needs can be met through books and reading. These same criteria can be applied to series and mass market books.

The Need for Security

Preschoolers' lives are intertwined with the extended family of *Sesame Street*. Its characters, like those of the Berenstain Bears and other mass market series, are familiar friends. American children have experienced the death of Mr. Hooper, Susan and Gordon's adoption of a baby, and consider the problem of "strangers" with Brother and Sister Bear.

The Need to Belong

What is mass marketed material if not *mass*? It is a great leveler. Most children, despite their differences in ethnicity or reading levels, have at least a tangential awareness of *Sesame Street*, Charlie Brown, *Star Wars*. This ties them together—they share this enthusiasm and knowledge. This is the Children's Culture.

The Need to Love and Be Loved

Tied into security, love and acceptance are plot elements in a number of these items—especially early childhood or younger elementary materials. *Sesame Street* and Mr. Rogers' books deal with love, friendship, and families. Even "Sweet Dreams" books address pre-adolescent longings for love and relationships.

The Need to Achieve

Many of these "supermarket" books deal with issues of accomplishment—even if it is something as seemingly pedestrian as tying a shoe or attaining bladder control. Certainly much of the appeal of a "Hardy Boys" or "Nancy Drew" book is the idea of the child—rather than the powerful adult—solving the mystery.

Play: the Need for Change

Reading can be the ultimate great escape. Examine your own reading habits. Many of us often select genre fiction, be it fantasy, regency, gothic, mystery, or even bodice ripper. Supermarket books can often provide the pleasure of relaxation, release. Nancy Drew, the Hardy Boys, "Sweet Valley High"—these are genre fiction, and if, IF, they meet basic criteria for appropriateness, they can be selected and offered to children.

Need for Aesthetic Satisfaction

True, many of these books are not beautiful by librarian standards, and they do not provide a highly vaunted aesthetic experience. In fact, they are often singularly ugly. However, because these supermarket books are cheap, accessible, and readily available, they are in many American homes. There is a certain thrill for many children (non-readers, reluctant readers, and even gifted) when they see a familiar book from the home library as part of a public library collection. In the case of pre-schoolers especially, there is also an element of object identification.

To further bolster my defense of these icons of popular culture, let me refer to an article by Peter Dickinson that appeared in *Children and Literature: Views and Reviews*, a collection edited by Virginia Haviland. Dickinson's article is titled "A Defense of Rubbish."

> I have always believed that children ought to be allowed to read a certain amount of rubbish. Sometimes quite a high proportion of their reading matter can healthfully consist of things that no sane adult would actually encourage them to read. . . . By rubbish I mean all forms of reading matter which contain to the adult eye no visible value, either aesthetic or educational.

Dickinson believes that the child should be given the "whole culture" and feels that a child has need of shared experience in that culture. While acknowledging the importance of each child's individuality, Dickinson states that a child "must not . . . feel that he is somehow set apart." He notes the importance of children "discovering things for themselves . . . This can only be done by random sampling on the part of children, and it is inevitable that a high portion of what they read will be rubbish . . . But in the process they will learn the art of comparison and subconsciously discover critical standards." Finally he asserts that children's needs for security and reassurance can be met by "rubbish": "One can often tell how happy or insecure a child is feeling simply by what he is reading. And sometimes he may need to reread something well known but which makes absolutely no intellectual or emotional demand."

I too am a believer that the cultural smorgasbord should be laid out before children. Nutritionists today tell parents to offer their children a wide variety of foods at the table. They counsel that over time a child will select a well balanced diet. I believe that if "supermarket" books are presented to children on an equal basis with "good" books, the "good" will drive out the "bad" in a child's reading experience.

It's given that certain types of books will circulate heavily—but in most cases they are filler, and in some cases, cultural junk food. But how else can we help children develop taste and discrimination? I know that many librarians believe strongly in NO JUNK. As a parent, I have met children who are denied junk food entirely. When offered an unsupervised choice between junk and "real" food, they will most often choose junk.

If you decide to open the door to popular materials in the children's room, will that door widen so that the collection grows out of control? Will it erode selection criteria so far that anything goes? How much responsibility do librarians have to the child, the parent, the community, the collection? And can they live with the selection decisions they have made?

In the Brooklyn Public Library, we consider these books for purchase. We see them as supplemental, high-interest ephemera. We see them as particularly useful in interesting and encouraging library use by children and families. We want our kids to be readers and library users. We want them to associate us with a positive experience. The inclusion of popular materials in library collections can assist in realizing these goals. It is certainly not our intention to trash our collections, or, most importantly, to select or highlight popular materials to the exclusion of, or in place of, traditional, "quality" books.

Since we view these books as ephemeral, it is generally our policy to prefer a paperback format, and the books are rarely, if ever, cataloged. Most branches merely place them, face out, on the Children's Carousel and they disappear. They are read and read until they disintegrate or are weeded because of poor condition. We have purchased some, notably the new "Curious George" books and some "Sesame Street" titles, in dumps. Many of the most popular items are listed regularly for replacement—and they are purchased by branch staff in fairly large quantities.

Is it the children's librarian's task to actively promote, introduce, and use these highly popular, high circulation items? I say no. The marketplace has already done an admirable job of marketing these books directly to children. Within the limits of time and resources, it is incumbent upon children's librarians to spend their energies on the special books, the ones that need to be introduced. By the time a toddler comes into your library, Bert and Ernie will need no introduction!

If you decide to experiment with highly popular ephemera, first make a careful assessment of your budget, collection, and community. Start small, and carefully select, monitor, and evaluate the efficacy of these materials within your total plan for collection development.

Highly popular materials do have a place in our collections. We can identify the best from the mass marketplace and successfully add them to our collections. I do not believe that it is selling out, abandoning a calling, or betraying a trust. With caution, care and selectivity, we can welcome these materials. We need to understand them on their own terms, and use them on OUR terms to meet OUR needs.

Future Tense:
Science Fiction Confronts the New Science

by Janice Antczak

The "Tomorrow Makers," Grant Fjermedal's term,[1] refers to scientists engaged in projects at the frontiers of their fields—robotics, genetic engineering, and artificial intelligence. The visionary, futuristic work of these people often appears to be the stuff of science fiction—and naturally, because the new science excites the imagination, it is fertile ground for the speculation of science fiction writers. Extrapolation from known scientific facts and advances in technology are hallmarks of the genre; as Steward Brand says, science and science fiction "are so blurred together they are practically one intellectual activity."[2]

Whereas much of the older science fiction conveyed a tone of the paramilitary, the pseudo-science, or the fantastic, many recently published juvenile and young adults science fiction titles contain an emphasis on and a connection with technological breakthroughs of our time—a concern with the dangers of technological developments as they pertain to the future of humankind, rather than the danger of an alien technology brought to bear on human life. Writers of SF stories for young readers—and many of today's SF authors are women—create youthful heroes of both sexes who journey to the far edges of science and the universe in entertaining stories which, by echoing progress reported by newspapers and scientific journals, also inform young readers. These books' connection with the new science allows young readers opportunities to journey, along with the young protagonists, to the world of the "Tomorrow Makers."

Genetic Engineering

The production, by scientists from Johns Hopkins and Auburn University in 1988, of a genetically altered carp that could grow up to 20 percent faster than a normal carp, was just one recent example of the developing uses of genetic engineering. Gene mixing/splicing has since been achieved in microbes and in plants, rodents and livestock. People have used applied biotechnology, such as fermentation or baking with yeast, since ancient times; but recent advances have enabled scientists working in recombinant DNA or gene splicing to remove genes from one organism and attach them to the DNA of another organism. A 1980 ruling by the U.S. Supreme Court permits companies to patent new forms of life.

While such scientific breakthroughs hold a promise for improved crops and better livestock to enhance our food supply, or for the development of cures for diseases, the advent of biotechnology has spawned a hot debate over its potentially harmful effects. Concerns are being voiced, for example, about the possibility of an escape of mutant strains which might result in environmental damage, or their deliberate use in biological warfare—or even in the creation of a race of superhumans.

All of these issues are now on the pages of juvenile/young adult science fiction books. Several published in the late '80s incorporate biotechnology into their plots. One such example is Pamela Sargent's *Alien Child*, set at the Kwalung-Ibarra Institute. The main characters, Nita and Sven (products of the Institute's work in *in vitro* fertilization and cryonics), are brought forth from the "cold room" and nurtured by the aliens Llipel and Llare. Nita and Sven represent a benign use of genetic engineering—the creating and storage of embryos to be presented, at the right time, to loving parents—but the author's message is decidedly mixed. By juxtaposing Nita and Sven's awakening knowledge of the horror and destruction brought upon the Earth by biological warfare, Sargent's thoughtful work explores both the hopes and the hazards of biotechnology.

In Annabel and Edgar Johnson's *The Danger Quotient*, genetic engineering sustains life 130 years after War Three. The novel takes place at a time when remnants of human civilization survive in deep shelter to avoid radiation and ozone depletion; biotechnology is necessary to support and create life. Continued existence is possible only by the "ingenuity of genetic engineers like Helmet Eddinger," who the author says has developed "new strains of hydroponic fruit, long-grain wheat that heads out in ten days, cows that produce triplets [and] superkids concocted in the test tube . . . to give us extra brain power." One of Eddinger's genetic hybrids, K/C-4(SCI), is designed to solve the problems threatening continued survival, but there is one design flaw. These superkids don't have a chance to enjoy longevity; premature aging in their teens claims them before they reach their early twenties. As Sargent does in *Alien Child*, the Johnsons provide readers plenty of opportunities to speculate about the use of biotechnology and how it might have an impact in the future.

Laurence Yep, known for his books about the Chinese-American experience, uses genetic engineering as the premise for the plot in *Monster Makers, Inc.* In this adventure, Rob

Kincaid's father hopes to make a fortune with MMI—"The best in genetic engineering." Mr. Kincaid has come up with some strange creations already, including an Adelbaran chomper (a giant worm used to aerate farm soil), a line of prehistoric pets (baby ankylosaurs and mini-mastodons), but his prize is a mini-Godzilla, which he had hoped would be a hit with tourists. "People out here are still leery of genetic engineering," says Kincaid. "But once we show them it's safe, we'll be rich."

Yep weaves a tale in which Rob and Shandi, a spunky young heiress, retrieve a rampaging Godzilla and fight nefarious aliens to once more make the planet Carefree worthy of its name. The lighthearted banter of the characters establishes a tone for the novel in which industrial intrigue and sabotage lend excitement. Genetic engineering is not seriously questioned here, but is treated as a facet of technology to be explored for both practical application and for profit.

John Forrester's *Bestiary Mountain* and *The Secret of the Round Beast* (the first two books in a trilogy concluded by *The Forbidden Beast*) each include genetic engineering as part of life after the chemical wars of the 2130s. Forrester writes that in the world of *Bestiary Mountain*, "too much feeling for plants and animals was something to be watched, [for] humankind had conquered the animals in the final wars that came after genetic engineering had given animals minds and hands . . ." Since that time genetic engineering in the space stations orbiting Luna produced "the animals bred in moon labs . . . for hunting by the workers. There had been lion-rams and rhino buffalo, tigers with horns, anything the geneticists could dream up and splice together out of DNA."

Ryland and Tava Langstrom are genetic engineers who have been outlawed for their work. Ryland wishes to continue to study the dune bears (the remaining beasts of the colony-world) and the DNA of telepathic animals—study which is forbidden by the government. Tava steals an earth-rocket outfitted as an exploratory genetics unit and returns back to Old Earth. There, she develops Kana—half-cat, half-human boy—as she works to restore animals "from cryogenic DNA banks on the moon islands" and to seek out animals she doesn't have in storage to "add to their numbers by cloning."

Forrester's second volume, *The Secret of the Round Beast*, continues the conflict. Other hybrid creatures—like the foxal, and various cat hybrids—emerge. On one side are the Langstroms, who represent the benevolent aspect of genetic engineering; on the other, Gorid Hawxhurst, the evil scientist whose objective is the creation of hybrids for the hunt. (His name suggests his brutal, sadistic nature.) More serious in tone than Yep's *Monster Makers, Inc.*, Forrester's trilogy still maintains a sense of adventure and romance, as it explores the conflict of Old Earth and its colonies caused by genetic manipulation.

Artificial Intelligence

Scientists in artificial intelligence (AI) laboratories around the globe are exploring the idea of downloading the contents of human brains into robotic bodies. At the Massachusetts Institute of Technology, Danny Hillis is working on a "connection machine," a non-sequential computer which would be able to do millions of things at once—more like a human brain than a mere computer. MIT's Carl Hewitt is exploring ways in which these parallel computers can advance the development of artificial intelligence to aid human beings to control their use of planet Earth. AI units would thus become the "caretakers" of the human race. In England, Kerry Joels, a fellow of the Royal Astronomical Society, believes robots will be made to look more like humans, as do the androids in *Blade Runner* and *The Terminator*.

Engineer Charles Lecht, of Lecht Sciences, Inc., claims that biochip technology could free the human race. Lecht, Hans Moravec of Pittsburgh's Carnegie-Mellon University, and Marvin Minsky of MIT envision "artificial experience" whereby one could, via headsets and sensors, explore the world without ever leaving home. Or, through the use of holography, a person living on the East Coast could dine with friends on the West Coast—or one could decorate one's homes with luxuries. All of this raises questions at once basic and fantastic: What is real? What is life? What is a human being?

Recent novels suggest that AI may be one of the more frequently used aspects of the new technology in science fiction for young readers. In the first two books of Forrester's trilogy, many of the ideas become part of the story. Some of *Bestiary Mountain*'s Overones, the robotic guardians of Old Earth and its colonies, are faceless and machinelike, but newer units are "partly organic and partly electronic creations." In *The Secret of the Round Beast*, the Overones have a technology which allows them to copy the neural imprints of humans and duplicate their thoughts: "a system called Software Input, which allows brain-to-brain processing." These elements of the novel sound much like the downloading of brain contents discussed by the AI scientists. Forrester's robots and androids, who once were to be soldiers and miners, the "caretakers," are now in charge. In an aside, Forrester says the robots "make wonderful bureaucrats" and are "perfect in middle management."

Ryland Langstrom discusses this with Marian Lytal, an engineer designing organic robots. "You're making the units more human?" Ryland asks. Marian replies, "it might be dangerous—as they get nearer us, they will understand us better. And they might decide to replace us." The robots/androids become obsessed with redesign and self-improvement, and their mission becomes one "to eliminate selected humans, just as fast as they think they can do without them." Forrester's novel echoes what Earl Joseph said, that "the door has been opened with artificial intelligence and recombinant DNA . . . There is some possibility of creating a human race that will be beyond humans."[3]

These ideas are also found in Sargent's *Alien Child*. The Kwalung-Ibarra Institute depends on robots and AI for its continued existence. "The intelligence's circuits were embedded in the walls and floors of the Institute. Through robots, the artificial intelligence maintained the Institute and the garden . . ." Nita realizes that her life "depended on the Institute's artificial intelligence and the technology that served it . . ." When she and Sven journey outside the Institute to find other humans, they travel to the nearest city and find that the only survivor is another artificial intelligence which says it has searched all over the Earth and has seen no other trace of humans. As Nita and Sven talk to it about the destruction, Nita realizes that "her people had used even the minds that served them to destroy themselves."

Other authors include AI in their vision of the future. Louise Lawrence, in *Moonwind*, had a cybernetic intelligence caring for Bethkan for the 10,000 orbital years she has been stranded on the moon. In George Zebrowski's *The Stars Will Speak*, each student is "given a personal AI" and "will pursue various subjects. The AI or a visiting scientist may occasionally suggest an assignment."

Ardath Mayhar's *A Place of Silver Silence* reflects Charles Lecht's ideas concerning biochip technology. Selected pairs of young people are "Linked" using "technology that came into being with the prototypes of the computers of today. The chip that will be put into your skulls is akin (though far more sophisticated) to those used in those primitive devices." The implanted chip, Mayhar explains, was first used by the military to link field commanders with superiors and computers. Later it was employed by teachers and students, and business managers and technicians. Mayhar writes: "When the interface between the microcomputer and microsurgery was first discovered in the late twenty-first century, there was much concern expressed as to the morality of using such techniques to teach (program) human beings." Eventually the attempt to use the technology with adults failed, and "genetically superior fetuses chosen for crèche nurturing were matched via computer and Linked at the age of ten, before being trained for their natural specialties."

While Mayhar's concept of the chip "Links" characters like Andraia and Josip both intellectually and emotionally, she develops alien characters who, in stark contrast, are non-technological and natural empaths. Mayhar also envisions the human tendency to use technology for destructive ends. As Andraia explains to the Deet: "We aren't particularly kind or wise or self-controlled. . . . We think only of ourselves, our interests, our short-term goals. We ruined our own world thousands of years ago. Why should we think we have the right to ruin yours?" Andraia is determined not to allow the peaceful planet of Argent to become another Terran colony, the proving ground for new military technology.

Robotics

Many of those in technology's forefront talk of space colonization as the only hope for the survival of the human race. In most visions of cities in space, robots again play a major role, often scouting new planets, converting (terraforming) them into suitable environments for humans. "These robots would be combination miners, refiners, extruders, and constructors," writes Fjermedal.[4]

Among the novels discussed above, both Forrester and Sargent use robots and AI to support life in space colonies. In *ORVIS*, H.M. Hoover (another of the very fine women writers of science fiction) introduces readers to one of these terraforming robots. ORVIS, an acronym for "Overland Reconnaissance Vehicle in Space," is a "self-educating" robot designed for "early deep space research" who can read, analyze and interpret and has extraordinary cumulative intelligence potential. Robots like ORVIS are considered obsolete and even dangerous; it has been ordered to junk itself at the Corona landfill. However, on its journey to the dump, it meets Toby West, a young girl who doesn't usually like robots. But she finds ORVIS intriguing because it is limping along on six legs and has no face, just a round turret—it looks like a machine. ORVIS is an old model and lacks the android qualities of the newer robots; it even speaks in a machine monotone. Although it is aged and obsolete, it appears to have a sense of self and dignity. While at the Spacer community, ORVIS finds there is little to say to the robotrac planting corn. As the robot travels with Toby and her friend Thaddeus, it begins to wonder about and experience the meaning of the words "care" and "feel." Like many of the scientists working on robotics, Hoover raises the question about robotic life and consciousness.

Are We Alone?

Questions about the development of robotic consciousness are not the only concerns about other life forms in the scientific community. For a long time, humans have wondered about life on other planets and the possibility of contact with alien species. Robert Foward reports in *Future Magic* on the Search for Extra-Terrestrial Intelligence (SETI) project, which for some years has been listening for radio signals from the stars.[5] Foward also discusses one scientist's hypothesis regarding the existence of tachyons, particles which (it is theorized) travel faster than the speed of light—and could therefore be used to send messages quickly through space and time. While present theories of physics suggest that tachyons could exist, their actuality has not been proven.

Such a notion is found in *The Stars Will Speak*, in which Lissa has, since the age of ten, been intrigued by the fact that "scientists were listening to signals from an alien civilization somewhere among the stars." She wants to help decipher these signals and has a feeling (as do some scientists today) that the radio signals are not aliens' primary mode of communication, but rather a means of commanding Earth's attention. To achieve her goal, she wishes to attend the Interstellar Institute, a highly selective school established by Adri Shastri, "who first picked up the alien signal in 2064." In what could be a reference to SETI's work, Lissa asks herself, "Why didn't we pick it up in the twentieth century? We were listening." In the 20 years of listening to the signal, Dr. Shastri has been searching for another frequency or more advanced means to decipher it. Lissa suggests tachyons, but realizes they are only hypothetical and have not been proven to exist. Dr. Shastri says that research in tachyons is on the brink of a breakthrough at a listening post on Mars. It is the success of this research that allows the stars to speak. Lissa realizes "tachyon signals [are] hurrying between galactic civilizations, exchanging the only thing in the universe worth trading—information, knowledge, unique viewpoints about the nature of life and the universe."

One important part of the signal is a warning to Earth of the danger of destruction from comets in the Opik-Oort Cloud. Here author Zebrowski refers to Jan Hendrik Oort, a Dutch astronomer who, based on speculations of the astronomer Ernst Opik, "proposed that a vast cloud of unseen comets surrounds the Sun."[6] Zebrowski extrapolates from theories proposed but not proven and provides scenarios which suggest that the future will prove them true.

Fact & Fantasy

Questions concerning the relationship between humans and machines and the role of technology in human life are part of the fact and fiction of contemporary existence. I wholly agree with George Williams, of Harvard University, who says in *The Tomorrow Makers*, "Science fiction is the imagination of society at the edge. It's informed science becoming fantastic and fanciful for the purpose of entertainment, but it might project a future possibility. So I don't think the imagination of science fiction writers is to be discounted."[7] Writers of science fiction for young readers continue to journey to the edge of technology, to create for their readers a future in which the dizzying, as-yet only partially realized scientific developments of our time are fully formed, wondrous and dangerous forces to be reckoned with.

Works Cited

Forrester, John. *Bestiary Mountain*. Bradbury, 1985; Starwanderer/Harper, 1987 pbk.
———. *The Secret of the Round Beast*. Bradbury, 1986; Starwanderer/Harper, 1988 pbk.
———. *The Forbidden Beast*. Bradbury, 1988; Starwanderer/Harper, 1990 pbk.
Hoover, H.M. *ORVIS*. Viking Kestrel, 1987.
Johnson, Annabel, and Edgar Johnson. *The Danger Quotient*. Harper Jr. Books, 1984; Starwanderer/Harper, 1987 pbk.
Lawrence, Louise. *Moonwind*. Harper Jr. Books, 1985; Starwanderer/Harper, 1987 pbk.
Mayhar, Ardath. *A Place of Silver Silence*. Millennium/Walker & Co., 1988.
Sargent, Pamela. *The Alien Child*. Harper, 1988.
Yep, Laurence. *Monster Makers, Inc.* Morrow, 1986; New American Library, 1987 pbk.
Zebrowski, George. *The Stars Will Speak*. Harper Jr. Books, 1985; Starwanderer/Harper, 1987 pbk.

Notes

1. Fjermedal, Grant. *The Tomorrow Makers: A Brave New World of Living-Brain Machines*, Tempus/Microsoft, 1986.
2. Brand, Stewart. *The Media Lab: Inventing the Future at MIT*, Viking, 1987. p. 225.
3. Quoted in Fjermedal, p. 213-14.
4. Fjermedal, p. 254
5. Foward, Robert L. *Future Magic*, Avon, 1988.
6. Sagan, Carl and Ann Druyan. *Comet*, Random House, 1985. p. 195.
7. Quoted In Fjermedal, p. 158.

Juggling
Popularity and Quality

by Barbara A. Genco, Eleanor K. MacDonald, & Betsy Hearne

As an aging baby boomer with a lifelong affinity for popular culture—be it TV, radio, movies, or rock 'n' roll, it is pretty near impossible for me to dismiss children's commercial television and movies as trash, pure and simple. Similarly, as a "thirtysomething" mom who can still sing the Flintstones theme song and one who once spent an entire summer reading the complete Nancy Drew and Sue Barton canons, it's even more difficult for me in my exalted role as librarian, book selector, parent, to declare (ex cathedra) that any and all media tie-in books are essentially, well, bad. I thought I might share with you some of the ideas and influences that have helped me choose between the "Twin Peaks" of popularity and quality in building collections for public library children's rooms.

Are some books inherently bad—junk food for the mind?

Are some books inherently good—the literary equivalent of an oat bran muffin?

I worry. Does buying *only* books widely recognized as "good" books make you a "good" librarian? If that is so, I guess I have to confess to you that my halo is tarnished.

Why? Because for my whole professional life, I have included some representative titles from the popular, high interest, mass media-based genres in collections.

My philosophy? Dorothy Broderick once described a personal philosophy as a "mix of idealism and pragmatism." (*An Introduction to Children's Work in Public Libraries*. H.W. Wilson, 1965, p. 13).

First, the pragmatism part: Are mass market, media-related books effective ways to satisfy children's reading needs? These products of mass culture are the kind of books that many kids love to read (and many librarians and parents love to hate). I will limit my remarks here to licensed character books, TV or movie tie-ins and/or novelizations. The books related to "Wonderworks," "Reading Rainbow," or "Long Ago and Far Away" fall into a different category.

The books I'm talking about are the ones you see in the book chain stores, in K-mart and Toys R Us. There seem to be hundreds of them—Sesame Street, muppet show characters, the newest Disney films, the most recently released movie blockbuster, hot trends like "New Kids on the Block," the pop singing group. They're everywhere. Everywhere? How about the children's room? In some libraries they are *not* there, even though the video is.

As a book selector for a children's room, how do you approach mass media tie-ins? I think we would all agree that it is relatively easier to evaluate and select material with which we are somewhat familiar. Our first response to mass media-based material is often skepticism. If these "books" are so popular, could they possibly have any value?

To further complicate our decision making is the depressing realization that sometimes high-quality books, the best books, don't circulate heavily. Working librarians must grudgingly admit that sometimes quality books just aren't reflective of kids' popular tastes, even though we are convinced of their place and value in our collections and (more importantly) in the hearts and minds of children.

When Anna Quindlen was still writing her "Life in the 30's" column for the *New York Times* I always felt she was eavesdropping on my life. The day she wrote about kids and TV I was certain ("Pity the Parent Who'd Deny a Child the Flintstones." *New York Times*, February 17, 1988, p. C3). In that column, Quindlen introduced the Enforcer—a character who "looks a little like the Grim Reaper, only shorter" who warns parents of newborns "NEVER feed this child processed foods. DO NOT clothe him in synthetics. And NEVER under pain of stunted verbal facility and coping skill permit him to watch more than an hour of television a day." (Sounds a little bit like the instructions for the care and feeding of the Gremlins!)

For me Quindlen's Enforcer is analogous to the quiet voice of the "good" librarian within, a voice that becomes stentorian when confronted with what *The Horn Book* once referred to as the "subliterary" genres. The Good Librarian/Enforcer says things like: "What happened to Quality? Do NOT buy books that condone, or celebrate TV or films. How will you ever encourage kids to read classics or honor winners if you trash and contaminate your collections with popular culture?"

Can we reach some accommodation, find some middle ground? I say yes. I am, however, acutely aware that many of you may not agree.

For some of us, popular culture seems as out of control as one of Sendak's Wild Things. But librarians can no longer merely pray that it will slouch away somewhere and leave us TV-free. Can we tame it?—only by meeting it unblinkingly head on.

We can learn to evaluate mass media-based books within the perimeters of their own genres, evaluate within their own type of (dare I say it?) "excellence." Now, I would be disingenuous if I tried to assert that a "Sesame Street" tie-in or the *Teen-age Mutant Ninja Turtle Storybook* was as fine an addition to your collection as *Lon Po Po* or *Sarah, Plain and Tall*. What I am suggesting is that they can coexist in a typical children's room. Each contributes something different to the collection even though the child may enjoy both.

What are the positives about these mass market materials? For starters, they are high interest. If you select some media tie-ins for your library, they have the power of the publicity machines behind them. For middle-school kids and preteens, there's another plus. They are invariably in the format of choice—paperback. They are inexpensive. They can effectively serve as what we once called "book bait"—the books that actively entice kids to pick them up and read them.

In his book *The Reluctant Reader*, Aidan Chambers (Pergamon, 1969) points out that this popular ephemera is most often exactly what the non-reader will embrace. They establish our credibility. They demonstrate that we know what is the talk of the school yard, the cafeteria, the school bus. We know what's hot.

Chambers counsels: "Work from the known to the unknown. From the accepted to the rejected. From the familiar to the formidable. From the soft edge of literature to the hard edge of bibliomania." (p. 131).

In the same book, Chambers speaks of the "Reluctant Librarian"—the one who refuses to move out to the world at large to encourage children to come in to the library. By extending his reasoning, if we consistently keep popular culture locked out, how can we ever reach out to the many kids whose first experience of children's literature consisted of supermarket fare? How can we reach out to kids whose genres of choice (admittedly perhaps because they've had no others) are comics, sports magazines, or movie novelization?

Are we reluctant librarians? Do we sabotage ourselves by excluding some of the most popular types of books currently produced for kids and, consequently, reinforce the rejection of libraries by reluctant readers? Could we, by limiting our collections to conventional library books, be actually working against our own best interests and intentions?

When we approach these troublesome subliterary genres, who are we? Are we acting as selectors or excluders? Are we librarians or enforcers? Does a child's right to free choice have a role in this discussion?

While it is true that providing a wide variety of choice may be financially and philosophically challenging for libraries, I think it pays off. Kids soon learn that their interests can be supported through the simple use of their library card whether its babysitting or horseback riding, hockey or the "New Kids on the Block."

If we are ever to begin to address the growing literacy crises, we need to provide opportunities for kids to become "self-identified" readers. If we want to support kids in this process, we must first respond to their reading choices and then help them expand and channel their interests. For me, this is the intersection of idealism and pragmatism.

The growth of children's book clubs and the astonishing increase in the number and variety of children's books in paperback format have had great effect on kids' choices. We can carve out a positive role for ourselves in this seemingly chaotic marketplace. Instead of relying on our stereotyped enforcer past, we can make a place where "high" and "low" cultures can coexist. Librarians, by judiciously selecting the best representative examples from the mass market place, can help children and their parents make informed choices. Both have traditionally looked to us as pathfinders through the forest of quality books. We can also lead them to the "best" through the jungle of popular culture.

The pull of mass culture has not left even the American Library Association unscathed. In fact, seeking to popularize our image and to break out of those old stereotypes, consider the ALA graphics catalog. How many of those featured celebrity readers are TV or movie stars? Garfield, Michael J. Fox, Glenn Close, Bill Cosby. ALA has unrelunctantly jumped on the media bandwagon. And what about those California Raisins! Talk about mass 'n' crass! (They began as characters in TV commercials. A library that hosts the Raisins while embracing "quality" or displays a Mickey Mouse or Garfield poster yet steadfastly refuses to buy books featuring these characters is in the throes of a schizophrenic episode!)

If you are selecting mass media tie-ins with the ultimate goal of boosting circulation, going heavily into popular culture will meet the goal, but only in the short run. For in the long run your collection will be warped and off balance. Your readers may never know the real Little Mermaid and will be convinced that the only Michelangelo is a Teen-age Mutant Ninja Turtle.

If your goal in selecting popular materials is to supplement your "quality" collection, to introduce and build readership, to help kids become self-identified readers, you just may achieve it. Someday, your collection may even achieve equilibrium between popularity and quality.

When we stop playing the role of cultural enforcers for society, we can find new ways to connect with some kids we might never have encountered—without standing in judgment, and with joy.—*Barbara A. Genco*

Books for the special child on one end of the spectrum; mass market titles on the other. Which should libraries choose? This is an old debate in our profession and the truth lies on both sides of the question. If that were not so, this issue would have been decided long ago. At some point, each of us will make our own series of decisions about the books we make available to the children we serve. But beyond the individual choice lies something else—a tradition of selectivity which is a hundred years old. Old values are always open to debate (as indeed they should be). As we enter our second century, librarians are under increasing pressure to amend this judgment. Let's examine and offer a rebuttal to some of the justifications given when quality is sacrificed to popular taste.

- *Libraries are funded by the public. You should give the public what it wants and these are the books kids ask for.*

Adults who ask for specific kinds of books are experienced readers who have already been exposed to a variety of materials. They are making choices based on informed and developed tastes. Children, on the other hand, don't know all that is available to them. Given a choice, they will *always* opt for something familiar. In the words of Frances, Russell Hoban's badger child, "Well, there are many different things to eat, and they taste many different ways. But when I have bread and jam I always know what I am getting and I am always pleased."

Children ask for these books because they are pre-sold. Someone else, usually a highly paid advertising specialist with a product to sell, has convinced them that this book is worth their time. Good parents consciously push their children into new choices: they encourage them to try unfamiliar activities, eat new foods, make new friends, and develop new skills. We should also say to children who are locked in a reading rut: "Try this one, you'll like it."

• *"Well, at least they're reading something."*

This is a very common argument. Would you give a child a steady diet of Twinkies and say, "Well, at least they're eating something"? We recognize that Twinkies are popular with kids and satisfy their immediate hunger, but these are empty calories, they provide no real substance and are lacking in the ingredients kids need to grow and stay healthy.

Let's watch out for "literary Twinkies," sugary, unrealistic books full of easy platitudes and canned morality; watered down versions of fairy tales from which all controversy and content have been removed; classics which have been abridged to the point that the author's unique voice has vanished.

When we say, "At least they're reading something," we act as if the choice was between something and nothing. Remember, the child came into the library looking for something to read (however reluctantly) and the choice is among different books.

We are in the library to provide a book for that child, and no one questions that libraries should own books that kids like. However, popular and mediocre are no synonyms. There are plenty of excellent writers and artists out there who write books kids love. Indeed, sheer readability is one of the hallmarks of a good children's book. Use the genius of an Arnold Lobel or a Beverly Cleary to give the kids confidence in *your* judgment. Then you can begin to encourage them to try more offbeat and increasingly challenging material.

• *"Well, I read a lot of junk when I was a kid and it didn't hurt me."*

This is a view shared by many—including Peter Dickinson, one of our most intellectually challenging authors. I'll admit that this statement is true for many people, including myself. But take a good look at the person saying this because that person is usually a real reader—probably even a compulsive reader. You may even be one yourself. We will read *anything*: novels, essays, magazines, newspapers, cereal boxes, bus benches, assembly directions on toy boxes. We read anytime we are not doing something else and often while we *are* doing something else. Given the variety of this kind of reading then the junk becomes only part of a rich and diverse mixture.

However, most kids aren't like this. Certainly the ones we worry about aren't like this. Most kids read an average of one book every two weeks and a lot of them read a lot less. This means the average child reads about 25 books a year. At that rate, it's possible for a child to emerge into the teen years and never read a significant book. If reading were nothing more than a physical skill that might be sufficient. Reading is more than a process, it's also an experience. Children who only read small numbers of mediocre books could miss altogether the true reading experience. Let's face it, kids who read very little can't afford the luxury of mediocrity.

• *The elitist demands of middle-class librarians are just not appropriate or relevant to the needs of inner-city or poor children.*

This is perhaps the argument where we feel the most vulnerable; few of us are elitist but we do fit solidly into the middle-class. Our profession has a long way to go before it fully represents the ethnic diversity of this country. But "appropriate" and "relevant" are the kinds of terms which can be both useful and intellectually insidious. What does "relevance" actually mean when we are speaking of individual children?

There's no question that it's important for children to see their own lives and experiences validated in the books they read. Therefore, it's as appropriate for a suburban white child to read Walter Dean Myers' *Scorpions* as for an inner-city child to read Tolkien's *The Lord of the Rings*. The suburban child needs to learn about the limited opportunities available to less fortunate children, in order to become a more empathetic adult. While inner-city children may not choose to relive the exact circumstances of their own lives, they will recognize Mordor for what it is. They may find in Frodo's final choice the courage to turn away from the seductive and easy power offered by drugs and violence. Both stories revolve around friendship, choice, and loss. It's presumptuous for us to assume we know which is the most appropriate for a particular child.

There is a strong interdiction in our profession against labeling books but I think we all do so unconsciously. "This is a good story for boys—or girls—or reluctant readers, or this is a book for 'the special child'." These are useful ways to categorize books for reader's advisory and we all keep mental lists in our heads. I do, however, think we have to be careful not to over-categorize or label material, and, above all, not to try to make matched pairs of books and children based on the child's ethnic origin or circumstance. Children would be properly resentful toward a librarian who only gave them books about characters like themselves.

What we should look for in the materials we choose is the connecting human element—the relevance of the story or information to our shared humanity. Any child who has deliberately broken a household rule can understand *The One-Eyed Cat*. Leon Garfield's street-smart beggars and apprentices are closer to tough inner-city kids than the children who are usually given his adventures.

I can sense the other part of this argument coming at this point. None of these are easy books to read. What about the child who, because of disrupted schooling, or an unstable home life or any of another dozen circumstances, cannot read at grade level? Can't we lower our standards on his or her behalf? We don't have to—there are excellent books at every level. It is not, in fact, any easier to read a mediocre book. Even the most unskilled reader can respond to the *ideas* expressed in quality literature.

To quote Sheila Egoff, "What the disadvantaged don't need surely is disadvantaged material." ("If That Don't Do No Good, That Won't Do No Harm: The Uses and Dangers of Mediocrity in Children's Reading," *School Library Journal*, October, 1972, p. 93-98).

The only advantage that mass market materials have over other materials is that they are familiar to children, not more relevant, not easier, just presold. Instant gratification will make us popular but by failing to push our own product we cheat the children most in need of it, with the least access to it.

Even in affluent cities like Beverly Hills we have large numbers of single parent families and homes where both parents work. Children in this circumstance have limited chance for conversation with adults and get much of their oral language from TV. We all know how limiting that can be, yet many mass market titles come directly from the screen with the same flat, generic language. These children need the added richness of good literature—starting with Mother Goose. Just think of the words embedded in something as simple as "Jack and Jill:" *fetch, crown, tumbling, trot,* and *caper.*

If the Mother Goose is beautifully illustrated, the child is doubly enriched. In homes barren of order and continuity, a beautiful picture book can be a child's first aesthetic experience. We must never underestimate the power of a single bit of beauty in a child's life. Remember the plate in *Blue Willow*?

> Only to Janey did the willow plate seem perfect. Only for her did it have the power to make drab things beautiful and to a life of dreary emptiness bring a feeling of wonder and delight. Bending over it now, she could feel the cool shade of willows, she could hear the tinkling of the little stream as it passed under the arched bridge, and all the quiet beauty of a Chinese garden was hers to enjoy. It was as if she had stepped inside the plant's blue borders into another world as real as her own and much more desirable.

Good collection development is a two-part commitment. First you purchase the best books you can find and then you sell the books to kids as if you were on a commission and got bonus points for the good stuff. Know your product before you start to sell it. Read reviews carefully. Look at every book before it goes on the shelf. Read as many books as you possibly can, even if you have to skim some of them. Kids don't read reviews and they don't have best-seller lists. They rely on the familiarity of the product (that's why mass market covers all look alike) or the personal endorsement of a peer or an adult they trust—a category you hope to fit into. They want to know what you thought about the book and you can't tell them if you haven't read it.

You only confuse patrons when you buy high quality material, then surround it with too many easy, popular choices.

You also make your job harder. It's hard to sell M.E. Kerr, Richard Peck, or even Paula Danziger, if you have every Sweet Valley High or Nancy Drew title. Can you convince those six-year olds (or their parents) to take Milne's *Winnie the Pooh*, or Marcia Brown's *Cinderella*, if you also have the more familiar Disney versions? I don't mean that you shouldn't offer a wide variety of choices—only that those choices be consistent with the standard the public has come to expect from libraries.

When I worked in a school library we had a boy who came in every week with his class, wandered around and seldom checked out anything. He would ask for things like *Nightmare on Elm Street* or *Halloween II*, partly to see how we'd react, partly because that's what he wanted to read. He told me he liked gory books, that he wanted something really "groddy." In a flash of inspiration I gave him Beowulf, the version with the Charles Keeping illustrations. Those illustrations sold the book and he not only read it, he loved it! He moved on to other ancient and "groddy" heroes, Cuchulain, Finn MacColl, King Arthur, and straight through Rosemary Sutcliffe. That wouldn't have happened if I had simply given him what he asked for.

Because they don't fit into any readily identifiable market, many quality books are *only* available to children in libraries. And patrons expect them to be there, it's part of our public image. Use that image—a lot of good librarians spent a long time developing it. Parents trust us, they see us as a source of excellence for their children. Yes, some may complain if we don't have a series they remember fondly from their own childhood, but on the whole they find our standards reassuring. It shows that we really care about their children and their reading choices.

We have incorporated new forms of media into our collections and embrace the new technologies which make the retrieval of information less cumbersome and therefore more accessible to children. But we must, above all, continue to boldly assert and affirm those basic values which have been identified with library service to children and are key to our success. If we do this, then every decision we make, every book we select, every child we talk to, becomes part of that success. Every time we compromise in the name of statistics, efficiency or external social values, we weaken our long term image.

Let's stop apologizing for our idealism, our love of literature, our commitment to both the physical act and sheer joy of reading. There are hundreds of authors and artists out there who go beyond the demands of the commercial market. They create from somewhere deep inside and give children a bit of themselves with every book. As long as we have them we don't need to compromise, we can continue to offer kids the real things.—*Eleanor K. MacDonald.*

I was showing a picture of the David statue to my nine-year-old one day. "It's by a great Italian artist, Michelangelo," I said. "Oh!" she exclaimed in surprise, "Was he named after the Teenage Mutant Ninja Turtle?"

What's high culture and what's popular culture? Which comes first, and how do they get separated? How did fairy tales, which used to be pop culture, become a subject for highbrows such as J.R.R. Tolkien and Bruno Bettelheim, who then imposed elitist definitions on them? Why do film and video animators, on the other hand, feel it necessary to "cuten up" fairly tales for popular consumption, when the basic story elements are so powerful already that slapstick just distracts rather than adds?

Well, if you've ever heard children's real subculture, you know it's more fierce than cute. Peter and Iona Opie's work collecting children's playground chants shows that children preserve a world apart from adults, and it is a world wicked with references to sex, violence, and obscenity. The Opies also show how children pass on their lore generation after generation, so that what a third grader sings while jumping rope today sometimes comes close to words and tunes from the 16th century. Names are substituted, melodies added; but popular culture is still a tenacious beast with its own beauty.

In studying the story of Beauty and the Beast through hundreds of years of versions, I found that no vulgarization could keep such a good story down. A doctoral student at the University of Chicago has shown how much Peter Pan's enduring popularity owes to the Greek god Pan. Another student has tracked the folk motifs that riddle the Teenage Mutant Ninja Turtle episodes. Another has traced the plots for dozens of series romances to discover that more revolve around four classic tale types. Transformation and quest motifs dominate popular literature, and there are tricksters lurking everywhere.

The energy, power, and tenacity of popular culture, whatever the medium, is undeniable. In an April 29, 1990 article in the *New York Times*, N.R. Kleinfield writes, "characters on TV and in comic strips can exhibit great vitality. Snoopy and his fellow Peanuts pals are in their 40th year. Betty Boop is looking good as she nears 60. Bugs Bunny turns 50 this year, and Warner Brothers is celebrating with its upcoming 'Box Office Bunny,' the bunny's first new film short in 26 years, and a blizzard of fresh Looney Tunes licensed products."

"Sales of Ninja Turtles goods, for instance, are estimated to have already surpassed $650 million, while Batman spinoffs have sold more than $500 million" (Kleinfield).

It's not just money at issue. Something in these fads speaks to emotions and always has. Popular culture has always been powerful. In 1284, after the English conquest of Wales, Edward I ordered all bards to be killed because they could so easily sway the people.

Does popular culture necessarily preclude other kinds of culture? I have spent 25 years promoting good literature for children; the ultimate faith in good literature must be in its power to give to and take from popular culture. Susan Roman, executive director of the Association for Library Service to Children, recently completed a study with conclusions that substantiate what many of us suspect. Given some enthusiastic guidance and a choice between high-quality fiction and formula series books, most young readers choose a mixture of both. We as adult critics should show as much wisdom.—*Betsy Hearne*

Gay Information: Out of the Closet

by Douglas Eric Anderson

As a teenager, when I first found myself attracted to other males, I discovered (after searching long) one sentence in one book in our local public library, which told me something like, "Many teenagers experience crushes on members of the same sex, but don't worry, it doesn't mean you're a homosexual." Period. Perhaps the authors intended to do a kindness to those who would pass through this phase to become "normal" heterosexual adults. But speaking for those who didn't become "normal," I feel an injustice was done to us. Why didn't they tell us we *might* be gay? They could have spared me years of tortured self-denial, of trying to persuade myself to get past this phase.

Fifteen years later, I find it appalling that most libraries are still only a little better supplied with in-depth, positive, accurate information on homosexuality and bisexuality for children and young adults. Moreover, even in cities with substantial lesbian and gay populations, precious few public libraries carry titles for the children of lesbians and gay men. And when it comes to fiction—well, most searchers in children's and YA collections might as well forget it.

As we speak of multiculturalism, let us remember that, in addition to those cultures that share a racial or ethnic bond, there are cultures determined by other differences—the so-called subcultures. These include American atheism, the gay and lesbian subculture, or the New Age movement. Most are so thoroughly overshadowed by the mainstream culture that children's and YA librarians consider them to be of little or no import.

But just as knowledge of dyslexia is vitally important to the second-graders whose worlds are dislocated by their difficulty in reading, so the preschooler whose mothers happen to be in love with one another, or the preteen whose father is arrested at an AIDS demonstration, or the teenage boy who can't get the quarterback off his mind, will find information on gay and lesbian issues to be vastly more important than the life cycle of a sphinx moth, or the Sweet Valley Ninja Turtles.

Too often I have heard colleagues reject all presentations in whatever light because "There's no demand for this." If thereby you mean "explicit requests," then there's no contesting the claim. Most lesbian and gay youth, or those who are simply unsure of their sexuality, are all too reasonably afraid of the reactions of others to their inquiries.

Similarly, a good case could be made in many libraries that there is no demand for books on menstruation; but a public library that would omit from its collections for children or young adults materials on menstruation would be tragically remiss.

Other reasons often given include the old standby, "There's nothing available." Any librarians worth their salt should have little difficulty finding excellent fiction and nonfiction titles available at any reading level, such as *Daddy's Roommate* by Michael Willhoite (Alyson), Nancy Garden's *Annie on My Mind* (Farrar), or *Gay: What Teenagers Should Know About Homosexuality and the AIDS Crisis* (Farrar). Librarians can approach the Gay and Lesbian Task Force of the American Library Association's Social Responsibilities Round Table for more recommendations.

"There is no gay community in [fill in the blank]," is another argument heard. Social scientists agree that at least ten percent of any population can be described as primarily homosexual, and an even larger percentage as bisexual. If you know of none in your community, it is most likely because these people are all in the closet, again for fear of the reactions of family or friends or employers. I grew up in a rural Pennsylvania town of fewer than 1000 people. Even in that conservative environment, I found at least 15 other gay or lesbian people among my acquaintances alone—and that figure doesn't include those who were so heavily closeted that no one could tell, or those I simply didn't know.

Some librarians cite possible community reaction; yet can a library that endorses the *Library Bill of Rights* seriously consider this a valid reason for rejecting a potential purchase? How many librarians were up in arms over the decision by many chain bookstores to remove Salman Rushdie's *The Satanic Verses* from their stores for just that reason?

Having worked as a librarian for nearly three years in a small town in Ohio, I can certainly understand the political and religious dynamics that may intimidate the librarian who has considered purchasing, say, Norma Klein's *Now That I Know* (Bantam), or Jane Futcher's *Crush* (Alyson); but if we do not let Jesse Helms and his ilk dictate which books we purchase for adults, it is hardly ethical to let them effectively censor our purchasing decisions for children and YAs.

Gay, lesbian, and bisexual teens and preteens make up a substantial percentage of our users. The children and siblings of gay, lesbian, and bisexual people make up an even larger percentage. Let us, as librarians committed to the principles of intellectual freedom, never swerve from our responsibility to serve this much-neglected segment of our population. Now more than ever, librarians know how important it is that people of the next generation see role models like themselves. We strive to present positive portrayals of women, people of color, the physically challenged, and members of other groups that have formerly been slighted or maligned. Let it be the same for those now growing up who are—or will be—lesbian, bisexual, or gay.

CD-ROM and At-Risk Students

A Path to Excellence

by Roxanne Baxter Mendrinos

Many educators have been reluctant and defensive about the integration of technology into the curriculum. One library media specialist stated that her superintendent was only interested in bells and whistles. He wanted to use a cutting edge technological project as a political tool to advance his career, regardless of its value or impact on student achievement.

Other educators feel that if students use technology, they read less, and do not develop critical thinking skills. In fact, one finds administrators, teachers, and library media specialists divided over the impact of technology on student achievement. The overriding impetus for its success appears to be that the mechanics of hardware and software are a motivating factor for students. Once the initial excitement wears off, so the thinking goes, the value is minimal.

My research on the use of CD-ROM technology for reference purposes in secondary school libraries stands in direct contradiction to this skepticism. High tech tools are the means for inciting a quiet revolution in the library media center environment. Information literacy is a process of critical, lateral, and branching thought strategies to seek, gather, retrieve, analyze, synthesize, evaluate, and apply information from all formats to solve problems. Being information literate is a life skill needed in elementary through graduate school, on the job, or in the home as one participates in life's decision making. This information literacy process is stimulated and perpetuated by the use of high tech tools.

CD-ROM for At-Risk Students

In the study of 381 secondary school library media specialists in Pennsylvania and Maine, 80 percent were using CD-ROM workstations, indicating a steady and continuous growth. In fact, library media specialists stated if they did not have a separate budget for this technology they would have used funds from their book budgets. The most profound educational outcome was that special education, learning disabled, and average students are not only more motivated but more productive using CD-ROM technology for reference.

CD-ROM expands students' thinking about the availability of different resources. Student productivity has increased because of CD-ROM's ease of use. Their research results have improved due to efficiency in accessing and retrieving a larger, relevant number of information sources. Perceivable outcomes mentioned by library media specialists in the use of CD-ROM technology for reference include the improvement of students' research skills, productivity, and critical thinking abilities.

Students are becoming more specific in what they are looking for as a result of the CD-ROM technology for reference. They are motivated to use more sources because they have clearer knowledge of which sources contain the information they need to fulfill their quest. They also know which subject headings can produce similar results in other indexes or catalogs.

Many library media specialists believe students are much more responsive to CD-ROM indexes than to print. Their observations indicate that all levels of students are increasing their use of the library media center, not just exemplary students. The division of topics into subtopics helps all students, especially average-level, those with special needs, and those with learning disabilities, in their search for information and in defining and redefining their research question.

The following passages from interviews with library media specialists capture the impact of the CD-ROM technology on students of differing ability levels.

> All levels are helped . . . not just your stellar students . . . Kids have been here in the past but have not really used the library to its potential and I think they are [doing so] a little bit more . . .

> I think that it is so important that ninth and tenth graders or middle of the road students who are not going to be doing a degree at Harvard have the ability to find the material they want with a minimum of fuss and bother . . . and they can do it by themselves . . . I think that . . . slower students would more readily use CD-ROM . . .

Library media centers that use CD-ROM technology tend to have larger periodical and microfiche collections. CD-ROM points the way for students to access, retrieve, and read information from more diverse formats.

Electronic tools such as CD-ROM do not represent information as being fixed and stagnant. Information is fluid, easily manipulated through the information literacy process. Students can view the search and the results on the screen in a visual way. The abstract becomes the concrete. The reasoning powers of the intellect interact with the sense of touch, sight, and sometimes hearing for a holistic learning experience.

In the electronic world as one is thinking, one is doing, concretely visualizing the thinking process. Learning is active. Students are engaged with the screen display. It is the visual integration and conception of ideas, keywords, and terms that is a critical learning stimulus for these groups of students. Electronic tools allow students to map concepts and ideas, to outline terms visually as well as abstractly, while being in control of the tactile manipulation of the data. The student is the navigator in the electronic sea of information.

This navigation breaks away from the traditional straight and linear course. It promotes divergent thinking and branching. It fosters the adventure of searching for connections, exploring and creating new constructs. It forges a new route to the knowledge path. At-risk students, those with special needs, learning disabled, and even average students may not be exposed to these tools of information literacy, thereby restricting their growth in the continuum of lifelong learning. Library media specialists remarked that, "CD-ROM helps students to think in concrete terms which is usually beneficial for a lower level student."

Special education students and staff have higher expectations using the CD-ROM technology. Mainstreamed and special education students use it by themselves and on their own. It overcomes previous learning barriers opening up a world of information to this group of former library nonusers.

CD-ROM vs. Other Indexes

Attitudes of library media specialists who use CD-ROM technology for reference and those who do not varied greatly. CD-ROM for reference is more popular than online databases or printed indexes. Foremost, it is student-oriented. Administrators and faculty like it because it is not strictly a librarian's tool. Library media specialists prefer it to online databases because it does not require additional staff, provides unlimited access with predictable costs, and utilizes the same thinking and learning strategies to access and retrieve information.

They prefer CD-ROM to a printed index because average students, those with special needs, and students with learning disabilities, have more access points to retrieve their information. Students and faculty get quick printed results—immediate gratification. They use the topics and subtopics found

---

Where in the World is Burkina Faso?

Chris was a disheveled, dark-haired seventh grader who often retreated from reality. He had an attention deficit disorder. His handwriting difficulties prevented him from transferring his thoughts adequately to paper. Chris attended Learning Center each day for help from the Special Needs teacher to overcome his learning disabilities. Chris was rebellious toward both his teachers and his peers.

His social studies teacher brought him to the Library Media Center to participate in an interdisciplinary high technology unit on the Third World. The country Chris chose was Upper Volta in Africa. After my classes on search strategies using print, CD-ROM, and online databases, Chris walked reluctantly over to the CD-ROM *Academic American Encyclopedia*. He typed in a word search on his topic, Upper Volta, and was faced with an index of articles containing the term. Recognizing the capital, Ouagandougou, he retrieved and printed the article. Considering his disabilities in both handwriting and thought processes, technology was a distinct advantage for him. However, the goal of the project was not a report which might encourage plagiarism. It was to be a personal essay involving analysis, evaluation, and a "what if" scenario seen through the eyes of a twelve-year-old living in that country.

The first sentence of the article about his country told him that it was no longer called Upper Volta, but Burkina Faso. Chris went back to the word search index of the CD-ROM encyclopedia to retrieve the article on Burkina Faso that he had first bypassed, and to search through other articles containing this term. This linking of lateral thought processes continued in InfoTrac's *Magazine Index Plus* as Chris's quest for current information, background, and an understanding of the country led him to research Burkina Faso. He related terms continuously—linking, connecting, and backtracking for leads on more information through the visual, concrete indexes of the CD-ROM technology. He was succeeding!

Chris was in the library mornings, during lunch, and after school comparing his notes and perceptions with his peers. He used the word processor to sort his ideas and perspectives, moving paragraphs, inserting and deleting his own comments. This was almost impossible for him without this technology, due to his handwriting disabilities.

One morning, he came in and asked to use DIALOG'S Magazine Index because the CD-ROM disks just weren't current enough. He wanted the recent census figures and up-to-date news on his country.

No longer an uninvolved, rebellious, and obstinate seventh grader, Chris was motivated to research current journals, newspapers, books and to retrieve full text articles through the availability of high technology pointing the way. The concrete visual connections provided guides to link him to new terms, and to help him think laterally. Chris's personal essay was one of five published and disseminated statewide as an outstanding example of multidisciplinary learning, combining high technology with critical and creative thinking.

This is one of many of the untold case studies of increased critical thinking abilities, productivity, and self-worth, resulting in personal internal and external student achievement.

in other sources. Library media specialists referred to full-text as one-stop shopping.

"Unfortunately, it's getting expensive and we have to justify it . . . When I discuss cutting the CD-ROMs to students and teachers, they are all aghast. 'Oh, you can't get rid of that, we use it too much.'"

The most popular CD-ROM databases in this study were MaineCat and Access Pennsylvania. These statewide databases foster resource sharing among school, public, academic, and special libraries throughout their respective states. They expand access to collections from over two million volumes in Maine to over 12 million volumes in Pennsylvania. This type of access promotes reading.

The most highly ranked commercial databases were electronic encyclopedias (Grolier's was first), magazine indexes (InfoTrac's *Magazine Index* was ranked first, followed by EBSCO), newspaper indexes, and educational abstracts. However, having the software and hardware available in the library media center will not achieve the outstanding educational outcomes in student achievement alone. Training is needed.

Inservice and Student Training

Faculty, administration, and students can all benefit from using these tools to their fullest advantage. Inservice training of faculty is critical to its successful implementation and efficient use within the curriculum. Training faculty increased the use of CD-ROM technology for reference in the specific disciplines, increased formal classroom instruction for students, and stimulated faculty to update and modify their curriculum. Faculty use for graduate, professional, and personal reasons also increased with training.

English and social studies teachers received more training and used such training more in their disciplines. Only 17 percent of the library media specialists surveyed introduced their science teachers to using CD-ROM databases for research. Those that received training also teamed with teachers for formal classroom instruction. However, only 53 percent of all the library media specialists providing CD-ROM for reference conducted inservice training.

There is a definite connection between training and curriculum use. Teachers who have been trained are more comfortable with the technology, opening up windows of opportunity between library media specialists and classroom teachers. Library media specialists become part of curriculum planning and classroom teachers better understand the importance of developing information-literate students, students who can access a wide variety of discipline-specific information using high tech tools. Inservice training has also encouraged team teaching and introduced interdisciplinary units of instruction.

Slightly more than three quarters of the library media specialists conducted formal instruction for the students. However, the average training period was 15 to 30 minutes long, hardly enough time to tackle information literacy and critical thinking. The library media specialists who spent a 45-minute to two-hour period in instruction were more inclined to check student search strategies. Formal classroom instruction is critical for students. Once trained, students not only use the technology for classroom assignments but also for their personal and leisure interests.

Begin with inservice training, then get into the classroom and team with the teacher. An electronic research tool can lie dormant or be improperly utilized at the expense of time, efficiency, and money invested if formal training is not provided.

School board approval of a library curriculum that includes CD-ROM searching for reference purposes increased the incidence of faculty training, especially in science. More classes also received formal instruction in the disciplines of English, social studies, science, and library skills with school board approval of the library curriculum. School board approval promotes active planning between library media specialists and classroom teachers in specific disciplines because high expectations have been established.

Implications

Library media specialists cannot be complacent or defensive in their role towards CD-ROM technology for reference. The Pennsylvania and Maine models of CD-ROM resource sharing provide for more equity in access and increased availability of resources. These state models have supported library media specialists who now feel comfortable with technology, expanding their use and understanding of the power of this tool to the educational program. Other states should replicate these models.

Educate your administration, special education director, and curriculum coordinator to the benefits of this technology. Its availability has a revitalizing effect on the topics in the curriculum, and expands the textbook learning environment. Graduate schools of education and library science should not only teach the mechanics of the hardware and the software but also focus on linkage to the curriculum and educational program.

Joan Winsor in the *Online Educator* (April 1987, p. 5) has the last word. "The mark of a good student of the future will be the ability to locate and manage information, skills in analytical and critical thinking, and an ability to cope with ambiguity."

History Comes Alive
The American Memory Project

by F. K. Rottmann

It is 1901. The scene is inside Mt. Auburn Prison, New York, and two men lead Leon F. Czolgosz, the man who assassinated President McKinley, to the electric chair. An official places a plank of lightbulbs on the chair to test the electricity. The bulbs light up and Czolgosz is strapped into the chair. A half-dozen men look on while the switch is thrown. Czolgosz's head and neck stretch toward the ceiling as he is slightly lifted off the seat by the electrical shock. The switch is turned on again and again, and with two more spasms, the man slumps over in his chair, dead.

A small group of students at David H. Hickman High School in Columbia, Missouri gasp as they observe this execution scene transmitted from a laser videodisc by an Apple Macintosh™ computer. One student remarks, "I can't believe that someone actually videotaped that."

Jenny Cox, librarian at Hickman, gently informs the students that what they just saw was not videotaped, but was, in fact, filmed by Thomas Edison. He used his invention, the kinetoscope (a peep-show instrument employing a cylinder, a magnifying glass, and a light source), the very first motion picture device. These high school students have been taken back in time through the use of the Library of Congress's American Memory Project (AMP), a program whose aim is ultimately to provide online, on-demand distribution of all types of collections to libraries across the nation.

Hickman High School is one of 14 school libraries currently participating in the AMP pilot program (see chart, p. 267). The Library of Congress (LC) began development of American Memory in 1990, and in May of 1991, 37 academic, public, special, and school libraries throughout the nation were selected to participate in the six-year-long pilot program.

Hickman, like the other schools, had to apply to receive the AMP, and also had to own most of the hardware necessary to run the program. As the recipient of the "National School Library Media Program for the Year Award" for 1989, and having been named "Best Missouri High School" by Columbia Teachers College in New York (partly because of its excellent media center), Hickman was readily accepted as one of the AMP pilot project participants. This was Hickman's first year as a project participant, and the school is eagerly anticipating another year of program use.

American Images

AMP now consists of seven LC primary-source collections: Cartoons about Congress, 1770-1981; Detroit Publishing Co. Photographs of the U.S., 1880-1920; Documents from the Continental Congress, 1774-1789; Films of President McKinley and the Pan American Exposition, 1901; Nation's Early Forum Sound Recordings, 1918-1920; Office of War Photographs, 1942-1943; World's Transportation Commission Photographs, 1894-1896; and Early Films of New York City, 1897-1906.

Coming very soon to AMP will be: African-American Pamphlets, 1820-1920; Civil War Photographs, 1861-1865; and First-Person Narratives of California's Early Years, 1849-1900.

The Library of Congress has chosen these collections for inclusion in the AMP prototype for several reasons. First of all, most of these unique materials have not been previously available to the public. By putting them into American Memory, they are being processed and cataloged as well. Also, these collections present no copyright problems. But, most of all, librarians of all types are for the first time able to provide access to this treasure of primary-source information through multimedia interactive video technology.

In Columbia, MO, American Memory is located in two schools, with one station per building at Hickman and Rockbridge High Schools. Librarian Jenny Cox says that the schools "make the most of what they have" by keeping AMP on a cart, and making it available for teachers to check out like any other piece of audiovisual equipment. She often takes the equipment to the classroom to demonstrate it herself, but even when it is parked in the library, it serves in an "attract mode" for curious students. Sometimes high schoolers visit the library just to play with the machine.

Cox firmly believes in in-service training for teachers and has conducted several workshops for Hickman's teaching staff since the program arrived. The system is primarily used by junior year American History, American Literature, and American Culture teachers and students. But, as the program expands, and people become more familiar with its capabilities, Cox feels that it could be used with a wider range of study areas, such as art, world history, geography, science, and English.

One problem with introducing the program, according to Columbia School District users, is that it arrived in the middle of the school year, and had to be set up and tested on various hardware platforms (Cox discovered that the Macintosh Classic was inadequate, so they had to move up to the Macintosh LC for faster processing). Teachers had to familiarize themselves with the program's contents and uses after lesson plans and curriculum for the year had already been planned. For example, in American History, the time period covered by the Continental Congress collection had already been studied in classes prior to the arrival of the equipment. This year, however, Cox is conducting summer workshops for teachers so that they will have time to integrate the AMP into next year's curriculum.

Another complaint about the program by high school users is that all of the collections are not yet available. LC has promised to deliver the three upcoming collections by the end of the summer. But the success of the present collections has only left librarians clamoring for more.

In a *Report of a Formative Evaluation of the American Memory Prototype* prepared in 1990 by Marcy C. Chobot for LC, the preliminary use of AMP was evaluated by three school libraries: Andrew Carnegie Middle School in Orangeville, California; Binghamton High School in Binghamton, New York; and Oakton High School in Vienna, Virginia. At Carnegie School, teacher Dave Matthews noted the limited size of the prototype database; and Kathy Hensen also mentioned that frequently there was not enough material on a given subject. An Oakton School teacher also had difficulty figuring out the scope of the American Memory collections.

Jenny Cox describes this problem of limited content by explaining that students in her school are most familiar with databases such as InfoTrac, which contain material on virtually any subject. Thus, when students search AMP, they have trouble adjusting to the limited subject matter available. They expect to be able to type in any subject which occurs to them, then have something appear on the screen. These problems only confirm the importance of librarians' role in educating students and teachers about the content and purpose of AMP well before the program is put into use in any school.

User-Friendly Software

One feature of AMP which has received very little criticism is the software which was developed by LC. William Priest, social studies coordinator at Rockbridge High, describes the software as very "user-friendly," and Dave Matthews of Carnegie School mentions in the formative evaluation that the interface was very well designed and intuitive. He even sent congratulations to the designers and programmers.

Programmers have provided interesting and creative ways to access the collections. For example, the opening menu of the program depicts the Library of Congress Reading Room, and places users in Washington D.C., with choices about which collections to access. In other collections, photographs and political cartoons are presented side-by-side with cataloging information.

One of the positive software features mentioned by Jenny

Cox is the fact that users can either select menus or "click buttons." On the Apple computer, all collections can be searched simultaneously. Or, one can go to the index to search alphabetically. Keyword and Boolean logic searching are also made easy, so that a novice can use the system.

Putting AMP to Work

One purpose of the pilot program is to find out exactly how schools will utilize AMP. Librarians, teachers, and students have discovered many and varied ways. In Hickman High School, students have used AMP to create their own newspapers or diaries of early America. Cox has created handouts from the project that explain how the program works. In other schools, several teachers in the early pilot program have transferred the videodisc images to videotape for student projects.

American Memory photographs have been used by teachers of English and American culture in high schools across the nation. At Rockbridge High, one American Culture teacher uses AMP to show buildings on an island in New York Harbor at the turn of the century. The specific buildings were mentioned in a piece of literature her class had studied. In Binghamton High School, an English teacher used AMP to illustrate the setting of the novel, *A Separate Peace* by John Knowles (Bantam, ISBN 0-553-28041-4), which is set during World War II. Another Binghamton teacher of creative writing used the program to illustrate how the time period of a setting affects a story by comparing current locations in Binghamton with the same sites depicted in AMP.

Political cartoons have been used in various ways. One history teacher selected a current cartoon, and then had his students search for cartoons in AMP that had the same theme. The lesson illustrated how history repeats itself. Another teacher printed out AMP cartoons and asked his students to make up their own captions. He then compared the students' captions with the originals. More specifically, political cartoons about Huey Long were used by an English class studying Robert Penn Warren's *All the King's Men* (Random, ISBN 0-394-40502-1).

The photographic collection on transportation contains everything from oxcarts to locomotives. Classes in technology have used this collection, and students in other classes working on reports on railroads, etc., have also found the transportation collection very useful. The Detroit Publishing Company photos of the U.S. contain photographs of each state capital. The Detroit collection has been used by various classes to depict small-town communities, clothing, and the lifestyle of a period.

Some other subjects which students have successfully searched on AMP include Henry Ford and the automobile, the sewing machine, the machine gun, and Robert J. Oppenheimer. One student in a world history class at Carnegie was able to use original photographs and bibliographic information from AMP to create an award-winning project about the invention of the printing press for National History Day.

Librarians and teachers who have tried AMP are already planning future uses. William Priest of Rockbridge High plans to build collections of materials around topics, and to download them to discs for use in the classroom. Teachers in Columbia (MO) are excited about using the Continental Congress collection and the Civil War Photo collection to illustrate those periods of history in the beginning of the next school year. Steve Carr of Blackstock Jr. High (Oxnard, CA) anticipates using the early diaries and letters of California to help students answer questions about why some towns during the gold rush became boom towns and why others went bust.

The Future of AMP

Librarians and teachers agree on the value of AMP in teaching high school students how to use primary source material. Most students are familiar with seeing history dramatized, or reading history that has been interpreted, or viewing reenactments. AMP presents the raw primary material, but it is then up to the students to use it, interpret it, dramatize it, etc. Librarians have found that students are often led to written material from American Memory. Teachers have given students historical questions or problems, and asked the students to look though AMP to reach their own theories or conclusions.

AMP is still in the prototype stage, and school libraries are taking an active part in the development and finetuning of it. Susan Veccia, leader of the Library of Congress user evaluation team for all sites, warns that it is still too early to detect trends or draw conclusions. But school librarians are now working with teachers to make the most of the program.

The future of AMP will be dependent upon congressional funding and approval at the end of the pilot program in 1995.

While the cost for hardware may now be prohibitive for many school libraries—a videodisc and CD-ROM player, high-speed computers, quality printers, etc.—it's clear that the electronic library will be the library of the future. In addition, students like it, are comfortable with it, and think it is fun.

The visual aspect of AMP is one of the main drawing cards for students. When the program is brought into a classroom, the technology itself quickly attracts the students' attention. But teachers and librarians always have a plan. William Priest can't wait until next year when the Continental Congress collection arrives, because he plans to "hook the kids in the very beginning with the broadsides." Before they realize it, Rockbridge High students will be learning to use primary resources for their own research.

Left on their own, students will inevitably be drawn to the more sensational aspects of the program, such as the execution scene of McKinley's assassin. With careful prodding from librarians and teachers, students could find themselves digging for more information: Who was this man who assassinated McKinley? Why did he do it? Who invented the electric chair? Additionally, students could be led to internalize the information: Is capital punishment justifiable? Would they flip the switch? AMP may not have all the answers, but it can provide the background for many of the important questions. Cox sees the American Memory Project as an opportunity for "a true partnership between media services and the curricular area."

Fourteen School Libraries Participating In American Memory

Andrew Carnegie Middle School, Orangeville, California.

Binghamton High School, Binghamton, New York.

Bismarck Public Schools, Bismarck, North Dakota.

Charles Blackstock Junior High School, Oxnard, California.

College Grove School, College Grove, Tennessee.

Columbia Public Schools, Columbia, Missouri.

East Central Independent School District, San Antonio, Texas.

Educational School District 113, Olympia, Washington.

Fox Hill Elementary School, Indianapolis, Indiana.

Gibraltar Area Schools, Fish Creek, Wisconsin.

Lubbock Independent School District, Lubbock, Texas.

Oakton High School, Vienna, Virginia.

Reed High School, Sparks, Nevada.

St. Mark's High School, Wilmington, Delaware.

Reading Images
Videos in the Library and Classroom

by Kay E. Vandergrift & Jane Anne Hannigan

I f reading is image-making, viewing is image-reading. The visual images which saturate the world of young people are a part, often a major part, of the tools they use to reflect upon and interpret their world. Videos are as important as books in confirming, illuminating, or extending the life experiences of those who perceive them. Perception is itself an interpretive act. Whether reading or viewing a story, perceivers both bring meaning to and take meaning from the symbol system in which that story is encoded. In the decoding process, therefore, readers recreate a unique and personal story. As young people watch film versions of other lives, they add shape and substance to their own.

For many young people, videos are the literature of choice. Librarians, parents, and teachers may not always be happy with this, but we must acknowledge it and take the same care in evaluating, selecting, and using videos as we do with books.[1]

We must also acknowledge that the range of technical and aesthetic qualities in video is as rich, varied, and complex as that of other media, including print. Videos are becoming increasingly important in library collections and in school curricula as more and more professionals learn to value films for what they can contribute to the informational and aesthetic needs of young people.

Video in the Curriculum

Schools incorporating integrated whole language programs may be more likely to accept that films and videos can enhance student learning just as print does. Unfortunately, however, too many still perceive of film only as an enticement to print (which it often is), as a filler, as a reward, or as an alternative to print for less able students. When such perceptions prevail, even teachers who use videos thoughtfully and effectively are sometimes made to feel guilty that they are demanding less, both of themselves and of their students. Until films are included on required "reading" lists and bibliographies and accepted as appropriate source material for school assignments, they will not truly be accepted as works of art in their own right. Videos can stimulate inquiry or inspire joy just as books do.

The wit and charm of Jane Austen's *Pride and Prejudice* (CBS/Fox Video) come alive in the BBC version and offer a valid interpretation of that classic that adolescents might thor-oughly enjoy. This video is often available in school or public libraries or in video stores and could be assigned as an alternate or additional version of this novel. When such videos are used in the classroom or library, the simultaneous sharing of that event helps to build a sense of community among students.[2] The best teaching incorporates alternative approaches and materials, making use of the unique characteristics and contributions of each while also accommodating various learning styles.

The skills and abilities needed to decode and interpret visual images are probably as demanding as those required for reading print. In fact, it is possible that they are even more demanding because the relationship between the "real" and the "imagined," between "visible" and "invisible" aspects of a created world are more difficult to discern. Good readers learn to read what is on the lines, between the lines, and beyond the lines in decoding print. Just so, do skilled viewers learn to look closely at and within images and at the juxtaposition of images. At the same time they must consider how sound, light, movement, and other aspects of filmic art are used to shape vision and enhance or inhibit personal interpretation.

Since many adults begin their selection of videos with those that originated from books, we have limited our discussion in this article to videos adapted from books.[3]

Three Categories

We examined three basic categories of book-based videos: traditional folk or fairy tales; modern short stories; and novels. There are many versions and variants of traditional tales on video, just as there are in print.[4] Some use animation or special effects to create the magic of these stories. Faerie Tale Theatre videos often incorporate a flippant tone and elaborate costumes in retelling familiar tales. *Cinderella* (Faerie Tale Theatre) combines clever contemporary humor in a traditional version of the tale. The makers of Davenport Films place old tales in more modern Appalachian settings. *Ashpet* (Davenport Films), for instance, is the Cinderella story set during World War II with a young soldier and a victory dance instead of the prince's ball. Ashpet's delicious fairy godmother is a local herbal woman who helps her stay in touch with her own heritage. Both stepsisters are well cast with one holding the focus of our attention throughout most of the film. Ashpet dominates only towards the end of the film, first at the dance and then when the young soldier comes to call. In this version of Cinderella, it is clear that Ashpet is her own person by the end of the film, a nice feminist touch. These videos emphasize the fact that Cinderella is a story which is, in many ways, more appropriate for young adults than for children.

Many modern short stories have also been depicted on video. *Jack of Hearts* (Journal Films/Altschul Group), based on a story by Isobel Huggan, convincingly presents young Elizabeth who must face her feelings of disgrace at being chosen to play the male role in a ballet recital. She feels big, awkward, and clumsy and is totally embarrassed by this situation. When the nasty but dainty Trudy leaps into her lap at the end of the dance, Elizabeth breaks down and insists on telling the audience she is a girl. It is Aunt Eadie who, like Elizabeth, is disapproved of, who deals with her disgrace and teaches Elizabeth to play poker as a means of releasing the emotion of the moment. The protagonist's glimpse of this grown-up rebel helps her to heal her heartache and begin to appreciate herself as a unique individual.

Many novels have been produced as video feature films either in animated or live action versions.[5] Sometimes excerpts from a novel are made into short films or a series of short films. This is the case with some of Beverly Cleary's books, from which several segments are available on separate videos. There is also a kind of video booktalk combining a narrator's introduction and filmed scenes to entice young people to read the book. Vincent Price introduces *The Ghost Belonged to Me* (Walt Disney Educational Media/Coronet/MTI Film & Video), a novel by Richard Peck, with obvious glee and his usual scary tone. This ten-minute video will have young people running to the shelves to get the book. Blossom Culp predicts that Alexander will see a ghost and soon it appears. He follows the ghost's instructions without knowing what he is doing or why. Viewers are left with more questions than answers and thus might lead to not only the reading of this and other books by Peck, but also to exploration of other ghosts.

The Transformation to Video

It is tempting to judge a book-based video on its faithful re-creation of the characters and events from the printed source. It is more important, however, to remain true to the spirit and the essence of the original and to recognize that, in order to do so, a film-maker may have to deviate from the original. Novels do not necessarily work as video scripts, and a great book does not necessarily make a great video. The development and importance of various compositional elements shift and change as stories are transformed from one medium to another.

It may be useful to recall that a film based on a novel, by the time it appears to an audience, has gone through a number of transformations. First, there is the story as written for original publication as a novel or short story; second, there is the film script developed from that; third, there is the embodiment of the scripted characters in the selection of a cast; fourth, there is the story as actually filmed; and fifth, there is the final edited version of the film. At each of these stages of film-making, the creators strive for both continuity and creativity. Too much continuity or coherence to the original may not only limit creative interpretation but could deny the unique possibilities of film as an aesthetic medium. An overabundance of creativity, on the other hand, could result in a marvelous film, but one that has little or no relationship to the original story. Thus, the successful book-based film seeks a balance between continuity and creativity. Ordinarily the director is considered the primary creator of film art, but in attempting to remain true to the spirit of the original, he or she becomes a cocreator with its author, whether or not that author has any direct input into the film.

Each transformation from print story to film both delimits and defines what is to follow. In the process of scripting, one selects from the original text those elements which can be represented through visual images and that the particular scriptwriter believes will most effectively convey the basic import and impact. The comedy, *The Hoboken Chicken Emergency* (Wonderworks), from the book by D. Manus Pinkwater, is a marvelous example of selecting the most obvious visual humor in the portrayal of Henrietta, the 266 pound chicken. The body language of the cast, including Henrietta, contributes to the laughter that results from the antics of the townspeople and the chicken.

Cast selection determines, at least in part, both the interpretation of various roles and audience response. The casting of Glenn Close as Sarah in *Sarah, Plain and Tall* (Hallmark), based on the novel by Patricia MacLachlan, focuses audience attention on her character and shifts the point of view from that of Anna to her stepmother.

Minor characters may also take on greater importance when they come to life through the actors or actresses who portray them. The humorous depiction of a young male classmate in *Molly's Pilgrim* (Phoenix/BFA Film & Video), based on Barbara Cohen's book, lightens the tone and serves almost as a character foil in contrast to the dramatic intensity of the young Russian immigrant who is the story's protagonist. Sometimes costuming or makeup provide the dimension that brings minor characters into viewers' consciousness and moves them from the background to the foreground of a story.

Style and Setting

When the assembled cast actually begins filming, the use of frame, visual composition, camera angles, light, color, sound, movement, and pacing reassembles elements from the original script to create a new version or variant of the story. The very act of framing an image singles it out and forces viewers to pay attention to what is inside and sometimes to imagine what might be beyond. Camera angles, use of light, shadow, and color serve as subtle instructions on how to interpret that image. Point of view may also be strengthened as the camera actually allows us to see what is seen by the protagonist. The eye of the camera, sometimes with the assistance of special effects, can also heighten the mood or tone. We are all familiar with the use of a soundtrack to establish these elements or to signal rising action or a shift in scene or time.

The significance of objects as symbols may at times be conveyed more powerfully and efficiently visually than through the printed word.

The setting into which an image is placed also contributes to viewers' perceptions and interpretations. Sometimes a novelist will leave a setting deliberately vague to allow readers to place the story in their own familiar contexts; but even when a particular setting is not an important aspect of the novel, it usually does not remain vague in a video.

In *Sounder* (Paramount Home Video), from the novel by William Armstrong, the harshness of the rural setting in which the family struggles for survival is softened by the eye of the camera revealing the lush beauty of nature. At the same time this setting stands in stark contrast to the grim conditions of the protagonists' lives. The mystery and suspense in *The House of Dies Drear* (Wonderworks) is intensified through the dark, shadowy images and the use of sound effects.

The pacing of *The Electric Grandmother* (Coronet/MTI Film & Video), a short story by Ray Bradbury, is part of the success of this film as the children grow older and reach the ages when they once again need the care of the title character. The robotic grandmother the family selected arrives when a helicopter drops a sarcophagus that young Agatha must open with her magical key, foreshadowing the opening of Agatha's own heart. The grandmother is marvelous as she flies the laundry from a kite and pours orange juice from her fingers. The concepts of love, death, and memory are explored eloquently in this visual translation of Bradbury's story.

Two Ways to Focus

Overwhelmed with the sheer numbers of book-based videos, we sought a way to reduce the numbers discussed and focus attention on key ideas. Thus, two foci determined the videos chosen for inclusion: videos whose stories developed or interpreted the imaginative, creative, or independent aspects of a protagonist's character; and a multiculturalism[6] that encourages examination of differences and seeks to eliminate conformity to a single model of being.[7]

Taking Care of Terrific (Wonderworks), based on the novel by Lois Lowry, combines both of these foci very powerfully. Enid, who wants to be called Cynthia, lives with busy professional parents and a befuddled housekeeper who love her but have very little time for her. She finds creative release in the park where she shares the music of the man called Hawk and just accepts the homelessness of the bag ladies. She babysits Joshua, who wants to be called Tom Terrific, and introduces him to the wonders of the park where they can be whoever they want to be. The late-night excursion on the lake with all the bag ladies in swan boats as Hawk plays "Stardust" is very moving. It is clear that each of these women are real human beings with a store of treasured memories. The alternate names the children adopt are symbolic of the park and the seeming lack of personal identity of all those who seek refuge there.

Runaway (Wonderworks), based on Felice Holman's *Slake's Limbo*, is a compelling interpretation of the novel which also deals both with creative, independent characters and with those who are different. Aremis Slake blames himself for the death of his friend Joseph and runs away to the New York subway to hide. Joseph and he had haunted the subway system in search of found objects which they used in the creation of free-form sculptures. Aremis chose Joseph as a friend although Joseph was mentally handicapped and spoke very little. The video places a great deal of strength in the characterization of Joseph and also in two other minor characters, the African-American Vietnam veteran who uses a wheelchair and the coffee-shop waitress. Survival is the obvious thread throughout, and the film reinforces this over and over. The found sculpture is a symbol for the beauty and joy that is a part of this child's life. What is clear in this interpretation, as in the book, is both the imagination of the children and the ability to value people for what they are.

The Sense of Self

Sarah is dismayed to be sent to visit her Aunt Claudia after being caught shoplifting in *Shoeshine Girl* (Coronet/MTI Video), based on the novel by Clyde Robert Bulla. She is an undisciplined youngster who has to face up to Aunt Claudia's rules and those of Al, the shoeshine man who employs her. Originally bitter and resentful, Sarah learns to care about her job and for the people around her and finally for herself as a person.

Jacob Have I Loved (Wonderworks), from the novel by Katherine Paterson, forces viewers to concentrate on the suffering of a young woman. Louise Bradshaw is jealous of her twin sister, Caroline, and is so consumed with hatred that she loses her own sense of self. The fishing community is critical in setting up the isolation Louise feels, and the music she loves is something she fights against just as she battles with her own demons.

In *The Haunting of Barney Palmer* (Wonderworks), based on *The Haunting* by Margaret Mahy, the difference is not one of culture but of paranormal powers. One sees Barney as a young, frightened child who is protective of a pregnant stepmother, terrified of his increasingly realistic dreams, and determined to find a way to cope with this strangeness. But it is the presence of his older sister Trudie and the final revelation of her powers that brings the engagement with potential evil to a climax. Both Barney and Trudie learn to accept their individual powers and to face life with a sense of joy, revealed in the playful sequences at the shore with Trudie and Uncle Cole swinging and all the children swimming. This is in contrast to Barney's use of a mask to hide behind as a visual metaphor in the opening shots and several times throughout the video. The visual representations of the powers are convincing, and the pace of this video should hold an audience to its conclusion.

When to risk one's own life for another human being is the theme of *Miracle at Moreaux* (Wonderworks), a touching interpretation of *Twenty and Ten* by Claire Hutchet Bishop. The story remains essentially intact although there are changes in both characters and plot to create dramatic tension. Three, rather than ten, Jewish children are saved from Nazi soldiers by the nun and children in a convent school near the border.

The film beautifully illustrates differences among people and the danger of believing terrible stories about others. The explanation of Hanukkah and the use of the lighted candle work well, both realistically and metaphorically.

Rudy Soto is the young protagonist who values the red-tailed hawk but does not yet grasp what it means to be a hawk in *Hawk, I'm Your Brother* (Byrd Baylor Family Video/Southwest Series). The heat and starkness of the reservation is convincingly conveyed in sequence after sequence and so is a respect for the land and its people.

Ramona: The Great Hair Argument (Churchill Films) is one of several videos adapted from the novel *Ramona and Her Mother* by Beverly Cleary. Beezus is wistfully eager to be attractive and appeal to her friends; all this, of course, to be accomplished with a fashionable haircut. Although Beezus is the focus of this story, Ramona is also learning about interaction with others. The Frankenstein sequence at the end of the film is very funny. When Ramona's friend comes to play, he declares that Ramona's haircut disqualifies her from playing Frankenstein.

Walter Small and his son Thomas uncover a variety of clues and lead viewers through a maze of suspenseful events, including meeting Mr. Pluto, in *The House of Dies Drear*, a novel by Virginia Hamilton. Both book and film encourage youngsters to inquire into events such as slavery, the abolitionist movement, the underground railroad, and ghosts. Hidden passages and secret doors are revealed and sounds abound in frightening cacophony. The gospel music is incorporated perfectly and adds a dimension of wholeness to the story. This video could be a useful tool to explore webbing concepts with young people, as it encourages curious young scholars to seek

---

Distributors

Byrd Baylor Family Video/Southwest Series, Inc., PO Box 2911, Tucson, AZ 85702

Churchill Films, 12210 Nebraska Ave., Los Angeles, CA 90025

Coronet/MTI Film & Video, 108 Wilmot Rd., Deerfield, IL 60015

Davenport Films, Rte. 1, Box 527, Delaplane, VA 22025

Faerie Tale Theatre, Playhouse Video, CBS/Fox Video, 39000 Seven Mile Rd., Livonia, MI 48152

Hallmark Hall of Fame, Box 419580, Kansas City, MO 64141

Journal Films/Altschul Group, 1560 Sherman Ave., Evanston, IL 60201

Paramount Home Video, 5555 Melrose Ave., Hollywood, CA 90038

Phoenix/BFA Videos, 468 Park Ave. S., New York, NY 10016

Walt Disney Educational Media, Coronet/MTI Film & Video, 108 Wilmot Road, Deerfield, IL 60015

Wonderworks, Public Media Video, 5547 N. Ravenswood Ave., Chicago, IL 60640

---

additional connections to and increased understanding of its content.

A Change of Perspective

An interesting set of videos addresses identical issues from various perspectives. The idea of being a perfect child is considered in *Charles* (Walt Disney Educational Media/Coronet/MTI Film & Video), *Konrad* (Wonderworks), and *How to Be a Perfect Person in Just Three Days* (Wonderworks). From a short story by Shirley Jackson, Charles is the delightful alter ego of Laurie, who creates Charles to embody his bad behavior during his first weeks in kindergarten. Viewers quickly guess what is going on, but the pacing is fast enough to keep them interested in seeing how the parents will finally face the truth. This film is best suited for young adult audiences.

Konrad, from a book by Christine Noestlinger, is fascinating in its creation of a very unusual family unit. Konrad is a factory-created "ideal child" who is mistakenly delivered to the imperfect and disorderly Bertie who eats tunafish salad with licorice sticks. Mr. Thomas captures Konrad's heart with music and becomes a third member of this wacky family.

Milo of *How To Be a Perfect Person in Just Three Days*, from a novel by Stephen Manes, is humorously believable as a real klutz. Weird Dr. Silverfish assigns a series of tasks to help Milo achieve perfection. He wears a broccoli necklace to learn humility and refrains from eating for a day, in spite of hunger and an outrageously noisy stomach, to exercise his willpower. These three videos portray differences while at the same time encouraging individualization, independence, and caring about others.

All of these videos and many others that are readily available, may help young people reach out to one another and recognize that differences are to be valued. The experience of sharing such videos enlarges the interpretive community to include those who are, at least temporarily, more comfortable with this medium than with print. It involves them in the crucial search for meaning in the activities of school or library. Respect for differences then extends from the virtual reality of a character in a film to the real life characters who share our world.

References

1. *From Page to Screen: Children's and Young Adult Books on Film and Video*, ed. by Joyce Moss and George Wilson (Gale, 1992) is an extensive listing of translations from book to film and should prove helpful in evaluating and selecting videos.

2. In some situations, according to the "fair-use" clauses of the copyright laws, "home use only" videos may be used in classrooms. We suggest that librarians and teachers check with individual distributors for information regarding performance rights.

3. The research for this article including viewing and evaluating 117 videos on a 52" Toshiba screen and derived from published novels, short stories, and folktales. Those videos selected for discussion are the ones we consider most

appropriate to the focus of this article. Animated and iconographic versions of picture books were not included.

4. It might prove useful to explore a variety of versions of currently popular Beauty and the Beast tale both in book and video format, such as *Beauty and the Beast* by Jean Cocteau (Janus Films/Embassy Home Entertainment); *Beauty and the Beast* by Shelley Duvall (CBS/Fox Video); *Beauty and the Beast* from the television series with Linda Hamilton and Ron Perlman (Republic Pictures Home Video); as well as *Beauty and the Beast* by Walt Disney Studios (Walt Disney Home Videos).

5. Among the best-known videos that have proved popular with children are *The Chronicles of Narnia* (Wonderworks), *The Secret Garden* (CBS/Fox Video), and *The Little Princess* (Wonderworks). *Anne of Green Gables* (Buena Vista Home Video) and *A Girl of the Limberlost* (Wonderworks) will attract viewers who admire the independence demonstrated by these heroines.

6. The authors accept a definition of culture as "learned behaviors." Therefore, "multiculturalism" refers to national, ethnic, gender, economic, social, or other groups presumed to influence individual behavior and/or behavioral expectations from others.

7. "*School Library Journal* published, during 1992, a series of annotated video lists on African-Americans (January), Native-Americans (May), Asian-Americans/Asians (September), and the Hispanics/Chicanos/Latinos (December)." The lists were compiled by Phyllis Levy Mandell and are also available as a set ($5) from *SLJ*'s reprint office. Contact Cathy Dionne, Cahners Reprint Services, 1350 E. Touhy Ave., Des Plaines, IL 60017; (800) 523-9654; FAX (708) 390-2779.

Periodicals by Fax
A Houston Experience

by Dorcas Hand and Barbara Weathers

The Houston Area Independent School Library Network (HAISLN) is an organization of local private school librarians. We meet twice a year for a program, and have gradually added projects that help us all to offer better library services to our individual schools. We include high schools, middle schools, elementary schools, and a few K-12 schools.

"Periodicals by Fax," was set up in Spring 1991 as an experiment to allow HAISLN's secondary schools to share the expenses and use of lesser used but needed periodicals. We conducted research about similar networks elsewhere, and wrote a detailed protocol to explain to all participants the expectations and responsibilities, and procedures of membership. The final page of the protocol is an agreement to participate which is to be signed by the head of school and the librarian at each participating campus. This insures that the administration is aware of, supports the network in concept, and allows the librarian to make appropriate decisions. The interested schools met to discuss the various issues, agreed on final wording, and the network was open for business in Spring 1991.

How We Began

The schools submitted their existing periodicals lists to one editor who compiled them into a Union List for HAISLN members. Then, each school agreed to be responsible for providing particular titles to the network for five years from the inception of the Fax Network. We also agreed on a list of titles which would be assumed to be held on each campus, and would not be eligible for fax support barring unusual circumstances. These titles are those which will be so widely used for research that copyright issues could not be respected, or those held for recreational browsing.

In the beginning, we agreed to use only our existing lists. Each school had built their serials list to complement their own curricular needs. The Union List provided all the members the collective curricular support of all the schools.

In Summer 1992, we compared our Union List with *Abridged Readers' Guide, Readers' Guide, Magazine Index,* and *InfoTrac.* At the October meeting, the group considered whether we should begin to build our collection to complete coverage of any one of these indexes. We hold 75 percent of the *Abridged Readers Guide* list. We decided to hold with our original choice, agreeing that for us the indexed titles not provided were marginal to all our curricula. We will consider in a future meeting how far back our coverage should go, bearing in mind space and format considerations. The second edition of the Union Serials List will reflect changes in all schools subscription lists, the addition of middle schools to the Fax Network.

Resolving Concerns

In early discussions of this project, many were concerned that their libraries might be unable to handle the number of requests for fax transmissions. We all have small staffs and many on-campus responsibilities. One reason for dividing the list was to spread the load evenly both in subscription costs and in person-hours spent responding to fax requests. We also hold as a long-range goal the addition of titles to our list which a few students at each campus might need occasionally, but which no one school can afford to support on its own. We will continue to spread the costs of subscriptions as equally as possible.

A second advance concern had to do with the variety in size of periodical collections at the various schools. Some schools are relatively wealthy with substantial holdings, while others are limited with small budgets. The larger libraries were concerned that they would be inundated with requests for the less common titles while they might not need the network for their own benefit. Our year-long trial actually proved that the benefit is mutual. The larger schools have more scholarly collections, but chose not to include *People Weekly*; it turns out that high school scholars sometimes need *People*.

The protocol spells out time limits for responding to requests which all the librarians felt they could honor. We remain a friendly group, and use the telephone whenever problems arise. If a school is inundated with in-house use at term paper time, the librarians can just call any fax requesters to say there's a delay.

Our initial intent in this network was to have fax machines in the libraries. But the schools were only just beginning to get them in their offices. So, we chose to approach the business manager or secretary to see if there would be any objections to the sending and receipt of library faxes. All the school offices were agreeable, and continue to be. Network usage has been only moderate to date, and the secretarial staff has not found it necessary to complain. Also, the administrations appreciate the money saving aspects of this collaboration.

We have chosen not to charge for the fax service, on the theory that all schools will participate at about the same level. So far, this has proven true. We have all the records required for copyright compliance, and could establish a fee structure if needed in the future. While we have not costed out the service precisely, we estimate the costs to be as follows for a hypothetical five-page article of $8^1/_2$" x 11" pages:

Sender
5 photocopies at $.04 ea. = $.20
staff time to locate 5 minutes
fax transmission 5 minutes

Receiver
fax paper 5 @ $.04 = $.20

Our assumptions include the absence of long distance charges, and the existence of a fax machine on the school campus.

How We Handle Copyright

A big concern of everyone in HAISLN and in the library literature is copyright. Our investigations support us in the establishment of the Fax Network:

1. The borrowing library is the one responsible for counting articles requested; the sender has no responsibility in this regard. A fax article counts the same as a photocopies article, and borrowers should not receive both a fax copy and a mailed photocopy as backup.
2. Borrowers should not request *in one year* more than five articles from the same periodical title from the previous five years. Five more articles from that journal may be requested the next year. An exception can be made for articles missing from the borrowers' own collection while a subscription is in effect.
3. Also, articles older than five years are not subject to the same limitations in receipt of copies; apparently, if a library is moderate in its requests for copies of these older articles, no copyright problems will ensue.
4. If a borrower sees that the limit is approaching, a subscription should be purchased, or additional articles purchased from University Microfilms International (UMI) or the journal directly are necessary, the network will recommend purchase, as everyone is busy and cannot support excessive fax requests.
5. If copies are supplied by fax for speed, they should *not* also be supplied by mail as backup. Fax transmission is fairly reliable, and telephone requests for retransmission work when the occasional article comes through illegible.
6. It has been suggested that if a network such as ours buys the subscription in the network name, then all network members could borrow freely from the journals bought in this way. However, ALA recommends caution in this approach. HAISLN would like to add a few esoteric titles to its union list to facilitate speedy response to student requests; given the limits stated in (2) above, we think there would probably be no problem. If a problem arises, we can write the journal directly for permission to make an exception or to pay for the additional copyright.

Future Plans

In Spring 1992, the eight high schools participating were surveyed about the effectiveness of the Fax Network. Six responded, and these were enthusiastic about continuation. Most felt that expansion to include HAISLN member middle schools would be appropriate. Some suggested subject areas in which to increase coverage, including African American publications and religious journals. We will further discuss the development of specialized areas on the various campuses. In October 1992, the Fax Network met to reexamine the protocol with the inclusion of nine middle schools in mind. Everyone continues to be enthusiastic, as we also consider establishing a fax committee to supervise Periodicals by Fax as we go along, to minimize large group meetings.

Our experience with this fax network has been that it was easy to begin and has been a wonderful addition to our individual school library programs. It has also provided the larger HAISLN group an ongoing reason to exist, beyond twice-yearly program meetings, and has contributed to all of our continuing library education. Other groups of schools may want to consider this low cost method of cooperation, so long as appropriate measures are taken to prevent copyright infringement.

Bibliography

Jackson, Mary E. "Library to Library." *Wilson Library Bulletin*, June 1989. Cites several fax projects and protocol examples.

Spitzer, Kathleen L. "Fax for Library Services." *ERIC Digest*. December 1991. Provides an overview of fax considerations, and a bibliography of ERIC documents.

Wilson, Mark. "How to Set Up a Telefacsimile Network—The Pennsylvania Libraries' Experience." *Online*. May 1988. Includes the protocol used as a model in Houston.

True Stories

- Audrey Smith's science project on the presence of DNA in leaves required an issue of *Science News* from 1990. Because the issue was missing from her own school's shelves, the Fax Network was used. An 8:15 a.m. request provided the article by fax by 9:43 that morning.
- A high school English teacher who is studying Chaucer chose to design the sophomore English research project around *The Canterbury Tales*. The Library had not anticipated the need for the *Chaucer Review*, and will use the Fax Network to support student research until the subscription and some back issues can be ordered.

Protocol, Houston Area Independent Schools Library Network
Updated October 1992

I. Purpose of the Network. The HAISLN "Periodical by Fax" Network is formed to assist all member schools to have the most access to the widest variety of periodicals at the least cost to each member by cooperatively selecting periodical titles among the member schools, and opening access among all participating libraries' periodical collections under the following guidelines. This Network began as a trial in Spring 1991 and was approved by the HAISLN membership for continuation at the Spring 1992 meeting. HAISLN member upper and middle school students and their faculties will be eligible for receipt of copied materials.

II. Purpose of Protocol. Many schools whose libraries are members of HAISLN have installed telefacsimile (fax) equipment to facilitate high speed document delivery among themselves and with other agencies. The intent of these guidelines is to establish a set of formal protocols to be used when sending interlibrary loan materials within the HAISLN Periodicals by Fax network. Schools without access to fax equipment can still participate, but the network would encourage them to acquire fax to speed document delivery both to other libraries and to their own students.

III. Cooperative Selection.

A. A Union List is made annually of the current serials holdings of all HAISLN member upper and middle libraries, including beginning dates for all holdings. A code will indicate the library which has agreed to be responsible for five years of back holdings of each title. (NOTE: In 1992-93, some titles originally deleted form network coverage and titles held by middle schools will not be so coded; the responsibility will be assigned after the Union List is compiled.) The list of journals will be re-evaluated annually and changed as agreed. The list will indicate members of record as of Nov. 1 of each year.

B. Schools not currently members must attend the annual Fall Periodicals by Fax meeting. New members unable to attend must make arrangements to meet with a returning member to be sure they understand the workings of the exchange.

C. In 1991, all libraries agreed that the network would not cover the following titles: *American Heritage, Car & Driver, Consumer Reports, Current History, Discover, Health,* local newspapers, *JOYS, Library Journal, Life, Nation, National Geographic, National Review, Natural History, New Republic, Popular Mechanics, Popular Photography, Popular Science, Psychology Today, School Library Journal, Science News, Seventeen, Smithsonian, Sports Illustrated, Texas Highways, Time, US News & World Report.* In October 1992, this pro-

tocol was amended to say that these titles will be available for back issues only. The network still assumes that each member will be responsible for subscriptions to any of these they feel essential to their own library program.

Participating libraries have selected 5-10 titles from their current holdings for which they agree to be responsible, and agree to supply to member libraries any requested citations from these titles. This has been done in cooperation with other members, and under the coordination of Kinkaid's library staff, to assure the broadest selection of titles. Each school also agrees to continue support of each title for 5 years from the initiation of the network. New members, especially middle schools, will be assigned appropriate responsibilities within the first year of membership.

II. Protocol.

Requests should be phoned to the sending member library before being submitted to other possible sources.

III. Requests

A. General Format

1. An abridged ILL form is supplied as an addendum to this document for use when requesting material via fax. The requesting library should complete a copy to use when phoning the request; the request form should NOT be faxed to the sending library. The sending library should record the request on the appropriate form. When the article is faxed, this abridged form will fit in the margin of a page to minimize pages of transmission. On completion of transmission, the photocopied article and the ILL request form should be stapled and filed for reference, and as a log of use of the system. By this method, schools will minimize network related transmissions, and nonlibrary staff and equipment use. Also, should the same article be requested by a second school, the photocopy would already exist.

2. All requests should include the particular librarian's name in case of any problems. See form.

B. Complete bibliographic and location verification is required before the request is phoned, and must be indicated on the request form. Requesting librarians should double check the student's citation against the index citation, and the location code in the HAISLN Union List for correctness to minimize error.

C. Copyright compliance must be noted on all photocopy requests. Also, the sending library should be sure the article includes complete citation data on the title page, hand written if not printed. The student will not be receiving the ILL form, and needs the complete information.

    D. No requests for searches or subject requests will be accepted.

    E. Should a requested document be received all or partly illegible, the requesting library should phone to request retransmission. The sending library will attempt one retransmission; if results are still unsatisfactory a photocopy will be mailed to the requesting school.

IV. Responses

    A. General Guidelines

       1. The sending library will provide telephone responses for any item which cannot be supplied for requests within the network, or any citation which seems not to provide the requested article.

       2. Libraries in the midst of end-of-term madness may find it necessary to suspend participation in the network for a brief period. Should this become necessary, they only need notify any requestors of a delay in supply of requested materials of up to one week.

       3. The sending library should provide a copy of the request with the supplied material, to verify the correctness of the article sent and to provide a record of receipt for the requesting library. These receipt copies should be filed appropriately, stapled to the original request as proof of receipt of a requested article and as part of the log of system use.

    B. Article Length.

       1. Articles more than 10 pages in length will not be sent via fax due to time constraints of clerical staff. Should an article of great length be

required and no other source known, special arrangements may be made by phone at the discretion of the sending library.

    C. Response Time Guidelines

       1. Fax requests will be filled within 24 hours. The sending library will notify the requesting library if this timetable cannot be met.

       2. Requests received before 11 AM daily can expect response the same day. Those received later than 11 AM will receive response the next school day.

       3. As stated above in III. Requests E., should a requested article be received in illegible form, the requesting library will phone to request retransmission. The sending library will try one time to retransmit more successfully. Should the results continue to be unsatisfactory, the sending library will mail a photocopy.

    D. Charges

       1. All charges for photocopies will be waived among HAISLN members. This policy will be reexamined annually to be sure all participants are using the system at comparable levels.

    E. Statistics

       1. Member libraries will keep accurate statistics of network use, both requests and responses. Participants should also keep records of journal requests by their own students unable to be satisfied either from their own holdings or those of the network; these titles will provide a list to include in future years.

    F. Sending libraries should retain the photocopy used to fax for one year for reference, for copyright compliance records, and for statistics.

VI. Revision. These guidelines will be reviewed annually by HAISLN Periodicals by Fax members.

Bring the Museum to the Media Center

by Beth Blenz-Clucas

Distance, time, and money prevent many schools from sponsoring frequent field trips to museums, even though these are among the most valuable out-of-school learning experiences students can have. Fortunately, many museum directors understand this and have come up with a way that the museum can come to the school if the school can't come to the museum.

A large number of major museums now offer lending and outreach programs that are designed to bring items from their collections directly into schools. In addition to full presentations, many institutions offer materials for loan that include artifacts, actual historical documents, audiovisual materials, teacher's guides, and displays. Through these programs, students get the kind of direct experience with museum materials that was once only possible by taking a field trip.

A natural liaison in the school-museum connection is the school library media specialist. In addition to providing special programs and displays of museum objects in the library, the media specialist can act as the link between museums and teachers by keeping informed about the different resources and programs that are available and by providing museum directors with information about the school's needs at all grade levels.

And, museum outreach isn't just for schools and school libraries. Many museums also count public libraries among their customers for special collections, display items, and educational programming.

Presentations

Ed Matthews, education curator of the Appleton Museum in Ocala, FL brings programs to schools on a regular basis, partly because of limited space for groups in the museum itself. Matthews recently presented a day-long program featuring the museum's collection of African masks and other artifacts to a kindergarten class. After viewing and touching the objects and hearing tapes of African folk music, the students made their own paper-plate masks, following the design examples Matthews provided.

"We don't have any classroom space at the museum right now, so these outreach programs are important," Matthews says. "By bringing part of the collection to the schools, students can become familiar with us, and they'll recognize what they see once they do come in."

In addition to serving as a next-best substitute for a mu-

seum trip, in-school programs can provide excellent preparation for an upcoming visit, helping students get the most out of the on-site experience. Curators from the National Portrait Gallery of the Smithsonian Institution bring tailored presentations to school groups before they visit the museum. And, the Smithsonian's Office of Elementary & Secondary Education offers comprehensive, low-cost summer seminars to help teachers (and media specialists) improve their knowledge about the various collections of the Smithsonian. The workshops cover such skills as understanding African-American art, teaching writing using museums, and using primary source materials to complement the history curriculum.

When a museum curator or volunteer makes a presentation to a school group, it is often geared directly to what the school has requested. The Lake County Museum in Wauconda, IL, recently created a multimedia program on pioneer history for the Woodview Primary School in nearby Grayslake, IL. Under the direction of the museum's education curator, Stacey Pyne, three sessions of third-graders learned about local pioneers while seeing and touching some of the settlers' belongings. Also featured were exhibit boxes on Native American life and other topics borrowed from the Field Museum of Natural History in Chicago. Students watched a video, *Patchwork* (Her Own Words Prod., 1989), that features the work of pioneer and contemporary quilters, then made their own "quilts" with fabric squares and glue.

In an unusual outreach program provided by the National Postal Museum in Hull, Quebec, elementary schoolchildren learn first-hand how their mail travels through the postal system. Presenters from the museum help young children stamp, sort and deliver letters to their classmates. Older students weigh parcels, estimate postage costs, and determine distribution routes. Francine Brousseau, who manages the program, says it is so popular that museum presenters are booked through the coming school year.

Lending Collections

You want to develop an exciting display on a theme but don't have the in-house resources to pull it off. Or, a teacher asks for your help in providing artifacts for a lesson on a specific period in history. Try checking out a nearby museum's lending collection.

Most major cultural museums in the United States and Canada have developed collections of materials for loan to schools. These collections are usually geared toward specific grade levels, and many include teacher's guides.

As the Woodview School discovered, the Field Museum of Natural History in Chicago had a wealth of materials on various world cultures (particularly Native Americans) that are available to schools under its Harris Educational Loan Program. For an annual registration fee of $20, schools may borrow up to five "exhibit cases," "experience boxes," or audiovisual materials at a time for three-week periods. As is typical of many museum lending programs, all materials must be picked up and returned to the museum.

Tibetan Masks and Colonial Quilts

The lending collection from the Newark (NJ) Museum includes such diverse objects as Tibetan masks and American colonial-era quilts. Though some of the objects are reproductions, many, like the Early American foot warmers and candle molds, are real. Helene Konkus, supervisor of the collection, says the materials are lent not only for classroom use, but often for exhibits in school and public libraries. Schools may register to borrow from the collection for a $25 to $30 annual fee ($10 for individual teachers). Loan periods are for two weeks.

The museum also offers "Outward Bound" programs that are brought into local schools, covering such topics as "Skulls and Skeletons" (on the pre-history of New Jersey) and "The African-American Experience in Newark." Each 45-minute program encourages student participation with artifacts to handle, games to play, and slides to view and discuss.

One school library media center that took advantage of the Newark Museum program was the one at the Betsy Ross School, which serves preschool through third-grade students in Mahwah, NJ. Media specialist Joan Kenney believes that an important part of her job is to introduce children to realia— objects from real life.

"The Newark Museum program provides wonderful realia for our students," Kenney says. "Most kids see so much every day that they don't truly *see* anything. When the museum materials come to our school, they are presented in such a concentrated, focused way that students really learn something. And, unlike a museum field trip, the kids can see the objects at their own level and touch them."

The borrowed museum materials are displayed in the school library along with related books from the collection. Kenney conducts brief introductory sessions for each of the classes, then allows students to examine the objects. "We can't keep the related books on the shelf after these sessions," she says.

One collection Kenney plans to borrow each year is the "Colonial Living" box, which includes a working miniature loom, an old wood carving, miniature rooms and furnishings from the era, and quilt samples. After viewing and handling the quilts, third-graders piece together their own quilt squares depicting something about their lives. Kenney then joins the squares into a large quilt that hangs in the school to commemorate the class as it goes on to middle school.

Traveling Trunks

Quilts are also an important part of the Kansas Museum of History's "Traveling Resource Trunks" program. Actual quilt samples along with videos, historical documents, and archival photographs make up the "Kansas Women and Their Quilts" trunk, designed for use with upper elementary-age students. Each of the museum's seven other trunks (which were developed in collaboration with teacher advisory panels) focuses on a specific theme in the cultural history of the state and Plains region, including the experiences of various ethnic groups. Students can try on pioneer clothes, play nineteenth-century children's games, and handle objects like those used by their great-great grandparents.

According to Mark Adam, outreach supervisor for the museum, the lending program is crucial in the largely rural Plains region. "With these trunks, a school can reach right across the state and see materials that are simply not available if you don't live in Topeka," Adam says.

Kansas schools and libraries have top priority in borrowing the trunks, but anyone else may reserve a trunk by agreeing to pay the round-trip shipping charges.

Smaller Than the Smithsonian

Smaller museums offer treasures for school use as well. At the Schingoethe Center for Native American Culture, part of Aurora University in Illinois, artifacts, audiovisual materials, and curriculum guides are collected in "discovery boxes" that are organized by region. According to curator Marcia Lautanen-Raleigh, the boxes are constantly circulating to local schools and libraries. The videos included in some boxes are extremely popular, she says, particularly ones with short running times that fit into a class period or hour-long program.

Many school libraries have borrowed Schingoethe Center materials for special displays. In October 1992, as the public debated the meaning of Columbus' landing in North America, the Friends of the Batavia (IL) Public Library borrowed several discovery boxes for a day celebrating Native American culture. Library patrons were able to handle artifacts and play traditional games as part of the event.

"The games were a good way to get people involved," says library trustee Barbara King. "We got a lot of people into the library who hadn't been there before, and everybody left with a bit more knowledge about Native American Culture."

Likewise, the "Grout to Go" Discovery Express Kits available from the Grout Museum of History & Science in Waterloo, IA, have proved popular with school and library borrowers. Under the general themes of "The Pioneers" and "Native Americans" among others, these kits are lent for two-week periods for a $20 user fee. Museum-quality artifacts, maps, mini-exhibits, and suggested activities are included, along with brief videos. New kits focusing on quilts and the one-room schoolhouses of Iowa pioneers are in the works, according to curator Robin Venter.

Plans for Expansion

Because of the growing popularity of outreach services, each of the museums mentioned in this article plans to add to its programs in the near future. And, school library media specialists will play a key role in advising museums about the particular needs of their schools.

"We're always trying to tie in the museum's materials with what's being taught in the classroom," say media specialist Joan Kenney. "Sometimes we don't hit it exactly right, but the kids always respond by wanting to read more about the subject."

Outreach and Lending Programs

For more information about the programs and collections mentioned in this article, contact:

Appleton Museum of Art
Ed Matthews, Education Curator
4333 E. Silver Spring Blvd.
Ocala, FL 32670
Phone: (904) 236-5050

Field Museum of Natural History
Harris Educational Loan Program
Roosevelt Rd. at Lake Shore Dr.
Chicago, IL 60605-2497
Phone: (312) 322-8853

Grout Museum of History & Science
Robin Venter, Education Director
503 South St.
Waterloo, IA 50701
Phone: (319) 234-6357

Kansas Museum of History
Mark Adam, Outreach Supervisor
6425 S.W. Sixth St.
Topeka, KS 66615-1099
Phone: (913) 272-8681

Lake County Museum
Stacey Pyne, Education Curator
27277 Forest Preserve Rd.
Wauconda, IL 60084
Phone: (708) 526-7878

National Postal Museum
Canadian Museum of Civilization
Francine Brousseau, Educational Programmes Manager
100 Laurier St., P.O. Box 3100, Station B
Hull, Quebec, J8X 4H2
CANADA

The Newark Museum
Education Department
Helene Konkus, Lending Collection Supervisor
49 Washington St., P.O. Box 540
Newark, NJ 07101-0540
Phone: (201) 596-6630

Schingoethe Center for Native American Cultures
Aurora University
Marcia Lautanen-Raleigh, Curator
347 S. Gladstone Ave.
Aurora, IL 60506-4892
Phone: (708) 844-5402

Smithsonian Institution Office of Elementary & Secondary Education
Ann Bay, Director
900 Jefferson Dr., S.W. Rm. 1163, MRC 402
Washington, DC 20560
Phone: (202) 357-2111

Tunneling through the Internet

by Carolyn Caywood

Back near the beginning of the Silicon Age, I used to play a computer game called Colossal Cave. It was one of many versions of Adventure, a treasure hunt for one. There were no pictures, not even a map. Exploring the cavern was a matter of moving in compass directions and up and down. When a room in the cave contained something of interest, I had to guess at the command to manipulate it. I remember thinking as I played that I was exercising a rarely used mental skill when I envisioned the twisting, three-dimensional paths through the cave and held them in my mind.

Now, I am rediscovering this skill as I explore the Internet using Gopher, an electronic document search tool. Like Colossal Cave, the Internet feels like an enormous maze full of blind alleys, paths that double back on themselves, and unexpected treasures. It is tempting to stay on the surface where the people are, chattering on e-mail and news-groups and getting answers to reference questions. But, that is only half of the Internet.

The Hunt for Information

A good way to learn how to get around the network's hidden caverns and discover what's there is Rick Gates's Internet Hunt, a monthly contest to find answers in electronic archives. (Past contests are archived as "The Internet Hunt" on NYSERNET under the heading "Search the Internet.") Last November, Gates tried a special hunt limited to K-12 students and got a dozen entries. The individual winner was a ninth-grader from Arizona, and other entrants included a home-schooler in Pennsylvania and a seventh- and eighth-grade girls team in Leonard, OK. They tackled such questions as the latest high temperature in Tegucigalpa and the top-of-the-chart recording on European MTV.

The Internet Hunt helped me start to identify treasures. One of my favorite destinations goes by the sinister name of **wiretap.spies.com**. It contains government documents from all over (including the Iroquois Confederacy), 162 electronically recorded books ranging from Shakespeare to the *CIA World Fact Book*, and a hoard of other stuff. Elsewhere, I've found indexes to song lyrics, archives of e-mail discussions, and even an archive of library policies.

Like any treasure hunt, one of the big questions becomes how to carry it all home. My instinctive response was to retrieve the documents, then download and print. I realized I was using an old paradigm on a new medium. Instead I needed to let go of ownership and trust access. As librarians begin to locate information on the Internet, we must learn what we have always expected our customers to understand: it isn't necessary to possess a book (or an electronic resource) in order to use it. There's another benefit to relinquishing ownership: timeliness. The archive on historic costume suppliers I printed out last year is now hopelessly out of date, but I can always consult the latest electronic version.

More Changes to Come

The benefits of electronic searching are rapidly multiplying, and electronic documents have the potential to offer far greater access than they do currently. I'm not quite sure of the value of having Shakespeare online when the reader has to scroll through his sonnets page by page, but imagine what it will be like when we can search by a half-remembered phrase. Add to that the ability to branch off and investigate a literary allusion, tracing it through other documents. This is the idea of hypertext: organizing materials not by physical location but by their intellectual relationships to each other. Dewey's goal of shelving like things together can be extended electronically beyond the linear into an infinite number of dimensions.

To prepare for this level of access, print documents are already being converted to electronic formats. Although there are different ideas on how to handle this, the goal of this conversion appears to be establishing an all-inclusive electronic collection. Selection will no longer mean choosing what to include, since collection development will be comprehensive. The concept of selection will change from acquisition to access—to determining, out of the universe of available knowledge, what is relevant to this inquiry from this customer and what will help extract the useful from a deluge of data.

Teens and the Internet

If, as Vice President Gore suggested at the 1991 ALA Midwinter Meeting, students will be able to download current research on dinosaurs or any other topic, then someone will have to help them find the materials they can understand and use. The K-12 Internet Hunt shows that a few students are capable of using today's Internet for specific facts, but we have a long way to go before the average teen will be able to use it for research. Until then, librarians need to be involved in creating access tools. Otherwise, we won't have information, but an unmanageable explosion.

Using the Internet for research is not a game, or another practice to fit into the existing structure, or even a way to make libraries look with-it—it is a basic change in the nature of library service. If librarians who serve youth leave its development to computer experts, or even to those in our profession who have more experience with information technology, we will have neither the skills nor the tools to make the Internet accessible to our customers.

A Delicate Balance

by Bruce Flanders

It all started out innocently enough. The library media co-ordinator for a school district in a university community called me recently to ask if I could provide an introductory seminar on use of the Internet for some of her secondary school librarians.

"Sure," I replied, "this is the sort of thing I do all the time." We set up a date for the seminar, and then she cautioned, "I thought I'd let you know that some of the district administrators may attend this meeting." (Uh oh, I thought, here it comes.) "The superintendent is very concerned about negative feedback if we provide student access to the Internet. Don't bring it up, but you should be prepared to field questions about pornographic materials on the Internet."

I thought I was going to be filling my usual role as Internet evangelist and educator. Now I was afraid I might be facing the Spanish Inquisition. To prepare for this potentially delicate encounter, I got in contact with quite a few school librarians via the telephone by posting some queries on the net. What I heard surprised and dismayed me: severe limitation or downright denial of student access to the Internet was prevalent. By any standard it is a nationwide problem of increasing significance; all technology-rich schools will eventually encounter this issue. There seems to be little consensus as to the most reasonable way to handle it now, but some of the comments I received provided encouragement that librarians, as usual, are engaged and ready to tackle the intellectually thorny issues of our times.

Eye of the Storm

What is there to fear? Oh, just a few innocuous things like unmoderated, uncensored alternative Usenet newsgroups such as alt.sex, password cracking programs, ftp sources for commercial software products, and humorous and erotic graphic image servers with X-rated material. Depending on your point of view, lots of goodies or lots of landmines for unwary librarians and administrators.

Steve Cisler focuses on the problem of youth access to inappropriate materials in his excellent paper, "Protection and the Internet."[1]

Educators who plan to offer Internet access immediately confront the challenge of Usenet and anonymous ftp files. There is a fairly strong consensus that the students must be protected from some of these discussions and some of the files. The reasoning comes in various flavors; some say that they personally don't find the material objectionable but if the conservative elements in the state found out, the project would be threatened or canceled. The nightmare they have is of some legislator waving around a raunchy GIF image "paid for with tax dollars and found on the State Educational Network," or reading some choice posting from alt.sex.furry.critters or alt.sex.necrophilia. This fear may be unfounded, but it tends to make some administrators restrain themselves and avoid all Usenet groups.

Yet, all the librarians with whom I communicated recognized that school libraries must participate in the information age in whatever form it takes, including the Internet. Many school librarians are so convinced that 99 percent of the resources on the net are essential to good education that they are willing to risk catching heat from an angry parent or active special interest group.

An almost universal response to my query was that school librarians must not only foresee, but anticipate misuse of Internet access by certain students. Kids will order things to be delivered to their home and billed to the school. They will send inappropriate (juvenile or malicious) e-mail messages—using the school's Internet address. As one media specialist put it, with the ragged edge of experience in her voice, "You name it, they'll try it." Yet, school librarians are survivors. You can't scare them anymore—they've been around children and young adults too much.

To help librarians chart their way through these issues, Judith Krug, director of ALA's Office for Intellectual Freedom, told me that the ALA Intellectual Freedom committee was currently discussing electronic access with a view toward issuing an official ALA position statement. Krug, who predicted "yet another unpopular position," had eminently practical advice to offer parents on the matter: "Talk to your kids, and go with your kids to the school library," she said. "See what's going on."

A Parent's Role

In talking with librarians about this issue, the question of the parent's role came up often. Steve Grant, library media teacher at La Jolla (CA) High School, commented,

Technology Code of Conduct
Bloomfield Hills (MI) Model High School, April 1992

Rights
- Students have the right to access the Internet to facilitate diversity and personal growth in technology, information gathering skills, and communication skills.
- Students have the right to use the following methods for retrieving information: file transfer protocol (FTP), telnet, and electronic mail (e-mail).
- Students have a *conditional* right to request newsgroups from the Internet in order to facilitate real-time learning with members of the network.
- Students have the *conditional* right to sign up for lists on the Internet.
- Students have the unconditional right to send e-mail to any member on the network. This right does not require prior approval.

Responsibilities
- The student exercising his/her right to use the Internet as an educational resource shall also accept the responsibility for all materials received under his/her user account. Only those students with prior experience or instruction shall be authorized to use the Internet.
- Students have the responsibility to monitor all materials received via the Internet under their user account.
- Students will accept the responsibility of keeping copyrighted software of any kind from entering the school via the Internet.
- Students will accept the responsibility of keeping all pornographic material, inappropriate text files, or files dangerous to the integrity of the network from entering the school via the Internet.
- It is the student's responsibility to make all subscriptions to newsgroups and lists known to the technology facilitator. Approval is required from the technology facilitator prior to requesting a newsgroup and/or list from the network.
- It is a facilitator's responsibility to maintain the privacy of students' electronic mail. The faculty has the responsibility to include a student in all acts of viewing, modifying, or removing that student's electronic mailbox.
- It is a student's responsibility to maintain the integrity of the private electronic mail system. the student has the responsibility to report all violations of privacy. Students are responsible for all mail received under their user accounts. Students have the responsibility to make only those contacts leading to some justifiable personal growth on the Internet. The student is responsible for making sure all e-mail received by him/her does not contain pornographic material, inappropriate information, or text-encoded files that are potentially dangerous to the integrity of the hardware on school premises.
- Students will be required to log all connections made while online with the network. All sessions outside the LAN network installed at the Model High School must be included in this log. All file transfers made while online with the network both within the LAN and outside the LAN must be included in this log.
- A student is responsible for keeping a log of all contacts made on the network. The full Internet address of correspondents on the network must be included in this log. A count of all mail received must be included in this log. The student is not responsible for logging the content of any mail received via the Internet.
- The technology facilitator will be responsible for placing a log book near each computer capable of accessing the network.
- The technology facilitator will be responsible for reviewing all audit trails created by the Novell 3.11 software and those logs found near each computer capable of accessing the Internet. The technology facilitator is responsible for determining and uncovering incorrect usage of the network and is also responsible for informing other faculty members and the student in question.
- The student is responsible for adhering to the Full Value Contract and using the Core Competency guidelines while online with the Internet.

While I firmly believe that school staff (including administrators) should not have the right to limit student access to materials (within certain limits of appropriateness—I think that providing access to *Hustler* in an elementary school library media center could reasonably be discouraged), I do believe that individual parents have the right to limit access to certain materials for their children only. Since the Internet is "wide open" and truly uncensored, it seems reasonable to allow parents the right to request that their own children not be allowed to access the Internet on library media center equipment. The converse also seems reasonable: that to protect the school district from possible lawsuits, a parent permission slip be required of students who will access the Internet on school time and equipment.[2]

Roger Melvin, academic programmer and systems analyst at Gonzaga University in Spokane, WA, addressed the hierarchy of individual rights. "I would be wary of any policy that places the 'right' of the student above the rights of the parents. . . . Isn't a public school administered by a school district made up of elected officials? So it would seem to me that a public school has no rights, just 'official orders,' if you will, which are subject to interpretation and change by the folks that elected the school board—you and me."[3]

Judy S. MacDonald, director of Media, Research, and Technologies at the Poudre School District in Fort Collins, CO, described the kind of constraints under which school libraries in her area have to operate.

> I do support intellectual freedom, but at times that conflicts with other mandates public schools must follow. For example, our selection and reconsideration policies contain phrases such as "age appropriate." Also, we just had an opinion from an attorney that even though circulation records in a public library are protected by the privacy act, parents have a right to request and receive in a timely manner student library records because of federal laws giving parents the right to monitor students' school records. Things are different in different environments.[4]

Many librarians feel strongly that access to information should be unrestricted and that Internet resources provide valuable information to K-12 students. Yet, schools work within certain restraints and must be sensitive to parental pressures.

Policies & Procedures

Several possible solutions to the problem of access are being tested. Diane Leupold, the coordinator of technical services for the Topeka (KS) Public School District, told me that, at least initially, librarians in Topeka secondary schools would supervise all dial-in sessions with the Internet. Other librarians noted that this had been considered as an option, but most told me that over the long haul, especially as Internet use expands in the school environment, constant supervision is unrealistic at best and intrusive at worst.

Several librarians mentioned that they train students on the use of Internet resources with menus, such as gopher servers, in the hope that this will screen out other objectionable Internet resources, or "channel" students to certain paths. But we all know that students are more clever than that. The Internet will defeat a cautious approach because its inherent structure can lead users anywhere on the net—given some skill, practice, and the perseverance of a 14-year-old.

The most common technique for shielding the school and its faculty from potential harm, as mentioned earlier, is the establishment of a system of parental permission forms for granting student access to the Internet. Linda A. Nichols, coordinator of the school library system for the Steuben-Allegany Board of Cooperative Educational Services in Bath, NY, stated, "We have schools that allow students to have Internet access after their parents have signed a permission form stating that they understand the school can't censor what their child might find. I think that it is much the same as the permission slips that parents sign so that their child can attend health classes dealing with reproduction."[5]

Numerous respondents mentioned the use of permission forms or ethics agreements. I was particularly impressed with the agreement put in place by Roger Ashley, media specialist and technology specialist at Model High School in Bloomfield Hills, MI—an agreement that he admitted was instrumental in securing school board support after his schools' Internet access was attacked in a lurid television exposé. (See previous page.)

Access Denied?

Now I was ready for my Internet seminar. When the school administrators posed the inevitable question—and they did—it was not a surprise nor was it all that uncomfortable. I didn't have the answers to all their questions, but at least I was able to anticipate some of their main points and have some cogent answers, thanks to librarians around the country who had taken the time to communicate with me on this difficult issue.

Although my presentation was geared to a school library audience, these issues are also relevant to children's and young adult specialists working in public libraries, as Patty Wright-Manassee, library school graduate student at the University of Washington, pointed out:

> Schools have always "withheld" information from children and quite frankly I feel very certain that they will continue. . . . Children in schools are a captive audience. However, the public library is a different scene entirely when it comes to children and intellectual freedom. I am curious about the access issues involved in public libraries because children have much more intellectual freedom in this environment. Currently the Internet is being accessed by children in only a few public libraries, but this number will grow quickly. . . . Will children have access to everything on the Internet at the public library?[6]

These questions will not go away. It is up to librarians to balance, as best they can, the often conflicting interests of students, parents, and the community, and to uphold the basic principles of open access to all information. I think this position is best stated by Aaron Smith, MLC/OCLC network librarian for the Michigan Library Consortium, Lansing, MI.

A basic problem with American education today is lack of respect for and belief in the individual. The educational system has to understand that people are able to make informed decisions themselves about what they can and cannot read; government and schools don't have to make these decisions for them. People (especially children and adolescents) need a great deal of freedom in order to learn and grow. Denying them access to the Internet because we're afraid they might read sex listservs is ridiculous. Look at the wealth of wonderful information we are denying these kids access to—and what are we as a society denying ourselves by not allowing them to add to this wealth of information over the Internet?[7]

Student access to inappropriate materials is only one question being raised about use of the Internet in schools. Another is the question of accuracy. With no quality control mechanism in place and the posting of information wide open to any-

one, how do teachers and librarians get students to analyze what they find and not assume that the medium is the authority? But, that's a question for another seminar.

References

1. Cisler, Steve (sac@apple.com), "Protection and the Internet," October 14, 1993. This document is available through anonymous ftp from ftp.apple.com.
2. Grant, Steve K. (sgrant@ctp.org), Denial of Internet access in school libraries (posting to LM_NET), November 23, 1993.
3. Melvin, Roger (roger@gonzaga.edu), Denial of Internet access in school libraries (posting to PACS-L), November 23, 1993.
4, MacDonald, Judy S., Denial of Internet access in school libraries (posting to LM_NET), November 23, 1993.
5. Nichols, Linda A. (lnichols@erie.bitnet), Internet access (private message), November 24, 1993.
6. Wright-Manassee, Patty, Information access and children (private message), November 23, 1993.
7. Smith, Aaron (smith@mlc.lib.mi.us), Student access to Internet (private message), November 23, 1993.

Part Six

Programs and Services

Want to see your school library collection used over the summer? How to build a portable puppet theater? Answers to these and other questions are included in this potpourri of practical, how-to-do-it articles and columns that have appeared in *SLJ* during the past four decades.

Mary K. Chelton's classic "BookTalking: You Can Do It" contains a wealth of pointers to give booktalks effectively. Charles Bunge advises breaking down age barriers in developing effective reference services. Distance education, automation, programs in Library Power schools, and the ubiquitous topic of flexible scheduling are all represented in this section.

Although the late Ralph R. Shaw disparaged the proliferation of "how to" articles in library literature with his aphorism "How I run my library good,"[1] we feel that these "how-to" are too promising to pass by.

---

[1] *Essays for Ralph Shaw*. Edited by Norman D. Stevens. Scarecrow Press, Inc. 1975. Page 208.

State Educational Agencies: Roles & Functions

by David R. Bender

Education today stresses differing teaching strategies, specific learning objectives, and measurable outcomes. This has led to great educational change. So, too, has come change in media programs at all levels—state, district, and school. Many people have, over the years, experienced many contact hours with their respective state departments of education media personnel. I believe that few persons fully understand the role which can be played by state media personnel. Likewise, many of the states' media components have grown and developed as a result of external happenings such as federal legislation and national association guidelines rather than a systematic, planned program.

It is the purpose of this article to discuss some ideas, views, and concerns relating to that portion of the media programming process which occurs at the state educational agency level. Much of the information in this article is based upon personal knowledge and experiences while working with two state education agencies and with state supervisors.

Research

My examination of the available literature turned up few items which describe what *is* actually occurring at the state level. Most articles describe what *should be* occurring and few descriptive program statements exist. A need exists for continuing research, evaluation, and study of state media programs. Those located include Ruth Ersted's article in *Library Trends*[1] which provides an excellent historical overview. A paper prepared by Mae Graham, titled "State Agency Responsibility for Developing Comprehensive Media District and Individual School Levels"[2] provides insight into several developments and possible directions for state level media personnel.

The 1969 *Standards for School Media Programs*[3] and *Media Programs: District and School*[4] provide much directional information for program development. There are numerous other documents which delineate adequately the roles and functions of district and school level services.

In November 1971, the Council of Chief State School Officers (CCSSO) passed a resolution which stated:

> One of the promising developments in the field of education over the past several years has been a nationwide move to integrate school libraries and technology services. This development provides a central source for

materials and professional assistance and a potential for reducing costs by eliminating duplication of facilities and services. Therefore, the Council favors the integration of library and educational technology services at all levels within the field of education.

In their 1961 booklet[5], the CCSSO released a statement on the responsibilities and functions of State Educational Agencies in the area of school library services. A policy and planning guide[6] published in 1964 offered direction in developing the use of new educational media from a state level prospective. But both of these documents are out-of-date and are badly in need of revision.

Brown, Norberg, and Srygley's chapter on "Media Services in State Departments of Education"[7] includes information on provisions, responsibilities, program suggestions, and two case studies. However, the content doesn't begin to present a comprehensive picture of current trends, conditions, and practices of state educational media programs.

Standards for Library Functions at the State Level[8] provides a statement on advising and supervising school media centers as an accepted state responsibility requiring coordination between public and school library/media agencies. Esther Carter's dissertation[9] describes the organization found in the 50 state departments of education media areas and the types of activities provided.

Services

Before examining the services provided by any agency, at whatever level of operation, there are several basic givens to be stated. The first given is that in order for learning resources and services to be effectively and efficiently provided to students and faculty engaged in the teaching/learning process, a team approach to media management and supervision must be created.

Secondly, just as students learn in varying ways and from exposure to varying types of materials in numerous formats, so do adults. Therefore, before any program of service can be undertaken, the clientele must be examined closely. This must be an ongoing process, capable of changing to meet varied needs, attitudes, and environments.

Next, a foundation must be established whereby the appropriateness of the service may be measured. Are State Agency personnel involved solely with housekeeping routines, or are opportunities provided for them to be involved with the planning and development of school media programs? The structure around this service oriented program will differ among the various states. Therefore, no single model can be developed which will be applicable to all. Greater sharing of ideas, program outlines, goals and objectives must be done. This implies that media professionals must be resourceful and learn to work within the system while seeking to meet the needs of those it is there to support, serve and encourage.

Fourth, media by themselves have no meaning until they are related to some curricular/program area. So, too, must state level media leadership seek to understand the needs of the people it serves in establishing its role.

Fifth, there must be some means for providing a record of what has occurred within any operational program area. The current literature on media supervision and management reveals numerous items regarding the building level media center program; fewer materials on the district level operation; and almost nothing concerning state level activities. Why is this so? What is happening in State Educational Agencies? Are people aware of programs, issues, trends, conditions, and services of State Agencies? Should there be concern about the role provided by state level media personnel? Can state level media areas provide effective program opportunities, or should this be left to other agencies?

The sixth, and last, given is that a clearer understanding of the responsibilities of State Educational Agencies needs to be stated. "The state is legally responsible for establishing and maintaining a system of education and the education agency prescribes by its legislature to provide leadership in the area of media programs."[10] Through the various state boards of education, policies and procedures are established which ensure and enhance the development of school media programs.

Programs and Functions

Most State Agencies have been forced into accountability either in program terms, budgetary considerations, or in combination. Any system that has developed is likely to have enumerable problems to be solved. Waiting for someone else to solve these problems will surely find media supervisors behind the times once again. Many planning systems have come and gone, some were worthwhile for educational settings, others were not. Too frequently education adopts a whole new system instead of adapting those portions applicable to real needs. State media personnel must be involved in the planning processes which will enable their program activities to be accountable. Planning activities, setting functional alternatives, selecting and establishing priorities, program implementation, and the designing of evaluation components are proper and necessary tasks which take commitment and involvement. Success with these tasks leads to accountability.

Media professionals come into contact with state media personnel in numerous ways. This exposure may be through federal programs, the completion of required forms and reports, the accreditation of a school program, the certification process, the occasional release of publications, or an infrequent inservice training opportunity. Everyone can add their own

unique experience to this brief list. These experiences raise various reactions, occasionally emotional, among those who have been exposed to one or all of these.

Various state departments of education have issued statements regarding the programs to be provided by the media area. Many State Agencies have or are supporting the unified media concept at the local, system or district, and state levels and recognize fully their obligation to provide leadership in the development of services which will further the growth of excellent media services for schools. For example, stated in the *Criteria for Modern School Media Programs,*[11] Maryland State Department of Education, Division of Library Development and Services, are 11 functions that illustrate one state's responsibility for program development. These items are:

1. To formulate long-range plans for the development of school media programs, including cooperative planning for regional and state services.

2. To provide advisory and consultative services to local school systems, particularly in the areas of new media services and technology and school media facilities.

3. To develop standards and guidelines for the improvement of media programs.

4. To provide programs of inservice education on the concepts and utilization of media to administrators, supervisors, media personnel, and teachers.

5. To develop proposals for needed research in media services.

6. To collect, analyze, and disseminate information on the scope and quality of media programs in the State.

7. To assist in the determination of qualifications for certification of media personnel.

8. To administer federal funds available for media programs.

9. To provide for the effective coordination of media services with the critical educational concerns of the State and local school systems.

10. To develop coordinated plans and policies with other personnel and agencies that will strengthen library media services for all citizens.

11. To act as a clearinghouse for information on library services in the State, and to foster interlibrary loan and cooperative arrangements with school, public, academic, or other libraries.

State level media services are built upon and must support system level and school level media operations. Below is a listing of those services which each system should provide to its schools; this could be either through contractual agreements or direct services.

1. Provision of inservice education programs in utilization of media.

2. Central purchasing, cataloging, and processing of materials for school media centers.

3. Provision of professional library collections and services for teachers.

4. Provision of additional materials to schools which are too small to provide adequately for the educational needs of students and teachers.

5. Loans of expensive or infrequently used materials.

6. Distribution of sample materials which schools may examine for possible local purchase.

7. Production of materials such as transparencies, slides, videotapes, audiotapes, prints, etc.

8. Maintenance of media equipment.

9. Provision of a central source for consumable media supplies.

10. Computer services for acquisition and processing of material for information retrieval.

11. Computer assisted instruction.

12. Television services which in addition to open circuit instructional television may include closed circuit television (CCTV) within the system and community antennae television (CATV) services where available in the community.[12]

A primary purpose of the media program in any school is to assist staff and students in acquiring needed information. Resources, both human and technical, must be provided. Materials collections should reflect use by individuals, small groups and large groups in the media center, classroom, or outside the school. To assist students and teachers in getting needed materials, the school provides access to a collection of media whose variety and scope are limited only by the program of the school and the abilities, interests, curiosities, and imagination of the media staff. Since no single institution is capable of acquiring or housing all needed resources, borrowing and other cooperative programming must be made with other agencies—neighboring school systems, public libraries, regional centers, colleges and universities, and so forth. State Agency media personnel should provide leadership in developing and extending cooperative activities.

Media Programs: District and School and other publications offer extensive lists of activities which make up a school or district level service component. These guidelines can serve as a planning document and an evaluative instrument against which program effectiveness may be measured.

As State Educational Agency media personnel develop programs of service, greater emphasis must be placed upon leadership, managerial, and supervisory functions. In any field undergoing change, clear directions for flexible program opportunities must be provided.

Supervisory Skills

Within many agencies a new or revamped program of services needs to be developed. New skills must be provided. Skills imply the performance and not the mere potential of an ability which can be developed, not necessarily inborn. Robert Katz[13] discusses three levels of skills which an effective administrator must develop:

Human—Leader's ability to work effectively as a group member and to build cooperative effort within the team he leads.

Technical—Leader's understanding of, and proficiency in, a specific kind of activity, particularly one involving methods, processes, procedures, and techniques.

Conceptual—Leader's ability to see the system as a whole; it includes recognizing how the various functions of the organization depend on one another, and how changes in any one part affect all the others; and it extends to visualizing the relationship of the individual unit to the field, community, and the political, social, and economic forces of the nation as a whole.

Each of these areas require further exploration, discussion, and development. During the 1972 Okoboji Leadership Conference one group further examined competencies according to these three skill areas which are needed by educational leaders.[14] It appears that this material has major implications for state level, system level, and school level media administrators.

State School Media Supervisors must stimulate and assist the media personnel in their states to become creative and resourceful change agents. Since personnel management and organizational planning are part of our skills, the above task should be simplified.

> 'Learn to use yourself in such a way that what you do makes a difference.' Accept your role as a leader in the unified media program with the sensitivity and vitality that it deserves, for it is only in this way that you will bring about change in the structure and change in the people. This is what leadership is all about.[15]

Several years ago Jane Hannigan, in addressing a group of media supervisors responsible for the development of district level services, stated that "in substantial measure, the conceptual framework of system-level supervision has been devised, rather than created."[16] This statement certainly describes the programs found in a few states. There are numerous reasons which can be offered for this; however, what frequently might be lacking from program development is staff commitment and involvement. Media professionals cannot sit back and accept what is given; they must be part of the planning process. Planning leads to stronger program development. We must begin to look to the future, using all available predictors, and develop strong state level media services that will have an effect upon the ultimate recipient—*the learner.*

References

1. Ersted, Ruth. "School Library Supervisors, National and State," *Library Trends* 1:333, January, 1953.

2. Graham, Mae. "State Agency Responsibilities for Developing Comprehensive Media District and Individual School Levels." Paper presented to participants of State Media Personnel Institute, Western Michigan University, Kalamazoo, Michigan, 1969.

3. American Association of School Librarians and Department of Audiovisual Instruction. *Standards for School Media Programs.* Chicago: American Library Association, and Washington, D.C.: National Education Association, 1969.

4. American Association of School Librarians and Association for Educational Communications and Technology. *Media Programs: District and School.* Chicago: American Library Association, 1975.

5. Council of Chief State School Officers. "Responsibilities of State Departments of Education for School Library Services." Washington, D.C.: Council of Chief State School Officers, 1961.

6. Council of Chief State School Officers. "State Department of Education Leadership in Developing the Use of New Educational Media." Washington, D.C.: Council of Chief State School Officers, 1964.

7. Brown, James W., Norberg, Kenneth D., and Srygley, Sara K. *Administering Educational Media: Instructional Technology and Library Services,* Second Edition, McGraw-Hill, Inc., 1972.

8. American Association of State Libraries and Standards Revision Committee. *Standards for Library Functions at the State Level.* Chicago: American Library Association, 1970.

9. Carter, Esther M. "The Organizational Structure for State School Library Supervisors and the Functions, Duties and Activities of State School Library Supervisors." Unpublished Ph.D. dissertation, Indiana University, 1971.

10. American Association of School Librarians and Association for Educational Communications and Technology. *Media Programs: District and School.* Chicago: American Library Association, 1975.

11. Maryland State Department of Education. *Criteria for Modern School Media Programs.* Baltimore, Maryland: The Department, 1971.

12. *Ibid.*

13. Katz, Robert L. "Skills of an Effective Administrator." *Harvard Business Review,* Jan.-Feb. 1955, pp. 33-42.

14. "Leadership Development for the Media Profession." Summary Report of the Eighteenth Annual Lake Okoboji Educational Media Leadership Conference, Milford, Iowa: 1972.

15. As stated by Elnora M. Portteus. "Leadership Implications of the United Media Concept." *Issues in Media Management.* David R. Bender, editor, Maryland State Department of Education, 1973.

16. Hannigan, Jane A. "The Role of Supervision in the United Media Program." *Issues in Media Management.* David R. Bender, editor, Maryland State Department of Education, 1973.

P.P. & P.R.

Two keys to circulation success

By Marcia Posner

PP and PR stand for Program Planning and Public Relations, two inseparable elements. Both PP and PR are necessary in attracting readers (and watchers or listeners) to the library. Your library may have a fantastic collection of books, realia, tapes, records, films and the like, but who will know about it except regular patrons? Successful Program Planning and Public Relations focuses on a wider community than just "regulars."

Librarians should take crash courses in PPPR. Here in the Library Science Department of Queens College, we try to combine workshop techniques with actual practice in planning and producing programs with all the accompanying print and written material that is essential to successful programing. The semester is divided into six workshop class sessions. For the balance of the semester, eight meetings are used for internship opportunities. After the sixth session, the class is divided into two groups: an in-class group (who produces programs in the classroom situation at regularly scheduled class time), and the out-of-class group (who were situated in participating libraries). Both groups turn in written assignments, either in person or by mail. Communication has to be maintained. The out-of-class group produces programs in a real-life library situation, while the in-class group has to simulate a real-life situation. Before the end of the term two class meetings are scheduled where both groups will be reunited to compare experiences and to hear a professional public relation consultant from a large library system speak on the topic "Public Relations and the Public Library." This experience allows both groups to realize that reading about PPPR is no substitute for doing it and that having a framework to use as a guide for initial attempts is helpful.

Community Surveys

The first step in PPPR is taking a survey.[1] How will you know for whom to program if you aren't aware of the various segments in your community? One librarian thought her library community was fairly homogeneous. Prevailed upon to make a survey of the community, she discovered a large "hidden" Italian population. *Her* library community *was* homogenous—inside the building. Alerted to the existence of the Italian Americans, the well-intentioned librarian hastened to make up for lost time. Soon the entire community was knee-deep in Italian culture: the library held musicales of opera recordings with librettos; poetry, art, and crafts sessions and of course, pasta parties. While the Italian patrons twirled and dipped to the strains of the Tarantella with their indigenous neighbors, who immediately signed up as library patrons, five Indian families recently arrived from Pakistan walked in, attracted by the green, white and red banners fluttering outside the library door. As she welcomed them, the now sensitized librarian immediately envisioned an Indian Festival.

Another librarian, encouraged to make a community survey, found an extremely Orthodox Jewish enclave within the community. They lived outside of walking distance to the library and seldom used it. The librarian persuaded her board of trustees to keep the library open on Sundays for the Orthodox Jewish fathers who were not at work and allowed to drive (forbidden to them on Saturdays). The result was an entirely new group of library patrons enrolled. The rest of the community used the library on Sundays also and good group interaction resulted.

Not all surveys result in ethnic discoveries. Some reveal that those story-hour kids you used to tell stories to are now teen-agers whom you never see except when they have to make school reports. Why not program just for them? The former story-hour mothers are older now and you may have school dropouts who would like to return to school or work if they knew where to begin. You can help them by programming to their specific needs. Try programming for nonintellectuals once in a while. Home repair, TV repair, plumbing, sewing and cooking, attract all kinds of people. When they find out that the library has many books on these subjects, they may become regular library patrons.

Program Sources

Now that you have got your target audience, where do you get your programs? When you survey the community, you should ask the question "Do you have an interest, hobby or avocation you would be willing to share with your neighbors?" You will be amazed at the numbers of resource people living right in your own community, eager to "do their thing." There will be amateur astronomers and astrologers; travelers who want to tell of their experiences and to show their slides and realia; rock hounds, shell collectors, stamp collectors, rug hookers, furniture refinishers, and so on. Sometimes people are either reticent about talking about themselves or think that their particular talent is so commonplace that they hesitate to mention it. Therefore it is sometimes helpful to compose suggested topics and leave some extra blank spaces on the survey. Then you only have to ask the survey recipients to indicate the area(s) in which they have some expertise.

Additional sources of programs are through local county, borough, city, state or even Federal government agencies. By checking the pages of a government organization handbook on each of the various levels of government, and calling the offices of those you decide upon, you may be able to get free resource people. These may include anyone from your Federal representative (making an appearance at an opportune time) to people supplied by local government who offer advice and instruction on repairs; canning; cooking; gardening; sewing, and health or safety topics.

Banks, insurance companies, real-estate companies, stockbrokers, lawyers, estate managers are all eager to offer or fund (sponsor) programs. Some large firms have their own public relations departments which make specific programs available to non-profit organizations. Large department stores like to co-sponsor programs, supply gifts for prizes for contests, and lend their personnel for decorating programs, fashion shows, and a variety of store-related subjects. Small local stores will often run programs in anticipation of receiving additional community business through exposure. A ski shop employee gave ski instructions in the library, after the librarian had shown a film on the excitement of skiing. He also brought along a selection of skis and ski clothing, although no sales were permitted in the library. Golf stores, tennis shops, bowling shops are usually connected with pros or may have one on their staff. A bookstore gave a program on the occult, (and incidentally many books on the occult circulated the next day). A health food store offered a program on the value of eating "organically." The possibilities are endless. Restaurants offer cooking demonstrations, as do authors of cookbooks, which brings us to another important source of free programs.

Book publishers will generally arrange for authors to speak, sometimes at no charge. Better-known authors are often available as speakers for a sliding fee rate arranged by their agents. Publishers will also send promotional material[2] such as bookmarks, book jackets, posters, mobiles, and the like. Sometimes they sponsor contests in which libraries may participate and offer the books on their lists as prizes. The craft book companies are prominent in this type of promotion.

Utilities offer programs—sometimes on your premises; sometimes on theirs. Chemical companies do too. Why not try large fabric concerns, those noted for having displays in cities and at World Fairs. How about tapping the oil companies? They are very concerned with their public image right now and will probably welcome the opportunity. Foreign consulates often offer programs to schools and libraries. They are also an excellent source for posters and give-aways. Don't forget to read the papers to see what other groups and organizations are scheduling.

Shows and contests offer a broad area of program resources. You can have craft shows, dog shows, cat shows, pet shows, art shows. . . . You can have cooking contests, limerick contests, poetry contests, bookmark contests. . . . ad infinitum. Remember to keep your sense of humor and perspective in holding these contests. The guiding principle is to be sincere, fair, but also to see that no one goes away unhappy or unappreciated. Library sponsored events in these areas need to be more benevolent than those sponsored by professional organizations. When you have contests, you need judges. Contact art organizations, music schools, galleries, high schools and colleges, publishers, town officials, and owners of retail stores with the necessary expertise. Contests need entry blanks which can be cut in half. The contestant keeps the upper part that has the rules, time, date, etc. printed on it. You keep the lower part which contains the contestant's name, address, phone number, age, sex, and type of entry (where applicable), also a notation of the fee payment. (In art shows there is often an entry fee charged which is used for buying additional prizes or paying judges if professional judges are required.) Search the yellow pages for firms selling award ribbons and call around as the prices vary greatly.

When you contact the local schools, keep in mind all those adult education teachers. They will usually give programs at the same rate they earn for teaching one evening, which is really nominal.

Although you are programing to community segments, remember to plan something having broad audience appeal at least twice a year. Art and pet shows are such programs. Certain kinds of film series are a possibility, or, for teens, live drama presented by a library sponsored school, or community "Way-Off Broadway" group, is another. Square dances or gourmet cooking programs usually draw varied community groups. One square dance was called the "Nine to Ninety" and it really was!

Record Keeping

So much for where to get programs. Once you start, they just keep multiplying. The problem is soon how to keep track of all of them, or, as we say in "libraryese," "Information Retrieval." The first thing to do is to invest in a large 6" x 8" file box, complete with cards and blank tab dividers. Then fill those blank tabs with any or more of the following categories: Spring, Summer, Winter, Fall, Children (age-levels), Young Mothers, Young Fathers, Young Married Couples, Young Parents, Young Women, Young Men, Middle-aged Women, Middle-aged Men, Middle-aged Couples, Senior Citizens—General, Senior Men, Senior Women; Music-operatic, Music-symphonic, Music-pop, Art, Arts and Crafts, Dance, Politics, Business, Sewing, Home Repairs, etc. etc. You may list the same resource under many different categories, but it is easier for you to locate them when they are listed under categories, rather than by name of resource.

Arrange your categories alphabetically, and subdivide them alphabetically under the broader categories. On each index card enter the following: title of program, name of contact person, address, phone number, goal of programs (to entertain, educate, inform, recreational . . .) target audience; source of program (where you first heard it from and where you found it); fee, and recommendations if any. Leave several lines for your evaluation of the program if you have previewed it. Leave several more lines for your evaluation after the program has been given.

These file boxes are for library use and also for public

information. It often happens that a girl scout leader requests information about a program featuring American Indians, or early-American crafts for a specific age group, or the *Cancer Care* group wants a program on how to care for the cancer patient in the home, or something on counseling the family how to treat the cancer patient. Perhaps an organization needs a program for fund-raising. If you carefully and systematically amass all the information you see or hear about and organize it in enough categories with plenty of cross-filing, you should be able to come up with the answer in just three minutes. You can publicize your program information service as "The Soft-Boiled Egg Program Service." Funny slogans humanize a library, and help you to spread a message through the community about your resources. Now that you have this wonderful fund of program resources (which you should check for currency twice a year), you must tell the local organizations about the new library service.

Getting Started

Now you have to either call the contact person or write to him. If your request is accepted, then the next step is to write a letter of confirmation. This letter will contain the subject of the anticipated program; the time; date; place; fee, if any; travel directions or travel arrangements and a request for instructions as to the kinds of audio visual devices, props or other equipment the speaker would like the library to provide. The second letter should be sent to the speaker so that he receives it at least one week prior to the engagement. You should reiterate the subject, time, place, travel arrangements and AV arrangements provided. The type of expected audience should also be stated as any topic can be presented on various levels. The name and phone number of the person in charge of the library program should be prominently placed on the letter in case the speaker has some new ideas or problems he/she wishes to discuss. *Every program person must have an alternative to a no-show program prepared,* a little act of his/her own, a sound-slide program always on hand in the library, have something because it may happen.

Keep a monthly record of all this "show-biz" on a large calendar, the back of each month having been converted to a page-size pocket. As soon as you confirm your program, write all the letters needed. The last letter to be sent is a simple "thank-you" acknowledging the audience's response to the program and your own reaction. Write at least three press releases and type them in duplicate. File the originals and insert the duplicates in the back pocket of each monthly calendar page when the letter or release must be mailed. Note the mailing date on the front of the calendar month, then you need only to dig into the pocket in order to retrieve the material. The same method should be used with all your PR materials: flyers, tickets, posters.

Publicity Materials

Now you are ready to tell the "Program Story." This rather rigid outline is intended only as a crutch until the PR writer hits his own stride, then it may be completely disregarded. You will need at least three press releases: one to inform the public that the library is planning a particular program, the sec-ond to remind the public that the program will be presented one week hence, and the third to show what a marvelous time was had at the program. This last should have black and white pictures or glossies to accompany it. Newspaper deadlines are often seven to 13 days prior to publication. Magazine deadlines can be months before. Learn all this and add the deadline information to your resource file. Your press releases are more apt to be accepted if they are couched in simple clear English and are to the point. If the editor has less work to do with your work he will accept it more readily. Let your first sentence be provocative. The second should contain the library's name and the name of the program. The third and fourth can tell something about the speaker's qualifications and the subject matter. The rest tells the time, place, date, whether tickets are needed, age limitations. Don't get flowery, but try to transmit *your* enthusiasm in the article.

To attract the public's attention you will need posters[3] placed in the library, in local stores and in banks. A good size for these is 11" x 14". They should be simple and bold, yet must contain: the program title, the library's name, the date, time and place; also ticket information if tickets are used. It appears that when tickets are required the programs appear more desirable in the eyes of the public. At the actual time of the program, you will find that those without tickets will turn up. Let them in if there is room.

Flyers are good publicity media too. They can be composed in an 8" x 10" format or smaller. They may be duplicated on a spirit duplicator, mimeographed, or preferably offset printed. Poster techniques also hold for flyers. Essentially it is a question of arranging all the necessary information (name of library, program title, time, place, date) in a pleasing composition with plenty of white (clean) space left. The flyer can be composed of bits and pieces of borrowed letters and illustrations, as long as they are black and white, with both electric stencil and photo offset. The finished product will not show any telltale signs of the fragments used to compose it. Colored paper is slightly more expensive but you may choose to use it for the actual printing. However, white must be used in the paste-up.

The next item is tickets. These may be run off easily on 3" x 5" index cards if your library owns a cardmaster mimeograph. If not, library supply houses have a 3" x 5" hand-stamp with replaceable letters and numbers. Or you can cover one 8" x 10" paper with sample tickets, have it photo offset, then cut the tickets apart.

An Important Note

Check all audiovisual equipment. Test it for sound by standing at the back of the room to listen. Test the room for darkness. Know where the drapery pulls, the light switches, and the public address switch are located. Have on hand heavy duty electric extension cords, three-prong plug adapters, extra equipment bulbs, a long slender insulated screw driver (useful for unjamming), and some splicing tape with a small plastic splicer. Even if only one mike is needed, have an extra one on hand. Live people get sick or get laryngitis but mechanical equipment is subject to many "last-minute no prior symptoms" ills, so the best medicine is to expect them and be prepared.

How-tos and No-No's

The program day finally arrives. The AV set-up has been tested beforehand. The chairs are arranged. The ambience in the library is perfect for the program. You have placed attractive posters, pictures cut from old magazines, and realia appropriate to the program on display. Library materials relevant to the program are prominently displayed on a separate table. Perhaps you have compiled a print bibliography of appropriate books for the audience. Maybe you have taped music playing while the audience gathers. Finally the time is here! You turn off the music. This signals to the audience that the program is about to begin. You must introduce the speaker. How do you do it?[4] The way in which the speaker is introduced is vital to the balance of the program. If you are enthusiastic, this will infuse both audience and speaker. If you sound bored, the listeners will be less receptive initially. Sometimes nervousness tightens up the throat muscles so much that the normal inflections of the voice flatten, and a bored delivery is the result. If you have that common tendency, find out beforehand. Practice speaking into a cassette recorder and listen to yourself. Then record your voice speaking to an imaginary friend about a movie you just saw and compare the voice quality and range. Naturalness is what you are striving for. If you remember that the audience is there to hear the speaker, not you, it will put you more at ease.

Here are some general rules in introducing a speaker: 1) If you are unacquainted with the speaker, take the time to talk to him before the meeting begins. 2) Set the stage with a few well chosen, brief (or borrowed) remarks. Above all, be enthusiastic and alive. 3) Introduce the speaker as if you yourself were eager to hear him. 4) Take time to frame your introduction of the speaker so that your presentation is not stereotyped. Remember these three words: "why," "what," and "who." a) Why is the speaker present? Because of his/her unique qualifications and background. Explain just enough to create interested expectation. b) What is the theme? Speak the title clearly and distinctly. c) If possible, do not mention the speaker's name until the very last words are spoken to spare the speaker embarrassment. Be sure that your pronunciation of the speaker's name is correct and distinctly spoken. 5) Be brutally brief—60 seconds tops for your introduction. 6) When making the transition from one speaker to the next: (if you have more than one speaker), listen carefully for one good point upon which you can graciously comment.

Here are some "no-no's." Don't try to be the main feature. (This is for the extroverted librarian.) This is not the time to establish a reputation as a humorist. Do not apologize for yourself (this is for the introverted librarian) or bring attention to yourself. Use cards, if you must, but never read a prepared introduction. When the speaker is performing, watch him; listen to him. Don't choose that time to count the audience. If refreshments are to be served do not allow either setting-up or clearing to be done during the performance. Do that before the program begins. If your scheduled speaker cannot come, and you are lucky enough to find a substitute so that you don't "have to go into your act," never call him a "substitute." Instead, briefly tell of the first speaker's inability to attend. Then describe how fortunate you are in obtaining the gracious services of the attending speaker and follow with the format of "why," "what," and "who."

OK—the program was a success. The audience has been inspired to borrow the books on display. Others are browsing through the shelves. Possibly they will ask questions of the staff, and certainly the staff will be needed to circulate the books. Does your staff take the same pride in the program's success as you do or are they annoyed at the extra work? A very important segment that you should survey is the library community itself.

If you had contacts or ideas for programs, don't you think the library staff will have other ideas? Perhaps some of them can become program source people. One clerk gave a fantastic program on dried flower arrangement and the incorporation of dried flowers into common household objects in order to make an uncommonly beautiful decorative object. Another demonstrated her expertise with herb cookery, while a third showed how to make homemade spaghetti and ravioli leaves. Do you involve the staff and the library director in your program planning,[5] or do you just spring your plans on them full-blown and expect them to cooperate? Work with your staff. Communicate. Make every program a joint effort and a joint success. Seek their advice. Thank them at the end of each program before the audience and always tell them how much you appreciate their support. You will find that you mean it. The greatest programs and the best PR means nothing if your library staff is discourteous or shows lack of knowledge as to what is going on. Making a point of actively involving staff in programing decisions precludes this from happening.

There are many refinements and techniques that have been omitted here, such as using PPPR in running a Budget-Vote campaign or establishing a Friends of the Library as the natural adjuncts of PPPR. All this can be explored in the literature.[6] Some of the suggestions here have necessarily been general, as conditions vary within each library and in each locale. Adapt those that suit you. By nature librarians are inventive. After all, research work can take the ingenuity of a detective. Cataloging demands skills such as imagination and perspective. A person who devotes so much time to books must have had a lively curiosity in order to have gotten so involved with books at all. Therefore, logically PPPR should come naturally to you. Just make the plunge and good luck.

Notes

1. ALA., *Studying the Community: A Basis for Planning Library Adult Education Services,* 1960.
2. Children's Book Council, Inc. *The Calendar,* all issues.
3. Coplan, Kate. *Effective Library Exhibits,* 2nd ed. Oceana, 1974.
4. Hull, Raymond. *Successful Public Speaking,* Arco, 1974.
5. Beal, George M., *et al., Leadership and Dynamic Group Action,* Iowa State Univ. Pr., 1962.
6. ALA *Friends of the Library,* 1962. Rice, Betty, "Structuring and Winning Bond and Budget Issues." *Public Relations For Public Libraries,* p. 96. Wilson, 1972.

Booktalking
You Can Do It

By Mary K. Chelton

Skill in booktalking remains one of the most valuable promotional devices YA librarians can have at hand to interest teenagers in the library. Once acquired, this skill can be adapted to floor work with individual readers, radio spots, booklist annotations, and class visits in the library or in the classroom. It can be combined with slide-tape, film, or musical presentations, and with outreach skills. Its limitations are set by YA librarians who either refuse to learn the technique, have never learned it (and judge it valueless even after learning it), or who remain inflexible in chosen methods of doing it. The best young adult librarians I have known, whether they see their book selection role as one of expanding horizons and literary tastes or of just giving kids what they want (and most of us usually fall somewhere in between), have a "hidden agenda" for promoting the love of reading for pleasure, and have found booktalks a superb way of doing that.

It should be said here that booktalking skills do not preempt professional abilities in programming, information and referral, traditional reference work, audiovisual collection building, or community outreach, as is often unjustly assumed of the YA specialty. It is my contention, however, that the public still assumes that libraries deal in books and our nonbook related skills and materials will win us no friends or financial support for other information or enrichment media unless librarians do traditional reader's advisory work very well.

In my opinion, the two simplest definitions of booktalks are Amelia Munson's, "The booktalk falls into place between storytelling and book reviewing, partakes of both and is unlike either," taken from *An Ample Field* (American Library Assn., 1950); the other is my own "A booktalk is a formal or informal presentation about a book or group of books designed to entice the listener into reading them."

Elaine Simpson, in her YA course at Rutgers, describes a booktalk as "That part of a librarian's visit to a classroom or during a class visit to the library devoted to presenting two or more books to the group. It is an art and a device by which the librarian tries to interest young people in all books in general and in some books in particular through a talk so carefully prepared as to seem spontaneous, in which he or she gives the subject, the flavor, and the appeal of each book presented." Simpson adds, "Indirectly through book talks we are able to show the teenager that he or she is welcome in the

school or public library, and that he or she has a place there. We are also able to identify ourselves as friends. . . ."

One of the axiomatic things about booktalking is that the talk is not to reveal everything about the book. This is a common beginner's mistake. Doris M. Cole's suggestion in "The Book Talk" in *Junior Plots* (Bowker, 1967) is that booktalks should give only an "enticing sample of the book's contents." In the same article, Margaret Edwards calls the sample "a little piece of pie so good that it tempts one to consume the whole concoction." Learning how to find and then how to present just the right sample is the essence of learning to booktalk. In her book, *The Fair Garden and the Swarm of Beasts* (Hawthorn, 1974), Edwards states that the objectives of booktalks are "to sell the idea of reading for pleasure; to introduce new ideas and new fields of reading; to develop an appreciation of style and character portrayal; lift the level of reading by introducing the best books the audience can read with pleasure; to humanize books, the library and the librarian."

To all of these objectives, I would add that booktalks keep librarians from becoming hypocrites who despair of their patrons' reading tastes while never reading for themselves or for their patrons.

There are probably as many types of booktalks as there are librarians doing them, but roughly they fall into long or short talks with interesting combinations of the two. A short talk, and the one which should be mastered first, usually presents only one title and lasts from 30 seconds to one minute. In it, the librarian tells listeners about something happening to someone in the book, without either divulging the entire plot or stringing along a variety of superlatives.
Examples:

> When BoJo was 17 and July was 16 and they'd been going steady all through high school, July got pregnant and they ran away and got married, even though both sets of parents were disgusted; July had to drop out of school; and BoJo gave up his college football scholarship. *Mr. and Mrs. Bo Jo Jones* will tell you how they made a go of a teenage marriage with three strikes against them.
>
> Even though Harold Krentz went totally blind as a child, his parents refused to send him to special schools,

and in *To Race The Wind,* he tells his true life story about how he played football, became a lawyer, got drafted into the army, and inspired the writing of *Butterflies Are Free.*

As a baby, she had been fried alive by alcoholic parents. By the time Laura was twelve and Dr. D'Ambrosio discovered her in an institution, she had been diagnosed as schizophrenic (the severest form of mental illness) had a long list of physical problems, and had never spoken a word. *No Language But a Cry* is about how he helped her.

It is obvious in these examples how easily short talks can be adapted to floor work, when a teen asks what the book's about, to annotated booklists, and to prerecorded radio spots. Depending on the use or situation, the booktalks can be shortened further or lengthened. "Booktalk" is probably too formal a word, but these short talks do demand that YA librarians discipline themselves to think constantly about the books they've read in terms of plot and the teen audience rather than literary quality or a strictly personal reaction. Kids want to know what happens in a book, what is so exciting about it that they should want to read it. Keeping out your own adjectives lets them feel that they make the decision to read the book, despite your predilection, rather than that the librarian is just pushing either personal favorites or some sort of "literary spinach" down their throats. In other words, let the book sell itself.

A long booktalk lasts ten to 15 minutes and usually emphasizes one particular section of one particular title, whether memorized or told in your own words but not read aloud. Some examples of good sections of books to use are the dead horse scene in *Red Sky at Morning,* the first day on the tubercular ward in *I'm Done Crying,* Albert Scully meeting Mrs. Woodfin for the first time and getting drunk in *The Dreamwatcher,* being fitted for braces and shoes in *Easy Walking,* the race at Riverside with no clutch in *Parnelli,* discovering that Madek has left him naked to die in the desert in *Death Watch,* or Capt. Lebrun's escape in *Escape From Colditz.* Long talks are more formal than short talks and are best used to follow up several short ones on the same theme or as a break in the middle of a variety of unrelated shorts.

Typing out a long talk, double-spaced, helps both with editing it and learning it, because no matter how closely you follow the author's words, there's usually a sentence or two which can be eliminated for an oral presentation. It also helps you incorporate an introduction, ending, and transitions from short talks into one coherent, packaged talk, rather than relying on your own memory. Typed talks can also be kept on file and used repeatedly by the same person or for training new talkers. It is possible to get stale or become dependent on out-of-date talks or, worse still, to forget all other sections of the book except the typed talk, but I have found that because a much-used talk is new to the audience it also remains fresh for the librarian, unless the subject matter is no longer relevant.

The major disagreement among the YA service experts is whether to memorize the long talk or not. Some feel the preparation is too hard, that it is too easy to forget a memorized talk in public, or that such talks are not adaptable enough for all types of audience situations. Some feel the kids will not be interested in so formal an approach or that the librarian will get stale and sound wooden if the same talk is given repeatedly. Others feel that memorization, at least once during a training session, is the only way new booktalkers can learn delivery and talk-cutting techniques against which to evolve their own individual styles later. Having been trained and having trained people by the memorization method, I find the latter to be true, for myself and for most beginners. I do believe, however, that there is no *one* way to do booktalks and that you should do what is comfortable for you—within the guidelines of experience outlined here—and what gets kids to read the books you talk about. It does seem illogical to reject a method just because it is difficult without trying it to see the results or how you might improve upon it.

The combination booktalk presentation can mean a combination of types of talks, librarians, books, genres, or media, and should generally not run more than 25 to 30 minutes. It is the most common type of presentation done for a teenage audience and is usually prearranged with the teacher or group leader to allow time for browsing, card registration, a film, discussion, questions, or just relaxing afterward. Examples would be interspersing poetry, cassette folk-rock lyrics, and short talks on a loneliness theme, or using themes like overcoming handicaps, teenagers in trouble, the future, love, etc.

Short talks could alternate with related slides of the books or the situations described, or of the library itself. Talks can be woven into a creative dramatic presentation or improvisation. If the theme is related to a particular curriculum unit, the combination of readable fun books with magazines, pamphlets, and reference works is valuable. With a little imagination, short talks can even be combined with a lesson on using the catalog. The combinations are limited only by your time, talent, ingenuity, and the audience response. It is always important to remember that your ultimate object in booktalking is to get the kids interested in reading the books you talk about. So if you get so AV-oriented that you are no longer connected with books or so entertaining that only your dramatic ability dazzles your audience, you may be missing the point.

Elaine Simpson further differentiates booktalks into the resource talk done by school librarians, which "is a supplement to a particular unit of work being done in a class, and its purpose is to show the useful, interesting, unusual materials available in the library on the subject"—done at the request of the teacher concerned—and the public library booktalk, which "is to show the great variety of materials and services available for all library users" and is not directed toward a specific subject. This distinction seems arbitrary to me with some of the popular curriculum topics now taught. It does seem unfair to ask public YA librarians to do only curriculum-related resource talks (which are extremely popular with teachers when they discover them) when a school librarian is available, but priorities must be decided by school and public YA librarians based on local circumstances, time, and talent, and should always be a fully cooperative, courteous, joint effort. The teenagers are the ultimate losers in territorial feuds between school and public librarians.

To prepare for booktalks and the accompanying reader's advisory floor work, YA librarians should read widely all types of books and subjects of interest to their teen patrons and keep track of what they have read. Writing a short talk on every title read on a 3" x 5" card is a good way to discipline yourself to think of books in terms of how you would present a particular title to a particular teenager. This also helps you keep the names of the characters straight—an eternal problem with teen novels—and the cards can be filed according to themes, which then helps train you in associating similar titles for talks, lists, and reader's advisory service.

The next step is to master talk delivery techniques in private, preferably in a formal training session where the rest of the group is as nervous as you are, and where videotape playback and group criticism are encouraged. The horrible shock of seeing your unconscious mannerisms on a television monitor corrects them faster than any other method I know, and addressing any audience will give you practice in pitching your voice properly.

If you are in a small, isolated library, have no one more experienced to work with you, and have not learned the technique in library school—an all too common problem among YA librarians—practice on your family or clerical staff and use a full-length mirror and a tape recorder if you have no access to video taping. A tape recorder can help you memorize a talk in addition to correcting mistakes, but there is a danger that learning your booktalk this way will make you bored with it before you ever give it for the first time. Since a formal group training workshop is so valuable in learning to booktalk, I feel isolated YA librarians should pressure local library schools to provide this as continuing education in extension programs and pressure library associations to give regional workshops and create videotapes of different booktalks which can be borrowed.

Once you feel you have mastered the cutting and delivery of a talk in the abstract and have read widely enough so that you won't be undone because a kid has already read one of the books you're prepared to talk about and you can't suggest another one, announce your availability to do this (with a prior agreement with your supervisors as to how often you'll be available) by letters and/or visits to teachers, curriculum supervisors and department heads, school librarians, principals, reading specialists, and youth workers. Be sure to state in the letter what you *will* and *will not* do, and I suggest that you always insist that the teacher or leader remain with the class or group. You are a guest, not a substitute, and it is extremely hard to be an entertaining booktalker as well as an authority figure at the same time. Classes are notorious for going berserk when they think an inexperienced substitute is on the

scene, and teachers who have never had booktalkers before are equally notorious for disappearing the whole period.

Be sure to state how long you will talk, usually 25 to 30 minutes and what you will do in any leftover time. If you will not do curriculum related talks, this is the place to say so, or to list which subjects or books you are prepared to talk about so they can be chosen in advance. English teachers will sometimes want you to discuss the literary merits of the books you talk about to reinforce their classroom objectives, and since it usually is disastrous to do this with booktalks, you can state this in your letter or in person as arrangements are finalized.

Another way to advertise yourself is to demonstrate the technique at faculty and department meetings and to invite teachers of other classes to observe you while you talk to a particular class.

Some schools assume that once you talk there you will never return and they will hit you with double classes and assemblies. So it is wise to state whether you will stay all day and talk to single classes successively or return at another convenient time. While I feel that assemblies are an awkward way to booktalk because of projection problems and the lack of personal eye contact, the Free Library of Philadelphia has perfected "On Your Own," a thirty minute multimedia assembly program featuring short films, slides, a tape of music and narration, and three librarians who present five short one-minute bookspots in person.

Ideally, the school librarian is the contact for the public YA librarian in neighboring schools and booktalk efforts should be coordinated through the school librarian.

A day or two before you are to appear, call to remind the person who invited you and check to see if circumstances have remained the same, and, if you're depending on school AV equipment, to make sure that the equipment is working and will be there when you need it. One piece of equipment you may need is some sort of podium if you're tall, and you can improvise with a dictionary stand or a pile of encyclopedias if necessary, on the spot, or carry a portable one with you. It's a useful crutch, and I suspect short people or those with photographic memories may scorn the use of such props.

You will find, as you booktalk more often, that the sheer public relations value of being so visible in the adolescent community makes rapport with them much easier because they remember you. "Hey, Miss, didn't I see you in my school the other day?" "Hey, what're you doing here?" Other youth service professionals will remember you also as a friendly helpful ally and often reciprocate with help at programs and recommend you as a resource person to others. Your own self-confidence grows immeasurably and you soon find that you're really not scared to talk to anybody anymore.

Best of all, though, is the immediate and immensely gratifying feedback from the kids who truly appreciate your presentation and will charge back to the library to get "the book about the guy who drank the blood" or say, in wonder, "Have you *really* read *all these books*?" or as one teen recently said, "that was a nice thing you did for us the other day."

There is almost no better way to let them know you're on their side than good booktalking, and I can only agree with Doris Cole who said, "Young people are the best, the most responsive audience in the world."

Titles Mentioned

Bradford, Richard. *Red Sky at Morning*. Lippincott, 1968.

Carr, John D. *Death Watch*. Macmillan, 1963.

D'Ambrosio, Richard. *No Language But a Cry*. Doubleday, 1970.

Ferris, Louanne. Edited by Beth Day. *I'm Done Crying*. M. Evans, 1969

Gershe, Leonard. *Butterflies Are Free*. Random, 1970.

Head, Ann. *Mr. and Mrs. Bo Jo Jones*. Putnam, 1967.

Krentz, Harold. *To Race the Wind: An Autobiography*. Putnam, 1972.

Libby, Bill. *Parnelli: A Story of Auto-Racing*. Dutton, 1969.

Lord, Walter. *Night to Remember*. Holt, 1955.

Nasaw, Jonathan. *Easy Walking*. Lippincott, 1975.

Reid, P. R. *Escape From Colditz*. Lippincott, 1973.

Tolstoy, Leo. *War and Peace*. Modern Lib.

Tyler, Anne. *Slipping Down Life*. Knopf, 1970.

Planning Problem-Free Book Fairs

by Carol Kline

A book fair or a book sale is a wonderful and wondrous event. Wonderful in its implications as a social, educational, and fund-raising event; wondrous that it ever comes to fruition. The idea that a book fair would be great fun and a satisfying fund-raising project, usually originates with the media specialist, teacher, principal, or parent, receiving literature describing a book fair program, from a book distributor. The book fair enthusiast enlists the aid of a volunteer committee which works within the framework of an existing organization—the library, a parent-teacher group, a class needing project funds, a school club, and a civic group.

The planning of a book fair is fraught with problems; the major ones being the choice of a distributor who will furnish the books for the school fair and the actual mechanics of running the fair (that is, defining responsibilities and finding appropriate space). To some extent the problems differ with each fair, whatever the choice of the distributor. Frequently, last year's fair, although it seemed successful while it was being held, in retrospect is judged to be a "flop." Either the selection was poor, the number of books too few or too many, or the logistics of running the fair was overwhelming. Book fair devotees are often tantalized by the thought of holding a "perfect" fair. However, since book fair committees, chairpersons, and school supervisors may change from year to year, it is not easy to build on past experience.

The sponsoring group may find that it will be easier to decide on the type of book fair and the choice of a book distributor when they answer for themselves the question, "Why are we having a book fair?" If the goal of the committee is primarily fund raising, then a chocolate sale may be more profitable. If a committee thinks of enlightenment, that only books of high literary quality merit inclusion in a book fair, then the sponsors must assume the responsibility for increasing the awareness of the students as to the desirability of the titles or accept the fact that a number of students will not be responsive to the sale. If the committee sees a book fair as an opportunity for students (readers and nonreaders) to browse and buy books for enrichment, fun, study, or the pure pleasure of buying a book on impulse, then the fair has a realistic goal.

The fair committee can achieve this goal with the help of a creative educational distributor—and earn money for a much desired educational purchase such as books, records, equipment, etc. Choosing a distributor who will best service the needs of a school is of paramount importance since it is the distributor's inventory on which you will base your fair. Keep in mind that most educational distributors warehouse and distribute books of many publishers and have no control over the list price of each book, the size of print, the cover art, or the number of books printed. Companies like Scholastic and Xerox, of course, publish and distribute their own books.

Some comparative shopping may be necessary to discover the differences in book fair offerings of the various distributors. To get a selection of books that will excite students to buy and read is both difficult and easy: the difficulty being in assessing the value of a distributor for your particular needs; the ease in being confident that you have a strong partner in a vender who is helping you to choose appropriate titles.

Whether you are buying at a local distributor or reserving a fair by mail, your shopping is always based on a preselected inventory. By asking questions you should be able to learn what titles are available to you; by subject, grade and reading level, or by publisher. One distributor may be a specialist in fairs for the elementary grades, another for the secondary schools. Generally, a selection that covers a broad range of subjects will fit the needs of a book fair audience. "Something for everyone," when you are trying to sell books, is a good slogan. The distributor who offers you a broad selection of titles from a variety of publishers is most likely committed to quality selling.

Many book distributors offer book fair programs that allow customers little choice in the selection of titles. Although this lack of choice may seem a limitation, in actuality, a book fair list that has been sensitively modified by the experienced distributor over a period of years, can be the foundation of a very successful fair. The creative educational distributor is constantly adding and deleting titles from his fair inventory; he is producing new lists and promotion that predict the trends in titles. Some titles become "hot" items when the media is heavily publicizing them. Whatever the format of the fair, the distributor should be flexible enough in his program so that if he is given sufficient notice, he can provide special titles or extra copies of a single title.

The expression, "nothing too much," may be true when you are choosing books from a wide choice of titles. A profusion of books, hundreds, even thousands, in the abstract is a lovely thought; in reality, inventorying, unpacking, displaying, and repacking enormous quantities of books, especially if the selection is mediocre, may be overwhelming and self-defeating. Too small a collection, even if the quality of selection is superb and suitable to the school's interest, may limit the success of your fair. Also, in a day where people think in quantity, a conservative number of titles may make a fair less attractive. A librarian who gives book talks can make a limited number of books appealing to readers in her audience; however, nonreaders need to be baited by some visual effect or by something in a book display that will be eye-catching.

Types of Fairs

Essentially there are two types of book fairs; the display-and-order fair and the multiple-copy fair. The number of titles and the number of books in each fair and the selection of books available will vary according to the programs of the various educational distributors. There are advantages and disadvantages to both types of fairs. In the display-and-order fair, generally consisting of 150 to 400 titles, single copies of each title are included in the display. The persons supervising the fair take orders and send them on to the distributor who is providing the books. Display copies are sold at the end of the fair. Where supervision or space is limited and/or shipping expenses are significant, the display-and-order fair is a good choice for a book sale. The handling of the books is minimal; the paperwork is somewhat detailed in that records of orders must be kept, duplicate sales slips collated, and books distributed to the students at a later date. Some of the impact of the sale is lost in that only a limited number of students can buy the display copies at the end of the fair while the majority of students must wait for their purchases.

The multiple-copy fair consists of 200 to 400 titles. Multiple copies of each title, generally three to five, sometimes as many as 15 of a title are included. The unpacking, inventorying, the setting up of hundreds of books, and the second inventorying and packing of the books at the end of the fair require much time, many helpers, and adequate space for both displays and the circulation of browsing students. A drawback to this fair is that large numbers of books can cause chaos if the sale is not well organized. At the end of the fair, the unsold books are returned to the distributor. The on-the-spot buying in this type of fair creates an excitement and enthusiasm that are infectious. When the multiple-copy method of selling is well organized, the fair is certain to be successful and usually more books are sold than in the display-and-order fairs.

Multiple-copy fairs are available in two other forms: bookmobile and portable cabinets. For the most part, the several distributors throughout the United States who offer bookmobile fairs use a large semi-trailer as the mobile housing for the book fair. Sundance Paperback Distributors in Littleton, Massachusetts, has bookmobiles which service the elementary schools in the state. These 32-foot semi-trailers hold approximately 6000 books or 600 titles. Truckers haul a trailer to a school and position it for two to four days so that the students are able to leave their classrooms and visit the van to buy books on the spot. This type of bookmobile fair eliminates inventorying, packing, and unpacking and so it frees volunteers

to help students select books. The educational distributors who have bookmobiles report enthusiastic support of the bookmobile fair, but extreme cold or hot weather can make the choice of a bookmobile fair less inviting.

The portable cabinet type of fair is becoming increasingly popular. This fair arrives in the school in the form of large, unfolding cabinets which contain multiple copies of about 250 to 300 titles. The cabinets can be locked after a day of selling and eliminate the need for table space. In a sense, the cabinets function as a room within a room. The number of distributors who have portable book cabinets, or for that matter, bookmobiles, is relatively few.

Getting Started

Before extensive planning for a book fair gets underway, one word of caution. The chairperson of the book fair should first meet with the principal or headmaster to discuss the plans and goals of the sponsoring group. The principal must approve the type of book fair and the dates of the sale. It can be very disappointing and inconvenient for parents, teachers, and students if a fair must be canceled because the supervisor has not been adequately informed of the book fair arrangements. Plan to schedule your fair on the school calendar early, not only to avoid conflicting events that would weaken the success of the fair, but also to find an opportunity for the sale during National Education or National Children's Book Week, during a community celebration, or a parent-teacher conference week. In this way the greatest number of parents will have an opportunity to choose books for their children and themselves.

With the approval of the principal, an established date set for the fair, and a definite idea of what the format of the fair will be, it is now time to enlist the aid of volunteers—interested parents, teachers, library aides, and students. When you have your committee of volunteers, you will be ready to define responsibilities. The number of people needed and the extent of their responsibility will depend on the type of fair, the number of days of the fair, and willingness and freedom of volunteers to participate. At this time you may want to set up a number of master forms that will outline your planning and job allocation. With each fair, Sundance sends out a sample of planning and publicity forms: (1) the Book Fair Committee Work Schedule, (2) the Daily Class Room Schedule, (3) the Daily Cash Report, (4) Suggested Copy for Radio Stations, (5) Suggested Bulletin to Parents, and, (6) Sample of Newspaper Copy, etc. A master checklist summarizes the planning of the fair.

In getting started, the book fair committee, in discussion with the distributor (personally, by telephone or mail), will wish the answers to a number of questions on the logistics of the fair. They are: (1) the space and number of volunteers required for the fair; (2) the newness, variety and number of titles needed for a specific student population; (3) the availability of titles within a certain price range; (4) the advisability of combining hardcover and paperback books in one sale; (5) the practicality of adding puzzles, games, posters, etc.; (6) the inclusion of professional literature and adult titles; (7) the possibility of reordering titles; and, (8) the return policy. The concerned distributor will be able to answer these questions and offer advice, based on a broad experience with book fairs.

The distributor may ask customers to give them a profile of the school; its population, grades, reading levels and interests, and physical facilities available for the fair. They will try to personalize a fair by taking into account the individuality of a particular student population and the desires of the school for special titles. In a typical fair, books on a variety of subjects should be included: humor, sports, mysteries and adventure, animals, activity and crafts, biography, science, classics, popular fiction and nonfiction, movie and TV tie-ins, picture books, etc. Certain types of books and authors are always popular: Judy Blume's books, humor, sports, mazes, and "search-a-word," Sesame Street, *Guinness' Book of World Records*, a new movie tie-in. The word dinosaur or monster in a title has a charismatic quality that young readers cannot ignore. And fortunately, children respond to marketing techniques so that they will buy books that they may not have imagined would be of any interest to them. A new Newbery or Caldecott title will win favor with the students if properly promoted by media specialists and teachers.

I feel strongly that lack of taste in selection can be a great weakness in a book fair offering; that if quality of selection is compromised, then the usefulness of a book fair to students and parents is limited The educational distributor, without adopting the role of censor, has an obligation to help educators obtain books of quality that will appeal to students and increase their desire to read.

Although my company offers book fair programs for grades K through 12, we find that our most successful fairs are at the elementary and middle school levels. Sponsors of a high school fair will find that there are a number of factors that may limit the success of their fair. High school students are mobile and so have access to book stores; older students are spending their own money, rather than their parents', and have numerous options for spending; high school students have developed tastes and are not greatly influenced by book lists and book talks; these students read adult literature (some of the most popular not being acceptable to the schools); and finally, pilferage may be more prevalent than in the elementary school.

Preparing for the Fair

Some general rules are as follows:

1. Choose a sponsor, select a chairperson, and define the responsibilities of the volunteers who will run the fair.
2. Reserve the book fair with the distributor six weeks before the event.
3. Arrange 2 to 4 days for the fair, at least six weeks in advance. A Parents' Evening should be planned during the first days of the fair.
4. Plan to use all available school and community promotional channels well in advance of the fair. There are many imaginative ways to publicize a book fair: newspaper releases; radio announcements; and invitations to parents, friends, and other schools will increase the community's awareness of the sale. Poster contests in which students advertise the fair by describing a book or the fair itself are fun for the students and will create excitement for the fair. Display cabinets with covers of the books, or some of the books themselves will emphasize the contents of the fair. Book talks can highlight individual titles, especially the classics, old and new, that need to be brought to the students' attention. Book lists, distributed to the parents, teachers, and students, will give the sale impetus. And remember that the teachers, themselves, need to be made as familiar as possible with the book fair titles.
5. Encourage student and teacher participation in the actual preparation and running of the fair.
6. Notify teachers ahead of time about the fair and arrange for them to bring their classes in.
7. Recruit a minimum of two volunteers to be on hand at all times to help the students with book selections.
8. Recruit two volunteers to supervise sales and to make change.
9. Arrange to have sufficient change on hand.

When the date of the event arrives, the persons responsible for receiving the books should be ready to inventory, unpack, and display the books. If the book fair is reserved with a local distributor, the book selection committee may decide to choose the books at a warehouse and to be responsible for arrangements for the books to be shipped to the school. The titles may be displayed by grade level, by subject category, by publisher, or randomly. Thinking of the fair as a mini-bookstore, with some order, but yet with an element of surprise disorder, is a good idea. Often, defining a book as belonging to a specific grade level offers the possibility of embarrassing a student and will keep him/her from purchasing books freely and happily. Displaying the books by subject category is the most popular method of presenting titles to students. Adult and professional titles are usually arranged separately from the rest of the book fair titles. Large signs posted over the table or displayed on the table can flag the subject categories.

Running the Fair

1. Find ways to share your enthusiasm about the fair merchandise with the students who come to browse.
2. Have available book lists and scrap paper so that students can note books in which they are interested.
3. Collect cash for each order taken.
4. Take orders for additional copies when the stock is depleted on a certain title. Use a two part sales slip; give one to the student, and keep one for your records.
5. Make a master order list of all titles in duplicate. Retain one list and send the second on to the distributor at the end of the fair.
6. Be certain that the cash box is attended at all times.
7. To discourage pilferage, ask students to leave coats, bags, books, etc., outside the fair area and use only one entrance and exit.
8. Arrange to either lock up the sales area at the end of the day or repack the books if necessary.

9. Tally sales and orders at the end of each day. Use a daily cash report sheet so that daily receipts are listed, accompanied by the initials of persons responsible for funds. Take all cash with you.

When your fair is over, the range of volunteer activity will vary with the type of fair. If the sale has been a display-and-order fair, then not only is there the necessity of collating orders but also the need for an orderly method of sending on to the distributor these orders and arranging to receive and distribute the books at a later date. If a book has been ordered from the distributor and is out of stock temporarily, then the decision must be made to inform the students that they may select other titles or set cash refunds. In all fairs, books that are being returned to the distributor must be inventoried and packed, either by price, publisher, title, or author, according to the distributor's instructions. When the fair is complete and all orders filled, then the distributor will invoice the sponsoring group. The invoice will indicate the total sales figure with the specified discount deducted. Generally, the invoice is payable within ten days.

Evaluation

After the completion of the fair the members of the book fair committee should meet for the purpose of evaluating objectively whether the originally stated goals of the fair have been achieved. The evaluation should be detailed enough so that it will become a working document for the next book fair committee.

The educational distributor who has selected and provided books for your fair will welcome your suggestions on how the fair can be improved. A good selection of books stimulates so much interest that increased reading enthusiasm is extended long after the fair. Both the librarian and the distributor will find that the challenge and efforts to bring worthwhile reading material to students are well worth the amount of time spent in good planning.

Piscataway's Puppet Program

by Lynn S. Hunter

Several years ago the Piscataway Public Libraries in New Jersey plunged into puppetry when a local organization donated an old puppet theater. Armed with a little book knowledge and a great deal of enthusiasm, the staff initiated summer puppetry workshops at two libraries—the John F. Kennedy Memorial Library and the New Market Branch Library.

A dozen children, ages eight to twelve, joined each workshop and met once a week for six weeks. The children selected plays to perform (folk and fairy tales were used so that the plots would be familiar and the children would not need to rely on a script). Two plays were selected for each workshop so that every child could have a part. The first two sessions were devoted to choosing parts and making simple hand puppets. For the next three weeks we rehearsed; while the children producing one play used the theater, the others worked on scenery and props.

We used a "learning through doing" approach—gradually teaching the children how to project their voices and handle the puppets as they rehearsed. We encouraged imagination and freedom of expression, and were rewarded by seeing very quiet children speak openly and quite wittily through their puppets. The last meeting of our workshop was a public performance of the children's plays at each branch.

The program, for me, was difficult—alternately exciting and exasperating—but it was worth it. The children thoroughly enjoyed the workshop and produced delightful plays. But the most extraordinary aspect of the program was the public response—more than one hundred people attended each performance. Never before had we had such a large turnout for a library program. At our cramped New Market Branch, people had to sit on tables or on the circulation and return desks!

As the staff and I became increasingly involved in puppetry, however, the general unwieldiness of the large, heavy theater (it consisted of three four foot by seven foot pieces of panelling framed with two- by four-inch lumber) became more and more of a problem. Three people were required to assemble the theater, and we had to transport the panelled sections in a borrowed station wagon. The theater itself was looking shabby from being bumped from place to place. The last straw came when we were asked to perform our Christmas show at a local hospital, and we had to haul our bulky theater upstairs, through narrow hallways, and into an elevator in order to reach the hospital's recreation room.

It was obvious that if we were to continue an active puppetry program we would need a theater that would: (1) be lightweight and easily portable; (2) be large enough to accommodate at least five people backstage; (3) fold up compactly enough to fit in an average size car; (4) be neat and attractive; (5) be easily transported and assembled by a single person if necessary; and, (6) fall within a reasonable cost range. We decided it would be most practical to design and build our own theater and after many weeks of planning, I drew up a basic design with the help of my husband, Alan.

Piscataway's puppet theater was built in one very long afternoon (approximately five hours); the fabric covering for the frame was donated by a local merchant and added during spare moments at the library. The result of our efforts is a theater eight feet tall, five feet long, and three feet deep, which can be folded into two packages (3 x 4 x 1/2 feet) that fit into my Volkswagon squareback. The theater is lightweight and simple enough for me to load, unload, and assemble unaided. And, putting personal bias aside as much as possible, it's quite handsome. The total cost of the project was $35. The cost breakdown is as follows:

Lumber for frame	$15
Hardware	4
Traverse rod with valance	10
Material for curtains	6
Total	$35

We now have had our new theater in operation for two years. It has seen countless rehearsals and performances, and has not yet required repairs. We have lent the theater to church youth groups and scout troops, and have taught them basic puppet construction and techniques. In return the groups gave puppet shows at the library. I have occasionally used the theater to teach library techniques to class groups (an owl helps a dog to find *Curious George*), or I simply hand a few puppets to a visiting group and let them "act out" library situations.

When Piscataway acquired a bookmobile, our summer puppet show went on the road, and we scheduled outdoor performances at several bookmobile stops. During a trial run, we were traumatized to discover that, when fully assembled, our theater was so light it took off like a kite when the wind blew!

After the initial shock wore off, we simply removed the curtains and crosspiece, and folded down the top half of the theater. We were left with a very simple but quite workable theater which was four feet high, and stable in a breeze. Scenery changes were done in full view of the audience, but that did not detract from the play. If anything, it added a casual, more intimate note.

My favorite venture into puppetry has been our Christmas puppet show. I have always been fond of traditions, and decided to "create" one for the library. So three years ago we used a script with a strong, lively plot and gave our first annual production of "Christmas at Creepy Castle" from Tom Tichenor's, *Folk Plays for Puppets You Can Make* (Abingdon, 1959). Each December when the show is given we add something new; spotlights, elaborate scenery, fresh costumes, etc. It's too early to tell, of course, but I would like to think that ten or fifteen years from now, the children of Piscataway will look forward to *Creepy Castle* at the library in the same way that we now look for *A Christmas Carol* on TV.

There are endless possibilities for using puppets in library programs. Puppetry requires very little money and very little space. (In our tiny branch library we put the theater between the stacks, and the audience sits on the floor.) Whether we are working directly with children or performing for them, the rewards are immense. The puppets become real for children—they speak to them (or through them) with heartwarming spontaneity.

It is my hope that other librarians who experiment with this creative and exciting field of puppetry or who adapt the ideas I've presented, will experience the same pleasure for their staff and generate the same enthusiasm among their public as we have at our library.

Effective School Visits—A Guide

by Elizabeth Huntoon

This outline was adapted from the "School Visiting Guide" prepared by the author for the Chicago Public Library.

How to Plan the School Visit

- Set an objective for each visit. Three possible examples are to seek better cooperation between library and teachers on homework assignments, to increase use of library's fiction collection by 4th and 5th graders, and to acquaint every child in the school with public library card registration procedures.
- Determine which style of school visit will best accomplish your objective.
- Read the previous years' school visit reports to alert yourself to problems, strengths, regulations, and size of school.
- Plan what you will talk about. Select books and public relations materials to stimulate interest. Be sure you have enough handouts for every classroom.
- If you plan to pass out applications, it is a good idea to inform the desk staff and, together, review procedures for library card registration, payment of fines, and replacement of lost cards.

How to Make Your Contact

Call the school at least two weeks ahead of time. State your name, which branch you represent, and tell them that you would like to visit the school. This person will usually put you in contact with the principal or vice-principal.

When you speak to the principal, be specific about *why* you wish to visit, to *whom* you will speak, and *for how long*. At this point, inquire about any special regulations you will be expected to follow. Confirm the date either by writing a letter stating what you have agreed to do during the visit or by telephoning a few days in advance.

What to Do at the School

Report to the office and introduce yourself to the clerk or secretary at the desk. Ask to be introduced to the person with whom you made the arrangements to thank that person.

The office clerk will usually give you a classroom roster and direct you to the classes or places you wish to visit. After the visit, check in at the office to tell the staff you are leaving and thank them for their cooperation. Many schools will give you a nametag but it's a good idea to have one to wear if they don't.

Topics to Discuss with the Principal

- Priorities and objectives of the school during the current year.
- Mutual areas of concern such as discipline, gangs, traffic hazards, and a change in enrollment.
- Special programs offered by the school. (Don't miss the opportunity to suggest ways the library might tie in with these programs.)
- Methods of teaching reading.
- PTA or parent group activities.
- Branch library program and facilities. (Mention the availability of the library to display children's art work.)

Topics to Discuss with the Librarian

- The school's curriculum and library materials.
- Specific reading interests of the students.
- The content of a typical class visit to the school library.
- New materials or collection strengths of the public library.
- New policies or services of the local library.
- Special programs such as creative dramatics or enrichment projects and the teachers who are involved in them.

Entering the Classroom

First, identify yourself. Although the teacher may be expecting you, you may be asked to come back after a test or lesson is finished.

Be sure to repeat your name and library several times during your presentation. You may also have available a 3 x 5 index card stating your name, position, branch, address, and phone number for the teacher to refer to.

Leave bookmarks, flyers, or other promotional materials with the teacher for display or handouts to remind the children to visit the library.

Do not overstay your allotted time(a visit should last from 10-15 minutes.

A Short Classroom Visit May Include

- An explanation of library card registration procedures. Bring along samples of the application, a type of required identification, and a sample library card. Define useful library terms. If you plan to supply applications have the teacher pass them out just before dismissal.
- Location of your library by address and landmarks that the children know. Be prepared to give walking directions from the school to the library.
- Invite the children to upcoming library programs and invite the teacher to bring the class for a scheduled visit.
- Do a short fingerplay or participation game or tell a short story.
- Ask the children what books they have enjoyed reading.
- Give short booktalks. Be sure to have enough library copies on hand to fill after-school requests.

Ideas For In-depth Visits

- Booktalks on a special topic the class is studying.
- Stories from a country that is being studied.
- Instruction on the *Reader's Guide*.
- Discussion of library materials that relate to a current class project.

How to Follow Up the Visit

- Mail immediately any materials or information you promised to send to the school.
- Write a letter thanking the principal for making your visit possible. Mention a school exhibit or program you observed that the library could help support.
- Write a school visit report. Include the person(s) or classes with whom you talked, what was discussed, and statistical information.
- Report orally to the branch head and to other staff members, perhaps at a staff meeting, so they are aware of your activities.
- Evaluate your visit in terms of your objective(s). You may not see immediate results but the information and observations gained from the visit will aid in planning the next visit.

Be aware of problems connected with school visits. Sometimes the school schedule has been rearranged because of a special program, so the time allotted to you is shortened. It may happen that the principal forgot to alert the teachers of your visit. A fire drill may interrupt you or a teacher may leave the room and fail to return by the time you have finished your presentation. Be flexible.

By following these easy guidelines, you should accomplish your major goal of school visiting—that is to remind students and teachers of your library's services and resources.

Steps to Cooperative YA Programming

by Fontayne Holmes & Carol Baldwin

The competition for young adults' time and attention in the Los Angeles, California area is terrific. While many teens do use the branch libraries to complete homework assignments and borrow books for recreational reading, many others in our highly mobile, fast-paced, multiethnic communities are not familiar with the public library and do not take advantage of its services. In order to introduce the resources of the public library to uninitiated teenagers, eleven YA librarians in the Hollywood branches of the Los Angeles Public Library work together to provide effective outreach programs.

One dreary fall morning two-and-a-half years ago as we discussed our frustrations about YA programming, the seeds of our solution to the problem of successful programming were planted. The key to that solution is cooperation. In the light of competition for YAs' attention and our strong commitment to outreach, we decided to work together to plan a program so fantastic that the kids would have to come.

We were very aware of the fact that for librarians in highly populated urban centers, young adult programming can often be more difficult than in smaller communities. In the big city, teenagers have easy access to many forms of sophisticated and appealing entertainment. Here in the Hollywood area, they are inundated by a myriad of stimuli—rock concerts, the latest movies, discotheques. In any given week in L.A., stars and superstars draw thousands and thousands of kids. Just recently, for example, they could choose among these entertainers: Zappa; Chicago; Helen Reddy; Journey; Bette Midler; Robin Trower; The Baby's; Black Oak; Blue Oyster Cult; The Beachboys; Earth, Wind and Fire; Aerosmith; Rod Stewart; and Queen.

We held our first program in May 1976. The topic was "Science Fiction and the Media." A UFO expert, a make-up specialist, and an animator participated and each gave a stimulating talk and demonstration. A panel of distinguished science fiction authors totally captivated the audience. To our amazement the program drew 350 fans from all over Southern California. A questionnaire substantiated that more than half were teenagers.

In the excitement of that day, and even in the calm evaluation sessions that followed, we considered ourselves lucky to have planned such a successful outreach program. We attributed our success to luck until last year when we presented our second cooperative effort, a "Comic and Cartooning Festival." Of the more than 600 fans who attended, two-thirds were teenagers. As we discussed and evaluated our second program, it struck us that our success was not due to luck at all but to cooperative programming. We call our formula for planning on a large scale, **STEP**: Special Interest Group; Think Big; Espirit d'Corps; Publicity.

Step 1: Special Interest Groups

Special interest groups are people bound together by a common concern or endeavor—stamp collectors, chess players, football fans, skiers, birdwatchers, science fiction buffs, hikers and backpackers, classic car refurbishers, cat lovers, tennis players, surfers, needlepointers, dirt bike enthusiasts, gourmet cooks, skateboarders, rock music devotees, and so on. They are people who love "to do their thing" and will drive scores of miles to hear speakers or to attend an event, convention, exhibit, swap meet, or show planned around their special interest. Teenagers belong to numerous special interest groups, especially ones related to hobbies, sports, cultural affiliations.

You don't have to be a specialist in the topic you choose. At the time we planned our science fiction program, our library had no resident SF specialist among us. Later, when we planned our comic and cartooning festival, we knew nothing about cartoonists and comic book artists and writers. But we did know that comic books are a hot item among teens who frequent our libraries. We met with one of the library's clerks who is an amateur cartoonist and he introduced us to the world of comic books. He began naming people we'd never heard of, and showing us newspaper and magazine articles that highlighted events in our own community.

After this introduction we began calling and writing the people involved and became increasingly familiar with the world of comics. We contacted organizations (the L.A. Science Fantasy Association and the Mythopoeic Society), newsletters (*Comic Journal, Fantasia*), convention planners (Comicon, Equicon: Filmcon, and Westercon), specialized bookstores (American Comic Book Company, Super Hero Shop, Change of Hobbit Speculative Fiction Bookshop, and Wonderworld Books), and private collectors in the field. Members of these groups helped find speakers, donated door prizes, judged contests, and disseminated information about these events.

These groups formed our core audience—they were real groupies who were intensely loyal to their heroes (the cartoonists) and glad for an opportunity to spend a day with them. The publicity drew in teens in our neighborhoods and other fans, but the core audience concept insured the huge success of our program. The "hard-core" devotees came in droves. They provided a sophistication often lacking in general audiences by asking profound questions, laughing at subtle jokes, and responding with the kind of interest that stimulates speakers and helps them give their best. We call it the "synergy effect."

Finding out about the insiders in a field of interest is easy. It just takes making the first few contacts and asking a lot of simple questions, all the while picking up on every name and organization mentioned.

Step 2: Think Big

In whatever special interest field you choose, ask the most popular artists or names to participate. To locate them, follow up on the leads given to you by clubs, organizations, newsletters, and interest-group contacts. Also use library bibliographic resources (e.g., *Who's Who in America*, regional Who's Who's, or *Writer's Directory*), and specialized directories (*Encyclopedia of Comic Books*) for addresses. Authors, artists, and other specialists are often enthusiastically responsive, especially when they know that the library program is being offered free to young people.

Considering the fact that we could not offer any honorarium to speakers, we were amazed by the impressive roster of science fiction writers who accepted the invitation to participate in our first program: A.E. Van Vogt (*Slan*), Larry Niven (*Ringworld*), Jerry Pournelle (*Lucifer's Hammer*), Alan Dean Foster ("Star Trek" logs), and George Clayton Johnson (*Logan's Run*). As for the comic and cartoon festival, we were grateful and excited when Don Rico, the dean of American comic book artists; Sergio Aragones, cartoonist for *Mad* books; Mark Evanier, cartoonist; Don Glut, writer for *Marvel* comics; Jack Kirby, creator of *The All American Boy*; and Mike Royer, writer for *Tarzan* comics, all agreed to appear. But we were really flabbergasted when one librarian announced that Sergio Aragones, *Mad*'s wacky cartoonist, was going to meet us for lunch during our planning stages. Sergio gave us lots of reassurance. He told us about the kinds of comic conventions he and his colleagues attend, guided us to film sources and comic book stores, and tactfully suggested that we ask a particular artist, in respect of his seniority, to moderate the program panel.

Fortunately many authors, artists, musicians, and other "celebrities" make their homes in Southern California. Yet many urban areas have a reservoir of talented specialists who can be called upon for YA programs.

Step 3: Develop Espirit d'Corps

The YA librarians of our region meet monthly to evaluate books, plan programs and school visits, and discuss matters pertinent to YA work. These meetings are free-wheeling brain-storming sessions when it comes to program planning.

As soon as a program idea comes up, someone volunteers to act upon it; nothing is assigned.

Volunteers follow through in every detail. For instance, a librarian who contacts a prospective speaker stays in touch with him or her prior to the event, to coordinate preliminary arrangements. The volunteer also finds out what equipment the speaker will need, obtains photos and biographical information for news releases, and escorts the guest from time of arrival to the program to departure. Finally, this volunteer is responsible for thanking the speaker for participating.

Step 4: Publicize Extensively

We all know that unless people hear about an event, no matter how appealing it may be, attendance will be disappointing. In urban areas publicity is a big challenge because information channels are glutted with announcements of competing attractions. That's why it is important to remember the special interest group concept. We distributed flyers in quantity to every known club and bookstore, and every organization related to our program theme. We sent news releases to specialized publications and newsletters covering that particular field of interest. For the comic/cartooning festival, we shared the work of sending news releases to 50 or 60 different sources.

To reach the general public we sent news releases to all local daily and weekly newspapers, including the *Los Angeles Times* Calendar section; to radio and TV stations (the KNXT Community Bulletin Board and KFWB, the all-news radio station); to high school and college newspapers (the UCLA *Daily Bruin* and the USC *Trojan*); and to local and regional magazines (*Los Angeles Magazine*, *New West*, and the Auto Club's *Westways*).

We also contacted several special TV and radio stations. As a result, one of our librarians was interviewed on a science fiction radio program.

Also, personal letters of invitation were sent to the mayor, city council members, the library administrators, and to all the young adult librarians in LAPL. Flyers were sent to public and school libraries throughout the metropolitan area (later we were happy to learn that more than half of the audience had learned about the programs by seeing a flyer at a library).

We believe the mass media publicity reinforced the significance of our events, however, and that publicity via libraries alone would have been insufficient. But the concept of the library as an information channel was given new credibility when we realized how many people had heard about the programs at our own agencies.

The STEP formula has worked for us. We wouldn't atttempt a large-scale program without following it. To implement the STEP formula, here is a checklist which incorporates all the details that are so easy to overlook in planning a big program unless you have experienced the difficulties resulting from their omission.

STEP by Step

1. Determine with whom you can work on a big program. Librarians in most cities belong to a library

system with colleagues readily available. At the first meeting, sell them on the advantages of cooperative programming—the reservoir of ideas, the shared workload, the division of responsibilties that eliminates any duplication of effort, and the public relations benefits.

2. Start planning six months in advance. It takes two or three months for the program to jell in your own minds, based on the conversations and inquiries with people in the field, so it is important to start early.

3. Select a program theme and formats (demonstrations, films, exhibits) that appeal to teenagers and relate to a special interest group. Delineate what you want the theme to include, but leave it open-ended so that the panelists can contribute. For example, we extended our "Comic and Cartooning Festival" beyond our original idea of featuring only comic books. But through the addition of cartooning we were able to reach out to artistic kids who were interested in a cartooning career.

4. Choose a date and time free from conflict with school schedules (holidays, final exams, proms, sports events, and graduation) and convenient for participants.

5. Decide where to hold the event and consider space requirements—the size of the main room, auxiliary rooms for various parallel activities, outdoor space, restrooms, kitchen, parking, and location. If you plan to use a library, another factor is its service hours and available staff.

6. Invite all the potential participants in advance to insure a full program. Many will say yes immediately. Some will give a tentative yes. Those who cannot attend will often recommend someone else in the field who may come.

7. Plan auxiliary events. We found that four hours is a long time for kids to sit still, and that holding two or three related events in separate rooms enables audiences to move around as they wish.

• At each event we showed films in a separate room all afternoon, repeating some of the films more than once. We obtained appropriate films through library and rental film catalogs. Some films were brought by the participants.

• In the small park area outside the library, various activities supplemented the main program. Booths were set up by fans and collectors for trading comic books and, at the S.F. fair, a "Star Trek" van was displayed in the park.

• We emplasized library resources; each librarian brought relevant books for circulation on an interlibrary loan basis.

• A major feature of the programs has been an art contest for junior and senior high students. School visits to art classses and contest flyer/entry blanks in the libraries and at the schools publicized the contest. We exhibited the entries and arranged for experts among the program participants to judge them just before the one o'clock opening of the fair. Prizes were awarded, and the winning entries were later showcased in the central library. Art contests are appropriate to our program themes, but other contests can be held for poetry, essay writing, dramatic presentations, or costumes (the best comic book superhero or the most way-out S.F. character).

8. Remember to publicize early. Many publications and monthly magazines have set early deadlines.

Designing and printing flyers takes time—our PR department requires six weeks. Flyers announcing our art contest were distributed far in advance of the program. Hundreds were taken by library patrons, yet we only received between 65 and 80 art entries. We realized that people pick up the contest entry-blank flyers in order to be informed of the event. So for our next cooperative YA program we intend to design three different types of flyers, a general one to announce the program, a contest flyer, and a final information flyer to be distributed one month before the program.

9. Two months before the program jot down all the equipment and staff the program will require. For our program, we obtained one 12' by 5' platform (to raise the speakers' table and chairs for good audience viewing), a public address system, 150 additional chairs, a tape recorder, two film projectors, one projection screen, one 35mm slide projector; and ten 3' by 5' folding tables for the booths.

Even with eleven libraries working, we needed additional staff members to check out the books, answer the telephone, help control the enthusiastic crowds of people, and assist in the clean-up effort.

10. Six to eight weeks before your program date reconfirm all speakers. When you know exactly who is coming you can determine the structure of the program. The specialties of the participants seem to naturally divide the program into categories. For the S.F. fair, five of the speakers were specialists in tangential S.F. areas. The authors appeared on a panel and talked about their careers, getting started, the challenges of their work, the creative process. The audience loved it when they continued on to discuss the theoretical concepts of speculative fiction. The authors stayed for the entire program—signing autographs and talking informally with small groups of fans. In the second half of the program the remaining speakers gave short presentations.

When your program is finalized you can then design the painted program. Ask a talented staff member or patron, the public relations department, or an artistic friend to do the artwork. Mad cartoonist Sergio Aragones designed the cover for our comic/cartooning fest in a matter of minutes at one of our meetings. The program was an inexpensively reproduced flyer folded in half and printed on both sides.

We cannot give exact costs on the 6000 publicity flyers, or 500 printed programs we used as they were included in the general publicity budgets of each branch library.

11. We are somewhat old-fashioned librarians—we're book oriented! So for each outreach program we prepared a topical, appropriate bibliography. For the first program we produced and distributed a union list of S.F. collections in libraries and bookstores located in Southern California. Included in the printed program of our second effort was a selected list of LAPL comic and cartooning books.

12. From the outset we wanted to find out about our audience to evaluate our outreach program. We decided to attach a very short questionnaire to the door-prize entry blank, hoping the prize would influence the kids to answer the questions: Do you use the public library? Which branch? Where did you hear about this program? What is your name, address, and school? They did answer them and at the monthly meeting following the program, the tabulated results gave us information on demographics, library usage, and the effect of our publicity.

13. Because we had no budget for prizes, we solicited local record, book, and T-shirt stores to donate art contest and door prizes. *Marvel* Comics (whom we wrote to) and Disney Productions (whom we telephoned) donated hundreds of new comic books for door prizes. Local comic book stores donated collectors' items, such as rare comic books and price-list books.

14. If you have the funds, take your speakers to lunch or dinner. If not, you might try setting up a wine and cheese reception for the program participants.

15. We wrote and posted a schedule to follow for the day of the program. Volunteers rotated one-hour shifts. The schedule included: two librarians at the entrance to hand out programs; two librarians to share the master of ceremonies duties; one librarian to operate the film projector; one librarian to tape the program and monitor the microphone; one librarian to watch the art exhibit; one librarian to handle the circulation desk; two librarians at the speakers' reception; and one librarian to photograph the events.

16. On the morning of the program we rearranged the library, placed directional signs and publicity banners outside the library, prepared the reception, tested all equipment, and took care of all unforeseen matters.

17. The feedback on our annual cooperative programs has been gratifying. Teenagers have come into each of our branch libraries to thank us for the programs and ask about the next one. As a result we've made many new friends who come to check out books and attend programs at our branch libraries.

The Measure of Success

Our annual YA happening has been inspirational. Rather than take the place of all other library program attempts, it spurs us on to present our individual programs for teenagers in the immediate communities surrounding our branches. By working together our group is able to share the enormous amount of work involved in planning and conducting a large-scale program for teenagers. We share the responsibility, the anxiety, and best of all, we share the great joy of knowing that our youngsters enjoy a well-planned event. If you haven't had the courage to undertake a big program before, cooperative planning through STEP can provide both incentive and a workable procedure.

Sure-Fire LMC Reports

by Patricia Howland

Sure-fire LMC Reports

Trying to use the wrong form for reporting your income tax is like trying to use the wrong form for reporting on library media center activities—both are unsatisfactory. The usual lesson plan forms for teachers simply are not appropriate for most library media functions and, more significantly, they are inadequate to the task of showing what actually occurs in a school library, especially an open-access library. Nonetheless, librarians are usually required to complete lesson plans. Furthermore, in this era of accountability, it is propitious that they should do so in order to convey to administration the library's functions and importance, and to plan and evaluate library programs. In short, whether or not lesson plans are required, library media specialists should find an effective method of reporting to administration.

It would be wise, therefore, to devise such a method that not only answers the need for administrators to know and to measure, but that also allows for adequate enumeration of significant library services, events, and activities. We've successfully used the following format as an alternative to traditional lesson plans. With modification for local needs, a similar format can be used by most library media centers.

Basically, there are eight components to this weekly report—1) Technical work; 2) Student-centered activities; 3) Class-centered activities; 4) Staff-centered activities; 5) Extra-library activities; 6) Statistics; 7) Unmet needs; and 8) Looking ahead.

To promote reading and understanding of the report by administrators, it is best to use the same format each week and, of course, to submit it promptly at the end of each week. Because this will be a report that you want your administrator to read, be sure to keep it brief—use outline form, follow a consistent format, and if it fits your style, don't be afraid to use some humor. A tip: It's helpful to keep a notebook for the report and jot down items each day—for even the best of us forget.

Technical Work

Write a brief description of the many underestimated or unknown technical chores which must be done to keep a library media center going: accessioning, cataloging, filing, inventories, repairs, ordering, etc.

1. Technical work
   a. Continued cataloging multimedia kits (3 in 1 hour)
   b. Inventoried library supplies (preparatory to budget work—2 hours by aide)
   c. Repaired filmstrips (2 hours—24 strips repaired by aide)
   d. Weeded A-F of fiction section; prepared about 50 books for discard (librarian and aide)
   e. Accessioned new professional materials (see list in faculty newsletter)

There is no need to belabor any given task; it is more useful to show the variety of work performed in a typical week, the time required, and whenever possible, its significance.

Student-centered Activities

Commonly called "floor work," student-centered activities are probably the most important work of any librarian—and the most difficult to document. Although it is impossible to show the full scope of this work, it is helpful to select and note specific examples, sometimes using the names of students and teachers.

2. Student-centered activities
   a. Worked on individual reading skills from Jones' special class.
   b. Helped new student council president to understand and use *Robert's Rules of Order.*
   c. Helped advance students from Smith's class with research outside the library—public library system, correspondence, state library, etc., on New York State history.
   d. Started Harold Walter on typing lessons (as planned with homeroom teacher)
   e. Worked with independent-study students from Harlow's class who made sound/slide presentations on mammals for science projects.

Again, it is more useful to show the variety of the work and its direct application to students and to the curriculum rather than attempt to describe every situation. (It would take volumes to document it all!)

Class-centered Activities

Scheduled library classes probably provide the opportunity for the most traditional lesson plans. Nonetheless, it is best to keep to the overall format of this report and to submit specific lesson plans as an addendum.

3. *Class-centered activities*
    a. Worked with Long's first-period class using library resources to investigate careers.
    b. Did questions for—and conducted—a quiz show contest between seventh and eighth grades.
    c. Worked with Schneider's class researching the '30s.
    d. Provided poetry-reading sessions for Owen's language arts classes.
    e. Introduced sources and research methods to Robinson's music classes for unit on biographies and musicians.

You may want to add addendum elaborating on specific technique and noting curriculum relationships.

Staff-centered Activities

The role of the library media specialist includes that of a curriculum planner and resource person for the faculty. Often this work affects only a small number of faculty members at a time, and the overall effect can be lost at the administrative level. However, it is such a significant and valued part of the professional librarian's work that special care must be taken to call this role to the attention of the administration. Those activities which demonstrate the role of the librarian as a vital member of the professional education team should be emphasized.

4. *Staff-centered activities*
    a. Worked with Brown's team to develop an inter-disciplinary unit on mythology. Designed library-center work for various level students.
    b. Made up list and collection of multi-media materials on botany for Clark.
    c. Attended an eighth-grade-team meeting to evaluate units on Europe (just completed) and to plan next unit on Africa.
    d. Participated in conference with Howard Klum's parents; recommended specific library activities for Howard.
    e. Prepared library "greetings" to inform teachers about new professional materials.

Other Activities

Oftentimes the librarian is—and should be—involved in programs and projects that are not major job duties, but which are significant and should be brought to the administration's attention.

5. *Extra-library activities*
    a. Attended Junior Chamber of Commerce meeting and presented a slide program on the role of the school library media specialist.
    b. Met with district Right-to-Read committee; staff will investigate the possibility of organizing a tutorial program for students.
    c. Addressed adult-education class on use of a library as a resource tool.
    d. Attended the school library media specialists' monthly meeting. Heard discussion on copyright.
    e. Met with PTA program committee to plan meeting on censorship.

Statistics

A simple "box score" or any other suitable abbreviated method of reporting can be used to report circulation and attendance statistics.

6. *Statistics*
    a. Circulation—fiction, nonfiction, non-book materials, professional materials
    b. Student attendance: (representative times/days)

Needs

Sometimes library media specialists hesitate to mention those things they cannot do, but it is essential to document these needs in order to provide both the information and the rationale for future planning, budgeting, and expansion. This includes indicating voids or shortages in the collection in addition to personnel and space shortages.

7. *Unmet needs*
    a. Unable to provide materials on copyright for faculty meeting due to short notice; will acquire information for teachers
    b. Insufficient materials on the Eastern Front on World War II for Sharpe who indicated he will be emphasizing this.
    c. Unable to schedule seventh-grade team to use wet carrels—too many out of order (*Help!* Please remember my previous request for repair).
    d. Had to postpone book talks in sixth-grade language arts classrooms due to aide's illness (no substitute aide available).

In your report, be sure to include plans for the coming week in complete lesson plans or a projected log.

8. *Looking ahead*
    a. See attached sheet for list of classes scheduled to use library.
    b. Tuesday, meet with sixth B team to discuss world studies project.
    c. Host district librarian's meeting Wednesday.

On first reading, this format may seem cumbersome but, in fact, it should take only one page. The significant point is that it more adequately portrays the scope, breadth, and depth of the library media specialists' work-week and illustrates how a LMC specialist supports the entire educational process.

Distance Education: Removing Barriers to Knowledge

by Daniel D. Barron

There are many people in the United States who are place bound—people whose jobs will not permit them to travel to schools of instruction, families with small children, those with physical disabilities. Many young people who live in small or rural communities where the financial base will not support a wide range of teachers are denied the promise of equal access to education. Constrained by the barrier of geography, these children, and the rest of the place bound, cannot attend tradional schools—teachers have to go to them.

Distance education, simply defined, is taking quality education to the people who need and want it. Distance education is to instruction what bookmobiles and branch libraries are to reading. We cannot guarantee that people who have books brought to their neighborhoods will read, but we know for sure that if these people do not have access to books they cannot choose to read. Likewise, if students don't have access to a physics teacher, if adults do not have access to basic literacy programs, or if those planning to become school library media specialists live too far away from institutions offering graduate courses in librarianship and information science, they cannot choose, at least formally, to prepare for this profession.

Basic television, cable TV, satellites, and computers are all being used by public and private institutions and agencies to provide more people with access to a greater number of programs than the world of institutionalized instruction has ever known. As it has evolved, the concept of distance education has been given a variety of different labels—correspondence study, extension teaching, open learning, and home study, to name a few. Distance education is best described by the subtitle of the *Online Journal of Distance Education* and *Communication*: "In the industrial age, we go to school. In the information age, school can come to us. This is the message implicit in the media and movement of distance education."

Background

Obviously, the concept of distance education is not new. Its roots can be traced back to the heroic efforts of educators who defied tradition and apathy to take education to those who were unable to participate in traditional schooling. Such crusaders took education into the slave cabins. In New England, Anna Eliot Ticknor used the mail to reach homebound women; she founded the Society to Encourage Studies at Home in 1873. In the 1920s, Ben Darrow pioneered the use of radio in

"The Little Red Schoolhouse of the Air" in Chicago, and in Iowa, J.L. Potter and E. B. Kurtz tested the power of television as an instructional delivery system during the early 1930s. William Harper, the first president of the University of Chicago, founded the first university-level correspondence teaching department in the late 1800's and is often referred to as the "Father of Correspondence Teaching." William Lighty and the University of Wisconsin are frequently cited for their commitment, in the early part of this century, to reach out to people for whom formal education would not otherwise be available.

Distance education in contemporary sociey has taken a number of new and exciting turns. One of the most notable is a result of the advantages in telecommunications technology—computers, cable television, and satellites. School administrators who once feared losing autonomy are now realizing that distance education can provide a host of resources to support the curriculum. Turf battles and bureaucratic stumbling blocks in top educational levels are being replaced by consortia and mutually beneficial agreements between and among institutions and agencies of education at all levels. As one educator said, "There is more than enough ignorance out there for all of us." Distance education is a new force in the battle against ignorance, and library media specialists have a critical part to play in its success.

Star Schools

Implementation of the Star Schools program has given the concept of distance education greater visibility. The Star Schools program is federally funded, with approximately 25 percent of the operating costs coming from local funds. Now funded for the second year, the project serves as a model for using technology as a means of reaching small or disadvantaged schools in isolated areas. Its primary goal is to develop and deliver courses for students in specific areas of the curriculum that suffer, on the local level, from a lack of faculty expertise. During the first year these courses for students included an introduction to Japanese (originating from Nebraska), probability and statistics (Kentucky), and German (Oklahoma). For many schools selected as sites for the project, this has meant purchasing satellite dishes and accompanying technology. In addition to courses for students in these selected schools, the project is providing opportunities for staff development—which, in the first year, included a course to help teachers teach advanced calculus, as well as a number of non-credit teleconferences.

Interestingly enough, the Star Schools program uses the term "partnerships" to describe the network of participants who are developing and delivering the courses. These partnerships are structured in a variety of cooperatives comprised of the local schools, state departments of education, colleges and universities, public television affiliates, public and private telecommunications services, and the other agencies from the private sector. The four partnerships are the Midlands Consortium, the Satellite Educational Resources Consortium (SERC), the Technical Education Research Centers (TERC), and the TI-IN Network, Inc (a private corporation).

Three of these partnerships use both satellite and television communications for instructional delivery. Most delivery systems use a live, interactive format with one-way audio and video to the receive site, with two-way audio between that site and the teacher at the originating site. TERC, the fourth partnership, is different in that it is based on computer-assisted communications and involves the networking of schools with participating scientists. This cooperative provides students with the opportunity to work directly with these professionals in developing experiments covering a wide variety of "real world" problems for discussion.

Program leaders identify and select exceptional teachers, who are asked to develop and deliver the courses. At the local level, a facilitator works directly with the students and a coordinator disseminates information materials. Since, in the pilot program stage, participation by schools is limited, each agency offers additional courses and services independent of the Star Schools effort.

Such careful planning and coordination among the partnerships has resulted in very successful models for instructional delivery. All reportedly have had excellent results: 97% of the principals involved in SERC, for example, indicated that they will continue as participants.

Beyond Star Schools

Distance education by no means ends with Star Schools. In fact, there are many distance education programs available. The Office of Technology Assessment is completing a study which will show that there are a tremendous number of distance education efforts going on, and that they involve all ages and categories of learners. Kindergarten through high school courses, adult basic education, basic literacy, undergraduate and graduate courses and programs, continuing education for business persons, engineers, teachers, lawyers, and other professionals, and a wide number of educational opportunities for the casual learner are available by way of television and other delivery systems.

In most states, the Public Broadcasting System (PBS) provides educational programming specifically for K-12 schools. Whether through a university or a state agency, local public television stations carry such classics as Sesame Street, The Electric Company, Reading Rainbow, and Think-About, as well as new programs like Dicho y Hecho and Mathnet. These programs are often accompanied with teachers' guides and other informational materials. In addition, free and inexpensive support materials can be obtained from the national office of PBS, and from such organizations or agencies as the Children's Television Workshop, the Corporation for Public Broadcasting and the American Library Association.

Other distance education opportunities are available to cable subscribers and owners of satellite dishes. Most of these offer off-air taping rights, teacher guides, suggestions for program and curriculum integration, and access to a staff member who is responsible for assisting schools in the use of general and specific programming. Among the stations available to cable subscibers is C-SPAN (the channel devoted to public-affairs), which has begun an educational program called "C-SPAN in the Classroom." Also, "Cable News Network," (CNN) offers "News Access," which provides materials created by the instructional designers and offers taping rights to "The Week in Review."

Whittle Communications' controversial "Channel One" news program, with its commercial inserts geared to high-school students, is only one component of a much larger effort by Whittle to provide educational programming to schools. Whittle also airs "The Classroom Channel." which runs commercial-free programs, and "The Educator's Channel," the offerings of which are specifically designed for staff development. Whittle provides free hardware and installation incentives for subscribers, but their methods—and especially, "Channel One"—continue to come under fire by local and state school boards.

The Discovery Channel, known for its excellent programs on nature, science, technology, and history, devotes an hour each day to help educators integrate their programs into their curriculum. The Learning Channel provides educational programming for children and adults. "The Electronic Library," two hours devoted primarily to middle and secondary schools in the areas of math, language, science, and the performing arts, is the Learning Channel's effort at making programs more useful in classroom instruction. The Mind Extension University, a 24-hour educational channel, also has a wide variety of educational programming; plans are underway to provide schools with special materials and services.

In addition, a number of universities such as Oklahoma and Kentucky and private sector companies such as the TI-IN network contract for courses to be delivered directly to schools.

Computer Networks

One of the chief advantages of distance education is that it provides a real proving ground for converging technologies. Television, which has been greatly exploited in this area, quickly comes to mind, but computer networks play an ever-increasing and important role in distance education. Often used for electronic mail and other types of communications between instructors and class members, computers may prove to be not only a means to educational programs, but rather a primary medium of delivery for some areas of study. While there are distance education opportunities such as MIX (McGraw-Hill Information Exchange), Nova University, and the Electronic University—all of which use computer networks——few are designed for K-12 education and few are offered in a course-related format. The National Geographic Society sponsors projects that involve schoolchildren performing real scientific experiments; Computer Pals provides a worldwide communications network for youngsters communicating with pen pals. A number of states, including New York, Georgia, Connecticut, Virginia, Pennsylvania, and West Virginia, are beginning to use computers in the curriculum for purposes beyond simple communications and information transfer.

Another important development that should be considered in relation to distance education is the availability of computer networks that provide access to library resources and other online information. Many states have multitype-library, computer-based networks in which school library media programs participate or to which they have access. Commercial information services such as DIALOG, BRS, and EINSTEIN are available to any school willing to make an investment in hardware which is simple and relatively inexpensive.

Most of the reform literature encourages educators to go beyond the textbook—and even beyond the classroom—to use a variety of resources to help children learn. All of us are constantly being told that problem-solving and higher-order thinking skills require information and resources for students to use. But here again, librarians are not directly named whenever suggestions and plans are made to help teachers to achieve these vital skills. For this and other equally valid reasons, the addition of new courses to the curriculum using television may be valuable; however, students and teachers will still need access to library and information resources. For the most advanced students, access to external information which permits a more detailed study of a research topic is even more critical.

Specialists' Current Role

Unfortunately, although all the leaders of the Star Schools program agreed that the library media specialist and the media program could play a very positive role in the program, the program has no specific guidelines for their involvement. Several persons told of library media specialists being involved in Star Schools, but none knew of any systematic effort to determine the overall participation of school library specialists in the project. Unless the specialists were facilitators (the local mentor or teacher for the class) or coordinators (the contact person for the school), their role was not recorded in the official monitoring and evaluation of the program's first year of operation.

For example, Sherry Deaton, media specialist at Wathena (KS) High School, had already latched onto the telecommunications wave before her school became a part of the Midlands Consortium partnership in the Star Schools program. Deaton's leadership, along with her principal's support, has brought not only Star Schools classes to her community (which she describes as "beautiful, but isolated"), but she also works with her teachers to use C-SPAN I and the Discovery Channel along with teleconferences produced by the nearby university. Despite some restrictions due to limited space, Deaton says that both students and teachers have enjoyed the experience and have learned from it. She has gotten a fax machine and is planning to implement a computer communications system. She urges other media specialists to take the lead "so that they can extract the best use of the distance education offerings."

In the small town of Tabor City in eastern North Carolina, Steve French, media coordinator at the local high school, has assumed a leadership role as both a facilitator and coordinator of the TI-IN Network's Latin course. Working with the Star Schools teacher, Cindy Pope, French negotiated a class project for nine students that culminated in the production of a videotape instead of the more traditional term paper. Complete with commercials of the period, the video (titled "Geraldo in Roma") is a great example of the creativity and communications skills that a media specialist can promote via TV instruction. French, who describes the experience as both exciting and rewarding, recognizes that the day-to-day operation of the media center requires some of the skills of the "librarian of yesteryear," combined with an obligation to help bring modern technology and innovative teaching methods into the school.

Star Schools and distance education are often associated with small, rural communities and rightly so, for it has been rural educators who have seen, firsthand, the consequences of isolation, and have been willing to break away from traditional classroom instruction. Detroit, Michigan is hardly rural, but that is where Paul Weaver, media specialist at Mumford High School, is assisting both students and faculty who participate in the Satellite Educational Resources Consortium. Weaver serves as the contact person, helping teachers incorporate technological resources in the classroom. He believes that the media specialist is the key contact person to bring all of the available technology to bear on educational problems.

In Hampton, Virginia, the schools are participating in the TERC partnership of Star Schools. Since the project is just getting underway this fall, there is little to report. The two media specialists involved—Elizabeth Green, director of Library Media and Records, and Ed Duckworth, the ITV Coordinator—have, working together at the district level, helped coordinate an effort that has brought CD-ROM, online searching, and a full range of television access to the Hampton schools. Both Green and Duckworth said that the project could not be successful without the strong commitment and enthusiasm of the building-level media specialists who help teachers integrate technology into their classes and assist students in their daily activities.

Specialists' Future Roles

Local needs and the degree to which the library media specialist is committed to the program will determine her or his role in a distance education program. The least desirable is that of facilitator of classroom activities. Because library media specialists don't have the reponsibility for specific classes, they are often recruited to serve in this capacity. Unless it is specifically mandated by the administration, a specialist should not accept such a role without a great deal of thought.

Some of the possible—and obvious—roles are:

- A *partnership role* with the teachers who are using distance education programs to provide the same support and integration that the school library media program offers more traditional delivery systems.
- A *contact and logistics* role to interface between the originating or coordinating agency and the school to distribute information and materials related to the distance education programming.
- A *technical support role* which grows logically out of the existing technological expertise expected of the library media specialist.
- An *information access role* that provides the school with the opportunity to use materials and information beyond the immediate collection through electronic access and other cooperatives developed by the library media specialist.
- A *leadership role* in which the library media specialist, by virtue of her or his expertise, can help others in the school make better use of existing, converging, and emerging technologies.

Professional Development

School library media specialists and librarians are essential components to the success of distance education and must not be left out of the movement. Many librarians, as readers may well be aware, find themselves place bound when it comes to continuing their professional growth. A limited number of graduate programs in library science, media, communication, and information technology make access to formal education difficult for some and totally impossible for others. Efforts are under way to help ease this situation for those who have access to cable and satellite systems.

During a preconference at the last Annual Conference of the American Library Association, 19 of the 60 ALA-accredited graduate schools with library and information science education programs met to begin organizing a consortial effort to provide distance education courses in this field. The consortium will be devoted to the development and delivery of pre-service and continuing education courses using cable, computer, and other communications technologies. Following an organizational meeting with the Association for Library and Information Science Education (ALISE), the consortium will begin enrolling charter members and initiate formal operations during the 1990 Annual Conference in Chicago.

In the meantime, the College of Library and Information Science at the University of South Carolina will offer a graduate-level course in school library media program management during the spring 1990 semester. In the summer of 1990, the college will offer two courses intended for recertification credits; these courses will be developed for school library media specialists as well as librarians serving children and young adults in public libraries. One of the courses will be devoted to the design, development, and implementation of literacy programs in libraries and library media centers. Graduate credit and continuing education units will be avilable for a limited number of participants, but the courses can be leased by other institutions of higher education and state agencies. These are available through the Mind Extension University and can be accessed by Jones Intercable subscribers as well as anyone with a satellite dish. For more information, contact Don Sutton, Director of Educational Services, The Mind Extension University, 9697 E. Mineral Avenue, Englewood, CO 80112 or call (800) 777-MIND.

Diminishing Barriers

Americans are justifiably proud of their efforts to ensure equal access to education for everyone. As we have progressed to better means of providing information, we have confronted many barriers to access such as race, gender, age, and physical disabilities. While we may not have completely overcome these barriers, they are diminishing. Today, distance education is being made possible through the availability of reasonably priced and more effective technology; both producers and distributors have worked together to bring attention to the concept of distance education as an educational innovation. Their efforts in publicizing the positive results of distance education have led to the allocation, by legislatures, of public funds for demonstration projects throughout the nation.

With the ever-increasing demands being placed on educators, we must use every resource at our disposal. School library media specialists and librarians can play a very important role in using and helping to shape distance education; they can serve as partners to others who are involved in it. Distance education also offers a new challenge to the leadership of our profession and allows everyone an opportunity to demonstrate how critical their involvement in formal and informal education is to every learner—no matter what barriers are imposed.

Bibliography

For a history or a more complete overview of distance education, see the following:

Darrow, Ben H. *Radio: The Assistant Teacher*. R.G. Adams and Co.,1932.

Diamond, Robert M. *A Guide to Instructional Television*. McGraw-Hill, 1964.

Jones, Maxine. *See, Hear, Interact: Beginning Developments in Two-Way Television*. Scarecrow Press, 1985.

Kurtz, E.B. *Pioneeering in Educational Television*:1932-1939, University of Iowa, 1959.

Mackenzie, Ossian and Edward L. Christensen, eds. *The Changing World of Correspondence Study*. The Pennsylvania State University Press, 1971.

Pinsel, Jerry. *A Summary of Telecommunications Efforts Involving Education Service Agencies and Others*. Report from the American Association of Educational Service Agencies, April 1988. For more information contact Walter Turner, AAESA, 1801 North Moore St., Arlington, VA 22209.

Office of Technology Assessment. *Links to Learning: A New Course for Education*. Report available later this year. Contact Linda Roberts, Project Director, OTA, U.S. Congress, Washington, DC 20510.

ERIC Documents

Barker, Bruce. *Interactive Satellites Instruction: How Can Rural Schools Benefit* (1986). [ED 274 499.]

Barker, Bruce. *An Evaluation of Interactive Satellite-Television as a Delivery System for High School Instruction* (1987). [ED 277 534.]

Barker, Bruce. *Using Interactive Technologies to Increase Course Offerings in Small and Rural Schools*. (1987). [ED 279 465.]

Bond, Sally. *Telecommunications-Based Distance Learning: A Guide for Educators* (1987). Southeastern Educational Improvement Lab, Research Triangle, NC [ED 287 474.]

Wall, Milan. *Information Technologies: Alternative Delivery for Rural Schools* (1985). Wall and Associates, Lincoln, NE. [ED 270 253.]

Star Schools Partnerships

Midlands Consortium, Malcom Phelps, 470 Student Union Building, Oklahoma State University, Stillwater, OK 74078. Sites are in Alabama, Kansas, Mississippi, Missouri and Oklahoma.

Satellite Educational Resources Consortium, Lee Monk, Southern Educational Communications Association (SECA), POB 50,008, Columbia, SC 29250. Sites in Alabama, Arkansas, Florida, Georgia, Kentucky, Louisiana, Mississippi, Nebraska, New Jersey, North Dakota, Pennsylvania, South Carolina, Texas, Wisconsin, and selected schools in Cleveland, Ohio and Detroit, Michigan.

Technical Education Research Centers, Peggy Kapisovsky, 1696 Massachusetts Ave., Cambridge, MA 02138. Sites in Massachusetts, Michigan, Minnesota, New York, Virginia, and "adjacent states."

TI-IN, Pamela Pease, 1000 Central Parkway North, Suite 190, San Antonio, TX 78232. Sites in Alabama, Arizona, California, Colorado, Illinois, Montana, Mississippi, Minnesota, Nebraska, North Carolina, North Dakota, Nevada, Oregon, South Dakota, Texas and Washington.

Commercial Programs & Services

The Public Broadcasting System

Children's Television Workshop, One Lincoln Plaza, New York, NY 10023. Offers teacher guides and other useful materials for use with Sesame Street, Electric Company, and Square One TV, a new math series.

Office of Education, Corporation for Public Broadcasting, 1111 Sixteenth St. NW, Washington, DC 20036. (202) 955-5100.

PBS Elementary/Secondary Service, 1320 Braddock Place, Alexandria, VA 22314-1698. Ask for information about "Learning File" and *PBS Video News*. The most important contact is the local PBS affiliate station. (800) 424-7963.

PIO/PBS American Library Association, 50 E. Huron Street, Chicago, IL 60611. Ask to be put on the mailing list for *PBS/Library Pipeline*.

Cable & Satellite Resources

C-SPAN (C-SPAN in the Classroom): C-SPAN, POB 75298, Washington, DC 20013. (800) 523-7586.

CNN (Newsroom): Contact Ann Skinner, c/o Media Management Services, Inc., 10 North Main Street, Suite 301, Yardley, PA 19067-9986. (800) 344-6219.

The Discovery Channel (Assignment Discovery): The Discovery Channel, Box AD, 8201 Corporate Drive, Landover, MD 20785. Ask about the "Assignment Discovery Educator's Kit." (800) 321-ITDC.

The Educational Network (Channel One, The Classroom Channel, and The Educators' Channel): Whittle Communications, 505 Market St., Knoxville, TN 37902. (615) 595-5100.

Lamb, Brian. *C-SPAN: America's Town Hall*. Acropolis Books, 1988. An excellent resource that describes the development and impact of C-SPAN's access to political and other social affairs.

The Learning Channel (The Electronic Library): Molly Breeden, Assistant Director of Educational Services, The Learning Channel, 1525 Wilson Blvd., Suite 550, Rosslyn, VA 22209. (800) 346-0032.

The Mind Extension University: Don Sutton, Executive Director, The Mind Extension University, 9697 E. Mineral Avenue, Englewood, CO 80112. (800) 777-MIND.

Computer-Related Resources

BRS Search Service, Maxwell Communications, Ltd., 1200 Rt. 7, Latham, NY 12110. (800) 468-0908.

Computer Pals, 4974 SW Galen, Lake Oswego, OR 97035.

Connected Education Inc., 92 Van Cortland Park South, No. 6F, Bronx, NY 10463. (212) 548-0435.

Dialog Information Services, Inc., 3460 Hillview Ave., Palo Alto, CA 94304. (800) 334-2564.

Einstein, Telebase, 763 Lancaster Ave., Bryn Mawr, PA 19010. (215) 526-2800.

Electronic University Network, 1150 Sansome St., San Francisco, CA 94111. (415) 956-7177.

MIX (McGraw-Hill Information Exchange): Steve Laliberte, EMS/McGraw-Hill, 9855 West 78th Street, Eden Prairie, MN 55344. (800) 622-6310.

National Geographic Kids Network, 17th and M Sts., Washington, DC 20036.

Additional Resources

ALA Video, 50 E. Huron St., Chicago, IL 60611. Distributors of the AASL/AECT-produced *Information Power* and *The School Administrator's Guide to Information Power* teleconferences. Also available in cassette format is *Library Video Magazine*, which is useful in continuing education activities.

Arts and Sciences Teleconference Service (ASTS), Oklahoma State Univ., 206 Life Science East, Stillwater, OK 74078. Ask about their satellite network, and ask to be put on their *Learning by Satellite Newslink* mailing list. (405) 624-5647.

KIDSNET, 6856 Eastern Ave. NW, Suite 208, Washington, DC 20012. (202) 291-1400.

National Center for Small Schools, Box 4110 Texas Tech University, Lubbock, TX 79409. Send requests to Dr, Bruce Barker. (806) 742-2337.

National University Teleconference Network (NUTN), 332 Student Union, Oklahoma State University, Stillwater, OK 74078. A service for developing and promoting teleconferences, this group provides useful information for faculty development as well as teleconferences of interest to some students. (405) 624-5191.

New Technology Consultants. *Satellite Programming Directory*. Available for $65 from NTC, P.O. Box 27044, Minneapolis, MN 55427.

Ostendorf, Virginia. *What Every Principal, Teacher and School Board Member Should Know About Distance Education* (1989). Virginia A. Ostendorf, Inc. This important resource should be purchased by any school that is considering implementing or expanding distance education.

Satellite Orbit. A monthly publication that contains informative articles and listings of all of the available programming using satellite dishes. Contact CommTek Publishing, 8330 Boone Blvd., Suite 600, Vienna, VA 22180. (800) 792-5541.

Editor's Note: Names, addresses, and telephone numbers may have changed since the original publication of this article, but they still provide a starting point for your research.

Learning at Home
Public Library Service to Homeschoolers

by Susan B. Madden

"**W**ould you be willing to arrange a story hour for 30 children aged seven to ten at 11 a.m.?"

"Can you help us find plans for a Biblical diorama?

"We need a copy of McGuffey's Reader, the latest Mary Pride book, and 36 more picture books for the family read-alouds plus that book you showed at the conference about 101 educational things to do with kids in the Puget Sound area."

If these requests spark a chord of recognition, you have obviously spent some time working with homeschooling and know what a delight and, sometimes, what a challenge it can be. I will try to offer here some definitions, statistics, and suggestions for public librarians working with homeschoolers. It is based on personal experience, but bolstered heavily by the superb work of King County Library System staff and Washington Homeschool Organization (WHO) members.

What is Homeschooling?

Homeschooling, the educating of one's offspring at home rather than the traditional public or private school, is a phenomenon of growing numbers and impact on the nation's public libraries. Both Toffler and Naisbitt in their respective books, *Future Shock* and *Megatrends*, anticipated significant increases in the numbers of home instructors. National statistics bear this out, from an estimated 10,000 in 1983 to a substantial 260,000 in 1986. In Washington State, partially due to "friendly" legislation, we have seen the home-educated student population increase from an estimated 500 in 1982 to 27,000 in 1987 and 15,000 in 1990.

It should be noted that statistics in this arena are always couched in cautious phraseology: "estimated," "approximately," and "about" are frequent modifiers. The reason for this is twofold. Children under eight are not included in school counts, yet an estimated 65 percent of homeschoolers fall in this category. Further, many parents who choose the homeschooling route are not eager to be involved in governmental surveys and enrollments. Many have been fined or found in violation of stringent laws at the local level dependent on their responses.

Research has shown that home instruction is more prevalent in the West and the South. It has given us a generic Homeschooler profile: middle class; white; at least one parent with a college degree; both boys and girls taught at home; the majority of the teaching done by the mother. The average homeschooled child begins around the age of six-and-a-half to eight and will continue in the program for two to three years.

On a much more local level, a recent survey in Whatcom County, Washington showed 93 percent of homeschoolers use the public library as an area source and 54 percent do so on a weekly basis (11 percent visit more than once a week!).

Why Do People Teach at Home?

The reasons why people choose home schooling are cited often in the literature, with the following being the most frequently given:

Religion/philosophy;
Avoid peer-pressure;
Greater parent-child contact;
Develops better self-concept;
Avoid peer competition;
Accomplish more academically;
Personalizes learning.

My personal experiences and observations are somewhat different:

Religious values;
Poor local schools (economically and educationally);
Busing (number of hours wasted and safety factors cited rather than racial biases);
"Different" kids (gifted, learning and/or physically disabled);
Environmental and historical concerns; (the historical model was home education until the Industrial Revolution. By 1918, compulsory school laws were passed in every state);
Learning styles and circadian rhythms can be fully utilized (total immersion in a subject is also possible):
Family togetherness (especially with siblings).

Most homeschoolers fall into two political/philosophical camps: those who follow John Holt's principles and precepts—the pedagogical; and those who agree with Ray Moore that public schools are filled with "secular humanist" curriculum—the ideological. No matter what motivates the homeschoolers, they are active library users and as such have precipitated some concerns on the part of various library workers.

Service to Homeschoolers

The following areas are concerns I have encountered over the past ten years.

- *Library Concern: Censorship.* Evolution, the occult, and age ratings or limits are often cited as problems.

Suggested Solution: Develop a working relationship with local homeschool groups. Give presentations on a broad variety of subjects (read-alouds, storytelling, etc.) but always include components on library policies, balanced collections, and readers' advisory services. Remember these parents do care, and they will accompany their children, so the burden of choice is where it should be (and so rarely is). Booktalks on perceived controversial titles can be very positive also, especially when you point out the educational/philosophical points that can be addressed by the subject matter or author's approach.

- *Library Concern: Subject Wipeout.* Just like all other class assignments, but here one family has taken everything available on a topic.

Suggested Solution: Maintain group/individual dialogue. Explain the problem and attempt to provide alternate subjects in corollary areas or formats. Use assignment alerts in the same manner as in traditional assignment situations.

- *Library Concern: Negative Staff Attitudes.* Child abuse, socialization problems, quality control, etc.

Suggested Solution: Sensitivity training sessions are useful, especially led in tandem with local homeschool folk. Proof of care, well-adjusted and comfortable kids make superb examples as do citations of the Colfax brothers at Harvard, overall high achievement test scores, and self-concept research studies.

- *Library Concern: Time/Energy Demands.* "They want too much."

Suggested Solution: Frequent use is a political plus but daily requests can drain. Utilize homeschool volunteers to alleviate time/energy demands in other areas (displays, bulletin boards, story hours, homework help, tutoring, etc.) Replicate programs or merge offerings with other educational groups when possible.

- *Library Concern: Technology Demands.* Regular requests for software, home modems, etc.

Suggested Solution: Tap into Homeschooler expertise and utilize it for the library. Develop a shared resource group with local schools and Friends groups. Get reviewing and donation activity from homeschoolers.

- *Library Concern: Administrative Limits.* "Too special a group, we can't cater to their exclusive needs."

Suggested Solution: Parents, children, and educational needs are usually part of the mission statement of most public libraries. Homeschoolers' needs are not exclusive but very common. These are factors that make this group easier to work with for service providers (always a key concern for administrators). They mainly use the library at off-peak hours. There is one student/assignment instead of 49. Parental supervision is constant: subject use is individual rather than state-wide.

But most importantly, whatever you provide for homeschoolers should equally be provided for all educators. If you remove the descriptor "Homeschooler" and insert "educator," it should effectively remove the exclusivity problem.

Library-Tested Ideas

So, what can the library do to make the homeschoolers welcome (if not catered to) at the library? The following list of ideas are all library tested, fairly easy, cost-free, and usable with all your clientele, not just homeschoolers.

Develop a Homeschool Vertical File Packet that includes local laws pertaining to homeschoolers (available from your State Superintendent of Instruction as well as from your local homeschool group—they may differ); a resource list of homeschooling groups; basic bibliographies and articles culled from the popular press; school district addresses, phone numbers, and names.

Offer library tours to individual families or groups. If such staffing is possible, have the reference librarian take the adults and the children's librarian take the kids, then converge for a mutual question and answer period.

Give Reference Workshops. Plan for an hour-plus hands-on session with basics; compare encyclopedias and dictionaries, demonstrate CD-ROM tools or different databases. Even time spent on catalog entries will be highly informative. It is a heady experience to have 25 or 30 adults avidly taking notes and asking questions about reference entries.

Create an educators' brochure that details services and procedures.

Ask for curriculum guides from your local school districts. These describe the various subjects and learning objectives of required courses and often offer supplemental materials and resources as well.

Offer traditional programs (story hours, films, crafts,, etc.) at nontraditional times. The 11:00 a.m. hour has proved to be the most popular, as have intergenerational programs at 7:00 p.m.

Provide displays of educational projects—art works, science fairs, student writings, etc.

Volunteer library and staff as proctor site for state and local educational tests.

Develop year-round reading/viewing clubs and broaden them to include adults as well as youth.

Advertise library book sales. Most educators, whether home or institutional, operate on tight budgets and very much appreciate book bargains.

Create an Educators' Bulletin Board, with meeting calendars, educational events in the community (don't forget library programs!), youth contests, new book/media reviews, student success stories (especially academic rather than sports).

Maintain involvement with local and regional homeschooling groups. Subscribe to a local or regional homeschool newsletter and try to provide a column or regular notes about materials, services, and programs at the library. Attend meetings bearing library card applications. Check first to see if that is okay and that the group is comfortable with your presence. Arrange for a library booth at a state homeschool convention. You might share with other libraries in the area. Try to get on the program as a presenter (Basic Home Reference Tools, Titles to Titillate Reluctant Teen Readers, Good Read-Alouds for Car Trips, etc.).

Provide materials that meet the needs of many other patrons: teaching methodologies, alternatives and mainstream; learning styles; home organization; literature and media guides; science projects. Then there are crafts, foreign languages, art, music instruction, cookery, sewing, woodworking, computers, intergenerational activity guides—in fact, just about every subject in your collection is grist for the homeschooling mill. All librarians and homeschoolers share this desire: Give us more books!

Put on an Educational Alternative program. Have a panel of private, public, and homeschooling educators discuss the pros and cons of their approaches. Provide display tables for exhibits and descriptive brochures. Anticipate high attendance and request heavy media coverage.

These ideas are just a sampling of what is possible. Sit down and brainstorm with your staff and local community folk. Not only will you develop superb programs and services for the homeschoolers; you will have raised your visibility in a positive way, discovered easily replicable ideas for other community groups (the disabled, business leaders, seniors, new immigrants, etc.) and, I hope, had lots of fun and experienced personal growth in the process. Enjoy!

Bibliography

Kohn, Alfie. "Home Schooling," *The Atlantic Monthly*, April, 1988, p. 23–25.

Avner, Jane. "Home Schoolers and the Public Library," *School Library Journal*, July 1989, p. 29–33.

Fisher, S. "ABC's of Serving Home Schoolers," *Christian Retailing*, May 15, 1989, p. 25–26.

Gemmer, Theresa. "Homeschoolers and the Public Library," *Aliki*, December, 1987, p. 96–98.

——— "The Library Response to Homeschooling," *Aliki*, March, 1991, p. 20–23.

Naisbitt, John. *Megatrends*. Warner. 1982.

Toffler, Alvin. *Future Shock*. Random, 1970.

Feinstein, Selwyn. "Domestic Lessons: Shunning the Schools," *Wall Street Journal*, p. 1, col. 1. October 6, 1986.

Send Your Books on Vacation

by Virginia Miehe, School Librarian, West Liberty Junior-Senior High School, Iowa

What do the school library media center's books do over the summer months: do they rest in the quiet of an empty building? Or do they, too, go on vacation? For the past three years at West Liberty (Iowa) Junior-Senior High School, the most popular young adult (YA) books have gone on summer vacation with the students.

The books have two travel options: they can either go home with a student for the summer, or they can circulate from the public library. Our school library media center sends its most popular books to the town's public library to be circulated over the summer. The public library does not have much of a demand for YA literature during the school year since most students use the school's collection. In the summer, when the school isn't circulating the books, it is logical to share with the public library's patrons. YA circulation over the summer months has grown every year (an increase of 1000 percent over three summers), and a book has never been lost or damaged through this program.

For the past two years, the library media center has checked out books to students over the summer. They can take as many as they want during the last week of school and return them in September. Most borrow three to eight books. The books are checked out in the usual manner and students are asked to read and sign a paper indicating that they will be held responsible for the materials. The first summer this was tried, only a small number of avid readers took advantage of the offer. Summer checkout had never been allowed before; one parent even contacted the library media specialist to make sure the books her daughter brought home were legitimately borrowed.

The following summer, circulation more than tripled, perhaps due to better promotion and word-of-mouth advertising. The library media specialist, student library aides, and teachers all helped spread the word. Faculty members took both recreational and professional materials for summer reading. The number of books checked out over vacation was comparable to a month's circulation during the school year. Loss has proved minimal (.5 percent), less than during the school year.

Publicizing the summer reading program, both over-the-summer checkout and public library circulation, was done through school announcements, faculty newsletter, and an article in the school newspaper. The public library announced the arrival of the YA books in its weekly column in the town newspaper. All of the junior and senior high English teachers invited the library media specialist to speak briefly to their classes about summer reading. A bookmark was distributed advertising both lending options and it included the library's hours. Students were encouraged to "take home an armload."

Unlike most travel plans, these two options involve almost no expense for the library media center or the students. Summer reading programs contribute to lifetime reading habits by showing young people that reading is a good way to spend leisure time. Too often summer reading promotions are aimed only at children of elementary school age. Young adults need to establish and continue good reading habits. A book lying on the porch swing or beside the bed is an accessible reminder that reading is a relaxing way to enjoy long summer days.

West Liberty is a consolidated rural Iowa school district encompassing three small towns and a large rural area. One can buy paperback books, magazines and newspapers at several places but there are no bookstores. One of the towns in the district has a public library which is open only 14 hours a week in the summer. All students are eligible to use the public library in the county seat, but there is no public transportation to get them there.

The library media center's collection is appropriate for adolescents; diverse in scope and free of charge. The books teens find in supermarkets, convenience stores, or mail chain bookstores may lack quality and diversity, even if teens have money and are willing to spend it on reading material. All of us are more willing to take a chance on a book, to try something different from what we usually read, if it's free.

Library media specialists should consider various ways to circulate the books during summer vacation. Another option might be to keep the media center open in the summer. If students are in the school during the summer months for other activities and classes, they could stop for new reading material as well.

Students eagerly look forward to summer vacation and extra time for relaxation and recreation. Books can be good companions while enjoying the sun at the beach, on long family trips in the backseat of the car, when staying up late at night, or while babysitting with young children, They can betaken in picnic baskets, tackle boxes, or bicycle bags.

Books should be at least as accessible as the family television. Melted ice cream on a few pages, a ruined book that fell over the side of a boat, or a novel left behind at the Holiday Inn in Tacoma would be preferable to the dust-covered books we usually find on the shelves when we return to school in the fall. Let's promote the idea that books are as much a part of a vacation as tennis balls, the beach, and sleeping late.

"An Unusual Contribution"

The Work of 1993 Grolier Award Winner Mike Printz

by Roger Sutton

Mike Printz, librarian at Topeka (KS) West High School and visiting instructor at Emporia State University is the winner of the 1993 Grolier Foundation Award. The award is given by the American Library Association "to a librarian who has made an unusual contribution to the stimulation and guidance of reading by children and young people." Here, Printz discusses his long career as a school librarian, some of the programs he has implemented, and his successful strategies for getting young adults hooked on reading.

You began your career as a high school English teacher, and then moved over to the library. What made you stay with it for almost 35 years?

PRINTZ: Well, probably a couple of things. One, I like the diversity of being a school librarian, so different from teaching five or six hours of English in a day. As a librarian, I have different things to do, different people to work with, and different challenges each hour of the day. Second, I've always loved to read and wanted a chance to be able to share that, to encourage young people to read and develop a love for books.

What kinds of books were you getting kids to read in your early days as a librarian?

PRINTZ: I especially remember the challenge of getting boys to read, which wasn't an easy task in those days. Henry Gregor Felsen wrote *Street Rod* (Random, 1953, OP) and *Hot Rod* (Dutton, 1949, OP), books that had some interest for boys. Then came that wonderful *Two and the Town* (Scribner, 1952, OP), which was, I think, one of the first stories that ever dealt with a high school couple who had to get married. Felsen maybe paved the way for young adult literature with that. Then for girls there were—I'm not trying to be sexist at all, but there were a lot of writers. There was Betty Cavanna, Rosamond du Jardin, Beverly Cleary, and *Seventeenth Summer* (Dodd, 1942) by Maureen Daly. Of course, I had them reading lots of adult books as well.

I remember when I was on the Best Books for Young Adults Committee (BBYA) with you, one of your big crusades was to get a lot of adult books on that list.

PRINTZ: It still is. I think we sometimes forget the mature, sensitive young adult who can handle adult books and has adult interests. I think it's important that we find the very best

of those books and writers—like Joanne Greenberg, for example, who writes books that really have an interest for mature young adults.

What do you do to get kids to read?

PRINTZ: I think the greatest thing for getting kids and books together is the booktalk. You can publish booklists, you can do displays, you can do all kinds of motivational things to get people to read. But there's nothing as great or as powerful as going into a classroom with a cartful of books and talking for 20 minutes about 30 or 40 books, then standing out of the way when students come up to get them. Of all the things I've ever done, that would have to be the greatest rush in the world. To be able to talk about books and turn somebody on; to have them come up and almost pull the book out of your hand or knock you over to pick up the book because they want to read.

What's your technique? Do you have any secrets?

PRINTZ: Well, I don't know if there are any secrets, but I try to find some element, some area of a book that picks up on an emotion or an event in somebody's life. Something that touches a responsive chord in a student and makes him or her want to read and share that kind of experience.

Do you let them check out the books right there when you talk?

PRINTZ: They check them out right there. You have to be able to let the books go *immediately*—that's the secret of a booktalk. I guess I'm not much of a purist, but if the books have just come in and you haven't had time to catalog them and put your little stamp and your tag on the back, you need to be able to let the kids take them anyway. I even get them to sign the inside of the book jacket. That way they can take the books immediately. They love the fact that the books are new and nobody's read them before.

You really caused a revolution at Best Books meetings when you started bringing in, very systematically, comments from kids. Until then it had been kind of hit or miss, where someone would say, "Oh, one of my kids read it, they liked it, they didn't like it." But you really started collecting what these kids had to say about these books. How did you do that?

PRINTZ: Well, I think that's very important. Some friends that I teach with are lovers of books, they let me come into their classrooms with books that have been nominated for BBYA, and I do some booktalks. I say, "You know, we really need your input. I'd like you to read some of these books and then I want you to write some comments for me. And when I share them at the Best Books meeting I'll say your name. I'll say this is what Mary thinks or this is what Joe thinks about this book." You have to make kids feel important. That's one way to do it. Another way is through an independent study program. I enroll six or seven kids a semester who do nothing but read for an hour a day. They come into the library at the beginning of the semester and I give them some guidelines. Then they read the books that are nominated and write for me all semester about what they think of them.

What do you think of their comments?

PRINTZ: I respect them very highly. Kids need to feel that you respect them as equals when it comes to their comments about books that have been written about them or for them. They need to know that what they say, what they write about a book, is important and that I trust their opinions as much as I do of my professional peers.

How do you establish relationships with teachers?

PRINTZ: The number one thing you need to say to teachers is, "Get rid of those awful textbooks." Textbooks are geared to the average student, and I'm not sure who the average student is. We need to throw that textbook out the window or only use it to start with. Let it be the guide to getting kids involved in all sorts of reading and sharing and research. For example, I'm doing this project right now with a mathematics teacher. He came to the library one day and said, "I get so tired of teaching math the same way all the time, but everybody says I have to do this to get through the textbook by the end of the year. I want to branch out. I wish there were a collection of science-fiction math stories I could give to my students. Then they could come up with some research topics from the stories." Not being a strong science fiction person, I called Sally Estes at *Booklist*, and she said, "Of course there's *Mathenauts* (Arbor House, 1987)." We bought a class set of the book, and it's been amazing to see what the kids reading those short stories have come up with. They are doing all kinds of research. They get on Dialog and get into some really scholarly professional journals. They get articles and books. With interlibrary loan the way it is today, we can get almost anything they need. To see that excitement happen in a mathematics class has been a real joy for me. You don't usually think there's much that the math department and the library can do together.

When you started your career, we were dealing with books and magazines, and now you have information in all kinds of formats. How did you introduce all that at Topeka West?

PRINTZ: Probably kicking and screaming, to begin with. One of the people who's had the greatest influence on my life as a librarian is Marilyn L. Miller. One of the first courses I took in library school at Emporia State was with her. And, I remember so well when she told us that we could not even compre-hend what was going to happen to information in our lifetime. No matter what it takes, you have to be on top of all the different formats of information. You need to help the kids find the information they need and you also need to teach them how to select the very best information. To wade through the materials that may not be good and develop some criteria for selecting the very best. For example, there's one database in Dialog called Papers, which has full-text retrieval of 30 or 35 daily newspapers from the mid-1980s through today. Students can enter a topic and get a bibliography of articles, and they can have those articles printed out for them within minutes. Then, they have to be able to sort through all that.

I have to give credit to another person, Linda Waddle, who has long been an advocate of Dialog and online searching for high school students. I went up to visit her library in Iowa in 1985, about two days after the *Titanic* was rediscovered (incidentally by a Kansan). I had a kid come into the library who wanted to read something about that, and I found two newspaper clippings from local papers. So Linda said, "I want to show you how to use Dialog." She got me into that newspaper database, I entered "Titanic" and the name of the Kansan who had led the expedition, and I had something like 34 articles in five minutes.

I knew that somehow I had to convince the people back home that we needed this. I said to our principal, "We have to have this. We have to have this tomorrow." And bless his heart, he said "Well, I've got a little money stored away here that I made from pop sales and a couple of other things. We'll try it for a year." And it started. You have to work with administrators that way. You have to convince them that this is something the kids need. At the end of the year he said, " We can't go backward. We have to continue this."

You said that the discovery of the Titanic *was " incidentally" by a Kansan, but I know that's not incidental to you at all. Some years ago, you wrote an article for* SLJ *about your Kansas oral history project ("In the YA corner, " April 1984, pp. 33-34). Could we talk about that?*

PRINTZ: I sometimes think the way we teach history to students is all wrong. We start with world history at the sophomore level, and then junior year they all take a course in American history, and if time allows we have local history. I think we need to work that around the other way and start with our own roots.

The oral history, project began in 1975 as we were getting ready to celebrate the bicentennial of this country. Our school district had some money ready to give to a school to celebrate the occasion with innovative programs, so we developed a program whereby seniors could enroll in a course in oral history. They would select a famous Kansan or an event in Kansas history and go out and interview anybody they could find who knew anything about that topic. Then they pulled all that together into a 30-minute documentary. We started with audiotape recorders and then went to videotape. Over the 16 or 17 years that we've had that project, we've probably covered about 200 topics with 300 or 400 kids traveling all over the United States to do their interviews. More kids researched

Kansans—famous Kansans—than they did events in Kansas history, and I think that's very important. Kids who grow up in the Midwest think that to make it big they've got to be on either coast. I contend that if you're willing to dream big enough and work hard enough, you can do anything you want to right here in Topeka, Kansas.

When the projects were finished, we gave them to the Kansas Historical Society, and they've been there for scholars to use. I think it's great for kids to realize that something they did in 1983 or '84 might be used 50 or 60 years from now. I think it gives them a sense of their place in history.

What kind of a staff do you have at Topeka West?

PRINTZ: I have a wonderful staff: I'm very fortunate. I have two people who have been with me for years—Kay Ping and Darlene Luellen. They are library clerks, and they have a real understanding of kids. Kay has worked with me for many years on the oral history program, working with the students on the editing and that sort of thing. And Darlene has an uncanny knack for finding kids who hurt in some way and reaching out to them with a lot of love and care.

I also have an outstanding co-librarian, Diane Goheen. She and I really work well together. I'm kind of an idea person and not really good with details. She is good with details and is also an idea person. She remembers kids' names, something I'm not really good at, and once the kids have worked with Diane they come back to her again and again. The first year she was there, Hazel Rochman's book *Somehow Tenderness Survives: Stories from Southern Africa* (Harper, 1988) came out. I read it and said, "Diane, you've got to read this book." She came back after she read it and said, "We've got to do something with this book in the school." So we went down to the principal and said, "Dr. Frazer, we know that every year in this school there's an ethnic week and we don't do a lot with it, but we'd like to volunteer to take over that week."

We had the whole school read the book, any class we could. I'm talking not just language arts and social studies classes, which read it eagerly, but we had speech and home ec. classes read it, and forensics classes did dramatic readings. We did a school-wide program on apartheid and were able to bring in some speakers Hazel recommended. I think if nothing else happened, we at least created an awareness of what apartheid was. Our student congress passed a bill that Coke machines would be taken out of Topeka West High School because of the Coca-Cola Company's presence in South Africa.

Another thing that happened was that the oral history kids who travelled all over the United States made a resolution they would never again stay at Holiday Inns, because Holiday Inn supported the South African government. One young black girl in our school who was very moved by Hazel's book got a job that summer with the state Department of Education as a clerical aide to earn some money to go to college. The state education departments of Kansas, Missouri, and Iowa, I believe, were planning a meeting in St. Louis and her responsibility was to make hotel reservations at a Holiday Inn there. On her second day on the job, she, to quote Shakespeare, "screwed her courage to the stickingplace," went to her supervisor and said, "I cannot morally make these hotel reservations." She told him why and they changed the place of the meeting. Well, I know that didn't hurt Holiday Inn and didn't hurt Coke, but the kids were taking some stands that I hadn't seen since the '70s when they were involved with the environment, Vietnam, things like that. They were taking some real stands on issues. And I think that's very important.

What kind of an ethnic mix do you have at Topeka West?

PRINTZ: Topeka, the home of *Brown vs. Board of Education*, has a neighborhood school system. And, you go to school in the neighborhood in which you live, although a minority student may go to any school he or she wishes until a racial balance has been reached. Of the 1,300 students, I imagine maybe 200 or 300 are minorities.

Do you see any tension because of that?

PRINTZ: Yes, I do. I've noticed it more in the last couple of years, but I'm not sure the tension is because of the minorities—I see tension because of violence and weapons. It bothers me that in the last year we've had 11 or 12 students expelled from our school because they were carrying loaded guns on campus. In fact, our school system has formed a separate school called "The Second Chance School." When you are caught with a loaded weapon you are expelled from your school and go to that school. There's an unbelievable lady there who teaches 16 to 18 kids. They go there for a semester a year and they come back to their original school. If they are caught with a gun or anything again they are expelled permanently.

It bothers me that we've come to that. I worked with some kids who had come back from the Second Chance program, and I think I failed them in some way because I wasn't able to spend the kind of time with them they needed. But, I learned a lot from them. I learned a lot about what it is to be alone, what it is to be ostracized, what it is to be watched by the school security people and administrators, what it's like to be watched by other kids' parents. And, I know they did something wrong. But sometimes it's hard to say "I did something wrong and I'd like to try to be better" when you don't have a lot of support to be better.

I've always believed that to work with kids you have to let them know you respect them. And if you respect them, then perhaps they will respect themselves, which I think is something very, very important. And, they will give that respect back to you. I think you get what you give. I believe that very strongly. I think it's simple. You just treat people the way you want to be treated, no matter how old they are.

Role Play: A Complicated Game

by Carolyn Caywood

Defining roles has been praised as a way to avoid the trap of trying to be all things to all people. Selecting roles focuses planning and makes evaluative measurement meaningful.

Unfortunately, library service to teenagers has never had its own set of roles. The presumption has been that the roles a library selects are supposed to be adaptable to an adolescent's needs, but this presumption may be failing the many young adults who stop using libraries when school work no longer requires it. Teenagers are not just students. They are also family members and friends, entrepreneurs and employees, consumers and activists. They may be faced with physical, political, or economic disadvantages. They are often desperate for self-understanding and growth.

Professional Guidelines

To assist librarians and their communities in setting roles to best serve their users, both the school and public library divisions of ALA have issued guidelines. *Information Power: Guidelines for School Library Media Programs* (ALA, 1988) focuses on the media specialist, rather than the media center, and defines and describes three roles: information specialist, teacher, and instructional consultant. Information specialist encompasses both facilitating access to materials and direct guidance in "identifying, locating, and interpreting information." As a teacher, the media specialist is responsible for instruction in the skills that will make students information-literate. Getting these skills and use of the collection integrated into the curriculum comprises the instructional consultant role.

Planning and Role Setting for Public Libraries (ALA, 1987) offers a menu of eight roles: community activities center, community information center, formal education support center, independent learning center, popular materials library, preschoolers' door to learning, reference library, and research center. Obviously, these roles overlap while relying on unnamed but essential library processes.

The official descriptions of these roles make several of them more restrictive than their names imply. A "sustained program of learning," for example, sounds pretty intimidating to a library user who just likes to read about the Civil War. The definition of research center emphasizes scholars, but in my experience, every library user seeking the information to create or fix something has called that research.

What public librarians have made of these eight choices is assessed in the July/August 1993 issue of *Public Libraries* in two articles. In "Confusing What Is Most Wanted with What Is Most Used," Kenneth Shearer reports: "The findings show that the library now emphasizes the role of circulating popular materials more than any other. However, the survey conducted by D'Elia shows that the support of formal education, independent learning, and readying preschoolers to learn top the public's list."

In an article by Charles McClure, one of the coauthors of *Planning and Role Setting*, he makes a case for revising the roles: "The existing ones are too traditional, somewhat out of date, and fail to include a range of service roles that are technologically oriented."

A New Definition

The eight public library roles seem to me to belong to three broad categories: learning, answers, and leisure. Those favored by the public in D'Elia's study clearly fall under the learning banner. The roles divide learning by who decides what is to be learned—the teacher or the learner. In the first instance, the librarian helps the learner find materials, shows how they are located, and, ideally, provides feedback or consultation to the teacher. The process works the same way when the learning is self-chosen except that the feedback is offered to the learner.

Though information service tends to lump them together, finding answers differs from supporting learning. In this case, process is not important to the library user, only the facts are. This is a legitimate library function but one that I think has been overemphasized in recent years. It is all too easy to confuse reference questions that need answers with those that require learning—and never more so than when the question is for an assignment.

Leisure reading often slides imperceptibly from escapism into learning. And, as is often the case with teens, leisure is spent in groups. At a summer meeting of regular teen library users, they identified desires that could be translated into new roles. They wanted an environment in which they could interact with each other, with enough structure to keep things from getting out of control, but without the limitations of a classroom. At the same time, they sought opportunities to exercise creativity and decision-making skills in ways that would foster civic pride. Social and volunteer center isn't on any list of library roles and doesn't have an obvious connection to books and information, but if teens (and adults) have this expectation of libraries, we need to think about its implications.

We know that libraries play many important roles for adolescents, but it can be hard to find them spelled out in the existing guidelines. Whether library service to teens needs its own roles or whether those for all users can encompass the specific needs of teens, it is time for a fresh examination of the real roles we play in our customers' lives.

The Media and the Message

How Librarians Can Bring Them into Focus

by David M. Considine

An extraordinary opportunity now exists for school library media specialists to increase the visibility and viability of their programs. By fusing their traditional role in reading, listening, and viewing guidance with the rapidly emerging movement in media education (also called "media Literacy"), media specialists can serve as the central force and focus in our schools not simply for teaching *with* media, but also for teaching *about* media. They can create a holistic educational response to the persuasiveness and pervasiveness of mass media in our society—and its potential impact on impressionable children and adolescents.

This opportunity has emerged from a nexus of events and issues converging at a historic juncture for both schools and society. Clearly, concern about the impact of mass media on young people is not new. The Payne Fund studies of the 1930s, for example, explored such issues as *Movies, Delinquency and Crime*.[1] The recent congressional hearings on television violence and the networks' attempts to attach warnings to their programs provide evidence that there is still widespread concern about the potential impact of the mass media on children.

Unfortunately, most of this concern centers on controlling or censoring the production of offensive messages rather than on the critical consumption of these messages. The development of critical viewing, thinking, and listening skills offers children greater protection and independence than do well-meaning attempts to control the content of music, movies, or television, which inevitably clash with First Amendment rights. When young people can recognize a stereotype, detect bias in news reporting, and understand how images can be offensive and demeaning to minorities, they are less likely to accept the value systems portrayed in media representations.

A Climate for Change

One of the most significant elements operating in favor of media education is the school reform and restructuring movement, which has shattered the institutional inertia of American education in the search for new paradigms. The evolutionary and transitional state that our schools are now in permits innovation and experimentation in terms of both *what* is taught and *how* it is taught. The examination of mandates, goals, outcomes, and core competencies now being embraced by school systems across the country makes it clear just how much things have begun to change.

In Oregon, for example, the state's Certificate of Initial Mastery Outcomes says students need to be able to:

- think critically, creatively, and reflectively;
- use current technology, including computers, to process and produce information;
- communicate through reading, writing, speaking, and listening, as well as through the integrated use of visual forms.[2]

Another Oregon document, the Core Applications for Living, requires that students:

- understand positive health habits and behaviors;
- interpret human experience through literature, fine arts, and performing arts;
- learn to deliberate on public issues.

In response to standards like these, school library media specialists working in Oregon are charged with helping students "develop the basic information gathering, evaluation, analysis, and communication skills they need to function in society" and providing instruction "to foster competence and stimulate interest in reading, viewing, and using information and ideas."[3]

Goals and outcomes articulated at the national level also suggest a major change in what schools now emphasize. *Turning Points*, a national report by the Carnegie Council on Adolescent Development, is of particular significance for school library media specialists working in middle schools. According to this report, middle schools should graduate students "who are literate . . . know how to think, lead a healthy life, behave ethically, and assume the responsibility of citizenship in a pluralistic society."[4]

As state and national organizations continue to outline the skills and competencies they believe students will need in the next century, very real opportunity exists for progressive school library media specialists to articulate and demonstrate the way in which media education is consistent and compatible with these emerging mandates. Research shows that change is much more likely to be adopted, integrated, and achieve critical mass when it emerges from the concerns of the stakeholders, rather than being imposed upon them. In short, by operating as change agents, school library media specialists can help administrators, teachers, and parents understand that media education is a competency that will facilitate the goals and objectives these stakeholders have already embraced.

The Literacy Link

Advocates of media education often refer to the discipline as "media literacy," emphasizing the need for educators to redefine literacy based on the increasingly iconic nature of information in our culture. And, since a growing number of states now regard communication or information skills as a core competency, it is logical that these skills be applied to all the information forms of our culture, not just print.

"We continue to think about literacy in the tightest, most constipated terms," wrote Elliot Eisner in *Educational Leadership*. "We need a more generous conception of what it means to know, and a wider conception of the courses of human understanding."[5]

Ernest Boyer, the former U.S. Commissioner on Education and President of the Carnegie Foundation for the Advancement of Teaching, has been even more specific about this need. "It is no longer enough to simply read and write," Boyer says. "Today's students must also become literate in the understanding of visual messages as well. Our children must learn how to spot a stereotype, isolate a social cliche and distinguish facts from propaganda, analysis from banter and important news from coverage."[6]

Perhaps the most advanced and sophisticated response to this age of visual communication is North Carolina's new K-12 information skills curriculum. This document clearly addresses the role of mass media in society and the role of educators in helping students understand its influence. "The sheer mass of information and variety of media formats challenges every learner to filter, interpret, accept and/or discard media messages." Intended to make students "lifelong learners and informed decision-makers," the curriculum is completely consistent with the broadly accepted definition of media literacy, which incudes the ability to access, analyze, evaluate, and produce information in a variety of forms.[7]

Voices from the Field

The need to teach students to comprehend and process pictorial information has received major attention recently in library science literature. In January 1993, *School Library Journal* featured a cover story called "Reading the Image" (pp. 20-25) by Kay E. Vandergrift and Jane Anne Hannigan. The authors argued, "If reading is image-making, viewing is image-reading. . . . The skill and abilities needed to decode and interpret visual images are probably as demanding as those required for reading print."

It is hardly surprising, therefore, to discover that publishers who serve the library science and educational media/technology market have begun to provide media education support materials. In 1991, Educational Technology Publications released *Media and You: An Elementary Media Literacy Curriculum.*[8] The following year, Libraries Unlimited published *Visual Messages: Integrating Imagery into Instruction—A Teaching Resource for Media and Visual Literacy.*[9]

By linking literacy to the changing information forms of the communication revolution, school library media specialists can articulate a compelling rationale for teaching students how to both comprehend and create visual messages, from the relative simplicity of the children's picture book to sophisticated computer graphics and multi-media productions. Far from belonging on the periphery of education, relegated to the status of an elective, the encoding and decoding skills inherent in media literacy are increasingly necessary in the real world of the workplace. This was evident in a recent report from the U.S. Department of Labor that addressed the information and technology skills workers will need in the 21st century. The report said: "Increasing numbers of people are now engaged in getting information and forming judgments by visual means. But even in colleges where students acquire a command of the written word, most are no good at dealing with oral and visual communication." The report also said that "the potential for visual culture to displace print culture is an idea with implications as profound as the shift from oral culture to print culture."[10]

The impact of technology on literacy is also addressed in *Dream Peddler*, a recent picture book by Gail Haley (Dutton, 1993). Set in the world of an eighteenth-century chapman, or seller of cheap books, the author states in cover notes that, just as the growth of printing challenged the oral tradition, "today's visual technology now challenges print."

Haley is not alone among authors and illustrators in her concern about visual messages in our culture. Robert McCloskey once said, "People must be trained to look and see; I find a great lack of visual perception."[11]

And, David Macaulay has articulated the need to develop pictorial proficiency, stating that its absence threatens to turn us into isolated, insensitive, incapable, and ultimately helpless victims of a world of increasing complexity and decreasing humanity."[12]

Macaulay's book *Black and White* (Houghton, 1990), which challenges readers young and old to find patterns and relationships in seemingly unrelated stories, is an excellent tool for developing critical viewing skills.

A Role in Civic Education

American education has always cherished the goal of fostering responsible citizenship. This means active participation in the democratic process and informed voting, which in turn requires an understanding of the way the media affects one's perception of candidates and issues. Since the major party conventions were first covered on television in 1952, image and visual persuasion have increasingly taken precedence over the serious analysis of issues and policies. Presidential historian Theodore White has said that television and the political process are now so closely connected that it is impossible to tell the story of one without also telling the story of the other.

In *Democracy without Citizens: Media and the Decay of American Politics*, Robert Entman cautions against celebrating the explosion of information in our culture. Access to information, particularly instant access as we saw in the Persian Gulf war, is not necessarily the same as understanding and comprehending what we see. In the case of politics, for example, Entman says, "Despite any improvement in access to news, Americans do not know more about politics than they did twenty years ago."[13]

According to Ben Bagdikian, author of *The Media Monopoly*, children need not only understand the form and content of the news they receive; they must also understand the institutional context in which it is both created and controlled. Bagdikian argues, "When fifty men and women chiefs of their corporations control more than half the ideas that reach 220 million Americans, it is time for Americans to examine the institutions from which they receive their daily picture of the world."[14]

If schools truly wish to foster responsible citizenship, curricula must address more than the three branches of government or who won an election. We must also direct children's attention to how elections are won. To study the political process without also studying the role of advertising and the news is to ignore the context in which electronic information both covers and creates candidates and public policy. Fortunately, there are a growing number of resources on this topic that school library media specialists can add to the collection and bring to the attention of teachers and school administrators.

A Role in Health Education

It is equally important to examine the cultural context in which children's values and behaviors with regard to health are created. The objectives of health education cannot be achieved without addressing the contradictions between what school teaches children and what the media teaches them. Whether the issue is self-image, diet, school violence, tobacco, pregnancy, or sex, the key concerns that health educators now face all require an understanding of media messages. In addition to simply understanding what the media tells young people, health educators must also provide students with frameworks and strategies that help them recognize the way advertising and other aspects of the media can affect their beliefs and behaviors.

School library media specialists who wish to document this issue for health educators have no shortage of materials to rely on. Recent research reports in the *Journal of the American Medical Association*, for example, have been highly critical of marketing that targets impressionable children and adolescents, including the "Joe the Camel" cigarette advertisements.[15]

Regulation of marketing aimed at the young was also recommended in 1992's *Fateful Choices* report published by the Carnegie Council on Adolescent Development. Among other things, the report noted that "by age 15, about a quarter of all young adolescents are engaged in behaviors that are harmful or dangerous to themselves and others."[16]

Teen sexuality is another issue that cannot be dealt with meaningfully without also looking at media influences. The Carnegie report concluded that the media (particularly television) "play a major role in modeling adolescent sexual behavior." And, a recent report in *The Journal of Adolescent Health Care* concluded that much of what adolescents learn about sexual activity from the media "does not depict the potentially unhealthy consequences of these behaviors and does not convey the need for sexual responsibility."[17]

An Abundance of Resources

There is perhaps nothing more daunting than the prospect of trying to promote change with little in the way of support materials. But, librarians who want to promote media education have an abundance of resources to turn to.

Media Education Support Organizations

The following groups are the leaders in the media education movement in the United States and Canada, providing everything from journals and newsletters to training sessions and in-service workshops.

Association for Media Literacy. Contact Barry Duncan, 40 McArthur Street, Weston, Ontario M9P 3M7. Duncan pioneered media education in the Ontario high school curriculum and heads an organization that has produced curriculum materials, a regular newsletter, and a series of outstanding international conferences at Guelph University.

Between the Lines. Production and analysis workshops conducted by two leaders in the field: Kathleen Tyner of Strategies for Media Literacy and Deborah Leverantz of the National Alliance of Media Educators. 1095 Market Street, San Francisco, CA 94103.

Center for Media and Values. Contact Elizabeth Thonan, 1962 South Shenandoah, Los Angeles, CA 90034. The group stresses media literacy within the context of Catholic education. Publishes *Media and Value* and distributes videotapes and other kits.

National Telemedia Council. Contact Marieli Rowe, NTC, 120 E. Wilson Street, Madison, WI 53703. One of the oldest media education groups in the country, now establishing major data clearinghouse. Publishes *Telemedium*, which features practical lesson tips for teachers and longer articles intended for school library media specialists.

Strategies for Media Literacy. Contact Kathleen Tyner, SML, 1095 Market Street, San Francisco, CA 94103. A constant presence in the field, with an important, practical newsletter and an endless source of current data related to media and society.

V.I.E.W. (Visual Information Education Workshops). Contact David Considine or Gail E. Haley, c/o Curriculum and Instruction, Appalachian State University, Boone, NC 28608. Provides in-service workshops for teachers and media specialists. Links media education to school reform and restructuring for grades K-12.

The media education movement has developed enormous momentum in the last two years. 1992 saw major conferences, think-tanks, and forums—including two major programs at the Annenberg School of Communication and the prestigious Aspen Institute. By 1993, media education workshops and lectures were showing up in library science and education media conferences from Seattle to San Juan. In the summer of 1993, Harvard University hosted a week-long institute on media education. The participants included library media personnel from across the country. Evaluations of the institute made it clear that this was an idea whose time had come. 1994 also looks promising. A major American conference co-hosted by the National Council of Teachers of English and the National Telemedia Council is scheduled for Madison, WI, in July. And, an international meeting in Spain is in the planning stages.

While the individuals and organizations promoting media education have a variety of approaches and methods, all agree that as the electronic environment expands, children must be given the skills to understand new information forms. Traditionally, American education has viewed the mass media negatively and has attempted to protect children by controlling what they watch. Those involved in the media education movement believe the time has come to concentrate not just on *what* children watch, but *how*. With media specialists and teachers serving as instructional intermediaries, children can learn to read today's new stories—and the technologies through which they are both sold and told—with full understanding.

References

1. Blumer, Herbert. *Movies, Delinquency and Crime*. New York: Macmillan Publishing Co., 1933.
2. Oregon State Board of Education. *Working Designs for Change*. Salem, OR: Oregon State Board of Education, 1993.
3. Oregon Educational Media Association. *Supplementing The Oregon Educational Act for the 21st Century through School Library Media Programs*. Beaverton, OR: Oregon Educational Media Association, 1993.
4. Carnegie Council on Adolescent Development. *Turning Points: Preparing American Youth for the 21st Century*. New York: Carnegie Corporation, 1989.
5. Eisner, Elliot. "What Really Counts in Schools," *Educational Leadership*, February 1991 (48:5), pp. 10-11, 14-17.
6. Boyer, Ernest L. Preface for *Television and America's Children: A Crisis of Neglect* by Edward Palmer. New York: Oxford University Press, 1988.
7. North Carolina Department of Public Instruction. *Standard Course of Study: Information Skills, K-12*. Raleigh, NC: North Carolina Dept. of Public Instruction, 1992.
8. Tyner, Kathleen and Donna Lloyd Kolkin. *Media and You: An Elementary Media Literacy Curriculum*. Englewood Cliffs, NJ: Educational Technology Publications, 1990.
9. Considine, David M. and Gail E. Haley. *Visual Messages: Integrating Imagery into Instruction*. Englewood, CO: Libraries Unlimited/Teacher Ideas Press, 1992.
10. Kirrane, Diane E. "Visual Learning," *Training and Development*, September 1992, p. 58.
11. Heins, Ethel. "From Mallards to Maine, A Conversation with Robert McCloskey," *Journal of Youth Services in Libraries*, Winter 1988 (1:2), pp. 187-193.
12. Macaulay, David. Caldecott Medal Acceptance Speech, *Journal of Youth Services in Libraries*. Summer 1991 (4:4), pp. 340-347.
13. Entman, Robert. *Democracy without Citizens: Media and the Decay of American Politics*. New York: Oxford University Press, 1989.
14. Bagdikian, Ben. *The Media Monopoly*. Boston: Beacon Press, 1990.
15. Fischer, P.M., et al. "Brand Logo Recognition by Children Ages 3 to 6: Mickey Mouse and Old Joe the Camel," *Journal of the American Medical Association*. December 11, 1991 (262:22) pp. 3145-3146.
16. Carnegie Council on Adolescent Development. *Fateful Choices: Healthy Youth for the 21st Century*. New York: Carnegie Corporation, 1992.
17. Brown, Jane et al. "Television and Adolescent Sexuality," *Journal of Adolescent Health Care*, January 1990, pp. 62-70.

Images of Information in a 21st Century High School

by Kim Carter

Souhegan High School (SHS) opened in 1992 with the purpose of preparing students for the twenty-first century. A planning team was hired to work for a year prior to the school's opening (in the newly defined school district of Amherst and Mont Vernon, NH) to develop a mission statement and to translate that philosophy into a functional reality. This team consisted of the principal, the dean of students, two division heads, and me, the school's information specialist.

The school's mission statement reads: "Souhegan High School aspires to be a community of learners born of respect, trust, and courage. We consciously commit ourselves:

- to support and engage an individual's unique gifts, passions, and intentions;
- to develop and empower the mind, body, and heart;
- to challenge and expand the comfortable limits of thought, tolerance, and performance;
- to inspire and honor the active stewardship of family, nation, and globe."

These are not just fancy words. There was a great deal of discussion with the school board and members of the community about these words. We keep the mission statement in front of us at all times. If you visit our school, you will immediately see it on the wall facing you as you enter.

A New Kind of Learning

SHS is a Coalition school, built on the nine principles of the Coalition of Essential Schools founded by Theodore R. Sizer of Brown University. (See sidebar on p. 337.) Among the elements that distinguish SHS, and Coalition schools in general, are the concepts of the student as worker and the teacher as coach; the use of essential questions to drive inquiry; and performance-based assessment through exhibitions and portfolios.

Other things that make SHS different include its commitments to heterogeneity and inclusionary education. Students of all abilities are placed in equal-sized classes, with everyone—including the severely challenged—sharing academic and social opportunities. Ninth and tenth grades are organized around teams, with four core teachers and approximately 80 students on each team. In addition, an "integration team" composed of teachers in the areas of art, music, theater, life skills, health and wellness, technology education, and computer skills works with the core teachers to integrate the fine, performing, and practical arts into every student's daily experiences.

Students earn honors designation through work individually contracted, not through attendance in special classes. Honors credit is available to any student maintaining a B average or better. Integrated seminar classes are required at the junior and senior levels that combine English with social or natural sciences. All students are required to complete a senior project in order to graduate. This entails the writing of a proposal based on a carefully formed question followed by active research, reflective writing, and an exhibition.

These practices have tremendous implications for the provision of information resources and the development of information literacy. As Sizer has said, "Not surprisingly, one good way to start designing an Essential school is to plan a library and let its shadow shape the rest."

Information is integral to the success of this exciting structure. All of the school's practices require access to an array of information sources and tools, and information skills are crucial for the kind of exploratory learning our students do. My role is to look closely at the implications of the school structure for information access, use, and instruction.

Layout of the Center

The physical layout of a learning space has significance beyond traffic patterns and usage needs. The arrangement of any space communicates many subtle, and some not so subtle, messages about what is valued there. In most school media centers, books are the focus. My original intention was to have technology command center stage at SHS, since ours would be a "high-tech" high school.

After visiting a media center with computers in the center of the room and books relegated to stacks in the outlying alcoves, however, I realized that something was missing: there was no celebration of the printed word. Perhaps I have not completely been able to let go of an old mindset, but I believe there is still a valid place for the book and other traditional types of resources in even the most modern school information center. The challenge is to strike an appropriate balance.

Following some ruminations on these ideas, I came to focus on the question of what we were indeed valuing in the information center. The answer was not information. Information is merely the means to the end, which is actually learning. I therefore made the decision to have the "environment of learning" be what people would notice upon entering the center.

As Richard Saul Wurman wrote in *Information Anxiety*, "Conversation is the beginning and end of knowledge . . . the full perfection of learning." The central visual focus of our information center is a conversation area with soft seating and magazine spinners. Of course, many other activities also contribute to learning and rely on information in one form or another. Our cataloging system reflects this by offering access at diverse points of need, rather than just one central catalog station. OPAC terminals are located in nonfiction, fiction, reference, and the study section. (In fact, any computer on the school network can access the OPAC.)

Technology can also be seen throughout the space. A separate room adjacent to the information center is the focal point for production work. Here, video editing and sound production equipment are available for student and staff use.

Collection Development

What does the collection look like in a twenty-first century high school? This question inevitably leads to another. How do students usually gain access to information? Do they use traditional resources, such as books, magazines, and videotapes, or technological resources such as CD-ROM, online databases, and software programs?

To gain a perspective on this, I sent a preliminary survey to school libraries in several states. I found that even in the very best, the real "high-tech" schools, the ratio of technological to traditional resources never surpassed 5 percent to 95 percent. And that was rare. In the business and work world, by contrast, I was cited ratios ranging from 50:50 to 80:20. In an attempt to design the information center with the future in mind, I opted for a 50:50 ratio of print to nonprint as a guideline, and I divided my budget accordingly

In addition to dividing the planned collection into print and nonprint, I also looked at purchases by the two main division areas—Humanities and Math/Science/Technology. For the humanities, I focused mostly on primary source materials such as journals and diaries. The math and science areas were developed using respected collection development resources such as *Science Books and Films* "Best" lists, *Senior High School Catalog*, and *School Library Journal* and *Booklist's* annual lists of best books, as well as teacher requests. I reserved approximately one quarter of the print startup budget for purchases throughout the first year so that I could meet teachers' and students' requests and needs as they arose. (I will continue to set some funds aside for this purpose each year.)

Fiction claims a larger share of the budget than is perhaps common in many high school library media centers. Literature is integrated into most curriculum areas, and we need a wide range of reading material as we work to meet the needs of students with varied abilities. We also support students' recreational reading as much as possible and try to coordinate these efforts with the local public library.

Nonprint acquisition has focused primarily on videodiscs, videotapes, and compact discs. A major investment has been the *Video Encyclopedia of the 20th Century* (CEL Educational Resources, 1986/1990), 83 hours of historic, primary-source film footage. Purchase of the site license for the *Video Encyclopedia* includes copyright clearance for student and staff production. Student exhibitions have already used this resource extensively.

All videotapes are previewed by staff and/or students before purchase—a time-consuming but extremely worthwhile process. An area that requires greater attention in the immediate future is music CDs, particularly those that support interdisciplinary units, and unabridged audiotape recordings of books, which support different learning modes and abilities.

The greatest deviation from the usual high school library collection can be seen in reference. As is true in any collection, this area requires constant evaluation and assessment. While some aspects of the reference collection look very familiar, others are very new, and some usual resources are missing entirely. For example, print encyclopedias are still an important part of the reference collection, but a conscious decision was made to omit literary criticism resources, challenging students to engage in more personal critique.

CD-ROM materials are by far the most heavily used of all our reference resources. As a new school, we had no back issues and had not invested in microfiche, so we purchased the full-image database of periodicals and indexing offered by University Microfilms, Inc., as Magazine Express. Another CD-ROM product that supports our curriculum is Ethnic Newswatch, which provides full text for over 100 alternative press publications representing a variety of perspectives and ethnic groups. (Publications in Spanish support our higher-level Spanish studies.)

This school year we implemented the Dialog database service. This is an important information resource specially for our Division II students (equivalent to 11th and 12th grades), who are involved in individual projects that require in-depth exploration. We also are exploring the possibility of getting involved with CD-I (Compact Disc-Interactive) resources as more educational programs become available.

The Technology Infrastructure

Some of the main components of our computer system include: 1) a fiber optic backbone network that links all areas of the school and provides the capacity for community links in the future; 2) A Digital VAX minicomputer, which allows computers of different families to share information easily, to "talk" to each other, regardless of whether they are Macintosh- or DOS-based; 3) an online catalog in the information center that is VAX-based and accessible from any school computer on the network; 4) computers for students and staff (primarily Macintosh, with a few DOS-based machines in selected locations).

One exciting component of our Macintosh computers is their ability to include "dynamic data"—video, animation, sound, and graphics—within regular applications such as word processing. This is an important component in the development of student portfolios.

Technology is much more than computers, however. We also have:

- a satellite dish, which allows students access to programs that would normally be cost-prohibitive in a school our size;
- a coaxial cable network, which allows for broadcast via cable or satellite to and from each classroom or key area within the school (classroom-to-community transmission is in the works);
- a telephone in each classroom that provides outside access and controls the playback of videotapes and videodiscs from machines located in the information center (five midband cable stations have been preempted for this purpose with the local cable company's permission);
- video projection capability, either in the theater or in a large group-instruction area with a 5' x 10' rear projection screen, allowing large groups of students to view instructional programs and exhibitions;
- graphing calculators and instruments such as motion probes and heat sensors that assist students in exploring concepts in calculus, physics, and chemistry.

Production equipment is another key component in SHS's application of technology. Videotape recording and editing equipment, computer-based media production, interactive media, scanning, graphic design, video still photography, video microscopy, and a powerful and flexible sound production system all provide a wide range of options. These capabilities are vitally important as we work to empower students to communicate through a variety of media and modes.

Instruction

Along with the use of these varied resources come tremendous implications for instructional practices. Boolean search strategy has become one of the most critical skill ar-

---

The Coalition of Essential Schools

The Coalition of Essential Schools, of which Souhegan High is a member, made front-page news in December 1993 when philanthropist Walter H. Annenberg announced he was donating $500 million to help improve public education in the United States. The Coalition was one of the first two organizations to benefit, with $50 million earmarked to support its reform projects.

Founded by Professor Theodore R. Sizer of Brown University, the Coalition is a network of more than 500 secondary public schools that have adopted a common system of school restructuring principles. The principles of Coalition schools (in abbreviated form) are:

1. The school should focus on helping adolescents learn to use their minds well. Schools should not attempt to be "comprehensive" if such a claim is made at the expense of the school's central intellectual purpose.

2. The school's goals should be simple: that each student master a limited number of essential skills and areas of knowledge. While these skills and areas will, to varying degrees, reflect the traditional academic disciplines, the program's design should be shaped by the intellectual and imaginative powers and competencies that students need, rather than necessarily be "subjects" as conventionally defined. The aphorism "Less Is More" should dominate.

3. The school's goals should apply to all students, while the means to these goals will vary as those students themselves vary. School practice should be tailor-made to meet the needs of every group or class of adolescents.

4. Teaching and learning should be personalized to the maximum feasible extent. Efforts should be directed toward a goal that no teacher have direct responsibility for more than 80 students. To capitalize on this personalization, decisions about the details of the course of study, the use of students' and teachers' time, and the choice of teaching materials and specific pedagogies must be unreservedly placed in the hands of the principal and staff.

5. The governing practical metaphor of the school should be student as worker, rather than the more familiar metaphor of teacher as deliverer of instructional services. Accordingly, a prominent pedagogy will be coaching, to provoke students to learn how to learn and thus to teach themselves.

6. Students of traditional high school age but not yet at appropriate levels of competence to enter secondary school studies will be provided intensive remedial work to assist them quickly to meet these standards. The diploma should be awarded upon a successful final demonstration of mastery for graduation—an "Exhibition."

7. The tone of the school should explicitly and self-consciously stress values of unanxious expectation . . . and parents should be treated as essential collaborators.

8. The principal and teachers should perceive themselves as generalists first (teachers and scholars in general education) and specialists second (experts in but one particular discipline). Staff should expect multiple obligations (teacher-counselor-manager) and a sense of commitment to the entire school.

9. Ultimate administrative and budget targets should include, in addition to total student loads per teacher of 80 or fewer pupils, substantial time for collective planning by teachers, competitive salaries for staff, and an ultimate per pupil cost not to exceed that at traditional schools by more than 10 percent. To accomplish this, administrative plans may have to show the phased reduction or elimination of some services now provided students in many traditional comprehensive secondary schools.

eas for all students (and staff!). The use of information technologies creates an exciting and dynamic interplay between technology and user: As the user tries to become more conscious of his or her search processes, the technology provides concrete, immediate feedback about the effectiveness of those processes. Integration of information literacy into all areas of the curriculum has always been essential. In this kind of school environment, the necessity for both information resources and integrated information skills instruction is self-evident.

Teachers are learning how to plan for this type of integration and are increasingly receptive to collaboration. Perhaps one of the most effective collaborative ventures during our first school year was a project built around the Billy Joel song *We Didn't Start the Fire* (1992), a chronological roll call of important historical events from the 1950s through the 1980s. In many ways, this project epitomized the concepts and practices that are the underpinnings of the Souhegan High School mission statement.

The chorus of the song says, "We didn't start the fire; it was always burning since the world's been turning. We didn't start the fire; though we didn't light it, we tried to fight it . . . " The following essential questions were posed to the students: Who started the fire? What is burning? What is the fire? Have any fires been put out?

A group of 85 ninth-graders spent six days on this unit. First, students needed to understand what all of the historical events mentioned in the song were in order to address the essential questions. Each of several sub-groups had to prepare a five-to fifteen-minute final exhibition that addressed one or more of the essential questions (or one they came up with themselves) and present their interpretation of the song. They had five days (4¹/2 hours each day) to complete the project, with the sixth day devoted to the exhibitions, which were viewed by the whole group and given peer evaluations.

All but one group chose to create a videotape for the final exhibition. The tapes exhibited a wide range of creativity, depicting everything from a 1950s version of *Wayne's World* to a hairdresser shop that was frequented by the famous in the mid-1960s. Several of the student productions incorporated film clips from the *Video Encyclopedia of the 20th Century*, and many students found occasion to explore new avenues for information sources. One teacher in the school who had a much-beloved collection of 45 r.p.m. records was tapped as an information source, as were a number of parents who were pleased to be interviewed about their involvements in and recollections of past events.

We are finding more and more that the use of presentation technologies is a critical learning outcome for this generation of students, particularly such skills as videotape recording and editing and using interactive media. The integration of presentation skills will continue to be a major focus of instruction in the coming school years.

Redefining Goals

As Souhegan High School continues to explore the meaning of effective education for the twenty-first century, the decisions and practices of the information center will continue to evolve. We are constantly questioning what our goals are and assessing the most effective ways of working toward these goals. This will be a continuing challenge as images of information shift with the tides of technological advances. In the twenty-first century, information will be, as former Secretary of State George Shultz once observed, "the international currency upon which fortunes will rise and fall."

References

Shultz, George. "The Shape, Scope, and Consequences of the Age of Information," *Department of State Bulletin*, May 1986.
Wurman, Richard Saul. *Information Anxiety*. New York: Bantam, 1989.

Responsive Reference Service

Breaking Down Age Barriers

by Charles A. Bunge

Children and young people are among those library patrons who need reference service the most. Many of the information sources they use have been designed for adults or are otherwise confusing and inaccessible. Yet, I have come to fear that some of the changes in reference services now being implemented and proposed in public and academic libraries only serve to further disadvantage this group. Advocates for youth must therefore redouble their efforts to establish and maintain dialogue with adult services librarians, reference managers, and library administrators to ensure that young library patrons get the reference help they need.

During the spring semester of 1993, I was on sabbatical leave from my normal duties as a professor at the University of Wisconsin-Madison School of Library and Information Studies, where I teach a variety of reference-oriented courses. As part of my sabbatical experience, I worked at the main reference desks of a medium-sized public library and a major university library. The experience allowed me to participate in, to observe, and to talk to reference librarians about services to children and young people in public and academic libraries. I also attended two conferences on "rethinking" reference services in the face of the changing environment in which such services are provided. I read widely, talked and corresponded with many librarians, and reflected on various aspects of reference services as well.

I came away from these exciting and rewarding experiences worried that current budget pressures and shifting priorities in public and academic libraries will lead to barriers to information for children and young people. I also became concerned that these barriers will negatively influence young patrons' attitudes and library use patterns for years to come.

Reference services, especially the answering of questions at the reference desk, are under serious scrutiny for change and redefinition. Such services occupy a lot of staff time, and library administrators look hungrily at those staff hours to meet demands for budget reductions and for reallocation to other functions and services. At best, reference staff sizes remain constant in the face of an ever-increasing volume of questions. On the one hand, expensive staff seem to be involved in answering a great many repetitive and routine questions. On the other hand, patrons with needs for in-depth service are not well-served because of the volume of questions and the hectic pace at the reference desk.

As I talked with library administrators and reference li-

brarians about responses to this situation, I found myself forced to define and defend the basic roles and values that reference services represent in libraries. One fundamental value of reference service, I believe, is *equity* in access to information. Reference service exists to provide personal service to help the less adroit, the less knowledgeable, the less skilled person find and use information that would otherwise not be accessible to him or her. Without reference service, the basic role of libraries, that of equalizing access to information and ideas for all people, will come to naught for some.

Obviously, children and young people are among those who most need implementation of this principle of equity and who can benefit the most from it. However, as managers and staffs of reference services in public and academic libraries cope with increasing budget and staffing pressures by tightening policies, focusing priorities, and generally "circling the wagons," these very important users (or potential users) can be left on the outside facing the barriers of exclusion, rather than getting assistance for better access. There are a number of areas in which I see this happening.

A Role in Reference Policies

Public libraries, along with school and academic libraries, are making dramatic changes in access to information. Many are adding CD-ROM information resources to their adult reference collections. Others are providing bibliographic and full-text access to periodical articles via their online public access catalogs. Some are becoming access points for the Internet. All of these developments have great potential for serving the information needs of children and young people, and all can produce needs for reference services.

These changes, along with the fact that most reference departments are making them with no additional staffing, are forcing public librarians to review and revise their reference service policy manuals. Unfortunately, some of the revisions and drafts that I have perused seem to have grown out of a "we *have* to cut back somewhere" attitude and to emphasize what the reference service will *not* do more than what it will do. While I have not seen any policy statements that explicitly discriminate against children or young people, restrictive treatment of certain categories of questions that are most frequently asked by young patrons (e.g., homework questions) can amount to the same thing. When the examples used for a general policy are ones associated with children, they can foster restrictive attitudes toward services to young people.

Youth services librarians can help keep the policies of general or adult reference services from discriminating against young users by becoming involved in the review and writing of such policies for their libraries. Sometimes those who are too close to the pressures of the immediate situation fail to see the inequity implicit in a policy that is proposed for what seem to be sound reasons. Youth specialists can remind policy writers (and those who interpret and implement policies) that the reference principle of equity demands that there be no categories or classes of library users or questions that receive differential responses. Perhaps your particular point of view will be helpful in framing policies so that limitations on responses to questions (if they are necessitated by limitations in staff time or other resources) are applied equally, to questions of all types and from all sources.

Such involvement might well have been a factor in one public library's reference policy statement that I saw recently. It said simply and directly, "Users of all ages and circumstances are to be treated with equal attention and with sensitivity to their particular needs." Another exemplary statement includes the words, "School assignment questions shall be handled in the same manner as any other question."

Seeing such policy statements, in contrast to the more restrictive ones to which I referred previously, gives me hope that one children's librarian with whom I corresponded on these matters was just having a bad day when she wrote, "In general, I think a young library user is much more likely to encounter resistance to service when sent from the children's department to the adult department *in his or her own public library* than between libraries or even across system boundaries!"

In at least one public library with which I am familiar, a children's librarian was invited to be part of the adult reference policies committee, but this is not always the case. Involvement in policy review and writing can be difficult for youth services librarians if they are generally cut off from the administration of adult services, perhaps to the point of not even knowing that reference policy review and writing is under way.

Opening and maintaining lines of communication between children's and adult services staff and administrators (from which involvement in policy formulation can evolve) is a long-term and continuing process. Youth specialists have told me that involving adult services staff in collaborative program planning (even in informal ways) can contribute to this process. Working together on displays for topics that cut across age levels, or jointly developing pathfinders for commonly researched topics, might establish a basis for continued communication on commonly held philosophies and goals.

Youth services librarians can also take steps to reduce the perception among adult services librarians that children and young people bring an undue or unnecessary volume of questions to the reference desk. Youth specialists need to become as familiar as possible with the information resources available in the public library's reference area so that referrals to this area are effective. Some school library media specialists

and public youth services librarians have collaborated with adult services staff to develop user guides and bibliographic instruction programs for young people that help to make them more adroit users of reference resources. This kind of effort is a benefit both to users and to harried reference librarians.

Multiple Service Points

Both academic and public librarians are trying to find ways to allow professional staff members to concentrate their time on complex or in-depth questions and to cut down the proportion of their time that is spent on routine questions. One common approach to solving this problem is to establish a directional or ready-reference desk that is the first point of contact for reference patrons, with referral of more complex questions to other service points. Frequently, this first point of contact is staffed by paraprofessionals, who are expected to refer appropriate questions to professional staff members.

Here, too, I have concerns that reference service to meet the needs of children and young people will suffer. I worry that questions from young patrons will automatically be treated as ready reference (or worse, as directional or trivial) and will not be referred as frequently as will similar questions from adults. I also worry that the training of the paraprofessionals who staff reference service points will not include skills and attitudes that are important for dealing with children and young people.

Youth services librarians can be valuable resource persons to public and academic librarians who are charged with restructuring reference service points, writing policies and procedures for such restructuring, and training reference staff members. Both school and public library youth specialists should pursue every opportunity to stay in contact with their adult services and academic library counterparts. Such contact can provide opportunities to remind these colleagues that today's youth have complex and pressing needs for access to information and that their treatment today can set the pattern for their use of reference services as higher education students and adults. Youth specialists might also volunteer to serve as resource persons for reference managers who are developing training programs for desk staffs.

"Primary Clientele"

As I talk with reference librarians and managers about how they are restructuring reference services, I hear a lot of talk about concentrating on the library's "primary clientele." It doesn't make sense, so the argument goes, to spend significant amounts of time serving the patrons of "other" libraries (or "other" service units) when there is not even enough time and staff to serve the needs of "our own" patrons adequately.

This attitude is cause for concern particularly in academic libraries, where one of the groups outside the primary clientele is elementary and high school students and where reference departments are feeling forced to adopt restrictive policies regarding services to them. (A participant in a conference I attended recently reported with sadness that staff shortages had forced his university library to drop a long-standing program of services to area high school honor students.) I have also encountered restrictive attitudes, if not stated policies, in public libraries whose longer hours or better resources attract questions from children and young people from surrounding communities.

Obviously, youth services librarians are sad to see such barriers to information imposed on their users, especially when such policies represent backward movement in library cooperation that has been developed through years of work. Nevertheless, the pressures and resource limitations out of which the restrictions arise are a fact of life. How might their impact on young people be minimized? Certainly, continued liaison and advocacy by school and public library youth specialists is one answer. Youth librarians can try to influence policy development by arguing for equity and point out that today's child is tomorrow's "primary" user, whose future attitudes and use patterns are being formed today.

In one community, a school library media specialist initiated a collaborative project to develop "self-help" options for young people in area libraries of all types. Students received printed or audiovisual introductions and guides to the libraries' resources and services, as well as tutorials and help screens for the online catalog and other electronic tools. (These could be especially useful at those ready reference "first point of contact" desks mentioned previously.) A number of school and children's librarians have developed elements in their bibliographic instruction programs that prepare their patrons to use "other" libraries with minimum need for reference assistance.

Teachers and parents sometimes encourage students to use academic libraries or larger public libraries before they have fully exploited the resources of their school or local public libraries, and without knowledge of the policies and procedures of these "other" libraries. Youth librarians should try to assist such teachers and parents in helping their charges to use library resources more effectively.

In many communities, youth specialists have participated in the development of a referral slip or "infopass" system among the libraries in their area. Such a process allows reference librarians in libraries with special resources to know that patrons have already used the resources of their primary libraries and need additional assistance. Infopass programs can also be a way for school libraries to offer their special resources to members of the community at large, thus improving attitudes among librarians of all types in the community. As I talked with librarians during my leave, I got the impression that such arrangements in some communities need to be rejuvenated and updated to increase their use and effectiveness.

Dialogue Is the Key

Many of the suggestions I have made here involve establishing and maintaining contact between youth specialists and reference librarians in adult services or academic libraries. This will not be easy for many youth librarians. Just getting to meet with colleagues from other types of libraries can be a serious problem. However, establishing a long-term goal of increasing such dialogue, along with building on small successes, can yield valuable results.

One way to make inroads is to watch for opportunities to offer resources and expertise to other libraries and their users. I recently heard about an effort by a school library media specialist to make resources in her library's professional collection available to teacher education students. This has led to a variety of other cooperative endeavors and has increased communication between school library media specialists and academic librarians in that area.

School library media programs have been using educational and communications technology for a long time and can offer considerable expertise and resources to other libraries and their users. In addition, youth specialists' experience in providing services to people with special needs could be a good basis for assisting adult services and academic colleagues who are facing similar challenges.

One children's librarian tells me that she has been successful at getting youth services managers and other colleagues to keep her informed of meetings they will be attending. She tells them her ideas and concerns, which they then share at the meetings, and receives reports on what took place. Another librarian I know watches for opportunities for information communication, such as car-pooling to meetings and social gatherings, and uses the relationships she forms in this way as a basis for continuing contacts.

By now, readers of this article may be thinking that all these suggestions ignore the fact that youth services librarians have their own pressures, staff limitations, and changing environments, and that they too can hardly bear to face yet another challenge. I can assure you that my youth services friends and colleagues continually remind me of these pressures! I believe that the changing environments of both adult reference services and youth services are part of a larger environment, wherein the very viability of our services, our libraries, and our profession are being called into question.

While the emerging electronic information revolution is offering greater and greater opportunities to find and use information, the financial resources that libraries have to guarantee equal access to those opportunities are increasingly limited in community after community. I deeply fear that children and young people will be among those who suffer most the inequities that can result from this situation. I hope these ideas will stimulate reflection, discussion, and action. All types of librarians must work together to ensure equal access to information for all.

The Power to Grow

Success Stories from the National Library Power Program

by Michael Sadowski

"**O**nce upon a time, there was a sadly neglected room on the third floor of P.S. 3. It had at one time been a library . . . " But, as the story goes, the room fell into disrepair over the years. The paint started to peel, the furniture became creaky and unstable, and the books got older and older as time wore on. Naturally, it wasn't long before the room was all but abandoned.

"Then some people arrived who knew a great deal about books!" explained an excited group of New York City elementary students. It was the grand opening of their new school library, revitalized by the National Library Power Program, and the students were telling the story of how it all began. Library Power painted the dreary room in bright, cheerful colors, installed inviting new furniture, put up new shelves, and—most important—helped fill the shelves with beautiful new books. The shining, new school library was officially unveiled May 12.

"Not too long ago we had a very bedraggled library with books dating back to the '60s, '50s, even '40s," said Principal Yve Douglass at the ceremony. "With Library Power's help, we've made it the kind of place that children love to come to and read."

Stuart Grodin, school-wide projects facilitator for the district, said, "Three years ago, parents didn't want to send their kids to P.S. 3. Now they're fighting to get in."

The National Program

P.S. 3, in Brooklyn's Bedford-Stuyvesant section (one of the city's toughest neighborhoods), is one of 137 schools participating in New York City's Library Power program, which is part of a $45 million national initiative supported by the DeWitt Wallace-Reader's Digest Fund. Library Power is now up and running in 13 cities and more than 300 schools around the country.

In addition to renovating spaces and supplementing local funds for books, Library Power provides mini-grants for special library-based projects and funds professional development activities for librarians and other members of the school community. This last element is key, since Library Power's mission goes far beyond refurbishing school libraries. "Library Power is not just library reform; it's school reform," says national project coordinator Ann Weeks (also executive director of the American Association of School Librarians and the Young Adult Library Services Association of ALA). "Our goal is to change the way teaching and learning happen in schools using the library as a foundation."

The amount of money allocated to each district for furniture, renovation, professional development, books, and special projects is about $1.2 million over a three-year implementation period. As a requirement for the grant, all Library Power schools must operate with a flexible schedule and must be staffed by full-time, certified school library media specialists. In many cities this has meant hiring additional librarians in order to qualify. In addition, all districts that receive Library Power book funds must match those funds dollar-for-dollar and must pay any of the labor costs incurred in the renovations. (Library Power pays for the materials.) Only elementary and middle schools may participate.

Since Library Power awards money not directly to school districts but to local education funds (groups that act as a funding bridge between school districts and potential local and national partners), only communities that have such funds have been eligible for the grants. But, according to Weeks, the project has created dozens of models that can now be replicated in other schools and districts.

Baton Rouge, LA: A Model of Collaboration

"Library Power has made our libraries warm and friendly places for children," says Baton Rouge Library Power director Evelyn Conerly. "Before they were dark, dismal, and crowded."

There are now 53 Library Power schools in Baton Rouge, more than in any other city outside New York. Only ten elementary and middle schools in Baton Rouge are not currently involved in the program.

In addition to $350,000 worth of new books and $200,000 worth of renovations, one of the most important changes Library Power has effected in Baton Rouge has been librarian/teacher collaboration. "Teachers and librarians are working together as an instructional team," Conerly said. "And librarians are integrally involved in curriculum decisions.

Along with an enhanced role for the librarian has come a greater emphasis on literature in all areas of instruction. The schools are using more trade books and fewer basal texts, and literature is being integrated into a variety of curriculum areas. A major initiative has involved the preparation of thematic units, which librarians have developed in collaboration with teachers to incorporate literature and other library materials into classroom lessons.

To help support the push toward collaboration and literature-based instruction, Library Power has funded extensive professional development for Baton Rouge librarians, teachers, and administrators. Every Library Power school has had to develop a list of professional development objectives, and there are two district-wide meetings for all school team members each year, as well as numerous school and district meetings.

Although it is in its third and final year of funding from DeWitt Wallace, Baton Rouge Library Power shows no signs of slowing down. "I believe Library Power will be institutionalized through support from the district," says Conerly. "We've changed our way of doing things, and people seem to like it better."

Cambridge, MA: Connecting Books & Authors

Before Library Power, the library in Cambridge's Peabody School had been a small room in a remote corner of the building. According to media specialist Holly Samuels, Library Power funding provided the impetus to create a much larger, more inviting library space that is literally the center of the school. "Now it looks like a library, and it looks up-to-date," Samuels says.

Samuels has used her Library Power funds to purchase the latest books and selected electronic materials such as the Electronic Bookshelf quiz, which is very popular with Peabody students. She says the enhanced collection has helped to encourage collaboration with teachers all the way down to the kindergarten level: "Teachers consult with me beforehand, and I help them tailor a project based on the resources the library has."

Author and illustrator visits have been another major success in Cambridge's Library Power schools. Ashley Bryan, Sook Nyul Choi, LaToya Hunter, and Giles Laroche are among those to have appeared recently in Library Power-sponsored programs.

In addition to district-wide professional development in such areas as technology, teaching resource skills, and flexible scheduling, each Cambridge Library Power school has received $1,000 for activities to involve other school players. This kind of internal outreach is important because it is not always easy getting teachers to go along with such ideas as collaborative planning and flexible scheduling.

"More and more teachers are coming into the library for collaborative projects," says Karen Arnold, media specialist at the Harrington School. "But, we still have to convince some people that flexible scheduling will be to their benefit. They can no longer just drop off a class to read a book."

Lynn, MA: Catalyst for Change

One of the primary purposes of Library Power is to serve as a catalyst for change. In the largely blue-collar city of Lynn, MA, this change can be seen not only in the school libraries, but in the entire school system and in many of Lynn's 80,000 residents.

"Schools had to make a commitment to get this grant," says Mary Long, the local Library Power director. To apply for the grant, Lynn schools had to have formed teams composed of the principal, two teachers, two parents, and a busi-

ness partner. Nine of the city's 18 elementary schools applied for the grants, and six received them.

Since Lynn had no librarians in its elementary schools, applying for the grant meant that the district would have to hire library media specialists, as well as promise to match book funds and pay for labor costs involved in the renovations. Despite the fact that library staffing had not been a high priority, however, Long is certain that the five library media specialists who have been hired to run the Library Power schools will be retained beyond the DeWitt Wallace funding period.

"Now that they've seen what Library Power can do, there's a strong desire on the part of teachers and principals here to make this work," Long says. "If you're going for institutionalization, you have to expect school districts to do it for themselves."

Lynn had originally planned to open two of its Library Power schools over each of the three years of the project. But, local enthusiasm was so strong that the plan was accelerated, and five of the six schools opened in the first year.

"This has been one of the most rewarding years in my 24 years of teaching," says Barbara Rozavsky, the media specialist at the Library Power-funded Ingalls School, the city's largest K-8 school. "Basically this room was a book depository, staffed by volunteers when and if possible." Now Rozavsky works on many collaborative projects with teachers.

Anne Carter, a fifth-grade teacher with whom Rozavsky has often collaborated, has an opinion that is not uncommon in Lynn: "Library Power is the best thing that's ever happened to this school."

New York City: An Enormous Undertaking

P.S. 3 is just one of the 137 success stories in the New York City Library Power project. By far the oldest and largest of the local programs, New York City Library Power began in 1988, four years before DeWitt Wallace decided to go national with the program. New York City Library Power is now a $7.2 million project that reaches about one in five of New York City's elementary schools.

As in P.S. 3, renovations to New York City Library Power schools involved painting, shelving, furniture, repairs, and redesign. "The existing spaces are old, but we try to make them as inviting as possible," says local Library Power director Sheila Salmon. "We try in each site to have spaces where kids can relax and where they can work in small groups."

New York Library Power also provides mini-grants for special projects. These include displays, guest lectures, and field trips to places like the Metropolitan Museum of Art.

According to Salmon, professional development efforts focus on how to run a library program, how to collaborate with teachers, and how to make the library a central part of the school. "We teach the librarians how to weed, how to merchandise, how to buy books—and we give every library a subscription to *School Library Journal*," she says.

Even though school district book funds have been cut back to $2.00 per pupil, Library Power is still matching $4.67 per pupil that the city used to provide. "It is difficult in a city the size of New York because the city has to leverage so much to participate," says Salmon.

Library Power officials hope the schools will find other funding sources and will adopt some of the positive changes permanently so that the success can continue. (The DeWitt Wallace funds run out this year in some schools.) Anita Strauss, Library Power associate director, says, "We're trying to give it momentum to carry on without us, to make the program so vital that no one would ever think of cutting it."

Library Power and school staff aren't the only ones who believe in the program. One of the painters working on a Library Power media center was so impressed by what he saw and heard about that he called the principal of his child's school and asked, "Why didn't you apply for Library Power?"

Paterson, NJ: Building Up from Rock Bottom

In Paterson, a multiethnic city of 140,000 residents in northern New Jersey, Library Power did much more than renovate school libraries—it provided the impetus to create libraries where none had existed before.

When the Paterson Education Fund applied for Library Power, the Paterson school system had hit rock bottom. The schools were in such dire condition that they were faced with a state takeover. Predictably, there were no full-time elementary library media specialists, but seven itinerant librarians who divided their time among the district's 32 elementary schools, working in spaces that could hardly be considered libraries.

"Everything was up for grabs," says the Fund's executive director, Irene Sterling. Applying for and winning a Library Power grant gave the Paterson schools a clear focus and an opportunity to begin building back up.

Library Power is now in 15 of Paterson's K-8 schools and is making a miraculous difference in many of them. Judy Finchler, media specialist in Paterson's School #15, says students are so enthusiastic about their new library that she has a waiting list for student volunteers. She has begun to work with teachers on collaborative projects, an option more and more teachers are choosing.

Luckily, one of the district's firm believers in the power of libraries is also a key decision maker, district superintendent Clarence Hoover. "In the ideal school, the library would be the hub of the building," Hoover says. "Curriculum planning, staff meetings, would have the librarian involved as a key person. We'd be well stocked with both technology and books, and we'd have year-round access for students and parents."

Hoover says that with or without Library Power, libraries are going to continue to be a central focus of education in Paterson, and the district will continue to have library media specialists. "It will not go back to the way it was," he says. "Libraries will not be treated as the stepchild of the system anymore."

Providence, RI: Supporting Diversity

Providence, RI, has a student population that is growing and becoming more ethnically diverse every year. Families whose first languages range from Spanish and Portuguese to Vietnamese and Khmer have immigrated to Providence in recent years.

"The diversity of our schools is one of our greatest assets—and creates one of our greatest areas of need," says Providence Library Power director Anne Hird. "We have responded by allocating funds for Spanish and other foreign-language materials."

The district's Library Power professional development activities also support this multicultural focus. Librarians (and sometimes teachers and principals) attend workshops on such topics as cultural sensitivity and multicultural literature. The programs are intended to make media specialists leaders in their schools, particularly in dealing with parents and students from different ethnic backgrounds.

Professional development activities also focus on encouraging librarians to develop partnerships with corporate sponsors and others. Library Power provides training on proposal writing, and local librarians have been successful in writing for grants and getting projects funded on their own.

"We're trying to plug people into community resources that will be there after Library Power," Hird says.

After the program in Providence officially ends, Hird expects the changes in schools to go on: "administrators now have an active interest in—and positive experiences with—the library. This has educated people about what to expect of libraries and library media specialists."

Rochester, NY: Saying No to Budget Cuts

In the winter of 1992, major budget cuts in Rochester, NY, resulted in the closing of all elementary libraries and the layoff of nearly three dozen librarians. Librarians and community groups launched a counteroffensive, and the libraries were reopened at the beginning of the next school year. This year Rochester schools face a similar cut, but library media services will remain intact thanks in large part to the Library Power program. "Library Power has greatly raised awareness about the important role of the library," says local Library Power director Suzanne Meyer.

By September 1994, Rochester will have 18 Library Power schools. In addition to renovations, collection enhancement, professional development, and special projects, one of the most significant changes the program has brought to Rochester is a greater respect for librarians and the role they can play in school restructuring.

"As the library is increasingly viewed as a resource rather than a scheduled break for teachers, we are beginning to see librarians involved in day-to-day teaching and learning," Meyer says. "In greater numbers than ever before, librarians are sitting in on curriculum and grade-level committees, serving as members of school-based planning teams, and are working with teachers, parent groups, and school administrators to make the library a true learning center."

One of Rochester's most zealous converts is the district superintendent, Manuel Rivera, who made the decision to cut school library services and staff in 1992. Now that he has seen what a difference school librarians can make with financial support, Rivera admits, "When I cut the librarians, I made a big mistake."

Tucson, AZ: The Power of Literature

Literature-based learning is a major thrust of the Library Power program in Tucson. One of the original sites (after New York), the program now encompasses 22 elementary schools and four middle schools.

"We believe in the power of literature," says program co-director Cyndi Giorgis. "It helps students learn empathy, journey through many worlds, and develop their imaginations." To that end, students in Tucson's Library Power schools do a lot of independent reading as well as read-aloud, book-sharing, readers' theatre, and choral reading activities. Librarians support teachers' use of literature in all subjects by preparing bibliographies and thematic units—"anything we can do to help them work with literature," Giorgis says. Literature is even used heavily in the district's staff development activities.

"There is an emphasis here on redefining the role of the library and the librarian through educating administrators," says Giorgis.

Library Power grants also help fund visits by authors and illustrators to schools to talk about the bookmaking process. As children learn more about language and illustration, they then begin producing their own books in school-based publishing centers.

Newer Sites

Library Power has been implemented in five additional sites over the past year, and changes are already starting to happen.

Chattanooga, TN: With seven elementary schools and five middle schools involved in the first year, Chattanooga Library Power plans to have all 32 of the city's elementary and middle schools on board within three years. A top priority here is working Library Power into school reform initiatives already in place. "Librarians will serve as catalysts for reform by helping teachers branch out beyond the classroom and the textbook," says director Barbara Stripling.

Cleveland, OH: Five elementary schools and two middle schools in Cleveland were made Library Power sites in December, 1993. After the three-year grant period, Cleveland will have a total of 24 program sites. Director Marian Usalis says Library Power media specialists are "more highly regarded as curriculum specialists and master teachers."

Dade County (Miami), FL: Ten elementary schools began with Library Power in November 1993, and more schools are scheduled to be announced this summer. A major success of the project has been the "Library Power Quest" contest, in which the *Miami Herald* and *El Nuevo Herald* newspapers published clues and encouraged students to seek answers in their libraries. The contest garnered 30,000 entries.

Denver, CO: "This is the heart and soul in this school," says principal Richard Jordan of the library at Baker Middle School, a new Library Power site. "It's both a hangout and a place where kids can come and begin to dream." The Denver metropolitan area will have 30 Library Power schools by the end of the program's third year.

Lincoln, NE: Lincoln has 28 schools currently participating in Library Power, 22 elementary and six middle schools. According to director Trixie Schmidt, collaboration has been the main focus. Every teacher in a Library Power school completes a self-assessment on his or her level of involvement in the library media program. Librarians and teachers also complete evaluations, and school professional development activities are designed to address the needs identified.

Planning sites: In Addition to the 13 implementation sites, Library Power planning grants of $20,000 each have been awarded to public education funds in nine cities: Atlanta; Berea, KY; McKeesport, PA; Nashville; New Haven, CT; Philadelphia; Raleigh, NC; San Francisco; and Washington, DC. The grants enable the local fund organizations to prepare proposals for implementing Library Power in their communities.

Life After Library Power

While all of this may sound too good to be true, there are of course a few problems associated with the Library Power program. Perhaps most pressing is the question of what school districts will do when the three-year grants run out. Before Library Power, many of the participating districts had histories of very poor support for school libraries. Nevertheless, Library Power officials remain confident that school administrators, boards of education, parents, and other community constituents will keep supporting school library services now that this project has helped to demonstrate their value.

"I have no doubt that this program is going to go on," says Paterson's Irene Sterling. "This project has really gotten people to change." Sterling expects that Paterson's full-time library media specialists will be kept on and that the district will continue allocating at least $25 per pupil annually for library materials. The Paterson Education Fund plans to seek additional outside funding sources to support school libraries, and the district plans to expand its program of library improvement into the city's high schools over the next few years.

Life without Library Power would be a bit tougher in New York City, where the per-pupil materials budget would be just $2.00. But, DeWitt Wallace has just announced an additional $4.8 million grant to continue funding the New York project, recognizing the great need that exists there.

Whether or not DeWitt Wallace will continue sponsoring Library Power sites beyond those already selected is another question. So far, the fund is committed to supporting the program through 1997, and continuation will depend largely on the results of a national evaluation due some time next year.

Of course, the most important measure of Library Power's success is the impact it has had on children. "When the program started, I couldn't believe how little access our kids had to books—it was as if they had never seen anything like this before," says Judy Finchler of Paterson. "Now they ask to spend their lunch hour in the library. The books here are well-used, often-renewed, and well-loved.

Flexible Access

Foundation for Student Achievement

by Mary D. Lankford

The report of the National Education Commission on Time and Learning, "Prisoners of Time," opens by saying:

> Learning in America is a prisoner of time. For the past 150 years, American public schools have held time constant and let learning vary. The rule, only rarely voiced, is simple: learn what you can in the time we make available. It should surprise no one that some bright, hard-working students do reasonably well. Everyone else—from the typical student to the dropout—runs into trouble. Time is learning's warden.

This statement, more than anything else I have read recently, reaffirms the need to give students flexible access to the school library. I urge all librarians to order a copy of this report *immediately*. It should be read by everyone working in education. My only criticism of the report is that not once in its 56 pages did I see the word "library." Once again, libraries are invisible. Although the word was not mentioned, however, I read library/librarian between the lines throughout the report.

In many elementary school libraries, students are still being held prisoners of time through the practice of rigid, lock-step schedules. These young time prisoners are missing the potential of a library program that may have all elements in place—except one. Excellent staff, facilities, and resources are not enough for a successful program. When the time spent in the library is dictated not by student need but by the clock, the "teachable moment" may never arrive. Opportunities for teachers and librarians to plan together are usually nonexistent. The time problem can be resolved by accepting, implementing, and promoting flexible access to the library.

Selling the Idea

We have had great success in our district with full implementation of flexible access in more than half of our elementary schools. Part of the reason for this is that we already had several positive factors in place:

1. We had full-time librarians on each elementary campus.
2. We had part-time clerical assistance.
3. We had central receiving and processing for library resources.
4. We were fully automated, had a union catalog, and encouraged inter-library loan.

5. We had expanded all our libraries' physical facilities. (See "Design for Change," *School Library Journal*, February 1994, pp. 20-24.)
6. We had employed librarians with outstanding teaching experience who also had leadership qualities.
7. Elementary school librarians were not "covering" for teachers' planning periods.

Even so, we had to overcome considerable challenges, particularly in people's attitudes. At the close of the 1992-93 school year, we provided a staff development session for all elementary librarians and principals to prepare them for the transition to flexible access. The consultant who conducted the session, Nancy Dobrot, explained that two factors are key to the successful implementation of the practice: both the librarian and the principal have to commit fully to supporting it.

Was everyone in favor of the transition at first? The body language at the training session was easy to interpret: legs crossed, arms folded, facial expressions indicating apprehension. It would be a while before this trepidation would change to enthusiasm.

The morning session, conducted for both principals and librarians, began to break down some of the barriers. Dobrot provided background information about flexible access, explained the necessity of providing students with new research techniques, and gave a report on the improvement of students' test scores where flexible access had been implemented. Dobrot, library coordinator of the Northside Independent School District in San Antonio, was certain, based on her district's success, that a key factor in the improvement of academic achievement is flexible access to the library, and one of her strongest selling tools was communicating this certainty to the participants.

The afternoon session included only the librarians and the consultant. This was a dialogue of "what ifs." What if one teacher doesn't want to bring her class to the library? What if a book is not checked out properly while I am working with a class? What if some library skills are not taught? What if I can't manage a schedule that is not scheduled? The overriding "what if" I kept hearing (though inaudible) was, "What happens if I give up *my* control in the library?"

What the participants eventually learned is that control of the library is not theirs to give away. The library and access

Testing and Flexible Access

Texas, like many other states, has implemented a statewide test, the Texas Assessment of Academic Achievement (TAAS), to determine student achievement. This assessment both extends and expands previous statewide tests, broadening the scope of content eligible for testing and emphasizing skill areas that improve a student's ability to think independently, read critically, write clearly, and solve problems logically in a real-world context.

In 1989, the Texas state legislature mandated that the TAAS program be expanded to include the subject areas of science and social studies. The TAAS social studies assessment is composed of both performance-based tasks and machine-scorable items. This spring, as a part of the assessment, students were asked to research real-world problems and issues using information supplied in, among other sources, *library reference materials*.

What a splendid opportunity for school librarians. Texas librarians, just like Texas teachers, had a choice. They could whine about this lemon of a test, the lack of materials on Texas, and say that the research task was too difficult for fourth grade students—or they could start construction of their lemonade stand.

One of the lemons students were given was the topic to be researched. The assignment was to compare the cultures and ethnic groups of Texas. Although a study of Texas is part of the fourth grade curriculum, much of the information on this topic is written for junior high school students.

Librarians, as resource people, stepped to the front of the line. They located cookbooks, books of games, publications from state organizations, and magazines that could be used in researching this topic. Resources were shared from building to building. It was, as Winston Churchill would have said, "our finest hour."

to its resources belong to all of us. Control does not rest in the hands of the person who knows the password to override the automation system. If you want to understand the benefits of giving up control, of empowering students and teachers, read *Zapp! in Education*. (See list of references below.) This book beautifully communicates the power gained by giving up power.

Keeping the Ball Rolling

In addition to the initial training session, I met throughout the summer and fall with site-based teams, grade-level chairpersons, librarians, and principals to discuss flexible access. How does it work? How do we resolve problems?

This last question is key to continued success. I know that as soon as you change one element in a program, you will have problems. But, I urged staff members not to toss out the concept when the first glitches appeared. As school began, our

"three Rs" were evident as we continued with staff development at each campus: reinforcing, reassuring, and reminding the staff that we were providing a framework to help students be successful users of information, literature, and knowledge.

Reaping the Rewards

Despite the initial apprehension, the lessons we all learned about flexible access over the last school year have turned most of the skeptics into believers. Teachers and librarians who reluctantly accepted the challenge have openly stated that they cannot imagine going back to a rigid schedule. Many librarians have said this was a most difficult year, but also the most rewarding year of their careers.

Among the lessons we have learned:

1. Flexible access is beneficial to the learner. If we want to create an environment to improve student learning, flexible access provides the necessary foundation for improvement. Rigid scheduling of classes into the school library each day or week only serves to destroy a program designed to give students information-gathering skills, an appreciation of literature, and activities to foster lifelong reading and library usage.

2. What is taught and learned in the library must not be separate from what is taught and learned in the classroom. One must be in sync with the other.

3. Multiple activities can successfully co-exist in the library, and more than one grade level or class can access resources simultaneously.

4. Flexible access results in no loss of control by the librarian. Instead (and in some cases for the first time), the librarian has become a full-fledged, integral part of the teaching and learning process, playing an essential role in curriculum planning.

5. Flexible access helps create students who are excited about learning and are able and eager to complete research projects. Students now design their search strategies in the classroom and use their time on task more efficiently when they arrive in the library. Students dig deeper into information, exceeding the expectations of their teachers. We even heard one second-grader say that he needed to return to the library for a better reference book. "I checked out an information book, and it is *not* a good information book," he said. "There is no index!"

6. Even kindergarteners and first graders can find their way to the library and independently check out their own books. Research skills do not begin in the fourth grade with a statewide test. They begin in the earliest primary grades with the skills of alphabetical order. Independent learning begins when students are allowed to work independently.

7. A library under siege by learners has a higher noise level, is not always in perfect order, and contains some worn out resources. But, such a library is also providing an environment for learning as we have never before witnessed.

8. Flexible access gives full visibility to the creative capabilities of librarians. The role of the librarian as teacher, organizer, leader, resource specialist, reading consultant, and curriculum wizard becomes obvious through planning sessions with teachers and other new responsibilities.

Sharing the Success

In one year we have not become experts. Our program is still evolving. In this first year, however, teachers and librarians from our flexible access schools presented programs outlining our success and how we solved problems for two neighboring districts and for our School Board of Trustees. We are proud of what we have accomplished in the space of one year and hope we can spread that success to other schools and other districts.

Jawaharlal Nehru said: "There are two things that have to happen before an idea catches on. One is that the idea should be good. The other is that it should fit in with the temper of the age. If it does not, even a good idea may well be passed by."

The idea of flexible access is good. The temper of our age is testing and discovering ways to escape the trap of time. The Commission's report concludes: "American students will have their best chance of success when they are no longer serving time, but when time is serving them."

Recommended Reading on Flexible Access

Buchanan, Jan. *Flexible Access Library Media Programs*. Englewood, CO: Libraries Unlimited, 1991. ISBN 0-87287-824-1; $24.50.

Dobrot, Nancy L., and Rosemary McCawley. *Beyond Flexible Scheduling: A Workshop Guide*. Castle Rock, CO: Hi Willow Research and Publishing, 1992. ISBN: 0-931560-44-9; $20.00.

Kroeker, Lois Hokanson. "Behind Schedule: A Survey of West Texas Schools," *School Library Journal*, December 1989: 24-28.

Loertscher, David V. *Taxonomies of the School Library Media Program*. Englewood, CO: Libraries Unlimited, 1988. ISBN: 0-87287-662-4; $26.50.

Ohlrich, Karen Browne. "Flexible Scheduling: The Dream vs. Reality," *School Library Journal*, May 1992: 35-38.

References

Prisoners of Time. Report of the National Education Commission on Time and Learning. Washington, DC, 1994. ISBN 0-16-043140-9.

Byham, William C. *Zapp! in Education: How Empowerment Can Improve the Quality of Instruction, and Student and Teacher Satisfaction*. New York: Fawcett Columbine, 1992. ISBN: 0-449-90796-1.

Part Seven
Forty Years of Issues

The concerns and issues of the past forty years of library service to the young have been well-discussed in the pages of *SLJ*. Many established library leaders articulated thoughtful reactions and sound advice. Many newcomers who entered the national arena of professional librarianship during the past ten years made part of their entree the sharing of their point of view or their concerns with bright, fresh ideas, or a different stand. In addition, the writings of specialists in related fields: newspaper reporters, researchers, and authors have appeared to broaden the scope of the journal. All of these contributors are represented in this section.

Discussions of children's vs. parents' rights, access for the young, patterns of expenditures for school library media centers, the creation controversy, and reports of research on reading and television, young adult use of community libraries, and the changing role of the central children's room in the American public library all found their way to discerning readers of *SLJ* during the four decades. These articles and others reprinted in this section still speak to librarians in the 1990s.

Censors and Their Tactics

by Jack Nelson

Shortly after the Civil War, a New York publisher advertised "books prepared for Southern schools by Southern authors, and therefore free from matter offensive to Southern people."

But times have changed, or have they? Regional texts have given way to books competing for a national market, so now the trick is to offend as few people as possible. The result is that many books lack vitality and controversial subjects are treated superficially or not at all.

Textbook publishers do not avoid information about controversial subjects because they believe this is the best way to promote education. They do it because in some cases it is not just the best way, but the only way, they can sell their products.

The publishers face a dilemma. Every time they show the courage to explore controversial subjects in depth, they risk economic setbacks caused by censorship forces. Even relatively minor matters can cost them sales. For example, in Bastrop, La., recently the school board, learning that the Macmillan Company planned a new line of readers in 1965 which would ignore an old taboo and show white and Negro children playing together, banned the books and urged the rest of the state to do likewise.

No matter how you slice it, it's still censorship

In our research for *The Censors and the Schools*, Gene Roberts and I found that the pressures for the elimination or censorship of "unpleasant" ideas or facts often come from diametrically opposed forces.

This has been a big factor in the treatment of the Negroes' plight. On the one hand, segregationists clamor to keep out of books pictures of Negroes and whites together, or any mention of an integrated society. On the other hand, the National Association for the Advancement of Colored People has demanded that facts it considers objectionable be excluded from books. As the NAACP has said, the outstanding accomplishments of many Negroes should be dealt with factually and truthfully in school books. But the plight of a majority of Negroes, the discrimination they still face, also should be told, with all the "unpleasant" facts included.

Are we to alter or ban American classics in literature because they contain Negro stereotypes? Or are we to teach them in the context and times in which they were written? After NAACP pressure, the New York City Board of Education dropped Mark Twain's *Huckleberry Finn* as a reading text in elementary and junior high schools, because of a central character in the classic, "Miss Watson's big nigger, named Jim."

In the words of the New York *Times*, "The truth is that *Huckleberry Finn* is one of the deadliest satires that was ever written on some of the nonsense that goes with inequality of the races.

What happens when Huck's conscience begins to trouble him about running off with another person's slave? Huck decided that if he doesn't undo this crime by letting Miss Watson know where Jim is, he will go to hell. But then he gets to 'thinking over the trip down the river; and I see Jim before me all the time; in the day and in the night time, sometimes moonlight, sometimes storms, and we afloating along talking and singing and laughing . . . and how good he always was.' So Huck tears up the note he was going to send to Miss Watson and then says to himself 'all right, then I'll go to hell.'"

There is too much emphasis today on deleting from a student's experiences, rather than expanding them. There is justification for pressure to expand the selection of books in school libraries and to include more facts in school books. There is no justification for attempts to ban books and to eliminate facts because they do not conform to some group's ideas about minority group interests, Americanism, or whatnot.

Rightwing censors have the lead

While the NAACP and, on occasion, other minority interest groups have campaigned for censorship of books, by far, the greatest pressure today emanates from rightwing sources, and is based on political ideology. Unlike the NAACP and other crusading organizations which, for the most part, work independently of each other, the rightwing groups distribute each other's propaganda and carry out concerted campaigns.

In San Antonio, Texas, last year, a legislative committee investigating school books for "subversive" contents heard from a score of witnesses armed with propaganda which had originated in Washington, D.C. and at least six different states—from the Watch Washington Club (Columbus, Ohio), the Teacher Publishing Co. (Dallas, Texas), America's Future (New Rochelle, N.Y.), the Independent American (New Orleans, La.), the Church League of America (Wheaton, Ill.), and Education Information, Inc. (Fullerton, Calif.). Not long before the Texas hearing, materials from these same sources, plus literature from the Daughters of the American Revolution, the Parents for Better Education in California, the Coalition of Patriotic Societies in Florida, and other groups, were used in an attack on books in Meriden, Connecticut.

While some of these groups have different axes to grind, they all find a common cause in the Communist menace as a domestic threat, so that you find a Southern segregationist juxtaposed with a Northern industrialist in a campaign for censorship. A segregationist equates integration with Communism and obligingly includes in the same category the income tax, social security, organized labor and other irritants of the ultraconservatives. An industrialist sees a Red hand in federal taxes and control of industry and business, and he obligingly ascribes the same danger to the Supreme Court decision outlawing segregation. You find a physician worried about socialized medicine, a minister troubled by "obscenities," and ordinary citizens concerned about the patriotism of other citizens. And they all blame it on Communism and together put up a solid front for their demands to censor and ban texts and library books.

One day last year a reporter investigating the activities of censorship groups in Texas called on a news service bureau at the state capital to ask what it had on file on J. Evetts Haley, leader of a militant rightwing organization called Texans for America. The blasé answer was, "Nothing. You can't take Haley seriously. He's not worth keeping a file on." Yet Haley and his Texans for America led successful censorship campaigns against texts and school library books, and helped spark a legislative investigation that turned into a witch-hunt.

Like the news service bureau, most of the Texas press gave Haley relatively little attention. Perhaps they thought a man who publicly advocated "hanging" Chief Justice Earl Warren and smeared Southern Methodist University as "being tainted with leftwingers" should not be taken seriously.

Whatever the reason for the scant attention given to the Haleyites and others who have clamored for censorship, the result has been that well organized forces attacking books in Texas have operated with little organized opposition, free of public scrutiny. And they have forced alterations in many textbooks, the banning of others, and the banning of many school library volumes.

In many other states the same thing has happened to some degree in recent years. During the past five years, school books have come under fire in nearly a third of the state legislatures.

The press plays it cool, or sometimes plays along

Unfortunately, some newspapers have editorially acquiesced in, and even supported, some of the book censorship campaigns. While Amarillo (Texas) College and four Amarillo high schools withdrew from libraries 10 novels including four Pulitzer Prize winners, the Amarillo *News-Globe* lauded the move in a front-page editorial and proclaimed its own guide for censorship: " . . . sentences too foul to print in the *News-Globe* are too foul for school libraries."

The Los Angeles (Calif.) *Herald and Express* (now the *Herald-Examiner*), in a series of articles opposing the adoption of 13 school books, warned that many phrases and terms were un-American and pro-Communist. It even found a subversive music book in which a song, "Swing the Shining Sickle," which it called "a ditty from behind the Iron Curtain," was found to have replaced, of all things, "God Bless America," in the new edition of the book! The truth was that the song had been composed in 1897 as an American harvest song relating to Thanksgiving.

The Jacksonville (Ala.) *News*, supporting the DAR's current book-banning campaign in Alabama, printed an editorial which, at first glance, I thought must be poking fun at the Daughters. The *News* noted that the DAR "exposes to Alabama parents a sample of socialism, first-grade style, which appears as a story in one of the basic first-grade readers . . . *The New Our New Friends* by Gray, published in 1956 by Scott Foresman." The *News* said the story, called "Ask for It," contains "an objectionable and destructive lesson" about a squirrel named Bobby who was not willing to work.

It seems that Bobby watched a nut roll out of a birdhouse every time a redbird (the *News* set "redbird" in boldface type) would tap on the door. Bobby tried the redbird's trick and it worked and then, in the words of the story, he thought, "I know how to get my dinner. All I have to do is ask for it." The *News* was shocked. It very soberly asked its readers, "Have you ever heard or read about a more subtle way of undermining the American system of work and profit and replacing it with a collectivist welfare system? Can you recall a socialistic idea more seductively presented to an innocent child?"

A little censorship goes a long way

I have cited a few specific examples of censorship campaigns to illustrate the scope of the censorship problems in schools, which the public still fails to recognize. No state escapes the effects of attacks on school books. When censors in Mississippi force a publisher to alter a textbook, that book is sold, as altered, in Missouri and other states.

Last year the Texas State Textbook Committee told a publishing firm it could not market its history book in Texas schools if it did not drop Vera Micheles Dean's name from a supplementary reading list. The publisher agreed to this forced censorship and commented, "Imagine objecting to Vera Dean. But in a case like this, we will have to sacrifice her name in all books. It would be too expensive to make a special edition just for Texas."

Publishers have also deleted references to other authors in order to compete in the big Texas textbook market, and one publishing firm went so far as to say it was "not only willing but anxious to delete any references" to the names of authors whose loyalty might be successfully questioned by the Texans for America.

Fighting back

In many parts of the country, teachers and school librarians have felt the direct sting of censorship attacks. Gene Roberts and I found that in most cases where teachers and librarians fought back and the press adequately covered the controversy, censorship efforts were thwarted. The same is true, of course, in textbook battles; censors score their most notable successes when they operate with little public exposure.

In Georgia recently a high school teacher was dismissed for making available to his students John Hersey's wartime novel, *A Bell for Adano*. The press gave the matter full coverage, and the teacher fought back. John Hersey was interviewed and was quoted as saying the teacher "has been done a grave injustice by self-appointed censors of the type who are not interested in what a book tries to say as a whole, but are only interested in words taken out of context."

In a page-one column in the Atlanta *Constitution*, publisher Ralph McGill, defending the teacher and the book, wrote in part:

"It is likely the average adult mind, preoccupied with its own guilts and memories of childhood, tends to over-protect to the point of absurdity. High school students never have been and certainly are not in our time unaware of the words, deeds, stupidities, weaknesses, and shabbiness of their communities. They know these as they know those in the community whom they regard as admirable, honest and trustworthy. They know the phonies and they know the whispered gossip. So, lucky is the youngster who has a teacher who tries to interest young minds in reading well written books by established writers— rather than leaving them with no values and direction at all and, therefore, prey to the pornographic and the suggestive."

The issue of Hersey's book and the Georgia teacher was debated editorially and at education meetings. The teacher was reinstated.

A newspaper survey showed that, unfortunately, school librarians in three other Georgia cities removed the book from their shelves to avoid possible criticism during the controversy. And one public librarian said she had not withdrawn the book, but added, "I've put it in a special place and haven't told anyone about it. Isn't that a good way to handle it?" However, librarians, educators and the press did overwhelmingly defend the book, and those who removed it have now returned it to the library shelves.

The point is that in our pursuit of the truth we need to operate with full exposure. Too often a librarian or a teacher quietly discontinues the use of a book—or never begins the use of it—because of pressure. Those who exert those pressures, and who are in fact perverting freedom of the press, would wilt under public scrutiny.

What is behind rightwing attacks?

Today's pattern of rightwing censorship activities—much of it aimed at library volumes as well as textbooks—evolved after World War II, as much of the country began to drift away from New Deal principles. The critics began to cry collectivism and Communism if they discerned statements which in any way could be twisted or distorted by interpretation into favorable disposition of TVA, socialized medicine, FEPC legislation, the United Nations or other such topics.

The dominant forces that bring this pressure today include the DAR, the John Birch Society, the New Rochelle-based America's Future, and many smaller groups. These organizations, through pressure, have managed to force restrictions on what students may read. And the public still is largely apathetic about such pressure.

The DAR, which regularly mails out a list of almost 170 textbooks it has determined to be "subversive," operates as a respectable patriotic organization whose own values seldom are publicly examined. In 1959, when the DAR first began mailing out its incredible blacklist of books, the American Library Association's *Newsletter on Intellectual Freedom* (Dec. '59) warned of censorship activities and declared, "Of all the programs by organized groups, the DAR textbook investigation, at both the state and national level, was the most specific . . . and the most threatening."

The Daughters' attacks on books need to be evaluated in light of their constant concern about Communist infiltration in religion, mental health programs, public schools and colleges, the Federal Government, metropolitan government, urban renewal, Christmas cards, and all international activities including cultural exchange. It should also be taken into account that the DAR circulated a long list of literature from other ultraconservative groups attacking fluoridations, the US Supreme Court, the Peace Corps, immigration, the UN, the National Council of Churches, the public school system, the National Education Association, and other aspects of American life.

Putting the pressure in perspective

Pressure groups are an integral part of our society and I am not suggesting that any steps be taken—even if such were possible—to restrict their censorship activities. But these groups and their charges need to be put in perspective for the public.

When, for example, America's Future literature is used in an attack on school books, it is important for the public to know that this organization's fears that the public school system, not just textbooks, is purposely subverting the nation's youth. An official of that organization has written:

"No one who has watched closely what has been going on in our public school system in America these past two decades can escape the feeling that something drastic—and rather terrible—has happened to it. What is more, it is rather difficult to believe that it has happened by accident, that there has not been a planned, slyly executed, and almost successful attempt to deliberately undereducate our children in order to make them into an unquestioning mass who would follow meekly those who wish to turn the American Republic into a socialistic society."

Now any group is entitled to harbor such fears about this country's schools, and even to use such fears as the basis for attacks on books. But the public, in evaluating these attacks, also should be aware of their basis in order to determine whether the group is judging a book on its merits or on the basis of its own fears and prejudices.

I suggest it is important for students themselves—those in elementary and high schools as well as in colleges—to be educated to the threats against unfettered reading. Those who fear that American youths are not capable of judging for themselves what is right and what is wrong condemn the very system they profess to support.

September 1965

A Clear and Present Danger
The Books—Or the Censors?

by Harry Bach

On January 9, 1963, the Lowndes County, Georgia, school board banned John Steinbeck's *East of Eden* from all its school libraries because objecting parents had described it as "vulgar trash." Members of the school board admitted they had not read the book.

Out in California about two years ago, the El Segundo High School suspended *The Reporter* and *The New Republic* from classroom use. The board ruled that the two magazines would be kept in the school library for use only by those students who had a teacher's permission to do so. School board president Charles Schumann chastised six social studies teachers for raising the question of bookbanning, which "subjected the community and board to ridicule and criticism."

In Los Angeles in October 1962, a Mrs. Lucinda Benge protested to the board of education that these social science textbooks contained planned Communist subversion: the *Real People Series* used in the 7th grade; the *Present in Perspective* and *Background of World Affairs* used in 12th grade; *Documents of American History* and *Heritage of America* in the 11th grade.

And in Connecticut, in November 1961, two Meriden citizens charged that the city's parents were financing the "subversion"—anything tending to undermine "faith and allegiance"—of their own school-age children with books with such subtitles as "Industrialization Brings Problems as well as Benefits" and "Congress Attempts to Curb the Trusts"; and Pearl Buck's works, because she had in 1941 appealed for help "on behalf of the Russian peoples." In this case a vigilant press and education officials took a strong stand.

This brief listing does not begin to include the protests that emerge continually in our schools against *1984, Catcher in the Rye*, works by Hemingway and Baldwin, or the bills that periodically near enactment. According to Jack Nelson's *The Censors and the Schools*, textbooks came under fire between 1957 and 1962 in nearly a third of the legislatures in states as far apart as California, Illinois, Texas, and Florida. In Texas a 1957 school censorship bill to outlaw books at variance with "morality, truth, justice, or patriotism" was killed in committee. In Alabama a bill was actually passed in 1953 prohibiting the use of any textbooks whose authors, contributors, and even *cited* authors were not certified by publishers as having no Communist affiliations. The act, however, was declared unconstitutional a year later.

The Texas legislature in 1962 established a textbook investigating committee to hold public hearings on charges of possible subversion and to ensure that the "American history course in the public schools emphasize in the textbooks our glowing and throbbing history of hearts and souls inspired by wonderful principles and traditions."

What were some of their demands? To:

Banish books that describe the United States as a democracy rather than a republic;

Remove books with favorable descriptions of the New Deal, the United Nations, the Tennessee Valley Authority, and Federal aid to just about anything;

Reject Webster's *New World Dictionary* because its definition of Communism does not call it "a world menace";

Remove the name of Albert Einstein from textbooks;

Eliminate books which "glorify" government control of economy and use only those praising capitalism;

Protest books which give "casual" treatment to Douglas MacArthur, or contain too little material on Nathan Hale, Patrick Henry and David Crockett;

Oppose books which refer students to works by O'Neill, Pearl Buck, Faulkner, Hemingway, Sinclair Lewis, Dreiser, and the historians Charles Beard, Henry Commager, and Bernard DeVoto.

Age of Anxiety

That book censorship should center so strongly on our schools is, of course, neither new nor surprising. As Paul Blanshard has pointed out, every group which has strong convictions about certain values wants the schools to indoctrinate their children with these ideas. In one generation the slavocracy of the South gave Southern children a flattering picture of slavery and Southern values; in the next, leaders of Christian fundamentalism tried to eliminate the "heresy" of evolution. Then the anti-British segments had their day; and in the 1920's socialism was a subject to be omitted entirely from history texts—at the same time that our public utility corporations began a drive to rewrite textbooks so that children would appreciate American private enterprise.

Since the end of World War II, many Americans have been uneasy about revolutions across the world, the growth in power of the Soviet Union, and the tensions of the Cold War. At home we are trying to cope with the mammoth problems of racial integration and urbanization, with all their dislocating effects. Youth, enjoying a freedom and mobility they have never known before, seem to be getting out of hand. These challenges have aroused passions and anxieties.

In all times of heightened uneasiness, tension, and frustration, people eager for simple certitudes reach for the most vulnerable enemy—if no individuals or groups which challenge their values, then at least the expression of threatening ideas in published literature. Removing "subversive" books from a library will undermine the Communist conspiracy; taking "obscene" books off the shelves will end juvenile delinquency.

Philosophically, censorship, whether official (based on law) or unofficial (ranging from persuasion to implacable economic or political pressure helped by the police) rests on the belief that those who can identify evil or error should be empowered to prevent their dissemination. "All silencing of discussion," said John Stuart Mill, "is an assumption of infallibility. While everyone well knows himself to be fallible, few think it necessary to take any precautions against their own fallibility, or admit the supposition that any opinion of which they feel very certain may be one of the examples of the error to which they acknowledge themselves to be liable." Opponents of censorship may believe as firmly in the same ideas but recognize that diametrically opposed views have often been held with equal certitude.

Legally, the First Amendment protects the liberties of speech, press, assembly and religious practice from any curbs except those that are based on a "clear and present danger" of substantive evil, to be determined by the courts. But the premise that published literature can present a "clear and present danger" is not easily demonstrable. Hence, it cannot be unequivocally shown that books promote juvenile delinquency, sex perversion, sadism, and divers other evils. Yet what evidence there is suggests the contrary. According to George W. Smyth, one of the nation's outstanding children's court judges, reading *difficulty* was among the 878 factors that had affected the troubled children before him; no reading matter of any kind had a place in that exhaustive listing.

It is strange that parents, educators, and organized groups should protest a few words in a few recent novels and display complete indifference to the efforts of entire industries—fashion and advertising, perfume and cosmetics—which work daily to stimulate sexual appetites. An even more important consideration—if we really wanted to preserve our young people's morals, might be to abolish the draft, even the armed forces, which in one or two GI bull sessions will teach the uninitiated more than all the works of Henry Miller.

Democracy thrives on open discussion and criticism, and school books certainly are not sacrosanct. Yet most agitators, Paul Blanshard cites, are not responsible critics concerned with quality, but vocal extremists who find treasonous any criticism of the United States in the past or any suggestions of needed improvement.

Brainwashing in the High Schools by E. Merrill Root, billed as an objective analysis of American history textbooks paralleling the Communist line, seems to be their Bible. According to the book the United States is losing the Cold War, largely because history textbooks have "brainwashed" students by distorting the truth and indoctrinating them with collectivist ideas. The Daughters of the American Revolution, also in the vanguard of this battle, approved only 15 of the 214 titles they examined. They unearthed "subversion" in books on music, geography, arithmetic, and biology. In music they noted too many work tunes and folk songs, not enough native and national airs. Many books were pronounced "guilty of special pleading from the liberals and internationalists" because the listings for *supplementary* study cited Ruth Benedict, Theodore H. White, Alan Lomax, Langston Hughes, Margaret Mead, Louis Untermeyer, and Bill Mauldin.

In 1958 the "America's Future" organization launched its "Operation Textbook." The president, Rudolf K. Scott acknowledged generously that "no American textbook publishers have stooped to subversion. There is no evidence of that and I don't like extremism. The whole thing of liberalism in the textbooks has been an evolution, taking place over the past decade or two. But we are going to change that. We have already had some influence and we ultimately will exercise a very considerable force in textbook publishing. Publishers have had a free hand too long. There were no qualified persons criticizing them. Now we are hurting the publisher where it hurts—in his pocketbook."

By late 1962 "America's Future" had mailed thousands of copies of reviews of more than 200 high school texts to educators, school board members, and many organizations. The common theme of these reviews include protests against literature on income tax, Social Security, TVA, labor unions, the UN, Democratic presidents, etc.

Easy Way Out: Self-Censorship

Unfortunately, the groups who should be exercising responsibility often fail to present a united front. Jack Nelson blames our communications media for not giving full reports on textbook controversies and censorship pressures, a neglect that has permitted censorship activity to flourish with little organized opposition. Publishers have not been notably cooperative in meeting these attacks. In fact, book salesmen have sometimes exploited unfounded attacks on a competitor's texts to increase their own sales. Authors and publishers are often silent, and capitulate in order to preserve their market. The result has been the dull, lifeless uniformity and masking of controversy for which textbooks are notorious and have been repeatedly criticized by Albert Alexander, Henry S. Commager, and Mark M. Krug, and others. By glossing over controversial issues and omitting important contexts, these books keep students from thinking critically, gaining insight into historical or civic issues and learning the skills of problem solving which are needed for intelligent and democratic choice. It is democracy itself that is threatened here.

In her famous study, *Book Selection and Censorship*, Marjorie Fiske found a shocking prevalence of self-censorship among California librarians and school administrators. Two thirds of the personnel who had a voice in book selection reported cases where the controversiality of a book or author resulted in a decision not to buy; one fifth of the people interviewed habitually avoided material known to be controversial or which they thought might create debate. In other cases, books which occasioned complaint were put on closed shelves.

Librarians and administrators who capitulate to outside pressures forget that it is hard to draw the line once you've started. Thomas Braden, chairman of the California Board of Education, has commented: "If you ban one book," he says, "equally good reasons can be provided for banning another. If one citizen's complaint that a book is objectionable is satisfied by removing it, then it is fair to satisfy other citizens who may find other books equally objectionable. Censorship is a seamless web."

"How to Resist"

Librarians under attack have been relying increasingly on several basic documents: the *Library Bill of Rights*, the *Freedom to Read* statement, and the statement *How Libraries and Schools Can Resist Censorship*. The first, a magnificent charter of literary freedom, has been used effectively against censorship claques in a number of cities. As a statement of library policy, it insists on the responsibility to provide materials on all points of view, regardless of the political news or private lives of their authors. The Westchester *Freedom to Read* statement, prepared jointly by the American Library Association Council and the American Book Publishers Council in 1952, asserts the necessity for making available a wide diversity of views, including unorthodox opinions which publishers and librarians do not necessarily endorse.

An especially useful statement "How Libraries and Schools Can Resist Censorship" was adopted by the American Library Association Council in February 1952. Acknowledging differences between school and public library collections, the statement affirms the school's freedom in meeting its professional responsibilities to the whole community, and it suggests these measures.

1. Maintain a definite, *written* policy for selecting books and other materials, approved by some administrative authority, and understood by the staff. Establish this policy without regard to attack.
2. Keep a file of precedents for titles likely to be questioned.
3. Have a clearly defined method for handling complaints: a requirement that each complaint be written, signed, and referred to an appropriate administrative authority before any action is taken.
4. Maintain continuous good relationships with civic, religious, and educational bodies, and participate in these agencies of community leadership.
5. When a complaint arises, be sure to report all the facts to the administration. A teacher or school librarian will go through the principal to the superintendent and school board, with full written information.
6. Seek the support of the local press immediately ("The freedom to read and the freedom of the press go hand in hand.") and inform local civic organizations of the facts, enlisting their support where possible.
7. Base your defense on the *principles* of freedom to read and the professional responsibility of librarians and teachers, rather than on the individual book. Laws on obscene, subversive, and otherwise controversial materials are subject to court interpretation, and removal of any book from public access should rest with the *courts*. The responsibility for using books in the schools must rest with those responsible for the educational aims of the school.

Inform the ALA Intellectual Freedom Committee, the NEA Commission on Professional Rights and Responsibilities, and other national and state committees involved with intellectual freedom. Even local efforts may enlist the support of local agencies.

Whether or not attempts at censorship in the schools will let up in years to come is understandably impossible to predict. We do not know what the political climate will be; we do not know what the moral climate will be; we do not know whether the American public will have a better understanding of the problem. We do know, however, that with the help of more books on the subject of censorship and publications such as the *Library Bill of Rights*, the *Freedom to Read Statement*, and the statement on *How Libraries and Schools Can Resist Censorship*, school administrators, teachers and librarians ought to be able to stand up to their destructive critics. Rather than capitulate or impose self-censorship as they have done in too many cases, let them make it impossible for censorship to become a "prominent part of school life." If pressure groups are allowed to determine the content of books, teaching in American schools will degenerate into indoctrination. The antidote to authoritarianism is not some form of American authoritarianism; the antidote is free inquiry.

References

Paul Blanshard, *The Right to Read: the Battle Against Censorship*, Boston, Beacon, 1955

Thomas Braden, "Trouble with Censorship." *California Librarian*, October, 1963

Marjorie Fiske, *Book Selection and Censorship*, Berkeley, University of California Press, 1959

Jack Nelson, *The Censors and the Schools*, New York, Little Brown, 1963

E. Merrill Root, *Brainwashing in the High Schools*, New York, Devin Adair Co., 1958.

Censorship Statements

Freedom to Read Statement, prepared by the Westchester Conference of the American Library Association and the American Book Publishers Council, May 2-3, 1953

How Libraries and Schools Can Resist Censorship, adopted February 1, 1962 by the Council of the American Library Association (See *ALA Bulletin*, March, 1962

Library Bill of Rights, adopted June 18, 1948; National Council of Teachers of English Anti-Censorship Resolution, adopted November, 1954

The Students' Right to Read, NCTE, 1962.

Sexuality in Books for Children
An Exchange

by Barbara Wersba and Josette Frank

It occurs to me that what we're talking about is political. We're talking about the control of one group of people by another group of people: namely, children by adults. We are not merely discussing what children should read about sex, but what they should *do* about sex—and the fascism implied by this is a bit mind-boggling. Yet somehow children tolerate us and go on doing the same things generation after generation: which is reading those "forbidden" books, and indulging in sexual activity—and surviving.

I would like to see more sex in children's books—starting with picture books and going right up to the young adult novels—but I would like to see it treated a different way. I have a friend who sat down with his 9-year-old son recently, and because he felt anxious about the child, proceeded to tell him all about sexual intercourse, abortion, venereal disease, contraception, and homosexuality. After an hour, this tiny child turned to his father and said, "Oh, Daddy, I know all about *that* because we get it in school. What I really want to know was—is it terrific?" Now, the one thing we don't seem to be able to tell children is, is it terrific? Or is it awful? Or can it be both? Is it beautiful? Is it degrading? Is it ridiculous? What I'm looking for here is what Dr. Mary Calderone so perfectly described as The Mystery. That's what is absent in our children's books, because it is absent in our adult books—especially in this decade. I think it's typical of our culture that we have leapt directly from Puritanism into pornography; pornography being the meshing and interworking of parts rather than people. What we rarely find in American fiction is the meshing and interworking of minds. Sex in human beings is psychological, not genital. Sex in human beings either succeeds or fails because of mental response. Sex in human beings is emotional. People respond to one another because of what is in their heads—and hearts.

However, if you examine the sales figures to see what books are selling on this subject, you will find that they are called *The Sensuous Man, The Sensuous Woman*—and at the bottom of the barrel is Dr. Reuben's shabby work, *Everything You Always Wanted To Know About Sex*. I find these books alarming because Americans are very sexually naive, and many people take such information literally. In *The Sensuous Woman*, written by "J", who will not give her name for good reason, she tells the female reader that she (the reader) is probably an ugly upright piano who, through fine tuning, could become a Steinway grand. Dr. Reuben's book describes the human body as a complex electrical system, which short-circuits occasionally. He describes master switches and explosions and fuse problems. The most shocking thing about these books is not the sexual information they impart—but the fact that they are discussing human beings in terms of pianos and electricity. And the fact that these books go into dozens and dozens of printings—all the while talking about parts rather than people—is terrifying to me.

The next thing I want to say is that the so-called New Liberalism in children's books just isn't there. I think what *is* there is the Old Morality disguised as the New Sex. In the old books, the boy and girl would go for a soda after a movie; in the new books, they smoke a little pot and go to bed. It's all very contemporary and a few four-letter words are tossed in. But when you examine these books closely, you find that the morality is still the same; that a judgmental quality pervades. Those who might have been homosexual, of course, go straight; those who were promiscuous are guilty; and if an adult has been attracted to a child, heaven help him. Recently, to my great fascination, I read a young adult novel in which a child seduces an adult. The adult is not at fault, and the child very much needs contact with him. I was tremendously impressed with this book until the last page—when (gratuitously) the author kills her adult character. I thought, "My God, what a price to pay for one orgasm." This writer, whether she knows it or not, has killed her adult character to conform to the Old Morality. But her book will be considered representative of the New Sex.

Children's books only reflect adult books—and adult books only reflect the culture. And as a culture we are still profoundly Puritanical. Our sexual evolution has emerged as a kind of ghastly pragmatism, a do-it-yourself car repair manual. We're very practical, we Americans, we believe in fixing things. If the car won't work, take it back to the shop. If your body won't work, read *The Sensuous Woman*. The pragmatism involved in all this assumes that bodies can be fixed the way cars and vacuum cleaners can be fixed. They cannot, because sex is still a mystery—like God.

I believe that it is up to the children's writer to take a chance and delve deeply into the subject of sex—even if it gets him into trouble. Because children today are not the children we were. They have television. They have seen Lee Harvey Oswald die before their eyes. They have seen murder in Vietnam. I connect Vietnam with this because I find it very strange that I eat dinner while I watch the news: gazing at wholesale slaughter while eating a good meal. There is something in me that is obviously dehumanized—and this, in turn, connects with the dehumanization of our sexual attitudes. There's something terribly tired—or perhaps it's dead—in us, because if we were alive, we would watch the television news and weep. We would consider what we were doing to our children with this disguised sexual Puritanism, and we would grieve for them because *our* lives were spoiled by sexual Puritanism. What we need to explore is not outer space, but inner space. And it is up to the artists and writers to do this.

I was thinking before I came home today that the book I most enjoyed as a child was *Wuthering Heights*, and the film I most enjoyed was *Wuthering Heights*. And it also occurred to me that there is more sex in *Wuthering Heights* than in *Portnoy's Complaint*. *Portnoy's Complaint*, which was well described by one critic as the *Moby Dick* of masturbation, also deals with how to fix the parts of the car, how to repair the vacuum cleaner. *Wuthering Heights*, by contrast, is an old-fashioned book—and to me, a hundred times more erotic. So you can see that I am not asking for graphic explicitness in children's books, but for depth and truth. I think the 19th Century Romantics knew things about sex that we don't. They knew that it implied distance and strangeness; that compatibility and closeness killed eroticism. People in 19th Century literature always had immense difficulties to overcome, miles to cross, social barriers to leap. In this way their books are not only romantic, but erotic—and better than ours.

Perhaps the real fault with our culture is that we lack reverence for life; that we are more concerned with things than people; and that The American Dream has murdered our sensibilities with its insistence on material happiness. Sexual happiness—human happiness—these are areas yet to be explored.

by Josette Frank

There is nothing new about discussion of sex education for children. Books purporting to tell children the "facts of life"—as it was then polite to call them—began appearing about the turn of the century. They were, for their time, brave books, though their "facts" were largely buried in euphemisms, and they were designed to be read quietly to the young child, seated on mother's lap, at twilight.

What *is* new, however, is the appearance of fiction for the teenager, or younger, dealing candidly (if that isn't an understatement) with the sexual activities of other teenagers. Stories about early sexual experiences, out-of-wedlock pregnancies, abortion vs. adoption, unwanted marriages—the whole gamut—are presented in so-called "young adult" books which reach down in readability to ten-year-olds. Perhaps it is time, now, to pause and consider.

The Child Study Association was, I believe, the first nation-wide organization to discuss with parents the sex education of their children. When I first joined the staff of the Association in 1923, they had already published a pamphlet and conducted parent discussion groups on this then highly prohibited subject. We gave what must have been the first radio talk on sex education—and I well remember our battle with the station censors who deleted from our script the mention of any parts of the body and especially the word "masturbation." We lost that battle but we gave the talk anyway, grateful that they allowed us to mention the word "sex." So much for history! In the intervening years we've learned that sex education involves more than words, more than "facts."

That the Child Study Association especially welcomes books for children which help them understand themselves and their world is evidenced by the fact that, ever since 1942, we have given an annual award to a book dealing with some of the realities children face in growing up. At that time (1942), when war and world holocaust were lapping at their feet, their books were filled with nothing but sweetness and light. The award was intended to emphasize the need for books about realities.

Now that this tide has turned, bringing flotsam and jetsam in books "telling it like it is" we have considered whether this award is now redundant. Yet, exactly because this new free-wheeling literature of realism is so uneven, it now seems urgent to honor those books which, in presenting realities and life problems, offer positive values and leave their young readers with hope and faith in themselves and in others.

Here I should explain that the Children's Book Committee of the Child Study Association, through whose heated weekly discussions many of these books pass, considers the age limit of its selected list as about age 13, since the older teens are already browsing in adult literature. This seems to put many of the so-called "young adult" books over-age for our listing. I confess, though, that sometimes we wonder whether, in deciding that a particular book is beyond our age range, we are merely copping out on a difficult decision.

On this point I want to quote from a paper by Dr. Mary Calderone. Pleading for greater freedom in sex education, she said, "learning about sex, being sexual and feeling sexual can and must be harmonized within the individual. At some time the thoughts, the feelings, the attitudes and the behavior must all come together in a congruent whole." For me the key phrase here is: *At some time*. And this is our dilemma. What time? And for which child? You look at a girl of 13 or 14 and you wonder. How much vicarious sexual experience is she ready for? How much can she take, or *should* she take? How much is too much? If she identified with the girl in *You Would If You Loved Me* (Avon, 1969) she is led to a very high point of sexual stimulation indeed. What will she do with her feelings thus aroused? Certainly it is reality. It is informative. It is authentic. But what will it do for the young reader? Actually, the girl in this story is a conscious tease. She comes through with her virginity intact and feels very virtuous therefore. But what about the boy? The author fails to make clear the real moral question of relationships here, and the reader is left with a false and confusing set of values.

We know that as adults we have to wrestle with our own

hang-ups in viewing young people's reading. But we cling to the hope of offering boys and girls something of positive value in their books. One asks of each book not, will it *damage* the young reader but rather, will it *benefit* him or her, and in what way? "Benefits" may come in many forms: information, emotional satisfaction, escape, expanded horizons, or just plain fun. Since the young cannot read *everything* in the limited time available, we hope the books they do read will be those which "stretch the mind and spirit."

Therefore when, in an otherwise conventional adventure tale, we come suddenly, without warning, to an episode in which a 13-year-old girl teaches a boy the way of what she calls "mating," we wonder how this can profit the young reader. Is it information he or she needs or can use at this point in maturing? Is it an integral part of the story or is it dragged in for titillation? When we give this book, or others like it, to a young teenager, are we, in effect, saying "Try it—you'll like it"?

In the last analysis, the criteria I would apply in the acceptability of books of high sexual content concerns the integrity of their purpose, their authenticity, their moral and social validity, and most important, the resolutions they offer. This is not to call for a so-called "happy ending." Rather it is to ask that the characters—especially those with whom the young reader will identify—come through their experiences, however grim or seamy, with a feeling that somehow he or she will cope. I believe it is not a healthy resolution when the heroine ends up on the human junk pile. The scare technique, I believe, profits the young reader nothing.

In contrast, I think of John Donovan's *I'll Get There—It Better Be Worth the Trip* (Dell, 1971). Here, for all their searing life experiences, there is health in both these boys—and the reader comes away knowing they have matured and learned to cope with their difficulties. Their homosexual experience is real, it is threatening and painful. It is handled with grace and insight. And the boys' own reactions are healthy and reassuring.

I think also of Irene Hunt's gently adolescing heroine in *Up a Road Slowly* (Follett, 1966). When, by chance, she comes upon a couple making love in the bushes—a boy and girl she knows—she steps back both physically and emotionally, with a feeling that she is not ready for this intimate knowledge. So the young reader can also step back from this episode, so delicately handled, reassured that it has left no scar on the girl they have come to care about.

Dr. Mary Calderone remembers from her own childhood a drama in which two adolescents, as she describes them, "took that one last step to each other and touched only their palms together, arms spread wide." And she says, "in those two moments I knew with my entire self what sex was all about." I doubt this experience would have been enhanced for the little girl she was then by a blueprint of sexual intercourse.

Reviewers frequently stress the "moral dilemma" faced by the characters in these books, and therefore shared with their readers. I have some question whether the dilemma is not *social* rather than *moral*. We are told that puberty tends to come at an earlier age in girls today. Certainly social sophistication does, too, to both boys and girls. We know there are cultures in which, at the onset of puberty, sexual intercourse is acceptable, even encouraged. But our culture makes no place, no provisions for its consequences. We have the sad story of 12- and 13-year-old girls coming to clinics for abortions. We have, too, the painful knowledge of venereal disease appearing in ever younger children.

True, these same children are exposed at all ages to movies, television, paperbacks, and news media setting forth lurid details of sexual activity and aberrations. Our children do not wear blinders. And of course they are curious. Yet in these media, as in the adult books earlier generations foraged in, they are confronted by the sexual behavior of adults. Here are feelings they don't share, people with whom they don't identify. In today's juvenile books it is *children* who are having the sexual experiences, experimenting with sexual behavior. It seems to me that here the impact is more real, more immediate, more compelling.

I confess I am thinking in terms of shielding children from unnecessary, premature, unhealthy sexual stimulation, beyond their present maturity and capacity to manage. Just when and how that capacity arrives cannot be defined for all children. Their exposure to sexual behavior in the omnipresent media most certainly hastens their information and their sophistication. Whether it hastens their *maturity* is an unanswered question. So also is the question of the effect of these sexual exposures on their healthy growth in attitudes and perceptions. This applies to books, and other mass media.

A father recently told me that he had accidentally come upon, in his 12-year-old daughter's bathrobe pocket, several of those so-called "bathroom" joke books—not juveniles, of course. He wasn't surprised, and neither was I. We agreed that she was probably enjoying the very clandestine aspect of it. But we agreed, too, that these are *not* the books her parents will give her.

Rightly or wrongly, I am convinced that there is a difference in impact between a book a child happens upon, or reads surreptitiously (like the forbidden books of my childhood), and one that is received with *commendation* from a parent, teacher or librarian—a so-called "approved" or recommended book. Therefore I feel that we adults—and this includes especially writers and editors—have a grave responsibility in commending books to children's attention, to give them books whose positive value we believe in. I do not consider this censorship. The children are free to read other books too, or to reject our suggestions.

But I dare to believe that children—even young teenagers—are impressed by the approval of adults whom they respect, and by the values they stress. Maybe the wish is father to the thought. Maybe I am whistling in the dark!

Certainly I do not have the answers to the serious questions I have raised here. But I am sure we should give them thought. The sexual maturing of the young in our culture today isn't all that simple.

Black English
The Politics of Translation

by June Jordan

We are in a political situation in America where, on the one hand, there are the powerful who control and, on the other hand, there are the powerless who pay the consequences.

In America, we are knuckling under the rapid loss of freedom of speech, freedom of the press. Too many people in this country deliberately seek to enforce a homogenized, complacent, barbarous society where *standard* means *right*, where *right* means *White*. Therefore, *non*standard means *sub*standard, and means *wrong*, and means *dangerous*, and will be punished, even unto the death of the spirit.

We are talking about power: and poetry and books—history books, novels, what-have-you—none of these can win against the schools, the teachers, the media, the fearful parents, and the elite of this country, unless we understand the power of these politics.

In America, the politics of language has become obvious around the globe: it is American power that invented and imposed upon our minds the Vietnam vocabulary of "making peace by making war," of murdering people and calling that "pacification," of "advisory personnel," "protective reaction," and even the 1972 Twelve Days of Christmas "carpet bombing." There is an obscenely long list of the lies and the euphemisms that have been printed and telecast in perfectly standard, grammatical, White English.

In America, the politics of language, the wilfull debasement of this human means to human communion has jeopardized the willingness of young people to believe *anything* they hear or read.

And what is anybody going to do about it? I suggest that, for one, we join forces to cherish and protect our various, multifoliate lives against pacification, homogenization, the silence of terror, and standards that despise and disregard the sanctity of each and every human life.

The Functions of Language

We can begin by looking at language. Because it brings us together, as folks, because it makes known the unknown strangers we otherwise remain to each other, because it is the naming of experience and, thereby, a possession of experience, and because names/language make possible a social statement of connection and lead these connections into social reality— for all these reasons, and more, language is a process of translation. Language is a process of translation whereby we learn and we tell who we are, and what we want, and what we need, believe, or why we tremble, or hide, or kill, or nurture and love. This is a political process, a process taking place on the basis of who has the power to use, abuse, accept or reject the words—the lingual messages—we must attempt to transmit to each other and/or against each other.

As a poet and writer, I deeply love and I deeply hate words. I love the infinite evidence and change and requirements and possibilities of language: every human use of words that is joyful, or honest, or new because experience is new, or old because each personal history testifies to inherited pleasures and/or inherited, collective memories of peril and pain.

But as a Black poet and writer, I hate words that cancel my name and my history and the freedom of my future. I hate the words that condemn and refuse the language of my people in America: I am talking about a language deriving from the Niger-Congo family of languages. I am talking about a language that joins with the Russian, Hungarian, and Arabic languages, among others, in eliminating the "present copula"— a verb interjected between subject and predicate. Or, to break that down a bit, I am talking about a language that will tell you simply "They Mine." (And, incidentally, if I tell you, "they mine," you don't have no kind of trouble understanding exactly what I mean, do you?)

As a Black poet and writer, I am proud of our Black, verbally bonding system born of our struggle to avoid annihilation—as Afro-America self, community, and culture. I am proud of this language that our continuing battle just *to be* has brought into currency. And so I hate the arrogant, prevailing rejection of this, our Afro-American language. And so I work, as poet and writer, against the eradication of this system, this language, this carrier of Black-survivor consciousness.

The Politics of Black English

The subject of "Black English" cannot intelligently separate from the subject of language as translation and translation as a political process distinguishing between the powerless and the powerful in no uncertain terms. Here are a few facts to illustrate my meaning.

1) Apparently, "Black English" needs defense even though it is demonstrably a language: a perfectly adequate, verbal means of communication that can be understood by any but the most outrightly standard racist.

2) On the other hand, where is the defense, who among the standard, grammatical, White English mainstreamers feels the need, even, to defend his imposition of his language on me and my children?

3) "Thou know'st the mask of night is on my face.
Else would a maiden blush bepaint my cheek
For that which thou has heard me speak tonight.
Fain would I dwell on form, fain, fain deny what I
have spoken: but farewell compliment!
Dost thou love me? I know thou wilt say 'Ay.'
And I will take thy word; yet, if thou swear'st
Thou mayst prove false; at lovers' perjuries,
They say, Jove laughs."
(*Romeo and Juliet* Act II, Scene II)

Now that ain hardly no kind of standard English. But just about every kid forced into school has to grapple with that particular rap. Why? Because the powers that control the language that controls the process of translation have decided that *Romeo and Juliet* is necessary, nay, *indispensable*, to passage through compulsory, public school education.

4) "You be different from the dead. All them tombstones tearing up the ground, look like a little city, like a small Manhattan, not exactly. Here is not the same. Here, you be bigger than the buildings, bigger than the little city. You be really different from the rest, the resting other ones. Moved in his arms, she make him feel like smiling. Him, his head an Afro-bush spread free beside the stones, headstones thinning in the heavy air. Him, a ready father, public lover, privately at last alone with her, with Angela, a half an hour walk from the hallway where they start out to hold themselves together in the noisy darkness, kissing, kissed him, kissed her, kissing.
Cemetery let them lie there belly close, their shoulders now undressed down to the color of the heat they feel, in lying close, their legs a strong disturbing of the dust. His own where, own place for living made for making love, the cemetery where nobody guard the dead."
(*His Own Where*, first page)

Now that ain no standard English, either. Both excerpts come from love stories about White and Black teenagers, respectively. But the Elizabethan, nonstandard English of *Romeo and Juliet* has been adjudged as something students should take and absorb. By contrast, Black, nonstandard language has been adjudged as *sub*-standard and even injurious to young readers.

I submit that these judgments are strictly political and that they should be recognized as political and resisted, accordingly.

But language and the politics of translation affect more than the censorship of literature; we are talking about power, and about the perpetuation of power.

White Power

In the compulsory public school situation, demonstration of such power is a daily event: Black and White children enter the so-called educational system. Once inside, the White child is rewarded for his mastery of his standard, White English—the language he learned at this mother's White and standard knee. But the Black child is punished for his mastery of his nonstandard Black English. Moreover, the White child received formal instruction in his standard English, and endless opportunities for the exercise and creative display of his language. But where is the elementary school course in Afro-American language, and where are the opportunities for the *accredited* exercise, and creative exploration, of Black language?

The two languages are not interchangeable. They cannot, nor do they attempt to communicate equal or identical thoughts, or feelings. And, since the experience to be conveyed is quite different, Black from White, these lingual dissimilarities should not surprise or worry anyone.

However, they are both communication systems with regularities, exceptions, and values governing their word designs. Both are equally liable to poor, good, better, and creative use. In short, they are both accessible to critical criteria such as clarity, force, message, tone, and imagination. Besides this, standard English is comprehensible to Black children, even as Black English is comprehensible to White teachers—supposing that the teachers are willing to make half the effort they demand of Black students.

Then what is the difficulty? The problem is that we are saying language, but really dealing with power. The word "standard" is just not the same as the word "technical" or "rural" or "straight." *Standard* means the rule, the norm. Anyone deviating from the standard is therefore "wrong." As a result, literally millions of Black children are "wrong" from the moment they begin to absorb and imitate the language of their Black lives. Is that an acceptable idea?

As thing stand, consequences of childhood fluency in Afro-American language are lamentably predictable; reading problems that worsen, course failure in diverse subjects dependent on reading skills, and a thoroughly wounded self-esteem. Afterwards, an abject school career is eclipsed by an abject life career. "Failing" English (Standard English) merely presages a "failure" of adult life. This, I submit, is a deliberate, political display of power to destroy the powerless.

Solutions

This punishment of Black children will continue until the legitimacy of Black language is fully acknowledged by all of us, Black and White. That will mean offering standard English as simply *The Second Language*. It will mean calling standard English studies "Second Language Studies" wherever that description accurately applies.

A sincere recognition of Black language as legitimate will mean formal instruction and encouragement in its use within the regular curriculum. It will mean the respectful approaching of Black children, *in the language of Black children*. It will mean an end to illegitimate, political use of language studies against Black life.

It is true that we need to acquire competence in the language of the powerful: Black children in America must acquire competence in standard English, if only for the sake of self-preservation. But I do not understand how anyone supposes that you will teach a child a new language by scorning and ridiculing and forcibly erasing his old, first language: all of his names for all the people and events of his black life prior to his entry into school.

I am one among a growing number of Black poets and writers dedicated to the preservation of Black language within our lives, and dedicated to the health of our children as they prepare themselves for life within this standard, White America which has despised even our speech and our prayers and our love.

As long as we shall survive Black, in this White America, we and our children require and deserve the power of Black language, Black history, Black literature, as well as the power of standard English, standard history, and standard, White literature.

To the extent that Black survival fails on these terms, it will be a political failure; it will be the result of our not recognizing and not revolting against the political uses of language to extinguish the people we want to be and the people we have been.

Politics is power. Language is political. And language, its reward, currency, punishment and/or eradication—is political in its meaning and in its consequence.

Recently, a White woman telephoned to ask me to appear on her television program; she felt free to tell me that if I sounded "black" then she would not "hire" me; language is power. That woman is powerful if she feels free to reject and strangle whoever will not mimic her—in language, values, goals. In fact, I answered her in this way: "You are a typical racist." And that is the political truth of the matter, as I see it, as I hope you will begin to see it; for no one has the right to control and sentence to poverty anyone—because he or she is different and proud and honest in his or her difference and his or her pride.

There is a need to understand Black language, per se: A young friend of mine went through some scarifying times, leaving her homeless. During this period of intense, relentless dread and abuse, she wrote poems, trying to cope. Here are two lines from her poetry: *"What have life meanted to me"* and, *"You are forgotten you use to existed."*

There is no adequate, standard English translation possible for either expression of her spirit because they are intrinsically Black language cries of extreme pain so telling that even the possibilities of meaning and existence have been formulated in a past tense that is emphatic, severe.

I deeply hope that more of us will want to learn and protect Black language. If we lose our fluency in our language, we may irreversibly forsake elements of the spirit that have provided for our survival.

Black language is not A Mistake, or A Verbal Deficiency. It is a system subsuming dialect/regional variations that leaves intact, nevertheless, a language that is invariable in fundamental respects. For example:

A) Black language practices minimal inflection of verb forms. (e.g.: *I go, we go, he go*; and *I be, you be, we be*, etc.) This is nonstandard and, also, an obviously more logical use of verbs. It is also evidence of a value system that considers the person/subject—the actor—more important than the act.

B) Consistency of syntax: for example, in Black English/Black language, the imperative case, the interrogative case, and the simple declarative case all occur within the same structural pattern. (e.g. *You going to the store*.) Depending on tone, that is a statement of mere fact, or a command, or a question.

C) Infrequent, irregular use of the possessive case. Therefore, in Black language, you say, "they house" at least as often as you might say, "their house."

D) Clear, logical use of multiple negatives within a single sentence, to express an unmistakably negative idea. (e.g. *You ain gone bother me in no way at no time no more, you hear?*)

E) Other logical consistencies, such as: *ours, his, theirs*, and, therefore, *mines*.

Black language is a political fact suffering from political persecution. Black language and Black literature are political facts persecuted by the same powerful political people in this country who feel bold to say, in perfectly standard, grammatical, White English: " . . . let each of us ask not just what will government do for me but what I can do for myself."

(Of course that declaration is quite entirely at odds with another, perfectly standard, American concept: " . . . government of the people, by the people, and for the people.") As the President has since made plain, his standard English exhortation to self-help means the deadly reduction of government aid to every program against poverty, poor housing, inadequate education, and poor health.

This is a time when those of us who believe in people, first, must become political, in every way possible; we must devise and pursue every means possible for survival as the people we are, as the people we want to become. For Afro-Americans, this certainly means that we must succeed in the preservation of our language.

Let us cherish its long service to us, as a people.

Let us halt the mutilation of abilities to manage the world through language. Let us cease the destruction of one language for the sake of another. Let us present standard English as merely a second language, whenever that is the case. And let us undertake these goals with full awareness that the stakes are truly the political stakes of the power to kill or the power to survive.

And, as for the children: let us welcome and applaud and promote the words they bring into our reality; in the struggle to reach each other, there can be no right or wrong words for our longing and our needs; there can only be the names that we trust and we try.

Book Reviews: Before & After

Zena Bailey Sutherland

On Reviewers

I think it is very important to realize that what goes into a review depends in part on the time in which the review is written as well as on the policies of the publication and the audience for whom it's published. Reviewers change in response to the times. I doubt that any reviewers achieve perfection. If we are honest, we can assess our strengths and weaknesses in much the same way we assess the strengths and weaknesses of a book.

On Requisites

A reviewer should have, I think:

- a wide acquaintance with children's literature
- the stability to remain objective
- the ability to see each book as a whole and report its balance of strengths and weaknesses
- the capacity to understand the uses to which a book will be put without becoming preoccupied with potential usage at the expense of consideration for literary quality. To me, literary quality is the most important aspect of a book.

On Content

You describe the book. You say whether or not you like it and why. You point out the strengths and weaknesses you see. You analyze it critically. That's it. Then, the librarian decides.

On Criticism vs. Reviewing

There has been a great deal of discussion, in print and wherever reviewing is talked about, on the difference between reviewing and criticism. I think there are some differences and some overlap. A critic is more concerned with an intensive personal examination of a book (or an aspect of a book) as literature. A reviewer is more concerned with telling the audience for his or her reviews what a given book is about, what factors made the book good or bad.

On Objectivity

A question I'm often asked is: "Doesn't it make it difficult to review a book objectively if the author or the editor is a friend?" It sure does. But, I think it is incumbent on the reviewer to be perfectly honest about every book. You don't need to review with your nails sharpened. You may be misguided, but you must always be honest.

On Bias

Reviewers have to watch themselves for bias toward a favored cause. For instance, if we are militantly feminist or espouse any other philosophy, we must sit back from our reviews and ask, "Is this book *really* good or is it because it promotes one of my pet causes that I think it is so good?"

On Censoring

Reviewers censor consciously or unconsciously in several ways. The most obvious form of censorship—although we prefer to call it "selection"—can be in what we do *not* choose to review.

Obviously, *Horn Book, Booklist*, and *The Bulletin of the Center for Children's Books* (for which I write the reviews) cannot review every book that's published. Therefore, there are a lot of books we don't review. As a result, I do a great deal of nail-biting about whether or not the omission of those books I haven't reviewed will be construed as censorship.

For instance, a new shipment of books comes in and I see that among ten titles, one of them is a book about new frontiers in medicine. Well, O.K., I know I'm going to do that one, not only because I like the subject, but because I feel I know something about it. (I started out as a premedical student, but the Depression killed that. I went to library school to become a medical librarian and I took a course in children's books and was hooked on books permanently.) If the rest of the shipment includes nonfiction on subjects on which I have varying amounts of knowledge, my choice of the one on medicine nevertheless has an element of censorship in the choosing.

There can be censorship involved in the way we review controversial books. I'll illustrate this with a story on myself. You know *Freddy's Book* (J. Neufeld, Random, 1973). You cannot read *Freddy's Book* without seeing the word "fuck" 500 times. Now how can you honestly write a review about this book—whether you are going to praise it, take the middle road and simply comment, or scathingly object to it—without using the word the book is all about? Well, I did. O.K., I weaseled in the review. Later that year, I was speaking at the University of Arizona and the program chairman asked me if I would talk about *Freddy's Book* since she was using it with her class in children's literature. I said I would.

Well, I was very conscious of the fact that I had weaseled in the review, but faced with an audience, I still felt sort of hesitant about using the word. The program chairman wanted me to, but I decided next morning to ask some older person. Male. (If that makes any difference.) He patted me reassuringly and said "I'm sure you can find some way around it." So I found some way around it, again. In the question period, one young man rose and asked, "How do you people [meaning people of my age] expect to understand us and the kids who follow us, to whom the word "fuck" means ever less, if you can't bring yourself to put it in a review or mention it when you're talking about it?" So, called on to defend the honor of my generation, I said, wording it perhaps too hastily, "Oh! I say 'fuck' all the time!" Guess who got in the papers.

Actually, when I wrote that review, when I weaseled, I was aware of the fact that I was being a censor. The self-awareness has to be there before you can start the process of stopping yourself.

On Prejudicial Reviewing

A reviewer can prejudice review users and throw the wrong light on a book by including one fact certain to attract attention. For example, at the 1974 National Council of Teachers of English Conference, an author told me she was very disappointed because she had written what she thought was the first children's book in which the mother of the child protagonist had a lesbian relationship; that is, the mother had separated from her husband and was living with another woman. The author said nobody got it. I said, "Yeah, somebody got it." I had thought seriously about whether or not to put my adult conclusions about this living arrangement in my review. I decided not to because it really wasn't what the book was about. Mentioning it would merely mislead users of the review, leading them possibly to talk about this suspected aspect exclusively.

Another form of prejudicial review statement is discussing a book's merit in terms of its price. I never say, and most reviewers won't say, "This used to be $3.95, but now at a higher price, it isn't worth it." Readers can judge what their budgets can bear.

Then, there is the prejudicial review commentary urged on reviewers by librarians. I've talked to other review editors over the last year and found that we've all experienced an increase in the sort of correspondence that begins, "I have always read and trusted your reviews, *but* . . . ." and on to a request to note the presence of any profanity. This is one of those cases where I think you can give, in a review, a wrong impression of the book and throw the review off balance.

The first such letter I ever got complained of blasphemy I'd failed to mention in my review of *Ellen Grae* (Vera & Bill Cleaver, Lippincott, 1967). Well, it just goes to show what a low character I am, but I couldn't remember any and I had to look it up. What I found was that an older girl, boarding in the same house as Ellen Grae, is just old enough to have be-

come conscious of her sex role in the old-fashioned way—sending off for cold cream samples, making up, trying to be sophisticated. One of her attempts at sophistication is to say, "Oh, God!" whenever she can. In this book the phrase contributes to characterization. I thought the characterization among the strengths of this book. To label this use of dialogue blasphemy would have skewed the review. I simply had to disagree with the librarian who wrote the letter about this sort of labeling as the function of the reviewer.

Each of us—editor, reviewer, librarian, teacher, or parent—has a different idea of what "protecting" children means. Each of us has a point at which we may say a book has gone too far; what we differ about is where that point is. And as long as each of us must make a judgment, whether the decision is to mention or not, to publish or not, to buy or not, it is incumbent on us to be aware that we are susceptible to playing a censorious or prejudicial role.

On Coverage

In 1967, I analyzed four children's book review sources used by most librarians—*Booklist, The Horn Book, The Bulletin of the Center for Children's Books* and *SLJ*. I turned up one statistic that interested me then and does still. Of the close to 3000 new children's books that had been published during the previous year, only 94 titles had been reviewed by all these review publications. It's a statistic better described as appalling rather than interesting. Although I can see all the problems attached to it even as I suggest it, I say that we need some sort of cooperative distribution of reviewing among the review sources. It really seems a shame that so many books get so little coverage.

There was a study done at the Graduate Library School of the University of Chicago by Judy Goldberger in which librarians were asked to talk about what they felt were the gaps in review coverage. Here's what they came up with:

- inadequate reviewing of foreign language books
- not enough reviews of new books about minority groups—especially Spanish surname, American Indian, and European-American ethnic groups.
- scanty reviewing of books from new or alternative presses
- too few reviews of books considered for their potential use by the visually handicapped
- not enough identification of high-interest, low-reading level books
- too few reviews of books not recommended for purchase
- too few suggestions for and too little comment on use of books in the home
- the time lag between the publication of books and the appearance of reviews.

All review agencies are concerned all the time about this lag. I must admit that I know many people in publishing and in library service who feel very strongly about it and I know why they do. I've never been able to see what the rush is. Children's books stay in print a long time and are read by succeeding waves of new children to whom the books are new. However, most of us try very hard to make our reviews as current as possible.

Since there is a clamor from publishers for current reviews, I wonder why it takes them so long to get new books to the libraries that order them. Since there is also a clamor from librarians for current reviews, I wonder why it takes them so long to get new books they've received to the shelves. All of the procedures—review scheduling, book ordering, shelf preparation—are very complicated. But, it's not just review scheduling procedures that cause the lag.

On Self-Perception

I guess, when I look at all of the problems of the children's book reviewer and all the pleasures (because it is a pleasure to see the new books), I think the advice I have for all who review, for all who select, is: We had better take our work seriously; we had better not take *ourselves* too seriously.

Volunteers? Yes!

by Elfrieda McCauley

I can recall peering suspiciously across my desk at our school system's first volunteer candidate, hoping my misgivings weren't showing. At the time—it was the late '60s—I didn't anticipate that she was the harbinger of 236 others who would be contributing upwards of 10,000 hours annually to the media services of the Greenwich Public Schools a few years later. Our small school system had just weathered a grueling inquisition at the hands of the town budget committee over an increased book budget request. Was she for us or against us? She had been last year's PTA president in one of our schools, she had the usual scout, church, Junior League, and American Assn. of University Women (AAUW) background, her husband was well-connected, and she knew at least two board of education members by first name. I wondered what she had in mind by volunteering to "Gray Lady" in my library for two mornings a week?

I worried about her motives but of course I welcomed her aboard. Looking back, I know now that any other decision would have been futile resistance on my part against an upswelling of popular involvement in the concerns of public education. This involvement by members of the community in local schools had its official beginning only a few years before and was on its way to becoming a full-blown movement of two million participants by the mid '70s. Interviews like the one I had described were taking place all across the land. And for the most part, they ended like mine did. In a single decade the number of volunteers in education has grown to upwards of 2.5 million and is still growing.

Last year, in the Greenwich Public Schools (it's suburban with 16 schools, 750 teachers, 11,000 students), 2,097 volunteers contributed a total of 50,752 hours to public education. At a cost to the school system of about $9000 and a little loving care, the dollar value of this auxiliary service at the modest rate of $3.50 an hour, was $177,632.

Volunteer Services

Volunteers tend circulation desks and perform technical processing tasks in the media centers. They create bulletin boards, letter directional signs, dry mount and laminate instructional materials, bind periodicals. They shelve books, compile booklists, tell stories, play games, help children find books, copy tapes, write overdue notices, process art prints and slides. In prescriptive learning centers they supervise the use of controlled readers, language masters, spellbinders, and other reading instruction devices. One of our volunteers serves as the adult advisor to a student book selection committee. About 70 have been intensively trained to operate closed-circuit television equipment, to tape off air, and operate video cameras and recorders in the classroom.

An additional 125 volunteer tutors give individual attention to children not performing well in group learning situations. Still others assist in the administration, health, and guidance offices—checking up on absenteeism, for instance. They help supervise field trips and athletic events. They are visiting lecturers in the classrooms, kindergarten assistants, homework helpers, tutors to children for whom English is a second language.

Most of our volunteers are women who may have children still in the system or recently graduated. They also include high school and college students and senior citizens. We have had an airplane pilot who gave us his free time, and a fireman who worked the night shift and shared his days with us. Business and professional persons and practitioners in the arts are listed in a human resource file and are on call for career days, book week programs, and special library/school events and programs.

Library media center volunteers lend hands where extra hands are needed and free the schedules of professionals, enabling them to be more responsible to the individual needs of children. They fill in wherever a need is articulated, in accordance with their variety of interests and abilities. In their turn, they come away from their media center involvement (we like to think) with a great understanding of our problems, including the financial ones, with which we wrestle.

Volunteerism

The arrival of citizen volunteers in education in the late '60s coincided with the erosion of student aides as a dependable and an educationally justifiable source of manpower in our school media centers. The elimination of study halls, the advent of advance placement courses, the open-ended school day, as well as the hollow ring of arguments in defense of library clubs served to decimate the ranks of student helpers traditionally made available to us. At the same time, our media center book budgets were going up and we were incorporating nonprint materials and equipment into our collections and a multitude of teacher and student services into our program. Greenwich was adding staff, too, but not fast enough to effect the smooth transition from being merely custodial to comprehensive full-service media centers. Assistance was offered by the emerging volunteer movement and we accepted their help, diffidently at first.

At the present time, school volunteers number 2,097 in Greenwich, and approximately 10 percent are volunteers in our school media centers. If this proportion is typical, there should be something like 250,000 school volunteers supplementing school services nationwide. That's a guess, of course. In some places the proportion is higher. Between 600-700 of Boston's 2000 school volunteers are library volunteers, for example. Of the 82 affiliates of the National School Volunteer Program listed in that organization's 1974 directory, twenty identified school libraries as a specific area of activity of their volunteer constituents. There are substantial numbers of school volunteers in Cleveland, Akron, Columbus, Dade and Orange Counties in Florida, Richmond, Virginia, Austin and Beaumont, Texas, San Diego and Long Beach in California, to name just a few communities. There is a growing body of literature to assist in the orientation of these new recruits to part-time library service.

This large and growing source of auxiliary personnel in school media centers is part of a nationwide school volunteer movement that is said to have had its official beginning in Bay City, Michigan in 1953, as a response to teacher shortages, overcrowding in the schools, and insistent demands for individualizing instruction. The coalescing of local groups into a national organization occurred in 1964 with the formation, with help from the Ford Foundation, of the National School Volunteer Program, Inc.

The movement picked up momentum with the now historic Right to Read address by former Commissioner of Education, James E. Allen, delivered before the 1969 Annual Convention of the National Association of School Boards of Education in which he invited the enlistment of people in business, industry, labor, and legislative bodies, civic and community groups, publishers, and communication media personnel to help professional educators make the ability to read a reality for all by the end of the '70s. The International Reading Association (IRA) issued a call for ten million volunteers to buttress reading instruction in the schools and, as the numbers grew, prepared guidelines for the volunteers' selection, training, and supervision. The Office of Education experimentally funded model volunteer training programs in five states through its Volunteers in Education effort. The Center for Urban Education was formed in 1970 to recruit inner-city adult volunteers for inner-city students.

The initial emphasis of the movement was on one-to-one tutoring in reading, mathematics, and in English as a second language. But inevitably school libraries, the lack of them, or their inadequacies, came into focus. An appallingly large number of schools below the secondary level had no school libraries at all, and it was not long before ingenious leaders of school and community found ways of using the Elementary and Secondary Education Act (ESEA) Title II funds in conjunction with volunteers to set up school libraries where none had existed before.

Boston, for example, had no elementary school libraries before 1966. That year, the School Volunteers of Boston aided by Ford Foundation funds, set about correcting the situation. At last count there were 75 in operation, staffed by between 600 and 700 volunteers, ten professional librarians, and some paid aides. Akron, likewise, had no libraries in the inner-city elementary school, and no means to initiate them. As a starter, the local Junior League volunteered the services of its membership and pledged $18,000 to staff, organize, and equip two inner-city school libraries over a two-year-period. In time, the two grew to 18, serving 12,000 children in formerly library-less schools.

Not all the accomplishments were as dramatic as these, but they are substantial. In University City, Missouri, which has libraries and librarians, volunteers supervise the use of tutorial instruction devices in prescriptive learning centers. In one way or another, more than half of that community's 300 volunteers are involved with instruction in reading, using the school libraries as their places of instruction. In Orange County, Florida, schools have media specialists, but no paid clerks. There, more than 100 library volunteers work in 65 elementary schools, performing clerical work, operating audio-visual equipment, and telling stories—always under the supervision of a professional. This is also the case in the schools of Richmond County, Ohio, where relieving the librarians of cataloging and processing chores has resulted in renewed vitality and increased use of the school libraries. At the Madison Comprehensive High School, in the same school district, a library for the use of adults in the adult education program is run completely by volunteers. The public library supplies the books and volunteers provide the staffing. There was no other way to do a job that needed doing.

Funding

Not all library professionals view the infiltration of volunteers into library management positions as desirable. For it is evident that national guidelines specifying that volunteers work under the supervision of professionals, not in place of them, have not always been strictly observed. In general, however, it would seem that librarians have opted to place the educational needs of children before self-interest. A recent example of this occurred in Connecticut last year when a consortium of the Connecticut School Library Association, the Elementary School Principals Association of Connecticut, and the State Department of Education, using undesignated Title II funds provided establishment grants to 67 Connecticut elementary schools that still lacked central libraries. "We hesitated to place our professional organization in the position of supporting media programs which are not professionally staffed," the chairperson of the Consortium wrote to her library association constituents. "However, we know no professional could deny children access to needed resources. Therefore, we put our concern for children before our concern for professional positions. . . ." (This appeared in a *SLJ* news story, October 1975, p. 66.)

Funding for the school volunteer programs has come from a variety of sources. The School Volunteers of Boston program got off the ground with the help of a Ford Foundation grant. Model City, Title I and II of ESEA financed some programs, the U.S. Office of Education's Educational Professions Development Act, Section 504, financed others. In most of the smaller communities, support has been indigenous: the Junior League, the AAUW, church groups, and local business and foundations pledged postage, telephone, stationery, and took care of other incidental costs needed to launch and keep the programs aloft. But as the number of volunteers grew, the position of a paid volunteer coordinator emerged as a program requirement. At first, borne by the cooperating organizations, this cost has been added to the school budgets of more and more communities.

In Orange County, where the volunteer movement is completing its fifth year, the program had its beginning with a three-year pilot program financed by the Junior League to cover the salary of a volunteer chairman, telephone, and office costs. After three years, the volunteer chairman's salary was assumed by the school board, but donations from local service groups and private foundations still pay other costs. In some communities, all operational costs of the volunteer program have been transferred to school budgets.

Coordination

In Greenwich, the coordinator of volunteers in the schools is a half-time paid professional who was a volunteer but is now a Board of Education employee. She functions as a liaison between volunteers and the school administration, and has responsibility for recruiting and screening, orientation and training, on-job-counselling for volunteers, in addition to keeping records. She is on easy terms with the school administration and teachers and is thoroughly familiar with the school program. At the same time, her ties within the community are deep and intimate.

She is sensitive to the motives that bring volunteers into the schools and is aware of their expected job satisfaction. She knows when to say no to filling a request that should be filled by a professional. She is able to anticipate personality conflicts before they happen, to transfer square pegs out of round holes, to exercise diplomacy in smoothing little dissatisfactions before they become problems beyond resolution.

In some communities there is also a volunteer advisory committee made up of representatives from those organizations who can recruit volunteers and teachers, principals and central school administrators. After getting a go ahead from the school board, the committee establishes game rules for the program. In my community the schools provide essential services, volunteers the extras. They are never used as substitutes for professionals. They work under the direction of teachers and teachers are held responsible for content and techniques. They do not perform professional tasks, though they may be called upon to carry out complex tasks, according to their special abilities and interests. They are expected to observe the same code of professional ethics as teachers with respect to confidential information they may be privy to in the exercise of their volunteer tasks.

It is the school system's responsibility to assess those needs that can be met by community volunteers. It is the volunteer coordinator, moving between school and community who finds willing people for the jobs that need doing, who interprets the school programs and policies to volunteers and explains the volunteer program guidelines to teachers seeking their services.

Motivation

The reasons why volunteers offer their services to the schools and to libraries within schools are many, and it behooves the library administrator to know them and to make personnel decisions regarding their deployment. Some volunteers become volunteers simply to get out of the house for a few hours, to talk to adults, to stimulate their minds, to do something useful. Or they want, surreptitiously, to share the school experiences from which, as their children grow up, they find themselves increasingly debarred. Some become volunteers to brush up their employment skills, to see if they like working outside the home and if they are still employable. For some, personal growth is important—they are looking for challenge and for an opportunity to learn new skills, to gain some new insights. Generally, they are mature, reliable, outgoing. They will want jobs not too overwhelming, not too pressing. They will look for the taste of success in the jobs they do and the joy of a job completed. They will want to feel it's a meaningful job, one worth doing. And to get credit for having a brain! Not a few want an assignment in a media center.

Librarians are better prepared than some other segments of the school community to define their auxiliary staff needs. They have been prepared by management experience and tradition to delegate tasks to untrained student helpers—very young student helpers, sometimes, and for their accomplishment to organize large jobs into short simple segments. Many librarians are not so accomplished at working with a professionally directed volunteer movement whose participants have general education and experience, though not professional expertise, often equal to their own. In my case, it didn't take many go arounds to realize that we were losing some of our best potential volunteers to jobs demanding a higher variety and higher grade of skills than those required to write overdue notices week after week, or type cards, or jacket books. To delegate to volunteers, regardless of their interests and abilities, only the simplest and most repetitive of library routines because that is what student aides did successfully is shortsighted and self-defeating.

Orientation

The librarian meets with the volunteer coordinator sometime in the spring to describe her volunteer needs for the following year. Where the volunteer program is extensive, it's a good idea to come to this meeting with job descriptions in hand. They will be useful both to the uncommitted volunteers and to the volunteer coordinator. In most communities, the recruiting and enlistment of community volunteers takes place during spring and summer, followed by a general orientation session late in September. The latter is generally an all-day event designed to acquaint volunteers with background information and purposes of the volunteer program, information about school policies and program, and some general caveats. For those who have not selected an area assignment, there may be a survey of the various opportunities for service, and there may be invitation to talk about what goes on in school media centers and what volunteers do and can do in them.

Reading tutors and tutors of foreign students attend additional training sessions, and so also, in some systems, do library volunteers, principally where the volunteers do not work directly under professional librarians and knowledge of library procedures is essential. In such situations professional direction, however remote, is provided through workshops, volunteer handbooks, and procedural guides. In some cases, Office of Education EDPA Section 504, funds have financed special library training courses for participants. More often, volunteers must go it alone after workshop sessions covering all aspects of the work they will be expected to carry out. In the instance previously cited, where 67 Connecticut school libraries were funded with no provisions for professional staffing, library management workshops were set up by the state school library association in cooperation with the state elementary principals' association.

In systems where volunteers work under a library professional, the general orientation session is followed by orientation in the school to which the volunteer is assigned. Specific job training is the responsibility of the school media center. In most cases a locally prepared handbook for volunteers helps them master the peculiarities of their assignments.

Volunteers work one morning a week, sometimes two, so an auxiliary staff may number in the twenties in some of our schools. Good organization is necessary if they are to be used effectively. Take time for a job interview. Find out who your volunteers are, what they probably can or cannot do, before making job assignments. Keep records of who does what, and when. The time to plan for your volunteers is *last week*, not when they come through the door and head for the coat closet.

Some of our volunteers prefer to do the same familiar things over and over whenever they come. Others like variety, with enough challenge to make the job interesting. Generally, it should be work that can be picked up and laid aside, to fit the volunteer's work schedule, should be moderately routine, with variety and change of pace built into the job.

Volunteers need space to work, comfortable seating, adequate lighting, a good typewriter, sufficient files. That's good sense, not just tender loving care.

Some volunteers prefer a quiet corner in the workroom. Some prefer to work at a table in the midst of the action, with sights and sounds of children all around them. Some like to work two-by-two, sharing transportation, a parking space and morning of work side-by-side. Why not? Volunteers come with various abilities, skills, talents, ages.

It is important to remember that the annual cycle for school volunteers does not necessarily coincide with the school year. Be flexible. Their numbers will dwindle before Thanksgiving and for a few weeks before and after Christmas. They go off with their husbands on off-season vacations, if the opportunity arises, and they stay at home—as they should—with sick children. They drop out at spring-cleaning time and are reluctant to begin the year until post-summer chores are done—well into September. They may decide they can handle a paying job and you may lose them to the business world about the time they have become indispensable to you. It will be your good fortune if they leave you to update their educational qualifications and reappear as a candidate for a library clerk or teacher-aide job, or even for a professional position in your system.

Remember that volunteers are auxiliary staff. They provide the extras: paid staff provide the essential services. If you find yourself saying that you can't run your media center without volunteers, you're in trouble.

Involvement

An important aspect of a successful volunteer program is maintaining morale. Most important is person to person contact. In our TV volunteer program where volunteers working in separate schools tend to be isolated from each other, a monthly newsletter keeps them in touch, informing participants about people and happenings within the program, about new equipment and in-service opportunities.

Volunteers should be reminded as often as it seems necessary that they are appreciated, and what they are doing, however personally thankless, is worthwhile. They are urged to participate, to the extent they will, in staff events. They become part of the staff, part of the school. Some of our staff give them small gifts at Christmas. Some schools arrange a luncheon, to which library volunteers are invited. In our larger schools there is an end of the year Thank You Day, with a tribute by the principal, refreshments, and a follow-up story in the newspaper.

Volunteers are encouraged to participate in workshops that are part of the in-service program for media personnel and teachers. Workshops on lettering, equipment operation, graphic techniques, puppetry, and television have extended the media skills of our volunteers, opening up avenues of creativeness and personal growth from which both the individual and the system benefit. The mutuality of benefits should not be overlooked.

One of the most popular and most demanding of volunteer assignments in Greenwich is that of television volunteer—the backbone of television services in our elementary schools. To qualify, our TV volunteers attend eight sequential workshop hours of instruction, followed by two more hours operating equipment under supervision. Thereafter, volunteers are part of the school's TV team functioning on their own, but under the general direction of a video coordinator. Throughout the year they upgrade their skills at brush-up workshops and special ones on television graphics, audio mixing, porta-pack and mini-studio equipment operation. The demands on their time and skills are heavy, yet morale in the program is high, for benefits accrue to both those who give and to whom those are given.

Benefits

Perhaps this is how we should view this new mass movement of adult participation in the affairs of our schools and media centers: not just in terms of the benefits for us derived from it because they're doing jobs in our schools that can't be done, for the time being, in any other way. At the same time, through us, volunteers are doing something for themselves: they are learning, growing, acquiring skills, doing worthwhile things that need doing, feeling good for having done them. So it should be. Properly nurtured, the volunteer movement in education—and volunteers in our school media centers—will be with us for a long time.

Bibliography

Carter, Barbara & Gloria Dapper. *Organizing School Volunteer Programs*. Citation: Scholastic, 1974.

———*School Volunteers: What They Do and How They Do It*. New York, Citation, 1972.

Goodman, Helen C. "The Library Volunteer." *Library Journal*, May 1, 1972, p. 1675–77.

"Guidelines for Using Volunteers in Libraries." *American Libraries*, April 1974, p. 407–08.

Jenkins, Harold. "Volunteers in the Future of Libraries." *Library Journal*, April 15, 1972, p. 1399-1403.

McGuire, Agnes C. "Volunteers Can Bring You the Help You Need," *School Management*, January 1974, p. 38-44ff.

Naylor, Harriet H. *Volunteers Today: Finding, Training and Working with Them*. Dryden, N.Y.: Dryden Assoc., 1973.

"Paraprofessionals and Reading." *The Reading Teacher*, December 1973.

Perkins, Bryce. *Getting Better Results from Substitutes, Teacher Aides and Volunteers*. Prentice-Hall, 1966.

School Volunteer, Arlington, Va., Education, U.S.A. Special Report. National School Public Relations Assn., 1973.

School Volunteers for Boston. Annual Report, 1972.

Volunteers in Education: a Handbook for Coordinators of Voluntary Programs. Philadelphia. Recruitment Leadership and Training Institute, Temple University, 1975.

Volunteer Aides Handbook: Media Center. Orange County Dept. of Education, Santa Ana, Calif., 1976.

Wehmeyer, Lillian Bierman. *The School Library Volunteer*. Libraries Unlimited, Inc., 1975.

West, Jeff. *Assisting in the Library: an Individualized Volunteer Education Module*. Dade County Public School, Miami, Fla., 1971.

Williams, Polly Franklin. *A Philosophical Approach for Volunteers*. U.S. Office of Education, Dept. of Health, Education and Welfare, 1974.

Still Playing It Safe:
Restricted Realism in Teen Novels

by Jane Abramson

There has been a lot of hoopla over the hard-hitting realism of juvenile fiction for older readers. Certainly there has been a dramatic change since the days when the gravest problem faced in teen fiction was whether the freshman heroine would get asked to the sock hop by the dreamy (sigh!) upperclassman. Now each new edition of *The Subject Guide to Children's Books in Print* (Bowker) boasts even longer listings on death, drugs, divorce; while publishers' catalogs attest to the latest inroads into teenage alcoholism, rape, homosexuality, et relevant al.

And yet, to borrow from the French maxim, the more realistic fiction changes, the more it stays the same. Taboos are lifted; restrictions still remain. The word "fuck" is now printable; scenes of love-making evidently are not. Judy Blume's *Forever* (Bradbury 1975), a tame mapping of first love charted strictly for adolescents, was nevertheless issued as an adult title, presumably because of the semi-explicit but decidedly soft-core sex scenes.

The restrictions on teen fiction result in books that succeed only in mirroring a slick surface realism that too often acts as a cover-up. It diverts readers. It disguises the fact that, at their core, most realistic novels are unrealistic and, far worse, dishonest. Books that seem to explore social change (alternate life styles, for example) end up reaffirming traditional mores. Books that set out to tackle painful experiences turn into weak testimonies to life's essential goodness.

There is plenty of evidence that conventional morality is still at work in teen novels that pretend otherwise. Besides bans on describing sex, attitudes about sex continue to be frighteningly unenlightened at times.

Throughout Dizenzo's *Why Me?: the Story of Jenny* (Avon, pap. 1976) there is an oddly ambivalent attitude toward Jenny, a teenage rape victim, as if the author were wagging a reproachful finger at her for breaking the code of all good girls—never to take a ride from a stranger. The implication is that perhaps Jenny deserved what she got.

Far more disturbing is Fritzhand's *Life Is a Lonely Place* (Evans, dist. by Lippincott, 1975), a truly nasty-minded exploitation of homosexuality. For reasons too ridiculous to recount, an unwarranted smear campaign is mounted accusing a young boy and his older writer friend of being "queer." Throughout the first person narrative, teenaged Tink constantly assures readers that he is a normal red-blooded boy, and just for good measure, the writer's wife, never before mentioned, is trotted out in the final chapter as if to quell any lingering doubts readers might have. The inference here is that, had the accusations been true, Tink would have deserved all the abuse heaped upon him—making this nothing more than a vindication of antiquated prejudices in twentieth-century drag.

In these days of divorce run rampart, the traditional roles of the family and of women (especially as mothers) are quite naturally called into question: the trouble is that the answers, as supplied in realistic books for teens, too often hedge the issues.

When her newly divorced mother skips off to pursue a college career, Jennifer Noel is prompted *To Live a Lie* (Atheneum, 1975): she tells new school friends her mother is dead. Mom, clearly the villain of the piece, is resurrected, however, when the ultimate, maternal purpose of her education is made known: she wants her degree so she can take back the kids and support them properly.

In Perl's *The Tell-Tale Summer of Tina C.* (Seabury, 1975) again it is Mom who has left the nest following the divorce, this time to shack up with a younger guy who does the cooking and cleaning. Terribly *au courant*? Not really, since Mom has married Peter, who, far from being a contented *hausfrau*, has ambitious plans for opening a gourmet cooking school.

Chester Aaron in *Hello to Bodega* (Atheneum, 1976) is another author who merely pays lip service to alternate life styles (here a California commune run by a Vietnam veteran). Although it's stated that Gil and Joanna "were, without ever having said the word or passed through the ritual, married," nevertheless, the book ends with them tying the knot—in a double ceremony, no less, with the commune's only other couple. The commune also conveniently folds before the wedding day so Joanna (pregnant) and Gil can set up house as a traditional nuclear family.

The gravest shortcomings of realistic fiction for older readers, however, is not its veiled support of conventional morality, but its failure to respect its audience. Two crucial facts are ignored. First of all, teenagers, even if their reading skills are limited, know if a book is trying to sell them a phony bill of goods. Secondly, adolescents are emotionally resilient: they can accept books about death or divorce—or whatever—without the reassurances and consolations offered in "problem fiction" for younger readers.

Yet the lion's share of realistic teen novels—even ones which specifically set out to deal with painful or problematic situations—persists in coddling readers with glib assurances.

For example, of all the recent titles on divorce Kin Platt's *Chloris and the Freaks* (Bradbury, 1975) is the only one where the breakup is not "for the best"; the only one without the facile optimism and tidy solutions that mark lesser efforts (e.g., Pfeffer's *Marly the Kid*, Doubleday, 1975, runs away from her "Lucretia Borgia" mother straight into the welcoming arms of Dad and new wife who doesn't blink twice at the prospect of a permanent stepchild).

Platt's heroine, astrology-nut Jenny, has no such easy out. During the course of a summer she finds herself watching helplessly while her worst fears about a family breakup are fulfilled. Her stepfather Fidel—the one bright star in Jenny's universe—is handed his walking papers; and Jenny is stuck with her childish mother and disturbed sister Chloris.

Platt honestly and compellingly addresses the feelings of powerlessness that are common to all adolescents; the frustrations of still being dependent upon adults, who, often as not, are undependable.

The mainstream of realistic fiction, however, continues to deny these facts. Instead, teenaged characters are shown as sure masters of their fates; authors look solely on the bright side of life and human nature; stories finish on a positive note. Witness the following statements: "Realism in (juvenile) fiction does not mean a story . . . ending unhappily. Relevant natural subjects . . . can perhaps provide a measure of hope or reassurance,"[1] and " . . . librarians and others evaluating YA literature should demand more than a cold rendering of reality. Honesty must be combined with hope, a hope that is life-affirming. . . ."[2]

Unfortunately, these guidelines only serve to enforce the pervading blandness of realistic fiction and to foster a cock-eyed optimism in stories whose happy endings do not jibe with anything that's gone before in the book. As evidence are the following two examples of supposedly realistic novels for pre-teen and teen readers.

Kaye's *Joanna All Alone* (Nelson, 1975) is just that—an only child whose upwardly mobile parents can't see past the next cocktail party. As a glimpse at loneliness this is fairly effective—until the sunny-side up ending when Mummy and Daddy rush home from a country weekend to announce that Jojo's dearest wish (for a baby brother or sister) is going to come true. Fade out on a happy family scene. . . .

In Shaw's *Call Me Al Raft* (Nelson, 1975) the hero spends a summer tracking down his father. All Al knows is that Dad was one of the many flings in the long and checkered career of ex-stripper Amanda L'Amour. Written in a flip-hip style and set in the familiar landscape of California freeways and roadside hangouts, this fudges any claim to realism by its ultra-goopy finale: Al, reunited with his dad, literally sails off into the sunset.

In contrast to these stories which conclude on such false notes of uplift, stand a few recent books, consistent and uncompromising, whose endings—downbeat to be sure—flow inexorably from characterization and events. They are all strong and jolting and do not condescend by offering bibliotherapeutic crutches to help readers "cope."

On balance, the critical reception of these novels has been hearteningly favorable; yet there exists a counter-current of wariness as to their appropriateness for a teenaged audience.

George Woods, for example, in the *New York Times* list of the best of the year's novels for older children bypasses S. E. Hinton's *Rumble Fish* (Delacorte, 1975), a powerful, raw portrait of a born loser. Fourteen-year-old Rusty James' hero worship of his older brother (the enigmatic, semi-psycho Motorcycle Boy) steers him straight into an emotional crack-up from which he never recovers. Although Rusty James recounts the events that led up to his brother's death, it is actually his own post-mortem that he's delivering. Readers can certainly handle the dead-end pessimism (they'll either empathize or feel lucky); yet Woods dismisses the book because it is about "death and disfiguration" and opts, instead for a "calm, placid story." Likewise, the cautious tagline for the review appearing in *The Bulletin of the Center for Children's Books* (December 1975) reads less like an evaluation than a warning that the book must be handled with extreme care: "Memorable but with no relief from depression, no note of hope. . . ."

Two other provocative novels, Platt's *Headman* (Greenwillow: Morrow, 1975) and Cormier's *The Chocolate War* (Pantheon, 1974) are also examples of what *Booklist* has cited as a trend towards "didactic negativity." Indeed, both heroes are caught in a "heads you win, tails you lose" setup. Each tries to buck the system only to be beaten down by it.

For Platt's Owen, the system is an ultra-violent section of L.A., where there's only safety in numbers, i.e., gangs. All his efforts to stay straight are futile (e.g., his first pay check from his job at a body shop is immediately stolen) and Owen eventually winds up on the wrong end of a switchblade.

For Jerry in *The Chocolate War*, the system is the tyranny of a boy's prep school run by a power-mad teacher and bullying secret society. He launches a one-man protest by refusing to participate in the school fund-raising drive. His crusade, however, is crushed and, as Jerry is carted off to the hospital, he realizes it was useless to try to "disturb the universe."

Both books are startling and stark looks at powerlessness. They do not shy away from the fact that there are situations where virtue does not have its reward and nice guys finish last. They qualify as good literature, because philosophy and plot have been dramatically welded together.

Both titles certainly have flaws: Platt overstates his theme of individual helplessness so that Owen can't seem to turn a corner without getting jumped or mugged; and Cormier underdevelops his characters (they're either lip-smacking villains or ineffectual wimps), but the books should not be faulted for the reasons listed in Betsy Hearne's attack on *The Chocolate War* in a *Booklist* Editorial (July 1, 1974).

Hearne charges that Cormier "manipulates readers into believing how rotten things are" and chides the book for not presenting "the whole truth." This dangerous criticism not only assumes that there *is* a "whole truth," a formula world vision with which all readers would agree and which all juvenile books should reflect, but that young readers are easily manipulated; that they are essentially *tabulae rasae* upon which the stamp of every book is indelibly printed. Rubbish! Adolescents are by nature questioning and this extends into their reading as well. They are quite capable of disagreeing with and discarding a book's message.

Adolescents are also manic; by turns ecstatic and desperate. They live at extremes; yet so few books written for them touch either emotional pole. Of course, there have never been any edicts against writing joyful books, and still there are a few truly exhilarating novels as there are ones which are deeply painful.

Oddly enough, the restrictions on teen fiction can occasionally work to the publisher's advantage. For example, Ann Moody's short stories, *Mr. Death* (Harper, 1975), interesting only in their grisliness and clearly aimed at adult sensibilities, received an undue amount of fanfare and critical attention when released as a juvenile title.

Unfortunately, the restrictions on teen fiction never work to the advantage of the readers. They result ultimately in books that are verisimilar but not truthful.

The pass-fail test for fiction of the realistic mode is not whether a picture of life has been duplicated which is superficially recognizable or falsely reassuring, but whether a vision of life has been created that is real in the sense of universal; a vision that *is* disturbing in the sense that it will arouse and move readers. And isn't that, after all, the purpose of literature?

References

1. M. C. Brei & M. A. Timms. "Realism: Honesty and Hope; Its Value in Books for Children and Young People." *Wisconsin Library Bulletin.* January 1974, p. 46.
2. Frances Hanckel & John Cunningham. "Can Young Gays Find Happiness in YA Books?" *Wilson Library Bulletin.* January 1976, p. 528.

Any Writer Who Follows Anyone Else's Guidelines Ought To Be In Advertising

by Nat Hentoff

In the early 1960s, Ursula Nordstrom asked if I'd be interested in writing a book for children. The notion had never occurred to me, but what proved tempting was Ursula's statement that, of course, I would have total freedom to write what I imagined. The result was *Jazz Country*, a novel about black music and the dues white boys have to pay to get inside that perilous land of marvels. The book has been read by black, white, Danish, Japanese—all kinds of kids. And for a time, I am delighted to say, it was stolen from a number of libraries more often than almost any other book.

That experience, for which I remain grateful to Ursula, was so much fun and so satisfying (because of all the letters I received from kids) that I have been writing novels for children ever since.

On the other hand, let us suppose that in the early 60s, I had been told by Ursula—or by a librarians' group—that as I wrote, I would have to remember that my book was going to be judged by the following guidelines:

> anti-racist/non-racist/racist (by omission/comission)
> anti-sexist/non-sexist/sexist
> anti-elitist/non-elitist/elitist
> anti-materialist/non-materialist/materialist
> anti-individualist/non-individualist/individualist
> anti-ageist/non-ageist/ageist
> anti-conformist/non-conformist/conformist
> anti-escapist/non-escapist/escapist
> builds positive images of females/minorities
> builds negative images of females/minorities
> inspires action vs. oppression/culturally authentic . . .

And then down in the corner, almost as an afterthought:

> literary quality/art quality.

Had anyone actually shown me such a set of guidelines, my first reaction would have been that I had suddenly been transported to Czechoslovakia or some such utterly stifling state. My second reaction would have been to ignore these externally dictated "standards" entirely because any writer who follows anyone else's guidelines ought to be in advertising.

Yet I did not invent that list. Those are the criteria by which children's books are judged by the Council on Interracial Books for Children, Inc. (CIBC) in their 1976 volume, *Human (and Anti-Human) Values in Children's Books: a Content Rating Instrument for Educators and Concerned Parents.*

Furthermore, these and similar criteria permeate the council's *Bulletin* and their public statements. To what end? Not only to sensitize parents, educators, and librarians to books that are "harmful" to children, but also to mount campaigns to censor those books.

Like certain Orwellian characters, the sepulchral representatives of the council deny that they are censors. For instance, in a letter to *School Library Journal* (January 1977, p. 4), Bradford Chambers, director of CIBC—that Watch and Ward Society—declares that he is encouraged at the realization "by many librarians that enlightened weeding and selection policies aimed at reducing racism and sexism do not constitute 'censoring.'"

One librarian's act of weeding can be a writer's shock of recognition that his or her books are being censored off the shelves. That is, if the weeding is not part of the normal process of making room for new books by removing those that kids no longer read but is rather a yielding to such slippery "guidelines" as those of the Council on Interracial Books for Children. The latter is censorship, as even a child can tell you.

Let me stipulate my agreement with the political goals of the council as they are stated on page 4 of *Human (and Anti-Human) Values.* . . . "We are advocates of a society which will be free of racism, sexism, ageism, classism, materialism, elitism, and other negative values." (Such other negative values as censorship, I would add.) I can make this stipulation not out of piety but on the basis of some thirty years of rather dogged if unspectacular work toward these ends as a democratic socialist involved in all kinds of movements to redistribute power in this land.

Politics, however, is not literature. And children ought to have access to the freest literature we can write for them. And literature must be freely conceived or it stiffens into propaganda (no matter how nobly intended) or into some other form of narrowing didacticism.

The council, however, is quite openly working toward the end of having "children's literature become a tool for the conscious promotion of human values that will lead to greater human liberation (*Human (and Anti-Human) Values* . . . p. 4)." I apologize for being obvious, but literature cannot breathe if it is forced to be utilitarian in this or any other sense. The council fundamentally misunderstands the act of imagination.

Recently, an internationally renowned writer for children commented about the council to me: "Of course, we should all be more tender and understanding toward the aged and we should work to shrive ourselves of racism and sexism, but when you impose guidelines like theirs on writing, you're strangling the imagination. And that means that you're limiting the ability of children to imagine. If all books for them were 'cleansed' according to these criteria, it would be the equivalent of giving them nothing to eat but white bread.

"To write according to such guidelines," this storyteller continued, "is to take the life out of what you do. Also the complexity, the ambivalence. And thereby the young reader gets no real sense of the wonders and terrors and unpredictabilities of living. Paradoxically, censors like the council clamor for 'truth' but are actually working to flatten children's reading experiences into the most misleading, simplistic kinds of untruth."

The writer quoted has never been attacked by the Council on Interracial Books for Children but nonetheless asked me not to disclose his or her identity. "Otherwise," the writer said, "they'll go after me. And that, of course, is another chilling effect of their work." In fact, no writer of books for children whom I spoke to in connection with this piece was willing to be identified, for all were fearful of the council.

I also talked—for nonattribution—to several former members of the council who supported CIBC in its early days but who left when the organization began to move toward its current function of righteous vigilanteism. "At the beginning," one of them, a black librarian, said, "the idea was to really open up opportunities for black writers, illustrators, publishers, and minority-owned bookstores. God knows, that needed to be done then, as it needs to be done now. But then the council changed course and turned into censors. That's when I left. I know damn well that if everybody doesn't have the freedom to express himself or herself, I'm going to be one of the first to lose mine."

Yet the council has a ready, if rather devious, rejoinder to such talk of indivisible freedoms. Their contention is that the publishing industry has long practiced "covert censorship." By that, Bradford Chambers says he means the kinds of venerable publishing criteria that result in an "underexposure of the views of women and Third World people." And he's right. For all the belated eagerness of many houses to publish books expressing just such views, the book industry as a whole is certainly still white-dominated. (By the way, the eagerness has so far led to an excess of virtuous pap and scarcely any literature. In the rush to repent, publishers have not sufficiently searched out truly creative tellers of tales who cannot be fitted into neat, sanitized, newly "proper" molds.)

However, the answer to what the council calls "covert censorship" is hardly the council's kind of book "elimination." At base, whatever the reasons of the expungers, all censorship is the same. It is suppression of speech and creates a climate in which creative imagination, the writer's and the child's, must hide to survive.

That the council does not understand the necessarily free ambience for children's literature is regularly evident in its

Bulletin as well in its procrustean rating systems for "worthy" books. For instance, in a recent issue of the *Bulletin* (vol. 8, no. 3) there is an article about the books that East German children are reading in grades one to six ("What Children Are Reading in GDR Schools" by Donna Garund-Sletack). The author focuses mainly on the "messages" these books convey about sex roles. For the most part, the books get high grades. Women are shown in a wider range of careers than in comparable American readers; children of both sexes exercise real responsibility; individualism is downplayed (no kidding!); all sorts of positive values are inculcated (such as helpfulness); respect for older people is "promoted"; there are plentiful tales of racial discrimination (the East Germans are against it); and by God, "an analysis of poverty and inequality is offered as early as in the first grade reader."

Nowhere in the article is there a hint that East German writers (whether their audiences are adults or children) who offend the state do not get published any more. Some are even given a chance to reflect on their "anti-human values" in prison.

Freedom of expression, however, is clearly not a focal passion of the Council on Interracial Books for Children. Correctness of perspective and attitude are its driving priorities as is stated in the council's pamphlet *10 Quick Ways to Analyze Children's Books for Racism and Sexism*:

No. 7: "Consider the Author's or Illustrator's Background." Look at the biographical material on the jacket. "A book that deals with the feelings and insights of women should be more carefully examined if it is written by a man." If it's written by Phyllis Schlafly, it also ought to be carefully examined. Obviously, blacks are likely to bring more to black themes, as Jews are to Jewish themes. But why not judge each book for itself, rather than order a line up before you read?

No. 9: "Watch for Loaded Words." Like what? "Chairman" instead of "chairperson." I would take twenty lashes rather than be forced to use so utterly graceless a word as "chairperson." And what does that make me, according to the council? A stone sexist, that's what.

And so it goes—"Check the Story Line," "Look at the Lifestyles," "Weigh the Relationships Between People," and so on. Fine for East Germany, if that's where you want to write, but no different here from the John Birch Society trying to hammer *its* values into books for children. Such groups are the enemies of any writer with self-respect.

Another dulling, constricting effect of the council's ardent work is that when successful, it produces its own stereotypes. During an appearance by representatives of the council at a February 1977 meeting in New York of the National Coalition Against Censorship, Mary K. Chelton, consultant on young adult services for the Westchester County Library System, made a good point about the council's addiction to labeling groups. She said that the council's view of racial minorities and women makes the groups emerge as monolithic, with each member of these groups in total accord on any matter that affects them. Describing herself as a feminist, she pointed out that she knows from personal experience that there is no unified perspective among feminists about what is most important to women now, or how best to achieve feminist ends, or even what the term "feminist" means.

The same is true of blacks, Chicanos, and all other so-called "Third World" people. It is no wonder the council considers "individualism" highly suspicious.

Yet there can be no literature without individualism—uncategorizable individualism—sometimes flaky, sometimes complexly rebellious, sometimes so stubbornly unassimilable as to make the child shout in recognition of himself. (Or herself. Or the chair he/she is personing.)

Collectivism is for politics. And if the council were to marshall its energies and foundation-financed resources for honestly political ends, I'd join it. Organize, bring pressure to greatly increase the numbers of "Third World" editors who will then find more non-white writers than white editors are likely to. (If only because they know a lot more.) Organize support for "Third World" publishing firms and bookstores. And by all means, hold sessions for librarians and editors on ways in which the children's booklists ought to be expanded (without censoring other books). There is still so little of value for children on the jazz life. Or on the turbulent, desperately complicated history of Puerto Rican independence movements. The list is huge.

But then leave the authors alone. Always leave authors alone. I'm not talking about editing for grammar and grace. But stay out of authors' quirkily individualistic heads in terms of what they write.

I am currently making notes for a novel, a successor to *This School Is Driving Me Crazy*. I am trying to imagine Sam, the maddeningly unregimentable hero, two years older. And there is a cohero, who is black. There are always blacks in my novels, and not once have I checked any of them out with the Council on Interracial Books for Children. I am trying to imagine the many intersecting reasons this black youngster, while witty, is so angry. Is he angry at the council because he is torn between collective and individual imperatives? That's a possibility. Maybe I'll be able to incorporate Bradford Chambers into the book. That's a real possibility.

And I am thinking of how the weather will be in certain scenes and trying to remember what it was like, in my teens, to be paralyzed at meeting a certain girl unexpectedly on the street. There will also be music in the books, and I am listening for those sounds. And there are voices I am after, rhythms, timbres. How do you put those into words? The council's guidelines do not tell me.

During this preliminary process and then as I write, I will have one of the council's precepts in mind: "It is the final *product* that counts—not the intent. We must be concerned above all with the effects of a book on the children who read it."

Exactly. Except that the council's concern with children is expressed through guarding them against any thoughts, characters, plot lines, words, and art work that might "harm" them. The council, of course, considers itself the arbiter of all that, having discovered, by innate virtue, the sole and correct party line.

My concern with children, on the other hand, is that they find in a book what they had never quite expected to see in print—elements of themselves, dreams they're not sure but what they too may have dreamed. And a chance, as many chances as I can give them, to play with their imagination. To stretch it and bend it and peer through and around it and make whatever connections are natural between the book and themselves, the life in the book and the life outside. And I want to make them care about the people in the book, and dig their foolishness, and maybe cry a little (I loved to cry over books when I was a kid). And I hope to get letters from readers. I will start a correspondence, as has happened after all the books before. And my correspondents will ask me all kinds of things, as I will them—none of which can be fitted into those grimly symmetrical checklist boxes so beloved by the Council on Interracial Books for Children.

Later, probably in a library, I will meet some of the readers of this new book, and will be astonished again at how marvelously, though sometimes hesitantly, different each one is. Whether they're all black, as in Brooklyn's Ocean Hill-Brownsville, or a motley, as in Tulsa. And I will look at them and think how truly stupid and destructive it is for anyone to stand guard over the ideas that may be offered to their lively minds.

What it comes down to is that the Council on Interracial Books for Children not only distrusts individualism ("should be discouraged as a highly negative force"), but it also greatly distrusts children.

And that is reason enough why the council should not be messing with children's literature.

Out of Patience—Indefinitely

by Audrey B. Eaglen

In the October 1977 issue of *School Library Journal*, Lillian Gerhardt wrote an editorial (p. 63) on publishers' increasing use of the euphemism "out of stock indefinitely" to describe book titles that for all practical purposes will never appear in print again, but which, for arcane reasons, these same publishers are loath to describe honestly as "out of print." The problems that such "flimflam" causes libraries are enormous and extremely costly, as anyone who has anything to do with book ordering or acquisitions is well aware.

After the editorial appeared, if our large library staff is any indication of others' reaction to it, there must have occurred a nationwide wave of head-nodding and rib-nudging among the tens of thousands of *SLJ* readers who knew exactly what Gerhardt was talking about. But there are myriad other problems facing libraries as they try to spend taxpayers' money as honestly and efficiently as possible in spite of ever-decreasing materials budgets and ever-increasing costs. Most of these problems relate directly to certain practices among publishers and the hoary myths that somewhere, sometime in the dim past, gave rise to them—practices that are a) very often unfair, b) frequently stupid, and c) sometimes dishonest—or at least they appear to be to anyone with a bit of common sense. The practices that most clearly reflect a, b, c, or any combination of them, relate to 1) discount, 2) delivery, and 3) a general belief that libraries really make up an insignificant part of the general book-purchasing market, a belief reinforced by both wildly misleading statistics (publishers' statistics, of course) and a century or more of librarians themselves accepting the (unproven and unprovable) "fact" of their insignificance in the larger world of the book industry. Just how unfair, stupid, and perhaps dishonest these practices have become can be more clearly seen by comparing the ways publishers deal with retail booksellers and the ways they deal with public and school libraries—comparisons that lead at least a few of us to believe that, in many instances, our public and school libraries (and thus our taxpayers) are inadvertently subsidizing several thousand retail booksellers.

Publishers' Statistics

According to *The Bowker Annual* (1977), our library system, Cuyahoga County Public Library (CCPL), ranked sixth among the nation's libraries in 1976, with a total operating budget of more than $11 million. Only one library in the U.S.

(New York Public) had a bigger library materials budget than ours, which was slightly more than 3\frac{1}{2}$ million, of which about 2\frac{1}{2}$ million was earmarked for books—no small potatoes in anyone's estimation, I would imagine.

On the other hand, I have a good friend who owns a decent-sized, very successful retail bookstore in this area. Her annual expenditure for books amounts to about $175,000, which is only about 7 percent of CCPL's yearly expenditure. Yet on trade hardbounds as well as trade and mass market paperbacks, her average discount is 40 percent; ours is 24 percent. Why? Here are some of the answers we get from publishers. 1) *Libraries do not spend as much on books as retail booksellers do, and* 2) *when they do spend these paltry sums, they usually buy single copies of titles, which are very costly for publishers to process.* Let's examine this by looking at the publishers' own figures.

There are 8,504 public libraries in the U.S., which, in 1976, spent $130.5 million on books, or an average of $16,500 per library. (School libraries spent another $170 million on books.) Retail book outlets add up to about 4600; their average annual expenditure for books per outlet is about $60,000 (a generous estimate) per year, or a total of $276 million, a figure that would seem to indicate that publishers' figures are right on target. But let's take a closer look at some of the things that must be considered in comparing the $130 million (public library) and the $276 million (retail bookseller) figures.

First, it is common practice for the retail bookseller to return, for full credit, any books unsold by a certain time—usually a year after purchase. The average percentage of trade books thus returned is 17.6; for mass market paperbacks it is 38.6. Both figures cut that $276 million down considerably. When a library buys a book it is returned only if it is defective or it is the wrong book or edition. In 1976, CCPL purchased 270,000 books; we returned exactly 5,557 of them, or less than one percent. In all but a few cases, it was the suppliers' fault that these books had to be returned: they were wrong titles, wrong editions, defective copies, extra copies, and so on. Common sense would tell most business people that there is a substantially greater cost of doing business with booksellers than with libraries; someone has to pay for opening those cartons of returns, re-storing them, issuing credits, doing all the fancy bookkeeping it all requires, and then finally dumping them on someone else!

Second, libraries (particularly smaller libraries) may order many single copies of titles, true, but do booksellers always order in enormous quantity? In a recent issue of *Publishers Weekly*, two of the American Booksellers Association's head honchos described the special order (invariably for a single copy) as "the backbone of the independent bookstore." As far as our system is concerned, single copy orders are the exception rather than the rule: on a recent juvenile book order, 3,964 books were ordered, and only 29 were single copy orders; on a recent adult order, 1,485 books were ordered, and only 11 orders were for single copies—hardly evidence to support the great single copy myth to which the publishers cling when describing library book buying.

There's one other reason for the survival of this myth, however, which is almost as amusing as it is infuriating. Many publishers believe in this so strongly that they refuse to send us more than one copy of a title. CCPL purchase orders clearly state, with arrows pointing to neat little boxes where the number of copies is printed, SHIP THIS QUANTITY. Let's say we order 84 copies of *Kitty Kat Kapers*. Someone at the Jones Publishing Company will say, apparently, "Poor CCPL's Honeywell 62 must be acting up again because a library never orders more than one copy of a title!" and the "84" is, maddeningly, changed by Jones Publishing to a "1." A recent small order we placed called for 4 titles, a total of 62 books; when the entire order came in a jiffy bag (4 books, 1 of each title), we knew the one-copy myth had struck again. But the infuriating thing is that the whole reordering process (and the same thing happened when we reordered) raises the cost of acquiring a book to almost four times the original cost. In this case, we ended up paying about $48 per book for books that should have cost us about $6 each—to say nothing of the costs to the publisher, which *we*, of course, will end up paying in higher prices on books next year.

Another factor that is rarely mentioned in connection with that oh-so-profitable $276 million figure for retail business is the cost of keeping the trade sales representative on the road, a cost that is now said to be more than $100 a day for each rep. I used to stop in my friend's bookstore several times a week on my way home from work. At least half the time she would be busy with a sales rep, so I'd look around and leave. Who calls on *me*? The Greenaway Plan, that's who! (Or the Standing Order Plan, or the Approval Plan, etc.) As we all know, under the Greenaway Plan, libraries receive one copy of all books published (except those costing over $15 in general) before publication date (more often after such date) at a "substantial" discount (sometimes 70 percent but more often 35 to 40 percent) for evaluation in view of possible purchase in quantity. Actually, the Greenaway Plan suits us fine, because few of us have the time or the inclination to deal with hordes of eager salespersons spending entire afternoons hawking their wares. But there is a rub: in the annals of poormouthing, publishers' names are writ largest when they talk about the enormous financial sacrifice the Greenaway Plan entails for them. I submit that it is one hell of a lot cheaper to send 8,504 libraries a few shipments of new titles each year even at 70 percent discount, than to have an army of sales reps calling on

each of those libraries several times a year. Yet, somehow, the cost of the sales rep is not figured in as a factor in doing business with the retailer and in tallying publishers' profits. Is it simply a matter again of the library subsidizing the retailer? (In all fairness, a few publishers do have library sales reps, some of whom are service-oriented enough that we deal directly with their companies rather than going to jobbers. They are the exception rather than the rule, however.)

Publishers have given us many more reasons for feeling that retail book business is somehow "better" than library book business: I have been told that library purchase orders are "funny"; that libraries pay too slowly; that libraries "nitpick" about broken corners on books, blank pages, oil smears, water damaged books, and smashed cartons, but the wildest answer I ever had as to why libraries are able to get a better discount from book jobbers than from book publishers (a mind-blowing economic concept—when the middleman can sell more cheaply than the producer) came from a vice president of the David McKay Company, who said, simply, "Because that's how we do it." I asked why; his response was, "Because that's how we've always done it." (Remember the Edsel?)

Perhaps no bookselling "technique" reflects publishers' attitudes toward libraries vs. retail booksellers as customers better than that demonstrated at the annual conferences of the American Library Association and the American Booksellers Association. Many librarians really seem to believe that publishers go all out at ALA meetings—parties, autographed books, neat buttons, free plastic (more like gossamer when you fill them up) bags, and an occasional free lunch. They probably also believe that publishers go all out every bit as much at ABA meetings. Why not? As one who has attended both, let me just mention a few differences; it was plastic bags at ALA in Detroit, but canvas totes at ABA in San Francisco; lovely cheeses and crackers at ALA, but great fat shrimp at ABA; autographed books which you pay for at ALA, but autographed books free at ABA (hardbounds yet!); cocktails in suite 1906 at ALA, but a major catered reception (one of many) in the Chinese Embassy at ABA. Get the picture, library people? It really isn't very pretty, not because we need shrimp and canvas totes or catered receptions, but because of what it says about how librarians are viewed by the people we, perforce, depend on so much.

Thoughts for Publishers

In *SLJ*'s editorial Gerhardt wrote, " . . . juvenile book publishers have been brooding aloud that their backlist titles aren't selling to libraries in anywhere near the numbers that they once did. Publishers question what's gone wrong." I would venture to guess that juvenile backlist titles aren't the *only* ones not selling to libraries as they once did, but that *all* titles are doing the same, and a lot more brooding is warranted, along with some concrete action. Suggestions for such action follow.

First, publishers ought to reexamine the whole discount structure and the *real* costs of doing business with libraries as compared with bookstores. My own library system is a large one with money to spend, but at no time are we ever given the discounts our retailer friends get. Small libraries, which buy little, do exist but there are also many small bookstore operations; the discrepancies between treatment of these two kinds of buyers are huge. Small libraries come out on the short end every time.

Second, publishers ought to examine very carefully just why libraries are buying fewer books each year and how much responsibility for this rests with the publishers themselves. In our case, the hidden cost of ordering a book, above and beyond its actual cost, is enormous. Nearly $3^1/$_2$ million was expended indirectly in 1976 to get and get into our branches some 270,000 books—for which the actual book expenditure was $2^1/$_2$ million—a total of $6 million. This comes to more than $22 per book, a figure that includes thousands of mass market, inexpensive paperbacks. When we can save some money by getting a better discount, by not having to reorder, by not having to take a debit or call a publisher or return a wrong title or spend months trying to locate part of a shipment lost by the U.S. Postal Service—when administrative costs of obtaining books decrease—more money will be spent on books. As an example, Gerhardt's thoughts about books being called "out of stock indefinitely" and how much publishers are losing by maintaining this quaint (to say the least) practice are not based on opinion, but on fact. If we order a $5 book from a publisher or wholesaler and the order is returned marked "OSI," we reorder from someone else; this increases the cost of the book by 400 percent. If, however, after one or two reorders, we never do get the book, we've spent a lot of money for nothing. We lose money, true, but so does the publisher, so why continue this ridiculous game of "out of stock indefinitely?" A spade should be called a spade, and "out of print" should be called just what it is—"OP," not "OSI."

Third, publishers might examine some of their delivery practices. An excuse for publishers' reluctance to deal with libraries has always been libraries' lateness in paying their bills. Yet in most cases, bills are not paid because the goods have never arrived or have arrived in bad condition. Not too long ago I received a book for review from *Library Journal*, sent "special delivery" from New York to Cleveland; it took 22 days for the book to reach me. Daily the newspapers carry "cute" stories about nondelivery of mail or mail delivered months and even years late, yet most publishers persist in using the U.S. Postal Service to deliver smaller shipments. We will not pay for books until we receive them in perfect condition. No intelligent consumer does otherwise. Yet when McGraw-Hill sends a shipment marked "one of 3" and one carton arrives one day, another two weeks later, and carton three five weeks later, courtesy of the U.S. mail, whose fault is it that we pay late? United Parcel Service (UPS) is not only extremely efficient, but in many cases is cheaper than the mail, so why not use UPS (especially since we pay the postage costs to most publishers with whom we deal)? Publishers also might make a special effort to hire packers who have mastered the fine art of counting to 100 or so; in 1976 we received 394 shipments that were short from 4 to 32 books, and 365 duplicate shipments—it's not that we mind the 365 cartons of freebies but that we know we'll pay for them in the long run one way or another!

Fourth, and perhaps most important, the real powers-that-be in most publishing houses ought to stop underestimating the intelligence of those of us who work in libraries. We can not only read but can often interpret their statistics; we know very well that our counterparts in the bookstores get higher discounts than we do for no reason that makes any economic sense at all; we know, as consumers, that we no more have to accept a $25 art book with broken corners than anyone has to accept a new Chevrolet with dented fenders; we know that the great "paper shortage" of several years ago resulted in an increase in the cost of the books we bought (a mystery, for example, went from $4.95 to $7.95), but that the actual cost of the paper, shortage and all, added only about 25¢ to the cost of producing most books; we know that "OSI" is a shuck, pure and simple; we know that by dealing with a decent wholesaler we can increase our discount from 10 to 25 percent at least; and we know a lot more.

Perhaps it really is this arrogant attitude at the top that most needs to be reexamined. One of the most infuriating experiences I have ever had in my job occurred three years ago. CCPL had participated in a Greenaway Plan with Thomas Y. Crowell Company for years—one copy of each new title, as usual, etc. One day a Greenaway shipment arrived, with an invoice for one copy of this, one copy of that, and 73 copies of an $8.95 book on condominiums. We chuckled for a while, then wrote to Crowell explaining what had happened. Crowell's answer came, and said, in effect, that this was completely impossible. So we called Crowell (at our expense) and said that it was hardly impossible since we had both an invoice for 73 copies of *Condominiums* and 73 actual copies of *Condominiums*. The person with whom we spoke said that was ridiculous and hung up the telephone. Six months, many letters and phone calls later, Crowell finally admitted that perhaps we were right, that perhaps they had erred, and graciously gave us permission to return 72 copies of the book (at our expense) to them. This is not an isolated instance; similar things have happened to us and to other libraries countless times. Granted, mistakes will happen, but I and my staff resent being treated like cretins when we try to rectify such errors. Most of the publishing people I have met—editors, library promotion people, salespeople—are sincerely concerned about what they are doing and are trying to do the best they can for libraries, but in the face of top-echelon stupidity such as we see every day, their jobs must be thankless at best.

Sobering Conclusions

The first reaction of any intelligent consumer faced with the situation we faced with Crowell, described above, would be to say never again will I buy a Crowell product. But libraries cannot usually do this; you can buy another car if your Chevy dealer's products aren't up to snuff, but each title on each publisher's list is unique and thus usually can't be replaced by another title from another company. So libraries must admit that they are a captive market; the patron really doesn't care whether you've had horrendous problems in getting a book or books from this publisher or that, but wants the book and has paid good money through his or her taxes for you to get it into your library. So what then?

Raise hell, that's what—through your own contacts,

through your library, and through your professional associations, local, state, and national. The latter, especially is important; ALA represents some 35,000 members, *all* of whom are affected by the practices I have described, yet where has ALA been in fighting for a better money deal for libraries? Copyright and free access and intellectual freedom may all be noble and knotty problems that ALA must cope with, but what good will it do to solve them if libraries can no longer afford the materials that provide the causes for concern in those areas in the first place? We all saw, a few years ago, just how ineffectual libraries and particularly library associations were in litigation when the whole matter of the price fixing on "library editions" came up (we are all still paying net prices for those editions more than 10 years later). But just as the citizens' consumer movement has acquired both voice and some real clout by fighting for consumers' rights, it is time that libraries and their associations began to fight back, too. If not, we may all find ourselves going the way of the dodo bird—and libraries are much too important for that to happen, as even our publisher friends must agree.

Déjà Vu from the Bridge

by Peggy Sullivan

Part I: Reviewing and Publishing

A few months ago, after some twenty years and some more than 100 reviews of books for *School Library Journal*, I submitted my final review. I had several reasons for giving up this interesting but demanding task. One was time. I kept feeling the constraints of deadlines more severely as I tried to do several things, and I also felt that there must be young people as anxious as I to achieve the distinction of reviewing for a publication.

Why should anyone write either reviews or articles? I can sum up four reasons I had for writing and reviewing on a regular basis: to test one's own ideas and reactions, to communicate with others, to repay the benefits one has gained from the writings of others, to develop and maintain a discipline that can be extended to other aspects of life and work.

As a reviewer, I felt—and I was assured by others—that I was always honest, usually well-informed, and appropriately succinct. I learned that publishers and editors did not easily or soon forget a negative review. One of them once passed word through a friend that "if Peggy Sullivan wants to keep in touch with new books and meet people, she needs to cut down on what she says. Writing critical reviews won't win her any friends." It may have lost me friends in publishing circles, but the bond it established with librarians, who appreciate criticism, more than compensated for that loss. I continued to review through several changes in my own career—children's librarian in a public library, supervisor of children's librarians, a library specialist in a school system, a project director and staff member of the American Library Association, doctoral student, library school faculty member, and, most recently, a public library administrator.

Books changed as much as I did. In the early years, there were career books that seem vapid indeed by today's standards, sought-after simple stories that have long since been outclassed by the charm of the *Little Bear* books and other easy readers that came along and family stories that served a purpose without pretension. In fact, it seems to me that pretension has increased considerably in children's books in these past decades. Plots dealing with death or social problems have increased in numbers without a comparable increase in the skill or subtlety of authors' writing them. Without embarrassment I'll repeat the question I asked the 1978 Newbery-

Caldecott Committee during their deliberations, "If Leslie had moved to Baltimore instead of dying, would we be considering *Bridge to Terabithia* for the Newbery Award?" I think not.

As my work took me further away from direct service to children, I thought I probably should quit reviewing, but I was reassured by those librarians working with children who said, "You hit the nail on the head! Keep it up!" It is ironic that many of them who have the know-how and the opportunities do not have the inclination to review or to write for publication. The library profession is all the poorer for it.

Several years ago, when a student told me she resented assignments of written work because she suspected the professor would take credit for publishing her work, I was so surprised that I blurted: "Copy your ideas when I don't have time to write down all my own? Why should I?" My candor was more convincing than my logic, and I know that she recognized me as no threat to her own reputation. However, to my knowledge, she has not written for publication. I could wish for more passion to publish, less concern for copying. And just in case anyone thinks that advances in age and status have provided me with the leisure for writing, let me assure them that I am writing these words on a lined, white tablet balanced on my knee in an airport lounge after a full day of observing and discussing a circulation control system and before taking a two-hour flight to my next stop where I will observe another system.

Librarians who work with youth in school and public libraries encounter a special kind of professional isolation. They often feel they are the lone spokespersons for youth or, especially in a school setting, for the unique values of libraries. Writing might initially increase that sense of isolation, because it requires personal confrontation with one's own background, judgments, and opinions. But eventually, it can provide a supple link with others who may respond either with the warmth of respect or the heat of disagreement. Both sources of heat should be welcome.

To me, it seems to be especially important for librarians working with youth to express themselves because they are being observed and studied by others. Mary Kingsbury (*SLJ*, November, 1978, p. 22) has noted that few librarians beyond their thirties continue to work with young people. And, Pauline Wilson and I, among others, have questioned what were the actual goals of librarians working with children. It behooves those librarians to state some of their own answers.

There is an interesting phenomenon which tends to impede communication between the practitioner in library work with youth and the observer or researcher. This person is set apart as soon as he enters academe as a library educator or goes into some aspect of general library administration no matter how long he may have worked with children or young people in libraries. I have done both, so I value all the more the continuing communication and support I have enjoyed with librarians who have continued in the field of library work with youth. But sometimes, I think that by alienating persons who have left their field, youth librarians have made unnecessary enemies for themselves. It should not be treason to become a general administrator. I know that my experience as a children's librarian and in school librarianship has made it possible for me to understand the special needs of these librarians for continuing education, their points of view on cooperation and networking, their need for recognition in their field as well as their need for career mobility.

Looking back upon rewarding experiences and looking forward to times when that experience will be useful in answering challenges, I am grateful. There is something pretentious in simple statements when they are repeated inappropriately, but Dag Hammarskjold's words are in my mind, "For all that has been, thanks. To all that will be, yes."

Part II: Goals of Public Library Service for Children

Some years ago, Lowell Martin wrote an article on cooperation between school and public libraries which he subtitled: "Or, Why Don't We Have Any?" It was not only eye-catching and provocative, but a very reasonable question to ask. A subtitle for this discussion of goals of children's services of public libraries might be: "Are We Sure We Have Any?" However, I would not do that because I believe that when conferees have heard all of the speakers and discussions planned, and when readers later have read all the papers, they will be convinced that, indeed, there are goals. If there were not, we could scarcely now all be so convinced of the importance of children's services that we would be gathered here, and there could not be the strong thread of agreement running through the presentations which, I predict, will be discernible. It is only in individual programs of service to children, perhaps only in the minds of individual librarians, that the question may not be satisfactorily answered. The most painful question is not whether librarianship has goals for public library service to children; it is whether or not each person responsible for providing that service has recognized, measurable, articulated goals for service. I think they do not.

There are several reasons why goals for children's services (and as I use that term throughout, I shall mean children's services in public libraries) are not often discussed. First, no matter how tough the budget crunch, or how minimal or thoughtless the planning of those services, no one ever says, "We are eliminating (or even cutting back) services to children." Instead, one hears, "We have found better delivery systems for service to the whole community," or "We are cutting out the frills," or "We are reducing the number of staff who don't provide direct service." I do not intend to suggest that

all such cuts have bad effects on the service actually given to children. A couple of years ago I asked a children's librarian in a public library system about the problems the system had had regarding the reduction of the number and status of children's consultants. She said, "Well, I'm sorry for those people, of course, but now I think I may be better able to get on with what I'm doing." When I asked why, she said, "Because I won't have to spend all my time preparing reports and getting approvals."

The reply of the children's librarian suggests another reason why we do not consider the goals of children's services often enough. For better or worse, children's librarians are so well recognized for their unique interests and abilities that their judgments on what services to children should be are seldom questioned. Because they tend to work in isolation, they seldom experience the cuts and thrusts, wins and losses, and the special joy of frequent discussions with colleagues who share their same interests and backgrounds. By the same token, they may develop an overly reverential deference to the person in their system or library community recognized as the defender or spokesperson for library services to children. Even I have recently been the object of such deference, and only the memory of my own irreverence for Kahlil Gilbran (O, speak to us of children's services, O Prophet! O, speak of filmstrips; O, speak of storytelling, O Prophet!) has helped me to keep me sane.

Traditions

Our rich tradition of leadership in public library service to children has developed because of people of courage and vision from earliest history, but we have too often attempted to adopt rather than adapt their vision. With the idea that we have inherited their courage, we have exercised it as intransigence or just bad temper. Ironically, the respect that librarianship for children has always received has generally allowed us to do these things. The conclusion, "But she's the children's librarian," has been used to compensate for the fact that "she" may be crazy, disorganized, unable to open a window or read a budget; and if she should be unable to work effectively with the children in the community, even that can be excused (because the children have changed)—nevertheless, the collective "we" say, "She certainly knows books!"

In a talk about goals, my emphasis on personality may seem misplaced, but I suggest that almost all the recognized goals for children's services have political bases (and politics is people), and have been accepted not just because of the toughness of their proponents, but because of their charm. It is our latter-day interpretation of the dicta of early leaders that has robbed them of their humanity. I worked once with a children's librarian who was an excellent storyteller, and who was even able to hold the interest of preschool children with stories like "The Poppyseed Cakes" without so much as a book jacket to distract the children from her oral interpretation. I asked her once why she never used picture books and she replied, "Miss God [her library school professor] said not to." Since she had gone to school at a time when the appropriateness and level of art of picture books for children were not as rich as they are today, there was probably good reason for that dictum, but to hold to it in a later era seems not only questionable but probably not at all what Miss God had in mind. In my own experience, I recall an early supervisor who cautioned me never to touch a child. I obeyed that dictum for a long time, or thought I did. But a day came when I glimpsed myself reflected in the door of the library with my arm around a child as he showed me an illustration from a book he had just borrowed. In a flash (or perhaps in a moment crystallized from a long period of growing awareness), I realized that my gesture was natural for me, as my supervisor's restraint was natural for her. This supervisor might still be shocked, but if she taught me well, her dictum should be satisfied in helping me to make my own decisions and to move, work and think in my own way.

It may be that the guidance and firmness which most of us received in generous abundance from training school teachers (later, library science teachers) and early supervisors have inhibited our decision-making and goal-setting skills. It may even be that the tradition of strong leadership among coordinators and supervisors has further inhibited the development of those skills. However, if that were true, or if those were the only inhibitions, we would be seeing today the setting and implementation of excellent goals for children's services in public libraries because we have moved away from those strong traditions. The fact is that goals are no clearer than they ever were; they are perhaps even less clearly articulated. The tradition of success and continuity has had its effect: in not having to justify initiation of children's services, we have failed to review and revise the goals which brought that service into existence, and we have arrived at what has been described as a mindless time of doing out of habit what we think is good, dropping what is not popular or relevant, and becoming less expert and experienced in the areas where children's librarians of earlier days made their most significant contributions.

Mindlessness—it is a harsh term for a sick condition, and I cringed when I first heard it applied to children's services today. Nevertheless, it has echoed in my mind as I have had several recent experiences with librarians working with children in public libraries. One I will share: I telephoned one of our branch libraries recently to ask exactly what equipment the children's librarian wanted for a program, why that rental of equipment was necessary, and what the nature of the program was. In the librarian's absence, one of her colleagues informed me coolly that she was a very good children's librarian and that if she said she needed something, she did, and if she planned a program, it would be a good one. Admiring the loyalty but still needing the information, I asked that the children's librarian return my call. When she did, she started out by saying that it certainly had not occurred to her in planning the program that a system like The Chicago Public Library would not have the equipment, and that she should not be blamed for the system's shortcomings. Fair enough; however, she continued by charging that no one in the administration understood what good programming was or how hard people like her worked. Eventually, and I think against her bet-

ter judgment, she answered my questions and I was able to present enough justification for her request that it could be honored. I found myself thinking again of Frances Clark Sayers's essay, "The Belligerent Profession," in which she praises the intransigence that is vital to innovation and success, and deplores the lackluster air of acceptance which she saw as characteristic of too many librarians.[1] I agree with her, but I do not believe that belligerence must replace tact, reason or competence in order to achieve good results.

What goals have to be personal (in the sense that they should be based on the needs of the people they are intended to serve) and should be developed from the individual commitments and drives of those who will implement them, they are eventually best stated in less personal terms, and need to be measured in some objective ways. Even when formal goals do not exist, the response to questions about why a specific book or series is not in a library collection, or why storytelling is no longer a regular part of the children's library program, cannot be answered satisfactorily by the statement that the children's librarian is competent and therefore should not be questioned.

Social Change & Libraries

There are reasons beyond the field of librarianship which have brought us to this time of mindlessness or assurance or fear or assertiveness—or, as Dickens might have seen it, a time of all those things mixed together. Social change is one of them. We always have had and always will have social change, but it has some interesting implications for children services in public libraries today. Before *outreach* was a word, much less a rallying cry or (later) a cliché, library services reached out to children. Librarians went where the children were—the parks, the schools, the streets, the isolated rural crossroads. And the outreach was warmly and widely directed to children as students, children as the best links to immigrant families, children as participants in culture, children as people. I have never seen a reference in the literature before World War II to the idea that we should provide a service to children because they would become future taxpayers, who could some day control our destinies and our library programs.

In the 1960s, when the idea of outreach was in its liveliest phase, the patterns followed were almost identical to the ones which children's librarians had set decades earlier. I remember reading in a library periodical about ways to win the support and discover the needs of people in a poverty area: get in touch with the teachers and the community leaders, invite them to the library by offering some program or exhibit they want, provide coffee even if you have to do it out of your own pocket, and then speak briefly to them, but allow plenty of time for discussion. Listen to them, said the article, and base your library program on what they say they need and want. It was and is good advice, but it was the same advice I had followed, instinctively, more than a decade earlier—and I was certainly not the first to do so. Service to children was indeed the classic success of the American public library, and its goals, as well as its techniques, were the classic means to achieve success, important not for its own sake but because success means accomplishment of purpose.

As outreach programs flourished, however, a new breed of librarian administered them. These librarians worked with children, yet did not think of themselves as children's librarians, and in many instances were philosophically and administratively separated from the mainstream of children's services. With some notable exceptions, persons responsible for service to children remained aloof from the guidance and supervision of these programs; the results were that the outreach librarians rediscovered goals and reinvented techniques for service and that those goals and techniques were seldom identified with the traditional service provided to children. Am I concerned about who should get the credit for all this? No. I mention it merely because this is one of several examples where service to children was actually provided and usually provided well, but where that aspect of service was never recognized as being under the traditional rubric of children's services. The recognized goals were usually stated so rigidly that outreach programs often reached around them rather than toward them, and did not openly recognize them at all.

Similarly, some aspects of library service to children have customarily been provided by other parts of the library, yet the goals have seldom acknowledged this. Telephone reference service supplied from a general or adult information area, selection and provision of nonprint media, and administration of the necessary services of registration and circulation are often dismissed, as though our goals and services were operative within time and space boundaries. I have also been intrigued to know that there are children's librarians who make no secret of their resentment of the occasional incursions into their rooms or use of their collections by librarians from other areas, but who manage to go off duty blithely leaving those rooms and collections unattended or attended only by formerly unwelcome colleagues. It is a puzzlement.

Schools & Public Libraries

Another puzzlement is the question of the relationship between public library service to children and schools. Here, too, there is a tradition that is cause for pride. It was children's librarians who first concerned themselves with the provision of library service to schools. Ways of doing so ranged from exhaustive programs of registration and either story-telling or providing book-talks throughout every school in the area, to the packing and sending of boxes of books for classroom use, to developing many strong relationships and programs of service for the teachers who became library stalwarts. The pattern became a little more mixed when school libraries began to develop. While children's librarians were among the first to become school librarians and to enrich those libraries with their traditions, ideals, techniques and goals, the loss has been in what the public library's program of children's service has been in relation to the schools.

No one should expect the relationship (or program of service) with a school which has its own library, however meager or grand, to be the same as that with a school which doesn't. Yet children's librarians have tended to go in one of two directions: either they have accepted a role as outside consultants or kibitzers to the work of the school library personnel, or they have simply ignored it and gone about their business as usual, i.e., their business as it used to be. Instead of seeing themselves and their services in relation to the school and its program of curriculum and instruction, they have too often settled for seeing themselves in relation only to the library program of the school. Examples of this are easy to cite. The perennial headaches of school assignments—from the horror of fruitless searches for information about the green scapular, to the placation of parents who are more concerned than their children about the need for citations in seven different media when the topic is the Panama Canal crisis—have been handed back to the school librarian, often (but seldom realistically) with the expectation that he or she will see that everything is straightened out. It is not that simple. Somewhere, a continuing link of communication needs to exist between the public library and the administration of the school, and to exist at all levels—branch library to neighborhood school, system to system. Schools are important not because they are sites for other libraries which have goals and programs basically similar to those of the public library, but because they are a place in society where the children whom public libraries are destined to serve receive much of their education.

The problem in regard to schools, as in regard to other aspects of society with which public libraries' children's services must deal, seems to be that when the schools themselves are active in areas which have traditionally been those of the public library, the public library has responded with not dynamism but withdrawal. "There's no need for me to tell stories any more; the kids get them in school," says the children's librarian, adding to sympathetic audiences that the quality of the story or the telling may not be as good—and that is reason enough for dropping a tradition. Thus, children's library programs have focused on daycare centers, nursery schools or camps. It is easier to find a new site than to attract and hold children's interest in the face of competition and distraction. The number of enthusiastic responses to the offerings of service from children's librarians in public libraries is so great and from so many sources—parents, teachers and senior adults, as well as the children themselves—that service to them can be demanding and satisfying enough to cause us to forget that this service may not achieve our goals. Some aspect of the goal-setting process must be concerned with priorities, and priorities must take into account the need to reach as many children as possible to give them an awareness of what libraries are all about. Special services may be devised and offered to children with special needs or those in unusual environments, but the goals should not be set without a clear idea of the need for some broad-based program of information about children's services for the entire public.

The word *information* has become a loaded one for those concerned with library service to children. In this respect, also, we have shrunk back rather than moved forward, as our goals might have us do. Because the provision of information services, data banks, referrals, etc. have tended to make libraries seem lopsidedly but resolutely committed to the presentation of facts rather than the encouragement of pleasure or even the development of culture, we have reacted by eschewing the idea of information as an important product of the public library. As I have said before, I believe the more reasonable approach is to stress that, for children, the provision of pleasure, encouragement of reading, enlargement of vocabulary, and development of a sense of fantasy or even of a sense of humor are informational services which the public library can provide in a unique, nonthreatening environment. We ought to take every opportunity to say this to the information-mongers who need to be reminded that personal development is the most significant kind of information process. Incorporation of this idea into our stated goals would put into perspective the true and natural relationship between library service to children and the great information programs of our day.

Measurement

No discussion of goals is complete without reference to some means of measuring their accomplishment. Measurement should be kept in mind throughout the entire goal-setting process. Sometimes, this results in choosing goals that can be measured readily, e.g., presenting a set number of programs or achieving some stated amount of circulation or use, but that at least is better than setting a goal which can then be discussed happily and theoretically because there is no reasonable way to measure progress toward it, much less achievement of it. The goals relating to quality are, of course, the more difficult ones to set and to measure. An interesting example is the incorporation of books of minimal quality into library collections with the intent that they will be as stepping-stones to something better, with no clear idea of how measurement of that development of taste will be accomplished. In the same way, we need cleaner statements of the success or failure of everything that is tried. Our recent history is strewn with abandoned projects which have been dropped by intuition, just as they were too often begun by intuition.

Having goals and measuring progress toward them are essential to the survival of children's services in public libraries. The development of them is not the esoteric or fanciful activity of people who like to play around with ideas or words. Rather, the development should be personal, in the sense that individuals will have to make the commitment and implement the goals, but social in the sense that the goals need to be stated in broad terms considering the audience. As the song says about peace—goals begin with me, but that is only the beginning.

Reference

1. Sayers, Frances Clark. "The Belligerent Profession." *American Library Philosophy: An Anthology*, (Shoe String Press, 1975).

How Long, Oh, Lord, Do We Roam in the Wilderness?

by Marilyn Miller

Happy 25th, *School Library Journal*. Like you, I'm celebrating my 25th year in library service. The first two years really don't count as "professional" library years since I didn't know then "how to run a library good." I hadn't had the courses—just a fascination for the potential of libraries and a love of books, and I was truly interested in working with young people. I found a supply catalog, figured out what the forms and gadgets were for, ordered what seemed usable in the school library, and established some routines and policies.

At the end of two years I knew for certain that kids were hungry for good books that spoke to them, entertained them, and provided them with a view of other worlds. I also knew that an enthusiastic person who had an interest in young people, as well as an interest in books, could have a marvelous time as a school librarian. So I went to library school and learned "how to run a library good." And, thanks to the University of Michigan's library school, I learned that to "run a library good," I had to keep on learning. I became aware that no library—regardless how small, where located, or patrons served—was a static institution. I embarked on my 25-year adventure as school librarian, state consultant, and library educator with *Junior Libraries*, which became *School Library Journal* when its name was changed in September of 1961, helping to point the way.

As I write, I am browsing through Vol. I, No. I of *Junior Libraries* with its features on comic books, the need for good libraries to teach reading, and articles on book exhibits and fairs. Scattered throughout are pictures of librarians I came to admire: Dilla MacBean, Christine Gilbert, Alice Brooks McGuire, Nancy Jane Day, and Carolyn Whitenack.

On the shelves in my office sit the entire 25-year run of *Junior Libraries* and *School Library Journal*. The temptation to dip into a few issues from each volume, especially the early years, is almost more than I can bear, for in those issues are articles by library notables such as Henne, Gaver, Ahlers, Rowell, Mahar, McGinnis, McJenkins, Nickel—professionals who gave outstanding leadership to school library development in the critical decades of the fifties and sixties. These were people who were willing to spend many hours acquainting newcomers to the profession, and they never seemed to complain about the hours spent in promoting what they believed in.

Whatever the future says about school library development during these critical decades, it must be noted that there was a cadre of dedicated school librarians in the postwar years who were deeply committed to the belief that the improvement of educational opportunity for young people included access to good school libraries. These librarians articulated their beliefs through their work on standards, federal legislation, improved higher education programs, professional associations, and research for a nation that needed freedom of inquiry, independent thinkers, creative adults, and many points of view.

So many exciting projects, activities, and developments came in the late fifties and sixties. School librarians did *good* things, and believed in their worth. Actually, the title of my article could be the cliché-slogan, "You've come a long way, baby!," but frankly, I worry that we have lost the momentum of the last decades. Now, what appears to be the basic reactive nature of school librarians has become overwhelming: the nature that easily accepts the service and support roles, and the following of the curriculum in purchase of materials, but not as easily the leadership role—that of planner, manager, and process person.

For some months now, as I have visited libraries and library media centers talking with library media specialists and supervisors, I have wondered, "How long, oh, Lord, do we roam in the wilderness?" We once had so much success in our grasp. Have we lost out, or will the pendulum swing again? But if it swings, do we have the leadership to move us to higher levels of program development and implementation? Do we have the leadership and the breadth of understanding and commitment among school librarians to implement, universally, the kinds of programs (in a few schools in each state) we have come to recognize for excellence?

I don't want to roam through my wilderness without some balance and tribute to what has been accomplished. So, in this response to the past 25 years, I plan to review significant events as well as identify some issues about which we should be concerned. The importance of school library events of the past 25 years will be assessed and described more objectively in the years 2000 plus. It is not untoward, however, to do a little personal reflection and second guessing on the historic developments that might be selected as vital to the present and to the future.

Surveying Significant Events

In order to check my views of the past 25 years and my concerns for the future, I turned to my colleagues in state level positions who are also members of the National Association of State Educational Media Professionals. The roster identified members from 34 states and Guam. At least one state consultant, or supervisor from each of the 34 states answered my call for help in identifying the three to five most significant events of the school library media field that occurred in the past 25 years. They were also asked to identify three to five of the most serious problems they believe face school library media program development in their states as well as in the nation, and to comment on their concerns and hopes for the future.

The survey was quite informal, and while a follow up, second-round ranking of the original list would be interesting and more scientific perhaps, the initial thoughts of my colleagues serve me well as beginning points on which to base my own reactions.

The five most important events in the past 25 years in the school library field nationwide are easy to list from the responses: Twenty-eight spoke to the importance of technology and the emerging field of media (and its use by the schools); 24 discussed the availability of federal funding; 16 cited the development of national standards; and 11 mentioned changes and developments in the professional preparation of school library media personnel.

My Choices

Although I agree as to the importance of these developments, I place the 1960 *Standards for School Library Programs* (ALA) first on my list of the most important events of the past 25 years. I have criticized (and still do) the document for its failure to adequately foresee the educational impact and use of audiovisual media, but *Standards . . .* is an example of a beautifully written, comprehensive, philosophical statement of the qualitative aspects of school library service. Its endorsement by other educational organizations, its style, and its comprehensive nature made it usable in interpreting library programs to parents, school boards, architects, legislators, and school administrators, or wherever it was needed. It served as a guide for the development of the state standards required by Title II of the Elementary and Secondary Education Act (ESEA), and it served as in-service education for thousands of school librarians and was *the* pre-service text for potential school librarians.

The philosophy of that document, and the document itself, provided ammunition and testimony for many activities and developments in the sixties (that decade when many of us surely thought the professional millennium had arrived). The School Library Development Project, the Knapp School Library project, ESEA Title II, and the broadening of the concept of the school library as a materials center all had a focus of support in *Standards for School Library Programs*. Let me explain here that I do heartily believe in *Media Programs: District and School's* (ALA/AECT, 1975) approach to provide programs in response to planning, and I appreciate the district-level recommendations it includes. But the newer document lacks a stylistic presentation that serves in the way the 1960 statement has (and still serves, the discerning professional).

My second choice, and not one respondent mentioned it, is the appointment of state school library supervisors in almost all 50 states in the sixties. The work of these supervisors in helping develop and implement state standards, the transition of libraries into media centers, and state plans for federal funding had a vital impact on school library development. Their many hours and miles spent traveling, and their numerous meetings with community groups, school boards, school faculties, and school librarians to talk about facilities, programs, certification, and accreditation, may not be totally appreciated today. However, those hours, miles, and meetings had a positive, cumulative national effect that will someday, I hope, be adequately evaluated and recorded.

The third item on my list of events is the development of communication technology and its subsequent impact on schools. Specifically, I note (in accord with my colleagues), the importance of the development of the school library media center, the introduction of the use of the computer and video in instruction, the concern for developing visual interpretation skills, the availability of facilities and programs for student production of materials, and classroom use of media.

I agree that federal funding is a significant development of the past 25 years, but I am interested in finding out how specific federal programs will be evaluated for their long-range impact on school media program development. I suspect the top credit will not go to ESEA Title II. Although the program has been very popular with school librarians and many congressmen, its impact on the qualitative aspects of program development nationwide may be hard to support—quantitative aspects are another matter.

I also feel that the identification of trends in the preparation and certification of personnel is highly significant. However, the implementation of those trends and the accomplishments of the products of those trends are another matter that will be discussed later in this article.

Consultants' Responses

Over half of the state consultants who identified the most significant events in school library media program development named, as the *most* significant, developments in media staff education programs and the establishment of state and regional standards. Federal funding was identified by 15, while 13 noted the development of "true" media centers; 11 noted the establishment of clementary centers and the provision of staff and services at the district and regional levels. School community recognition of the role of the media program was identified by 10 state leaders.

Although not considered as significant by a large number, 7 did list the provision of supervision at the state level; 6 listed the mergers of school library and audiovisual state associations into one organization.

In citing media staff education and preparation programs as significant, supervisors particularly noted the changes in state certification requirements recognizing the need for preparation in librarianship and audiovisual technology, and the trend towards demonstration of competencies as part of the certification process.

One supervisor noted the development of a state master plan for education, a foundation program, and performance expectations as the most important staffing events of the past 25 years. Another noted the development of a career ladder concept from the two-year college degree or certificate through the Master of Library Science. Still another described a move to licensing; another noted the provision of staff development programs for media specialists through master inservice plans. Others noted the current availability of newly established and recently accredited ALA library education programs as most important to staff development in their states.

Undoubtedly, the concern (in most states) for the provision of improved professional education programs is an important development, but there is still a long way to go. Prospective school library media specialists in many parts of the country still find themselves outside the pale in AL accredited programs. (Indeed, I believe history will show that the ALA accreditation process has been too easy on graduate library schools which claim to maintain adequate programs for preparing school librarians, but obviously do not.) Truth in advertising, related to certification requirements for school personnel, is not available in all graduate library school catalogs or through counseling efforts. Indeed, we really know very little about library/media education programs for school personnel. Although it is doubtful that we can, we may be able to identify the sites of most programs. However, important aspects such as quality control in terms of resources available to faculty, faculty credentials, and the caliber of instructional opportunities are suspect. Most shockingly, we don't know much about the overall caliber of the end products of these programs. What we need are humane, literate, knowledgeable, liberally educated men and women who have, in addition to teaching competence, specific knowledge of the organization and management of school library media programs. However history may show that the roots of our failures are in our personnel.

We need to look for instance, at our willingness to approve of undergraduate majors in library science who, with required courses in teacher education, have sacrificed—without realizing what the college or university has done to them—courses in the liberal arts. Lowered and lowering academic standards, the lack of infusion of new blood into the field, and the failure to develop the concepts and idealism of professionalism are plagues upon us now. Added to these factors are frightfully (and frighteningly) low salaries for elementary and secondary teachers in many, many states. And, school discipline problems, which are keeping bright young people from the field, are encouraging many of our best to leave building-level jobs.

When asked to describe the serious problems currently facing media program development in their states, supervisors spoke of losses, retrenchments, failures in funding, staff, standards, and a loss of leadership from both media personnel and school administrative personnel.

Thirty-six responses described concerns with dropping enrollments, inflation, and subsequent loss of professional staff at both building and district levels. Others noted the decrease in categorical, federal aid programs as changes occurred in the management of ESEA. Six responses noted the failure to secure state mandates for minimum staffing, budgets, and collections in school libraries.

While the effects of inflation and falling enrollments are indeed devastating (and one hates to predict the long-time effects of these events), eight responses spoke to even more ominous concerns.

The long-time effect of the lowering of regional and state accreditation standards reported by supervisors could be one of the most serious of all developments. Add to this (1) the low certification requirements, (2) the failure of some states in developing a certification structure and requirements that reflect the contemporary roles of media specialists, and (3) the continued resistance of local school systems to appoint certified personnel, and the picture becomes very gloomy.

An issue no one has tackled publicly, to my knowledge, is the growing number of private schools in this country, including the "white flight" schools. Undoubtedly, their growth will exacerbate the funding problems of public schools which depend on the local tax dollar. In one state, private schools lobbyists have managed to get legislative exemption from some state mandated requirements supervised by the State Department of Public Instruction. These developments are serious as we talk about quality library media collections, programs, and services for all students. One would expect public libraries to be as concerned about the thousands of children in these schools.

Supervisors' Concerns

Certainly not unrelated to the concern for the losses I just described, is the supervisors' worry over the following: poor leadership; a lack of understanding of the role of media programs; lack of foresight and commitment; and apathy on the part of school administrators and leaders as well as media personnel.

Ten respondents mentioned the isolation, in their schools, of the school library media specialists through the specialists' failure in developing positive and aggressive self-images and their failure in demonstrating that they can facilitate more effective communication opportunities for learners.

One supervisor spoke bitterly of the complacency of library media specialists who have arrived in terms of good facilities, collections, and budgets, but who do not reach out to demonstrate their value to children or their roles in the schools. Three supervisors were concerned that personnel were not "keeping up" with modern technology, especially in the rural areas of their states. School library media specialists were not communicating innovative ideas and techniques for involving students in learning through media. Other respondents noted that the school library was no longer the priority of the state department of public instruction; they bemoaned the lack of leadership—not only at the state level, but at the regional and district levels.

Undoubtedly, the growth in numbers of district level supervisors has been a significant part of school library media development in the past 25 years. Many positions were created to deal with funds made available under ESEA II, one of that program's creditable effects. The burgeoning pool of materials available for selection, increased number of building level positions to be supervised, and the need for facilities all contributed to the growth in number of appointments.

When there were competent professionals who understood the role of the media center and their own responsibilities and opportunities as leaders and managers, there were many fine district programs developed. The cutting of these positions in many states (mentioned in the survey by some state supervisors) could be the cruelest blow to continued development of good programs. Building-level programs could be adapted and adjusted temporarily to budget cuts, but without the advocacy, interpretation, and planning at the district level, these programs will continue to suffer due to lack of funds.

Studies of the "whys" of these losses would be revealing. Are district level supervisors victims of their own short-sightedness? For example, their failure to look ahead demonstrates again the reactive nature of school librarians. Are they victims of politics?

How many supervisors are like those described in Ruth Otzman's study of media directors? Otzman isolated certain learned personal tendencies that previous research indicated could differentiate between leaders and nonleaders, and she surveyed a state's media directors to determine who possessed leadership capabilities. She concluded that media directors in that particular state did not appear to be strong leadership types, and, more important, they did not indicate extensive involvement, or a desire for it as far as carrying out district level job responsibilities defined by various national and state recommendations.[1]

Another interesting question for the study of supervisory losses is determining to what extent building level school librarians mobilized to fight for the retention of that position.

Two-thirds of the state supervisors cited the development of the "true" media center and the recognition of the role of the media program as significant in their states. Undoubtedly the philosophical description of the true media center exists, as do definitions and descriptions of the role of the media specialist. These descriptions will stand as we prepare people to assume positions in schools. I am a firm believer that the major purpose of media, media programs, and media people in schools is to assist in the implementation of curriculum and teaching and learning. There is no doubt in my mind that the school library media specialist who combines this implementation function with the traditional role of the librarian (as information and materials specialist and manager) is in a position of intellectual power in the school.

From My Viewpoint . . .

But, as might be expected, I have some concerns. I actually see few completely developed bona fide school library media centers where children or young adults and their teachers move among materials, hardware, and production facilities as motivated by interest or need. I know there are many shining examples throughout the country because I have read about many of them, and I have seen a few of them as I go about my work and travels. What I see most often is painful to describe. I visit many facilities that are *called* school library media centers, but they function as such only in a most superficial or cursory way. Audiovisual media are usually segregated by format—and it is often necessary to ask how and where students find and use audiovisual media. Personnel are busy developing "library skills" programs in isolation from the curriculum. And the students, especially in the high schools, are doing little individual inquiry or developing projects with the knowledge and coplanning of the school librarian or the school library media specialist.

The findings of two studies reinforce my concerns about high-school library programs. In 1974, I conducted a study of high-school seniors in 25 southwestern Michigan high schools to ascertain their opinions on the accessibility of school library media resources.[2] The schools were representative of schools throughout the country: small, large, urban, suburban, rural, inner-city. The students surveyed and interviewed reflected typical representative backgrounds and aspirations: college bound, technical school bound, middle class, affluent, good students, mediocre students, poor students.

Findings revealed that a large majority of the seniors identified themselves as nonusers of the school-library media center. Subsequent interviews revealed that a small number of the respondents characterized themselves as *users* of *other* libraries but as nonreaders—except for paperback and magazine reading. (The equation, by the young, of paperbacks with "nonreading," and "difficult or unattractive" with hardcover books constantly intrigues me). The survey also revealed that a very large number of students did not know whether audiovisual materials were available, could circulate, or be produced. Some students believed that audiovisual resources were less accessible to students than were print materials. They also believed student access to television, videotaped materials and production facilities was limited. According to these students, study halls and scheduled classwork sessions in the media center were the major avenues of access to the media center, and assignments the greatest motivation for use. They believed the circulation procedures for print did not extend to circulating audiovisual materials. The students expressed a desire for more teacher effort in recommending resources for classwork; they believed neither teachers nor librarians recommended materials for recreational and personal use.

In a follow-up study, Alida L. Geppert administered a two-part student survey to library media specialists in the same 25 high schools attended by the students. She found a difference of opinion between the students' perceptions of the accessibility of resources and the media specialists' perceptions of student access to resources on 27 survey items, or 51.9 percent of the total.[3] Media specialists disagreed with students on several items. They believed circulation policies on reference materials were flexible; that students had access to reserve shelves; that recordings, visual media, and AV equipment was accessible. They further disagreed with students in asserting that equipment storage was convenient, that students did know of the existence of the microfilm and videotaped materials; and that students did have access to production facilities.

Media specialists and students did agree however that

encouragement for students to use the center was greater for classwork than for recreational or personal use. (These findings also support my concern for the diminishing young adult services and programs in public libraries.)

In the second part of the Geppert study, librarians were asked various questions on circulation and user policies. Some findings in the subsequent profile were very revealing. In response to questions on how students learned about the availability of recordings, filmstrips, and other visual media, over 75 percent of the librarians responded "the card catalog." When asked how students learned what audiovisual equipment was available for their use, the replies were: "word of mouth" (60 percent); "from teachers" (56 percent); and "browse" (8 percent). The students reported that all equipment for their use was located in special storage.

When librarians were asked about student knowledge of the availability of reserve collections: 56 percent reported that students find out from teachers; four percent reported that they find out by asking; and 16 percent reported that students could find out from the card catalog. The majority of students in these schools find out about the availability of videotaped materials by asking teachers or media staff members.

These are incredible findings. And, as Geppert concluded, a major task for directors of school library media centers and staff is finding ways to improve and evaluate the communication process between users and media center staff. If "true" media center programs and services are to emerge and exist, media specialists at *all* levels must begin to concentrate their efforts on individualization; options for teaching and learners; new patterns of organization of facilities and materials; "gut-level" evaluation of services, programs (and communication of them); useful documentation of inadequacies, etc. The "back to basics" movement and budget cuts for materials are not acceptable excuses for the failure to improve performance in these areas.

Library Education

Although 11 supervisors mentioned the changes and developments in the preservice education of school-library media specialists as significant, positive developments in their states, eight spoke to their current concerns about library media education programs. They worried about the lack of professional preparation of school library media personnel, the need for continuing education, the need for institutions of higher education to prepare people who can develop programs for the twentieth century.

Others referred to, or alluded to, continuing dichotomies in the "demands" of librarianship and instructional technology. They spoke of their desire for "finding a stable ground between the librarian and the media person for certification purposes," education to be developed for the unified approach to the use of library media centers, and for an end to the separation of librarianship and audiovisual at the university level which carries over to performance of those educated in divided programs.

In speaking of improved educational programs at the professional preparation level, it is important to include the 25-year ongoing concern that teacher education programs devote little or no attention to the role of the library media center in the total educational process.

Future Developments

Asking state supervisors to look to the future was a logical last step in the short questionnaire. To encourage both positive and worrisome predictions, I asked them to list those possibilities which looked exciting and those which appeared discouraging.

Supervisors did not offer many exciting possibilities for the future. The majority of responses centered around technology and what could happen with its use: computers in many forms, video in its many forms, and other new communication options. They spoke of alternative message design and delivery systems, instructional television, cable, satellites. They spoke of networking and individualization of instruction. One consultant spoke hopefully of "technology capabilities to enhance individualization and curriculum support." Another spoke of the "wave of the future—the media specialist as a true instructional developer and instructional leader." And another believed "inflation will force closer cooperation between media personnel and classroom teachers to provide needed materials and services to students." Two believed interagency cooperation will be an exciting development, while another believed younger, more competent people entering the field would improve the quality of media programs.

Communications technology is exciting to contemplate. the patient, tireless computer, coupled with its stolid obedience to the creativity (or the lack of it) in the programmer, make it a force that cannot be denied in an era of public criticism of the accountability of traditional teaching strategies. The potential of well-designed and produced instructional television is equally promising.

Teaching and learning options are constantly being developed. But will library media people expand their horizons to lead in this era of communications technology? It doesn't take visits to many schools to collect evidence of the ignorance and disregard of appropriate and productive strategies for the best use of new forms of communications. (Fiddlesticks! We can also find evidence of similar misuse of print. Let's face it!)

The question has to be asked again, "Are present media staffs willing and able to work with the demands and potential of these new systems?" If the answer is "Yes," when are they going to begin on a much wider scale than I see in practice? If the answer is "No," where is the national focus for preparing them to do so? Present professional organizational leadership? Present professional library education programs? Present undergraduate or graduate library and audiovisual media programs? I think not. Perhaps this statement by a midwestern supervisor best sums this concern: "I think maybe there is a place in the schools for some person who is not yet trained—will our present people be expected to do jobs for which they are not qualified?"

In articulating their concerns for the future, supervisors repeated some of their present problems already mentioned such as monetary constraints underscored by inflation, declining enrollments, and closing down of programs. Some spoke further of leadership failures by media specialists themselves, and the need to develop public awareness, and professional education problems. One summed up his concern bluntly: "The future is bleak."

A few, however, spoke to issues for the future, not previously discussed, and they are worth recording for consideration. One supervisor noted a concern over the lack of forceful direction coming from the national level for supervisory personnel including the United States Office of Education [most recently changed to the Department of Education] and the appropriate national associations. Others worried about the leadership capability of the national professional associations and wondered if these organizations could survive. "The American Association of School Librarians," noted a supervisor "lacks a positive force in the organizational structure of ALA. Its leadership is not strong enough on regional and state levels and local school media personnel don't feel that there are real benefits for them in being members of national organizations."

Lack of interest in multitype library networking by school-library media personnel, as expressed by another consultant, is worrisome in this day of cooperative relationships and reduced resources for independent operations.

All expressed concerns are viable and should be addressed more thoroughly in coming months, but I would add censorship and access to resources—both should have been much higher on the list of concerns. While listed in one or two responses, the area of intellectual freedom was not predominant in the replies to my survey. The results of the activities of organized groups (Henne reports 40 such groups), as well as unorganized efforts, can be seen as widespread self-censorship by librarians and as the failure of school librarians to seek ties with other community libraries in mounting public information campaigns to defend access to information by the young. The lack of both intellectual and physical defenses of the right of access to information and materials by the young is frightening.

Priorities for the 80s

So, where does this leave us on the eve of the decade so promisingly described earlier in the seventies by Jetter[4] and Kingsbury?[5] I'm not sure. I do not view myself as a pessimist or as a prophet. As mentioned earlier, I am a firm believer in the potential of the media program and the intellectual power of the school librarian who can function in the hybrid world of the modern view of the school library. I also believe we expect far too much from *one* professional manning a school library. And, as Clark[6] noted in her fine state of the art article in the June 1979, *American Libraries* (must reading for us all), national guidelines have not been helpful to those schools needing assistance in developing priorities for media programs since they do not have enough staff (or energy, financial resources, or ability) to implement the complete package of recommendations.

I don't have any splendid new recommendations, but I do wish school librarians would involve themselves more in the total library world both in their communities and in state and national professional organizations. The fight against censorship, the development of community library resources, the interpretation to the community of the necessity of breadth of access to materials and services for all ages can best be done by the total library community.

I wish (1) that school librarians will be more diligent about pursuit of in-service educational opportunities for themselves; (2) that district supervisors and school administrators be more diligent in their evaluation process of staff performance and growth and development; (3) that those same people, district supervisors and administrators, would reevaluate their hiring requirements for media personnel and be more careful in the appointment process; (4) that somehow we could develop a system for the national planning of school library development.

But in the meantime, I wish all of us, instead of continuing to roam in the wilderness, would reconsider our work and reavow our intent to consider the students—the children or adolescents—first. Let's put them at the center of our planning. The instructional program with its facilities, curricula, teaching strategies, and teachers comes next. The librarian in the school (I use librarian here because the term implies more than a mere media specialist) functions as a teacher and, therefore, is one of the integrators of the instructional system and the students. A school librarian is, of course, much more than a teacher. As a librarian, he or she is also a professional who believes in the absolute necessity of access to information as a basis for life in a democracy. And most of all, the school librarian believes in the potential of the library as an idea and as an institution that offers the opportunity for lifelong, self-education—regardless of the way its resources are stored and retrieved.

For those of us who view youth as our national treasure and our tomorrow, what better way to serve their future than as a librarian who functions also as a teacher and as a media specialist?

References

1. Ruth Zalewski Otzman, "A Study of the Extent to Which Media Leaders in Michigan Possess Certain Leader Need Dispositions (Ph.D. diss., Western Michigan University, 1978).
2. Marilyn L. Miller, "Student Access to School Library Resources as Viewed by High School Seniors in Southwestern Michigan Schools Accredited by the North Central Association of Colleges and Schools" (Ph.D. diss., The University of Michigan, 1976).
3. Alida L. Geppert, "Student Accessibility to School Library Media Center Resources As Viewed by Media Specialists and Compared to Students in Southwestern Michigan Secondary Schools" (Ph.D. diss., Western Michigan University, 1975).

4. Margaret Ann Jetter, "Role of School Library Media Specialist in 1980," in *Futurism and School Media Development*, eds. Marilyn L. Miller and Alida L. Geppert (*Proceedings of the Higher Education Institute*, 1974, Kalamazoo, Michigan: Western Michigan University, 1975), pp. 143-50.

5. Mary Kingsbury, "The Future of School Library Media Centers—Preliminary Report," in *Proceedings of the Higher Education Institute*, pp. 137-142.

6. Geraldine Clark, "Echoes of 60s Advocacy in the School Media Center of the 80s," in *American Libraries* (June 1979), pp. 369-372.

Standards & Free Access—
Equal but Separate

by Linda R. Silver

If the International Year of the Child has any messages for librarians, it should be to remind us just how far removed we are from the survival edge of childhood. While all of us are aware of the plight of most of the world's children, including some in our own country, there is little we can do through our jobs to change the physical and spiritual misery in which appallingly large numbers of them struggle to grow up.

Books do not ease hunger. Information has no immediate effect on the daily ravages of neglect and ill health. Story hours and other programs provide momentary relief at best from abuse and deprivation. To the children among the world's refugees, whose numbers are now the largest since the second World War, or to the victims of political atrocities, library service must figure very low on a list of needs. Amid all the IYC celebrations creeps the chilling realization that to many of the world's young, life is no less than what Isaac Bashevis Singer has called it: "a slaughterhouse . . . a nightmare."

This is the somber perspective from which public library service to children, especially during the International Year of the Child, should be viewed. When all the fun and games, the folk dances and nationality crafts programs, the foreign language lessons and foreign book displays are over, time remains to ask: "What are we doing? What are we here for? Does any of it matter?"

Children's Services and Civilization

The "culture of narcissism," as Christopher Lasch terms contemporary society, has trivialized institutional goals and public expectations. But library service to children earned its reputation as the "glory" of the American public library system precisely because its goals were high, its purposes clear and its responses vigorous and effective. Now, as then, libraries are symbols of a civilized society, for civilization begins only after survival needs are met. If children's librarians are removed from the survival edge of childhood, it is because libraries themselves are addressed to needs that proceed from an absence of chaos and a reasonable guarantee of survival. Established by a civilized society, libraries support civilization by preserving and providing some of the resources that humankind needs to hold back the dark.

The "luxury" of books, information, and library services—which indeed are luxuries to children whose very survival is precarious—are some of the essentials needed for civilized existence. Once assured, the *quality* of that existence then becomes important. How well do libraries provide the essentials? Are they available to all children or only to select groups? Are they provided with intelligence, tact, and respect? And perhaps most important, what do we hope will be the result of the books and information on the children who partake of them? The late Spanish cellist, Pablo Casals, phrased the question this way:

> Each second we live is a new and unique moment of the universe, a moment that never was before and never will be again. And what do we teach our children . . . ? We teach them that two and two make four, and that Paris is the capital of France. When will we also teach them what they are? We should say to each of them: Do you know what you are? You are a marvel. You are unique. In all of the world there is no other child exactly like you. In the millions of years that have passed there has never been another child like you. And look at your body— what a wonder it is! Your legs, your arms, your cunning fingers, the way you move! You may become a Shakespeare, a Michelangelo, a Beethoven. You have the capacity for anything. Yes, you are a marvel. And when you grow up, can you then harm another who is, like you, a marvel? You must work—we must all work—to make this world worthy of its children.[1]

Differently as it may be expressed, one might venture to guess that this idea is shared by the vast majority of children's librarians. But *how* ideals are translated into action is a thornier matter than it once was and among children's librarians, as among all librarians, philosophies and responses differ.

The Issue of Reevaluation

Glancing back over the library literature of the past 10 years, one notices shifts in emphasis and points of view. In the late '60s and early '70s there was much debate about the issue of reevaluation—the removal from library collections of materials that had come to be regarded as socially or morally retrograde. What was seen as the social responsibility of librarians to remove racist and sexist books from their collections was called censorship by others who believed that intellectual freedom perforce allowed all attitudes, no matter how offensive they might be. Answering the assertion that all ideas are equal in the sight of the First Amendment, Dorothy Broderick wrote: "The whole concept of social responsibilities implies value judgments—some things are right and some are wrong . . . In modern jargon, that is known as an elitist point of view, and elitist is a very dirty word, indeed."[2]

From reevaluation—or what to take out of libraries—to the selection process—or what to put in libraries—requires just a slight shift of focus and both sides of the reevaluation debate found a common target in selection standards. To many intellectual freedom purists, librarians have no right to judge because those judgments sometimes result in the exclusion of books from libraries and thereby violate their authors' rights to be heard. To many social responsibilities advocates, librarians have no right to judge because those judgments sometimes result in the exclusion of popular books, and thereby cast elitist aspersions on people's taste. Despite their differences, both points of view resulted in an attack on selection standards that were already being looked at uneasily by administrators interested in winning taxpayers' approval by hardly ever failing to meet their demands.

Book evaluation and selection has long been considered a major part of the children's librarian's job. Therefore, the multipronged attack on standards, almost all of it spoken in the name of high principles, hit children's services hard. Because the attack coincided with a growing concern for children's rights, the selection process had added to the charges leveled against it another that placed selection standards in opposition to the right of children to free access to library materials.

Books on Demand vs. Judging Books

To many children's librarians who have always believed in standards and in free access and who have tried to uphold both principles, it is difficult to see the two in opposition. But to those who do find them inimical, the argument is as follows: Standards are elitist because they make value judgments about children's reading interests and tastes. To tell a child that the library doesn't own a desired book does damage to the child's self-image and to the library's "credibility as a nonjudgment agency." Children have a right to pursue whatever interests them and adults do not have the right to inflict their own values on children. Even though children are not yet taxpayers, they are citizens and entitled to expect a tax supported institution to supply what they demand. Because, as children, they lack the economic power to buy what the library doesn't have, the children's librarian has more of a duty than ever to provide it for them. Selection standards put the importance of literary quality above the interests of children, and collections based on literary quality tend to be safe, but meaningless. Furthermore, poor quality books have no ill-effects on the child's growth into a mature human being, and it doesn't matter what children read so long as they read something.

Librarians who believe in standards counter by saying that this argument is off the mark. Making value judgments about people is elitist perhaps, but making value judgments about books is a professional responsibility and a fulfillment of the public trust. No one has the right to expect instant gratification for all wants, and part of the children's librarian's challenge is to find books that are interesting substitutes for those not in the collection. Rather than violating children's rights, a librarian who chooses books with regard to their honesty and literary integrity is upholding the child's right to concerned and intelligent adult guidance. Instead of representing a safe or "protectionist" philosophy, selection by literary standards provides books that will help children test values and question the status quo. Furthermore, a steady diet of bad books does have ill-effects on the child's growth into a mature human being and it *does* matter what children read.

Two Points of View on the Child

Although these two points of view may seem like polar opposites, they have their similarities. Both have the child in mind, although their concept of "the child" varies. Both profess a concern for the values of library service, although they interpret these values differently. And both consist almost entirely of articles of faith, assumptions about children and books that have yet to be proved or disproved by solid research. The tone of moral self-righteousness that often marks the first and the tone of fuddy-duddiness that sometimes marks the second tend to add emotional clutter to a debate that calls for open-mindedness and hard thinking. Phrases like "credibility as a nonjudgmental agency" and "meaningful developmental growth" are but two examples of the jargon that replaces reason with verbosity and dialogue with table pounding. "Hier stehe Ich" may have been an appropriate response to the Diet of Worms but it doesn't make for good library service to children and young people, who are frequently forgotten amidst all the sloganeering.

The Question of Intellectual Freedom

A question to be asked about the standards versus free access controversy is if it has anything to do with intellectual freedom at all. There has been little or no outcry among adult services librarians to admit the likes of *Hustler* or hardcore porn into their collections, despite the fact that a readership for such does exist. Here, obviously, principles of intellectual freedom are moderated by a concern for the public good. Yet recognition of this has not extended to children's librarians, whose attempts to serve the "public good" of their charges have been labeled as a protectionist imposition of moral standards and as censorship. Neither is the concern for the reader's self-image too apparent when it comes to the outer limits of adult literature. When sadomasochistic romances or child seduction novels, both of which are published in abundance, are rejected because they fall below the level of public library acceptability, do adult services people suffer the same pangs about damaging their patrons' sense of self when they lament the effects of excluded books on children? If they do, they are unusually quiet about expressing them. It is interesting to observe how selectively principles can be applied.

Are Children Served or Betrayed

Perhaps the difficulty some have with the standards versus free access issue is because it is not a valid issue. Literary standards focus on the book: free access concerns which persons may use the book once it is in the library. The latter is an intellectual freedom issue but the former is not. Creating a *cause célèbre* where none exists may be the last refuge of the bored, but it has wasted countless hours that might have been better spent pondering each of these fundamentally important topics in its properly separate place.

The charge of elitism, made against selection by literary standards (i.e., value judgments), also bears scrutiny. What could be more elitist than the assumption that the "silliest, sleaziest or most salacious," in Lillian Gerhardt's words, is the most attractive to the young? The dewy-eyed image of young people as some sort of noble savages, fully capable of applying reason and discernment to every idea and experience, is put into perspective by Christopher Lasch when he says:

> When elders make no demands on the young, they make it almost impossible for the young to grow up. 'The betrayal of youth . . . starts from the assumption that (they) are only interested in wallowing in their own subjectivity . . . ' In the name of egalitarianism (reformers) preserve the most insidious form of elitism, which in one guise or another holds the masses incapable of intellectual exertion.[3]

Lasch's chapter, "Schooling and the New Illiteracy," in *The Culture of Narcissism* should be must reading for every librarian working with young people, because it reveals some of the myths by which many well-meaning adults have betrayed those whose rights they advocate and purport to defend.

The Responsibility To Set Standards

Although the current standards versus free access debate has emerged from the reevaluation controversy of a few years ago, it may also be traced to more historical roots. "What right have we to judge?," which could serve as a motto for the opponents of selection standards, is generally regarded (at least

by those who adhere to it) as a symbol of enlightened library service. Because standards are mistakenly associated on the one hand with a conservative impulse to keep the lower orders in their place and on the other hand with the perpetuation of an obsolete literary culture, the opponents of standards pride themselves on being in the vanguard of progressive or, when it was stylish, radical change. Yet Lester Asheim, in an article in *Library Trends*, suggests that the public's image of librarians as "inoffensive, nonassertive, compliant" is a result of librarians' *traditional* "self-effacing evasion of decision-making responsibility ('Who am I to say what a person ought to read: I'm only a librarian.') and their unwillingness to face the consequences if their professional ideals were carried out in practice."[4] The reluctance, indeed refusal, to judge represents a retreat into the timorous past far more than it reflects any great or courageous leap forward.

It remains very doubtful then whether selection standards have any invidious connection with children's rights. Insuring that children are provided with free access to all library materials is a battle that is far from being won, but attacking standards is a diversionary action. With all the genuine injustices perpetrated against the young everywhere, the International Year of the Child provided a good time for librarians to begin to clear their sights, define what the *real* problems facing children's services are, and do all that is within their particular province to make the world worthy of its children.

Notes

1. Pablo Casals, *Joys and Sorrows* (New York: Simon and Schuster, 1970).
2. Dorothy Broderick, "Censorship Reevaluated," *School Library Journal* (November 1971).
3. Christopher Lasch, *The Culture of Narcissism* (New York: W. W. Norton, 1978).
4. Lester Asheim, "Librarians as Professionals," *Library Trends* (Winter, 1978).

Children's Rights, Parents' Rights—
A Librarian's Dilemma

by Margaret Mary Kimmel

Some people refer to children as the resource of a nation, tomorrow's promise, the hope of civilization. Others label children as juvenile delinquents, welfare recipients, tax burdens, or wards of the state. Still other groups think only in terms of noisy-Robert, Sarah-who-sings, or Matthew-of-blond-curls with an angelic smile and the soul of a fiend. However that perception is shaped—whether by parent or family, by court or social institution or merely by an interested observer—it is adults who do the defining, limiting, and evaluating. This relationship between child and adult has its roots in ancient tradition as well as in 20th-century family life style. Definitions of children, who they are, their rights and obligations, and their relationship to the rest of the community are complicated by social, economic, even political considerations. Few would deny, however, the necessity for caring for the young.

The notion that children have rights before the law is a relatively modern phenomenon and one that needs a good deal of exploration—whether by interested observers or militant advocates. The purpose of this paper, then, is to briefly review the status of children and the law and to look at the child and the family in interaction with other social institutions.

As representatives of such a social institution providing a wide range of information services, librarians must specifically examine some questions relating children and their families to the information environment that we provide for them. It is important to stress the relationship of children in their family setting. Children do not exist in a vacuum, and it is their relationship to others in a community that must be clarified for us—for within that relationship lies crucial questions defining the scope of our services.

The definition of the term "children" may be viewed as a legal classification describing individuals under 18 or 21. Legal terminology suggests that "infancy" or "minority" persons have a special status that determines their rights and duties before the law and dramatizes their powerless position. This legal definition suggests some of the vagaries between children and the law, however, for the status of a minor may differ from state to state, even from crime to crime within the same jurisdiction. In some areas, for instance, individuals under 18 or 21 may be tried in criminal court for such serious crimes as homicide, but in other instances are relegated to the juvenile court where their fate is decided for them.

Most historians agree that before the 19th century, children were viewed as the property of their parents or guardians and had little or no rights at all, only the obligation to serve and be respectful. The few cases brought before the English Chancery Court laid the groundwork for the concept of *parens patriae*, the intervention of another authority when the guardian abused his power to chastise a child. By 1817, when the poet Shelley was denied custody of his children on the grounds of his behavior and his beliefs, the intervention of the state was a more accepted practice by society as a whole. Since we have inherited so much from English common law, this concept of the right of the state to intervene is an important one to note. There are some exceptions to this, especially in the American experimentation with adoption, common-law marriages, and in the relative relaxation of laws pertaining to illegitimacy.[1]

The social historian, Phillippe Aires, claims that Rousseau and Locke essentially invented the concept of childhood.[2] Before Locke, children were accepted as small adults and were given little or no special treatment. Viewed as economic assets, they were valued for their contribution to the welfare of the family. While some dispute Aires's theory, few deny that in the 19th century the industrial revolution, urbanization, and growing efforts at education and emancipation provided the background and impetus for the concern for children. The exploited social situations and grim physical conditions of youth on the streets, in slavery, in mills, or cotton fields were cause for reform.

Two strains of legislation are observable from these early efforts. One may be defined as structural reform, the other as a deviancy-control approach. In the first approach to legislation, the efforts at expansion of the educational system and development of child labor laws may be seen as dominating efforts. In promoting a classless society where democratic process demanded literacy as a priority, reformers found themselves faced with the task of forcing sometimes unwilling youth and parents into the classroom and sometimes unwilling taxpayers to assume the burden of educating all young people. As early as 1647, the Massachusetts General Court enacted a law that required the establishment of different types of schools when a town grew to a certain size. Although the towns assumed that parents would teach their young the basics of reading and writing, it was obviously necessary to support the establishment of schools for those families who could not or would not provide such learning. The phrases "for the sake of the children" or "in the best interests of the child" typify early efforts to clarify society's right to intervene between children and their legal guardians.

The second theme became apparent in the latter half of the 19th century as a part of the expansion of social services and a movement to save the deserving poor. Part of this effort was directed toward children, promoting an individualistic approach to reform, rather than a structural one. Those most closely involved in this so-called child-rescue movement were often women who claimed that they best provide the firm authority and human warmth which the abandoned, the orphaned, and the wayward seemed to lack. These "child savers" (a term used by Anthony Platt in his book by the same name) attempted to defend the values of traditional family life and to emphasize the necessity for the proper socialization of children. The role of women in this effort was obvious since, as these 19th-century reformers contended, "women were more genteel than men, better equipped to protect the innocence of children and more capable of regulating their education and recreation."[3]

The efforts of these women reformers were significant in maintaining the prestige of middle-class women in a society that was rapidly changing, but these efforts also provided legitimate career opportunities for women. The strength of the movement to save the "deserving poor" was enhanced by a workable, stable, administrative system in which caretakers assumed the role of professionals and sought community sanction for their work. The volunteer was replaced by an individual who became part of a structural organization with institutional loyalties, whose efforts on behalf of the client vied with keeping "statistics which would justify their continued existence and warrant increases in personnel and budget."[4] The new role of the social worker, for instance, combined elements of an old role as defender of family life with that of a new one—social servant. Work with social agencies was not only "fitting" for women but, additionally, it was an instrument of emancipation that allowed women to leave their homes yet remain in a socially acceptable situation.

In terms of child protection standards, then, a subtle but profound change began to occur. The individualistic approach to save the deserving child shifted general community responsibility to governmental agencies. The juvenile court was deemed the appropriate instrument of intervention—enforcing policy and interrupting patterns of daily living—and children came to have separate and special status. The system defined conformity as the dominant principle of reform.

In the last 10 to 15 years, social conditions have again forced a reconsideration of the status of children and their place in the community. Civil rights activism and the women's movement have forced a reevaluation and reconsideration of many segments of society whose interests have been overlooked. The so-called children's rights movement is only one aspect of the growing concern about the case of children before the law. John Holt, in his *Escape from Childhood*, for example, suggests that children must have the same rights and

responsibilities as adults. This theme is echoed by Richard Farson, who claims that children are forced into an "unnatural state" by adults who attempt to curtail their growth and impose restrictions.

Marian Wright Edelman, on the other hand, declares that much of the children's liberation talk is "just hogwash." The Children's Defense Fund, established in 1973, is a national, non-profit, public charity that seeks to provide systematic advocacy for children. There are some instances where children should have adult rights, Edelman contends, and it must be determined which instances those are and which children need them. She continues, "But children are not adults. They need protection and nurturing. . . . My five-year-old should not be liberated and my four-year-old is not capable of managing his own money. The institutional disregard of children is pervasive and destructive, but I question whether the liberationists are raising the issue in the most helpful way."[5]

These two arguments exemplify the approaches that summarize the position taken by leaders in the field. One is to extend all adult legal rights to children in areas of jurisdictional disputes, health and welfare cases, education, discipline, work or legal immunity. The other approach insists that children have special interests and needs that should be recognized as rights.

There is an absence of fair, workable, realistic standards for limiting parental discretion and guiding state intervention. There is also a failure to evaluate a child's independent interests, allowing competent children to speak for themselves.

It is necessary to pause a moment and consider the term "right" in itself. The *Oxford English Dictionary* described a legal right as an enforceable claim to the possession of property or authority or to the enjoyment of privileges or immunities. One must make a distinction, then, between legal rights and political or moral demands that have not been formally recognized by the law and have the status of needs or interests, not rights.

The extension of adult legal rights to children is a complex question, but it may be the most significant challenge to confront the movement to reform the child's place before the law. Such reform might involve, for instance, extending certain adult criminal rights to children even when those children are not in the adult court system. For example, trial by jury is not permitted in today's juvenile courts. It would involve the possibility for children to request medical care without parental consent, or might provide the child with legal representation in any situation where his or her interests are involved.

One of the most complicated aspects is also one urgently in need of reform—that of juvenile court proceedings involving those cases that apply strictly to children because they are children. In these so-called status offenses children are labeled "Persons In Need of Supervision" (or PINS). Because of their status alone, children may be detained for truancy or running away from home, disobedience of "reasonable" orders at home or school, or "improper" sexual behavior. They may also be held in protective care for being found in a railway or truck terminal, keeping late hours, or using profane language. For such offenses, the "custodial care" provided by the juvenile court often means jail or police lockups. In New York State, for instance, the Carnegie Commission estimates that in 1971 100,000 young people were in jail. Forty-three percent of them were status offenders. Furthermore, it has been noted that there are more girls than boys declared status offenders, and that children in this category are more often held for longer periods than others.[6]

In some cases, rights have been granted to children in exactly the form provided for adults. In cases involving voting, for instance, the age limits have been lowered to 18, and all rights and privileges have been granted to young people. In other instances, however, legislation is interpreted or tailored to the perceived characteristics of children. A case in point is *In Re Gault* (1967). Gault provides for due process guarantees, specifically:

1. Notice to both parent and child in time to prepare a defense, including a "sufficient statement of charge";
2. Right to counsel (and provision of counsel if necessary);
3. Right to remain silent—"privilege against self-incrimination"; and
4. Right to confrontation and cross-examination of witnesses.[7]

Implementation of *Gault*, however, finds lawyers still applying more stringent standards of interpretation to children, not because the courts have constrained them to do so, but because their clients are children. Although adult clients might be advised how to avoid punishment, lawyers are reluctant to help children "beat the rap." It has been suggested that the participation of lawyers in juvenile court is likely to make the system more orderly and efficient, but not substantially more fair or benevolent.

The second approach to children before the law accepts the assumption that children have some special and unique interests and needs above and beyond legal rights now granted to them. But these claims, drawn from natural law and moral philosophy, are based on needs not yet considered legal rights for anyone in our system. How can one group or agency enforce the right of a child to grow up in a world free from war? Or who is to define and enforce the right to be wanted? Or who is to define and enforce the child's right to learn? to information?

It is here that the dilemma of the librarian becomes apparent. Library service to children has traditionally been a part of a movement to save the child, to protect and defend the individual and the family as an institution. Child protection has traditionally encompassed the tasks of both salvation and re-education, as though the child lives in sin and must be redeemed. Together with the older law of parent and child laid down over seven centuries, these two themes form the modern legal framework for the definition and implementation of permissible standards of behavior by and toward children.

But like other social institutions, we must now ask whether children are to be treated as status offenders, restricted from service and materials simply because they are children. Or do children deserve all the privileges and service given to other segments of the population—interlibrary loan and access to a total collection?

There are some very difficult questions involved in either approach that need study and definition. For many years, the service to children in public and school libraries has subscribed to the education theory that one learns best by doing. "Have you looked it up in the card catalog?" is not unfamiliar to anyone setting foot in a library, but for children we have devised games, quizzes, and hunts to introduce various sources and help the young help themselves. Librarians and educators have sought to provide the answers and devise methods for children to find out just what we want them to know.

A controversial title, *Freddy's Book*, suggests a number of approaches to information-seeking patterns that a child may employ. Without debating the merits of the book, it is interesting to note that when Freddy's search for information takes him to the public library (after the failure of his mother and his friends at school to clarify his question), Freddy is once more stymied because the librarian deems his request inappropriate.

On the other hand, there is an equally tough set of questions evolving from a stand that suggests "all information for all children all the time." For one thing, children are faced with a knowledge/technology explosion as vast as the one that overwhelms adults. Children, too, need a filter, a manager of information, and relatively few of them can afford the services of Xerox Corporation, whose series of commercials offered to select, organize, and disseminate information.

At the same time, the recognition of the worth of good writing, illustration, artistically developed film, sound recordings of quality and integrity are value judgments that librarians make every day and automatically pass on to the clients serviced, adult or child.

These value judgments must be recognized as such, and defenses for or against such disparate titles as *Dr. Dolittle* or the Nancy Drew series must accept both the responsibility of such judgments and the limitations imposed. The difficulty of defining access, selection, and guidance is magnified by community factors, by the relatively undefined nature of the relationship between social institutions and parent intervention. Does the parental request for *Show Me* supersede thoughtful, evaluative professional judgment that rejected a titled labeled by one reviewer as "a mixture of 'corn' and 'porn'"? Are librarians obliged to respond to community demand to add a favorite, well-loved book, such as *Little Black Sambo*.

These questions about the rights of children are not new. Kate Douglas Wiggin in 1899 asked:

> Who owns the child? If a parent owns him—mind, body, and soul—we must adopt one line of argument; if, as a human being, he owns himself, we must adopt another. In my thought, the parent is simply a divinely appointed guardian, who acts for his child until he attains what we call the age of discretion—that highly uncertain period which arrives very late in life with some persons, and not at all with others.[8]

Three quarters of a century later, we still ponder these problems.

The Carnegie Commission on Children states bluntly that there are no affirmative rights in common or constitutional law for the minimum essentials needed for children and their families to survive, to grow, to flourish. Standing alone, the law cannot provide all requirements of a healthy, happy child. Love and nurturing are the foundations most of us expect beyond any legal mandate. It can be the source of some controls, some opportunities, but the library, like other social institutions must face the questions now. The Chilean poet Mistral declares:

> Many things can wait. The child cannot. Right now his hip bones are being formed, his blood is being made, his senses being developed. To him we cannot say tomorrow. His name is today.

References

1. Margaret K. Rosenheim, "The Child and the Law," in *200 Years of Children*, edited by Edith Grotberg (Washington, D.C.: U.S. Department of Health, Education, and Welfare: Office of Human Development, Office of Child Development, 1977), pp. 423-86.
2. Phillippe Aires. *Centuries of Childhood: A Social History of Family Life* (New York: Random House, 1965).
3. Anthony Platt, *The Child Savers*, rev. ed. (Chicago: University of Chicago Press, 1977).
4. Ibid., p. 78.
5. Margie Casady, "Society's Pushed-Out Children," *Psychology Today* 58 (1975).
6. Kenneth Keniston and the Carnegie Council on Children, *All Our Children: The American Family Under Pressure* (New York: Harcourt Brace Jovanovich, 1977), p. 195.
7. Hillary Rodman, "Children under the Law," *Harvard Educational Review* 43, no. 4 (1973): 56.
8. Kate Douglas Wiggin, *Children's Rights* (Boston: Houghton Mifflin, 1899), pp. 4-5.

Bibliography

Adams, Paul, et. al. *Children's Rights*. New York: Praeger Publishers, 1971.

Aires, Phillippe. *Centuries of Childhood: A Social History of Family Life*. New York: Random House, 1965.

Casady, Margie. "Society's Pushed-Out Children." *Psychology Today*, June 1975, pp. 57-65.

Edelman, Marian Wright. "In Defense of Children's Rights." *Yale Alumni Magazine and Journal*, February 1978, pp. 14-16.

Farson, Richard. *Birthrights*. New York: Macmillan, 1974.

Gottlieb, David. *Children's Liberation*. Englewood Cliffs, N.J.: Prentice-Hall, 1973.

Gross, Beatrice, and Gross, Ronald, eds. *The Children's Rights Movement*. Garden City, N.Y.: Anchor Press, 1977.

Holt, John. *Escape from Childhood*. New York: Dutton, 1974.

Keniston, Kenneth, and the Carnegie Council on Children. *All Our Children: The American Family under Pressure*. New York: Harcourt Brace Jovanovich, 1977.

Lubove, Roy. *The Professional Altruist*. New York: Atheneum, 1975.

Platt, Anthony. "Maternal Justice." In *The Child Savers*. Rev. ed., pp. 75-100. Chicago: University of Chicago Press, 1977.

Rodman, Hillary. "Children under the Law." *Harvard Educational Review* 43, no. 4 (1973): 487-514.

Rosenheim, Margaret K. "The Child and the Law," in *200 Years of Children*. Edited by Edith Grotberg, Washington, D.C.: U.S. Department of Health, Education and Welfare; Office of Human Development, Office of Child Development, 1977.

Senn, Milton. *Speaking Out for America's Children*. New Haven: Yale University Press, 1977.

Wiggin, Kate Douglas. *Children's Rights: A Book of Nursery Logic*. Boston: Houghton Mifflin, 1899.

Librarians as Political Activists

by Ethel Manheimer

In post-Proposition 13 California, many librarians were jolted into action when they realized that their libraries and jobs could be decimated through other people's actions. When Californians voted themselves a substantial property-tax reduction in June 1978, sharply curtailed budgets were to affect libraries, both school and public, in most cities, towns and counties. Schools faced the additional financial constraints that resulted from declining enrollment. Library closings—as well as reductions in service, staff, hours, and book budgets—have been described and well documented in the library press.

Less well known are some California success stories—situations in which action by librarians and the community at the local level enabled libraries to maintain their positions or even grow, in spite of the general shrinkage of local budgets in the state.

Most recently, the city of Berkeley voted for a new tax that will totally fund the operation of the Berkeley Public Library at pre-Proposition 13 levels, with a small inflation factor added. The library's budget is now independent of the city's general fund and the library is no longer in competition with other city services (such as police, fire, health, recreation) for dwindling revenue.

How did Berkeley become the first and only community in California to levy a new tax on itself in order to rebuild and maintain a quality library program? Part of the answer lies in the nature of the community, its dependence on the library, and the library's success in meeting the community's needs. A city of 110,000 in which 45 percent of the population have active library cards, Berkeley's per capita circulation is triple the average for the state.

But this relationship between the community and the library is not enough to explain the passage of Measure E (the local tax bill) in these times of voter antipathy to government and taxation. This came about in a city where a sharp political split resulted in public opposition to the measure, where the city's major newspaper editorialized against the measure, where the Chamber of Commerce opposed it, and where the approval of two-thirds of the electorate was needed to pass the bill. The support given by the sponsoring political party—Berkeley Citizens Action—was vital, but victory at the polls can be attributed to a campaign characterized by the close cooperation of three distinct groups: The Friends of the Berkeley Public Library, the library's Board of Trustees, and the library staff. The board unanimously supported the measure, and individual members participated effectively in public debates. The Friends kicked off the campaign with a $5000 contribution; the unpaid campaign manager and other Friends worked vigorously and untiringly through the eight weeks of election activities. The significant and unstinting work of the librarians and other staff members gave the campaign much of its energy and effectiveness.

Motivated, inspired, and led by library director, Regina U. Minudri, the staff of the Berkeley Public Library gave up many hours of their own time (no electioneering on the job) to plan events and strategy, to raise money, to do the nitty-gritty work of campaigning (and to enjoy a victory celebration). Though most of us were politically inexperienced and naive, we learned quickly, and we discovered that our skills and competencies as librarians were transferable to the political arena and stood us in good stead as campaigners. What did we actually do in the campaign? We researched library history; we wrote letters to the editor; we helped compose campaign literature; we scanned voter lists to find names of library patrons, supporters, and friends; we folded, stuffed, addressed envelopes; we walked precincts dropping literature (i.e., went door-to-door through preselected neighborhoods leaving our campaign literature and urging anyone who'd talk with us to vote for the measure); we distributed our literature at supermarkets, at churches, at concerts, meetings and fairs, we "sniped" signs; we telephoned friends and strangers asking for their endorsement of the measure and for contributions to finance our campaign; walked to work wearing signboards, taking different, heavily trafficked routes each day; we stood at tables outside the libraries giving information and soliciting funds; we spoke at meetings of senior citizen groups, of parents' organizations, of church and civic groups, of any group that would let us in.

On election day, we got up at 4:00 A.M. to walk precincts again. This time, we went in cooperation with the political party that put Measure E on the ballot, hanging voter cards on every doorknob in town so every Berkeleyan left home election morning with a reminder to vote "Yes on E" and with the address of her/his polling place. When the polls opened and again after work, we went and stood the legal 100 feet from polling places, greeted voters, and reminded them to vote for the libraries.

Why did the librarians and other library staff get so involved, give as much time, energy, and money to this campaign? Particularly, we wondered, why did the staff working with young people (traditionally or stereotypically the most reticent, politically) become activists? How was their activism affecting their lives, both personally and at work? What benefits accrued to Linda Perkins, supervising program librarian for Young People's Service, and to staff members, Joan Akawie, Jean Leiby, Carol Naito, Heo Park, Martha Shogren, as they gave up much of their leisure time for two months?

Commitment to the library and its mission, to their coworkers and to the community as well as a desire to "fight back" against the effects of Proposition 13 stimulated these young people's librarians' participation. For the most part, they were glad they got involved. They felt that their effort, as part of a committed working group, was important to the campaign and could make a difference in the election's outcome. They expressed satisfaction with the large number of their colleagues who were working (but felt disappointment and some tension at work with those who were doing nothing for the campaign or grumbling); they were gratified by the number of friends and library supporters who joined in at work meetings and other campaign efforts.

Working with other people at concrete tasks was energizing; "joining in the fight makes you feel good" even though there was also anxiety and sleeplessness. All the librarians we talked to felt the hardest and most unpleasant task they performed in the campaign was asking for money. Several expressed disappointment that so few librarians from schools and from other library systems joined in. Said one Berkeley librarian, "We're all part of the library movement; I hope I'll respond when other libraries need help." These young people's librarians enjoyed working with and getting to know community people and colleagues from all the departments and branches of the library. All were leery of involvement with the city's political parties and the partisan issues on the ballot. Without exception, before knowing if Measure E would win or lose, these young people's librarians knew that if another campaign for library funding became necessary they'd be active campaigners again. Jean Leiby summed it up, "It's the only way you can make your voice heard."

Mount Diablo USD Organizes Union

For the past two years, librarians in the Mount Diablo Unified School District (Contra Costa County) have been making their voices heard. Drastic personnel cuts were announced by their board in July 1978; newly instituted collective bargaining required their sympathetic supervisor to hew to the management position; the librarians knew their own immediate action was necessary to save the library program. The librarians organized themselves into Library Staff United (LSU), an ad hoc group separate from their grade level staff organization. They became their own advocates, delivering their message to teachers and administrators, to their teachers' association officers, to parents and to the board. LSU asked the California Media and Library Educators Association (CMLEA) and the American Association of School Librarians (AASL) for advice and action; both groups came through with infor-

mation, letters and telegrams of support to the administrators and board members, and Alice Fite, executive secretary of AASL, visited the district to help. LSU, at its own expense, retained an attorney knowledgeable in the laws pertaining to education and school libraries. But it has been the constant activity of LSU and the individual librarians in it that made the difference.

Under the leadership of LSU's first two presidents, Lynn Pryer and Laurene Martin, the group has used a variety of strategies including the assignment of a number of librarians to be at each school board meeting, so that their specialty is always represented. They've asked parents and teachers who are supportive of library service to write letters to newspapers and to call board members. Out of this appeal, a parent, Jan Fezatte, organized a parents advocates group to support better library services in the district. The librarians met with administrators to tell them what librarians do in the schools and how the libraries fit into and serve the total curriculum. For one of many library presentations to the board, LSU organized an authors' night with the cooperation of local writers. On the evening of a school board meeting, a dinner for the writers and the board members was followed by an autographing session for students. A huge turnout of students and their parents graphically displayed to the board the vitality and significance of the librarians' literature programs.

Through LSU, the librarians have mutual support and problem solving assistance, strengthening their own skills and the program. They prepared and publicized a library curriculum continuum, which, though never adopted by the board, informed the entire district of their plan of instruction. LSU worked even more closely with the teachers' association than they had before—some became building representatives—resulting in greater recognition of the librarians as teachers.

What does LSU have to show for its herculean efforts? During the first year, the board retained three-and-one-half elementary library positions they'd planned to eliminate through attrition. In the secondary schools, the librarians were involved in planning the realignment of a reduced clerical staff. Since then, a new board attempted to eliminate elementary librarians, but LSU and its now numerous library supporters were ready for the threat; the board was convinced and the program was saved. When eight schools were closed recently, the parents of many transferring students exerted pressure on the district to provide better library facilities or services in the new schools their children would attend.

Clearly the Mount Diablo Unified School District librarians are devoting many after-school hours to LSU's planning and activities. They've gone out to the community, provided information about their program, and found the support they needed to keep their programs alive and save their jobs.

A Matter of Survival

How many librarians have remained aloof from all political involvement, feeling the issues were too remote or that they should not take an active role? How many believe that "my involvement won't make any difference, or "what will be, will be," or that politics is a dirty business? How many other reasons have we given ourselves to justify doing nothing in the political arena? If we think libraries are worth fighting for, then we librarians must lead the fight. Insofar as libraries are funded by citizens to serve the citizens and must compete with other public services for revenue, it is clear that we must generate our support from the citizenry in the political arena. And, as Betty McDavid, past president of CMLEA, Northern Section, said, "It's a never-ending job. There are always new people, new groups to whom we must communicate our message."

It has been said that libraries have no natural enemies, but neither do they have natural political allies. It is up to us librarians to recruit our allies. Alice B. Ihrig once pointed out that "the political process turns the good will enjoyed by libraries into the ultimate support dollars."* The day of the low profile is over. Librarians must be politically aware and politically adept in order to survive in the decade of the '80s and beyond.

---

*Ihrig, Alice B. "Librarians and the Political Process," in *As Much to Learn as to Teach* (Shoe String, 1979), (p. 83-93)

Legacies for Youth:
Ethnic and Cultural Diversity in Books

by Spencer G. Shaw

In every age and culture, one of the most significant events to occur is the departure of children and young adults from their homes into the gradually expanding environments of the school, the community, and, eventually, the world.

As they travel beyond the family unit, several forces emerge to shape the lives of the young. These forces have several aspects: (1) they are multi-dimensional, allowing exposure to all expressions of experience that will affect the physical, mental, emotional, social, aesthetic, and humane spheres; (2) they reveal a growing recognition of the ethnic and cultural diversities existing among peer groups that are different from a family's traditional mode of life; (3) they bring into sharp focus the quality of interactions between children and young adults and educators and librarians in schools and libraries; and (4) they determine what impact varying socioeconomic neighborhoods and the universe beyond may have on children and young adults.

One might ask whether these forces will overwhelm the young to the point of stultifying their imagination, harnessing their creativity, debasing their heritage, stifling their dreams, or confusing their sense of identity. Or, as harbingers of the 21st Century, will children and young adults find in these forces positive elements that will enable them to retain their individuality with a sense of dignity and pride in their ethnic and cultural heritages?

Children and young adults must be challenged to explore the inner, spatial frontiers of the mind and of the spirit—these realms must be nourished with a *compatible* emphasis upon the humanities and the arts as librarians turn libraries into the "information centers" of the future.

Research in early children's literature provides disturbing findings. In 1930, Bruno Lasker, in his searing study *Race Attitudes in Children*, set forth a prophetic warning:

> Generation after generation, we see them pass by—children who are given the stones of fictitious stereotypes when they ask for the bread of knowledge, children of all races and all nationalities made the potential cannon-fodder of future wars because they are not permitted to develop in themselves those qualities of mind that make for a sense of fair play, for mutual appreciation, for mental flexibility in response to changing situations. It is to these children, burdened with the material costs of past wars and with the inheritance of limited social attitudes, that society owes its greatest unacknowledged debt.[1]

A Look Backward

Literature has been and continues to be significant in the educational, informational, recreational, and aesthetic pursuits of children and young adults. Probe into the past! Study books written for the young that may have reflected ethnic and cultural diversities.

Prior to World War II, if we were to visit a school or public library, we would have noticed a dearth of books stressing multicultural themes. Young patrons of that era failed to find fictional role models worthy of emulation or with whom they could identify. Instead, for almost fifty years, authors and publishers appeared more interested in trying to build a foundation for international understanding with stories about children of other lands.

I recall the *Peeps at Many Lands* series and other literary works in which the children of other countries were presented, euphemistically, as "cousins". According to authorities Julia Sauer and Rebecca Caudill, the characters in books of this type fostered feelings of superiority within American children. Also, children who read these stories developed an "intolerant" tolerance, with the result that they acquired "an inflated sense of their personal and collective prowess as opposed to the ability and the prowess of people of other countries. . . ."[2]

How many of you were brought up with the *Twin* series by Lucy Fitch Perkins, who tried, in her patronizing style, to perform a herculean service in introducing American children to their counterparts of other lands. When she attempted to introduce these same children to their young black fellow citizens in the United States, however, she failed miserably—her own racial biases overpowered her skills as a writer. This was glaringly evident in *The Pickaninny Twins*, a title which flaunted a disparaging label. Analyzing these and similar books concerned with building international friendships, Sauer stated:

> We have worked for twenty-two years on the belief that we could build some sort of international friendship through children's books. It has stimulated the production of an enormous supply of "background" books on other lands. We are surfeited with them. For some few we are grateful. Far too many are unsuccessful in that the plot or story and the life of the people are completely unfused.[3]

Such conditioning of young children's minds by publishers and authors was not restricted to American fiction. It probably was repeated in many other countries where literature for children and young adults was published.

In the 1974 May Hill Arbuthnot Honor Lecture at the University of Washington, Ivan Southall, the noted Australian author, made this observation:

> From our English comics we learned the fundamental truths of life: for instance, people with yellow skins were inscrutable and cunning, people with brown skins were childlike and apt to run amok, people with black skins were savages but, if tamed, made useful carriers of heavy loads on great expeditions of discovery by Englishmen. It was in order for black people to be pictured without clothes; after all, they didn't know what clothes were and didn't count, somehow. But white nudity was unimaginable, except in solid marble or in ill-lit galleries on very old paintings. The white body was so sacred it was not proper to look at your own.[4]

From such reminders of past literary contributions and their effects upon impressionable young minds, Southall concludes:

> If you raise a dozen or a million children or ten million children on falsehoods and phonies and trivialities—through your own ignorance or indifference or deliberate intention—you end up with a substantial number of grown persons who need to be sustained by lies and illusions and cheap sentimentalities because they cannot live with truth or be bothered by the effort of comprehension art demands. Switch on the box and there it is to see. In terms of humane wastage you dare not ever think about it. Man bent upon poisoning himself.[5]

While such ill-fated publishing ventures were indoctrinating youth with a false sense of superiority based upon favored cultural groups, few stories that depicted ethnic minorities fostered any feelings of pride. In the *Early Settler* stories, the emphasis was on the scalping Indian:

> He was the personification of all that was bloody and terrible, with an eye on scalps and a tomahawk ready for all white people, especially women and children. *The Matchlock Gun* is this type of story. In none of [the stories] was there any hint that the Indian might have some justification for harrying the white settlers. No mention is made of the period when treaty after treaty was broken with the Indians and they were driven ruthlessly off their land, farther and farther West to poorer and poorer lands.[6]

For years the literary diet of all children, black and white, of stories depicting what was mistakenly believed by many to be the "black experience," was mainly two well-known tales (now grossly mislabeled "classics"). The characters *Little Black Sambo* (Helen Bannerman) and *Epaminondas* (Sara Bryant) have had opposite effects upon children of both races. White children find the two boys endearing and delightful (in a patronizing manner). But for many black children, the stories have resulted in a lack of a positive identity. In too many instances, a black child becomes "Sambo" or "Epaminondas" in the cruel exchange of taunts and name-calling in the classroom, on the playground, or in the streets.

(Parenthetically, it is a sad commentary to realize how many "insensitive" teachers and librarians still use these stories with their young listeners. They deem them "charming tales" to amuse and entertain young children. When questioned as to the validity of the continued use of these stories, their responses include questionable rationales: "removing them for storytelling borders on censorship," or, "I enjoyed them when I was young and they never hurt me.")

Equally pernicious are the poorly contrived, formula-written series produced by the Stratemeyer Syndicate—*Nancy Drew, The Hardy Boys, The Bobbsey Twins*. Filled with racial and cultural biases, these "fictional assembly-line products" served to implant subliminally, upon impressionable minds, deeply etched caricatured images that assumed realistic characteristics. Now, sanctioned and shelved in too many library collections, these never-ending series retain their popularity with today's readers. Although some blatant racial and cultural overtones have been softened or eliminated, the series' lack of literary merit and social values leaves much to be desired. Furthermore, a librarian's competence and skill in book evaluation and selection and reading guidance must come into question when these are promoted as approved reading.

The white curtain of silence about books for American children, written with a disregard for honest portrayals of minorities, equally affected other ethnic groups. Thus, the Spanish-speaking and Spanish-surnamed characters were often depicted as indolent, illiterate, and dirty—always wearing an oversized sombrero and usually pictured asleep. Asians (Chinese and Japanese) were inscrutable, sneaky, given to treachery, and considered a "yellow peril". The Italians were noisy, oily, law violators. The Jews were conniving, money-hungry, heartless.

Fortunately, during the years following World War II, a ferment of change prevailed. Underlying all spheres of society, cultures, and social orders, a burgeoning stream of social consciousness emerged. In the sixties and seventies, more strident, justifiable demands from still-unaccepted ethnic minorities required drastic attitudinal changes and resulted in new directions.

Consider some of the agents forcing these changes to occur:

1. Recognition of the fact that when children and young adults come into larger environments they do not come empty-handed; they bring with them a *sense of identity*, and *ethnic background* in which they take pride, and a *social status*. These are the words of a young Mexican-American when he exclaims:

> Who am I? I am a product of myself. I am a product of you and my ancestors. We came to California long before the Pilgrims landed at Plymouth Rock. We settled California and the Southwestern part of the United

States, including the present states of Arizona, New Mexico, Colorado and Texas. We built the missions; we cultivated the ranches. We were at the Alamo in Texas, both inside and outside. You know we owned California—that is, until gold was found there.

Who am I? I'm a human being. I have the same hopes you have, the same fears, the same desires, the same concerns, the same abilities; and I want the same chance that you have to be an individual. Who am I? In reality I am who you want me to be.

2. Endowed with varying degrees of identity, the young also possess legacies which are derived from an *ethnic* and *cultural* heritage. The importance of such a dual inheritance cannot be overlooked or minimized. With the legacy of *ethnicity* there are embraced the cultural, racial, religious, and linguistic traditions of a people. When these individuals with similar identifications come together to form into groups, they share a unique social and cultural heritage which they pass on to their children from one generation to the next.

Maya Angelou, in her commencement address to the graduating students at predominantly black Spelman College in Atlanta, Georgia, proclaimed:

You are phenomenal. The reason you are phenomenal is because you come from a phenomenal people. When you get into the marketplace, whether it is the academic world or the industrial, or business, corporate, or the arts, it is wise to remember where you came from and then you can use your past as the mirror so that you can see yourself. You have come well from a very healthy, a lusty people, a people loving life and loving love.[8]

One important factor indicative of every cultural group is that no single group can be considered monolithic, possessing a uniform, intractible characteristic. Rather, within each, children and adults are uniquely different human beings, possessing varying degrees of potential for development.

It is incumbent upon teachers and librarians to refrain from generalizing about any one group, or focussing on a single individual as one who represents or speaks for an entire cultural group. Authors and publishers must also recognize this fact; too often in recent publications, too many stories about ethnic minorities are over-burdened with the most negative aspects of human existence—poverty, life in the ghetto or in the worst areas of the inner city, drugs, broken families, absentee fathers, gangs, failure to assimilate into the larger society, incorrect use of the English language, alcoholism, and a false dependency upon a benign "benefactor" from the majority culture.

Michael Novak, a contributor to the *Harvard Encyclopedia of American Ethnic Groups*, in his thought-provoking essay entitled "Pluralism: A Humanistic Perspective," states:

Generalizations about cultural characteristics . . . observe four other conditions. *First*, in most complex cultures more than one set of cultural ideals is available; *second*, cultures are normally open to change, so that new types of cultural heroes regularly emerge; *third*, the function of cultural ideals is not to describe all members of a society but rather to single out, to promote, and to reward certain forms of behavior; *fourth*, each individual appropriates the ideals of a culture in a free and distinctive way, sometimes by rebelling against them, resisting them, muting them, or playing counterpoint against them. Without denying the force of distinctive cultural ideals upon the whole everyday life of cultures, it is important to see the wide range of liberty exercised by individuals within them. It is a mistake to apply to individuals the generalizations that attempt to define the working ideals of a culture; this mistake is properly called stereotyping.

3. A third catalytic agent that has helped to raise the levels of social consciousness has occurred in the field of education. In several instances there has been a "head-on" collision with intransigent, procrustean teaching methods and library procedures which ignore diverse traditions and customs in a vain attempt to homogenize learners and users. This has led to protests, confusion, disarray, and possible failures among ethnic minority youth.

In an *educational* and *library renaissance* in which an effort is made to feed the mind of each child and young adult, a framework is needed upon which the *values*, the *customs*, the *traditions* of all youth may be interwoven. From such a source a meaningful structure may be derived which will help learners and library users to avoid a culture shock in the process of evolving a meaningful scientific, humane, spiritual view of life. If this framework is not made available, the very act negates one of the premises set forth in *A Nation at Risk* by the National Commission on Excellence in Education.

All, regardless of race or class or economic status, are entitled to a fair chance and to the tools for developing their individual powers of mind and spirit to the utmost. This promise means that all children by virtue of their own efforts, competently guided, can hope to attain the mature and informed judgment needed to secure gainful employment and to manage their own lives, thereby serving not only their own interests but also the progress of society itself.

. . . at the heart of the Learning Society are educational opportunities extending far beyond the traditional institutions of learning, our schools and colleges. They extend into *homes* and *workplaces*; into *libraries* and *art galleries*, *museums* and *science centers*; indeed into every place where the individual can develop and mature in work and life. In our view, formal schooling in youth is the essential foundation for learning throughout one's life. But without lifelong learning, one's skills will become rapidly dated.[9]

This graphic description of educational opportunities that extend far beyond the conventional school curriculum may be termed "the societal curriculum," a concept introduced by Dr. Carlos E. Cortes, who defines it thus: "The 'societal curriculum' is that massive, ongoing, informal curriculum of family, peer groups, neighborhoods, mass media, and other socializing forces that 'educate' us through our lives."[10]

4. Among the catalytic agents mentioned in the Commission's report and alluded to by Cortes was the library, with its vast array of materials that vary in form, function, and versatility. Among such materials is *literature*, which may be used as a means to reinforce ethnic and cultural diversities. Novak in his essay reinforces this view:

> In American life . . . both literary materials and methods of 'participant observation' . . . are among our best sources for understanding the impact of ethnicity upon our inner lives.

> . . . many books reveal the quite different instincts, attitudes, aspirations, and perceptions that actually motivate diverse individuals in our midst.[11]

A Look Ahead

Building upon the best representations from the past, editors, publishers, authors, and illustrators have combined their creative talents to enrich the lives of young readers with works of merit. From among the plethora of titles which have deluged the market care must be taken to discourage the acceptance of any book which is purely "message-oriented", contrived, and unrealistic, lacking in literary quality and social values, and resulting in new stereotypes.

Creators of fictional and information books that depict different cultural groups must reveal in their writing a perceptive understanding of and sensitivity to their subject, an honesty and accuracy in the portrayal of characters and situations, plausible themes and insights into the ways of life that will extend the horizons of readers, thus permitting an untarnished growth of appreciation for others different from themselves. In this regard, Jean Karl notes:

> What kinds of books do we give the child who lives in today's multi-ethnic society? We give him books in which he can see himself and know his own value, and we give him books that help him to understand that others are different and that differences are good. . . .

> The best books are the books that show society as it is. The welfare child, the child of militant parents, the child of the streets, the middle-class child, the wealthy child— all need to be in books, representing all the cultures and sub-cultures of society. There must be nonfiction that speaks to any and every interest a child may have. We need histories of the Spanish-speaking in America, of the Negro in America; we must have books in Spanish and in other languages as well—African dialects, Asian

languages—whatever will make the children feel at home with themselves and with others. The heroes of every culture must be available in books so each race may take pride in its own people and come to respect the virtues of others. If such books are done and they are good, they will be bought. If they are bad, they should be ignored.[12]

From the emergence of literature that portrays ethnic and cultural groups have come two noticeable phenomena, one *positive*, and the other *negative*.

The positive aspect has been the publishers' recognition, *finally*, of the fact that there are capable and well-qualified authors and illustrators among ethnic minorities, whose contributions can and are extending the richness of the fields of literature for all children and young adults. These creative individuals with their insights into the very depths of a culture are bringing new dimensions that have been lacking. From the expressed thoughts of some of these authors there is fashioned a rich mosaic that reveals inner searchings of the intellect and the human spirit; these are eloquent, personal testaments.

Laurence Yep, cited for his excellent books, *Dragonwings* and *Child of the Owl*:

> You should always write about what you know; the things you have seen and the things you have thought and, above all, the things you have felt, so that I set my novel in the smaller, quieter Chinatown in which I grew up, before the immigration laws were made fairer in October 1965 so more Asians could enter . . . Chinatown is not so much a place as a state of mind— or to be more accurate, a state of heart—and it is this state of mind and of heart that I have tried to explain as much to myself as to others. But, the heart is a difficult place to enter, let along describe, unless one wears some sort of disguise . . . it has been my aim to counter various stereotypes as presented in the media. I wanted to show that Chinese-Americans are human beings upon whom America has had a unique effect.[13]

Pura Belpré, storyteller, collector of Puerto Rican folktales—*The Once in Puerto Rico*; *Perez and Martina*; *The Tiger and the Rabbi: and Other Tales*:

> Writing on multi-ethnic themes has become a necessity these days when the search for identity permeates the atmosphere involving a large segment of the population. The responsibilities of an author dealing with these themes are great and of utmost importance. In his hands rests the presentation of a group of human beings to the reader, who will form his own ideas according to the image the author projects. Whether the author is part of the ethnic group or an outsider writing about it, he has the same responsibility toward the group and the reader . . .

> Cities are the theatres wherein these people live out their lives. Some live in comfort away from slums and ghettos. Others in their very midst, victims of economic

conditions and prejudices, are living in their poverty with dignity, preserving their family structures, their cultures and traditions, and their faiths, hopes, and, yes, even their humor. Here then, is living source material for eyes to see, ears to hear, and hearts to understand. Let it be used, in any form or fashion, with dignity and truthfulness that it deserves. This is, after all, the duty and responsibility of the author who chooses to deal with it.[14]

Jamake Highwater, a distinguished cultural anthropologist, author—*Many Smokes, Many Moons, a Chronology of American Indian History Through Indian Art*; *Anpao, an American Indian Odyssey*; *The Sun He Dies*:

It is very unfashionable at the moment to suggest that all people are *not* the same. It is equally unpopular to insist that we can learn more about a culture from its differences than from its similarities to other cultures, and that the basis of human nature is probably more visible in human diversity than in the relatively few ways in which we are fundamentally the same . . . In the process of trying to unify the world we must be exceedingly careful not to destroy the diversity of the many cultures of man that give human life meaning, focus and vitality . . .

Today we are beginning to look into the ideas of groups outside the dominant culture, and we are finding different kinds of "truth" that make the world we live in far bigger than we ever dreamed it could be— for the greatest distance between people is not geographical space but culture.[15]

Yoshida Uchida, prominent author, collector of Japanese folktales—*The Dancing Kettle and Other Japanese Folk Tales*; *Journey to Topaz*; *Sumi and the Great Journey Home*; *The Forever Christmas Tree*:

All my books have been about Japan and its children or about Japanese-Americans because I felt I would make the best contribution in this area. I wanted American children to become familiar with the marvelous Japanese folk tales I had heard in my childhood. I wanted them to read about Japanese children, learning to understand and respect differences in customs and cultures, but realizing also that basically human beings are alike the world over, with similar joys and hopes.

I have also written of fathers who were potters or artists or carnation growers or landscape gardeners to develop awareness of life and occupations perhaps not as familiar as the usual father who comes home from the office.[16]

Lorenz Graham, noted novelist, biographer, author— *North Town*; *South Town*; *Song of the Boat*; *How God Fix Jonah*; *John Brown: A Cry for Freedom*:

As a Negro I grew up with fears and hatreds for white

people and came to understanding of these destructive emotions only after being outside the United States and separated from the 'race problem'. I concluded that people, all people, should be brought to better understanding of other people.

For this I work and write . . . My personal problem with publishers has been the difference between my images and theirs. Publishers have told me that my characters, African and Negro, are 'too much like white people'. And I say, 'If you look closely you will see that people are people.'[17]

Walter Dean Myers, popular author of *It Ain't All of Nothing*; *The Dragon Takes a Wife*; *The Young Landlords*; *Won't Know Till I Get There*:

Editors are often hampered by pre-conceived attitudes, arising from their (typically) white, middle-class backgrounds. Editors tend to view books by black authors in terms of "the ghetto" or the "ghetto child".

Myers insists that these terms are not appropriate when applied to his books. He sees himself as a storyteller, writing about the black community and "good, lovable kids." To a degree he conceded that his first book, *Fast Sam*, was written in response to Claude Brown's *Manchild in a Promised Land*. Myers revealed that he had lived four blocks from Brown in Harlem and that he did not recognize the neighborhood or experiences portrayed in Brown's book. Part of his urge to write, Myers joked, is that he simply does not trust anyone else to record the black experience for him. He deplored the notion that because his books are primarily about black children, they are only for black children.

Observing that there are more similarities than differences between young white and black children, he strongly objected to the attitude he perceived librarians have: refusing to buy his books if their schools do not have significant black populations. Myers compared this to not purchasing Dickens' novels because there are no nineteenth-century English children in the schools.[18]

An Impediment to Advancement

While we extol these advances, we realize that there is a great challenge before us as we near the start of a new century. Once again, a threatening wind is sweeping across the land, causing the pendulum of ethnic and cultural progress to swing back as the forces of conservatism and bigotry seek to corrode the democratic ideal.

For the past several years there has been a noticeable decrease in books that portray ethnic and cultural minority groups as other subjects are becoming the concern of publishers. In addition, the wave of "social consciousness" has been supplanted by a more dangerous, negative phenomenon—*censorship*.

Pertinent to our concern regarding representations of ethnic and cultural diversities—legacies in literature for children and young adults—are the growing numbers of books that have become "problem books." Some have been censored and removed from library open stacks. Others have not been selected for purchase by librarians and educators. A few have been purchased by librarians and kept in "closed shelves", "restricted" collections or the librarians' office.

A Call for Commitment

Regardless of these censorship skirmishes, we cannot be deterred in our efforts to give children and young adults books and media that will enable them to forge a sense of identity, a feeling of self-worth, a pride in their ethnicity, a respect for their heritage—all rightful legacies for children and youth.

References

1. Lasker, Bruno. *Race Attitudes in Children.* Henry Holt & Co., 1929, p. 384.
2. Caudill, Rebecca. "Books Are Bridges," *Illinois Libraries*, Vol. 29, No. 2., February, 1947, p. 76.
3. Sauer, Julia. "Making the World Safe for the Janey Larkins," *Library Journal*, Vol. 66, January 1, 1941, p. 51.
4. Southall, Ivan. "Real Adventure Belongs to Us," in *A Journey of Discovery, on Writing for Children.* Macmillan, 1976, p. 69.
5. Ibid., p. 79.
6. Arbuthnot, May Hill. *Children and Books.* Scott, Foresman, 1947, p. 384.
7. Martinez, Gilbert. "Spanish Speaking American Children and Children's Books," in Harold Tanzyer and Jean Karl, eds. *Reading, Children's Books and Our Pluralistic So-ciety.* International Reading Association, 1972, p. 20.
8. Angelou, Maya. "Commencement Address at Spelman College, Atlanta, Ga." *Time Magazine*, June 20, 1983, p. 55.
9. The National Commission on Excellence in Education. "A Nation at Risk: the Imperative for Educational Reform." *The Chronicle of Higher Education*, May 4, 1983, p. 11.
10. Cortes, Dr. Carlos E. "The Societal Curriculum and the School Curriculum." *Educational Leadership*, Vol. 36, No. 7, April, 1979, p. 475.
11. Novak, Michael. "Pluralism: A Humanistic Perspective," in Stephan Thernstrom, ed. *Harvard Encyclopedia of American Ethnic Groups.* Harvard University Press, 1980, p. 779.
12. Karl, Jean. "What Does It Mean," in Harold Tanzyer and Jean Karl, eds. op. cit. p. 78, 79.
13. Yep, Laurence. *Child of the Owl.* Harper & Row, 1977, p. 216, 217.
14. Belpre, Pura. "Who Speaks for a Culture," in Harold Tanzyer and Jean Karl, eds. op. cit. p. 28.
15. Highwater, Jamake. *Many Smokes, Many Moons: a Chronology of American Indian History Through Indian Art.* Lippincott, 1978, p. 13, 14.
16. "Uchida, Yoshida 1921-" in Anne Commire, *Something About the Author: Facts and Pictures About Contemporary Authors and Illustrators of Books for Young People*, Vol. 1, 1971, p. 219.
17. "Graham, Lorenz, 1902-" in Anne Commire, op. cit., Vol. 2, 1971, p. 122-123.
18. "Myers, Walter Dean." *Catholic Library World*, Sept. 1981, p. 74.

"A Nation at Risk"
& The Library Community's Response

by Gale Eaton

In April 1983, a report to then-United States Secretary of Education Terrel H. Bell warned that American education had declined to a level at which our national "prosperity, security, and civility" were endangered. The report, *A Nation at Risk: The Imperative for Educational Reform* was issued as "an Open Letter to the American People" and received wide press coverage. Its language was urgent: "If an unfriendly foreign power had attempted to impose on America the mediocre educational performance that exists today, we might well have viewed it as an act of war." It was deliberately brief, selective, and readable, without footnotes. Its authors, the National Commission on Excellence in Education (NCEE) believed that "their [members'] purpose would be best served if their report didn't look like (1) a federal report or (2) a research report."

The Commission's aim was to focus public attention on the nation's schools and energize public support for school reform. From the mass of testimony received, it chose statistics that dramatized the weaknesses of contemporary American education: unfavorable comparison between American and foreign student achievement; declining College Board scores; and high levels of adult illiteracy. The figures cited, the Commission claimed, served as indicators of a "declining trend . . . that stems more from weakness of purpose, confusion of vision, underuse of talent, and lack of leadership, than from conditions beyond our control."

The Commission made five general recommendations for reform, with more-detailed suggestions for implementation. Briefly summarized, they state that: (1) school curricula should be strengthened, especially in the "five new basics"—English, mathematics, social studies, science, and computer science; (2) time should be used more effectively and, if necessary, school days and years should be lengthened; (3) high school graduation requirements and college entrance requirements should be more stringent; (4) steps should be taken to make teaching a more desirable profession; and (5) the public should demand more effective leadership from educators and elected officials.

In general, response to *A Nation At Risk* was varied. President Reagan, in his April 30th address to the nation, welcomed the report as support for his own policy of decreased federal spending. He called attention to the years of educational decline—"years when the federal presence in education grew and grew." The *Cincinnati Enquirer*, sharing the more general perception that educational reforms will be costly, declared that "Americans would be more inclined to increase their investment in education if they had some assurance that the billions already spent were supporting a system capable of more than mediocrity." Elsewhere in the media there were calls for better tax bases. *USA Today* announced that increased local, state, and federal expenditures would be "worth it."

Partly due to the timing of the report's release, the Commission succeeded in attracting extraordinary publicity for education. Educational reform was already high on the nation's agenda. *A Nation at Risk* was one of several '84 reports which emphasized a need for higher educational standards and for regaining public confidence in the schools. Other reports were *Action for Excellence* by the Task Force on Education for Economic Growth: *Educating Americans for the 21st Century* by the Commission on Precollege Education in Mathematics, Science, & Technology; *The Paideia Proposal: An Educational Manifesto* by Mortimer Adler; *High School* by Ernest Boyer; and *A Place Called School* by John I. Goodlad.

Secretary Bell recognized the current concern and said that the NCEE was created in response to a "widespread public perception that something is seriously remiss in our educational system." Although Bell felt that the NCEE report was "the firebrand that ignited the national campaign for educational improvement," the campaign for educational excellence was already underway. In many areas of the country, state officials and members of local school districts had not only perceived failures in schools, but had taken steps to reform them. *Newsweek*, in May 1983, reported a dozen governors were working to boost education, 27 states were making efforts to raise university admissions requirements, and a number of schools were introducing programs that were intellectually challenging and stimulating for students.

A Nation at Risk was effective in attracting attention and support partly because it said what people wanted to hear. It was effective, too, because of its narrow focus and heightened style. Members of the NCEE were well aware that educational problems do not begin in high school. NCEE's charter directed it to pay special attention to teenage youth; they did so by concentrating on high school education. *A Nation at Risk* dramatizes the need for reform at one level of education and does not discuss other levels in any detail, but it certainly does not rule out support for reform at other levels. The concentration is on "five new basics" and consideration of other subject areas is omitted.

Problems highlighted in the report and the measures recommended for improvement are significant, but limited. Because issues are presented in a simplified and rhetorical form, the report can readily be used as a political tool, either in implementing reforms at the local or state level, or in raising the funds necessary for implementation.

By April 1984, a year after its official release, an estimated 400,000 copies of *A Nation at Risk* had been distributed, and it is estimated that as many as five million people read it. With pride, Secretary Bell summarized its effects as of that date:

> All 50 states now have education task forces that follow the example set by the National Commission on Excellence in Education. At last count, 44 states are in the process of raising their high school graduation requirements; 20 states are considering a longer school day or year; 13 states are in various stages of adopting master teacher plans; 42 states are reexamining their laws governing teacher preparation and certification; and 36 states are seeking ways to address teacher shortages in such critical fields as science, mathematics, and computer technology.

It is difficult to know how much educational improvement can be attributed to any one call for reform, but it's probably safe to say that many positive changes initiated following the publication of *A Nation at Risk* can be attributed to problems identified, and recommendations outlined, in it.

Controversy & Criticism

Perhaps NCEE's greatest achievement was the production of a report that was widely visible and discussed, both in the media and in the professional literature. *A Nation at Risk* provoked controversy and was criticized for its heightened, "sensationalist" language and its many omissions. Some critics pointed out practical obstacles to reform—the difficulties of funding longer school years, or the problems of reconciling new teacher-incentive plans to old teacher contracts and collective bargaining procedures. Others were disturbed by the report's underlying philosophy. *A Nation at Risk* is not a partisan report. Nevertheless, commissioned under a conservative administration, it is political in both its origins and its potential uses. The *Wall Street Journal* called it "a profoundly conservative document."

NCEE expressed a solid commitment to equity as well as to excellence, but took the position that equal access to a mediocre education is no more useful to the disadvantaged than to the average or gifted student. Liberal educators feared that excellence could be harmful to some: raised standards would force less-gifted students to drop out. Some were disturbed also by the report's attention to education as a source of national economic and military strength. With the shift of emphasis from education for the needs of students to education for the needs of the nation, they feared that students with special needs would suffer.

Any call for the education of capable independent thinkers is, by implication, a call for adequate libraries; inquiry cannot be carried on without resources. The report, however, did not make this connection explicit.

The first response from the library community was a criticism of one glaring omission—scant mention was made of the contribution of libraries to education. *School Library Journal* reported that "the library community was dismayed and astonished to discover that the Commission's recommendations for improvement lacked substantive reference to the role of libraries and that the report centered on secondary and post-secondary education."

The Commission may simply have taken library support as a given, as it did elementary school education. The library community felt that this omission could be both politically and economically damaging. The missions of libraries and schools are mutually supportive, but in many communities schools and public libraries are in competition for limited financial resources. Media centers must compete with other school programs for a share of limited funds.

Because *A Nation at Risk* attracted national attention to educational issues, librarians had an opportunity and a rationale to publicize their role in education. For school library media centers and public libraries serving high school students, the need was particularly urgent. These were the institutions which could make the most direct contributions to high school reforms. At the same time, they stood to lose the most if their contributions were not recognized.

Delayed Reaction

The library response was slow. *A Nation at Risk* was released in April, and available to the public on request by May. Even before its release, the report was widely expected by the education community. For more than a year, the Commission had been sponsoring hearings, symposia, and panel discussions. It had commissioned papers and solicited testimony from experts around the country. Neither the American Library Association nor its divisions concerned with schools and education used that time to prepare a response to the report.

Eventually, action on the matter was prompted by Virginia H. Mathews, a member of the American Association of School Librarians who arrived at the June 1983 ALA Annual Conference with a position paper for AASL's consideration and possible endorsement. By a close analysis of the NCEE report's implications for school libraries, Mathews laid the groundwork for a focused AASL response.

At its meeting during the Los Angeles conference, AASL's Executive Committee forwarded Mathews' paper to the ALA's Legislation Committee. It then went to ALA's Executive Board and was presented in Council's last session on June 29. In the process, Mathews' intent was broadened almost beyond recognition, and the proposed AASL statement became the nucleus of a general response from the American Library Association. Incoming ALA President Brooke Sheldon appointed a Task Force on Excellence in Education to investigate the issues on behalf of the association at large, and report at the 1984 ALA Midwinter Meeting. At the Annual Conference in

Dallas in June 1984, the Task Force distributed its findings in a pamphlet titled, *Realities: Educational Reform in a Learning Society.*

Realities, however, was one of two major documents to emerge from the library community's consideration of the NCEE report. The second, published a month later by the U.S. Department of Education, was *Alliance for Excellence: Librarians Respond to A Nation at Risk.* This had been prepared under the auspices of the Department's Center for Libraries and Education Improvement. Representatives of virtually every segment of the profession were involved. Like members of the original Commission, they had gathered information for recommendations through a series of seminars. Five issue-papers served as bases for discussion of network, school, public, academic, and special library responses. ALA published these papers in *Libraries and the Learning Society.*

Comparisons of Reports

Realities and *Alliance for Excellence* were intended to be political tools. They were meant, like *A Nation at Risk,* to sway public opinion and to influence the allocation of funds. The ALA Task Force stated specifically that *Realities* spoke "to public decision-makers and others who provide resources to libraries." The booklets were a reply to *A Nation at Risk,* and sought to rectify the omission of libraries and augment the recommendations.

The professional leaders who framed the library reports accepted a double task: to make an effective case for libraries, and to do so in the context of the discussion on educational reform. The resulting documents are impressive, but flawed. Both *Realities* and *Alliance for Excellence* are handsomely designed booklets. They should be distributed with pride to school boards, city councils, and state legislatures around the country. Both demand more of readers, however, than does the NCEE report.

Realities is short and clearly organized, but its prose is unexpectedly difficult. *Alliance for Excellence* follows the outline of *A Nation at Risk,* but adds recommendations in new categories and is significantly longer. In addition, *A Nation at Risk* freely uses emotional language, whereas the two library reports attempt to be objective and to accentuate the positive. Compared to the NCEE report, however, they seem vague, partly due to their broadened focus. *A Nation at Risk* is about high schools; it calls for a society in which learning is respected and young people are challenged to intellectual achievement. *Realities* and *Alliance for Excellence* both envision a society in which learning at all levels is supported and facilitated; they are about library service to every age group and sector of society, by every kind of library. *Realities* "bangs away at four basic points: learning begins before schooling; good schools require good libraries; people in a learning society need libraries throughout their lives; and public support of libraries is an investment in people and communities." (*American Libraries,* Jul./Aug. 1984)

Alliance for Excellence includes recommendations in support of adult literacy programs and upgraded education for librarianship. This inclusiveness may be good for the profession. No single element of the library community appears to be in competition with others for funding. They appear to state "We are collegial; we recognize each others' importance."

What the library reports have sacrificed for collegiality is a clear focus. Library networks and education for librarianship are not irrelevant to the issue of library service to high school students, but their relevance is indirect. Local citizens and administrators who handle funds may not understand this, and librarians who use *Realities* or *Alliance for Excellence* in a budget fight may have to mark salient points to identify them for lay readers.

Another factor contributing to the vagueness of the reports from the library communities is veiled disagreement. *A Nation at Risk* is the expression of a conservative viewpoint. *Realities* and *Alliance for Excellence* are written in support of it. Both wholeheartedly endorse the goals of the NCEE. Their only overt criticism of the earlier report is that it failed to mention the importance of library contributions to educational reform.

Yet, *Realities* and *Alliance for Excellence* are essentially liberal documents. Their tone is remarkably different from that of *A Nation at Risk. Realities* gives voice to such liberal concerns as the "reader's right to privacy," and the mandated availability of state and federal government documents "through library networks." Even certain key phrases are used differently. In referring to the "global village," for instance, NCEE tells us that we "live among determined, well-educated, and strongly motivated competitors." *Alliance for Excellence* places us "in a global village" with quite a different ambience, where it sees us as "neighbors to all humanity." The meaning of the phrase has shifted.

The difference in underlying philosophy is particularly apparent in the standards section of *Alliance for Excellence.* NCEE was concerned that undemanding high school graduation and college admissions requirements, combined with grade inflation, had communicated to students a message that society expected little of them, or even that academic excellence was not important. Its recommendation of more rigorous and measurable standards was intended to stimulate achievement. *Alliance for Excellence* shifts the focus from student to institutional achievement, recommending "that libraries, associations, state educational and library agencies, and accrediting organizations adopt more rigorous and measurable standards for school library media services." These standards "should be performance-based and founded on clear, solid research." This tacit admission that the research is not yet entirely in place constitutes a challenge of sorts, but to the profession, rather than to young people.

Like *A Nation at Risk,* the library reports make recommendations which are expensive to implement. *A Nation at Risk* calls, not only for financial expenditures, but also for structural change in the nation's school systems, and even a reordering of society's attitudes and priorities. Whatever its faults, it does not offer a Band-Aid approach to reform. It involves a critical reevaluation of the purpose of education.

Effectiveness

Realities and *Alliance for Excellence* both make many constructive suggestions but seem to be primarily concerned with money. *Realities*, in both tone and substance, evokes the service orientation of librarianship. It is virtually a litany of community enterprises which libraries support, might support, or could support if they themselves were better supported. Most institutional shortcomings are attributed to inadequate funding, and a majority of the report's recommendations are either for increased government funding of library programs or for the establishment of state and federal regulations favoring such programs.

Alliance for Excellence calls for assessment of the nation's school library media centers and public libraries, and for research and data collection to make that assessment more reliable.

Both reports stop far short of proposing a major critical review of the library profession. Perhaps it is safer to avoid public criticism of libraries. Schooling in this country is compulsory, and the schools, however much lambasted, will limp along. For most of us, library attendance has always been optional. If library funding, too, could be seen as optional, then perhaps any critical examination of institutional effectiveness is dangerous, offering ammunition to those who might discontinue fiscal support. Accentuation of the positive may be the only safe course.

Yet, by choosing to respond so positively to NCEE's report, the library community put itself at a disadvantage. Comparisons between the reports are inevitable, and *A Nation at Risk* is an effectively written document. Its basic plot—we have fallen from grace and doom is upon us, we must repent and be saved—is one which has served prophets for thousands of years. Certainly it has more kick than *Realities* and *Alliance for Excellence*, which avoid the appearance of negativity as much as possible. It's difficult to accentuate the positive in support of a jeremiad and still appear relevant.

The effectiveness of *Realities* and *Alliance for Excellence* as documents, then, is impaired by several factors. Some of these factors should have been strengths: e.g., inclusiveness, idealism, and a positive attitude. They appear to be weaknesses in the response to *A Nation at Risk* because they do not fit easily into the agenda set by the NCEE report. The inclusiveness of the library reports broadens their focus and diminishes their immediate impact on readers. Their positive support for the NCEE report creates an awkward context for the advocacy of the library professional's ideals.

Realities and *Alliance for Excellence's* effectiveness as political tools depends on the use librarians make of them. As of October 1984, approximately 10,000 copies of *Alliance for Excellence* and 15,000 of *Realities* had been distributed; both have since been reprinted. In Rhode Island, a two-day workshop focused on the recommendations of both reports, "exploring how all libraries can be linked more effectively with citizen and community resources." The Texas Library Association has made use of *Realities*.

At the national level, ALA has appointed an ad hoc Coordinating Committee on *Realities* and *Alliance for Excellence* (CCRAX), with Virginia Mathews as chair, to coordinate the implementation of the two reports. At the 1985 Midwinter Conference in Washington, D.C., CCRAX presented for discussion its first draft of a Family-Library Learning Partnership Bill, focusing on service to children though both school and public libraries.

In Retrospect

The library response to *A Nation at Risk* has not yet exhausted its potential, and much may yet be accomplished. Yet, even while we applaud the successes of *Realities* and *Alliance for Excellence*, we should learn what we can from their partial failure.

First, for maximum impact, they should have been released far sooner. Ideally, librarians should have seen *A Nation at Risk* coming. They might then have persuaded the Commissioners to include recommendations for library support, or, failing that, they might have been able to prepare their response in advance. Lack of previous planning delayed the library response. So, too, did the very extensiveness of the planning which became necessary when it was decided to make the library response representative of the entire profession rather than of the one or two divisions most concerned. The inclusive nature of the library reports was thus doubly expensive in loss of timeliness as well as in blurring of focus.

A second lesson to be gleaned from the experience is *caution*. It may be wise to pause before launching an ALA-wide initiative in response to a passing occasion, such as publication (and publicizing) of a government report. In this instance, a brief statement from a concerned division might have provided members more quickly with a political tool more specific to their needs. Rapid dissemination and active use by members could have made a document like AASL's two-page "School Library Media Programs and Their Role in Schooling" more effective than an elaborately produced pamphlet.

Finally, an effort on the scale of *Realities* or *Alliance for Excellence* might better have been mounted as a direct expression of the profession's own ideals and purposes, not a reaction to an agenda set from outside the profession. Libraries exist for the education of youth, but not only for that. They collect and transfer information for other purposes as well. *A Nation at Risk* offered a coherent, if controversial, view of high school education. The library response, partly because it was a response, could not do the same for librarianship.

Librarians have a responsibility, not only to provide effective library service, but to make the library visible in the community, to ensure its use, and to advocate its continued support. *Realities* and *Alliance for Excellence* are steps in this direction, but they should not be the last steps. Librarians must prepare for tomorrow's needs, assess resources, and work towards formulating strategies in the best creative spirit of the profession.

References

"Action on *Realities*," *American Libraries* 15 (Dec. 1984): 811, 815.

American Library Association Task Force on Excellence in Education. *Realities*. ALA, 1984.

Bell, Terrel H. "American Education at a Crossroads," *Phi Delta Kappan* 65 (April 1984): 531.

Brandt, Roy. "On Excellence and Mediocrity: A Conversation with Milton Goldberg," *Educational Leadership* 41 (March 1984): 18.

Lewis, Anne C. "*A Nation at Risk:* One Year Later," *Phi Delta Kappan* 65 (April 1984): 515.

Libraries and the Learning Society: Papers in Response to A Nation at Risk. American Library Association, 1984.

"Library Professionals to Specify Libraries' Impact on Education," *School Library Journal* 30 (Nov. 1983): 10.

Mathews, Virginia H. "Implementing *Alliance for Excellence* and *Realities*: Libraries' Partnership in a Learning Society," *The Bowker Annual*, 30th ed. (R.R. Bowker, 1985), p. 77.

"National Committee on Excellence Cites Problems in U.S. Education, *School Library Journal* 29 (Aug. 1983): 8-9.

"Newspaper Reaction to the Report on Excellence in Education," *The Chronicle of Higher Education* 26 (May 11, 1983): 9.

Passow, A. Harry. "Tackling the Reform Reports of the 1980's," *Phi Delta Kappan* 65 (June 1984); 676.

Reagan, Ronald. "The President's Radio Address to the Nation on Education," *American Education* 19 (June 1983): 4.

"R.I. Citizens, Librarians Get Down to *Realities*," *American Libraries* 15 (July/August 1984): 490.

"Sheldon and Shubert Counter *Nation at Risk* with *Realities*," *American Libraries* 15 (July/Auguust 1984): 490.

Tanner, Daniel. "The American High School at the Crossroads," *Educational Leadership* 41 (March 1984): 6.

U.S. Department of Education. Libraries and the Learning Society Advisory Board. *Alliance for Excellence: Librarians Respond to A Nation at Risk*, July 1984.

U.S. Department of Education. National Commission on Excellence in Education. *A Nation at Risk: The Imperative for Educational Reform*, April 1983.

Williams, Dennis A., *et al.*, "Can the Schools Be Saved?" *Newsweek* 101 (May 9, 1983).

Reaching the Unserved
Libraries Can Attack Illiteracy

by Sue McCleaf Nespeca

Libraries are ushering in the new decade proclaiming 1990 "International Literacy Year" and 1991 "Year of the Lifetime Reader." We have seen an increasing emphasis on family literacy—buzzwords for the '90s. Libraries must change service patterns to try to help solve the problems of illiteracy and aliteracy (the lack of a desire to read). Although some libraries are making attempts to reach children who do not frequent the library, the vast majority continue to concentrate all their efforts on serving children who already are library users. In addition, the practice of converting an entire staff to "generalists," now endorsed by several large library systems in the U.S., only discourages librarians who have special talents and an interest in working with children from taking additional course work in this area.

In my travels to libraries throughout Ohio and in conferences and workshops in other states, I have often overheard children's librarians discussing the library programs they do each week—often with a certain amount of braggadocio.

"How many storytimes do you do each week?"

"I'm doing eight right now—three for toddlers and five for preschoolers, and I still have a waiting list."

These comments seldom vary, and when they do it's only in the number of programs. I hear librarians talking about craft programs, programs involving magicians, and summer reading clubs. Occasionally they mention computer clubs, reader's theaters or puppetry. Of course, there is nothing wrong with these programs. They are certainly needed, and they serve their purpose by encouraging children to read. But who is being served in those eight storytimes each week? I believe that most children who come to those programs that we spend so much time planning and executing need little encouragement to read. By and large, they are bought by parents who already read to them at home and who would probably come to the library anyway (though quite possibly without as much regularity).

This observation will probably provoke controversy since, in output measures, storytimes have been proven to increase circulation (which in most libraries translates to dollars). Isn't it true that every library director likes to see high circulation statistics, especially when trying to justify budget increases? And, doesn't every children's librarian strive to increase circulation? If we want to help stem the growth of illiteracy and convert aliterates, especially children who are educationally at risk, we need to reach all children. To do this, we must go to those children who do not walk through our doors. What are librarians serving children doing to make contact with the vast numbers of unserved children—those they need to reach most?

Obviously, there are problems over which we have no control. Children may lack transportation. Parents may not have access to public transportation and may not be able to bring their children to the library. Also, in this age of single parents and dual-income families, many parents don't have time or are not motivated to bring their children to storytimes. Even if they did find time, they may find that the library closed early or is open only on certain evenings.

Children's librarians must look for ways to overcome barriers in their communities. Teachers and media specialists see all school-age children. Do you, a public librarian, know your area school library media specialists and meet with them on a regular basis? Do you keep local teachers informed about new literature and suggest good books for them to read aloud? Have you contacted home schools to invite families to the library? Do you know which high schools or vocational schools teach child care or family living classes? Are you aware of classes for pregnant teens, and have you talked to the girls about the importance of reading to infants. Have you spoken to participants at your local Red Cross babysitting clinic? Have you ever held a storytime with an interpreter on hand for the deaf, or talked about library materials such as tapes, records, and braille books to those who may need such materials? Have you tried giving a storytime at a shelter for the homeless or for battered persons? Have you attended classes for illiterate adults who are learning to read, and recommended books on tape for them to use with their children?

By now, most of you want to scream, "Time out! I don't have time to do outreach programs!" Yet many librarians will find the time to do eight storytimes each week. If each storytime session draws 25 children, the total number of children reached is 200, with large blocks of time used to plan, set up, and execute these programs. In approximately the same amount of preparation time that one story hour takes, a librarian can demonstrate the use of picture books to 30 early childhood educators who each work with 25 children. The joys of picture books could then reach 750 children!

We can work with teachers or caregivers to reach the many preschoolers who are in day care of early childhood centers, and those school-age children who are being taught at home. We can develop outreach programs to take to well-baby clinics, child development centers, family health centers, community centers, social service agencies, or children's hospitals. We can also approach foster parents' groups or organizations for single parents such as Parents Without Partners. Even more important, we can deposit paperback collections or packets with read-aloud suggestions at welfare centers or places where food stamps are issued. We can arrange for bookmobiles to stop at early childhood centers or day care centers, family day care homes, or at housing projects where low-income families live.

Children enrolled in day care or preschool centers have additional problems. Because seat belts are mandated in certain states, and because these centers have limited modes of transportation, trips to the library by preschool groups are few or nonexistent. I believe that some libraries actually discourage such centers from bringing children to the library on a regular basis, or limit them to a certain number of visits in one year—or they don't really encourage storytime attendance.

Several library systems have dealt with these problems, often in a large-scale way. One of the most successful programs is Project LEAP (Library's Educational Alternative for Preschoolers), a service of Cuyahoga County Public Library in Cleveland. Through this program, the library circulates storytime and puppet kits to early childhood centers, conducts workshops for the personnel, distributes newsletters, and trains day care and preschool staff in storytime skills.

In Prince George's County (MD) Library System's WEE CARE program, staff members visit family day care homes. Pioneer Library System in Rochester, NY, circulates learning kits to preschool and day care centers. Denver (CO) Public Library's "Magic Bus" takes books to the centers. New York Public Library's Early Childhood Resource and Information Center is designed for adults who live with, work with or study about children from birth to age five. Lee County Library System in Fort Myers, Florida, has a circulating library housed at the Lee County Child Care Office for teachers to borrow books that their preschoolers can take home. What better way to get books into the hands of children of non-reading parents?

Although most of the programs mentioned above require funds—either a Library Services and Construction Act (LSCA) grant or foundation funding—there are other ways to serve early childhood centers or day care homes on a smaller scale. Since day care and preschool centers don't have much money to buy books, you might meet with your library director to draw up some special circulation rules, possibly granting an institutional library card which will allow teachers at these centers to check out a large number of books with limited or no fines, similar to special loan privileges for public school teachers.

Finding out about local homes in which caregivers will take in young children may be difficult, but in most states, caregivers are licensed and you can contact regional licensing agents to obtain a list of these homes. I recommend that you keep a file of all centers and preschools (with contact

people listed) in your library. This information can be compiled in booklets for referral purposes or for mailing publicity about library programs.

A good way to reach early childhood educators is through newsletters, programs and workshops. One of my most successful ventures was a program for early childhood educators in which the importance of sharing books was stressed and various methods of storytelling were demonstrated. I remain active in my local chapter of the National Association for the Education of Young Children and often speak about storytelling or new children's books at their workshops—or, I present simple puppetry ideas for accompanying stories or rhymes. I also do storytelling at the Week of the Young Child Festival, which reaches hundreds of children in the community each year. Both Baltimore County Public Library (in Towson, MD) and Seattle's King County Library System distribute newsletters to preschool teachers and/or day care providers.

Many librarians continue to expend large amounts of time organizing summer reading programs, which tend to reach children who are already turned on to books. Librarians get caught up in the trappings of summer reading programs—the number of books read or who gets to add to the bookworm stretching around the wall of the children's room. Incentives are given to encourage top readers. Few reluctant readers or children who rarely come to the library sign up for these programs or receive any special encouragement to come regularly. Children of working parents attend day care centers or are with babysitters.

We can find some of these non-library users by going to where the children are: a park, swimming pool, recreational center, child care center, camp or a summer class for remedial students. Then, instead of rewarding children who join up for the number of books read, we can reward them for "continued" reading—whether it be 10 pages of a book or even a book beneath their grade level. Before school closes for the summer months, we can contact teachers to ask which students would profit if a letter on the necessity of retaining reading skills over the summer vacation were mailed to their parents. Or, why not recruit grandparents or volunteers to help with read-aloud sessions in the library over the summer?

Libraries can attack illiteracy and aliteracy. By expanding or improving two popular programs—story hours and summer reading programs—we can reach a vast number of children who do not use the library. Hopefully many suggestions I've given can be implemented. I realize that no one library or system can possibly implement all of them. Both time and budget constraints are definitely problems that need to be addressed. Library directors and trustees must realize that in order to serve all the children in the community, an increase in the staff of the children's department is necessary.

Librarians should contact their state libraries to ask about federal funding under LSCA. For example, The Library Literacy Programs (Title VI) is a discretionary grant program administered by the Office of Library Programs, U.S. Department of Education, Washington, DC 20208-5570. In the five-year reauthorization of LSCA, signed into law on March 15, there were programmatic changes in LSCA I, II, and III: new are Title VII (for evaluation and assessment of LSCA) and Title VIII (for Library Learning Centers with provision for Family Learning Centers and Library Literacy Centers). Under Public Library Services (Section 9), Intergenerational Library Services was expanded to include assisting libraries in developing programs in which adult volunteers assist in "developing afterschool literacy and reading skills programs for unsupervised school children during afterschool hours." Childcare Library Outreach was also expanded to include "assisting libraries in providing mobile library services and programs to child-care providers or child-care centers which are licensed or certified by the State, or otherwise meet the requirements of State law." Part A in the new Title VIII, Family Learning Centers, authorizes discretionary grants of up to $200,000 to local public libraries "to expand and improve opportunities for lifetime learning and the involvement of the Nation's families as partners in their children's education by providing comprehensive, family-oriented library services."

Part B, Library Literacy Centers, calls for the establishment of model library literacy centers to aid adults. Another interesting provision is found under Interlibrary Cooperation and Resource Sharing: "Public and school libraries which cooperate to make school library resources available to the public during periods when school is not in session may be reimbursed for such expense."

More specialists trained to work with young children must be hired, not generalists. Larger systems should consider adding an early childhood specialist to the staff, or more important, a Children's Outreach Librarian who is responsible for setting up some of the programs described above and working with community organizations dedicated to eradicating illiteracy. Library organizations at the national and state levels must strive harder to work with other organizations which serve children. Joint conferences of librarians and early childhood educators, particularly at the state level, could be a start. Only by joining efforts will we begin to reach the unserved child.

The Color of Censorship

by Kenneth F. Kister

If you think about it, practically every hue in the color spectrum can be found in our attitudes toward censorship. Red is for the redneck who does not read or think much but knows what is good—and not good—for the rest of us. White is for the pure of heart and mind, usually a latter-day knight whose challenge in life is to save thee and me from a host of hydra-headed evils that beset the world. Blue is for the bluenose, whose consuming passion is sniffing out smut, to say nothing of purple language, in an effort to halt the imminent downfall of Western civilization.

Across the nation, the rednecks and white knights and bluenoses are having a field day, energized by a plethora of causes ranging from naughty photographs in a Robert Mapplethorpe exhibition to a constitutional amendment banning flag burning.

In Florida, these colorful characters, on the march throughout the 1980s, have been zealous, determined, and devastatingly effective. For instance, Chaucer's "Miller's Tale" and Aristophanes' *Lysistrata* have been banished from the schools of Columbia County after a long, bitter struggle that ended up in the Supreme Court. In a similar case, a wholesale assault on some of our most revered literary classics from Shakespeare to Tennessee Williams occurred in Bay County's schools, and the wounds inflicted remain open today. Fundamentalist Christian groups all over the state have tried, sometimes successfully, to shield the populace from the alleged blasphemies in the film, *The Last Temptation of Christ*. The state legislature, no shrinking violet when it comes to red-hot political issues that get headlines but cost no green, could not resist getting into the act several years ago by passing an "obscene" bumper-sticker law that has police officers ticketing vehicles sporting such messages as "RUSSIA SUCKS" and "51 PERCENT SWEETHEART, 49 PERCENT BITCH." As we enter the 1990s, the rap group 2 Live Crew has garnered national attention as its album *As Nasty As They Wanna Be* was declared obscene in Florida, the first time in U.S. history that a musical group has been so gagged.

How do you color censorship?

For patriotic-sounding organizations like the American Family Association, an extralegal pressure group that has declared war on *Playboy* and similar "pornographic" magazines, censorship is red, white, and blue, all rolled into one. Interestingly, groups at the opposite end of the civil liberties spectrum like People for the American Way (who vigorously challenge censorship in the educational system) also view themselves as protecting traditional American values.

Then there are those, again in both camps of the censorship debate, who are pink with embarrassment over juvenile excesses some writers, film-makers, and entertainers take with the freedoms they have. Foul-mouthed Eddie Murphy and Andrew Dice Clay come readily to mind.

And, of course, let us not forget the color yellow, reserved for those who are unwilling to speak out and stand up for their convictions, no matter which side they espouse.

How do you color censorship?

Many librarians, myself included, tend to see censorship in black or white terms. All those perceived to be censors are bad; all who oppose censorship are good. We have no patience with those who would try to restrict or suppress words, images, and ideas they find abhorrent. The problem is, as in most of life, black or white paradigms tend to be overly simplistic and often wrong.

Perhaps the most appropriate color for censorship is gray.

True, gray is not as distinctive or definite as red or white or blue or purple or pink or black or yellow, but it does convey a sense of the professional, intellectual, ethical, moral, political, and legal ambiguities that frequently characterize censorship problems.

Consider, for instance, the complaint about a book on witchcraft in a Florida elementary school media center. As sometimes happens, a youngster checked out the book, took it home, read it, and then showed it to his mother, who, upon inspection, found it to be objectionable. In this case, the book discussed devil worship, one page containing a line written backwards, which when held up to a mirror spelled out a pledge to Satan. After alerting the media, the boy's mother loudly condemned the book and demanded that it be removed from the media center.

A review, or reconsideration, committee comprised of the school's media specialist and several parents (but not the complainant) examined the book. Unfortunately, the book lacked positive reviews, did not appear on any recommended lists, was written and published by a press of uncertain reputation, and by all accounts seemed well beyond the reading comprehension of the typical elementary-school student. In sum, it became clear that the book should not have been acquired in the first place. The incident was resolved by placing the book on a restricted shelf and requiring parental permission to check it out. Despite public protestations about being excluded from the reconsideration process, the child's mother who brought the complaint accepted this compromise.

How would you color this case? Both the American Association of School Librarians and the American Library Association condemn restricted shelves and closed collections as "major barriers between students and resources." Are restricted shelves sometimes necessary? Are they sometimes a reasonable compromise between parental concern and access to sensitive library materials? Or are they always shameful cop-outs? Wouldn't the media specialist in this instance have been wiser to admit a selection mistake and simply withdraw the book? Color this case gray.

Or consider a recent case involving meeting-room policy at one of the Florida's largest public library systems. A group called Concerned Women of America (CWA), described in news clips as both a "religious" and an "anti-abortion" organization, requested use of a meeting room at the main library for a program that would include both a prayer service and discussion of prolife political strategy. Library personnel initially rejected the request, citing a standing policy that prohibited political and religious groups from meeting in the library. When CWA instigated legal action, the library administration promptly changed its policy. Just as promptly, the group dropped its lawsuit.

How to color this case? Was the library wrong to change its policy? Did the administration cave in to pressure exerted by an aggressive special-interest group? Has some cardinal principle of intellectual freedom been breached by permitting this group, and presumably others like it, to meet in the library? Should the Ku Klux Klan and like organizations be allowed to use the library's meeting rooms? Is the library to be congratulated for rewriting a restrictive policy that mocked open access to library facilities, to say nothing of the democratic process? Let's color this one gray, too.

Consider one more case. Although it only indirectly involved media specialists and librarians, the incident points up a different problem for those of us who like to view censorship as strictly a black or white affair. The problem is, what happens when someone cries censorship and it's not true?

The case began when a reading teacher in Florida reported that the school's principal confiscated multiple copies of a book the teacher was using with a seventh-grade remedial reading class. After the incident, the teacher contacted various state and national organizations opposed to censorship, as well as print and broadcast media serving the area, pointing out that the book in question, a novel, is considered a contemporary classic and that complaints about passages concerning rape and incest (that led to the principal's action) were to-

tally unjustified. National anticensorship groups, newspaper accounts, and a local television piece immediately condemned, either directly or by implication, this act of "censorship"—without bothering to investigate further.

Closer examination of the facts of the case, however, revealed that there was more to the story than the teacher cared to admit. First, the disputed book was an adult novel being used to teach seventh-grade students reading below grade level. Moreover, despite the teacher's assertions to the contrary, the book remained available in both the school library and various sites in the county public library system. What on the face of it appeared to be a case of blatant censorship turned out rather to be a professional disagreement between a strong-willed teacher and principal over what constitutes appropriate curriculum materials for remedial reading students. The principal prevailed, but at a price. As one neutral observer privately suggested, the teacher's cry of censorship was motivated by a desire for revenge against the principal for questioning the teacher's judgment.

Censorship? A question of academic freedom? A dispute over curriculum materials? Color the incident very dark gray.

The message in the cases briefly described here? Listen; don't jump to easy conclusions; get and study the facts; be wary of the many land mines that go with the territory. Be prepared to concede that sometimes the censor might have a point worth hearing. Sometimes, much as we hate to admit it, librarians and media specialists do make errors.

Obviously, this is not to suggest that we throw out or water down the *School Library Bill of Rights, Library Bill of Rights,* etc. and appease the censor. Not at all. Librarians and media specialists must continue to articulate the bedrock principles of intellectual freedom and vigorously oppose censorship in all its guises. Rather, I am suggesting that we all need to look for shades of gray when confronting censorship activists, issues, and incidents.

Several years ago, Will Manley, in his "Facing the Public" column in *Wilson Library Bulletin* (January 1986; p. 41), addressed another side of the question this way: "The irony is that one of the main tenets of intellectual freedom is that both sides of an issue should be represented. However, intellectual freedom is the most one-sided issue in the profession. It is an issue that really needs to be opened up, because there is a tremendous gap between what many practicing librarians facing the public every day think about intellectual freedom and what they say they think. There are legitimate limits to intellectual freedom in the public library, and we should be able to talk about those limits. After all, intellectual freedom advocates preach that all sides of an issue need to be aired." Of course, the same goes for school libraries and media centers.

How do you color censorship?

Is Privacy Reserved for Adults?

Children's Rights at the Public Library

by Janet Hildebrand

Do parents have the right to know the answer to "What has my child checked out?" When a computerized circulation system takes over library records, borrowing information becomes easily accessible by patron name. How does this change in availability of information affect children? Whose "right" do we respect when parent and child are in conflict? How does the library decide?

Computer technology introduces complex professional and procedural questions that relate to the intellectual freedom of young people. The professional community now faces unavoidable decisions that directly concern children, their right to privacy, responsibility, and freedom to use library materials. What will children learn as a result of these decisions by libraries?

The Contra Costa County Library in California has gone through an evolutionary process that started a year and a half ago with confusion over these new problems. That was followed by legal consultation, staff debate, and finally the formulation of policies, procedures, and a public relations flyer. All of these support the child's right to privacy. How did this policy in Contra Costa County evolve, and why is it significant?

Is Privacy Reserved for Adults?

In the June 1990 *School Library Journal* editorial, Lillian N. Gerhardt states: " . . . the whole idea of privacy in our society seems reserved to adults." Certainly, as a professional group librarians have successfully defended the right of the public to privacy of records to prevent the Federal Bureau of Investigation, the police, city hall, and others from official snooping.

As librarians and as adults, we do hold dear our own rights, and it is not hard for us to identify with our adult patrons. If a woman borrowed the title *How to Do Your Own Divorce in California*, we can easily imagine that she may wish privately to explore her options before discussing her feelings with her spouse. Her interest in the material may or may not be indicative of her future decisions, but in either case she would not want the library to reveal her private search. If the library did breach her trust and thus intervene in her relationship, she might reconsider before checking out library materials again. She might also sue since an implied privileged contract has been violated.

Clearly, the library's role is to provide access to material and to ensure absolute anonymity. Few would question that we must leave to the adult patron and her family the responsibility for communicating and negotiating with each other. The library's charge is to maintain the integrity of the relationship with that patron—and as professionals we must consistently prove ourselves to be trustworthy.

Nevertheless, we may be confused when faced with the parent-child relationship. To whom, then, is the library responsible? The child possessing a library card is the cardholder of record. However, in many libraries the parent has traditionally been asked to sign as the financially responsible party, although libraries vary widely as to the age for which this is required. Does the parent have the right to know what the child borrows? In fact, do libraries possess the legal right to deny a parent such information?

A Step Back for Children?

In Contra Costa County, California, public expectation changed overnight with the advent of the computerized circulation system over a year ago. The public knows, or imagines, what computers can do.

To aggravate the situation, the original computer program allowed all borrowing information, current materials as well as those overdue, to appear on all circulation terminals throughout the 22-outlet system. At times, the pressure on staff to provide the information on the computer screen was intense. Furthermore, the staff in this situation is usually clerical and less versed in professional ethics issues.

For staff, whole new dilemmas arose. Obviously some information must be conveyed to help patrons conduct their business with the library—but what kind of information, and to whom? How do we know with certainty we are giving the information to the right person? Suddenly we would not be physically limited in the information that could be provided, and, for the first time, staff and library policy would have to draw the lines and make these judgments.

Amidst the many new problems grew a nagging concern that this big step ahead for our library system might be a step back for some children. Under the old circulation system—which microfilmed checkouts in order of transaction, the library could not access circulation information by patron. This mechanical limitation provided borrowers of all ages with privacy protection, and the public understood and accepted this limitation. The old system inadvertently protected all equally. Would we now only protect adults? The library was forced to take a position.

Legal Counsel

To begin to sort out this confusion, the Contra Costa County Library asked County Counsel (the attorney for county departments) to respond to specific questions and provide legal interpretation of California state law and case law. In the final analysis, the city or county attorney will have to defend the policy the library has adopted. Since state laws and court history vary widely from state to state, the local interpretation can differ within the same state or county. Libraries must therefore work with their own legal counsel from the beginning.

We posed two specific questions to County Counsel. "Can the Library give parents information about the books their children check out?" and "Can the Library establish an age at which the right of confidentiality begins?" In short, the guidance we received was as follows. Because the California Government Code, section 6267 (part of the Public Records Act), does not specify age, it therefore applies to all ages of cardholders. " . . . Absent a person's written authorization, or an order of the Superior Court, no one, including a minor's parents, has a right to know what a person checks out of a public library."

Legal consultation may differ in other California jurisdictions, but this response gave the Contra Costa County Library a clear mandate to protect a child's right to privacy. Once legal advice is sought, it must be carried out in policy.

Building a Philosophical Base

For three months following this response, library staff on all levels discussed how to carry out the intent of the law through library policy and procedures, which went through three different draft stages. It sounds very clear-cut to say: "All cardholders are entitled to receive equal privacy protection." But how exactly do staff members deal with requests for borrowing information?

At this point in the formulation process, it is desirable for staff to have opportunities to talk out all fears and objections. This subject stirs the emotions, and conflicted feelings are common, even among staff who clearly support privacy protection for adults.

It is vital that staff understand how privacy protection fulfills a need in the lives of children. A staff member who does not believe in the legal and ethical correctness of the policy will experience more difficulty and discomfort in carrying it out than a staff member who personally embraces it. Honoring privacy is a concrete expression of respect for another person. We need to start out with a belief that it is desirable for adults in our society to allow children to experience privacy and respect.

In discussion with our own staff and other professionals, three major concerns typically emerge. These areas involve questions of financial responsibility, the age of our youngest cardholders, and the role of the parent in guiding a child's reading choices.

Financial Responsibility

To many librarians and library staff members, the issues of the privacy rights of children and the financial responsibility of the parent seem to be intimately interwoven. They are actually separate issues, however.

First, let us examine this from the library's perspective. Traditionally, the reason we have required the parent to sign for a child was to try to control losses and recover the cost of lost books. However, computerization now allows us to detect delinquent accounts much earlier and to stop loans to a person who has a book overdue or has accumulated fines. Furthermore, this system works equally well for borrowers of all ages.

Librarians all know a few adult patrons who have not returned many items and to whom the library has lost large amounts of money. But in my experience, children who fail to return materials usually follow a family pattern—their parents, too, exhibit similar habits. Now the computer stops all abuses. Libraries have a cap on losses, and the need for another party to be "financially responsible" is less important.

Next, let us look at what happens in the parent-child relationship under such a policy. "How can we expect the parent to pay for something without knowing what he or she is paying for?" is a common argument. However, this is unlikely to happen for several reasons. In our library, all overdue notices and bills are mailed in a sealed envelope directly to the cardholder, regardless of age. The child then has three options:

(1) Most children will ask the parent for help in paying their bills and clearing their records so they can continue to borrow materials. Usually, then, the parent will ask to see the bill and will know what is being paid for. This is part of the bargain between the child and the parent.

(2) A few children, however, will want to have their privacy, even if it means they cannot clear up their borrowing records and will be denied more books. Each of us as adults may choose to do this. So why not allow a child to have that choice and learn from it?

(3) Some children, on the other hand, may decide to use allowance money to pay their own bills privately. These children opt for both continued library use and privacy.

As adults, we have all of these choices. Children have an essential need to make these same choices, and to have control over those choices.

Individuals within the Family

Past library practice further suggests a precedent for treating the financial responsibility of family members individually. When one member of a family has a blocked borrowing account, that does not transfer to another member of the family. A child would usually not be told he could not borrow a book because his older sister has overdue materials. Nor is a parent with a clear record blocked from borrowing when a child in the family has overdue material. Except in rare instances, the borrowing privileges of family members are seldom linked.

The Contra Costa County Library does not use a collection agency. However, the Santa Clara County Library (California), with similar policies about privacy, does use such an agency. This system received a legal interpretation from its county counsel that also directed the formulation of policy to protect the privacy of all cardholders, including children. Their registration of borrowers includes birthdate, and the collection agency does not pursue children's accounts. Borrowers of all ages are given ample time to find lost books. On the first occurrence of a delinquent account charges are forgiven and the policy reexplained. On subsequent debts the client may pay in small amounts over a period of time. Even pennies are accepted. In rare cases, to help children restore their borrowing privileges, the Santa Clara County Library allows children to "work off" their debts to the library through assigned tasks. The child may clear a borrowing record in this manner with or without a parent's knowledge.

This sets a creative example for how libraries can deal directly with the child user, providing options that a child can manage and an opportunity to learn.

The Youngest Cardholders

A second area of concern centers on the age of our youngest cardholders. In Contra Costa County, we issue a library card to any child who can write his or her name. For some children this can be as young as four years old. Four-year-olds cannot read overdue notices or the written forms requesting a printout of their borrowing record. Why not allow parents of young children to see records directly? Some staff anticipated embarrassment if forced to withhold information from the parent of a preschooler.

County Counsel interpreted state law thus: "There is no legal authority establishing an age at which the right of confidentiality begins, and there is no legal authority granting the library the right to establish such an age." The confidentiality aspect is not a policy choice. We are carrying out the law. However, the age at which we issue a library card is a policy choice, and different libraries set this age at different levels. Some issue cards at a younger age than we do, and some older.

It is true that the very young may not understand how to return books in three weeks or that fines will be charged if they are not returned. Yet when children reach the big moment when they can write their own names and receive their own library cards, it is a memorable and important day. They feel very grownup! At this point, children lack a mature understanding of that responsibility, but they have a first taste of how it begins. The concept of responsibility is not one we just wake up with one day. It begins with a small seed at an early age, and it grows slowly from experiences throughout life.

Learning Respect for Privacy

The same is true for the concept of privacy—knowing one's own right to privacy and respecting the privacy of others grows out of the experience of having one's own privacy respected. When the library deals directly with a child to impart information about a borrowing account, that child experiences a first taste of privacy.

The child is not in conflict with the parent over library use at this age, so in practical terms it does not block the parent from finding the books that are due and keeping the account clear. In interacting with the child, the staff member can say: "Our records show there are still two books that aren't back yet. As soon as you bring back these last two books, you'll be able to take out some more. Do you want me to discuss this with your mother or dad so they can help you look for them at home?"

In a moment of extreme recalcitrance, a preschooler might deny permission, in which case I would talk to the child privately, list the names of the books, offer to write them down, and suggest that later the child might ask a parent to help. Some staff members have worried that the experience could frighten or overwhelm a preschooler, but the adults in the situation set the tone. A light and matter-of-fact tone is appropriate and natural, and a child this age is able to participate.

Young children will hardly ever exclude parents from involvement in their dealings with the library. However, by the time it is important to a child to keep something private, the child has begun to realize that the process allows some choices. At this stage, children begin to exercise those choices.

The Need for Privacy

As with adult patrons, library staff must remember that we cannot guess children's privacy needs by the nature of the materials. If a child checks out a book about how to live with an alcoholic parent, we may guess that there is a fear of physical danger if the parent is told. Or it could be as simple as a child fearing that a parent will say a desired book is "too easy." Whether fear of anger or anticipation of embarrassment, a child's feelings cannot be second-guessed by anyone.

In some cases, it may not be the parent that the child is embarrassed about. When a parent asks, it tends to be in a very public situation, and maybe the child does not want nearby classmates to hear. The parent will be less likely to notice that the class bully is within earshot. Children know the personalities, and the overdue title about which they are likely to be teased. Only the child is 100 percent sensitive to the child.

The Role of the Parent

This leads to a third area of concern and confusion. "Don't we tell parents to be involved in their child's reading and borrowing? Aren't we preventing them from doing that?"

We have always advised parents to guide their child's reading choices within their own family, but the methods we have recommended were to visit the library with the child, select books together, read aloud in the family, and discuss books with each other. If there are materials they do not want their child to check out, we tell them to advise their child of this. We have never advised that they carry out their role by examining circulation records, nor have we ever made this possible in Contra Costa County.

As in the example of the woman considering divorce, it is a family matter how parent and child communicate about borrowing habits, something to be decided between them. The library's role is to provide access to materials for all and to ensure absolute privacy. It is our responsibility to maintain the integrity of our relationship with each individual cardholder, so each continues to trust. This must include children. A child experiences the same feelings an adult does when that trust is broken, and a child will think twice before checking out materials again.

Handling the Patron

While an understanding of these concepts will help staff to implement policy effectively, clearly they also need specific procedures to follow, both in giving appropriate information to the right person and in refusing inappropriate requests. Our procedures even include a routine question to ask, and what actions are required in response to different answers.

In addition, staff need a public relations flyer to help explain privacy rights to all clients. Our flyer "Your Rights to Privacy" gives the text of the law and explains what information is available and to whom. A statement about parent and child is included as a natural part of this explanation of privacy protection.

The most important procedural decision the Contra Costa County Library made was to reprogram the computer so that current borrowings would no longer appear on terminals; only overdue information appears. In the interest of better protecting users of all ages, we consciously stepped back from the state of full information to one of limited availability.

The public can accept that the information is not on the computer screen at all, more easily than they can accept that the information is displayed but that the staff member will not release it. Staff follow explicit procedures for the handling of overdue information, which is given only to the cardholder.

The Bottom Line

As attorney Roger Funk explained in a California Library Association conference program in November 1990, the concept that the child has rights apart from parents or family is a new idea to many parents and may be hard for them to understand or accept. Furthermore, the legal precedents are not clear. Local legal interpretation has been the basis of Contra Costa County Library policy.

However, barriers such as these have never stopped librarians from fighting tirelessly for legislation and even issuing legal challenges in the commitment to secure and protect access and privacy for adults. The right of a child to access and privacy deserves an equally pro-active stance from the profession.

This idea may seem radical because it is new. Our computers have forced us to begin dialogue and conscious decision making. However, the concept of a child's right to privacy lies well within the mandate of public libraries to provide free access to everyone of every age. Our policy is in keeping with this intent and brings expression to the position that children have a right to privacy no matter what they borrow.

It has been a year since we implemented our policy and procedures in the Contra Costa County Library System, and our staff has been surprised that the throngs of angry parents they had imagined have not materialized. A few people have been upset now and then, but most have accepted our policies, even though we have the full range of extreme liberal to fundamental conservative opinion in our county. When the privacy issue for children is mentioned to people, they either go away scratching their heads, or they seem amused and rather pleased.

Perhaps on some level, in our very computerized society, people are relieved to know that they can trust the library. The bottom line is that children need privacy as much as adults do. I am pleased that at the Contra Costa County Library we are keeping children's trust.

Read My Lips: Copyright

by Robin Pennock

There is a distinct paradox in media specialists' roles in schools across the United States, and it comes vividly into view when the subject is copyright. On the one hand, media specialists have become Teachers' Friends—sources of support, materials, camaraderie, and supplies. On the other hand, most media specialists are charged by their administrators with overseeing copyright compliance, scarcely a role designed to win popularity contests. To make the situation even worse, those very administrators who turn over the copyright hot potato to their media specialists are sometimes the worst offenders themselves.

Educators, normally so strident in their insistence on values ("Keep your eyes on your own paper"), sometimes do not equate violating copyright laws with illegality, cheating, and unethical behavior. Regrettably or not, it is most frequently the media specialists who are appointed to show them the error of their ways. As both a media specialist and as an elementary school principal, I have fought this battle. I offer some tips for enforcing the copyright laws and living to tell about it.

• **Clarify the administration's expectations early in the year**. If you are indeed to be the one to monitor copyright, find out how far the administration expects you to go in furthering the cause. A good solution is for media specialists to be responsible for posting all notifications and explaining to the staff the intent and virtue of the law, then leaving any outright confrontation to the administration.

• **Do a presentation early in the year explaining the copyright law and how it applies to your school's situation**. I think the three most abused areas of copyright compliance in a school are illegally copying literature to mass-produce "room sets;" illegally copying computer software to mass-produce computer sets; and illegally copying off the air. Be sure to include paraprofessionals in your presentation. Often we present this information to the teachers, but the paraprofessionals are the ones who actually do the duplicating.

• **Be prepared with an answer for the commonly advanced reasons for ignoring copyright**. There seems to be an underlying impression that the publishing corporations responsible for these materials make millions and millions of dollars each year, and copyright infringement is a sort of "Robin Hood" activity, robbing from the rich and giving to the poor schools. In reality, the people likely to be hurt are the author, the composer, and the creator. Second, some violators feel that running off those extra workbook sheets is such a small violation that it will not be caught. I tried to counter this at my school by asking if the teachers really knew all their students' family members and whether or not they were lawyers for large corporations. The final excuse centers on the paucity of resources of most publicly supported school systems. There is no easy, quick answer to this excuse, except to state that robbing banks is not more excusable if the robber is poor.

• **Use local examples, if available, of people who can be hurt by copyright violation**. Is there a teacher on the staff who has published an article or who hopes to see a children's book in print? Ask that person to give testimony to the importance of copyright in the protection of the integrity of the creative process.

• **Offer help in working out copyright problems**. Many corporations are willing to grant reproduction rights, particularly if you have been a steady consumer of their wares. It is not reasonable to purchase one workbook at each grade level, then expect anybody to grant permission for its duplication. However, off-air taping, the reproduction of only a part of a book, and the donation of musical scores have been granted in the past to those who have the foresight and courtesy to ask permission. Make yourself available to help in this process.

• **Let your administration know from the start what you will be telling staff about copyright**. If you encounter problems with your administration you will have to decide how to deal with the situation. The start would certainly be a heart-to-heart talk, followed by several articles you have found on copyright violators and the particularly nasty things that have happened to them. Beyond this, research your district's policy manual for copyright statements. Finally, many state departments of education have adopted stringent standards supporting copyright laws. All of these resources can be shown to your administration.

• **Do not be afraid to present the copyright issue as an ethical concern**. Just because children may "benefit" to the extent that they have a few more workbook pages to fill in does not excuse professionals who knowingly break the law.

• **Remember to explain the "fair" in the Fair Use doctrine**. Basically, such uses as excerpts for the purposes of literary criticism or comment, scholarship, and research are protected under the fair use clause. A basic of the doctrine, however, is the assumption of good faith; that is, that the user is not trying to circumvent copyright. Therefore, there are no hard and fast rules regarding fair use. The nature of the work, what parts and how much of the original is being copied, what effects the duplication will have on commercial rights—all of these factors have an impact on fair use.

Old habits are hard to break. Many schools have maintained a pattern over the years of copyright violations. As we become more technologically sophisticated, it becomes easier to violate the law. As professionals dedicated to nurturing creativity in our customer, however, we must make our stand for upholding copyright laws.

The Many Faces in Children's Books

by Ann Cameron, Keiko Narahashi, Mildred Pitts Walter, & David Wisniewski

Four creators contend with the biggest problems in providing books that reflect multicultural diversity: how and why they work at showing children the ways in which people are different—and the same.

"The Many Faces in Children's Books" was the title of a preconference at the 1991 annual conference of the American Library Association, sponsored by its division, the Association for Library Service to Children. The intent of the program was to celebrate the multicultural diversity to be found in contemporary children's literature.

Four authors and illustrators presented their views of what "cultural diversity" means and its importance to their books. *School Library Journal* excerpted the presentations (with the speakers' permission) in order to illuminate some of the issues and challenges arising from the new emphasis by educators to recognize and to appreciate the cultural heritage attached to the "many faces" of this country.

Ann Cameron

I grew up in a little town in northern Wisconsin. My parents owned what had been a 40-acre farm, and until I was six no other children lived nearby. When I was four, I used to go out to the road a little before sundown and sit on the sawhorse that supported the mailbox. Then I would count the cars as they went by. There were seldom more than three or four. When they had passed I would watch the sun, and wonder where it went, and what those places were like where it was still light. I wanted to follow the sun and see everything it saw, and I told myself I would, one day.

Now, most of the year I live in Guatemala. My next door neighbor is a Mayan Indian. His name is Rufino Juracan de Leon. Neither Rufino, nor his wife, nor his children, nor his children's children have ever been to school. Rufino can't read, but he is fluent in two languages, Spanish and Cachiquel. Cachiquel is one of 23 languages spoken in Guatemala, and I am trying to learn it. However, it's a formidable and very local language—its pronunciation changes when you travel more than three miles in any direction.

My neighbor Rufino's house is built against my west wall. I wake in the morning to music on his radio and the scraping sound of homemade ice cream being churned. Rufino's son-in-law, Abelino, makes ice cream every day and sells it from a cart on the street. Soon after I'm awake, Rufino leads his

four enormous cows out through the corridor that runs through the center of his house, and takes them to his fields to graze.

I could view Rufino as an ignorant, unlettered man. On the other hand, he could view me as a total incompetent. Despite 20 years in school, I'm not perfectly bilingual, as Rufino is. I don't know how to build a house, and he's built several. I don't know anything about farming, or just how and when to irrigate a field by hand, throwing precise sprays of water from a bowl. I don't get up at five in the morning to start the ground corn cooking, as his wife does, and I make a very tattered tortilla. I can't shell dried corn from the cob by twisting it in my hands the way his wife and daughters do. The one time I tried it, I wasn't strong enough to break off even a single kernel—a useless woman, in short.

It would seem that Rufino and I have almost nothing in common. One day, however, when we were talking, Rufino gave me his view of life. "We are all the same," he said. "We are all human beings. We are all equal, and we need to respect each other." Rufino and I have had very different lives, but when I try to sum up what I want to say in my children's stories, it turns out Rufino has said it.

But is there such a thing as simply "a human perspective"? In terms of books, can authors write authentically about people who are not like them? Can readers fairly judge books about people from cultures they don't know? Don't our backgrounds crucially affect, if not entirely distort, how we see things?

I just received a letter from a nine-year-old in Texas who described herself this way. "My name is Nicole Ferretti and my dad is a player for the Dallas Sidekicks. . . . I have two sisters, a mom, a stepmom, and a dad. My stepmom's name is Barbara, my mom's Gloucia, my small stepsister's Stephanie, and my bigger sister Ericka. We are Brazilians except my stepmom and my stepsister."

So who is Nicole? She is a Texan, she's an American, she's a Brazilian. It sounds like she might have had some Italians among her grandparents or great-grandparents. She herself is a one-person multiculture.

When in 1929, my mother, a Swedish-Norwegian Lutheran, eloped with my dad, a Scottish Catholic, and went home to Chippewa Falls, Wisconsin to meet his family, her mother-in-law wept. No one would speak to my Lutheran mother, except my dad's brother, who went up to her, gave her a kiss, and said, "Welcome to the family." Sixty years later, my family includes Dutch-American nieces, newborn Irish American-Mexican cousins, and a blonde step-granddaughter who is one-quarter Hawaiian and one-quarter Chinese. Every day she plays with little Saudi Arabians who, like her, are living in Virginia. One of my dearest friends was part African, part Spanish, and part Mayan Indian. He was also a Guatemalan, a U.S. citizen, and a New Yorker. What was he? American Indian? Black or white?

If you recall the 1990 U.S. Census, you'll remember being asked to fill in a question about your race—to say whether you are white, black, Asian, American Indian, or "other." It does not surprise me that in the census more than ten million people listed themselves as "other." In fact, "other" is the second fastest growing ethnic group in the United States. The census-takers also don't surprise me much. They consider that the people who said they are "other" made a mistake, and they are allocating the "others" to the four traditional categories.

To return to children's literature— What entitles any writer to draw the portrait of a culture or cultures? What qualified a reader to judge that portrait? For me, the answer in both cases is the same—knowledge, imagination, and sympathy. Our license to create and to judge is not a particular experience, a particular racial or national background. It is our humanness.

Our humanness tells us when a book is confronting us with stereotypes and noble abstractions. It tells us when a book is introducing us to real human beings, different from us, strange to us, but full of that aliveness that all people everywhere, good or bad, really have.

Among many Americans, old style racism and ethnocentricity is dead. But there are new misunderstandings about ethnicity and identity. Many of us assume that ethnicity is a simple thing. Many of us assume that it divides the world into airtight racial compartments. Some of us believe that only such compartments offer authentic windows on life, and our only license to comment on it.

I've heard of Chinese-American writers whose work was published when it dealt with Chinese-American themes but went unpublished when it dealt with American society at large. And I've heard of a black writer who wrote a teenage novel which her publisher rejected, saying, "Well, we might take it if you put more black characters in it."

Despite our multicultural society, we are still, in new ways, denying experience and pigeonholing people. We forget that identity is not a box we are stuck in; it is roots we grow from. We forget that identity is not only what we come from. It is what we reach toward.

Often we talk about whether child readers can identify with unfamiliar characters and places. We forget that all of us are born incomplete, desperate to become larger, to know a wider world. For each of us, all kinds of people for all kinds of places can contribute to our wholeness. In the end for each of us, what wholeness means will be an individual thing.

What is central to us, however, should include the recognition of shared humanity—the importance of being human. Being human includes competence and learning, friendship and loyalty, knowing what we stand for and what we stand against. Being human includes knowing what cruelty is—and being able to recognize it and oppose it even when we find it in ourselves. That is what our best children's books, multicultural or otherwise, teach.

My stories about Julian began because a South African friend named Julian told me stories about his childhood, beginning with a pudding that he and his little brother Huey ate when they weren't supposed to. I thought it was a universal story, something that might have happened to nearly every single child on the face of the earth.

Starting from that story I began to create my Julian as an Everychild—a child living in an unspecified anywhere, who has adventures within the reach of any child. My books describe daily life in Julian's family. His is an ordinary but special family—a family where adults listen to children and help them understand the world; a family where children and adults both learn to respect each other and themselves; a family where children and adults admit and overcome their fears.

Hidden fears come up a lot in stories about Julian because unadmitted fears are a problem for most children. The problem is made worse because children are generally unaware that adults have fears, too. So a child who reads the Julian books will learn that adults can get scared, just like them.

I put fear into my stories for other reasons, too. Up to a point it is fun and exciting. More seriously, unacknowledged fear, especially the fear that we or somebody else is "no good," is the most insidious source of disrespect for self and others. If we can relieve this fear in children, we can do a lot to eliminate racism.

All kinds of children like Julian's family. The response to the book that moved me most, though, was from a seventh-grade white girl in Texas. My books about Julian were her favorites. At the time I met her she had no home. She was living in a shelter for abused children. Why did she like the books so well? She was not black. She had not grown up in a home like Julian's. On the other hand, neither, had I.

Or, I should say, my home was only occasionally like Julian's. At other times, I didn't know what was going on or why my parents fought so bitterly, or when violence might erupt, or how not to hate myself for my powerlessness. In children's fiction I found families that made sense. I turned to books so that I could believe in the possibility of harmony and in my own power of understanding life. From books I read I created inside myself a model of what good human relationships are, of what a happy family might be.

The books had authority. I knew they could be relied on. The grownup society had printed them. They had put covers on them and everything. They had put them in the library, a building so big that even my parents in their fights could not have knocked it over. Books, and the steady, sturdy library that provided them, gave me faith that there was more to the world than what I saw at home, and that I could survive.

I look at the United States now and see tremendous multicultural richness—but also broken and struggling families to whom each day our government offers less help. I read about libraries in poor neighborhoods closing, other libraries reducing their hours.

In some damaged families, books about people who love each other may be a child's only lifeline to the future. I pray this lifeline will continue to reach our children. I earnestly hope my books may form a strand of it.—*Ann Cameron*

Keiko Narahashi

I have thought quite a lot about what difference, if any, my being Japanese made in my books. It wasn't obvious until I started thinking about what it is that motivates me when I am working on a children's picture book and how these motives are directly related to my having grown up Japanese in this country.

My family moved to America when I was six years old. Being the only Japanese child other than my brother in the entire state of North Carolina—or so it seemed at the time—I learned to be observant. I had to study the native customs so I could fit in.

Life was so different for me anyhow, having two eccentric people as parents, that being Japanese seemed to me to be just one more thing that set me apart. To other people, it was the defining factor. To them, the reason I had to go home immediately after school to practice the piano all afternoon was related to being Japanese, not having a television was due to our being Japanese, and even my ability to draw seemed to have something to do with my being Japanese.

I took this all pretty much for granted: at home we spoke Japanese and at school, I spoke English; at home we ate miso soup and seaweed, and at school I ate collard greens and grits. You could say that I was fairly well assimilated, at least on the surface.

In the sixth grade, I was bussed from an all-but-one white school (I was, of course, the "one") to an all black school. While this did broaden my circle of friends, I was still the only Japanese kid on the block. After an initial period of clinging to the known and familiar, I began to realize that I wasn't any more aligned with white children than with black children. I think that was the year that I began to see that I really *was* different, that my experience was unique, at least in Durham, North Carolina.

I found myself caught in a sort of limbo. I didn't think of myself as American, but neither did I think of myself as Japanese. I knew this because I couldn't bring myself to say "we" and "us," instead of "them" and "they," when talking about the Americans or the Japanese. It is a sign, I suppose, of how much of an outsider I really was that I felt that it would be presumptuous of me to say, "we, the Americans," or to speak of "*our* country." Yet when I heard the phrase, "Japanese-American," my reaction was to turn around to see who they were talking about.

I think that a major theme of growing up an outsider is that there are bits and pieces of you all over. Everyone knows a different part of you, but no one knows the whole story. This may be the general experience of growing up—I can only speak for myself. However, it was also a problem of racial identification. At home, my parents saw me as Japanese, while every day I was being "Americanized" in a way that they couldn't understand. Yet, when others did assume that I *was* Americanized, I resented it. I felt patronized.

Later, while at art school, I began to work these things out. There, I began to learn how truly Japanese I was and how indebted to Japanese art I am for the way I see things. Initially, I was reluctant to acknowledge this because I did not want to be pigeonholed by my race, especially in my drawing and painting. I felt with much pride that my art was to be a completely personal and unique vision. I remember one teacher complimenting me on some brushwork in a drawing by saying, "You're naturally good at it because you're Japanese." I was *so* deeply offended!

But sometime in my last year, it began to dawn on me that perhaps my being Japanese had something to do with why I had so much trouble with the Western ideas of art. It wasn't that I couldn't understand them, exactly. I just couldn't see their relevance to the kinds of pictures that *I* wanted to make. It was such a relief to discover that, after all, it might be cultural differences rather than ineptness, or a lack of understanding on my part. Finally, I began to accept these differences and to see my being Japanese as a source of pride.

Working on picture books has also been a series of discoveries. Recently, my first book, *I Have a Friend*, was published in Japan. The Japanese editor there told me that it reminded her of her own childhood and that the Japan of that time didn't exist anymore. She said that looking at the book brought up tremendously nostalgic feelings for her. It made me feel a bit like Rip Van Winkle. All this time, the Japan of my childhood had remained encapsulated in my mind whereas the real Japan had gone through so many changes. It was quite a shock.

Lately, I have become more and more interested in injecting bits and pieces of my own childhood feelings and experiences into books. I had always thought that these experiences were irrelevant to American audiences. It is only recently that I have felt that my background, my memories *are* legitimate to use, and that they could be appreciated by American children of all kinds. After all, you don't have to have grown up Japanese in North Carolina to know what alienation is.

When I am working on a book, I always have in the back of my mind the children who do not quite belong. It is my way of including them. Without inclusiveness, all the morality tales and uplifting messages are not going to sink in, they are not going to speak to these children. The interest in this country in different cultures and stories of these cultures is wonderful, though it may seem at times like the latest marketing trend. Not only does it open up other worlds for everyone, for those of us growing up outside of the American dream, it says to us, "Your experience counts, it is important too." And that is a good thing to hear when you're growing up.—*Keiko Narahashi*

Mildred Pitts Walter

As a writer creating within the black experience, I feel that I have a special opportunity during this phase of African-American history. At this time when we are clarifying our own identity, I face the exciting task of exploring, understanding, then recording our way of life as it has changed and developed through struggle.

It is exciting being a writer or author even though the root word of "author" is the word authority, a very heavy duty word. In West Africa, the counterpart of the writer is the griot. Many families whose members all live together in one compound have their own griot. The griot knows that family's history very well: its glories, its defeats, everything there is to know about all the members of that family. This historical knowledge becomes the stuff out of which the stories and legends are made. With this information the griot informs, entertains, and keeps alive the rituals, rites, and traditions that are sacred within that family. Therefore the griot is both revered and feared.

The writer is the image maker, and the successful one achieves the ability to stand outside herself, apart, while remaining an integral part of her people. The writer, as the griot, knows the history, the myths, rites, rituals, and traditions— the underlying fabric that makes a people unique and dynamic. She is the visionary, the one who knows where the people have come from, where they are at the moment, and where they can possibly go. She informs, entertains, and preserves the rites, rituals, and sacred traditions of her people.

As the griot, writers, too, are looked upon with awe. I think they have a sixth sense that helps them understand things and people better. I believe they are feared. Don't you think so, or is that just part of my African superstition? Seriously, writers are image makers. I believe the best images are made when the writer creates within the experiences of her people. Images will not ring true when created outside the experiences of the image maker. Those images will not invoke memory. Memory is necessary to examine first assumptions, or suppositions. Memory is also necessary for one to become thoughtful and to grow into awareness of self.

If there is any one theme that runs through my work it is the dynamics of choice, courage, and change—ingredients for the creation of thoughtfulness and self-awareness. The ability to accept a choice (whether it is a popular one or not) is measured in courage. The greater the courage to accept the choice, the greater the possibility for change. Action for change that affects the life of all living things positively will inevitably create thoughtfulness in the person. Thoughtfulness will assist in the creation of self-awareness.

I use the dynamics of choice, courage, and change in my books so that all readers can, through the experience of black characters become thoughtful; and so that African-American readers, through those experiences, can not only become thoughtful, but aware of themselves as well.

There is not a large body of children's literature that clarifies and crystallizes images of African-Americans in their everyday experiences. Therefore, I create images for all children within and outside of the black experience.

To African-American children I bring characters who in the home, in the street, and in the institutions, act and react the way they do. They see, and hear themselves, their relatives, and their friends, and can form opinions about who they really are. But more than that I try to remind them that they have a viable history. Knowing this they just might begin to ask serious questions, to explore and discover that they come from a long line of people whose lives did not begin with slavery in the western world. Slavery is only one event out of the many in their history. The shame of that event is not theirs, but belongs to those who enslaved them.

I hope other children who read my books will see that we are, as human beings, very much alike, but culturally different, and that to be different is all right. Difference is the spice that brings the taste of excitement to life. How dreary life would be if there was no color in our world; if everything were the same size and shape. Thank goodness we are not the same. We are equal, for equality does not mean sameness. Apples and oranges are different but equally fruit. I think of the children I write for I have hope that they will come away from books with renewed spirits. I hope they will learn that they are their brothers' and sisters' keepers and that the universe is their home. They are responsible to keep that home clean, healthy, safe and in good shape for their children and children's children.

Is it too much to hope that they will make wise choices and once they have chosen that they will have the courage to act to use their knowledge and technology to bring in a new millennium not rife with greed, bigotry, poverty, disease, and war? I think not. It is the writer who makes dreams and the dreamers who make those dreams come true.—*Mildred Pitts Walter*

David Wisniewski

When I was a circus clown, my partner and I came up with a new routine: the watch repair gag. He would proudly show his oversize watch to the audience, then discover to his horror that it didn't work. At that moment, I would set up my watch repair stand two feet away and proceed to happily bang the top of it with a huge rubber mallet.

He'd give me the watch to fix and, after a moment of professional appraisal "WHAM!" I'd give him back a big flat watch. "Hey!" he'd shout. "Look what you did to my watch! it won't even fit my hand!"

I'd compare the big flat watch with his hand. Then I put his hand on the watch repair stand and "WHAM!" gave him a big flat hand to match his watch.

We performed this gag for two years throughout the United States and it never failed to get a great reaction. Everybody laughed. Not just the Swiss; not just the employees of Timex. Everybody.

That was our job: to make *everybody* laugh. It never occurred to us to formulate a gag that would only appeal to a certain segment of the audience. A good thing, too, because I don't think the boss would have understood.

After the circus, I became a puppeteer; first with a parks department, then with my wife in our own company. We were based in Prince George's County, Maryland, a jurisdiction outside Washington D.C. noted for ethnic diversity and rough-and-tumble audiences. In the course of preparing shows, we pored over collections of myths and folklore. The tales we eventually chose included stories from the Middle East, Africa and the Orient, as well as a sprinkling of Kipling and less familiar efforts by Hans Christian Andersen and the Brothers Grimm. The productions based on these stories were all successful, even in the "tough" schools. (One principal dubbed us "the SWAT team of children's entertainment".)

Again, everybody was entertained. Everybody, because, again, that was our job. It never occurred to us to design a production for less than *all* the audience. To be sure, the production had an ethnic origin and carried the necessary cultural details of race, costume, music, and custom. But ethnicity was a detail, not an overriding concern, for this multihued audience. What mattered most was the resourceful hero, the spunky heroine, the hilarious trickster, the detailed cast of supporting characters, a plot with dash and originality—in short, a good story.

It still matters most, because the thrill and mystery and humor and wonder of a tale well told transcend the culture of its birth, the society of its listeners, and the origin of its teller.

I bring this perspective to the children's books that I write and illustrate. When asked what audience I envision for them, I would have to reply, "Everybody!" I'm used to working for the whole audience.

The first step in this process is to decide upon a worthwhile idea to communicate; a widely held, if not universal, point of view that can infuse a story with a moral or spiritual center. Then the search begins for the people, place, and period that will naturally support the idea. After thoroughly researching the culture, a story is written, one that has (I hope) absorbed the character of a people and its beliefs into its very structure.

In *The Warrior and the Wise Man* the twin sons of the emperor must gather the five magical elements that the world is made of in order to determine who will rule next. The warrior brother uses blind force to wrest each element from its guardian demon; his wise brother uses reason and patience. In examining the inferiority of brute strength against the superiority of rational thought, what better setting is there than ancient Japan, where the fierce samurai and the serene Buddhist monk existed side by side.

In *Elfwyn's Saga*, a blind child overcomes and destroys the mesmerizing crystal that has captivated her people with its impossible visions of wealth and beauty, leading them to abandon the everyday duties and responsibilities upon which their existence depends. How can you accomplish anything of importance, this story asks, if you spend all your time with the enjoyably trivial? The danger of distraction had to have dire and immediate consequences, hence its placement in the harsh Viking settlements of tenth century Iceland.

In the new *Rain Player*, a young boy insists on determining his own fate rather than relying on the predictions of his rulers. Because he acts on his own ideas rather than passively accepting the thought of the majority, he wins an almost impossible match against the rain god, ending a drought that would have destroyed his people. Few civilizations were as fate-oriented as the ancient Mayan, and this story of being a first-rate thinker (rather than a second-rate accepter of thought) found a comfortable home there.

Why new stories to carry these ideas?—because authentic folktales don't usually possess the structure to accommodate them, and to adapt one to the other would do service to neither. Also, many genuine folktales take little notice of the details of their own culture. The culture was, after all, a daily occurrence. The most fascinating facts of community, religion, behavior, and locale were often taken for granted and not necessarily woven into the fabric of a story. Without the surrounding richness of its society, an authentic folktale is sometimes like a fine jewel without a setting. Creating an original story allows me to make societal detail an intrinsic part of it, both visually and verbally.

I considered the cultural aspect of these stories as very important but secondary to the universality of their underlying messages. At the most, I thought that the cultural content might lead a reader to the nonfiction side of the library, to find out more about samurai swords, Viking ships, Mayan temples, and the splendid peoples who produced them.

This was brought home to me very clearly during a booktalk for an inner city reading group in Baltimore. I was asked where I got my ideas from. And I replied, aside from wanting to communicate a deeply held conviction, that sometimes a single compelling fact would set my mind rolling in the direction of a story.

"Did you know," I asked, "that Mongol warriors cut deep scars in their cheeks to stop their beards from growing and to make themselves look more hideous?"

"Eeeeeoooo . . ." they said.

"Did you know," I continued, "that, in certain parts of Tibet, sticking your tongue out is the polite way of saying 'hello'?"

"Eeeeeoooo . . . " they said.

"And do you know what the major import of the African city of Timbuktoo was?"

"Gold?" they asked. "Silk? Spices?"

"No," I replied. "Books! One of the great universities of Africa was there, so the merchants imported more books than anything else." At this, the audience burst into a round of spontaneous applause, not for anything that I said or did, but the reality of this simple historical fact. When the books of Timbuktoo, which have long since crumbled to dust, get this type of reaction, you know that a deep hunger exists within children. How can such yearning for validation and self-worth be fulfilled? Certainly here is something that we, as authors and illustrators and publishers and librarians, can supply: moments of possibility so luminous that they change lives.

Sociologists recognize five major institutions in organized social life: the family, the economy, education, law and government, and religion and morality. If one of these institutions goes through change, it is the generally accepted theory that the others modify themselves to adjust for that change. But if all these systems undergo rapid, fundamental change at the same time (which our cultural organizations have been doing for the last 30 years), then society itself becomes unstable.

The audience we serve—the *whole* audience we serve— is probably the most susceptible to that instability. But this is where multicultural books can be of most value; by acquainting individual minds with the transcendent truths proven by the past, by fostering respect for the tribes and nations and races that lived them, and by discovering a common humanity, in a moment of luminous possibility, within the pages of a book.—*David Wisniewski*

Put It In Writing

by Dianne McAfee Hopkins

A national intellectual freedom study was conducted by questionnaire in Spring 1990, focused on public secondary schools and challenges to library media center (LMC) materials as reported by the school's library media specialist.[1] The study looked specifically at the factors that mattered in whether the outcome to challenged LMC material was retention, restriction, or removal.[2] (See box, p. 434 for methodology used in the survey).

Six Outcome Factors

Overall, there were six general factors which were found to influence the outcome of challenges to LMC materials:

- the existence of a school board-approved district materials selection policy and the degree to which it was used when LMC materials were challenged;
- the school environment, including the influence and power of the school principal and the support of classroom teachers;
- the community environment, through support received outside the school district in which a challenge occurred;
- the initiator of the challenge;
- selected characteristics of the library media specialist including gross degrees of dogmatism and internal/external locus of control;
- complaint background, including whether there was active support for retention or removal of materials, and whether the challenge was oral or written.

Oral vs. Written Challenges

The great majority of reported challenges were oral. One finding particularly stood out: oral challenges fared differently from written challenges. Oral challenges were more likely to result in removal than written challenges, while written challenges were more likely to result in retention than oral challenges (Table 2). This articles focuses on the differences between oral and written challenges as revealed in the national intellectual freedom study, and as reported by the library media specialists who experience the challenges.

Differences in oral and written challenges were found for aspects of each of the six general factors known to relate to challenge outcomes. The discussion that follows reflects statistical test examinations. Statistical analyses included chi square analyses (used to determine if the proportions between rows or columns of tables are statistically significant or due purely to chance) or analyses of variance (used to test the statistical significance of the response level), as appropriate. Where findings indicate differences in form of complaint, they represent statistical significance at the $p<.05$ level (This means there is a five percent probability that the researcher will reject a hypothesis that is actually true). I offer here a discussion of the findings at U.S. secondary level library media centers with challenges, and some recommendations.

The term "oral complaint" refers to challenges submitted verbally only, while the term "written complaint" includes challenges submitted only in writing as well as challenges initially submitted verbally and later submitted in writing.

What Was Found

Characteristics of the Library Media Specialists: Female respondents were more likely to report that challenges were oral, with 74.2 percent reporting challenges to be oral, compared to 62.6 percent of male respondents (Table 3).

Materials Selection Policy Use: The literature of the profession is replete with recommendations noting the importance of a school board-approved written materials selection policy. Library media specialists are also urged in the literature to see that the policy is followed during a challenge. The national study found the use of the policy to make a difference in overall retention of challenged LMC materials. Closer examination of the data found that there was more use of the policy when challenges were written. In fact, when challenges were written, the policy was reported to be used in full almost half the time. In oral complaints, almost half the time, the policy was reported as not being used at all (Table 4).

School Environment: Internal support received within the school or district was found to relate to the overall retention of challenged LMC materials. When examined more closely, it was found that the support of the principal as well as teachers for retention was higher for challenges that were written than for those that were oral only. For support of the principal, on a scale of 1-6, with 6 indicating the highest level of support which was "partnership role," 58.4 percent of those with oral challenges selected a 5 or 6 compared to 72.5 percent of those with written challenges (Table 5). Similarly, for teachers, 73.3 percent of those with oral challenges selected a scale of 5-6 compared to 91.8 percent of those with written challenges.

Table 1
Results of LMC Material Challenges

Outcome	Frequency
Retained	317 (44.2%)
Restricted	131 (18.2%)
Removed	158 (22%)
Other	112 15.6%
Total	718 100%

Assistance sought within the school or district by the library media specialist also varied according to whether complaints were written or oral. When challenges were written, library media specialists were more likely to seek support. On a scale of 1-6, with 6 indicating much assistance sought, 13 percent of those with oral challenges selected 5 or 6, compared to 45 percent of those with written challenges (Table 6).

Assistance received during the challenge process differed according to the form of complaint. Those with written complaints were more likely to receive assistance from others inside the district than those with oral complaints. Library media specialists with oral complaints received some type of assistance 62 percent of the time, compared to those with written complaints, who reported receiving some type of assistance 87.4 percent of the time. There was more assistance provided for written complaints by all others named in the questionnaire, including other library media specialists in the district, district library media coordinator, principal, local teachers organization, and others. Thus, whether the challenge was oral or written made a difference in the support that was received within a school or district.

Community Environment: Support received from the community was found to be an overall factor in the retention of challenged library media materials. While most respondents generally indicated that they did not seek assistance outside the district regardless of whether the challenge was oral or written, differences could be seen here, as well. Of those with oral challenges. 93.2 percent reported seeking no assistance outside the district compared to 75.7 percent of those with written challenges. Library media specialists who indicated they sought a great deal of assistance from outside the district were limited. On a scale of 1-6, where 6 indicated much assistance sought, 2.2 percent of those with oral challenges selected scales of either 5 or 6, compared to 10.4 percent of those with written challenges (Table 7). Thus, while most respondents clearly did not seek assistance outside the district when material was challenged, those with written challenges were more likely to do so than those with oral challenges.

Library media specialists with written complaints were more likely to receive assistance outside the district than those with oral complaints. Overall, written complaints received some form of outside assistance 30.3 percent of the time, compared to oral complaints, which received some outside assistance 12.1 percent of the time. There was more assistance provided for written complaints from library media specialists outside the district, local public library and/or public library system staff, state professional library or media associations, as well as state Departments of Public Instruction/Education. No differences in support by form of complaint were found for state teachers' organizations or national organizations. Thus, whether the challenge was oral or written related to differences in support received from persons or groups outside the district.

Whether the challenge was oral or written was looked at in terms of local media awareness of the challenge. In the overall study, it was found that few outside the school or district were aware that a challenge to LMC materials had occurred. The majority of respondents indicated that local media were not aware of the challenge regardless of whether the media were newspapers, radio, or television. However, the local media were more likely to be aware of a challenge if the challenge had been submitted in writing. Those with oral challenges indicated there was no knowledge of the complaint from local media 97.8 percent of the time compared to 85.4 percent of those with written challenges. Those with oral challenges indicated there was extensive knowledge 1.4 percent of the time, compared to 6.3 percent of those with written challenges.

Initiator: In overall findings, the person who initiated the challenge made a difference in the outcome of challenges. Principals and teachers were more likely to have their challenges result in removal than parents, whose challenges were more likely to result in retention. An examination of the initiator of the challenge and form of complaint also showed differences between oral and written complaints. Challenges initiated by district administrators, the principal, or teacher(s) were more likely to be oral challenges when compared to parents or conservative groups that challenged materials.

For example, 80 percent of challenges from district administrators were oral, 93.6 percent of challenges from principals were oral, and 88.7 percent of challenges from teachers were oral. This compares to 67 percent of challenges from

Table 2
Form of Complaint and Outcome

Complaint	Retain	Restrict	Remove	Total
Oral	212 49.1%	95 22%	125 28.9%	432 100%
Written	103 60.9%	35 20.7%	31 18.3%	169 99.9%
Total	315 52.4%	130 21.6%	156 26.0%	601 100%

$X\!\!\OE\,(2, N = 601) = 8.60967$, P<.05

Table 3
Gender and Form of Complaint

Gender	Oral	Written	Total
Female	465	162	627
	74.2%	25.8%	100%
Male	57	34	91
	62.6%	37.4%	100%
Total	522	196	718
	72.7%	27.3%	100%

XŒ (1,N = 718) = 5.31879, P<.05

parents and 47.1 percent of challenges from conservative groups reported as oral (Table 8).

Complaint Background: In the overall study, it was found that where there was active support for retention, there was a greater likelihood that challenged LMC material would be retained. Similarly, where there was active support for removal, the material was more likely to be removed. Form of complaint was also examined in terms of whether there was active support for retention and removal. Written challenges were more likely to generate active support for retention than oral challenges. Of those with written challenges 20.5 percent indicated there was no support for retention, compared to 43.6 percent of those with oral challenges. Similarly, 37.8 percent of those with written challenges indicated a high level of support for retention, compared to 10.6 percent of those with oral challenges (Table 9).

Other Categories: The form of complaint was not statistically significant for other categories including school or district enrollment sizes, number of library media specialists, level of school, i.e., middle, junior, senior high school, or active support for removal. Statistical significance was also not

found for education level, age, or racial background of the library media specialist.

Results

The form of complaint was found to make a significant difference in many aspects of the challenge process for secondary school level LMC challenges. Oral and written challenges differed in some important ways in terms of the materials selection policy, school environment, community environment, challenge initiator, and characteristics of the library media specialist. The study found that most challenges to LMC materials at the secondary level were made orally and that oral challenges were more likely to result in removal than written challenges. The study found that women were more likely to receive oral challenges than men. It found that challenges from district administrators, principals, and teachers were more likely to be made orally, and that these internal challenges were more likely to result in removal. Yet, materials selection policies were more likely to be used when challenges were written. In addition, support for the retention of challenged materials from persons/organizations within or outside the district was greater for written challenges. In fact, library media specialists were more likely tó seek support when challenges were written. While there was little likelihood that local media would learn of any LMC challenges, challenges had a great chance of being known, when they were written.

Implications

What does all this mean?

- It means that due process is more likely for challenges that are submitted in writing, and that the result of due

Table 4
Policy Use and Form of Complaint

Scale	Oral	Written	Total
1	212	25	237
not used at all	45.2%	14%	36.6%
2	56	16	72
	11.9%	9%	11.1%
3	46	16	62
	9.8%	9%	9.6%
4	31	14	45
	6.6%	7.9%	7.0%
5	44	22	66
	9.4%	12.4%	10.2%
6	80	85	165
used fully	17.1%	47.8%	25.5%
Total	469	178	647
	100%	100.1%	100%

XŒ (1,N = 718) = 5.31879, P<.05

Table 5
Principal Support and Form of Complaint

Scale	Oral	Written	Total
1	68	11	79
not supportive	14.8%	5.9%	12.2%
2	30	9	39
	6.5%	4.8%	6.1%
3	46	14	60
	10%	7.5%	9.3%
4	47	17	64
	10.2%	9.1%	9.9%
5	66	33	99
	14.4%	17.7%	15.4%
6	202	102	304
partnership role	44%	54.8%	47.1%
Total	459	186	645
	99.9%	99.8%	100%

Analysis of variance:
F(13.9365, df = 1,643) = P<.05

Table 6
Assistance Sought within the School or District and Form of Complaint

Scale	Oral	Written	Total
1	296	47	343
no assistance sought	57.9%	25.1%	49.1%
2	44	19	63
	8.6%	10.2%	9.0%
3	50	12	62
	9.8%	6.4%	8.9%
4	55	25	80
	10.8%	13.4%	11.5%
5	33	33	66
	6.5%	17.7%	9.5%
6	33	51	84
much assistance sought	6.5%	27.3%	12.0%
Total	511	187	698
	100.1%	100.1%	100%

Analysis of variance:
$F(103.8636, df = 1,696) = P<.05$

process is more likely to be retention of LMC materials on open shelves.

- The study raises questions about internal challenges to LMC materials made by district administrators, principals, and teachers. Are materials selection policies intended to exclude school administrators or faculty, or is there the expectation that a challenge is only "serious" enough to be placed in writing if someone outside the school community initiates a challenge?
- Does pressure come to bear more heavily on the library media specialist when the challenge is internal? What can the library media specialist learn from these findings?

Recommendations

Based on the results of my study, I made the following recommendations:

(1) Examine your district's materials selection policy carefully. Is the wording inclusive enough to show that challenges initiated by administrators, teachers, and other school personnel are to be included in reconsideration steps outlined in the policy? If not, contact your state library or media association and/or LMC consultants at the Department of Public Instruction/Education. Seek a critique of the current policy as well as sample policies to review.

(2) Assure, possibly through in-service opportunities, that principals and teachers are aware that the policy is intended for all who challenge the appropriateness of LMC materials.

(3) Take every challenge to LMC materials, whether oral or written, seriously.

(4) Follow the reconsideration section of the policy fully. After initial discussion with the complainant, if concern still exists, have the complaint submitted in writing.

(5) Seek support when an oral or written challenge occurs. Have a clear understanding of the type of support that may be available. Be certain to communicate your expectations. For example, if you wish the discussion to be confidential, say so.

(6) Remember, communication at all levels is necessary to assure that challenges are handled in an effective, objective manner.

(7) Recognize that as a library media specialist, you can be the key person in shaping the outcome of challenges to library media center materials.

References

1. The primary funding for this study was provided by the U.S. Department of Education, Office of Educational Research and Improvement, Library Programs. Additional support was provided by Encyclopedia Britannica, Inc., The Institute on Race and Ethnicity, University of Wisconsin System, and the Graduate School, University of Wisconsin, Madison. The research consultant for the study was Douglas L. Zweizig, Professor, School of Library and Information Studies, University of Wisconsin-Madison.

   A paper based on this study received the 1992 Association for Library and Information Science Education (ALISE) Research Paper Award.
2. The study is reported in articles by the author in several library and information science journals, including: "Challenge to Materials in Secondary School Library Media Centers: Results of a National Study." *Journal of Youth Services in Libraries* 4 (Winter 1991); 131-40.
"A Conceptual Model of Factors Influencing the Outcome of Challenges to Library Materials in Secondary School Settings." *The Library Quarterly* 63 (January 1993).

Table 7
Outside Assistance Sought and Form of Complaint

Scale	Oral	Written	Total
1	481	146	627
no assistance sought	93.2%	75.7%	88.4%
2	13	7	20
	2.5%	3.6%	2.8%
3	1	5	6
	.2%	2.6%	.8%
4	10	15	25
	1.9%	7.8%	3.5%
5	6	12	18
	1.2%	6.2%	2.5%
6	5	8	13
much assistance sought	1%	4.2%	1.8%
Total	516	193	709
	100%	101.1%	99.8%

Analysis of variance:
$F(45.9880, df = 1,707) = P<.05$

Table 8			
Initiator and Form of Complaint			
Initiator	Oral	Written	Total
School Board Member	5 62.5%	3 37.5%	8 100%
Liberal Group	1 100%	0 0%	1 100%
District Administrators	12 80%	3 20%	15 100%
Principal	44 93.6%	3 6.4%	47 100%
Teacher(s)	86 88.7%	11 11.3%	97 100%
Parent(s)	308 67%	152 33%	460 100%
Conservative Group	8 47.1%	9 52.9%	17 100%
Other	59 79.7%	15 20.3%	74 100%
Total	523 72.7%	196 27.3%	719 100%

XŒ (7,N = 719) = 39.16232, P<.05

"Perspectives of Secondary Level Library Media Specialists About Material Challenges." *School Library Media Quarterly* 21 (Fall 1992), p. 15-23.

Individual copies of the full U.S. Department of Education report, which includes the questionnaire, are available for $20 from School of Library and Information Studies, University of Wisconsin-Madison, Helen C. White Hall, 600 N. Park St., Madison, WI 53706; Title: "Factors Influencing Materials in Secondary School Libraries: Report of a National Study." Also available in ERIC ED 338266.

Table 9			
Active Support for Retention and Form of Complaint			
Scale	Oral	Written	Total
1 no support	129 43.6%	32 20.5%	161 35.6%
2	23 7.8%	6 3.9%	29 6.4%
3	20 6.8%	22 14.1%	42 9.3%
4	29 9.8%	10 6.4%	39 8.6%
5	34 11.5%	27 17.3%	61 13.5%
6 high level of support	61 20.6%	69 37.8%	120 26.5%
Total	296 100.1%	156 100%	452 99.9%

Analysis of variance:
$F(30.0659, df = 1,450) = P<.05$

Survey Methodology

A proportionate, stratified sample of 6,557 schools in grades seven or higher from each state in the United States was sent an initial questionnaire about whether challenges to LMC materials had occurred. The resulting response rate was 72 percent, with 4,736 returning the completed questionnaire. Of these, 4,625 answered a question about LMC material complaints. It was found that 35.9 percent or 1,661 library media specialists reported that one or more challenges to library media center materials occurred during the school years 1986-87, 1987-88, or 1988-89. No challenges during the three year period were reported by 64.1 percent or 2,964 of the respondents. Thus, about one secondary school library media specialist out of three reported experiencing one or more challenges to LMC materials within the three year period studied.

To answer the more complex question of the factors that made a difference in whether challenges resulted in materials' retention, restriction, or removal, those library media specialists reporting challenges received a more detailed questionnaire that sought information about the most recent challenge that had been resolved between September 1987 and Spring 1990. Of the 1,171 or 70 percent who responded, 739 reported challenges and of this group, 606 indicated that challenges to material resulted in retention, restriction, or removal. Results are listed in Table 1. When only the outcomes—retained, restricted, or removed—were examined, 52.2 percent of materials were retained, 21.6 percent of materials were restricted, and 26.1 percent were removed.

Whole Language
A Movement Out of Sync

by Lou Willett Stanek

Remember the little girl who had a little curl right in the middle of her forehead? "When she was good, she was very, very good; but when she was bad, she was horrid." While interviewing teachers and librarians for a book on whole language, those familiar lines often played in my head.

In some schools, dream teams exist where everyone from the administration down through the ranks believes in the philosophy of whole language and understands the practices and the shifting of staff roles it requires. Curriculum planning is a joint effort between teachers and librarians, a reasonable time schedule is worked out, and everyone knows what will be expected of him or her—including who will order the books for what grades. Teachers and librarians present a united front and articulate their goals to parents, encouraging them to become involved in the project. In the best of all possible situations, the public librarian completes the loop.

Unfortunately, this is not the case everywhere. There are schools where bureaucrats mandate the whole language approach without supporting the staff or providing the funds needed for in-service training or books. Worse still are schools where *attitude* problems prevail—where some professionals think their colleagues' knowledge and contributions diminish their own.

These are just the kind of "sticky wickets" that are keeping many whole language programs from achieving their important goals. Of course, the players in these conflicts are not deliberately trying to undermine the cause; they are simply responding to a number of negative factors that make the going difficult for everyone involved.

Teacher Training

On too many college campuses, there is one children's literature class dubbed "Kiddie Lit," and the person who teaches it gets less respect than Dan Quayle at a spelling bee. Even where adequate courses are offered, meeting requirements for certification often leaves education students few, if any, electives. The need to complete a battery of required courses, coupled with the desire to be knowledgeable about children's literature, leaves these student teachers caught in a beastly Catch-22. With tuition costs soaring and trainees already facing whopping student loans, asking them to remain in school for another semester is not a fair option.

Teachers with one children's literature course on their transcripts—if they were lucky—come into a school system where they are told they will teach thematically, across the disciplines, from a literature-based curriculum. Already intimidated by an inadequate background in books and research resources, the teacher dashes to the library for help.

"I'm going to teach a unit on farms . . . "

"Of course you know *Time to Go* and *Once Upon Mac-Donald's Farm*?" the librarian says, growing in the teacher's mind until the librarian appears to look down his or her nose while picking beans off Jack's stalk.

"Uh . . . no . . . "

The teacher thinks the librarian is haughty. The librarian's suspicion that teachers don't read is confirmed. Righteous indignation rules the day.

"Teachers and librarians have to hold the premise above the pettiness," says Bernice Cullinan, author of *Literature and the Child* (HBJ). "When a librarian gets on her high horse and a teacher has to reveal her ignorance, the scene is set for conflict."

Overteaching a Good Book

Some people may have found the scenario that Grace Ruth presented in a recent preconference sponsored by the Association for Library Service to Children to be a bit farfetched. Ruth, director of youth services at San Francisco Public Library, asked librarians how they would handle a request from a teacher who wanted 30 copies of *Charlotte's Web* (Harper & Row), not just for a unit on spiders, but also to cover spelling, grammar, and friendship. Many librarians, on the other hand, probably think Ruth has been eavesdropping at their schools.

Hearing how much was being piled on books like her *Tuck Everlasting* (Farrar), Natalie Babbitt warned that a good story can collapse if it's made to bear too much weight. Babbitt feels that, under the pretext of "a new approach," stories are being used in the same dry, boring way in which workbooks were used before being relegated to the curriculum cemetery.

When literature is being twisted every which way to make a point, this is not the best use of a good book. On the other hand, when authors and librarians talk about simply letting children enjoy a good story, I doubt that this is precisely what they mean. There has to be a happy medium.

In *Aspects of a Novel* (HBJ), E.M. Forster said that "the king died and then the queen died" is a story—a narrative of events arranged in their time sequence. "The king died and then the queen died of a broken heart" is a *plot*. In a story we say, "And then what happened?" In a plot, we ask "*Why* did that happen, and *what does it mean?*"

In good whole language classrooms, teachers' goals are to lead children to another intellectual level, armed with the tools not only to ask why Winnie chose to help the Tucks, but also *how* the author created the suspense. How did she persuade readers to be on Winnie's and the Tucks' side without telling them how to think?

Most important, the students in these classrooms are able to nip back to their own experiences, remembering when they were faced with a decision and either choice meant they would lose something. These children are being encouraged to think like writers, which not only helps to build their self-esteem and increases their appreciation for literature, but alleviates some of the awe and fear they might have about writing stories themselves.

When children understand that a character in a book has to have a motivation, just as they do when they make their own decisions, does this mean they all will be able to write great books? Probably not. But at the every least, they will learn to read like insiders, gain some self-perception, and not be afraid of a blank piece of paper and a pencil.

Curriculum Planning

After a rousing curriculum planning session where the second grade teachers have come up with an exciting cross-disciplinary idea based on the environment, three of them descend upon the librarian, who has spent the day preparing a second-grade booktalk on Jon Scieszka's *Knights of the Kitchen Table* (Viking), putting up a display, and hosting a storytelling session on time travel.

"If you had just told me you were doing the environment, I could have . . . "

"Well, you might have let us know Scieszka had a new book . . . "

After working hard all day, the teachers and the librarian leave school thinking, "What's the use?"

Sara Miller, director of library services at Rye (NY) Country Day School, understands both the librarian's and the teacher's point of view. Miller, who also has a master's degree in education, says, "It takes two to do the whole language waltz. When the librarian is not on the curriculum planning committee and does not centralize the book orders, children are sometimes asked to read the same story over and over in different grades."

No child deserves to grow up not having had the chance to read *Alice in Wonderland* (Putnam), *Bridge to Terabithia* (Crowell), or *Sarah, Plain and Tall* (Harper & Row)—but as a class project, once is enough. It is a waste of limited resources when the fourth grade teacher orders 30 copies of the same book the fifth grade teacher has in her classroom library, but it happens.

Sins of the Publishers

Still another threat to high-quality whole language instruction is that some (not all, but some) rapacious publishers' marketing departments prey on teachers' weaknesses. They stick whole language labels on clunkers, offer silly or expensive aids, and, deplorably, sell simplistic guides that distort whole language principles and practices.

There are even reports of some teachers who use the guides but have not read the stories. If this indeed happens, these teachers must be the ones who got through college with Cliff's Notes. Back then, of course, they were only cheating themselves—now the crime is greater. Guides are supposed to be supplements, not substitutes. Having recently designed whole language guides for the books of authors like Patricia MacLachlan, Norma Mazer, Bruce Brooks, and M.E. Kerr, I always hope the children and teachers enjoy digging deeper into these writers' stories as much as I do.

What Is Being Done?

Criticizing is easier than creating, recognizing problems is a snap compared to solving them. Perhaps the best testimony to the whole language movement is in the effort the believers are expending to meet the challenges, resolve the conflicts, and save the day.

Take the Teachers as Readers Book Groups sponsored by the Association of American Publishers in conjunction with the International Reading Association. School districts can apply for grants ($500-700, with an additional $100 for groups where a superintendent, school board member, or community member is a participant) to buy multiple copies of children's books. Teachers meet regularly to discuss the books, reviews, and professional literature. The books are then donated to schools. As their students do, participants learn more about the authors and keep response logs or journals. They become better whole language teachers for the experience.

The whole language approach depends upon secure, flexible people with generous natures who realize that giving and changing takes nothing away from who you are or were. In my research, corroborated by other studies such as Linda Leonard Lamme and Linda Ledbetter's survey of Florida schools and Cullinan's national review of reading initiative (see references), I found programs that were "very, very good."

Teacher and librarian teams begin by brainstorming courses of study together. Knowing what is coming, the librarian can then prepare author files and collect cross-disciplinary materials and supplementary community and media resources. Occasionally the librarians and teachers switch roles. Librarians teach, offering in-service sessions to update teachers on new books and to teach storytelling techniques. They also give booktalks in the classroom. So do public librarians, who also either sit in on curriculum planning meetings or are given copies of the plan in order to anticipate requests.

The Future

Any school or public librarian who still resists whole language should be warned: this phenomenon is not going away.

Those who don't join the force soon may be left totally unprepared for the demand that is sure to come.

The guideline in *Information Power* calling for "service at the point of need" must be taken just as seriously as a doctor's hippocratic oath. It is both the librarian's and the teacher's task to resolve whatever conflicts and problems are hampering their whole language efforts in order to meet this need—because when whole language works, it works wonders.

References

Babbitt, Natalie. "Protecting Children's Literature." *The Horn Book Magazine*, November/December 1990.

Carroll, Lewis. *Alice in Wonderland*. Putnam; ISBN 0-448-18983-6, $10.95

Cullinan, Bernice. "Latching on to Literature: Reading Initiatives Take Hold." *School Library Journal*, April 1989.

———. *Literature and the Child*, 2nd ed. HBJ, 1989; ISBN 0-15-551112-2, $2.50.

Fiday, Beverly and David. *Time to Go*. 1990. HBJ; ISBN 0-15-200608-7, $14.95.

Gammell, Stephen. *Once Upon MacDonald's Farm*. 1990. Macmillan; ISBN 0-689-71379-7, $3.95.

Information Power: Guidelines for School Library Media Programs. American Library Association, 1988; ISBN 0-8389-3352-1, $15.00.

Lamme, Linda Leonard, and Ledbetter, Linda. "Libraries: The Heart of Whole Language." *Language Arts*, Vol. 67, no. 7 (November 1990).

MacLachlan, Patricia. *Sarah, Plain and Tall*. Harper & Row, 1986; ISBN 0-06-024102-0, $10.89.

Patterson, Katherine. *Bridge to Terabithia*. Crowell, 1972; ISBN 0-690-01359-0, $13.95

Scieszka, Jon. *Knights of the Kitchen Table*. Viking, 1991; ISBN 0-670-83622-2, $10.95.

White, E.B. *Charlotte's Web*. Harper & Row, 1974; ISBN 0-06-440055-7, $3.50.

Presumed Influence

by Carolyn Caywood

Several weeks ago I attended a Bill of Rights symposium at the College of William and Mary. One of the panelists, a law professor, expressed his belief that there is a causal relationship between the "free speech" in songs like Ice-T's "Cop Killer" and youth violence, even though there is little solid evidence to support such a relationship in court. The professor is not alone among his legal colleagues in having this opinion.

According to an October 1991 article in *Crime and Delinquency*, "The Presumption of Influence: Recent Responses to Popular Music Subcultures" by Jill Leslie Rosenbaum and Lorraine Prinsky, minors on probation in California are sometimes required to comply with a list of "Rules to De-punk or De-metal." These rules regulate both teens' appearance and their contact with music that the courts fear could inspire antisocial behavior.

The same article describes an experiment in which a researcher, posing as a concerned father, called numerous facilities with treatment programs for adolescents. The "father" described a hypothetical teen who had no symptoms of mental illness, drug abuse, criminal behavior, or even bad grades, but who dressed like a punk, kept his room a mess, and listened to heavy metal music. Personnel at 83 percent of the facilities said the teen required hospitalization.

Clearly, parental advisory stickers are merely the most common expression of a widespread belief that certain kinds of music can turn an otherwise normal teen into a criminal or psychopath. The belief that music can have a subversive influence is nothing new. Examples span American history, from laws forbidding slaves to play drums to the uproar over Elvis Presley's black-influenced sounds (and gyrating hips) just a few decades ago. Television has intensified this belief, first by adding dress and behavior to the list of things that fuel parents' worries, then by creating fantasy visions to accompany the music. At the same time, the idea of brainwashing has entered pop psychology to bolster the supposition that, while the older generation's favorite music did no harm, what teens enjoy now is dangerous.

For both oppressed minorities and for each generation's young people, music helps to create a cultural identity. The frustrations of having less than equal rights are echoed in their music. It is not surprising that the music of minority cultures usually enters the mainstream by way of teens.

Part of this controversial music's appeal for adolescents seems to be that it is disturbing to parents, thereby proclaiming teens' separateness. Also, the tensions involved in learning new social skills based on sexual attraction are both masked and intensified by music. The perennial need for teens to search for identity as they take on new social roles guarantees that music will always be the focus of generational conflict.

Even though, as Rosenbaum and Prinsky state, "there is no research demonstrating a connection between punk and heavy metal music and delinquency," the controversy over this music is being acted out aggressively. Those who see record labeling as an invasion of their rights are told it is just consumer information. Syndicated columnist Mike Royko recently compared it to labeling Twinkies. He apparently saw no difference between a list of ingredients and a judgment on those ingredients. Parental advisory labels imply that there must be something dangerous in the contents. Some stores refuse to carry labeled recordings, limiting everyone's access.

Those who bravely defend print against censorship may feel on shaky ground when it comes to recordings. After all, it is only audiovisual materials that our society has felt the need to label. Sound and images are believed to have more power than mere words. It seems odd, then, that the frequency with which certain words are used is one of the justifications for labeling. In any case, the underlying presumption is that the teenage listener or viewer cannot think critically about the messages expressed in music and will be hypnotized by them. If people who will have adult responsibilities in just a few years are this vulnerable, we have a much bigger problem than music.

Librarians need to be aware of the fears many parents have about teens and their music. If we try to avoid them by avoiding the music, we will be telling teens that we are just another institution that doesn't trust them. Thoughtful selection policies provide for both music that is part of the collective teen identity and music that can foster the development of individual tastes.

Discussion of the library's music collection with parents and teens should not be postponed until there is a complaint. The video *Dangerous Songs: Censors, Rock and the First Amendment* (American School Publishers, 1991) provides a short, stimulating introduction to the issue for parents. In a congenial setting, many teens are eager to talk about what particular songs mean to them. Parents may discover that the messages they fear are not being interpreted in the way they suspect. Discussions with teens also allow parents to share their values instead of just their anger and distaste.

It isn't necessary, nor is it wise, for adults to embrace teens' music, since that would destroy the distance that teens are seeking. We can, however, cultivate respect for teenagers' right to have their own tastes and trust that they are not about to be brainwashed by a song.

Technology Is Not Enough

by Valerie J. Wilford

The Technology for Education Act (S.1040) represents a bold and dramatic legislative response to the National Education Goals. This is a significant piece of legislation that represents a major structural reorganization.

I applaud, appreciate, and support the recognition and inclusion of the nation's library media centers and school library media specialists as an integral, essential element—a partner—in the educational infrastructure. If we are committed to achieving the National Education Goals, the need for strong and vital school library media programs is clear.

In order for our nation to achieve a 90 percent graduation rate, a *perfect* adult literacy rate, and national leadership in math and science by the year 2000, students will need to develop the ability to access, evaluate, and use information. Providing and ensuring access to information and resources is a long-standing responsibility and commitment of school library media specialists.

Technology is playing and will continue to play a key role in providing access to the information critical to the development of tomorrow's leaders. The recent revolution in information and instructional technologies has provided school library media specialists with unprecedented opportunities and challenges as they provide leadership for the incorporation of educational technologies into schools' curricular programs.

Yes, technology will play an important part in the achievement of our nation's goals—but it is not the only part. A blend of technology, access to a wide variety of resources, and vital school library media programs will be required.

Funding available for education in our local school districts has declined. Every decision to spend money takes on increased importance. There is often a strong temptation to buy new technology to satisfy our desire to be "on the cutting edge."

I commend you on the inclusion of two of the elements from S. 266, the Elementary and Secondary School Library Media Act, in S. 1040. [See "A Call for Progress" by Sen. Paul Simon, *SLJ*, April 1993, pp. 26-29.] But technology is only one element in the solution. An essential component of S. 266 has been ignored—the need for strong school library media collections and programs.

Programs "At Risk"

The reality is that our nation's school library media programs are "at risk." Funding for school library media centers has declined significantly over the last ten years.

The Elementary and Secondary Education Act of 1965 provided targeted, separate funding for school library media programs and resources. During the last dozen years, however, all funding for school programs was merged into the block grants of Chapter 2. As a result of this consolidation, funding for school libraries declined dramatically. And, I might add, total funding for the Chapter 2 block grant program has decreased in the past several years.

"Expenditures for Resources in School Library Media Centers FY 1989-1990," the fifth in a series of *School Library Journal* reports [by Marilyn L. Miller and Marilyn Shontz], summarizes expenditures for public and private school library resources in the United States. The report documents the steady and continued erosion of funding to school library media programs. An update of the survey is under way now, and preliminary data reveal an even more deplorable situation. [The sixth biennial report appeared in the October 1993 issue of *SLJ*, pp. 25-36.]

In my own state, during the spring of 1993, the Illinois School Library Media Association conducted a study of Illinois public and private school library media center collections in the areas of astronomy, space science, and the solar system; general biology and ecology; and human anatomy, physiology, and hygiene. The results of the study have not yet been published, but I would like to share just a few of the highlights of that research with you.

- The Illinois survey data document the national trend that funding for school library media center programs has eroded over the past decade.
- Illinois school library media center collections in the topical areas surveyed are old, reflecting funding of the late 1960s and early 1970s.
- Sixteen percent of the respondents reported that they spent less than $3.00 per student for library media resources in 1991-92. The average cost of a book in 1991 was $13.07 at the elementary level and $42.12 at the secondary level. Thus, a $3.00 per student expenditure in 1991 would buy less than one-fourth of an elementary book and less than one-tenth of a secondary title.
- Eighty-eight percent of the respondents reported that astronomy, space science, and the solar system were part of their school curriculum, but 45 percent have fewer than 20 titles on these topics. Forty-three percent have

fewer than six books published between 1990 and 1993 about these subjects. Sixty-six percent responded that they have more than 20 titles published before 1970, 23 years ago.

Today's students require a wide variety of resources, not only books and periodicals, in order to be information literate. Access to information in newer formats such as CD-ROM, video, and computer software, while crucial, is priced out of the reach of a majority of school libraries.

School Libraries = Achievement

Two studies, both published in 1993, explored the contribution of the school library media center (SLMC) to student achievement and the value of free reading. [See "Objective: Achievement," *SLJ*, May 1993, pp. 30-33.] Findings from the Colorado study [by Keith Curry Lance et al.] include:

- The size of an SLMC's staff and collection is the best school predictor of academic achievement.
- Students who score higher on standardized tests tend to come from schools with more SLMC staff and more books, periodicals, and videos—regardless of other factors, including economic ones.
- School library media expenditures affect SLMC staff and collection size and, in turn, academic achievement. Conclusions from Stephen Krashen's study, *The Power of Reading*, include:
- Voluntary reading is the best predictor of reading comprehension, vocabulary growth, spelling ability, grammatical usage, and writing style.
- Access to SLMCs results in more voluntary reading by students.
- Having a school library media specialist makes a difference in the amount of voluntary reading done.
- Larger school library collections and longer hours increase both curriculum and amount read.

The Central Role of Librarians

Within the school setting, it is often librarians, more than those in any other disciplines, who have embraced and enhanced automation. They did this *not* to make their jobs easier. In fact, automation opens up so many opportunities and makes so much possible that the librarian's job is more complex now than it ever was. It is ever so much easier to simply say, "I'm sorry, but we don't have that," and move on to other things than it is to master the intricacies of remote database searching.

But librarians *did* embrace and enhance automation, and they did it because of their commitment to the concept of equal access to information. What started years and years ago as library-to-library sharing through the exchange of handwritten requests has evolved into the instantaneous transmission of full-text documents from sites all over the world. But the bottom line has never changed for an instant—access to information, for absolutely everyone who needs it.

Indeed, the school office uses automation to prepare schedules and compute grades; various "technologically-minded instructors" make available computer programs to enhance their curricula (those programs usually are ordered by, cataloged by, demonstrated by, housed by, and maintained by librarians), and more and more students use computers for word processing.

But it is librarians who have consistently and doggedly led the way in the application of automated systems to enhance learning. And all of this research, development, and application has been done with the understanding that one of the primary purposes of library automation is for resource sharing.

At this moment, thanks to the insistence, creativity, and philosophical foundations of American librarians, the student in tiny Henry-Senachwine High School in Henry, IL, has virtually the same access to the same materials as the student in the Sidwell Friends School in Washington, DC.

Librarians are justly proud of this. But there is another side to this story—and it is the side of the story that you must concern yourself with the most.

Something to Share

In just the past few years, the focus of library service has changed so dramatically, so rapidly, that now it oftentimes is easier to secure hardware and software than it is to keep on the shelves an updated collection of books. Foundations continue to fund innovative uses of technology, and the PTA is zealously collecting enough soup can labels to get the school district a new computer. And all of that is wonderful—but what about the books, the resources, the sharing in resource sharing?

Consider again Henry-Senachwine High School. Here is a school library with a collection of fewer than 5,000 volumes, most of which are so dated as to be virtually worthless. It is little wonder that when the Henry-Senachwine Library was able through grant funds and great local effort to secure a computer and a modem, the school principal and the school board member present at the installation were elated. Now their students would have access to library collections through Illinois and throughout the United States. In the ten minutes it took to hook up the computer, the students in this school went from access to 5,000 dated volumes to the entire collections of 36 colleges and universities in Illinois, to the collections of major metropolitan libraries, even to more than 28 million records of the Library of Congress now accessible through the Internet.

But, in the midst of all this excitement, there was one individual who had reservations—the school library media specialist, Katie Grumbine, who has been at the school long enough to remember when this year's seniors were starting kindergarten, had tears in her eyes when these final connections were made. More than anyone else in the room, she knew the significance of what was happening.

But her first words to me had nothing to do with what databases she could search, what possibilities now were hers. Her very first question was, "But what can *we* possibly have to share, to give back, to loan to other libraries?"

And there it is. That attitude is the norm among librarians. Were it not the norm, we never would have gotten this far. We never would have reached this level of resource sharing. We never would have had librarians so eager to allow remote access to their collections. We never would have seen this incredible development of library automation. System designers are not in the business of creating systems that will not be used. The sophistication of the systems that have been developed attests to this attitude—there is among librarians a market for the tools of sharing.

But as Katie Grumbine realized, in order for this to make any sense at all, we must have something to share. Katie Grumbine now has the ability to essentially eliminate her book budget and rely on the collections of others. But that will never happen. Indeed, Katie will devote even more time, energy, and expertise to the development of her collection, and she will participate wholeheartedly in coordinated collection development—programs designed to enhance the cooperative planning of and sharing of materials.

Stretching the Federal Dollar

In 1968, federal dollars were used to put a collection of books in libraries A, B, C, and D. Students in libraries A, B, C, and D then had access to the very latest print information. That program in 1968 was a tremendous boon to school libraries and to education.

But here is the remarkable thing. Resource sharing is built on a foundation in which school libraries (like all libraries) strive to meet the basic needs of their students and teachers at the local level and then share with one another those resources required. Because of librarians' commitment to equal access to information, adherence to the provisions of copyright restrictions, and the automated resource sharing systems thereby engendered, federal dollars for school library resources in 1993 will go much, *much* further than in 1968. Is there any other area of government spending that can make the same claim?

In 1993, federal dollars can be spent to put a collection of resources in library A, a *different* collection in library B, still a different collection in library C, and yet another collection in library D. Through automated systems for resource sharing, through fax technology, through the Internet, each collection will be accessible to each library. Moreover, each

collection will also be accessible to libraries E, F, G, H, and all the rest.

A Call to Action

As you deliberate and design a legislative response appropriate to the achievement of the nation's educational goals:

- I implore you to guarantee student access to the wide variety of school library media center resources and skills that will enable them to become *life-long learners*.
- I ask you to reexamine the components of S. 266, the Elementary and Secondary School Library Media Act.
- I ask you to recognize legislatively that [as Miller and Shontz state], "library media centers and their collections are not fixed assets. Adequate local educational programs cannot be developed unless a wide variety of learning resources are regularly replaced and updated."

References

1. American Association of School Librarians and the Association for Educational Communications and Technology. *Information Power: Guidelines for School Library Media Programs.* Chicago: American Library Association, 1988.
2. *Library and Book Trade Almanac, 1990-1991.* New York: R.R. Bowker Co.
3. Krashen, Stephen, *The Power of Reading.* Englewood, CO: Libraries Unlimited, 1993.
4. Lance, Keith Curry, Lynda Welborn, and Christine Hamilton-Pennell. *The Impact of School Library Media Centers on Academic Achievement.* Castle Rock, CO: Hi Willow Research and Publishing, 1993.
5. Loertscher, David V. "Objective: Achievement. Solution: School Libraries," *School Library Journal,* May 1993, pp. 30-33.
6. Miller, Marilyn L., and Marilyn Shontz. "Expenditures for Resources in School Library Media Centers FY 1989-1990," *School Library Journal,* August 1991, pp. 32-43.
7. New American Schools Development Corporation. *Designs for a New Generation of American Schools.* Arlington, VA: NASDC, 1991.

We're All in This Together

by Virginia H. Mathews

The Elementary and Secondary School Library Media Act was introduced into the Senate in 1992 by Sens. Paul Simon (D-IL) and Paul Sarbanes (D-MD) and into the House of Representatives by Rep. Jack Reed (D-RI). It calls for categorical federal funding for school library media materials and programs, the kind of targeted funding that has been lacking since the 1970s.

The provisions of the school library bill have recently been included in the reauthorization of the Elementary and Secondary Education Act (ESEA), a wide-ranging piece of federal education legislation, by the House of Representatives. ESEA was approved by the House on March 24 and is currently before the Senate. After passing the Senate, the legislation still must be signed by the president and funded during the appropriations process in order to take effect

Why should the passage of the Elementary and Secondary School Library Media Act, and the major and immediate improvement in school libraries it would create, be a priority for all librarians, regardless of the type of library? Because the current funding of school libraries affects the future perception and funding of all other libraries for decades to come!

As a College Librarian:

You are the immediate beneficiary of good student bibliographic instruction, which begins in quality schools in the elementary grades. Students exposed to good school library programs understand that, although no one person can ever know more than a fraction of all there is to know, knowledge exists and can be found; that resource-based learning is essential to fulfilling our highest expectations of our own abilities and talents; and that competence in information searching and independent learning is the most useful insurance anyone can have against changing jobs and social and economic structures. The knowledgeable demands on college libraries that such students bring with them from their school experience can give you leverage for collection building, more qualified staff, equipment, and a higher budget.

As a Reference Librarian:

You will meet out-of-school young adults, some of the 60 percent who do not go on to formal higher education. Many will have urgent information needs and will not know how to fill them. The attitude they bring to asking for, looking for, finding, and using information—their attitude toward you and

what you can do for them—will have been formed largely by what they learned, or did not learn, in school libraries at the elementary and secondary level. Their facility with print and electronic tools, or lack of it, will make our work either more satisfying or harder and more frustrating. Their contribution to the economy as workers and to the community as parents and voters may have a direct effect upon your job and the conditions under which you work.

As a Public Library Administrator:

You have much to gain or lose depending upon the school libraries in your district. The habit of reading for enjoyment and of lifelong learning is fostered from the earliest grades by school libraries when they are the genuine, professionally staffed, quality article. The products of schools with good libraries and those without them will sit on your city councils and state legislatures, they will run your local businesses and civic clubs, and they will become reporters for your news media. They will vote. School libraries are the training grounds for those who will use and support your library.

And remember: the key word for the 1990s and probably far beyond is *change*. Population mobility, cultural diversity, and the rising economic power of many of those who experienced the poorest school libraries in their youth will change your community, the personnel pool from which you select your staff, your clientele, and your budget. The quality of the school libraries in your community and state is very much your business, but so too is the quality of those in other parts of the country.

As a Special Librarian:

You will be able to see a difference in your clientele if school libraries over the next few years fail to do their jobs for lack of staff and resources. Many school libraries have had no new materials in science, social studies, biography, and other areas for several years—some as long as a decade. Clerks and volunteers are running a book check-out business that hardly qualifies as library service.

Business people, engineers, the myriad professionals who use (and urge management to support) your services may scarcely know what they need to know and how to get it. They may be unaware of your role as an information intermediary and facilitator if they were not trained in an adequate school library when they were young.

Remember, too, that many of your clients in the future

will come from multicultural backgrounds; school libraries could have been their only exposure to library services if they grew up in inner-city neighborhoods, poor rural areas, or reservations with little or no community library presence.

We had better make adequate funds for school libraries our concern *now*. We are all in this together.

The Race for the School Library Dollar

by Drs. Marilyn L. Miller & Marilyn L. Shontz

School library media specialists are increasing the pace of providing access to electronic resources, especially to e-mail and the Internet, according to our most recent survey of school library expenditures, the seventh in a series of *School Library Journal* reports. These reports summarize specific developments during 1993-94 in public and private school library media programs in the United States.

Book expenditures—the slow and steady equivalent of Aesop's tortoise—are not faring as well. Technology, the upstart hare, is demanding more and more from a limited purse. The largest portion of library media center (LMC) budgets has traditionally been devoted to books, but book collection dollars continue to remain static; budgets are not growing enough to buy new books, replace older ones, *and* purchase the necessary resources for the move to access information electronically.

In brief, expenditures for all types of non-book resources *combined*—for example, computer software, CD-ROMs, AV, and microforms—now come close to what LMCs spend for books.

We found healthy signs in other aspects of LMC programs; active reading motivation programs in both elementary LMCs and classrooms, planning for the achievement of Goals 2000, and relatively stable staffing patterns, especially welcome after a big decrease two years ago. Library media specialists (LMS) are taking on a variety of challenges: increasingly diverse programming, difficult funding problems, and more complex professional development, especially technology training.

What the Survey Offers

The purpose of this series, begun in 1983, has been to provide *SLJ* readers with an up-to-date account (as well as a longitudinal review) of national trends in LMC expenditures, thus providing a way to compare local expenditures, services, and programs with a national norm.

All of the *SLJ* reports have focused attention on the status of school library collections, expenditures, staffing, and instructional involvement. In addition, we have reported the steady escalation of LMC use of computers for management and program development and the emergence of telecommunications in LMCs.

Each report also adds current data on one or more previ-ously unstudied aspects of library media programs. In the current report we describe the availability of selected reading motivation programs in elementary LMCs, the types of staff development programs being selected, and the rapidly growing use of the Internet and e-mail in schools by students and teachers.

All references to LMCs and staff in this report refer *only* to those schools that subscribe to *SLJ*. All tables reflect data from both public and private schools. We are reporting no separate data for private schools since we received responses for only 65 private schools, reflecting 10 percent of the total survey response. For survey methodology, see box on page 453.

Survey Highlights

We've noted some of the survey's most significant findings in the following guide.

Respondents (Tables 1-3, 13)

We asked respondents to identify their gender and to describe themselves in terms of certification, educational background, full or part-time status, years of experience in the field of K-12 education as well as in librarianship, and salary. **Table 13** summarizes some of these data.

Tables 1 through 3 describe demographic characteristics of the respondents. In **Table 1**, we see a few percent gain compared to the previous survey in respondents who identified themselves in the "other" category and a four percent dip in elementary school respondents. The latter represents almost a 10 percent drop in the elementary response rate since the 1991-92 survey. **Table 2** shows two percent fewer LMSs working in the Northeast and three percent fewer in the West, while the South shows a five percent increase. **Table 3** shows the greatest change in the enrollment categories—a three percent drop in the number of LMCs service schools with 500-699 students.

Expenditures (Tables 4-8)

Table 4 presents mean and median expenditures for all resources. This accounting does not consider district or regional funding, or services from other sources.

As usual, we requested information on expenditures from local, federal, and gift monies, including those from fundraising, increasingly common in schools. "Local" is de-

Table 1	Table 2	Table 3
RESPONDENTS BY GRADE LEVEL	**RESPONDENTS BY CENSUS REGION**	**RESPONDENTS BY ENROLLMENT**

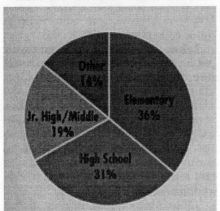

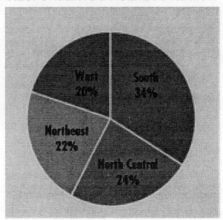

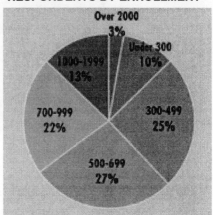

fined as money allocated by local school boards, states, and/or counties that fund all or part of local school expenses and are administered through a local education agency (LEA). Nearly 50 percent of the respondents reported receiving gifts or resources from fundraising, with the median reported as $1,125. **Table 4** also reveals that while the median expenditure per LMC for books is $5,000, the combined expenditures for AV resources and equipment and computer resources and equipment total $4,800. By adding $990 per LMC for microforms, it becomes apparent that books no longer represent the majority of LMC expenditures. Federal funding is still available for some schools from the Education Consolidation and Improvement Act of 1981 (ECIA), commonly known as block grants. About one third of the respondents reported receiving a median sum of $2,000. The amount of federal funds expended on specific resources is so small however, that we are not reporting those categories.

Tables 5 through 8 summarize public and private school expenditures of local funds for books (includes preprocessing costs), AV (includes videotape purchases, rentals, and leasing), periodicals (includes magazines, journals, and newspapers for both student and professional use), software (includes online fees and technical processing), CD-ROMs, and microforms.

Table 5 reports mean and median amounts spent in 1993-94 per school while **Table 7** offers the same information per pupil. **Table 6** compares median expenditures per school from 1984-1994 while **Table 8** looks at the same expenditures per pupil.

Table 5 displays the inequities among expenditures for resources. Far more is still spent on books—a mean of $5,362 per school and a median of $4,000—than on non-print resources considered *separately*. The range between the mean and median is significant for each type of resource. For example, the disparity between mean and median CD-ROM expenditures calls attention to the gulf between "high-tech" schools (defined for this survey as those that have both an automated circulating system and catalog) and those that can buy few resources or none at all.

Table 6 reports modest increases per school for resources. The largest increase is $177 per school for microforms, while book expenditures increased $68, AV resources, $17, periodicals, $13, and software by a mere $10.

Table 8 shows per pupil median increases since 1992 to be extremely modest in light of rising costs. Per pupil expenditures for books still represent the latest national per pupil expenditures. Expenditures for the rest of the categories range from $0.14 for microforms and $0.17 for periodicals to $0.21 for software and $0.22 for AV.

Book spending has gone up slightly from 1984 to 1994, taking into account a 37.1 percent increase in inflation. When the 1984 per school expenditure of $2,263 for books is adjusted to 1994 money, the real gain in median expenditures for books is $900. However, this gain is a chimera when we take into account continually increasing book prices and growing demand for computer resources, periodicals, and diverse subject matter. For example, the 1995 *Bowker Annual* reported the average cost of juvenile hardbacks to be $14.44, an adult novel, $20.85, and a volume of general works, $55.54. An increase of $900, therefore will have no visible impact on the collection.

Collections/Programs (Tables 9-12)

Regardless of how the data are presented, the state of school library book collections in the U.S. continues to worsen.

Table 4
MEAN & MEDIAN EXPENDITURES
ALL RESOURCES, 1993-94 (all funding sources)

EXPENDITURES	NUMBER RESPONDING	MEAN	MEDIAN
Total Local Funds	590	$12,950	$9,587
Total Federal Funds	213	3,569	2,000
Total Gift Funds	330	2,675	1,125
Total All Funds			
Books	576	6,299	5,000
Periodicals	568	1,529	1,000
Microforms	130	1,380	990
AV Resources/Equipment	498	3,209	2,000
Computer Resources/Equipment	447	5,423	2,800
Total Expenditures	590	$15,499	$11,745

Table 5
MEAN & MEDIAN EXPENDITURES PER SCHOOL FOR LMC RESOURCES, 1993–94 (LOCAL FUNDS ONLY)

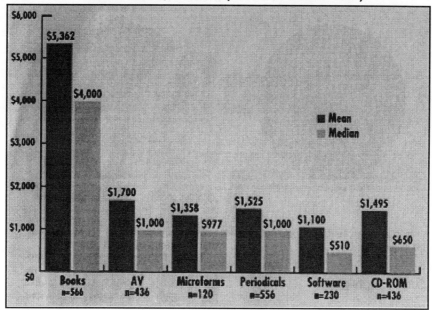

Table 6
MEDIAN EXPENDITURES PER SCHOOL FOR LMC RESOURCES, 1984–1994 (LOCAL FUNDS ONLY)

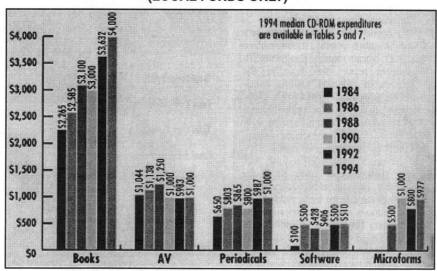

Two years ago we reported that book collections were stagnant. Today, book collections are becoming totally inadequate to serve the goals and objectives of school library media programs that support reading programs. Only 35 percent of teachers surveyed in the federal 1990-91 *Schools and Staffing Survey* (see box on page 453 for more information) believe that their library/media materials are adequate.

Tables 9-11 present collection size and expenditures reported categorically by school level, region, and enrollment. Expenditures from all sources—local, federal, gifts, and fundraising—are shown as Total Materials Expenditures (TME). TME is reported at the bottom of each table for purposes of comparison. TME reflects *all* expenditures for resources including AV equipment, computer hardware, online services, rentals, leasing, supplies and maintenance, but excludes salaries.

Table 9 displays data by school level. Schools in the "other" category added 400 books to their collections, followed by elementary schools adding 393 and middle and senior high schools adding 300. Because each level discarded at least half as many books as they bought, little progress is being made in even maintaining, much less expanding collection size. TME in high schools, as expected, and the "other" category is slightly higher than the other two levels, but books for the secondary level cost so much more that this higher expenditure does not indicate progress toward larger collections.

As has been true in most of the *SLJ* reports, the largest book collections are in the North Central and Northeast re-

Table 7
MEAN & MEDIAN EXPENDITURES PER PUPIL FOR LMC RESOURCES, 1993–94
(LOCAL FUNDS ONLY)

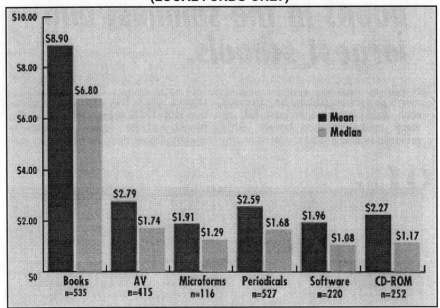

Table 8
MEAN & MEDIAN EXPENDITURES PER PUPIL FOR LMC RESOURCES, 1984–1994
(LOCAL FUNDS ONLY)

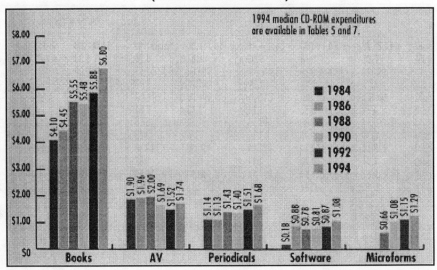

gions. **Table 10** reports that LMCs in the North Central region average 10,800 volumes, and those in the Northeast, 10,729. Schools in both the South and West reported 10,000-volume collections on average. When examined by region, local mean expenditures for books do not exceed $5,000 in any school. As usual, median TME figures for schools in the Northeast remain the highest at $23.46 per student.

Table 10 also reveals that LMCs in all regions, except the West, spend more money on CD-ROMs than on software. Schools in the South and Northeast spend more funds on non-book resources than on books. In the North Central region, LMC collection expenditures are almost equally divided between book and non-book resources.

Although not shown in **Table 11**, only LMSs in schools serving fewer than 125 students purchased one book per child to add to the collection. In small schools, a 50 percent discard rate and inadequate budgets are having a negative impact on the quality and quantity of book resources. In half the enrollment categories—those servicing 300-499 students and those serving 500-699—expenditures for non-book resources surpass those for books. Large schools (1,000+ students) have dismal resource budgets. Median expenditures for schools enrolling more than 2,000 students total $8,500. Of that $8,500, or $11.44 TME per pupil, $3.43 is spent for books.

Resource-based Learning. Some schools are adopting a resource-based learning approach as the primary way of teaching, with less emphasis on textbooks and more on using the variety of resources usually found in LMCs. We asked library

Table 9
LMC COLLECTION SIZE & LOCAL EXPENDITURES BY SCHOOL LEVEL, 1993-94

	ELEMENTARY n=231		JR. HIGH/MIDDLE n=120		SENIOR HIGH n=195		OTHER n=87	
	median	mean	median	mean	median	mean	median	mean
Size of Book Collection	9,000	9,691	10,000	10,450	12,200	14,063	10,000	12,300
Volumes Added, 1993-94	393	460	300	454	300	396	400	542
Number of Books per Pupil	17	20	15	17	19	16	21	29
Volumes Discarded, 1993-94	150	412	100	285	107	384	183	345
Size of AV Collection	375	694	276	683	300	971	150	505
Number of AV Items Added, 1993-94	10	24	5	54	1	16	3	13
Number of AV Items per Pupil	0.70	1.40	0.38	1.02	0.40	1.23	0.35	0.91
AV Items Discarded, 1993-94	3	52	0	63	5	56	2	23
Size of Video Collection	100	153	119	184	200	304	130	283
Videos Added, 1993-94	18	30	20	42	20	92	15	24
Videos per Pupil	0.21	0.29	0.19	0.29	0.25	0.43	0.24	0.56
Videos Discarded, 1993-94	0	4	0	21	0	6	0	5
Size of Software Collection	70	195	24	93	15	65	28	73
Software Added, 1993-94	3	15	2	14	1	6	1	9
Software per Pupil	0.15	0.43	0.04	0.14	0.02	0.09	0.05	0.15
Software Discarded, 1993-94	0.00	2.59	0.00	0.99	0.00	2.54	0.00	5.94
Size of CD-ROM Collection	7	10	8	11	8	13	6	9
CD-ROMs Added, 1993-94	3	6	3	5	3	5	3	6
CD-ROMs per Pupil	0.01	0.02	0.01	0.02	0.01	0.02	0.01	0.02
CD-ROMs Discarded, 1993-94	0.00	0.01	0.00	0.45	0.00	0.07	0.00	0.06
Expenditures								
Books	$3,608.00	$4,222.92	$4,290.00	$6,264.78	$4,710.00	$6,091.40	$4,000.00	$5,353.13
Books per Pupil	6.74	7.87	6.76	9.83	6.67	8.20	8.33	12.07
Periodicals	600.00	680.22	1,200.00	1,366.99	2,000.00	2,563.57	1,060.00	1,503.43
Periodicals per Pupil	1.10	1.37	1.89	2.30	2.72	3.67	2.19	3.17
Microforms	520.00	560.75	661.00	842.85	1,000.00	1,511.07	1,450.000	1,744.64
Microforms per Pupil	1.02	1.42	0.92	1.24	1.30	1.81	1.72	3.89
AV Materials	914.00	1,298.19	1,000.00	1,697.58	1,021.00	2,158.10	845.00	1,767.68
AV Materials per Pupil	1.74	2.59	1.55	2.60	1.74	2.93	1.91	3.33
Software	685.00	978.63	452.00	936.45	450.00	1,180.58	500.00	1,390.03
Software per Pupil	1.36	1.84	0.78	1.41	0.63	1.67	1.10	3.85
CD-ROMs	300.00	466.82	624.50	1,016.98	1,500.00	2,414.56	600.00	1,112.42
CD-ROMs per Pupil	0.70	0.99	0.86	1.87	1.75	3.18	1.37	2.21
*Total Materials Expenditures	$9,537.00	$11,407.45	$11,087.00	$14,909.88	$15,650.00	$20,189.16	$12,300.00	$16,399.05
TME per Pupil	$17.53	$22.08	$18.00	$24.69	$20.68	$27.13	$27.19	$39.39

*See p. 447 for explanation of TME

media specialists to comment on this approach in their schools and to evaluate the impact on their collections. In 55 percent of the schools, at least some teachers are using this teaching technique, and in 13 percent, the whole school is using it. All those reporting resource-based learning noted that extra funds are being allocated to teachers or the LMC for additional resources. We also tried to ascertain the impact of this teaching strategy on the collection. Only four percent reported no significant change in use. Others reported a 16 percent increase in the use of nonfiction; CD-ROM/computers, 12 percent; and fiction, 11 percent.

Goals 2000. We asked respondents to tell us whether their school districts are developing programs and activities related to the Goals 2000: Educate America Act. We found an emphasis on Goals 2000 activities in school districts with 25,000 or more students. Thirty-two percent reported that activities are now underway; 41 percent report that they are in the planning stage for the next one to three years; and 27 percent report no activities being planned.

Reading Motivation. We also asked LMSs to identify special reading motivation programs or techniques used by teachers and/or the LMS. **Table 12** lists types of reading and lit-

Table 10
LMC COLLECTION SIZE & LOCAL EXPENDITURES BY REGION, 1993-94

	NORTHEAST n=140		SOUTH n=219		NORTH CENTRAL n=152		WEST n=124	
	median	mean	median	mean	median	mean	median	mean
Size of Book Collection	10,729	12,579	10,000	10,779	10,800	12,431	10,000	10,621
Volumes Added, 1993-94	350	430	324	488	307	450	409	320
Number of Books per Pupil	19	23	15	19	18	21	17	19
Volumes Discarded, 1993-94	100	466	150	340	150	370	100	318
Size of AV Collection	395	872	400	771	300	884	100	406
Number of AV Items Added, 1993-94	2	13	9	29	5	39	3	17
Number of AV Items per Pupil	.56	1.46	.60	1.14	.54	1.44	.20	.66
AV Items Discarded, 1993-94	5	121	2	38	5	31	0	21
Size of Video Collection	111	186	180	280	122	204	78	182
Videos Added, 1993-94	15	32	25	45	15	32	10	21
Videos per Pupil	.19	.31	.27	.45	.24	.36	.13	.28
Videos Discarded, 1993-94	0	2	0	4	0	8	0	22
Size of Software Collection	25	104	40	127	35	135	12	97
Software Added, 1993-94	1	8	2	17	3	9	1	7
Software per Pupil	.03	.21	.06	.23	.05	.29	.02	.19
Software Discarded, 1993-94	0	4	0	3	0	3	0	2
Size of CD-ROM Collection	8	12	7	14	9	7	7	9
CD-ROMs Added, 1993-94	3	5	3	6	3	5	3	5
CD-ROMs per Pupil	.01	.02	.01	.02	.01	.02	.01	.02
CD-ROMs Discarded, 1993-94	.00	.05	.00	.02	.00	.14	.00	.03
Expenditures								
Books	$4,975.00	$6,138.38	$3,952.50	$5,702.46	$4,000.00	$4,632.40	$4,200.00	$4,767.36
Books per Pupil	8.65	10.53	5.99	9.14	6.25	7.80	7.56	8.04
Periodicals	1,142.00	1,812.41	978.00	1,317.67	1,300.00	1,840.69	800.00	1,174.74
Periodicals per Pupil	2.18	2.92	1.41	2.16	2.30	3.09	1.31	2.38
Microforms	1,550.00	2,312.50	1,066.00	1,382.10	527.00	828.72	980.00	1,178.13
Microforms per Pupil	1.90	2.65	1.49	1.87	0.70	1.24	1.14	2.06
AV Materials	1,235.00	1,928.64	770.00	1461.10	1,000.00	2,030.22	600.00	1,402.15
AV Materials per Pupil	2.50	3.33	1.26	2.22	2.00	3.35	1.36	2.46
Software	600.00	1,042.49	600.00	1,148.44	550.00	879.53	450.00	1,386.02
Software per Pupil	1.36	1.92	1.07	2.27	1.02	1.61	0.81	1.98
CD-ROMs	800.00	1,711.67	1,000.00	1,880.21	493.50	1,216.18	599.50	1,086.88
CD-ROMs per Pupil	1.52	2.31	1.17	2.76	0.82	2.15	1.01	1.70
*Total Material Expenditures	$12,000.00	$16,006.78	$11,609.00	$15,790.75	$11,850.00	$15,587.47	$11,512.50	$14,330.41
TME per Pupil	$23.46	$26.37	$17.38	$26.82	$19.94	$26.66	$19.17	$25.78

*See p. 447 for Explanation of TME

eracy activities and allows comparison between leadership by the library media specialist or classroom teacher. The top five LMC programs are booktalks, read-alouds, storytelling, author visits, and sustained silent reading (SSR). The most popular programs managed by teachers are exactly the same except that peer tutoring replaces author visits. We're pleased to see that many library media specialists are also trying family literacy reading programs, peer tutoring, and comics and graphic novels.

Human Resources (Table 13)

Staffing. Staffing 1994 was relatively stable as compared with 1992, which saw significant staff loss. **Table 13** illustrates that one media specialist per school is the average across the board. The number of student assistants has dropped slightly in middle school LMCs, and elementary schools and those in the "other" category report using no student assistants. High school library media specialists continue to report using four student assistants on average per LMC.

Full-time Salaries. Salaries for elementary library media specialists remain unchanged from 1991-92 as do their average number of years of experience. Middle School LMSs saw a $4,000 salary increase and have, on average, one year less experience. High school MSs report an increase of $2,000 and

Table 11
LMC COLLECTION SIZE & LOCAL EXPENDITURES BY ENROLLMENT, 1993-94

	UNDER 300 STUDENTS n=65		300-499 STUDENTS n=156		500-699 STUDENTS n=169		700-999 STUDENTS n=135		1,000-1,999 STUDENTS n=81		2,000 AND UP n=19	
	median	mean	mean	median	mean	median	mean	median	median	mean	median	mean
Size of Book Collection	7,000	8,583	9,694	8,024	10,784	10,000	11,907	11,000	14,000	16,120	20,154	21,470
Volumes Added, 1993-94	250	288	355	300	433	350	515	450	500	650	521	699
Number of Books per Pupil	33	42	24	21	18	17	15	14	11	12	8	9
Volumes Discarded, 1993-94	125	277	265	100	442	150	389	120	200	440	90	547
Size of AV Collection	150	318	479	200	848	350	821	388	400	978	300	1,296
Number of AV Items Added, 1993-94	2	24	16	5	30	6	23	5	7	23	3	102
Number of AV Items per Pupil	.58	1.73	1.91	.51	1.42	.60	1.02	.50	.32	.77	.12	.51
AV Items Discarded, 1993-94	3	28	26	2	45	1	104	4	8	34	15	79
Size of Video Collection	76	111	163	100	201	120	264	171	210	342	400	516
Videos Added, 1993-94	10	31	30	15	31	20	31	20	27	41	30	119
Videos per Pupil	.32	.60	.41	.25	.34	.20	.33	.22	.19	.26	.16	.21
Videos Discarded, 1993-94	0	36	3	0	3	0	4	0	0	14	0	18
Size of Software Collection	15	115	126	30	137	40	122	25	17	67	48	100
Software Added, 1993-94	0	11	8	1	13	2	18	2	0	5	4	7
Software per Pupil	.06	.48	.30	.08	.24	.06	.15	.03	.01	.05	.02	.04
Software Discarded, 1993-94	.00	.86	1.90	.00	2.00	.00	4.00	.00	.00	4.00	.00	.18
Size of CD-ROM Collection	6	9	10	6	11	8	9	7	9	19	13	21
CD-ROMs Added, 1993-94	2	5	5	3	6	4	5	3	3	5	4	11
CD-ROMs per Pupil	.03	.04	.03	.01	.02	.01	.01	.01	.01	.01	.01	.01
CD-ROMs Discarded, 1993-94	.00	.07	.05	.00	.38	.00	.03	.00	.00	.13	.00	.16
Expenditures												
Books	$2,500.00	$2,926.10	$3,967.92	$3,004.50	$4,845.07	$4,183.00	$6,617.27	$5,241.50	$6,000.00	$7,554.65	$8,500.00	$11,233.72
Books per Pupil	12.09	14.94	9.94	7.90	8.25	7.20	8.26	6.26	4.26	5.86	3.43	4.75
Periodicals	800.00	1,059.08	1,247.88	796.00	1,243.23	900.00	1670.01	1,300.00	1,800.00	2,338.45	2,467.58	3,5116.94
Periodicals per Pupil	4.29	5.34	3.19	1.90	2.09	1.44	2.04	1.58	1.38	1.78	0.99	1.43
Microforms	500.00	959.29	1,240.17	901.00	981.00	730.00	1,185.94	800.00	1,450.00	1,662.27	2,037.50	3,036.38
Microforms per Pupil	1.91	4.27	3.11	2.27	1.62	1.07	1.42	1.03	1.26	1.27	0.88	1.15
AV Materials	602.00	956.02	1,286.77	800.00	1,540.64	939.00	1,873.01	1,325.00	1,550.00	2,629.88	2,690.00	3,078.36
AV Materials per Pupil	2.73	5.07	3.20	1.98	2.60	1.62	2.28	1.57	1.24	2.02	1.00	1.22
Software	300.00	618.18	861.77	600.00	1254.60	817.00	1,081.39	500.00	600.00	1,634.94	300.00	1,114.46
Software per Pupil	1.88	4.39	2.16	1.50	2.09	1.34	1.35	0.63	0.48	1.28	0.12	0.43
CD-ROMs	375.00	776.92	1,185.95	600.00	1,019.08	500.00	1,407.48	747.50	1,575.50	2,641.07	3,750.00	3,488.92
CD-ROMs per Pupil	1.77	4.39	2.99	1.43	1.72	0.85	1.73	0.85	1.81	1.91	1.67	1.48
*Total Material Expenditures	$6,866.50	$9,559.35	$18,683.87	$9,748.00	$14,638.64	$10,848.00	$17,363.61	$13,073.00	$17,200.00	$21,864.03	$28,888.50	$31,800.22
TME per Pupil	$35.26	$50.30	$47.03	$24.89	$24.94	$19.08	$21.47	$15.77	$13.82	$16.40	$11.44	$13.24

*See p. 447 for Explanation of TME

one more year of experience. Likewise, those working in "other" LMCs report a $2,000 increase, but have an additional two years of experience on average. Full-time LMS salaries range from a low of $6,200 (this is not a misprint!) to a high of $77,000, with a median salary of $36,278.

Since technology plays such a big part in changing the environment for LMSs and demands new services and programs, we asked respondents to identify staff development activities in which they had participated in the past two years. Seventy-five percent explored instructional design/consulting with teachers; LMC automation/computer applications, 73 percent; CD-ROM technology/applications, 72 percent; and integration of information/computer skills into curricular areas, 71 percent. Forty-four percent had e-mail training while another 40 percent participated in Internet inservice training. Training for online searching drew 39 percent of the respondents.

Technology (Tables 14-15)

The development of technology in LMCs continues to be impressive. **Tables 14 and 15** show that technology continues to dominate collection development and LMCs.

As **Table 14** illustrates, the most pervasive technology for delivering information to LMCs is cable television—60 percent of respondents use it. Library media specialists have also made determined efforts to integrate CD-ROMs into their collections. Forty-eight percent have CD-ROM indexes available while 78 percent provide CD-ROM encyclopedias and other books. Thirty-six percent have extra funds to purchase CD-ROMs, up from 24 percent two years ago. The availability of OPACs has doubled in two years; the remainder of respondents have plans to develop them. Data for computerized circulation systems is comparable—64 percent report access to such technology. The number of LMCs providing both OPACs and computerized circulation systems has risen to 57 percent. Access to online databases also continues to grow. The availability of fax machines in LMCs has doubled as has access elsewhere in school buildings. The number of LMCs with videodisc technology is unchanged; about one-third of schools are using it.

We asked for more specific information this time about LMC participation in networks. **Table 14** reports that 70 percent of respondents belong to a network and, of that group, 37 percent are in electronic networks. Since a major purpose of networks is to increase access to external resources for teachers and students, we asked respondents to identify interlibrary loan sources. Public libraries and district resource centers top the list, followed by regional resources, college and university libraries, and state resources, in that order. Of great interest, though not shown in the table, is that 34 percent of LMSs use the Internet to locate resources for teachers; 28 percent do the same for students.

No less impressive is that teachers and students in 25 percent of the LMCs have Internet access and e-mail. One of the most encouraging findings in **Table 14** is extra funding, even

if minimal, for a variety of computer technologies. Thirty-nine percent reported extra funding for software, 36 percent had additional funding for CD-ROMs, and 21 percent snared more money for online/telecommunications activities.

Table 15 displays the continuing increase in use of computers. Seventy-six percent of LMSs use them to manage overdues, followed by circulation, 64 percent; inventory, 61 percent; and cataloging, 60 percent. Forty-four percent use them for telecommunications activities, including the Internet, on-line resources, and e-mail.

Curriculum Planning (Table 16)

Though not reported in **Table 16**, 77 percent plan weekly, either formally or informally, with teachers to integrate LMC resources and services into the curriculum. This is a significant decrease from 92 percent in 1992. The current data shows, however, that LMSs are spending more time planning (3.88 mean number of hours a week) than two years ago (3.60 hours per week). This increase is laudable and essential as LMCs add electronic resources. Only slightly more than 29 percent of the teachers contacted in the federal 1990-91 *Schools and Staffing Survey* (see box on page 453 for more information) "strongly agreed" that they plan curricula with the school library media specialist. Our goals, therefore, of a collaborative curriculum will continue to be thwarted until we can successfully communicate the value of cooperative planning.

District Leadership (Table 17)

Over the years we've found that respondents who work with a district-level media coordinator (as compared to those who do not) see little impact of that relationship on collections or expenditures. We've seen, however, that district coordinators do have an impact on policies, media advisory committees, electronic resources, and planning. This year is no exception. The percentage of respondents having access to district-level coordination is unchanged from 1992. Twenty-nine percent report full-time district support, 13 percent report part-time coordination, and 52 percent have no coordinator. Although not shown in Table 17, the data reveals that schools *with* full-time district-level media coordinators have one LMS and one part-time clerk; schools with part-time district coordinators have one LMS and one clerk. Schools without district-level support have the opposite situation—a part-time LMS and a full-time clerk.

Table 17 compares policies, services, planning, and use of technology in schools with and without district-level coordination. We see a clear statistical relationship between district coordinators and 1) the use of a library media advisory committee, 2) curriculum planning with teachers for integrated instruction, 3) the use of cable television in the LMC, 4) the availability of an automated circulation system and/or catalog, and 5) plans to develop a local area network. Interestingly, schools without a coordinator are *more* likely to have access to a fax machine than those with a full-time coordinator.

There are other notable elements to study in Table 17. The

percentage of LMCs with selection policies at schools with coordinators remains high—86 percent. The availability of a telephone in the LMC for voice communication is nearly unchanged in all three categories of district-level assistance since 1992. The 1994 data shows that 80 percent of the schools without coordination have telephones, compared to 86 percent with part-time coordinators and 83 percent with full-time coordinators. The use of flexible scheduling is also fairly consistent across all levels of district coordination. Forty-six percent of part-time district-coordinated schools use some form of flexible scheduling as compared to 43 percent with full-time coordinators. Forty-one percent without coordinators are moving toward this type of schooling.

The Race Isn't Over Yet

School library media specialists are clearly moving LMCs into the 21st century, with electronic resources and telecommunications at the forefront of education. At the same time, many elementary library media specialists are successfully blending the traditional emphasis on reading and literature programs with the demands of an electronic world. Whether this news is good or bad depends on one's philosophy. Is the bucket half full or half empty? Those who believe in the half-full perspective can take heart knowing that there are so many active library media programs. Those who believe in the half-empty view can start reinvigorating an interest across the country in providing students with quality library media programs.

METHODOLOGY

In September 1994, a questionnaire was mailed to 1,570 school library media centers chosen by systematic random sampling from the *SLJ* school-based subscription list covering 50 states. Questionnaires were mailed only to subscribers who indicated either the name of a school or some form of the title "school library media specialist" in their address. Two subsequent mailings were sent to non-respondents. By December, 674 responses, 45 percent of the sample, had been received: 635 responses were usable. The 1993-94 usable response rate was lower than that available for the 1991-92 report.

Each response was checked for accuracy, then coded and entered into the computer. Data analysis was done using the Statistical Package for the Social Sciences (SPSS). Measures of central tendency (means and medians) were produced for all of the budget items listed on the survey. Chi square and ANOVA tests were used in statistical analysis of data presented in Table 17. For purposes of this study, both means and medians are reported, wherever appropriate, to give a more accurate description of the data. The means allow for comparisons with earlier studies that have used this measure; the medians indicate accurately the expenditures reported by most LMCs.

Although the mean (or average) is the descriptive statistic most commonly used in studies of this type, analysis of the data showed that much of it was skewed upward because a few respondents reported spending extremely large amounts for various kinds of library material. With a wide data distribution like this, the few large scores make the mean a less desirable measure of central tendency because they cause it to be unrealistically large.

In instances where the data was skewed, simply to report the mean would be misleading. For example, in response to a request asking for the size of school video collections, five respondents reported having at least 9,000 videotapes in their collections. On the other hand, 25 respondents reported no videotapes in their collections. The data for this question produces a mean of 222.4 videos per LMC while the median is 125.

FOR MORE STATISTICAL DATA

Previous *Expenditures for Resources in School Library Media Centers* have been published in the following *School Library Journal* issues: October 1983, May 1985, June/July 1987, June 1989, August 1991, and October 1993. In April 1994, *SLJ* published a second report from the 1991-92 data. "Inside High-Tech School Library Media Centers: Problems and Possibilities" compared selected data from LMCs that had automated circulation systems and catalogs to those without such technology.

DATA FROM THE FEDERAL GOVERNMENT

Since the publication in 1960 of *Standards for School Library Programs* (American Association of School Librarians/ALA), the U.S. Department of Education has published three sets of statistics on school library media programs. The final report of *Statistics of Public and Private School Library Media Centers, 1985-86* (National Center for Education Statistics) was extremely useful and still stands as the most complete picture of conditions in school library media programs. In the 1990-91 *Schools and Staffing Survey* conducted by the National Center for Education Statistics, school administrators identified whether a school library media center was available in their schools and whether the center was staffed. Data related to these two items as well as others are available in *School Library Media Centers in the United States: 1990-91* (U.S. Department of Education, National Center for Education Statistics, Office of Educational Research and Improvement, Washington D.C.: U.S. Government Printing Office, 1994).

Table 12
READING & LITERACY INVOLVEMENT IN SCHOOLS & LMCs, 1993–94
(Total number of respondents per activity)

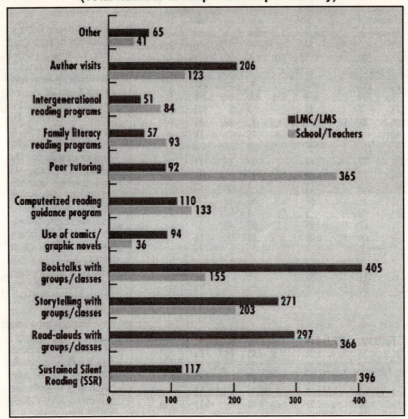

Table 13
SCHOOL LIBRARY MEDIA SPECIALISTS: EXPERIENCE, SALARY, & SUPPORTING STAFF, 1993-94

	ELEMENTARY		MIDDLE/JR. HIGH		SENIOR HIGH		OTHER		ALL SCHOOLS	
	median	mean	median	mean	median	mean	median	mean	median	mean
# Media Specialists in School	1.00	0.92	1.00	1.00	1.00	1.24	1.00	1.05	1.00	1.05
Years Experience in K-12 Schools	19	18	20	19	21	20	17	16	20	19
Years Experience Library/Media	12	13	14	14	16	16	12	12	14	14
Salary of Head Media Specialist	$37,000	$37,484	$39,000	$39,775	$37,500	$39,006	$29,828	$29,000	$36,277	$37,425
# Students Assistants	0.00	4.28	3.00	7.03	4.00	7.07	0.00	4.86	1.00	5.72
# Support Staff/Paid Clerks	0.50	0.58	0.50	0.70	1.00	0.99	0.50	0.64	0.50	0.74
# Adult Volunteers	2.00	3.92	0.00	1.68	0.00	0.65	1.00	4.07	0.00	2.54

Table 14
LMCs & TECHNOLOGY, 1993-94

	NUMBER RESPONDING	PERCENT
Additional Funds Provided for:		
Software	235	38.9
Online/Telecommunications	127	21.3
CD-ROM	213	35.5
Interactive Video	86	14.9
Technical Processing Services	69	11.9
Network Activities	49	8.1
LMC Uses Cable TV	370	59.5
Uses Videodisc Technology	201	33.2
Has Online Catalog on Site	294	46.9
Plans an Online Catalog	180	66.9
Has Computerized Circulation System on Site	401	64.5
Plans a Computerized Circulation	124	69.3
Has Local Area Network	237	38.8
Plans to Develop Local Area Network	95	20.2
Has Wide Area Network	147	44.0
Plans to Develop Wide Area Network	129	33.0
Member of a Library Network	422	69.6
Library Network Linked Electronically	179	36.8
Telephone	506	81.9
LMC Has Access to Fax Machine:		
in LMC	88	14.3
in School	334	54.2
No Access	194	31.5
Is "High Tech" (see p. 446 for definition)	289	56.9
Student Access to Electronic Databases:		
On Site Online/Telecommunications	231	40.0
CD-ROM Indexes	282	48.4
CD-ROM Books/Encyclopedias	477	77.7
Internet	144	25.0
E-mail	145	25.3

Table 15
COMPUTER USE IN LMC MANAGEMENT, 1984–1994

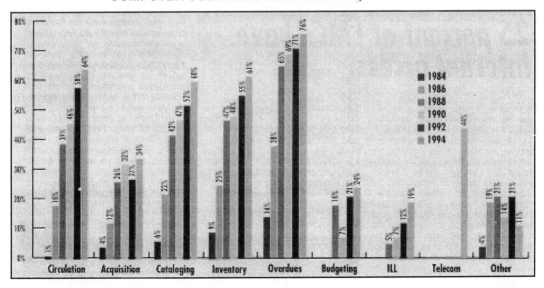

Table 16
LMS/TEACHER INSTRUCTIONAL PLANNING BY GRADE LEVELS, 1993-94

	Mean # Hours Formal Instructional Planning	Mean # Hours Informal Instructional Planning	Mean # Hours Total Planning
Elementary	1.04 (n=198)	2.26 (n=2110	3.30 (n=196)
Jr. High/Middle	1.61 (n=97)	2.82 (n=108)	4.50 (n=97)
High School	1.45 (n=166)	2.90 (n=183)	4.37 (n=165)
Other	0.94 (n=66)	2.62 (n=78)	3.52 (n=65)
All Schools	1.26 (n=528)	2.61 (n=581)	3.88 (n=524)

Table 17
SCHOOLS WITH & WITHOUT DISTRICT LEVEL MEDIA COORDINATORS: LMC CHARACTERISTICS, 1993-94

	WITH FULL-TIME n=193		WITH PART-TIME n=83		WITHOUT n=335	
	count	percent	count	percent	count	percent
*Library Media Advisory Committee	72	38	27	33	61	18
Selection Policy	165	87	71	~87	262	79
*Planning with Teachers for Integrated Instruction	148	79	61	74	221	68
Member of Library Network	131	45	58	71	322	69
Added Funds for Network Participation	15	8	6	8	27	8
Telephone	157	83	70	86	262	80
*Cable TV	131	69	51	62	183	56
Online Library	91	48	45	54	149	45
Plans for Online Library	52	69	19	61	104	68
*Automatic Circulation System on Site	141	74	55	66	193	59
Plans for Automated Circulation System	27	77	13	57	81	71
Local Area Network	67	37	35	44	126	39
*Plans to Develop Local Area Network	41	27	12	19	40	17
Wide Area Network	49	47	15	34	81	46
Plans to Develop Wide Area Network	39	35	18	33	67	32
Telecommunications/Online Access on Site	79	45	34	44	113	37
CD-ROM Access on Site	151	32	69	14	258	54
*Fax Machine in School or Library	120	64	48	58	236	73
Internet Access on Site	49	28	17	22	72	24
E-mail Access on Site	49	28	23	30	23	29
*LMC is "High Tech" (See p. 446 for definition)	91	66	44	62	145	52
Resource-based Instruction	33	17	8	10	35	11
Flexible Scheduling	81	43	38	46	133	41

*statistically significant at p=.05

Epilogue

40 Years . . . Onward & Upward

by Lillian N. Gerhardt

With this issue, *School Library Journal, The Magazine of Children's Young Adult & School Librarians* begins the celebration of its 40th anniversary of continuous publication and growth in service to its readers.

It was in July 1954 that the content of *SLJ*'s first issue was in preparation for the printers. It was published with a cover date of September 1954 (and for six years thereafter) under the title of *Junior Libraries*, which had grown up in the back pages of *Library Journal*.

SLJ started with nine issues per year and now publishes twelve issues year-round. It began with nearly no subscribers and now goes to 42,000 every month. Each issue is read by over 100,000 readers—mostly librarians serving children and adolescents in schools and public libraries.

When you reach your 40th birthday, self-help manuals often advise you to take stock—to look back and to plan ahead. As editors, looking backward at *SLJ*'s first 40 years has been a defining and vitalizing exercise. Thousands of specialized magazines have been founded since 1954—and thousands have ceased publication within a few months or years. The survival difference for *SLJ* has been its steadfast concentration on the concerns of its readers.

While *SLJ* carries the advertising of those who wish to attract sales from librarians, *SLJ*'s news, articles, and reviews are written by and for librarians. While *SLJ*'s contributors often address major issues in the politics of education, library service, and child development, the bulk of our articles and columns over 40 years have centered on the practical issues in managing library collections for children and young adults—what to purchase, how to use it, and how to survive long days and budgets that aren't (and never have been) big enough to allow *SLJ*'s readers to work as effectively as they

know how to with young library customers.

Looking ahead over the next 40 years, the editors know that there will be no shortage of material for *SLJ*'s content. Many of the same dilemmas that faced our first corps of readers have only changed in size and shape and still deserve discussion and re-thinking: how to recruit and train a new generation of librarians; how to stretch inadequate funds; what to buy and what to pitch from a collection; how to try out something new and how to rediscover the value of something old; how to examine and affect the social, political, and economic forces that impel or impact our profession; how to deploy services and materials to engage, support, and strengthen young readers.

Not everybody in library service sees the last—or next—40 years the same way. We invited a number of leaders in library services to answer one of the following questions:

- What have been the major issues facing librarians and libraries over the past several decades?
- How has public library service to children changed?
- How have schools and school library service changed?
- How has the censorship issue evolved over the years?
- How has the customer profile in libraries changed?
- How have changes in young customers' interests, family values, or reading levels affected library service?
- What changes have you seen in children's books?
- As we approach the year 2000, how do you see the roles of the library and the librarian changing?

Now it's *your* turn. Pick a question and send us your answer for publication in *your SLJ*. We will publish responses later in this anniversary year. Help your colleagues think about what has been and—more importantly—what can be.

In Service To Youth

by Lillian N. Gerhardt

1 954. President Dwight David Eisenhower nominated L. Quincy Mumford, President of the American Library Association, to be Librarian of Congress, the first professionally-trained librarian to hold that post. The United States Supreme Court ruled that the notion of "separate but equal" school facilities was unconstitutional in the landmark decision, *Brown v. Board of Education.* Ernest Hemingway won the Nobel Prize for Literature. The Atomic Energy Commission announced that the hydrogen bomb was attainable. During the waning days of the anti-communist fervor he helped create, Sen. Joseph R. McCarthy was censured by his colleagues for conduct "contrary to Senate traditions." Charles Lindbergh received the Pulitzer Prize in biography for *The Spirit of St. Louis.*

And on September 15, *Library Journal* began publishing *Junior Libraries*, a monthly section of news, feature articles, and book reviews that would appear in every mid-month issue. *Junior Libraries* (renamed *School Library Journal* in 1961) remained a part of *LJ* until 1975.

In honor of *SLJ*'s ruby anniversary, the editors have asked several leaders in the field of youth librarianship to share their perspectives on the last 40 years and their predictions for the next 40.

What have been the major issues facing libraries and librarians over the past several decades?

Margaret Bush: It seems to me there have been five big issues: a shortage of librarians, the interlibrary sharing of resources, intellectual freedom, the rapid expansion of information and technology, and persistent problems with funding.

The recurring shortage of librarians improves at times in some areas and then worsens. As a profession we've worked to improve salaries and sharpen our image. We've mounted recruiting efforts and opened more library schools. Now we've watched the closing of some of our oldest, most prestigious schools. Unless we can make salaries attractive enough to persuade folks to move beyond their immediate geographic region to study and work, the shortage will certainly continue to plague us.

The notion of resource sharing has been a driving force in shaping library services. The stand-alone library, meeting the needs of customers through its own collections, has extended its reach through interlibrary loan, reciprocal borrowing, and the establishment of library consortia and networks.

Rapidly developing technology provides so many new opportunities for locating and transmitting information. We have barely begun to examine and understand the effects of telecommunications and the many electronic formats on reference service and collection development.

One of librarianship's most fundamental philosophical tenets, freedom of expression and inquiry, is eternally under challenge. From decade to decade we experience new manifestations of intolerance toward the freedom of speech. Today many librarians, being a socially responsible lot, are caught in the muddle of political correctness. Intellectual freedom is always the issue that prods our conscience.

Money, my final issue, stirs our worry (and rightly so), since the supply of funds doesn't grow as quickly as our needs. Most of us have found fundraising to be a very desirable, even mandatory, professional skill in today's world. It's a safe bet that this will become ever more true over the next 40 years.

Virginia Mathews: Unfortunately, I think we're behind where we were 25 or 30 years ago in terms of school library service. When we got categorical federal funding for school libraries in 1965-66, we were already in the process of building up service. The fact that we haven't had categorical funding over the past two decades has been terrible, especially for elementary school libraries. Most are a decade or two behind in their collections, and their condition is just pitiful.

As for school librarians, there are too few of them. Many have been let go or put back into classrooms, or they're serving two or three buildings at a time. The major issue we face now is figuring out how to make up for this terrible gap so that we can move forward. The confusion in which many schools find themselves—proposed reforms and shrinking public confidence and support—makes it doubly hard for school libraries to operate.

As for youth services in public libraries, I see a kind of renaissance going on. I see a renewed fighting spirit among public library children's and youth specialists as they realize the roles they play in greater social issues such as crime, poverty, child development, parent involvement, and drug abuse. Public library cooperation with Head Start [which has just been written into reauthorization of the federal funded program] is just one example. Of course, budget problems exist for public libraries, too, but public librarians have impressed me over the years with their refusal to give in.

I know there is a general assumption in the field that technology is revolutionizing things, but I frankly think this has gone a bit overboard. Some people are even suggesting that libraries will no longer exist in the future as a *place* to go—that everyone will simply access information from their homes. I think youth librarians are going to be the ones to prove this theory wrong. There will always be a need for libraries as places where people go for restoration and social and intellectual contract, as well as information.

Marilyn L. Miller: We've been struggling with two major issues over the past 40 years. Our failure to deal with them adequately during changing times continues to keep us from reaching our potential.

First, we're still not able to interpret effectively what school library media center programs are and can be. Beginning with Frances Henne's powerful, definitive mission statement in the preface to the 1945 standards, *School Libraries for Today and Tomorrow*, we have developed powerful philosophical and descriptive statements about school library programs and what they do. No other aspect of the field has done this as well as we have. However, we simply haven't been able to mount and sustain the national initiatives to demonstrate outcomes, document contributions, and define relationships to educational improvement that are peculiar to good library media programs.

Second, the quality of professional education remains a challenge for us. At first we didn't have enough personnel. Again, we developed position papers, produced documentation, conducted national projects, and we recruited and prepared thousands of librarians. But, the issue has always been that of recruiting and producing entry-level personnel who will be change agents. The multimedia movement has given way to communications technology, but the ability of our personnel to move into a role of instructional consultant in an information age dominated by video and computers is being challenged. And, once again we are hearing the threat, "If we don't do it (this time installing modems instead of changing light-bulbs) . . . someone else will."

Those who doubt this is an issue should review the archaic certification requirements in many states, note the absence of library education programs in many states, count the numbers of ALA- or NCATE-accredited programs that have folded (remembering that the majority of our personnel come from the latter programs), and observe the numbers of library media specialists who still have rigid scheduling, avoid planning with teachers to improve classroom instruction, and refuse to assume responsibility for staff development in the use of library resources.

How has public library service to children changed?

Peggy Sullivan: When I saw my first issue of *Junior Libraries*, I was one of three children's librarians working in a branch of the Kansas City (MO) Public Library.

By today's standards, we were probably overstaffed, and we spent a lot of time on very clerical routines: checking out books (or an occasional item from the vertical file) with a date stamp on the end of a pencil, sorting the picture books on their tight little shelves, or typing out overdue notices. However, since there were no school librarians in the ten elementary and junior high schools that we served, we also had classes in the library on a regular schedule, chose books to send them, and planned and conducted weekly story hours, attended mostly by children in the fourth through sixth grades.

Every month when all of us from children's rooms throughout the city went "down to Main" for a meeting, we passed around and ordered any new books reviewed that month. At one of those meetings, Vera Prout, supervisor of children's work, expressed her delight that the awful book by that New Yorker, *Charlotte's Web*, had not won the Newbery medal. I didn't comprehend her hostility, but I don't think I had voted for it myself. If any of us there had supported it, she surely didn't tell Miss Prout.

Do I think youth work has changed since 1953? Yes, yes, yes! For the better? Yes, in many ways. For the worse? Yes, that too.

How have schools and school library service changed?

Mike Printz: *School Library Journal* was just four years old when I subscribed for the first time. Books have always been bonds between librarians and young adults, but there have been distinct changes in school library services over the last 36 years that I have served in this profession. First is the advent of various forms of technology. Some have been gimmicky, but online searching of Dialog databases, electronic reference tools on CD-ROM, and statewide, online catalogs have made up-to-date, reliable sources available immediately, so students never leave the library empty-handed.

Books, however, are still a power because of fiction authors like S.E. Hinton, Gary Paulsen, Chris Crutcher, and Bruce Brooks, whose novels speak to young adults and enrich their lives. The work of nonfiction editors like Jeanne Vestal has brought responsible, accurate titles into the library, titles that not only provide information but create a sense of awe and wonder. Hazel Rochman's works on multiculturalism have helped us transcend basic studies of individual cultures to an awareness of the human condition in all peoples. Changes have been positive, and during the next 40 years school libraries will again lead the way in providing the best from the information explosion.

Jean C. Lowrie: *School Library Journal*'s span of 40 years covers the remarkable growth period of school libraries since World War II. It was during the late '40s and early '50s that programs for enriched service through library media centers came into their own.

A look at some of the literature and early research from that period indicates such earthshattering concepts as audiovisual materials in the library, the utilization of library books instead of basal readers or textbooks, open hours for the library (flexible scheduling), curriculum enrichment through regular planning with classroom teachers, projects that involve administrators and parents, an exploration of community resources along with the traditional teaching of library skills, and an appreciation for good books. These were all a part of the 1950s and '60s as school librarians began to assume real visibility in the educational program.

Librarians have taken advantage of the changes that have come with the information/technological revolution. Less time spent on cataloging and processing materials means more release time to plan, search online databases, provide individual student instruction, and expand research studies to promote greater support for educational programs.

> ## Fast Facts
>
> Culled from several sources, including *Statistics of Public-School libraries, 1953-54* (U.S. Department of Health, Education, and Welfare) and "Expenditures for Resources in School Library Media Centers, FY 1991-92" (*SLJ*, October 1993, pp. 26-36), and *Digest of Education Statistics, 1993* (U.S. Department of Education), the numbers below provide a quick comparison of a few school library statistics from 1954 and the most current data available.
>
> Average price of a juvenile book, 1954: $2.50
> *Average price of a juvenile book, 1994: $14.66*
>
> Librarians in public schools, 1954: 30,753
> *Librarians in public schools, 1991: 49,718*
>
> Library expenditures per pupil—
>   Books, 1954: $ .67
>   *Books, 1992: $5.85*
>
>   Audiovisual materials, 1954: $ .14
>   *Audiovisual materials, 1992: $1.52*
>
>   Periodicals, 1954: $. 09
>   *Periodicals, 1992: $1.51*
>
> Public schools with libraries, 1954: 46,880 (36.3%)
> *Public schools with libraries, 1985: 73,352 (93.5%)*
>
> Average number of books per pupil, 1954: 5.2
> *Average number of books per pupil, 1992: 18.15*
>
> Children's books published, 1954: 1,342
> *Children's books published, 1993: 5,062*

The next decades produced an increase in national research and innovative demonstration projects that not only influenced school libraries in the United States but became the models for many in other countries. It seems clear that the exciting changes of these past 40 years are the result of library personnel being able to capitalize on the changes in our educational, social, and scientific environment. But, the basic constant in all this is still *service*.

How has the censorship issue evolved over the years?

Judith F. Krug: Traditionally and historically, materials have been challenged or censored because of their political, religious, or sexual content. But the focal points of challenges have changed dramatically over the last 40 years. They have, in fact, followed new issues as these arise in the public arena.

In the mid-1960s, as the civil rights movement took hold, libraries began to receive challenges that focused on the alleged racism in materials. In the late '60s, as a result of the women's movement, challenges of sexism increased. In the '70s, challenges to materials because of religious content decreased until they were almost nonexistent. Indeed, for almost

15 years it was considered unsophisticated to complain about materials because of their religious content.

Then came Ronald Reagan's election in 1980. Among other things, Reagan reestablished the credibility of religion, and over the next few years, an increasing number of materials were challenged because of their *lack* of religious content or because of the blasphemous manner in which they treated religion. In the late '80s, complaints about materials said to "promote" witchcraft or similar topics spawned the greatest number of challenges. Complaints about the sexual content of materials, however, remained a close second. It's really hard to get kids away from the "good parts" of books!

Also during the 1980s, would-be censors began to focus on books dealing with homosexuality. There were some challenges early in the decade, as AIDS became a major issue of public concern and focused attention on homosexuality. Nevertheless, despite this focus, our database reveals that in 1991, we only had 40 complaints about homosexual content. But, 1991 also brought the demise of the Soviet Union. With the disintegration of the "evil empire," the American public lost its favorite scapegoat of 45 years. What, then, could possibly take its place? The answer was not long in coming—homosexuality. In 1992, we recorded 64 challenges to gay materials and, in 1993, 111. As of this writing, the number of challenges to gay materials in 1994 stands at 37. What will be the next area targeted? Stay tuned . . .

Evie Wilson-Lingbloom: The evolution of censorship contains "something old, something new." We still have challenges over explicit sex, frank language, free access, and the right of students to express their opinions in their student publications or by their appearance and clothing. Some of the most courageous folks I've been privileged to work with during the past 30 years have been not only the youth services librarians who have "hung tough" for free access, but also the administrators who have backed us up. In 1979 at the Finkelstein Library in Spring Valley, NY, library director Sam Simon supported YA librarian Larry Parisi and the publication of an article on substance abuse at a local junior high school that appeared in *Teenage Express*, the YA advisory group's free expression publication.

Around 1990, as cassettes and CDs replaced the record disc, and as hard rock, grunge, and rap became more angry and reactive, parental concern escalated. Currently, some of the biggest media challenges are aimed at rap music and its lyrics. For nearly two years, Tom Mayer and Jonalyn Woolf-Ivory, administrators for the Sno-Isle Regional Library System in Marysville, WA, have been standing firm in support of media librarian Pat Shaw to protect youth access to rap recordings. While many musical artists and styles of music and dance can be trendy, it seems likely that rap will be around for quite a while, as will the anger, frustration, and injustice its lyrics express.

Looking to the future, we must protect the access of young people with limited budgets to the wealth of information on the Internet and on databases such as Dialog, which are increasingly fee-based.

How has the customer profile in libraries changed?

Maria Salvadore: Perhaps it's not the customer who has changed but the needs of those who use library services to children. There is an increased awareness of the importance and lasting impact of early literature experiences for children, the importance of the parent's role in providing those, and a heightened sensitivity to the needs of the adult who may not read fluently. As a result, children's services in libraries provide a broader range of service for both younger and older customers.

Storytime and outreach efforts specifically target the very young child. Library programs for infants (up to age two) are as accepted as preschool storytimes. Children's librarians routinely introduce parents, teachers, and other adults to children's literature and to ways of selecting literature appropriate for a broad age range.

In many cases, the range of children's books available encourages the adult who doesn't read easily to successfully share books with children. In developing family literacy programs for these customers, children's librarians often work with adult basic education specialists to help make reading a family affair.

There have also been other changes. Children and their families speak many languages; families now include grandparents or other relatives; and these families don't necessarily live in houses or apartments but sometimes in shelters or transitional housing. Because many children live in single parent homes or have working parents, children's services librarians have noted an increase in group visits to the library, visits that require programs and activities for larger numbers of children.

Children's services librarians must be able to assess and respond to these changing customer needs, adapting their services to better serve a diverse population.

Ruth M. Hadlow: From the 1950s onward, the influence of television and movies and marked social changes have been reflected more and more in the worldliness and restlessness of many children.

Today, most young people are the products of a multimedia-impacted society. Among preschoolers and primary-aged children especially, this has resulted in their being very visually oriented and wanting action-filled activities. Attention spans are limited compared to those of children several decades ago. For many of these boys and girls and their older siblings, continued exposure to violence, fragmented family patterns, and increased mobility result in a lack of concentration, in either a detachment or an urgent need for attention, and in low self-esteem.

Children and younger teens are showing greater interest in such subjects as suicide, drugs, guns, gangs, and sexual activity, resulting in a foreshortened view of the future and a need for instant gratification.

Most children need and want a sense of belonging and self-respect; they are eager to learn, they enjoy a good laugh. These have always been basic. Today's customers, however, whether children, parents, or teachers, are conditioned by many conflicting values and bombarded with fast-developing technology. They challenge the children's librarian more than ever to be creative, innovative, and flexible.

How have changes in young customers' interests, family values, or reading levels affected library service?

Margaret Mary Kimmel: Headlines in newspapers and on the evening news attest to a crisis in the lives of our children. The chaos of the streets spills into our libraries and schools. What is going on may not be new, but it appears to be more pervasive.

One aspect of change is the rapid escalation of technology affecting how we learn and how we communicate with each other. The amazing growth of the Internet, for example, has made the exchange of ideas and news and bits and bytes of our lives even more immediate and more remote than the CNN coverage that brought SCUD missiles into our living rooms.

What remains the same is the mandate for working with children and young people that we have always accepted: to provide these youngsters with hope, the stuff of dreams, the power of story. We all need these stories more than ever to give meaning to the "instantness" of it all; we need the time and perspective that story provides to motivate young learners. As the marketplace demands more basic skills, the concern about declining literacy skills grows, and we need to give young learners the heart to accept the challenge of learning.

As this century turns into the next, we may need to review our history and look at what we were doing as the nineteenth century gave way to the twentieth. Masses of immigrant children in pockets of urban chaos found librarians telling stories and sending boxes of books to settlement houses and orphanages. Does it sound more familiar if we say "inner city" and "homeless shelters"? What must remain constant is our commitment to reaching out to those who don't even know they need us. We must be there not just to answer questions, but to explore possibilities in an ever-changing world.

Pam Klipsch: Library service has changed from an emphasis on print to a multimedia approach. We are now servicing customers who have been subjected to a barrage of images from mass media and advertising since infancy.

The media has also made young customers aware of the world and its problems at a younger age. Libraries now provide information resources that treat, in a more frank and forthright fashion, a broader range of issues for younger and younger readers. Fiction, too, reflects an awareness of tensions and anxieties once thought the province of adults. One can trace changes in attitudes by comparing popular authors: from Eleanor Estes to Betty Cavanna, to Beverly Cleary and Judy Blume, to Betsy Byars and Cynthia Voigt.

Libraries today often participate in cooperative efforts with other youth service agencies to provide services to families and neighborhoods disrupted by economic and social problems. Like these other agencies, libraries are being asked to serve as surrogates for absent or overburdened parents and as substitute extended families for children who have little regular contact with caring adults.

The decline in young customers' reading skills particularly affects readers' advisory services. The leisurely enjoyment of books is one of the most endangered pleasures of childhood and adolescence. Young people still struggling to develop decoding skills have no time or inclination to explore subtleties of plot, characterization, or style. They will attempt only the short, simple, and straightforward. While there are many wonderful books that fit these criteria, there are many more books that are equally wonderful and effectively lost to all but a lucky few.

What changes have you seen in children's books?

Margaret Hodges: In 1953 when I began to work in the Boys and Girls Room at the Carnegie Library in Pittsburgh, the collection was already rich in picture books illustrated by classic artists in the field: Beatrix Potter, Walter Crane, Randolph Caldecott, Kate Greenaway, and others loved and revered by children who passed down their books from generation to generation. William Nicholson's *Clever Bill* (1929) achieved the feat of telling a story almost entirely through pictures. Another landmark was Wanda Gag's *Millions of Cats* (1928), which gave vitality and freshness to illustrations done in black and white. New and distinguished artists turned their attention to children's book illustration when photo-offset lithography made beautiful books inexpensive and therefore feasible for printing in large quantities.

During the 1940s, serious book-length critiques appeared on illustrators and their work. Meanwhile, black-and-white picture books, like *The Story of Ferdinand* and *Make Way for Ducklings*, continued to compete successfully for children's favor with pictures in color.

But by the 1960s, with color TV in the majority of American homes, picture books began to rely almost exclusively on color. Meanwhile, picture books that had cost under $5 now cost $15. And, a flood of artists with backgrounds ranging from commercial art to fine art were submitting samples of their work to a rapidly growing number of publishers. A staggering output of picture books now vie for attention each year, and it becomes difficult, at least for me, to distinguish one artist from another. Only a few strong individuals stand out as exceptions.

While the picture book has been traditionally intended for the youngest children, a welcome new development is the picture book for older children. Partly because fewer parents read, reading for pleasure is a way of life undreamed of by many children today. At the same time, television has made them more visually aware. With strong plots and subtleties of thought and atmosphere, the rich talents of today's artists are attracting a new audience in the upper grades and offering easy access to literature, where that help is most needed.

If this trend continues, the picture book will have a bright and greatly expanded future.

As we approach the year 2000, how do you see the roles of the library and the librarian changing?

Jennifer Gallant: In the 21st century, many library collections will exist in part electronically. As information becomes more accessible through new linkups, the role of the librarian becomes increasingly important. If we don't want to end up as the blacksmiths of the next century, our role will have to evolve to reflect the changes brought about by technology and automation. Librarians of the next century will be innovators in the creation and application of technology. They will be teachers and guides in the use of this technology. they will be providers of "open access" to information for youth as that access becomes a necessity for survival. They will be expert locators and retrievers of relevant information for a society that may be overwhelmed by data.

The readers' advisory role of the librarian will likewise evolve. Youth services librarians in particular deal with generations that are not print-oriented but media-oriented. Images replace words as the preferred mode of communication, and librarians must be experts in multimedia materials.

Librarians will have to compete with other service sectors during the next century. Our existence will depend on the quality of the service we provide and on the availability of funding, which relies in turn on the continuing perception that libraries are a public "good" and "necessity." In that last thought, there is the hope that libraries and librarians will continue to transmit to future generations an appreciation for the cultural knowledge and history of mankind. The 21st century would be richer for it.

Jacqueline Mancall: Complexity is the name of the game. It is the challenge that faces library services: books will continue as they are; delivery modes will expand; new information formats will continue to develop; demands for information services will increase. Because of the growing complexity of the information environment, librarians will be even more essential. Gaining intellectual access to information will be paramount regardless of where or how it is stored.

For all youth service librarians, this means continuing our strong service orientation and developing differentiated staffing models for libraries with distinct and unique areas of specialization.

For school library media specialists this also means focusing on the teaching and learning process, becoming learning specialists and equal partners on teaching/learning teams, and mentoring and coaching students and teachers.

Several trends will enable the above changes to occur. These include the emergence of information technologies that will change the look of the school, the library, and the classroom. The delivery of information to youth and all caregivers, including teachers, will be expanded by the Internet. There will be a growing awareness among school library media specialists of the importance of being an access specialist as well as a collection specialist. And, educational institutions and professional associations will focus on supporting career-long professional development programs.

We can look forward to a time of excitement, rapid change, growing complexity, and continuous career development.

Virginia McKee: Too quickly, we will turn the corner into the 21st century. Libraries will continue to exist, but their roles will have expanded and adapted to meet the changing technology.

Certainly, customers of all ages will have access to information via an array of electronic media and may have only to turn it on in their own homes. But we already know about the staggering amount of information and the myriad of sources that exist today. As the resources and the paths to those resources expand, librarians will be the ones who continue to work with young customers to guide them toward and assist them in selecting those most appropriate to their questions.

Introducing literature to children and their caregivers is one role that I see remaining with the library and the librarian. Reading will not become a lost art. The customers of high-tech equipment will need to be able to read and interpret the information they find. Libraries will continue to select, purchase, and house the books that bring both joy and information to readers, and it will be librarians who share their knowledge of the best of these books, from the glorious picture book to the complex novel or informational book.

We will turn that corner in just a few years, and we will continue to realize that "Kids Need Libraries" every bit as much as they do today.

The Way It Was
School Library Service in 1954

In the *Statistics of Public-School Libraries, 1953-54*, nearly all public schools reported some type of library service, but only 36 percent said they had a centralized school library. Forty-seven percent of the schools offered their students classroom collections that were maintained by teachers, and 11 percent said they received some "other" type of library service. The remainder had no library service at all.

"Other" could mean anything from service by a county school library to personal service by local public librarians to being a stop on a bookmobile route.

In response to the 1953-54 survey, a respondent from the Natrona County Public Library in Casper, WY, described that library's version of "other":

Twice a year, in September and in January, we supply each grade teacher in the city school system with a box of library books suitable to her age group, allowing about one book per pupil. A school truck delivers these boxes to the various schools and returns the ones they have been using. Teachers may keep the books for the four-month period, or they may return them and exchange them for different ones in between the scheduled deliveries. Teachers may also come and select books on special subjects for us in their classes.

Twelve grade schools are supplied in the above manner. Two others, which are located near the library, send pupils for books for class use. In addition, rural teachers throughout the county may take books for their schools and exchange them as often as they wish.

In the same survey, the coordinator of school libraries in the heavily agricultural county of Fresno, CA, talked about the demands of providing library service to dozens of schools in a county that encompasses many districts:

You can gather from our statistics that we work under pressure. But full compensation comes with the knowledge that we are meeting well the varied needs of a highly varied school population in Fresno County—the right book for the "child who moves with the crops"—and the right book for the especially favored child of our suburban districts, multiplied many times over, for the many in between.

Index

Mary McClelland School, Wayne, IN 56

Maryland 34, 53, 139, 190, 219, 290, 415

Maryland State Department of Education 290

Masee, May 5, 163

mass market books 249–50, 255–59

mass media 331

Massachusetts 23, 67, 129, 208, 243, 247, 302, 343, 367, 368

materials for bilingual education 129

materials for exceptional children 117

materials use 84

mathematics 47, 48

Mathews, Virginia 40, 98, 410, 412, 443, 460

Matthews, Ed 277

maturity levels 9

Mayhar, Ardath 252

McDermott, Gerald 232

McDonald, Dwight 52

McElderry, Margaret 153, 160

McGill, Ralph 353

McGuffey readers 11

McLuan, Marshall 173, 174–75

McNeil, Robert 88

Means, Florence 110

media education 331–34

media education support organizations 333

media literacy 331–34

media management 289–90

media specialist, role of 63, 156, 318

media supervisors, role of 291

Media Library for Preschoolers, Erie Public Library, PA 131, 132–133, 135, 136

media-related books 255–59

mediocrity in children's books 65–69

Melcher, Dan 3

Melcher, Frederic G 3

Melvin, Roger 284

Michigan 23, 63, 283, 284, 317, 367, 389

Michigan Library Consortium 285

Midlands Consortium 316, 317

Miller, Mary Agnes 134

Mind Extension University 316, 318

Minnesota 157

minorities in children's books 404–07

minors, information services to 13

Minudri, Regina 7, 41, 400

Mississippi 352

Missouri 265–266, 352, 367

Monteith Library Project 63

Montessori 131, 135

Moon, Eric 13

Moore, Anne Carroll 5, 160–162

Moore, Ray 321

Moore, Raymond and Dorothy 138–39

Mount Diablo Unified School District, CA 401

multiculturalism 260, 270, 272

multimedia approach 463, 464, 465

Munson, Amelia 297

museum outreach 277–79

Museum of Modern Art, Houston, TX 173

music, effect on adolescents 438

music, teen 463

Myers, Walter Dean 407

N

Naisbitt, John 138, 321

Narahashi, Keiko 427

national information policy 13, 14

National Advisory Commission on Libraries 62

National Advisory Committee on Dyslexia and Related Reading Disorders 189

National Advisory Council for Bilingual Education 128

National Association for Retarded Citizens 116

National Association for the Advancement of Colored People (NAACP) 351

National Association for the Education of Young Children 168, 415

National Association of School Boards of Education 367

National Association of State Educational Media Professionals 387

National Center for Education Statistics 102, 453

National Center on Educational Media and Materials for the Handicapped (NCEMMH) 117, 119

National Clearinghouse on Bilingual Education 129

National Coalition Against Censorship 375

National Commission on Excellence in Education 405, 406, 409–10

National Commission on Libraries and Information Science 203

National Commission on Reading 165

National Commission on Time and Learning 346

National Council for the Accreditation of Teacher Education 100

National Council of Churches 353

National Council of Teachers of English 229, 232, 334, 364

National Defense Education Act 47, 48, 49, 51

National Education Association 48, 49, 50, 353, 356

National Education Goals 440

National Education Week 302

National Endowment for the Humanities 128

National Institute on Education 165

National Instructional Materials Information Center (NIMIC) 117

National Library Power Program 342–45

National Library Week 40, 50, 143

National Organization for Women 12

National Portrait Gallery, Smithsonian Institution 277

National Postal Museum, Hull, Quebec 277

National Research and Education Network (NREN) 37

National School Volunteer Program 267

National Telemedia Council 334

Native Americans 109–111

Natrona County Public Library, Casper, WY 466

Nebraska 315, 345

networking 80, 121, 217–20, 390, 391

networking, periodicals 273–76

networks 96, 315–316, 411, 452

Nevins, Allan 52

New Hampshire 335

New Jersey 47, 63, 278, 305, 335

New Mexico 405

New York 54, 57, 127, 130, 219, 250, 266, 317, 351, 415

New York City 342, 343

New York Public Library 34, 160–64, 208, 377

New York Public Library, Early Childhood Resource and Information Center 131, 134–35

Newark Museum, NJ 278

Newbery-Caldecott Committee 381

Newman, Audrey 48

Noestlinger, Christine 271

non-fiction, accuracy in 68, 109–111

non-print 190–92, 203, 268–72, 336

North Carolina 317, 427

Northern Pacific Railroad 110

Northside Elementary School, Middleton, WI 118

training, in service 41, 60, 63, 71, 72, 155, 264, 265, 387–88
training, of school librarians 62, 63
training, student 264
translation, children's books in 184–86

U

U. S. Committee for UNICEF 208, 209
U. S. Department of Labor 332
U. S. Department of Education 102, 391, 411, 415, 433, 434, 453
U. S. Office of Education 47, 59, 62, 64, 126, 128, 367, 368, 391
U. S. Supreme Court 76–7, 139, 353, 418
Uchida, Yoshida 407
Usenet 282
user satisfaction 84
Utley, Robert 110

V

Van Orsdel, Darrell 219
Victor, Edward 79
video 265–67, 268–72, 336
Virginia 317, 367
visual literacy 88, 173, 205, 230–34, 332
visual media 173–75
vocational education 47, 48

volunteer programs, funding 367–68
volunteer services 366, 369
volunteers 366–70
Volunteers in Education 367

W

Walter, Mildred Pitts 427–28
Warren, Mary 110, 111
Washington 47, 54, 56, 57, 140, 219, 321, 415, 463
Washington Homeschool Organization 321
Weeks, Ann 342
Wessells, Helen 3
West, Jessamyn 53
West Liberty Junior-Senior High, IA 324
West Virginia 47, 317
Westlake, OH 225–27
Weston Woods 232, 233
White, Burton 131
White, E. B. 193, 196
White House Conference on Library and Information Service, Second 37, 98, 99, 103
whole language 435–47
William Lyon School, Orange County, CA 142
Wisconsin 23, 219, 334

Wisniewski, David 428–29
Wizelius, Ingemar 184
Wojciechowska, Maia 112
Wolf, Anna w. M. 191
Wolff, Gertrude 3
Women's National Book Association 49
Woods, George 372
Works Progress Administration (WPA) 160
Wright-Manassee, Patty 284
Wyoming 466

XYZ

Yahgan 109
Yale Family Television Research and Consultation Center 221
Year of the Lifetime Reader 414
Yep, Laurence 251–52, 406
young adult reading 236–38
young adult services 41, 104, 153–54, 112–14, 176–80, 297–300, 309–12, 324–25, 329–30
Young Adult Library Services Association (ALA) 35, 98, 100, 342
Young Adult Services Division (ALA) 153, 237
Young Americans Act 98
Zebrowski, George 253, 254
Zolotow, Charlotte 194, 195

Additional Titles of Interest

CULTURALLY DIVERSE LIBRARY COLLECTIONS FOR CHILDREN
By Herman L. Totten and Risa W. Brown

A single source bibliography to help school library media specialists diversify their collections with African American, Hispanic American, Asian American, and Native American books. Includes full bibliographic data, suggested ages or grades, and a brief annotation for nonfiction, biography, folk tales, and fiction, reference books, and scholarly works.

"Succinct and informative." *Booklist*

" . . . well-organized . . . valuable for its scope, currency, and subject index." *School Library Journal*

"A comprehensive, annotated guide to building a multiethnic children's collection." *Reference & Research Books News*

1-55570-140-X. 1994. 6 x 9. 304 pp. $35.00.

CULTURALLY DIVERSE LIBRARY COLLECTIONS FOR YOUTH
By Herman L. Totten, Risa W. Brown, and Carolyn Garner

Young adult and school librarians can look here to find recommended books and videos about African American, Hispanic, Asian, and Native American cultures. Nonfiction, biography, folk tales, reference books, and scholarly works. Each title is annotated with full bibliographic data and suggested ages and grades. Relevant adult ethnic books are also evaluated for use in school.

" . . . should prove valuable as a selection tool for public, middle school, and high school libraries." *Booklist*

1-55570-141-8. 1996. 6 x 9. 220 pp. $35.00.

THE INTERNET FOR TEACHERS AND SCHOOL LIBRARY MEDIA SPECIALISTS:
Today's Applications, Tomorrow's Prospects
Edited by Edward J. Valauskas and Monica Ertel

Wondering how other schools incorporate the Internet into their curricula? Look here for successful Internet programs used in elementary, middle, and high schools to teach math, science, history, literature, music, and more. Program descriptions are written by the faculty members and/or school library media specialists involved. Each contains goals and results; budget, technical, and curricular information.

"Actual school programs provide many teaching ideas." *Technology & Learning*

1-55570-239-2. 1996. 6 x 9. 231 pp. $35.00.

INVITING CHILDREN'S AUTHORS AND ILLUSTRATORS:
A How-To-Do-It Manual for School and Public Librarians
By Kathy East

" . . . helpful information on every aspect of inviting an author or illustrator . . . equally pertinent to the school or public library visit." *Voice of Youth Advocates*

" . . . covers everything librarians and teachers need to know." *Book Links*

"A smart purchase." *Booklist*

" . . . furnishes the details to insure a successful visit. The emphasis on communication is powerful." *School Library Journal*

1-55570-182-5. 1995. 8 1/2 x 11. 127 pp. $32.50.

LAPSIT SERVICES FOR THE VERY YOUNG:
A How-To-Do-It Manual
By Linda L. Ernst

The value of library service for the very young (birth to 24 months) is being increasingly recognized. Here is a basic, right-on-target guide that will enable readers to provide excellent LAPSIT service in their libraries.

"Includes excellent bibliographies and resource lists. Best of all are sample programs . . . a solid title for all public libraries." *School Library Journal*

"Libraries considering programming for babies and toddlers will find this a practical guide." *Booklist*

1-55570-185-X. 1995. 8 1/2 x 11. 136 pp. $32.50.

LIBRARY SERVICES FOR CHILDREN AND YOUTH:
Dollars & Sense
Edited By Virginia H. Mathews

" . . . will help library directors and front-line youth service librarians defend and support their services to young people." *Journal of Youth Services in Libraries*

"Use this book to educate yourself on current library thinking and projects. Use it as an eye-opener for new ideas and a change in thinking. But most of all . . . use it to actively develop missions and goals to promote library service to children and young adults." *VOYA*

1-55570-176-0. 1994. 8 1/2 x 11. 70 pp. $19.95.

PROTECTING THE RIGHT TO READ:
A How-To-Do-It Manual for School and Public Librarians
By Ann K. Symons and Charles Harmon

" . . . delivers even more than it promises in an easy-to-use format. . . . a well-organized, concise, and pragmatic guide . . . including electronic media and the Internet." *School Library Journal*

" . . . information-packed . . . covers every key intellectual freedom issue . . . a valuable resource." *Library Journal*

"An essential resource." *VOYA*

"The chapter on intellectual freedom and the Internet (a subject not covered in the latest ALA Manual) will prove particularly useful . . . " *Emergency Librarian*

1-55570-216-3. 1995. 8 1/2 x 11. 220 pp. $39.95.

RUNNING A SCHOOL LIBRARY MEDIA CENTER:
A How-To-Do-It Manual
By Barbara L Stein and Risa W. Brown

"Quick to read and easy to use . . . offers lots of practical advice . . . " *Booklist*

" . . . there is counsel here on every aspect of school librar-ies for the beginning librarian." *American Libraries*

1-55570-100-0. 1992. 8 1/2 x 11. 160 pp. $35.00.

SERVING FAMILIES AND CHILDREN THROUGH PARTNERSHIPS:
A How-To-Do-It Manual for Librarians
By Sandra Feinberg and Sari Feldman

This innovative manual explains how to forge new partnerships with local agencies and organizations in order to design a family-centered community environment. Covered are developing library-based family support services; changing libraries to meet the needs of changing families; providing parent education and support; exploring new partnerships to create new services; developing strategies for services, and building resource collections for families (including the Internet and public access bulletin boards).

"For libraries seeking to develop contacts in the community and to provide a unique learning experience for children and families." *Library Journal*

1-55570-227-9. 1996. 8 1/2 x 11. 266 pp. $39.95.

Publication dates, prices, and number of pages for new titles may be estimates and are subject to change.

To order or request further information, contact:
Neal-Schuman Publishers
100 Varick Street, New York, NY 10013
212-925-8650
or fax toll free—1-800-584-2414